# MODERN METHODS OF VALUATION

# MODERN METHODS OF VALUATION

*Note to Second Impression of Sixth Edition*

As stated in the Preface, the present Sixth Edition was in print before the coming into operation of the consolidating provisions of the Town & Country Planning Act, 1971. Consequently certain statutory references, mainly in Chapters 18 and 19, are now out of date.

Tables of Comparison showing the mode in which earlier enactments are dealt with by the Town & Country Planning Act, 1971, and the Sections of the Act corresponding to provisions in earlier Acts, have been compiled by the Department of the Environment and are published by H.M. Stationery Office price 40p.

These should readily enable corrections to be made to the references to earlier Acts in the Chapters in question and also in Appendices B1, B2 and D–Or, in place of Chapters 18 and 19, readers may find it more convenient to refer to Chapters 20–22 of "Compulsory Purchase and Compensation" (Fifth Edition) by Lawrance and Moore, published by the Estates Gazette, which cover the same ground.

Since the Sixth Edition was printed other legislation has also been enacted. The two principal Acts are: The Housing Finance Act, 1972, which mainly affects Chapter 13, (Residential Properties), and The Finance Act, 1972, which mainly affects Chapter 15, (Valuations for Probate) and Chapter 17, (Capital Gains Tax): it also alters Appendix E, (The Scale of Estate Duty). These and any further legislation changes will be dealt with in detail when a new edition of the book is prepared.

## CORRIGENDA

Page 14    paragraph 7, second line for "change" read "chance".

Page 50    for Page 52 read Page 48

Page 55    paragraph 2, second line for "At" read "As".

Page 81    answer to example: Profit rent in present interest for "£3,100" read "£1,300".

Page 174    paragraph 6, fourth line for "be" read "by".

Page 180    example—Valuation—costs of redevelopment—for "£160" read "£260".

Page 206    line 1, for "two years" read "seven years".

Page 246    paragraph 4, line 3 for "£25,000" read "£35,000".

Page 270    Footnote for "1969" read "1968".

Page 272    line 3, for "gain" read "disposals".

Page 276    Footnote 2, line 2 for "heed" read "held", and in line 3 for "before" read "after".

Page 280    Add to footnote "The time apportionment method is not available where the disposal price of land includes development value".

Page 326    last line, delete "arterial".

# MODERN METHODS OF VALUATION

## OF

## LAND, HOUSES AND BUILDINGS

BY

### DAVID M. LAWRANCE

*B.Sc. (Estate Management) Lond. (Gold Medallist); Fellow and Gold Medallist of the Royal Institution of Chartered Surveyors; Fellow of the Institute of Arbitrators; of Gray's Inn, Barrister-at-Law.*

### W. H. REES

*B.Sc. (Estate Management) London.; Fellow and Prizeman of the Royal Institution of Chartered Surveyors; Member of the Rating Surveyors Association.*

AND

### W. BRITTON

*B.Sc. (Estate Management) Lond.; Fellow of the Royal Institution of Chartered Surveyors.*

---

THE ESTATES GAZETTE LIMITED

151 WARDOUR STREET · LONDON · W1V 4BN

*SIXTH EDITION, 1971*
Reprinted 1972
Reprinted 1974

Reproduced and printed by photolithography and bound in
Great Britain at The Pitman Press, Bath

# PREFACE TO THE SIXTH EDITION

THE OBJECT of this book is to combine within a reasonable compass a detailed study of the principles governing the valuation of land and buildings with an account of the application of these principles to everyday problems met with in practice. In this way we hope that it may be of value to both the student and the practitioner.

Since the last edition of this book was published there has been a mass of new legislation affecting town and country planning, rating and income and capital gains taxes amongst other matters. In consequence of this and other changes, many Chapters have had to be completely re-written. Although Betterment Levy has been abolished a chapter on valuations for this purpose has been included since many cases remain to be settled. As the book was already in print before the passing of the Town and Country Planning Act, 1971, it has not been possible to revise references to earlier Town Planning legislation. But since the new Act is a consolidating one only, and contains a table showing the derivation of its sections from previous Town Planning Acts, it is hoped that this will not cause undue inconvenience to readers.

Except in the case of some references in the Chapters on Licensed Premises and Minerals, units are given in metric measurement and the shillings and pence in previous editions have been replaced by decimal currency: income tax is stated as a percentage.

The book is divided into two parts as in the Fifth Edition, largely for the benefit of students. Those studying for examinations in Elementary Valuations will mainly be concerned with Part 1, which deals with basic principles and the construction and use of Valuation Tables. Advanced Students and practitioners will mainly be concerned with Part 2, where the application of statutory provisions is considered.

Once again we wish to express our thanks to all our many colleagues for their help and assistance. They include Mr. R. E. Clark, F.R.I.C.S., for revising the Chapters on the Valuation of Life Interest, Rating and Capital Gains Tax; Mr. P. D. Wood, F.R.I.C.S., Member of the C.A.A.V., for revising the Chapter on Agricultural Properties; Mr. J. P. Lambert, T.D., F.R.I.C.S., for the revision of the Chapter on Licensed Premises; Mr. J. C. Rackham, B.Sc., F.R.I.C.S., for revising the Chapter on Minerals; and Mr. T. A. Johnson, B.Sc., F.R.I.C.S., for writing the Chapter on Betterment Levy.

D. M. LAWRANCE

W. H. REES

W. BRITTON

London, 1971

v

# TABLE OF CONTENTS

## PART 1

vii

# Appendices

# Chapter 1

## Principles of Valuation

### 1. GENERALLY

THE SERVICES of a valuer may be sought by anyone with an interest in, or contemplating a transaction involving, land and buildings. For example, a valuer may be required to advise a vendor on the price he should ask for his property, a prospective tenant on the annual rent he should pay, a mortgagee on the value of the security and on the mortgage loan he can advance and a person dispossessed under compulsory powers on the compensation he can claim.

Knowledge of the purpose for which his valuation is required is usually vital to the valuer, for the value of a particular interest in landed property is not necessarily the same for all purposes. In many cases the valuer will also require to know details of the circumstances of the person for whom the valuation is being prepared because the value of a particular interest may be different to different individuals according to, for example, their liability to income tax.

In the majority of cases, however, the primary concern of the valuer is to estimate the market value; that is the capital sum or the annual rental which at a particular time, on specified terms and subject to legislation, should be asked or paid for a particular interest in property.

It might reasonably be asked next, what are the special characteristics of landed property which make the services of a person with special knowledge desirable, or in many cases essential, in dealing with it? There are three primary reasons: —

    (i) Imperfections in the property market.

    (ii) The heterogeneity of landed property and the interests which can exist therein.

    (iii) Legal factors.

The need for special knowledge of the law relating to landed property will become apparent in later Chapters; the varied interests which can exist in landed property are considered in Chapter 4.

The nature of landed property, the methods of conducting transactions in it and the information available on the transactions, all contribute to the imperfection of competition in the landed property market. Apart from structural differences in any building, each piece of landed property is unique by reason of location. The majority of transactions in the property market are conducted privately and even if the results of the transactions were available they would not be particularly helpful in the absence of detailed information on such matters as the extent and state of the buildings and the tenure. The degree of imperfection does, however, differ in different parts of the market. First-class shop investments, for example, are fairly homogeneous and this fact will decrease the imperfection of competition in the market for them. The greater than average degree of homogeneity lies in the tenants of such properties rather than the properties themselves, but the tenant is probably of greater significance than the property.

It is, perhaps, misleading to talk of the property market as though it were a single entity. In fact, there are a number of markets, some local and some national, a few of which are becoming international. For example, residential properties required for occupation are normally dealt with locally. A man looking for a house to live in is rarely indifferent to its location because it must be conveniently situated usually in relation to his place of work. The market for first class investments on the other hand, is national. This type of property appeals to large institutions such as insurance companies who are largely indifferent to the situation of the property. The market for development properties can be local, national or international. Small bare sites suitable for the erection of a few houses are of interest to small local developers, larger sites to larger organisations operating in a much wider area. Redevelopment of central areas, if it is to be undertaken privately, requires such large funds that only organisations of at least national status can command them.

## 2.  A DEFINITION OF VALUE

Much paper can be, and indeed has been, consumed in discussing and defining value. It is not intended here to contribute to this particular store of literature but merely to provide a definition which will serve the present purpose.

The market value or market price of a particular interest in landed property may be defined as the amount of money which can be obtained for the interest at a particular time from persons able and willing to purchase it. Value is not intrinsic but results from estimates, made subjectively by able and willing purchasers, of the benefit or satisfaction they will derive from the interest. The valuer must, therefore, in order to value an interest, be able to assess the probable estimates of benefit of potential purchasers.

A potential purchaser is a man who proposes to tie up a certain amount of capital in land or in land and buildings, and there are three main angles from which he may view the transaction. Firstly, if he wishes to occupy the property he will be concerned with the benefits, commercial or social, which he anticipates deriving from that occupation. Secondly, he may regard the property as an investment capable of yielding an annual return in the form of income. Thirdly, his motive may be speculation; that is, buying at one price now he hopes to sell at a higher price at some time in the future and thus make a capital gain. These motives are not, however, mutually exclusive and a transaction may be entered into with more than one motive in mind. In any case the price which the purchaser will be prepared to pay at any given time will be influenced largely by the supply of that particular type of property and the extent of the demand for it. Supply and demand are discussed at length in the next two Sections of this Chapter but it might be noted here that demand must be effective; that is, that the desire to possess should be translatable into the action of purchasing.

Although the aim of the valuer is to provide an estimate of market value, it should not be assumed that the valuer's estimate of value and the market price or market value will always be the same. Different valuers could well place different values on a particular interest at a particular time because they are making estimates and there is normally room, within certain limits, for differences of opinion. In the majority of cases this is the most serious difference which should arise between competent valuers in times of stable market conditions because market prices result from estimates of value made by vendors and purchasers on the basis of prices previously paid for other similar interests; but in times when market conditions are not stable more serious differences may arise. In such unstable times the valuer's estimate of value will be based on prices previously paid but he must adjust this basis to allow for the changes since the previous transactions took place. The accuracy of his estimate will, therefore, depend on his knowledge of the changes and his skill in quantifying their effect. More serious differences may also arise where the valuer is making statutory valuations in hypothetical market conditions.

## 3. DEMAND, SUPPLY AND PRICE

It is axiomatic that quantity bought is equal to quantity sold regardless of price. This does not mean, however, that price is unimportant. Demand and supply are in fact equated at any particular time by some level of price. Other things being equal, at any given time, any increase in demand or decrease in supply will cause price to rise; conversely, any decrease in demand or increase in supply will cause price to fall. Therefore, whatever the given demand and supply, in a freely operating market, price will ration the supply and match it to the demand

Price has, however, a wider role. If, over a longer period, price remains persistently high in relation to the cost of producing more of the thing in question, it will call forth increased supplies which will gradually have the effect of pulling price down again to a long-run normal or equilibrium level. Conversely, if price remains persistently low it will serve to diminish supplies forthcoming which will pull price up again to an equilibrium level. Price, therefore, acts also as an indicator and an incentive.

The extent of price changes caused by changes in demand or supply will depend upon the price elasticity of supply or demand. Thus, if supply is highly elastic, a change in demand can be matched quickly and smoothly by an expansion of supply and the price change, if any, will be small. Conversely, if supply is highly inelastic, a change in demand cannot be matched quickly and smoothly by an expansion in supply, thus the price change will be more marked. If demand is elastic, a change in supply will quickly generate an appropriate contraction or expansion in demand and the price change, if any, will be small; but if demand is inelastic this means that any change in supply is likely to generate a contraction or expansion in demand less quickly and the price change will be more marked.

This is a simple statement of economic laws which are applicable to all types of commodity or service, but to consider their application to a particular type of commodity or service it is necessary to look at the special characteristics of the commodity or service in question.

It is proposed, therefore, to look next at some of the principal factors which affect the demand for, and the supply of, landed property.

### 4. Demand for, and Supply of, Landed Property

The term landed property covers such a wide range of types of land and buildings and interests therein that generalisation is difficult but it is correct to say that, generally, the demand for, and the supply of, landed property are relatively inelastic with respect to price changes.

The most important single factor restricting the supply of land and buildings at the present time is planning. There are, of course, natural limitations on the supply of land. Firstly, the overall supply of land is fixed and, secondly, the supply of land suitable for particular purposes is limited, but these natural limitations are overshadowed by planning limitations.

The powers of the planner are considered in more detail in Part 2 but the following are the most important in this particular context: —

(1) The power to allocate land for particular uses; for example, agricultural use or residential use. This allocation is shown in the development plans which have been prepared for the whole of the country. Thus, it would not normally be possible to erect a factory on a bare site in an area allocated for residential use.

(2) The power to restrict changes in the use of buildings. For example, before the use of a house can be changed to offices planning permission must be obtained and this permission will not usually be forthcoming unless the change is in accordance with the provisions of the development plan for the area.

(3) The power to restrict the intensity of use of land. Thus the owner of a bare site in an area allocated for residential use is not free to choose between erecting on it, for example, a four-storey or a fifteen-storey block of flats. This power may be exercisable also by means of building regulations.

To illustrate the operation of these powers in practice, assume that in a particular area in which all available office space is already taken up, there is an increase in demand for office space. This increased demand might be met by an increased supply in three ways. Suitable buildings at present used for other purposes might be converted for use as offices, suitable bare sites might be developed by the erection of office blocks, and buildings which are not fully utilising their sites might be demolished so that larger office blocks could be erected. But planning may affect all three possibilities.

In the extreme case it might be that, although suitable buildings are available for conversion, planning permission for the change of use is not forthcoming; although bare sites are available, none is in an area zoned for office use in the development plan and although existing buildings do not fully utilise their sites, they provide the maximum floor space the planner will permit. In such a case, in both short and long run, the effect of the increase in demand will be to increase the price of the existing office space to the point at which the high price so reduces demand as to equate it once again with the fixed supply.

In a less extreme case it would be possible to increase the supply by one or more of the three methods but some, perhaps considerable, time would elapse before any increased supply was available. In the case of conversion of existing buildings it would be necessary to obtain planning permission, dispossess any tenants and carry out any necessary works of conversion. The time taken would depend on the administrative speed of the planning authority, the security of tenure of the tenants and the extent of the works.

With the other methods planning permission would again have to be obtained and with the penultimate method any tenants of the existing buildings dispossessed and the buildings demolished. The erection of the new buildings would take about one to two years. Thus, in this less extreme case the effect of the increase in demand would be to increase the price of the existing space in the short run. In the long run as the new space becomes available the price would tend to fall. If the increased supply was sufficient to satisfy the whole of the increased demand the price might return to its former level but if, as is more likely in practice, the increased supply was insufficient the new equilibrium price would be higher than the old.

A reduction in the supply of buildings is difficult to achieve; the existing stock of buildings can only be reduced by demolition or change of use and the loss involved in failing to complete buildings already started would almost certainly be higher than the loss resulting from a fall in price.

It has already been observed that the demand for land and buildings is also generally inelastic but the degree of inelasticity will depend to some extent on the purpose for which the land and buildings are held.

Elasticity of demand for any commodity or service depends on whether the commodity or service is regarded as a necessity or a luxury and the existence of satisfactory substitutes.

Take, for example, the demand for landed property for residential occupation. This, viewed as a whole, can generally be regarded as a necessity and no satisfactory substitutes exist. Thus, an increase in the price of living accommodation would probably not result in any marked contraction in demand because a particular standard of such accommodation is regarded as a necessity and a caravan or a tent would not, to the majority of people, offer a satisfactory substitute. This would not, however, be true in less prosperous times than this country has enjoyed over the last few years. In such times, an increase in price would probably, subject to legal restrictions on sub-division and over-crowding, lead to economies in the use of living space.

The importance of the difference between the desire of a prospective purchaser to possess a property and his ability to translate that desire into the actuality of purchasing was mentioned earlier, but further elaboration is desirable at this stage. The majority of purchases of landed property are not effected wholly by the use of the purchaser's own capital. To take houses as an example, the purchaser will normally pay only a small proportion of the purchase price out of his own capital and the remainder he borrows by way of mortgage from a financial institution such as a building society or an insurance company. In some cases this will be done because the purchaser prefers to invest the remainder of his capital elsewhere but in many cases the purchaser has insufficient capital to pay the whole of the purchase price although his income is sufficient to pay interest on the mortgage loan and to repay the capital gradually over a long period of years. Therefore, the ability of the majority of prospective purchasers of houses to make their demand effective depends on obtaining the necessary loan from a financial institution. In recent years these financial institutions have rarely had sufficient funds available to satisfy the whole of the demand for loans from prospective purchasers. They have, therefore, laid down priorities and they have determined these priorities primarily in terms of the security offered. The nature of a mortgage is considered elsewhere but the point of significance at this stage is that the main security for the loan is the interest in the property in respect of which the loan is granted. Thus, the financial institutions have given priority to new houses. This has meant that, although in most areas demand for houses has been at a sufficiently high level to absorb all types of houses for sale, new and recently erected houses would be taken up first, then inter-war houses and finally, if any mortgage money was still available, the pre-1919 houses. This became a sufficiently serious problem for the Government to make Exchequer funds available to certain building societies to enable them to make advances on pre-1919 houses. The policy of financial institutions such as building societies has, therefore, an important bearing on the demand for certain types of landed property.

Legislation often affects, either directly or indirectly, the demand for landed property. The various statutes affecting different types of landed property are considered in detail in Part 2 but as an example at this stage, the demand for smaller or poorer types of residential accommodation is directly affected by the Rent Acts which restrict the income which the owner may derive from his property. The same type of property may also be affected indirectly by legislation restricting immigration.

The other principal factors affecting the demand for landed property are mainly long term so that their effects are felt only gradually over a long period of years.

Some of the effects of planning in relation to the supply of land and buildings have been noted but planning may also have important effects on the demand side. The creation of new towns, the extension of existing towns to accommodate overspill from the large conurbations and the redevelopment of central shopping areas are examples of positive planning which may increase demand in and around the areas concerned although it may reduce demand in other areas.

Changes in the overall size, the location and the composition of the population will affect the demand for landed property. An overall increase in population, particularly if accompanied by an increase in prosperity as it has been in recent years, will increase the demand for most types of landed property. The increased population must be housed and its increased demands for necessities and luxuries will have to be met through the medium of such properties as shops, factories, offices, schools and playing fields. The movement of population from one part of the country to another will have the dual effect of increasing demand in the reception area and reducing it in the area of origin. Changes in the composition of the population also have important effects. For example, a reduction in family size will increase the demand for separate dwelling units and an increasing proportion of retired people will increase the demand for bungalows in the favoured retirement areas such as the South Coast.

Improvements in transport facilities have encouraged people who work in towns to commute, sometimes over very long distances. As the number of commuters increases the transport facilities may become overburdened and the process may be reversed.

## 5. LANDED PROPERTY AS AN INVESTMENT

Any purchase of an interest in landed property can be regarded as an investment. There is, firstly, the straightforward case of the purchase of an interest in a property which is to be let to someone in order to provide the benefit of an income. But purchase for occupation is also an investment, the benefit in this case being the annual value of the occupation. A businessman, for example, may make a conscious choice between investing his capital in purchasing a property for occupation for his business or alternatively renting a similar property, owned by someone else, so that he can invest his capital elsewhere. The point can be further illustrated by considering a case where a businessman has at some time in the past made the choice of investing part of his business capital by purchasing business premises for occupation. If he now wishes to realise the capital tied up in the property and invest it elsewhere in the business he might enter into a lease-back or a mortgage transaction. In the lease-back transaction he will sell his interest in the property but take the property back on lease paying the annual value by way of rent. In the mortgage transaction he obtains a loan on the security of his interest in the property paying annual interest on the loan.

Purchase for speculation is also an investment but with the object of obtaining a capital gain rather than an income flow.

The methods of valuation employed by the valuer are discussed at length in Chapter 9 but the consideration of landed property as an investment leads to the introduction of one of these methods. the investment method.

The investment method of valuation consists of finding the present capital value of a future income flow discounted at an appropriate rate of interest.

In order to perform a valuation by this method it is, therefore, necessary to know, or to be able to estimate, the income which the property will produce and the appropriate rate of interest at which to discount that income. The operation of the method can best be illustrated by starting at the answer. For example, if a purchaser has paid £3,000 for an interest in a property and the rate of interest he may expect on his capital is 5 per cent he must be able to anticipate that he will derive from the property the benefit of a perpetual annual income of £150, that is 5 per cent of £3,000 calculated

$$\frac{5}{100} \times \frac{3000}{1} = 150.$$

Now to reverse this mathematical process, if it can be anticipated that a perpetual annual income of £150 will be derived from a particular property and the appropriate rate of interest at which this income should be discounted is 5 per cent, the present capital value will be £3,000, calculated: —

$$\frac{100}{5} \times \frac{150}{1} = 3,000$$

The multiplier applied to the income to arrive at the capital value, in the example above $\frac{100}{5}$ or 20, is known as "Years' Purchase" or the "Present Value of £1 per annum".

Where the income is perpetual, as in the example above, the appropriate Years' Purchase can be found as shown by dividing 100 by the rate of interest, thus: —

Rate of interest $-5\% - $ Y.P. $= \dfrac{100}{5} = 20$

,, ,, ,, $-4\% - $ Y.P. $= \dfrac{100}{4} = 25$

,, ,, ,, $-6\% - $ Y.P. $= \dfrac{100}{6} = 16 \cdot 67$

Where the income is not perpetual the calculation of years' purchase is more complex and such cases are dealt with in Chapter 5.

# *Chapter 2*

## Interest Rates

### 1. GENERALLY

IN CHAPTER 1 it was shown that, in order to use the investment method of valuation, the valuer must determine the rate of interest appropriate to the particular interest in property being valued. He will normally do this by an analysis of previous market transactions. The valuer is not, however, merely an analyst. He must have a clear idea not only of what the market is doing but also why the market is doing it and, if he is to advise adequately on the quality of the investment, what the market is likely to do in the future. He should, therefore, have some knowledge of the levels of interest rates on most types of investment and of the principal factors which influence them.

This Chapter is concerned with these points and in it will be considered the principles governing interest rates generally and interest rates on the main types of landed property.

Before considering these matters, however, it is necessary to dispose of one preliminary point which may be a source of confusion to the student.

### 2. NOMINAL AND REAL RATES OF INTEREST

The nominal rate of interest, or dividend, from an investment is the annual return to the investor in respect of every £100 face value of the stock. Where stock is selling at its face value, that is at par, the nominal rate of interest and the real rate of interest, or yield, are the same. Thus, to take a Government Security as an example, the nominal rate of interest on 2½ per cent Consolidated Stock is fixed at 2½ per cent, that is £2·50 interest will be received each year for each £100 face value of the stock held. If the stock is selling at £100 for each £100 face value, an investor will receive £2·50 interest each year for every £100 invested which gives a yield of 2½ per cent. But assume now that £100 face value of 2½ per cent Consols is selling at £40, or 60 below par. Each £40 of capital actually invested would be earning £2·50 interest annually

$$\therefore \text{ Yield} = \frac{2 \cdot 5}{40} \times \frac{100}{1} = 6 \cdot 25 \text{ or } 6\tfrac{1}{4}\%$$

If a large industrial concern declares a dividend of, say, 25 per cent on its Ordinary shares but the price of each £1 share on the market is £4

$$\therefore \text{Yield} = \frac{25}{400} \times \frac{100}{1} = 6 \cdot 25 \text{ or } 6\tfrac{1}{4}\%$$

If the price of these shares in the following year had risen to £6·25 and the same dividend of 25 per cent had been declared

$$\therefore \text{Yield} = \frac{25}{625} \times \frac{100}{1} = 4\%$$

From these examples two important points can be seen:—

(i) That a comparison of incomes receivable from various types of investment can only be made on the basis of yields and that nominal rates of interest derived from face values are of no significance for this purpose.

(ii) That a rise or fall in the price of a security involves a change in the yield of that security.

### 3. Principles Governing Yields from Investments

The precise nature of interest and the relationship between, and the level of, long-term, medium-term and short-term rates of interest are subjects for the economist and are not dealt with in this book. The valuer is interested primarily in long-term securities and the relative yields from them. He is interested in why the investor requires investment A to yield 6 per cent, investment B to yield 3 per cent and investment C to yield 12 per cent.

A reasonably simple explanation of the many complex matters that the investor must take into account in determining the yield he requires from an investment, can be derived from the creation, firstly, of an imaginary situation. For this purpose the following assumptions are made: —

(i) That the real value of money is being maintained over a reasonable period of years—that is, that £1 will purchase the same quantity of goods in, say, 10 years' time as it will now; and, either

(ii) there is no taxation or that the rates of tax are so moderate as not to influence the investor significantly; or

(iii) the system of taxation is such that taxes bear as heavily on capital as on income.

In these circumstances the yield required by the investor would depend on: —

(a) the security and regularity of the income;

(b) the security of the capital;

(c) the liquidity of the capital; and

(d) the costs of transfer, i.e., the costs of putting the capital in in the first instance and of taking it out subsequently.

Thus, the greater the security of capital and income, the greater the certainty of the income being received regularly, the greater the ease with which the investor can turn his investment into cash and the lower the costs of transfer, the lower will be the yield he requires.

Therefore, if investment D offered a guaranteed income payable at regular intervals, no possibility of loss of capital and the loan repayable in cash immediately on request at no cost to the investor, the investor would require the minimum yield necessary to induce him to allow the borrower to use his capital. If investment E offered the same terms as investment D except that six months' notice was required before the capital could be withdrawn, the investor would require a yield sufficiently higher than the minimum to offset this difference. If investment F offered the same terms as investment E except that there was some risk of fluctuation in, or non-payment sometimes of, the income, the investor would require a still higher yield.

Broadly speaking, therefore, in this imaginary situation the greater the risks the investor is required to take with his money and the greater the cost to him of lending it, the higher the rate of interest he will have to be paid in order to induce him to part with it.

Now this imaginary situation must be adjusted to make it accord more closely with actual conditions in recent years.

With regard to the first assumption, that of money maintaining its real value, this does not happen during periods of inflation. Thus, if an investor investing during a period of inflation is guaranteed a secure income of, say, £100 a year, if the value of the pound is halved in 10 years, his "secure" income will in 10 years' time have a real value of only £50 a year. So also if "security" of capital means merely that if he invests £1,000 now he can withdraw £1,000 when he wishes, the real value of his capital would be halved over a period of 10 years. If, in these circumstances, 10 per cent, that is an income of £100 a year from an investment of £1,000, is a reasonable yield, the investor should be prepared to accept a lower rate of interest from an investment which will protect his capital and income from the erosion of inflation. Thus, he might be prepared to accept a yield of 5 per cent now on an investment of £1,000 if there is a reasonable chance that (i) the income of £50 a year now will have doubled to £100 a year in 10 years' time thus maintaining its real value, and (ii) that the capital of £1,000 will increase to £2,000 in 10 years' time thus maintaining its real value. An investment which offers the investor the opportunity of maintaining the real value of capital and income in this way is described as a "hedge against inflation".

The second and third assumptions for the imaginary situation related to the level and incidence of taxation. Until 1962 there was no tax on capital during life but there was a tax on capital on death, estate duty. Estate duty, which is still levied, may at its highest rate take 80 per cent of the deceased's estate. In this situation there was a strong incentive to prefer capital gains to income during life but to avoid the accumulation of capital in the hands of one person in such a way as to render it liable for estate duty at a high rate on death. As death is an uncertain occurrence, nice judgements were required.

The Finance Act, 1962, introduced a short-term capital gains tax for gains realised within three years in the case of landed property and six months in the case of other investments. Such short-term gains were subjected to income tax and not to a special capital tax.

The Finance Act, 1965, introduced a long term capital gains tax and modified the short-term gains provisions of the 1962 Act. The main modification to be noted here is the time for realisation of short-term gains which was made 12 months. Capital gains realised after 12 months, with the exception of those arising from development value of landed property, were subjected to long-term gains tax at a rate for individuals of 30 per cent.

Section 55 of the Finance Act, 1971, abolished short-term capital gains tax.

Gains arising from the development value of landed property were subject to betterment levy under the provisions of the Land Commission Act, 1967, but this was abolished as from 22 July, 1970, and such gains are now treated as other capital gains.

The present standard rate of income tax is 38·75 per cent and individuals with incomes exceeding £2,000 may be obliged to pay an additional income tax known as surtax which, at its highest rate, is 50p in the £. Thus, in the extreme case, a gross addition of £1 to a high income could after deduction of income tax and surtax, provide the individual with a net increase of only 11·25p.

Thus, to revert to the last example, if the investor is offered a reasonable change of his capital of £1,000 not just maintaining its real value in the period of 10 years, but of it appreciating in real value, he would be prepared to accept now a yield lower than 5 per cent.

The four principles governing yields enumerated above, adapted to meet conditions of inflation and high income taxation have, in fact, governed yields in the investment market in this country in recent years. This is apparent on examination of yields from different types of security during this period. British Government securities, which in times of stable prices and moderate taxation have been described as the "ideal security" offering the minimum yield because they are practically riskless, are at the time of writing yielding about 9 per cent, which is higher than the yield on many ordinary shares. There are many reasons for the fall in price, and consequent increase in yield, of Government securities, but one of the most important is that neither the capital invested in them nor the income issuing from them is secure in real terms. The lower yields on ordinary shares in, for example, many industrial concerns and property companies, can be accounted for by the security in real terms which they offer and, in many cases, the probability of substantial capital appreciation. On the other hand the yields from shares in tea and rubber companies are normally well in excess of those from Government securities, reflecting the insecurity of this type of company due to the instability of the Far East where their main capital assets are situated.

## 4. YIELDS FROM LANDED PROPERTY INVESTMENTS

A prospective investor in landed property will be aware of the other forms of investment available and of the yields he can expect from them. He will, therefore, judge the yield he requires from a landed property investment by comparison with the yields from other types of investment such as insurance and stocks and shares. The principles governing yields discussed in Section 3 are, therefore, applicable to landed property in the same way as to other forms of investments. However, landed property has certain special features which will be considered before looking at the yields from the main types of landed property.

Firstly, there is the question of management. The investor has no management problems with, for example, Government securities as he will receive his income by cheque every six months. With most types of landed property, however, some management is involved. The actual cost of management of landed property is allowed for in computing the net income[1] but, where, in addition to being costly, management is also troublesome, the investor will require a higher yield to compensate for this.

The second special feature of landed property relates to liquidity of capital and costs of transfer. Ordinary shares, for example, can normally be bought or sold through a stock exchange very rapidly and the transfer costs are a very small percentage of the capital involved. A transaction in landed property, however, is normally a fairly lengthy process and the costs of transfer, mainly legal fees and stamp duty, are high.

The last of the special features is legislation. Legislation does, of course, impinge on many types of investment but its effects, direct or indirect, on landed property are frequently of major significance. The Rent Acts and the Town and Country Planning Act, provide excellent examples. The former limit the amount of rent which can be charged for certain categories of dwelling-house and the latter severely restricts the uses to which a property can be put.

---

[1] See Chapter 7

There is more than one type of interest in landed property[2] and different interests in the same property may have different yields. The yields considered below are from freehold interests in the type of property concerned. It is important to note that the yields given merely indicate the appropriate range for the particular type of property at the time of writing. The general level of yields from all types of investment or from landed property investments only may change and there are often substantial variations between yields from landed property investments of the same type. The age and condition of the buildings are also factors which influence the yield. Other things being equal, the older the building and the poorer the condition of it, the higher will be the yield. This information cannot, therefore, be applied to actual valuations where the yield must be determined in accordance with market information.

*Agricultural Land.* Analysis of market transactions shows an enormous variation in yields but a normal range is 3 to 5 per cent. Farms are normally a good investment with special tax advantages. For reasons which are considered in Chapter 11 rents passing on many farms are below the full rental values, thus an investor has scope to secure his income in real terms by increasing the rent. Government support of the agricultural industry also gives security to both capital and income. There are numerous income tax concessions in relation to agricultural properties although two important concessions were terminated by the Finance Act, 1960. The first related to the setting off of losses made in a business against future profits whether or not the business was being run on a commercial basis and the second to the setting off of losses in agriculture against profits from another type of business. Estate duty on agricultural properties is charged at 45 per cent below the rate applicable to other types of property.

The possibility of Britain entering the Common Market is another factor to be borne in mind, particularly in relation to agricultural properties.

*Shops.* A normal range of yields is 7 to 10 per cent, the lower figure being applicable to shops in first-class positions occupied by national retail organisations and the higher to shops in secondary positions occupied by small traders. Position and type of tenant are vital factors in judging a shop as an investment and these matters are dealt with in detail in Chapter 14. The substantial increase in the volume of retail trading in recent years has has been a vital factor in determining yields from shop investments. The high level of demand for shops resulting from this has kept rents moving upwards at a sufficient rate to secure income and capital in real terms and, indeed, in many cases to show a substantial appreciation.

---

[2] See Chapter 4.

*Offices.* A normal range of yields is from 7 to 9 per cent. The lowest yield would be expected from a modern block let to a single tenant who shoulders the management burden. The same block let in suites where the owner is responsible for a considerable amount of management, including the provisions of such services as lifts and central heating, would yield a slightly higher rate, say 7½ per cent. The highest yield would be expected from an old block let in suites and lacking modern amenities. As is apparent from the low yield, good office property is considered a good invest-ment. In areas where the demand for modern accommodation has been running at a high level for a number of years, rents have been increasing at a sufficient rate to provide a secure invest-ment in real terms with a substantial appreciation.

*Factories.* Until recent years factories have not been a popular investment and the range of yields, 7 to 12 per cent, to some extent reflects past unpopularity. Many factories, unlike most shops and offices, are suited only to the purposes of a single trade or a small range of trades. If such a factory becomes vacant the number of prospective tenants is severely restricted, thus the income is insecure. The majority of factories built since 1945 have been single storey buildings suitable for a wide range of trades and the demand in most areas for factories of this type has been sufficient to keep rents moving upwards with the same results as on shops and modern offices.

There are certain income tax concessions on industrial properties by way of capital allowances and, in a limited range of cases, an estate duty concession the same as that on agricultural properties can be obtained.

*Residential Properties.* This expression covers a very wide range of properties and some sub-classification is required before even the broadest generalisation on yields can be made.

With the tenement type of residential property the yield is high, up to about 14 per cent. Properties of this type will frequently be rent restricted, there is a great deal of legislation imposing onerous obligations on owners relating to repair, cleanliness and other matters, and many tenants may be unreliable in payment of rent. Capital and income are not, therefore, secure in any terms, income may not be regular and the property may be difficult to sell.

Blocks of flats, on the other hand, particularly if they are modern, are a good investment and will yield about 8 per cent.

The majority of houses are either local authority owned or owner-occupied but a large number of smaller houses are held for investment purposes and yield in the range, 6 to 12 per cent. These smaller houses are normally of a sufficiently low rateable value to be rent restricted and it is this factor of rent restriction which in some cases justifies the low yield. If a tenant, who is enjoying occupation of this type of house at a low statutorily controlled rent, leaves the house, prospective occupiers will be prepared to pay the full market value with vacant possession. This is invariably well in excess of the value while the property is controlled, providing the owner with a substantial capital appreciation. The higher yields will be obtained in the case of the older and poorer types of house.

*Ground Rents.* A ground rent is a rent reserved under a building lease in respect of the bare land without buildings. If buildings have been erected on the land since the lease was granted the ground rent is called a secured ground rent but until buildings erected it is called an unsecured ground rent. Building leases are normally granted for a long term, 99 years being fairly common.

Secured ground rents where the lease has many years to run yield in the range 7 to 14 per cent. Where the rent is a fixed amount throughout the term it is comparable in many ways with Government securities and the yield will be similar to, but slightly higher than, that on 2½ per cent Consols. The investor obtains better security in real terms where the lease provides for upward revision of the rent at reasonable intervals and such an investment would provide a lower yield than where the rent is a fixed amount. The amount of the rent is also a significant factor. A single rent of a few pounds may be unsaleable unless the occupier is in the market.

The yield on unsecured ground rents of about 8 per cent is an exception to the general rule that yields on landed property are those appropriate to long-term securities. The cost to a developer of obtaining the necessary short-term finance for the period between taking the land and completing development on it is the determining factor.

## 5. Changes in Interest Rates

The landed property investment market normally responds to change less rapidly than other investment markets. The reason for this is probably the length of time taken to transfer ownership and the high costs of transfer. If, for example, circumstances are such that it is felt desirable to hold a greater proportion of assets in cash than hitherto, Stock Exchange securities can be realised immediately even if some loss is incurred. Landed property, however, cannot be realised with anything like the same speed. If, therefore, the change in preference is temporary the landed property investment market may remain unmoved while other markets are reacting violently.

The landed property investment market will respond to longer term changes. Thus, yields on landed property are now generally higher than they were during the post-1945 "cheap money" era.

# Chapter 3

## Rental Value and Net Income

### 1. GENERALLY

IN ORDER to value a property by the investment method, two things must be known. Firstly, the net income which the property will produce and secondly, the rate of interest appropriate to the property from which the Years' Purchase can be found. The factors determining the yields from investments in landed property were discussed in Chapter 2. This Chapter is concerned with the factors affecting net income and the methods used in ascertaining it.

### 2. NET INCOME

Many types of property are let on terms which require the landlord to bear the cost of certain outgoings such as repairs and rates. To arrive at the net income in such a case the outgoings must be deducted from the rent paid.[1]

If the tenant undertakes to bear the cost of all outgoings whatsoever with the exception of income tax, which is a general charge on all incomes whatever their source, the rent is known as "net rent". "Net rental value" is the rent which may reasonably be expected to be obtained in the open market on the same terms as "net rent".

At this stage, therefore, where reference is made to "rent" it is to be understood that "net rent" is intended.

Rent may be defined as "an annual or periodic payment for the use of land or of land and buildings." In fixing the rental value of a property a valuer is largely influenced in practice by the evidence he can find of rents actually paid, not only for the property being valued, but also for comparable properties in the same district. But it is essential that he should appreciate the economic factors which govern those rents. Knowledge of economic factors may not be necessary for the immediate purpose of his valuation, but it is vital in understanding fluctuations in rental value, and in advising on the reasonableness or otherwise of existing rents and market prices.

---

[1] The usual outgoings in connection with land and buildings are outlined in Chapter 7 and further considered in the Chapters dealing with particular types of property.

### 3. Economic Factors Affecting Rent

(a) *Supply and Demand.*—In Chapter 1 it was observed that the general laws of supply and demand govern capital values and that value is not an intrinsic characteristic.

Variations in capital value may be due either to changes in rental value or to changes in the return that may be expected from a particular type of investment. Either or both of these factors may operate at the same time.

For example, shops in an improving position may increase in rental value over a period of years. At the same time, there may be changes in the investment market which cause that particular type of security to be less well regarded; a higher yield will be expected and consequently a lower Years' Purchase will have to be applied to the net rent to arrive at the capital value. The net result may be that whilst the rental value has increased, the capital value remains unchanged.

*Example.*—

| | | | | |
|---|---|---|---|---|
| Rental Value today... | £1,000 | Rental Value 5 years hence ... ... | £1,400 |
| Years' Purchase (Y.P.) to show 7% yield... | 14 | Years' Purchase (Y.P.) to show 10% yield... | 10 |
| Capital Value ... | £14,000 | Capital Value ... | £14,000 |

Both changes in rental value and changes in the yield required from property investments are the result of the operation of the laws of supply and demand. In the first case the influence of demand and supply is on the income which the property can produce. In the second case it is on the Years' Purchase which investors will give for the right to receive that income. In either case any variation has a direct bearing on the capital value of the property.

In this Chapter we are concerned with the influence of supply and demand on *rental value*.

When we say that value depends on supply and demand, it must be remembered that demand means the *effective* demand at a given price. Many people may desire a certain property or type of property, but all or many of them may be unwilling to satisfy that desire if the price is above the level which in money value expresses the strength of their desire.

In a similar way, supply means the *effective* supply at a given price in the market, not the total of a particular type of property in existence. In a particular shopping centre there may be perhaps thirty shops of a very similar type; of these the owners of twenty do not wish to let. The effective supply consists of the other ten shops whose owners are willing to let.

The demand is derived from potential tenants who have weighed the advantages and disadvantages of the shops offered against other properties elsewhere.

The prevailing level of rents will be determined by the inter-action of supply and demand, or what is referred to as the "higgling of the market." If there is a large or increasing demand for a certain type of property, rents are likely to increase; if the demand is a falling one, rents will diminish.

As pointed out in Chapter 1, in two important respects landed property can be distinguished from other types of commodity in that the supply of land is to a large extent a fixed one and that in the case of buildings supply may respond only slowly to changes in demand.

(b) *Demand Factors.*—It is obvious that the factor of the greatest importance in fixing rent is demand.

The demand for land and buildings is a basic one in human society, as it derives from two essential needs of the community: —

(i) The need for living accommodation.
(ii) The need for land, or land and buildings, for industrial and commercial enterprise—including the agricultural industry.

The demand for any particular property, or for a particular class of property, will be influenced by a number of factors, which it will be convenient to consider under appropriate headings.

*General Level of Prosperity.*—This is perhaps the most important of the factors governing demand.

When times are good and business is thriving, values will tend to increase. There will be a demand for additional accommodation for new and expanding enterprises. There will be a corresponding increase in the money available for new and improved housing accommodation and for additional amenities in connection therewith.

The increase in rental values will not necessarily be exactly comparable to the increase in the general standard of living. It may not apply to all types of property and its extent may vary in different parts of the country owing to the influence of other factors.

Experience in this and other countries has shown, however, that rental values generally show a steady upward tendency in times of increasing prosperity.

*Population Changes.*—Times of increasing prosperity have in the past been associated with the factor of a growing population.

The supply of land being limited, it is obvious that an increase in demand due to increased prosperity or increase of population will tend to increase values. On the other hand, when these causes cease to operate or diminish in intensity values will tend to fall.

Increase in population will, in the first place, influence the demand for housing, but indirectly will affect many other types of property the need for which is dependent upon the population in the locality —as, for instance, retail shops.

Movements of population may produce locally the same effect on rental values as a general increase or decrease. In Southern England since 1945 the general upward movement of rents due partly to increasing local populations and the high level of prosperity, has been accelerated by migration from the North.

*Changes in Character of Demand.*—Demand, in addition to being variable in quantity, may vary in quality. Associated with an increase in the standard of living, there is a change in the character of the demand for many types of property.

With regard to housing accommodation, many amenities are taken for granted today which thirty years ago would have been regarded as refinements only to be expected in the highest class of residence.

Similar factors operate in relation to industrial and commercial properties. The increased standard of factory legislation or technical improvements in the layout, design and equipment of buildings for such purposes tend to cause many buildings to become obsolete and so diminish the rental value.

*Rent as a Proportion of Income.*—In relation to residential property, the rent paid may be expressed as a proportion of the income of the family occupying the property. It is obvious that in a free market, the general level of rents for a particular type of living accommodation will be related to the general level of income of the type of person occupying that accommodation. There will, of course, be substantial variations in individual cases owing to different views on the relative importance of living accommodation, motor cars and television sets. However, in this country, there is not, and has not been for many years, a free market in living accommodation to rent. Thus, although statistics are available showing the relationship between rent and income, they are of little assistance to the valuer even as background information.

There is, however, a free market in residential properties for sale and a useful parallel today in relation to capital, not rental, values is that building societies in determining an appropriate mortgage loan assume that an individual should not pay more than one-quarter of his income on mortgage repayments plus rates.

*Rent as a Proportion of the Profit Margin.*—Both commercial or industrial properties and land used for farming are occupied as a rule by tenants who expect to make a profit out of their occupation, and that expectation of profit will determine the rent that such a tenant is prepared to pay.

Out of his gross earnings, he has first to meet his expenses; from the gross profit that is left, he will require remuneration for his own labour, and interest on the capital that he has to provide; the balance that is left is the margin that the tenant is prepared to pay in rent and rates. Obviously, no hard and fast rule can be laid down as to the proportion which rent will form of profit, but the expectation of profit is the primary cause of the tenant's demand and the total amount of rent and rates he will be prepared to pay will be influenced by this estimate of the future trend of his receipts and expenses and the profit he requires for himself.

*Competitive Demand.*—Certain types of premises may be adapted for use by more than one trade or for more than one purpose, and there will be a potential demand from a larger number of possible tenants. For instance, a block of property in a convenient position in a large town may be suitable either as offices or for light industrial purposes. In a particular locality the demand for office accommodation and the rent that can consequently be expected to be paid for that purpose may be more, or less, than the demand, and the consequent rent that can be expected, for industrial purposes.

In a free market it would be expected that the enterprise yielding the largest margin out of profits for the payment of rent would obtain the use of the premises. For where there are competing demands for various purposes properties will tend to be put to the most profitable use. In practice the operation of this rule may be affected by the fact that the use to which the property may be put will probably be restricted by town planning legislation.

(c) *Supply Factors.*—It has already been stated that land differs from other commodities in being to a large extent fixed in amount. This limit on the amount of land available is the most important of those factors which govern supply.

*Limitation of Supply.*—At any one time there will be in the country a certain quantity of land suitable for agricultural purposes and a certain quantity of accommodation suitable for industrial, commercial and residential purposes.

If these quantities were entirely static, the rents would be affected only by changes in demand. In fact, they are not static, but respond, although slowly, to changes in demand. There is, ultimately, only a certain quantity of land available for all purposes, but increase in demand will cause changes in the use to which land is put.

In agriculture, conditions of increasing prosperity will bring into cultivation additional land which previously it was not profitable to work. Conversely, in bad times land will go out of cultivation and revert to waste land. Similarly, increasing demand will render it profitable for additional accommodation to be built for commercial and residential uses and the supply of accommodation will be increased by new buildings until the demand is satisfied. Both of these statements assume that the market is working freely. In fact, at the present time, the Government is committed to supporting agriculture in bad times; thus, land which might have gone out of use may continue to be used although the use is uneconomic. Also in relation to building for residential use, there is at present in the London area a large unsatisfied demand for living accommodation. This demand can be met by new building only to the extent that land is granted consent for residential development.

The increase in rents that would occur if the supply remained unchanged will be modified by additions to the supply. But it was pointed out in Chapter 1 that adjustments in the supply of land and buildings are necessarily made slowly in comparison with other commodities.

Where there is a tendency for the demand to fall, the supply will not adjust itself very quickly; building operations may well continue beyond the peak of the demand period and some time may elapse before the expansion in building work is checked by a fall in demand.

It would enlarge the scope of this book unduly to discuss the various causes of inelasticity in supply. But the principal ones are probably—(i) the fact that building development is a long-term enterprise, i.e., one where the period between the initiation of a scheme and completion of the product is comparatively lengthy; and (ii) the difficulty involved in endeavouring to forecast demand in any locality.

The above considerations introduce the subject of what economists call " marginal land."

In the instance given of land being brought into cultivation for agricultural purposes, there will come a point where land is only just worth the trouble of cultivation. Its situation, fertility or other factors will render it just possible for the profit margin available as a result of cultivation to recoup the tenant for his enterprise and for the use of his capital. There will, however, be no margin for rent. This will be " no-rent " land or marginal land.

It is obvious that land better adapted for its purpose will be used first and yield a rent, but that also, with increasing demand, the margin will be pushed farther out and land previously not worth cultivation will come into use.

Similar considerations will apply to other types of property. For instance, there will be marginal land in connection with building development. A piece of land may be so situated that if a house is built on it, the rent likely to be obtained will just cover interest on the cost of construction, but leave no balance for the land. With a growth of development, the margin will spread outwards, the rent likely to be obtained for the house will increase, and the land will yield a rent.

Land may have reached its optimum value for one purpose and be marginal land for another purpose. For example, land in the vicinity of a town may have a high rental value for market garden purposes and have reached its maximum utility for agricultural purposes. For building purposes it may be unripe for development—in other words, " sub-marginal "—or it may be capable of development, but incapable of yielding a building rent—in other words, "marginal." Such a case is rare today.

From the practical point of view, it is unlikely that land will be developed immediately it appears to have improved a little beyond its marginal point. Some margin of error in the forecast of demand will have to be allowed for, and no prudent developer would be likely to embark on development unless there is reasonable prospect of profit.

*Relation of Cost to Supply.*—Another factor which may influence supply is the question of cost.

If, at any time, values as determined by market conditions are less than cost, the provision of new buildings will be checked, or may even cease, and building will not recommence until the disparity is removed.

Thus, in the years immediately preceding the 1939–45 war, there was a considerable increase in the number of residential flats in and around London. In some areas the demand appeared to have been overtaken by supply and rents had fallen. At the same time costs had increased, and in such areas it was no longer very profitable to build flats. There was, accordingly, a contraction in the rate cf building.

The disparity which may exist at any time between cost and value may be subsequently removed either by a reduction in cost or by an increase in demand. Over a very long period it might even be modified by the non-replacement of obsolete buildings, which might in time bring about an excess of demand over supply and a consequent increase in value.

## 4. DETERMINATION OF RENTAL VALUE

(a) *Generally.*—It has already been pointed out that in estimating the capital value of a property from an investment point of view the valuer must usually first determine its rental value.

In doing so he will have regard to the trend of values in the locality and to those general factors affecting rent which were considered in Section 3 of this Chapter. The latter will form, as it were, the general background of his valuation, although he may not be concerned to investigate in detail all the points referred to when dealing with an individual property.

The two factors most likely to influence his judgment are—

(i) the rents paid for other similar properties, and

(ii) the rent, if any, at which the property itself is let.

In most cases it will be assumed that the rental value at the time when the valuation is made—and consequently the net income from the property—will continue unchanged in the future. Experience proves that this is not necessarily the case and changes in value may result in the rent rising or falling over a period. But, in the absence of special factors indicating an abnormal future change in rental value, the assumption is reasonable, as normal changes either upwards or downwards are reflected in the rate per cent which an investment is expected to yield.

For example, in the case of offices let at inclusive rents, where there may in the future be some variation in the amount of the outgoings or changes in the actual rents, and no provision is made in the lease or leases for increases to be passed on to the tenants, these risks are met by using a higher rate per cent as the basis of valuation than would be used for such properties let on lease for a long term at exclusive rents. Where the rent of a property appears to be well secured and likely to be below the rental value in the future, the rate per cent which the investment is expected to yield is correspondingly reduced.

Future variations in rental value may sometimes arise from the fact that the premises producing the income may be old, so that it may be anticipated that their useful life is limited. Together with the likelihood of a fall in rental value there may be a possibility that in the future considerable expense may be incurred either in rebuilding or in modernisation. In such cases the rate per cent which the investment will be expected to yield will be increased and the Years' Purchase to be applied to the net income correspondingly reduced.

In general, therefore, it may be said that if rental value is likely to increase, a higher Years' Purchase will be applied; while if there is a doubt of the present level of rent being maintained, the Years' Purchase will be reduced to cover the risk.

Where a future change in rental value is reasonably certain it should, of course, be taken into account by a variation in the net rent to which the Years' Purchase is to be applied. For example, a valuation may be required of a shop which is offered for sale freehold subject to a lease being granted to an intending lessee on terms which have been agreed. These terms provide for an increase in rent every seven years. It has been ascertained that many similar shops in the immediate vicinity are let on leases for 7, 14 and 21 years with a provision for a substantial increase in the rents at the end of each 7 year period. Assuming that the position is an improving one and that the valuer is satisfied that such increasing rents are justified, he will be correct in assuming that the shop with which he is dealing can be let on similar terms, and he will take future increases in rent into account in preparing his valuation.

The method of dealing with such varying incomes from property will be considered in detail in Chapter 6.

(b) *Basis of the Rent actually paid.*—Where premises are let at a rent and the letting is a recent one, the rent actually paid is usually the best possible evidence of rental value.

But the valuer should always check this rent with the prevailing rents for similar properties in the vicinity or, where comparison with neighbouring properties is for some reason difficult, with the rents paid for similar properties in comparable positions elsewhere.

There are many reasons why the rent paid for a property may be less than the rental value. For instance, a premium may have been paid for the lease, or the lease may have been granted in consideration of the surrender of the unexpired term of a previous lease. The lessee may have covenanted to carry out improvements to the premises or to forgo compensation due to him from the landlord. In many cases the rental value may have increased since the existing lease was granted. Differences between rent paid and rental value may also be accounted for by the relationship between lessor and lessee, e.g., father to son.

If, as a result of the valuer's investigations, he is satisfied that the actual rent paid is a fair one, he will adopt it as the basis of his valuation, will ascertain what outgoings, if any, are borne by the landlord and by making a deduction in respect thereof will arrive at net rental value.

If, in his opinion, the true rental value exceeds the rent paid under the existing lease his valuation will be made in two stages. The first stage will be the capitalisation of the present net income for the remainder of the term at a rate of interest lower than the normal to allow for the increased security. The second stage will be the capitalisation of the full rental value after the end of the term at the full rate of interest appropriate to the property.

If, on the other hand, he considers that the rent fixed by the present lease or tenancy is in excess of the true rental value, he will have to allow for the fact that the tenant, at the first opportunity, may refuse to continue the tenancy at the present rent, and also for the possible risk, in the case of business premises, that the tenant may fail and that the premises will remain vacant until a new tenant can be found.

As a general rule, any excess of actual rent over estimated fair rental value may be regarded as indicating a certain lack of security in the income from the property. But it must be borne in mind that rent is secured not only by the value of the premises but also by the tenant's covenant to pay, and a valuer may sometimes be justified in regarding the tenant's covenant as adequate security for a rent in excess of true rental value.

An example of such cases is where a shop is let on long lease to some such substantial concern as one of the large multiple stores. Here, the value of the goodwill the tenants have created will make them reluctant to terminate the tenancy, even if they have the right to do so by a break in the lease. Where there is no such break, they will in any case be bound by their covenant to pay. Since rent is a first charge, ranking even before debenture interest, and since such a concern will have ample financial resources behind it, the security of the income is assured.

(c) *Comparison of Rents.*—It has been suggested that the actual rent paid should be checked by comparison with the general level of values in the district. Not only is this desirable where the rent is considered to be *prima facie* a fair one, but it is obviously essential where premises are vacant or let on old leases at rents considerably below true rental value.

In such circumstances the valuer has to rely upon the evidence provided by the actual letting of other similar properties. His skill and judgment come into play in estimating the rental value of the premises under consideration in the light of such evidence. He must have regard not only to the rents of other properties that are let, but also to the dates when the rents were fixed, to the age and condition of the buildings as compared with that with which he is concerned, and to the amount of similar accommodation in the vicinity to be let or sold.

In many cases, as for instance similar shops in a parade, it may be a fairly simple matter to compare an unlet property with several that are let and to assume, for example, that since the latter command a rent of £500 a year on lease it is reasonable to assume the same rental value for the shop under consideration which is similar to them in all respects.

But where the vacant premises are more extensive and there are differences of planning and accommodation to be taken into account in comparing them with other similar properties, it is necessary to reduce rents to the basis of some convenient " unit of comparison " which will vary according to the type of property under consideration.

For example, it may be desired to ascertain the rental value of a factory having a total floor space of 1000 square metres (m²). Analysis of the rents of other similar factories in the neighbourhood reveals that factories with an area of 500 m², or thereabouts, are let at rents equivalent to £3 per m² of floor space, whereas other factories with an area of 2000 m², or thereabouts, are let at rents of £2 per m² of floor space. After giving consideration to the situation, the building and all other relevant factors, it may be reasonable to assume that the rental value of the factory in question should be calculated on a basis of £2·50 per m² of floor space.

The unit chosen for comparison in the past varied throughout the country. In the north of England it was usual to find valuers using the unit of a square yard, while sometimes the unit chosen was a "square" i.e., 10 ft. × 10 ft. In the south a square foot was used.

The method of measuring also varies. Thus, some valuers exclude the areas occupied by lavatories, corridors, etc.; others work on external measurements of buildings, some including the space occupied by walls, others not. To avoid ambiguity, the basis employed should always be given when quoting the area of a building—e.g., 1040 m² of effective working floor space. It is of course vital that analysis of rentals of similar properties and the subsequent calculation to find rental value of the property under consideration should be on the same basis.

When quoting rental figures the amount per annum should always be qualified by reference to such terms of the lease as the liability for rates, repairs and insurances, and by reference to the length of the term. The date of the valuation should also be given. For example, if the rental value of premises is reported at £500 per annum, this will mean little to the recipient. The report should state that the rental value " at the present time is at or about £500 per annum (five hundred pounds per annum) on lease for a term of seven years on the assumption that the lessee will be responsible for all repairs and outgoings including fire insurance premium." Reference to a rent or rental value in terms of amount per unit is always unwise.

In making comparisons, it must be remembered that the terms of the lettings of different classes of property vary considerably. It is convenient, therefore, to compare similar premises on the basis of rents on the terms usually applicable to that type of property. Good shop property is usually let on terms where the tenant is liable for all outgoings including rates, repairs and insurance. Thus, net rents are compared on this type of property. With blocks of offices let in suites, however, the tenant is usually liable for internal repairs to the suite and rates and the landlord for external repairs, repairs to common parts and insurance. The landlord provides services such as lifts, central heating and porters, but these are dealt with separately by means of a service charge on the tenants. Thus, rents used for comparing different suites of offices would be inclusive of external repairs, repairs to common parts and insurance. Having arrived at the rental value of the office block on this basis, the net income would be arrived at by deducting the outgoings which are included in the rents and for which the landlord is liable.

*Example.*—A prospective tenant of a suite of offices on the fourth floor of a modern building with a total floor space of 250 m² requires advice on the rent which should be paid on a seven years' lease.

The tenant will be responsible for rates and internal repairs to the suite. The landlord will be responsible for external repairs, repairs to common parts and insurance. Adequate services are provided, for which a reasonable additional charge will be made.

The following particulars are available of other recent lettings on the same terms in similar buildings, all of suites of rooms:

| Floor | Area in m² | Rent £ | Rent £ per m² |
|-------|-----------|--------|---------------|
| 1st   | 200       | 3,200  | £16           |
|       | 300       | 4,500  | £15           |
| 2nd   | 150       | 1,800  | £12           |
| 3rd   | 160       | 2,000  | £12·50        |
| 5th   | 400       | 5,000  | £12·50        |
| 6th   | 500       | 6,500  | £13           |
| 7th   | 200       | 2,500  | £12·50        |

*Estimate of Rent Payable.*—As the particulars relate to lettings on the same terms as that proposed, it is unnecessary for purposes of comparison to consider the outgoings borne by the landlord or to arrive at net rental values.

The broad picture which emerges from the evidence is that the highest rents are paid on the 1st floor but thereafter, the rents are approximately the same. This is what would be expected in modern buildings with adequate high speed lifts. In older buildings with inadequate lifts or no lifts, the higher the floor the lower the rent. The inconsistencies in the rents may be due merely to market imperfections or to differences in light or noise.

Subject to an inspection of the offices under consideration so that due weight can be given to any differences in quality and amenities, a reasonable rent would appear to be, say, £12·50 per m² or £3,125 per annum.

The different methods used in practice for fixing rent by comparison are referred to in more detail in later chapters dealing with various classes of property.

(*d*) *Rent in relation to Cost.*—A careful analysis of rent will show that, except in the case of undeveloped land, it is made up of two things—(i) an annual payment for the use of the land itself, and (ii) an annual payment for the use of capital expended on it in the form of buildings, improvements, etc.

This aspect of rent is seldom consciously present in the mind of either landlord or tenant. A prospective tenant, for instance, thinks of the house or shop he proposes to occupy in terms of land and buildings combined. The land will give him the advantages attaching to a certain situation; the buildings will provide him with accommodation in the form of rooms, floor space, etc. He thinks of the rent as the annual sum it is worth his while to pay for that amount and type of accommodation in that particular situation. But the valuer has from time to time to think in terms of (i) the rental value of the land, and (ii) the rental value of the buildings, etc., upon it.

That part of the rent which represents a payment for the use of buildings and other improvements should in normal cases consist of a reasonable return by way of interest on the owner's capital expenditure. What may be regarded as a reasonable return will depend upon the type of property in which the capital is sunk. But as between two properties of the same type there is likely to be little variation in the rate of interest expected.

*Example.*—A owns two pieces of land, one in a good shopping street in the centre of a small provincial town and one in a somewhat inferior position. On both these sites he has erected shop premises costing £6,000.

The first shop is leased for 14 years at a net rent of £800. The second is leased on the same terms at £600. Analyse these rents.

*Analysis.*

It is probable that the owner will expect approximately the same rate of interest from capital expended on either site. Assuming 8 per cent to be a fair return in the circumstances, that part of the rent which represents a payment for the use of the building will in both cases be £480. Then:—

*Shop No.* 1.

| | |
|---|---:|
| Net Rack Rent　　...　　...　　...　　... | £800 |
| Payment for use of buildings, 8% on £6,000... | 480 |
| *Payment for use of land* | £320 |

*Shop No. 2.*

| | | | | | |
|---|---|---|---|---|---|
| Net Rack Rent | ... | ... | ... | ... | £600 |
| Payment for use of buildings, 8 % on £6,000... | | | | | 480 |

*Payment for use of land*          £120

It is plain that the difference in rental between the two shops lies in the value of the land. The higher rent of the first shop is due to the advantage of situation of site No. 1, as compared with site No. 2, and its effect on the profits which prospective tenants are likely to make from their occupation of the premises.

A possible method of estimating the rent of a property is to reverse the process shown in the above analysis and to add to the rental value of the site a fair percentage on the cost of any buildings, etc., erected on it.

Where freehold land has been purchased, the usual practice is to take a percentage—say 7 per cent—on the purchase price. For instance, assume that in the above example site No. 1 was bought for £4,500, the rack rent might be estimated as follows:—

7 % on £4,500 (value of land)          — £315

8 % on £6,000 (cost of buildings)      — £480

*Net Rack Rent* — £795

The use of this method requires considerable care and experience. A price paid or a rent fixed for land some years ago may be misleading as a guide to its present rental value. The cost of building may have altered considerably since the premises were erected; also capital spent on buildings is not always laid out in the manner likely to give the best return. In any case, the method is an estimate of what the landlord may expect the property to be worth, whereas rents are finally determined by what prospective tenants are able and willing to pay.

For all these reasons it is very desirable that an estimate of rent based on a percentage of the cost of land and buildings should be checked where possible by comparison with rents actually paid for other similar buildings.

This method of estimating rental value is probably more often resorted to in valuing for rating than for other purposes.

## 5. EFFECT OF CAPITAL IMPROVEMENTS ON RENTAL VALUE

Since, in most cases, an owner is not likely to spend capital on his property unless he anticipates a fair return by way of increased rent, it is usually reasonable to assume that money spent on improvements or additions to a property will increase the rental value by an amount approximating to simple interest at a reasonable rate on the sum expended. The rate per cent at which the increase is calculated will naturally depend upon the type of property.

Since, however, the real test of rental value is not what the owner expects to obtain for his premises, but what tenants are prepared to pay for the accommodation offered, in practice any estimate of increased rental value should be carefully checked by comparison with the rents obtained for other premises to which similar additions or improvements have been made.

Capital expenditure is only likely to increase rental value where it is judicious and suited to the type of property in question. For example, a man may make additions or alterations to his house which are quite out of keeping with the general character of the neighbourhood and are designed solely to satisfy some personal whim or hobby. So long as he continues to occupy the premises he may consider he is getting an adequate return on his money in the shape of personal enjoyment, but there will be no increase in the rental value of the premises since the work is unlikely to appeal to the needs or tastes of prospective tenants.

Again, expenditure may be made with the sole object of benefiting the occupier's trade—as, for instance, where a manufacturer spends a considerable sum in adapting premises to the needs of his particular business. In this case the occupier may expect to see an adequate return on his capital in the form of increased profits, but it is unlikely that the expenditure will affect the rental value unless, of course, it is of a type which would appeal to any tenant of the class likely to occupy the premises—as, for instance, where property on a good shopping street is fitted up by the occupier with a new shop front or improved showrooms.

On the other hand, the increase in rental value due to capital expenditure may considerably exceed the normal rate of simple interest on the sum expended in those cases where the site has not hitherto been fully developed or where it is to some extent encumbered by obsolescent or unsuitable buildings. For example, a site in the business quarter of a flourishing town may be covered by old, ill-planned and inconvenient premises. If by a wise expenditure of capital the owner can improve these premises so as to make them worthy of their situation, he should secure an increase in rental value which will not only include a reasonable return on the capital sum expended, but also a certain amount of rental value which has been latent in the site and which will have been released by the development.

*Example.*—Somewhat old-fashioned premises on a good shopping street are let at a rent of £800, which is a fair one for the premises as they stand. The occupier, who has a long lease of the premises, proposes to spend £2,500 on a new shop front, additional showroom accommodation and other improvements.

These works will make the premises equal in every respect to adjoining shops which readily let at £1,100 p.a.

| | | |
|---|---:|---:|
| Probable rental after improvements | | £1,100 |
| Present rental value ... ... ... | £800 | |
| Normal return on capital expenditure of £2,500—8% on £2,500 ... | 200 | 1,000 |
| Increase in rent due to release of latent site value ... ... ... | —— | —— |
| | | £100 |

In this case the total increase in rental value (£300) represents a return of 12% on the capital sum expended.

Since rental value is determined by what tenants are prepared to pay for the accommodation offered, it follows that any capital expenditure on premises will have precisely the same effect on rental value whether the money is spent by the freeholder or by a lessee who has only a limited interest in the premises.

For instance, suppose that premises are worth £500 p.a. and the expenditure by the freeholder of £500 on improvements will increase the rental value to £550; a prospective tenant will certainly not pay more than £550 for identical premises next door where the same works have been carried out by a lessee whose term expires in thirty years' time.

Since, however, the lessee's interest in the premises will cease altogether when his lease runs out, the true annual cost of the improvement to him will be greater than the increased rent he can hope to obtain for it.

# Chapter 4

## Interests in Land

### 1. GENERALLY

THE TWO principal interests in land or land and buildings with which the valuer is concerned are known respectively as freehold and leasehold.

To the valuer the term freehold implies a property which the owner holds absolutely and in perpetuity, and of which he is either in physical possession or in receipt of rents arising from leases or tenancies which have been created out of the freehold interest.

In law the term freehold has a wider meaning and extends to entailed interests and interests for life. The legal term for the valuer's conception of freehold is "The fee simple absolute in possession."

In the following sections it will be convenient to consider first the position of the freeholder who is in physical possession of his property, and then to note the nature and incidence of the various types of leasehold interest which may be created out of the freehold. Later it will be explained how successive interests in property— "entailed interests"; "life interests"; "reversions and remainders" —may sometimes arise under wills or settlements.

### 2. FREEHOLDS

Freehold is the highest form of ownership known to English law. Under the Crown the freeholder is the absolute owner of the property, and is sometimes said to be able to do what he likes with his land, subject only to the law of the land and to the rights of others. His ownership of the property is a perpetual one—buildings may become worn out, the use and character of the property may change, but the land remains the permanent property of the freeholder and his successors.

As the freeholder is absolute owner of his property, he usually holds it without any payment in the nature of rent. But in some parts of the country freeholds will be found to be subject to annual payments known as "rentcharges," "fee farm rents" or "chief rents." These usually arise through a vendor of freehold property agreeing to accept a rentcharge usually in perpetuity but sometimes for a limited term in lieu of the whole, or sometimes part, of the full purchase price. Although the rentcharge owner has the right, in the event of non-payment, to enter and take the rents and profits of the

35

land until arrears are satisfied, a freehold subject to a charge of this kind still ranks in law as a fee simple absolute in possession.[1]  In most deeds creating such rentcharges there is a power of absolute re-entry where the rent has been in arrear for two years.

A rentcharge or fee farm rent will be treated as an outgoing in arriving at the net income of the freehold for valuation purposes; while the interest of the rentcharge owner will usually rank as an exceptionally well secured one, since the rentcharge is commonly a very small fraction of the net rental of the land and buildings on which it is secured, but it is subject to depreciation in real terms due to inflation.

The statement that the freeholder may do as he likes with his property implies that he may develop it, sell or transfer it, or create lesser interests in it, without the consent of any other person. But important modifications of these powers may be imposed (i) by the law of the land, and (ii) by the rights of others.

During a state of national emergency the Crown may be given the most drastic rights of user and possession over the property of its subjects, while even in normal times there are numerous Acts of Parliament whereby an owner can be forced to sell his land to Government departments, local authorities or statutory undertakings for various public purposes.  The freeholder's right to develop his land as he pleases is now subject to the necessity of first obtaining planning permission under the Town and Country Planning Act, 1962; Public Health Acts, Housing Acts, local Acts and building regulations may also restrict the erection or reconstruction of buildings or compel the owner to keep them in a state of good repair and sanitation.  Further, the Leasehold Reform Act, 1967, gives certain leaseholders of residential property the right to require the freeholder to sell his interest to them.

The freeholder's power to do as he likes with his property is further limited by the fact that in doing so he must not interfere with the natural rights of others as, for instance, by depriving his neighbour's land of support or polluting or diminishing the flow of a stream.  In some cases, too, a freeholder's control of his property is diminished by the fact that some other owner has acquired an easement over his property or is entitled to the benefit of covenants restricting the use of it.

It is beyond the scope of this book to deal in detail with the subject of easements.  But it may be stated briefly that an easement is in the nature of a curtailment of an owner's natural rights whereby he may be obliged to submit to some use of his land by another owner or to refrain from some use of it himself.  Thus, a neighbouring owner may have a right of way across the freeholder's

---

[1] Law of Property (Amendment) Act, 1926, Schedule.

land, or an easement of light attached to adjoining buildings may prevent the freeholder from so building on his land as seriously to diminish the access of light to the windows in that building.

On the other hand, the freeholder may enjoy easements or other rights over the land of another which increase the value of his own land, or he may benefit from restrictive covenants imposed on adjoining land.

The question of restrictive covenants will be considered in more detail in a later Section of this Chapter.

The power of the freeholder to create lesser interests in the property leads to the consideration of tenancies and leases. It commonly happens that the freeholder, instead of occupying the property himself, grants the exclusive possession of the premises to another for a certain period, usually in consideration of the payment of rent.

Such a letting may be for quite a short period—yearly, monthly or weekly—the tenancy continuing indefinitely until terminated by notice from either side. Or it may be for any definite period of years, ranging from the three-yearly " agreement " to the 99 or 999 years' building lease.

The term " lease " really extends to all lettings passing an estate or interest in land, by whatever means the letting may be made, and for whatever period the lease is granted. But in the case of short-term tenancies or leases the lessee seldom has any valuable interest in the property owing to the shortness of his term and the fact that he is usually paying the full rental value which the premises are worth. The valuation of leasehold interests is therefore usually confined to those cases where property is leased for an appreciable term of years and where the rent reserved under the lease is less than the rental value, so that the lessee is enjoying a " profit rent " from his possession of the property.

Before considering such cases we may usefully remind ourselves of the position, from a valuation point of view, of the freeholder who has created some lesser interest out of his freehold estate.

A freeholder who grants leases or tenancies retains the right at common law to regain physical possession of his property when these leases or tenancies come to an end. This is known as his " reversion." It has already been indicated in Chapter 3 that rents reserved under leases of property may at any given time prove to be above or below the true rental value of the property. In these cases the valuer of the freeholder's interest must consider both the net income receivable for the remainder of the term of the lease and also the net income obtainable when the freeholder comes into his reversion. The sum of the capital values of these two sets of income represents the value of the freehold subject to the lesser interest which has been granted out of it.

The common law right of a freeholder to regain physical possession of his property at the end of a lease granted by him is now much restricted by legislation, the most important statutes being the Rent Acts, the Landlord and Tenant Act, 1954, the Agricultural Holdings Act, 1948 and the Leasehold Reform Act, 1967. The provisions contained in these Acts are considered in greater detail in later Chapters.

### 3. LEASEHOLDS

A leasehold interest in property is one which is held on lease for a term of years, subject to the payment of an annual rent and to the observance of covenants contained in the lease. The person who grants the lease is called the " lessor " and the person who takes it the " lessee " or " leaseholder." If the rent which the lessee has covenanted to pay is less than the true rental value of the premises, the lessee will be in receipt of a net income from the property the capitalised value of which, for the balance of his term, will represent the market value of his leasehold interest. Even if the lessee is paying the full rental value of the property this interest may have some value in that it confers a right on him to occupy the premises for the unexpired term of his lease and may enable him to claim a new lease or to continue in possession at the end of his term under the legislation mentioned in the last paragraph of the preceding Section of this Chapter. If he is paying a rent above the full value, the lease will have a negative value owing to the liability which it creates.

The following are the principal types of lease by which such interests may be created.

(i) *Building Leases.*—These are leases of land ripe for building under which the lessee undertakes to pay a yearly *ground rent,* to erect suitable buildings upon the land, and to keep those buildings in repair and pay all outgoings in connection with them throughout the term. The *ground rent* represents the rental value of the bare site at the time the lease is granted, and the difference between this and the net rent obtainable from the buildings when erected will constitute the lessee's *profit rent* or *net income.*

Building leases are usually granted for terms of 99 years in London and the South. Terms of nine hundred and ninety-nine years are more common in the North and are found occasionally in other parts of the country. Lesser terms than 99 years are met with, but it is obvious that no would-be leaseholder will incur the expense of erecting buildings unless he is granted a reasonably long term in which to enjoy the use of them. On the termination of a building lease, the freeholder enjoys a reversion not only to the land, but also to the buildings which the lessee has erected and maintained, subject to the lessee's rights under the Landlord and Tenant Act, 1954, or under other similar legislation.

In the case of leaseholders of residential property it has been stated that the principle is that the buildings belong to the lessee and the land to the lessor.[2] From this principle flow the statutory provisions in the Leasehold Reform Act, 1967, that qualified leaseholders have the right either to continue to occupy the land at a modern ground rent on the termination of their lease, or to compel the sale to them of the freehold interest.

(ii) *Occupation Leases.*—This term is applied to a lease of land and buildings for occupation by the lessee. The length of the lease varies according to the type of property. Dwelling-houses are often leased for fairly short terms, such as three or five years, or if a long term, such as twenty-one years, is granted, the lessee usually has the option of determining it at the end of the seventh or fourteenth year. Modern shops are commonly let on seven, fourteen or twenty-one year leases. But longer terms may be arranged in the case of shops or other business premises where the lessees are of considerable financial standing or where a heavy capital outlay is incurred at the start of the lease and shorter terms may be appropriate in the case of older properties.

Where the rent reserved under an occupation lease represents the full rental value of land and buildings, or near it, it is called a *rack rent.* Where it is less than the full rental value, although obviously not a ground rent, it is called a *head rent.* It is on the difference between the head rent and the net rack rental value of the premises that the value (if any) of the leaseholder's interest depends in the case of an occupation lease.

The term *head rent* is also used to distinguish the rent paid to the freeholder from other rents paid in respect of the same property by sublessees.

It is sometimes found, for example in new towns, that lessors grant leases on what are known as *rising rents.* For example, a shop may be leased for 21 years at a rent of £500 per annum for the first seven years, £600 for the next seven and £700 for the balance of the term.

In order to counteract the loss due to inflation in real income derived from a rent reserved in a long lease, in the last twenty-five years the practice of incorporating " rent revision " clauses in such leases has become prevalent. These take various forms but in the case of ground leases, such clauses often provide for the landlord to have an option, on giving notice to the tenant so to do, to increase the ground rent payable after certain years of the term, for example in the case of a lease for 99 years, at the end of the 33rd and 66th years. The rent to be paid on the exercise of such an option is to be agreed between the landlord and tenant or in default of agreement, to be a specified fraction (for example one quarter) of the then net rack rental value fixed by arbitration. In all cases the landlord endeavours to have such a clause worded to provide an upward and not a downward revision.

---

[2] Cmnd. 2916, Leasehold Reform in England and Wales, Pa. 3.

(iii) *Subleases.*—Subject to the terms of his headlease—which may require the consent of the lessor—a leaseholder may sublease the property for any less term than he himself holds, either at the same rent or at any other figure he may be able to obtain. In this way the head lessee himself becomes entitled to a " reversion " on the falling in of the sublease. Often this reversion will be a purely nominal one of a few days only. Thus, a head lessee having fourteen years of his lease still unexpired may sublease the property at an improved rent for a term of fourteen years less ten days. The reservation of a few days reversion is necessary to preserve the nature of the sublease. An attempt to lease for the full term would have the effect of an assignment, not a sublease.

A sublessee may also have the right to continue to occupy the property under the Landlord and Tenant Act, 1954, or under other similar legislation.

Where a lessee has been granted a 99 or 999 year lease of building land at a ground rent he may sublease the land, as a whole or in smaller plots, either at the same rent as he himself pays, in which case the new rent is known as a *leasehold ground rent,* or, as is usually the case, at a higher rent than that reserved in his own lease, in which case the rent is known as an *improved ground rent.*

(iv) *Leases for Life.*—It was possible at one time to grant leases for the duration of the life of the lessee or some other person. By the Law of Property Act, 1925, these " leases for life " now take effect as leases for ninety years determinable on the death of the party in question by one month's notice from either side expiring on one of the usual quarter days.

This provision of the Law of Property Act has little practical effect on the duration of such a lease. For it is obvious that if the premises are held at less than their true rental value the lessor will take the first opportunity of terminating the lease on the lessee's death. While if the lessee was paying a higher rent than the premises were worth, his personal representatives will be equally anxious to determine.

From a valuation standpoint, therefore, the period of the lease may still be safely regarded as that of the lessee's life.

*Leasehold Interests Generally.*—A lessee is very much more restricted in his dealings with the property than is a freeholder. In many cases he will be under express covenant to keep the premises in good repair and redecorate internally and externally at stated intervals. Usually he cannot carry out alterations or structural improvements to the property without first consulting his lessor, and possibly covenanting to reinstate the premises in their original condition at the end of the term, nor sublease or assign his interest without first obtaining his landlord's consent, although that consent cannot be unreasonably withheld.

If the lessee subleases, even though the sublease contains precisely the same covenants as his own lease, there is still the risk of his incurring liability to his lessor if the sublessee fails to keep his part of the bargain. While if he assigns he may still be held liable on his express covenants—such as the covenant to repair—should his assignee prove to be a "man of straw."

For these and other reasons leaseholds are less attractive to the investor than freeholds and the income from a leasehold interest in a particular class of property will usually be capitalised at a higher rate per cent than would be used for a freehold interest in the same property. The difference may be one-half to two per cent; the lower the freehold rate the lower the increase for a leasehold interest in the same property.

## 4. RESTRICTIVE COVENANTS

It has already been pointed out that freehold land may be subject to restrictions as to user imposed in some previous conveyance. Thus, common restrictions prevent land being used for business purposes or prohibit the erection of houses costing less than a stipulated figure.

Similar restrictions are often inserted in leases. For instance, the lessee of house property may covenant not to use the premises except as a private dwelling-house, or the lessee of shop premises may covenant not to use them for any offensive trade, or to use them only for one particular type of trade.

Restrictions on the user of land are sometimes imposed solely for the benefit of other land which the vendor is retaining. In other cases they are intended to safeguard the general development of property in an area. For example, where a building estate is sold in freehold plots to various purchasers, each purchaser usually enters into the same covenants as regards the use of his land.

In the latter type of case the covenants are frequently mutually enforceable between the various purchasers and their successors in title, so that the owner of any one plot may compel the observance of the restrictions by the owner of any other plot.

Restrictive covenants which are reasonable in character may help to maintain values over a particular area, such as a building estate. But in some cases—particularly when imposed a considerable number of years ago—they may restrict the normal development of a property and detract from its value.

There are circumstances in which the right to enforce restrictive covenants may be lost. For example, if the party entitled to enforce them has for many years acquiesced in open breaches of the covenant, or has consented to a breach of covenant on one occasion in such a way as to suggest that other breaches will be disregarded, or if the character of the neighbourhood has so entirely changed that it would be inequitable to insist on a rigorous observance of the covenant.

There are also statutory means by which a modification or removal of restrictive covenants may be obtained.

The Housing Act,[3] enables any interested persons or the local authority to apply to the County Court for permission to disregard covenants which would prevent houses being converted into maisonettes. Sanction may be given by the court to abrogate covenants in leases or restrictions on freeholds if satisfied that changes in the neighbourhood render it reasonable to do so, and that, while the house is unlettable as a single house, it would readily let if converted into two or more tenements.

Under the Law of Property Act, 1925,[4] the Lands Tribunal may wholly or partially modify or discharge restrictive covenants on freeholds if satisfied that by reason of changes in the character of the property or the neighbourhood, or other material circumstances, the restrictions ought to be deemed obsolete or that their continuance would obstruct the reasonable use of the land for public or private purposes without securing practical benefits to other persons. These powers also extend to restrictive covenants on leaseholds where the original term was for over 40 years of which at least 25 years have elapsed.[5]

The Lands Tribunal may make such order as it deems proper for the payment of compensation to any person entitled to the benefit of the restrictions who is likely to suffer loss in consequence of the removal or modification of the restrictions.

The 1925 Act also gives power to the court to declare whether land is, or is not, affected by restrictions and whether restrictions are enforceable, and, if so, by whom. This is a valuable provision which enables many difficulties to be removed where the existence of restrictions or the right to enforce them is uncertain.

## 5. SUCCESSIVE INTERESTS IN PROPERTY

Provisions are frequently made in settlements by deed or by will whereby, so far as the law permits, the future succession to property is controlled.

A common example is the creation of an " entailed interest " in freehold or long leasehold property whereby the property is settled on a certain person for life and after his death on his eldest son and the heirs of his body. In this way the property will descend from generation to generation unless the entail is barred or unless heirs fail, in which latter case the land will revert to the heirs of the original grantor.

---

[3] Housing Act, 1957, Sec. 165.
[4] Section 84 as amended by Lands Tribunal Act, 1949, Section 1 (4), and Law of Property Act, 1969, Section 28.
[5] Landlord and Tenant Act, 1954, Section 52.

Under this and other forms of settlement certain persons may be entitled, either alone or jointly with others, to successive life interests in a property, the absolute ownership finally passing to some other person who is called the *remainderman*. In most cases the " remainderman," or his heirs, will ultimately succeed to the property after the falling in of the intermediate interests. But sometimes a party may be entitled to succeed to a property only subject to certain conditions—for example, that he is still living at the termination of the immediately preceding life interest; in this case the interest is spoken of as a *contingent remainder*. In law, life interests and future interests in property rank as equitable interests not legal estates. But from a valuation point of view the distinction is of little consequence. To a valuer the problem they present is that of finding the capital value of an income receivable for the duration of a life or lives, or the capital value of an income for a term of years or in perpetuity receivable after the lapse of a previous life interest.

The valuation of such interests by the use of the Life Tables will be considered in a later Chapter.

Under the Settled Land Act, 1925, a person enjoying the interest of *tenant for life* may sell the whole freehold or leasehold interest in the settled property, the capital money being paid to trustees and settled to the same uses as was the land itself. A valuer advising on a sale of this description is concerned not with the value of the party's life interest, but with the market value of the freehold or leasehold property which is the subject of the settlement.

## 6. SHARES IN PROPERTY

In the past, land was sometimes held in shares by several persons, either by way of *joint tenancy* or *tenancy-in-common*.

In the case of *joint tenancy* the parties had equal and undivided shares in the same property, and if one joint tenant died his share passed to the surviving joint tenants.

In the case of a *tenancy-in-common* the shares were undivided, but not necessarily equal. Thus, one tenant-in-common might hold a fourth share in the property, another a half share, and so on. Moreover, there was no benefit of survivorship, as in the case of joint tenancies, for if one tenant-in-common died his share passed to his heir and not to the surviving tenants-in-common. Of the two forms of holding, the tenancy-in-common was the more usual.

The shares of the joint owners were known as *undivided shares* because none could lay claim to any particular portion of the property but all shared in the enjoyment of the whole.

Under the Law of Property Act, 1925, the holding of undivided shares in the legal estate in land is abolished. In future, where a joint tenancy or tenancy-in-common exists, the legal estate of the property as a whole will be vested in a trustee or trustees for sale, the owners of the shares being entitled to their respective proportions of the proceeds of sale and of the net income from the land pending sale.

From a valuation standpoint there is little change in the nature of the interest to be valued. The owner of a share in property no longer has any legal estate in the land but he is entitled to all the benefits of ownership; such as participation in the rents and profits and a share of the capital sum realised by the property on sale. The best method of procedure is therefore to value the property as a whole and assign an appropriate fraction of the total to the value of the party's share.

It is generally recognised, however, that a share in property is less attractive to prospective investors than absolute ownership, owing to the very limited control which the owner of the share has over the property as a whole. To allow for this factor a deduction of say 10 per cent is often made from the estimated value of the share.

Thus, if the freehold value of a certain property is £2,000, the value of a quarter share in that property might be estimated as follows: —

| | |
|---|---:|
| One-quarter of £2,000    ...      ...      ...      ... | £500 |
| *Deduct* 10% to allow for the restricted demand for this type of investment ...      ...      ... | 50 |
| Market Value of Owner's share ...      ...      ... | £450 |

The suggested figure of 10 per cent is merely the normal allowance. There is nothing fixed or arbitrary about it. If there are many shares in the property or if the property is of a type, such as building land, where sole ownership and control of development is particularly desirable, a higher allowance than 10 per cent may be justified. On the other hand, if the interest is of a purely investment character—such as a half share in long-term freehold ground rents —a deduction of 10 per cent may be considered excessive.

The size of the share should also be considered when deciding on the percentage deduction. As a rule, the smaller the share, the larger should be the deduction.

# Chapter 5

## Nature and Use of Valuation Tables

### 1. GENERALLY

IT IS the valuer's business to make a carefully considered estimate of the worth of a property.

In making that estimate he must come to certain conclusions regarding the property—for instance, as to the net income it can produce, as to the likelihood of that income increasing or decreasing in the future, as to the possibility of future liabilities in connection with the property, and as to the rate per cent at which a prospective purchaser is likely to require interest on his capital.

The accuracy of his conclusions on these and other points will depend on the extent of his skill, judgment and practical experience. It is then the function of the valuation tables to enable the valuer, by a simple mathematical process, to express his conclusions as a figure of estimated value.

The object of the valuation tables is thus to save the valuer time and reduce the risk of error involved in elaborate mathematical calculations. Proficiency in their use can never be a substitute for practical experience of the property market or real appreciation of the factors which influence value; but it will assist the valuer very substantially in his work.

The mathematical construction of the valuation tables and the formulae on which they are based are considered in Appendix A. The subject of this Chapter is the nature of the various tables, what the figures in them represent and how they are commonly used in practice.

It should be emphasised, however, that all the tables which the valuer uses are based on the principle of compound interest.

It is for this reason that the following sections deal first with the "Amount of £1 Table"—the table of compound interest—instead of following the order in which the tables are arranged in "Parry's Valuation Tables" and other works.

### 2. AMOUNT OF £1 TABLE
#### (Pp. 89–105 of Parry's Valuation Tables[1])

The figures in this table are simply figures of compound interest. They represent the amount to which one pound, invested at various

---

[1] Ninth Edition, published by The Estates Gazette, Ltd., price £4·00 (post free).

rates of compound interest, will accumulate over any given number of years.

Such a calculation could, of course, be made without the use of tables, as shown by the following example.

*Example.*—To what amount will £1 invested at 5 per cent compound interest accumulate in three years?

*Answer.*—

| | Principal. | Interest. | Total. |
|---|---|---|---|
| Amount at end of 1 year (£1 plus interest @ 5% on £1)...    ...£1· | | £·05 | £1·05 |
| Amount at end of 2 years (£1·05 plus interest @ 5% on £1·05) £1·05 | | £·0525 | £1·1025 |
| Amount at end of 3 years (£1·1025 plus interest @ 5% on £1·1025) ...    ...£1·1025 | | £·0551 | £1·1576 |

The above process is obviously a laborious one and it is a great saving of time to be able to take the appropriate figure, direct from the valuation tables.

The importance of the Amount of £1 Table lies mainly in the fact that it has been used as the basis for the construction of the other valuation tables.

In practice the table is sometimes useful in calculating the loss of interest involved where capital sums are expended on a property which, for the time being, is unproductive of income.

*Example.*—A building estate was purchased for £50,000. A sum of £10,000 was spent at once on roads and other costs of development. During a period of five years no return was received from the property. What was the total cost of this property to the purchaser at the end of the five years assuming interest at 6 per cent?

*Answer.*—If the owner had not tied up £60,000 in the purchase and development of this land, he could presumably have invested that sum in some other investment producing interest at 6 per cent and have allowed capital and income to accumulate at compound interest. The cost of the property to him is therefore the sum to which £60,000 might have accumulated in 5 years at 6 per cent compound interest.

| | | |
|---|---|---|
| Capital sum invested      ...    ... | £60,000 |
| Amt. of £1 in 5 years @ 6% ... | 1·3382 |
| | |
| Cost to purchaser, say      ...    ... | £80,000 |

### 3.  PRESENT VALUE OF £1 TABLE
(Pp. 57–76 of Parry's Valuation Tables)

The figures in this table are the inverse of those in the Amount of £1 Table. Whereas the latter table shows the amount to which £1 will accumulate at compound interest over any given number of years, the Present Value of £1 Table shows the sum which invested now at compound interest will amount to £1 in so many years' time.

The figures in the table are the reciprocals of those in the Amount of £1 Table—i.e., it is possible to obtain any required figure of Present Value of £1 by dividing unity by the corresponding figure of Amount of £1.

*Example.*—What sum invested now will, at 5 per cent compound interest, accumulate to £1 in six years' time?

*Answer.*—

Let V equal the sum in question.

V × Amt. of £1 in 6 years @ 5% = £1

$$\therefore V = \frac{1}{\text{Amt. of £1 in 6 yrs. @ 5\%}}$$

$$= \frac{1}{1 \cdot 340}$$

$$= \cdot 7462154$$

It is, however, very much quicker to take the figure direct from the Present Value of £1 Table.

The Present Value of £1 Table is widely used in practice for calculating the value at the present time of sums receivable in the future and in making allowances for future expenditure in connection with property.

The value at the present day of the right to receive a capital sum in the future is governed by the fact that whatever capital is invested in purchasing that right will be unproductive until the right matures. So that if £x is spent in purchasing the right to receive £100 in three years' time, it follows that for those three years the purchaser's capital will be showing no return, whereas if the £x had been invested in some other security it might, during those three years, have been earning compound interest. The price which the purchaser can fairly afford to pay, therefore, is that sum which, with compound interest on it at a given rate per cent, will amount to £100 in three years' time.

*Example.*—What is the present value of the right to receive £100 in three years' time assuming that the purchaser will require a 5 per cent return on his money?

*Answer.*—Let V = sum which the purchaser can afford to pay. He will be losing compound interest on this sum during the three years he will have to wait before he receives the £100.

V must therefore be such a sum as, together with compound interest at 5 per cent, will in three years' time equal £100.
V × Amt. of £1 in 3 years @ 5% = £100.

$$\therefore V = \frac{£100}{\text{Amt. of £1 in 3 yrs. @ 5\%}}$$

$$= \frac{£100}{1 \cdot 1576}$$

$$= £86 \cdot 38$$

The above method has been used to show the principle involved. The same result would be obtained direct from the Present Value of £1 Table as follows:—

| | |
|---|---|
| Sum receivable ... ... ... | £100 |
| P.V. £1 in 3 years @ 5% ... | ·8638376 |
| *Present Value* | £86·38 |

The process of making allowance for the fact that a sum is not receivable or will not be expended until some time in the future is known as " deferring " or " discounting " that sum. In the above example £86·38 might be described as the present value of £100 " deferred three years at five per cent ".

Since, in the case of sums receivable in the future, the valuer is concerned with the temporary loss of interest on capital invested in their purchase, the rate per cent at which their value is deferred should generally correspond to that which an investor might expect from the particular type of security if in immediate possession. In other words, the rate should be a " remunerative " one.

*Example.*—What is the present market value of the reversion to a freehold property let for a term of five years at a peppercorn rent but worth £350 per annum? Similar property in possession and let at its full market value has recently changed hands on a 5 per cent basis.

*Answer.*—

| | | | | | |
|---|---|---|---|---|---|
| *Value in five years time* | | | | | |
| Full rental value ... | ... | ... | ... | £350 | p.a. |
| Y.P. in perp. @ 5% | ... | ... | ... | 20 | |
| | | | | £7,000 | |
| P.V. £1 in 5 years @ 5% ... | ... | ... | ·783 | | |
| | | *Present Value* | | £5,481 | |

In the above example, the capital value of the interest increases in five years from £5,481 to £7,000, In most cases a purchaser acquiring the interest now for £5,481 and selling it in five years time for £7,000 would not be liable to pay income tax on the capital appreciation of £1,519. This characteristic is an advantage to any investor liable to income tax but it is particularly valuable to those also liable to surtax. A surtax payer gains little net monetary advantage from an increase in income. If, for example, he is paying combined surtax and income tax at the highest rate of 88·75% his net gain from a gross income increase of £100 will be just over £11.

Capital gains are liable to tax as such but capital gains tax is at present charged at 30%. Thus, on a capital gain of £100 the investor will be left, after capital gains tax, with a net gain of £70.

Thus, any investor liable to income tax at a rate exceeding 30% would prefer a capital gain to an increase in income and this preference will increase the higher the rate at which income is taxed.

When an investment offering a capital gain comes on to the market, competition between investors who can derive particular advantage from it may be such that the price it fetches is in excess of the figure obtained by the use of the Present Value of £1 in the manner shown in the example. Theoretically, the price could increase to just below the point at which the tax advantage is entirely discounted but it is unlikely that the market will be sufficiently competitive for this to happen. Some allowance can, however, be made for this factor by the use of the Present Value of £1 adjusted for tax. Such tables are in the coloured section of the valuation tables; for example, on pages 175–180 will be found the Present Value of £1 at varying rates of interest adjusted for tax at 35%.[2]

Reference has been made in earlier Chapters to incomes as being " net ". For valuation purposes this means that the income is free of all outgoings with the exception of income tax, which is a charge on all incomes.[3] Although this is the normal basis on which valuations are made, they could be made on the basis that the income was free of all outgoings *including* income tax. As far as constant incomes receivable in perpetuity are concerned no difference would arise between valuations made upon the usually accepted basis and those made upon the true net basis.

*Example.*—Shop premises A, let at a fair rent of £400 per annum, free of all outgoings other than income tax, have recently been sold for £5,000 freehold. Analyse this transaction to value the freehold interest in shop premises B, let at a fair rent of £475 per annum on the same basis.

---

[2] This matter is discussed in further detail in Appendix A.16.
[3] This point is further discussed in Section 7 of this Chapter.

*Analysis on usual basis.—i.e., disregarding income tax—*
Rate of interest on Shop A—

$$\frac{£5,000}{£400} = 12 \cdot 5 \text{ Y.P.} = 8\%.$$

*Application to Shop B—*

| | | | | | |
|---|---|---|---|---|---|
| Rent reserved | ... | ... | ... | ... | £475 p.a. |
| Y.P. in perp. @ 8% | ... | ... | ... | | 12·5 |
| | | | *Present Value* | | £5,937·5 |

*Analysis on a " true net " basis—*
Taking income tax at 50%.
Rate of interest on Shop A

$$\frac{£5,000}{£200} = 25 \text{ Y.P.} = 4\%.$$

*Application to Shop B—*

| | | | | | |
|---|---|---|---|---|---|
| Rent reserved | ... | ... | ... | ... | £475 p.a. |
| *Less* tax at 50% | ... | ... | ... | | 237·5 |
| " True net " income | ... | ... | ... | | 237·5 |
| Y.P. in perp. @ 4% | ... | ... | ... | | 25 |
| | | | *Present Value* | | £5,937·5 |

In cases of varying incomes, however, the results will not be the same in each case. Referring to the example on page 52 the valuation adopting the "true net" approach and using a tax rate of 40%, is:—

*Value in five years time—*

| | | | | | |
|---|---|---|---|---|---|
| Full rental value | ... | ... | ... | ... | £350 p.a. |
| *Less* tax at 40% | ... | ... | ... | | 140 |
| " True net " income | ... | ... | ... | | £210 p.a. |
| Y.P. in perp. @ 3% | ... | ... | ... | | 33·33 |
| | | | | | £7,000 |
| P.V. £1 in 5 years @ 3% | | ... | ... | | ·863 |
| | | | *Present Value* | | £6,041 |

It will be observed that while this figure does not agree with the first answer of £5,481, it does agree if the Present Value of £1 is adjusted for tax. It is sometimes argued that the " true net " method should, therefore, be adopted, but it is doubtful if there is sufficient evidence from market transactions to warrant this as a general rule. If a figure of Present Value of £1 adjusted for tax is used it seems logical to allow for the effect of capital gains tax.[4]

Where the sum for which allowance has to be made is a future expense *in the nature of a liability which cannot be avoided,* the valuer is not concerned with the question of loss of interest on capital invested, but rather with the rate per cent at which a fund can be accumulated to meet the expense. A future capital liability can be provided for either by the setting aside of an annual amount in the form of a sinking fund, or by the investment of a lump sum which at compound interest will accumulate to the required amount in the given period. The first method will be discussed in Section 5 of this Chapter. The second method can be effected through an insurance company by what is known as a single premium policy.

Unless the amount of the single premium is fairly considerable, the rate of compound interest on it allowed by insurance companies is low. It is therefore sounder, as a rule, to defer sums to meet liabilities in the future at a low " accumulative " rate rather than at the " remunerative " rate at which interest on capital is taken.

> *Example.*—A freehold factory was let two years ago to substantial tenants on a 40 years' lease at a rent of £1,350 per annum. The premises are in good repair, and the tenants are under full repairing covenants, but the owner has covenanted with the lessees that, after four years of the lease have expired, he will rebuild, in fire-resisting construction, a staircase which is now of wood at a cost of £1,000, also that after a further period of four years, he will rebuild the chimney shaft at a cost of £2,000, and that two years later (i.e., when the lease has 30 years unexpired) he will replace a wooden fence with a brick wall. This will cost £1,000.
>
> Assuming that the works in question are necessary to maintain the present rent, and that no higher rent may be expected when the lease comes to an end, what is the value of the freehold interest?

*Valuation—*

| | | | | | |
|---|---|---|---|---|---|
| Net Rental Value (with improvements) | ... | ... | £1,350 | | |
| Y.P. perp. @ 8% ... | ... | ... | ... | ... | 12½ |
| | | | | | £16,875 |
| *Deduct cost of:* | | | | | |
| Fire-resisting staircase | ... | ... £1,000 | | | |
| P.V. £1 in 2 years @ 2½% | ... | ... ·952 | 952 | | |

---

[4] See Appendix A.16.

|  |  |  |  |  |  |
|---|---|---|---|---|---|
| *Chimney shaft* | ... | ... | ... £2,000 |  |  |
| P.V. £1 in 6 years @ 2½% | ... | ... | ·862 | 1,724 |  |
| *New brick wall* | ... | ... | ... £1,000 |  |  |
| P.V. £1 in 8 years @ 2½% | ... | ... | ·821 | 821 | 3,497 |

*Value of Freehold Interest, say* ... £13,375

An exception to the above general rule occurs in cases where the future capital expense can be met out of moneys arising from the property itself, in which case there will be no need to provide for it by investment of a single premium at a low rate of interest and the sum can be deferred at the appropriate " remunerative " rate.

Where, as is frequently the case, future expenditure is of a kind which is optional—as distinct from a liability which cannot be avoided—it is probably preferable to allow for it at the higher (remunerative) rate, since in this type of case it is thought that the investor would not set aside a sum to accumulate at a low rate of interest—e.g., in a single premium policy.

> *Example.*—Old warehouse premises are let at £200 per annum exclusive on a full repairing and insuring lease now having 30 years unexpired. This rent is about half the present rental value. At the end of the lease it will be necessary, if the present rental value is to be maintained, to renovate the building at a cost (today) of £3,000. What is the value of the free-holder's interest?

*Valuation—*

*Next* 30 *years.*

|  |  |  |  |  |  |
|---|---|---|---|---|---|
| Rent reserved | ... | ... | ... | £200 p.a. |  |
| Y.P. 30 years @ 8% | ... | ... | ... | 11·26 |  |
|  |  |  |  |  | £2,252 |
| *Reversion to* | ... | ... | ... | £400 p.a. |  |
| Y.P. in perp. @ 10% | ... | ... | ... | 10 |  |
|  |  |  |  | £4,000 |  |
| *Deduct* cost of renovation ... | ... | ... | £3,000 |  |  |
|  |  |  |  | £1,000 |  |
| P.V. £1 in 30 years @ 10% | ... | ... | ·057 |  |  |
|  |  |  |  |  | 57 |

*Present Value of Freeholder's Interest*     £2,309

*Note.*—The same value is obtained for the reversion if it is valued as follows:—

| | | | | | | |
|---|---|---|---|---|---|---|
| *Reversion to* ... .. .. ... ... | | | | | £400 p.a. | |
| Y.P. in perp. @ 10% deferred 30 years ... | | | | | ·57 | |
| | | | | | £228 | |
| *Deduct* cost of renovation ... | | ... | £3,000 | | | |
| P.V. £1 in 30 years @ 10% | | ... | ... | | ·057 | |
| | | | | | £171 | |
| | | | | | | £57 |

Where the sum required is a comparatively large proportion of the value of the whole interest, and the period of deferment is a comparatively long one, the use of the low (accumulative) rate of interest may even give a negative value.

### 4.   AMOUNT OF £1 PER ANNUM
### (Pp. 107–120 of Parry's Valuation Tables)

The figures in this table represent the amount to which a series of deposits of £1 at the end of each year will accumulate in a given period at a given rate of compound interest.

A calculation in that precise form does not often come within the scope of a valuer's practice; but the table may be of use to him in calculating the total expense involved over a period of years where annual outgoings are incurred in connection with a property which is for the time being unproductive.

The following example serves to illustrate this use and also to emphasise the distinction between the nature and use of this table and the Amount of £1 table.

*Example.*—A new plantation of timber trees will reach maturity in 80 years' time. The original cost of planting was £10 per ha. The annual expenses average 20p per ha. What will be the total cost per ha. by the time the timber matures, ignoring any interest on the value of the land and assuming that interest is required on other outstanding capital at 5 per cent?

*Answer.*—The £10 per ha. spent on planting is in the nature of a lump sum which will remain unproductive over a period of 80 years. Its cost to the owner is represented by the sum to which it might have accumulated if it had been invested during that period at compound interest. This part of the calculation requires the use of the Amount of £1 Table.

The expenditure of 20p per ha. on upkeep is an annual payment which will also bring no return during a period of 80 years. Its cost to the owner is represented by the sum to which a series of such annual payments might have accumulated if placed in some form of investment bearing compound interest. Here it will be necessary to use the Amount of £1 per annum Table.

| | | | | | |
|---|---|---|---|---|---|
| Original capital outlay per ha. | ... | ... | £10 | | |
| *Amount of* £1 in 80 years @ 5% | ... | ... | 49·56 | | |
| | | | | | £495·6 |
| Annual cost per ha. | ... ... ... | ... | £0·2 | | |
| *Amount of* £1 *per annum* in 80 years @ 5% | ... | 971·229 | | | |
| | | | | | 194·2 |

*Total cost per ha. for period of maturity*  £690

## 5. ANNUAL SINKING FUND
### (Pp. 77–87 of Parry's Valuation Tables)

This table is the inverse of the Amount of £1 per annum Table. Instead of showing the sum to which a series of deposits of £1 will accumulate over a given period, it shows the sum which must be deposited annually at compound interest in order to produce £1 in so many years' time. The figures in the one table are the reciprocals of those in the other, just as the figures in the P.V. of £1 Table are the reciprocals of those in the Amount of £1 Table. Thus, any required figure of Annual Sinking Fund can be found by dividing unity by the corresponding figure of Amount of £1 per annum, or vice versa.

The table is of direct use to the valuer when it is required to know what sum ought to be set aside annually out of income in order to meet some capital expense accruing due in the future, such as a possible claim for dilapidations on the termination of a lease or a sum likely to be required for the rebuilding or reconstruction of premises.

The provision of a sinking fund to meet future capital liabilities, although often neglected by owners in practice, avoids the embarrassment of having to meet the whole of a considerable expense out of a single year's income and enables the owner to see precisely how much of the annual return from the property he can afford to treat as spendable income.

*Example.*—An investor recently purchased for £10,000 a freehold property which it is estimated will yield a net income of £500 for the next 30 years. At the end of that time it will be necessary to rebuild at a cost of £8,000 in order to maintain the income. How should the owner provide for this and what will be the result on the percentage yield of his investment?

*Answer.*—The owner may provide for the cost of rebuilding by means of an annual sinking fund accumulating at, say, 2½ per cent over the next 30 years, as follows: —

| | | | | | |
|---|---|---|---|---|---|
| Cost of rebuilding | ... ... | ... | ... | £8,000 | |
| Annual sinking fund to produce £1 in 30 years @ 2½% | ... ... ... | ... | ... | ·023 | |

*Sinking fund required* ... £184 p.a.

The owner's true income for the next 30 years will therefore be (£500 – £184) £316 only, representing a return of 3·2 per cent on the purchase price instead of the 5 per cent which the investment might appear to be yielding.

The necessary provision may be made by means of a sinking fund policy taken out with an insurance company. At the annual payments on such a policy are comparatively small and a considerable amount of office work is involved on the part of the company, the rate of compound interest allowed on the annual deposits is low, approximately $1\frac{3}{4}$ per cent to $2\frac{1}{2}$ per cent net.

If the sum to be set aside annually is considerable, it is possible that an owner may find opportunity for the accumulation of it in his own business, or in some other investment, at a higher rate of interest than that usually allowed by an insurance company. It is probable that in most cases purchasers will be inclined to take this fact into account in considering the investment value of property, since otherwise the cost of allowing for replacement of capital on ordinary sinking fund terms becomes prohibitive.

It is proposed in the examples which follow to adopt $2\frac{1}{2}$ per cent net as a reasonable average figure where sinking fund is concerned.

The Annual Sinking Fund tables on pages 77–80 of the valuation tables are compiled on a net basis—that is assuming that the accumulations of interest on the sinking fund are free of income tax.

The allowance for income tax on interest on sinking fund accumulations which is made by using a net rate of interest should not be confused with the entirely separate adjustment for income tax on the sinking fund element of income which is made when using dual rate Years' Purchase. This latter point is dealt with in Section 7 of this Chapter.

### 6. Present Value of £1 per annum or Years' Purchase Table

#### (Dual Rate pp. 1–25, Single Rate pp. 27–39 of Parry's Valuation Tables)

It was explained earlier that the main purpose of this table is to enable the valuer, when using the investment method, to estimate the present capital value of an income receivable in perpetuity or for a given number of years.

The figures in the table show, at varying rates of interest, what sum might reasonably be paid for a series of sums of £1 receivable at the end of each of a given number of successive years. By applying the appropriate figure from the table to the net income of the property the valuer arrives at his estimate of market value.

Where the income is perpetual the appropriate figure of Years' Purchase can be found by dividing 100 by the rate of interest appropriate to the property, or by dividing unity by the interest on £1 in one year at the appropriate rate per cent. Thus, Years' Purchase in perpetuity can be expressed as

$$\frac{100}{\text{Rate per cent}} \quad \text{or} \quad \frac{1}{i}$$

But where the income is receivable for a limited term only, as with a leasehold interest, the relationship between Years' Purchase and the rate of interest is more complex.

For example, if a certain property producing a perpetual net income of £500 per annum can fairly be regarded as a 5 per cent investment, a purchaser can afford to pay (£500 × 20 Y.P.) £10,000 for it. Assume now that the income is receivable for 30 years only but that 5 per cent is still a reasonable return. In this case a purchaser could not afford to pay £10,000, for if he did so, although the income of £500 would represent 5 per cent on the purchase price throughout the term, at the end of the 30 years his interest in the property would cease and he would then lose both capital and income.

A lower Years' Purchase will, therefore, be required to capitalise the terminable income but at the same time the rate of interest must not be interfered with. If the rate of interest is merely increased to give the lower Years' Purchase necessary, it is no longer performing only its proper function as an indicator of the relative merits of different investments, it is also being required to function as an indicator of the period during which the income will be received. In order to leave the rate of interest to perform only its proper function, it is necessary to make the incomes comparable in terms of time. This can be achieved by allowing an amount out of the terminable income to be set aside annually as a sinking fund, sufficient to accumulate during the term to the capital originally invested. If this is done the purchaser, having paid £x for the interest in the first instance, will receive the income during the term and set aside out of that income a sinking fund, so that at the end of the term the sinking fund will have accumulated to the original capital of £x. In this way the terminable income has been perpetuated and is, therefore, directly comparable with the perpetual income.

Thus, the formula for finding the Present Value of £1 per annum

for a terminable income is $\dfrac{1}{i + s}$, i being the interest on £1 in one

year at the appropriate rate per cent and s being the sinking fund
to replace £1 at the end of the term.

The next question is at what rate of interest should the annual
sinking fund be assumed to accumulate? Again, the proper function of the rate of interest, that of indicating the relative merits
of different investments, is the prime consideration. It was
explained in Section 5 of this Chapter that sinking fund arrangements can be made by means of a sinking fund policy with an
insurance company. The interest on such a policy is low because
the investment is riskless and as near trouble-free as possible.
If it is assumed that the sinking fund is arranged in this way, all
of the risks attached to the actual investment in the property will
be reflected, as they should be, in the rate of interest the purchaser
requires on the capital invested.

These two assumptions, (a) that a sinking fund is set aside and
(b) that the rate of interest at which the sinking fund accumulates
is the rate appropriate to a riskless and trouble-free investment,
are in no way invalidated by the fact that many investors make
sinking fund provisions in some way other than through a leasehold
redemption policy or that many investors make no sinking fund
provision at all.

*Example.*—What is the value of a leasehold property producing
a net income of £500 for the next 70 years assuming that a
purchaser requires a return of 5 per cent on his money and
that provision is made for a sinking fund for redemption of
capital at 2½ per cent?

*Answer*—

Interest on £1 in 1 year @ 5%      = ·05
S.F. to produce £1 in 70 years @ 2½%  ·0053971

Y.P. 70 years @ 5% & 2½% $= \dfrac{1}{i + s}$

$$= \dfrac{1}{·05 + ·0053971}$$

$$= 18·051$$

| *Valuation*— | Net income ... | £500 |
|---|---|---|
| P.V. of £1 p.a. or Y.P. 70 years @ 5 and 2½% | | 18·051 |
| | *Value* ... | £9,025 |

*Note.*—In practice the figure of 18·051 could have been obtained direct from the table of P.V. of £1 p.a. @ 5 and 2½% in Parry's Tables.

*Proof.*—The fact that the estimated purchase price does allow both for interest on capital and also for sinking fund may be shown as follows:—

| | | |
|---|---|---|
| Interest on £9,025 @ 5% (£9,025 × ·05)  ...  ... | | £451 |
| Sinking fund to produce £9,025 in 70 years at 2½% (£9,025 × ·0053971)  ...  ...  ...  ... | | 49 |
| | *Income from property*  ... | £500 |

The Years' Purchase used in the above example is called a dual rate Years' Purchase because two different rates of interest are used. The first rate (5% in the example) is called the " remunerative " rate, and the second (2½%) is called the " accumulative " rate.

Except where the income from freehold property is likely seriously to depreciate in the future, dual rate figures should not be used in any calculation involved in the valuation of a freehold interest.[5] For instance, a freehold property may be let at £100 for the next ten years with the prospect of an income of £150 thereafter in perpetuity. It is unnecessary in this case to take the Years' Purchase for the first ten years on a dual rate basis, because although the £100 considered alone is receivable for ten years only, a perpetual income follows and the necessity for replacing the capital value of the first ten years does not arise.

The derivation of the appropriate Years' Purchase for use in such cases, called single rate Years' Purchase is best illustrated by the use of the Present Value of £1. Single rate Years' Purchase gives the present value of a series of instalments of income of £1 and it can be built up by summing up the Present Values of £1.

*Example.*—What is the present value on a 6 per cent basis of freehold shop premises let on lease with 3 years unexpired, at a net rent of £1,000 per annum? The rental value is estimated to be £1,500 per annum.

*Valuation*—

1*st* 3 *years*

| | | | | |
|---|---|---|---|---|
| First year's rent  ...  ... | £1,000 | | | |
| P.V. £1 in 1 year @ 6%  ... | ·943 | £943 | | |
| Second year's rent  ...  ... | £1,000 | | | |
| P.V. £1 in 2 years @ 6%  ... | ·89 | £890 | | |
| Third year's rent  ...  ... | £1,000 | | | |
| P.V. £1 in 3 years @ 6%  ... | ·84 | 840 | £2,673 |

---

[5] See Pages 60 and 61.

| *Reversion to* | Rental value | £1,500 p.a. | |
|---|---|---|---|
| Y.P. in perp. @ 6% ... ... | | 16·67 | |
| | | £25,005 | |
| P.V. £1 in 3 years @ 6% ... | | ·84 | 21,004 |
| | *Present Value* | | £23,677 |

The value of the first 3 years could have been determined more simply by the use of the single rate Years' Purchase table as follows: —

*Valuation—*

| 1*st* 3 *years* | Rent reserved | £1,000 p.a. | |
|---|---|---|---|
| Y.P. 3 years @ 6% | ... | 2·673 | £2,673 |
| *Reversion*—as before | ... ... | | 21,004 |
| | *Present Value* | | £23,677 |

In Appendix A, in which the derivation of the various tables is considered, it is shown that single rate Years' Purchase can be calculated from two formulae. The first is $\dfrac{1 - \text{Present Value of £1.}}{i}$

Thus, to calculate the single Years' Purchase for 3 years at 6%—

$$\frac{1 - \text{P.V. £1 in 3 years @ 6\%}}{·06}$$

$$= \frac{1 - ·8396}{·06}$$

$$= \frac{·1604}{·06}$$

$$= \underline{2·673}$$

The second is the same formula as that for dual rate Years' Purchase which is $\dfrac{1}{i + S}$. Thus, to calculate the same Years' Purchase as above

$$\frac{1}{·06 + \text{S.F. to produce £1 in 3 years @ 6\%}}$$

$$= \frac{1}{·06 + ·3141}$$

$$= \frac{1}{·3741}$$

$$= \underline{2·673}$$

In practice it is usual for the income for the next 3 years to be valued at a lower rate of interest than that used to capitalise the full rental value in reversion as the rent reserved under the lease is better secured, being below the full rental value. If 5 per cent is used to capitalise the rent reserved and 6 per cent for the reversion, the calculation becomes: —

| | | |
|---|---|---|
| Rent reserved ... ... ... ... | £1,000 p.a. | |
| Y.P. 3 years @ 5% ... ... ... | 2·723 | |
| | ——— | £2,723 |
| Reversion to full value ... ... ... | £1,500 p.a. | |
| Y.P. in perp. @ 6% deferred 3 years ... | 14 | |
| | ——— | £21,000 |
| | | |
| *Present Value* ... | | £23,723 |

A second approach to the same valuation would be to value the income of £1,000 per annum in perpetuity and to add to that the present value of the increase of £500 per annum receivable in perpetuity after 3 years. The main difficulty with this method is the selection of an appropriate rate of interest for the increased rent on reversion. Assume, however, that 9 per cent is appropriate.

*Valuation—*

| | | |
|---|---|---|
| Rent receivable in perpetuity ... ... | £1,000 p.a. | |
| Y.P. in perp. @ 5% ... ... ... | 20 | |
| | ——— | £20,000 |
| Increase receivable in perpetuity after | | |
| 3 years ... ... ... ... | £500 p.a. | |
| Y.P. in perp. @ 9% deferred 3 years ... | 8·58 | 4,290 |
| | | |
| | | £24,290 |

It is obvious that as the bottom layer of income (£1,000 p.a.) has been treated as well secured throughout, the top layer (£500 p.a.) superimposed in 3 years' time must be treated as less well secured than when the whole of the income on reversion (£1,500 p.a.) was valued at 6 per cent by the first method. It would be difficult to substantiate the choice of the rate of interest used to capitalise the increase in income by analysis as this is usually done taking the income as a whole but it can be calculated mathematically.[6]

Where the income from freehold property is likely seriously to depreciate in the future, so that the greater part of the capital is lost at the end of a given term of years, dual rate figures may reasonably be used in the calculation. For instance, suppose that existing premises are likely to produce an income of £100 for the next twenty years, after which the building must be pulled down, leaving the rental value of the bare site at, say, £20. It would be proper in that case to capitalise the income of £100 for the next

---

[6] See Appendix A.16.

twenty years on a dual rate basis, since a large proportion of the income will cease entirely at the end of that period, and it is therefore necessary to make adequate provision for replacement of part of the capital spent in purchasing it. The amount of capital replaced in such a case is not necessarily the amount by which the capital value falls between the date of purchase and the date of the cessation of the income for the term. Thus taking the facts quoted above, the calculation is:—

| | | |
|---|---|---|
| Income for next 20 years ...      ...      ... | £100 p.a. | |
| Y.P. 20 years @ 8 and 2½%      ...      ... | 8·39 | |
| | | £839 |
| Reversion to site value of      ...      ... | £20 p.a. | |
| Y.P. in perp. @ 6% deferred 20 years ... | 5·20 | |
| | | £104 |
| | | £943 |

In 20 years' time, provided that the existing conditions remain the same, the value of the freeholder's interest will be:—

| | | |
|---|---|---|
| Rental value      ...      ...      ...      ... | £20 p.a. | |
| Y.P. in perp. @ 6%      ...      ...      ... | 16·67 | |
| | | £333 |

The depreciation in value over the next 20 years will therefore be £943 – £333, i.e., £610, whereas the above calculation provides for replacement of £839.

An alternative approach which partially overcomes this difficulty is shown below:

| | | | |
|---|---|---|---|
| Terminable portion of present income | £80 p.a. | | |
| Y.P. 20 years @ 8 and 2½%      ... | 8·39 | | |
| | | £671 | |
| Continuing portion of present income | £20 p.a. | | |
| Y.P. 20 years @ 8%      ...      ... | 9·82 | 196 | |
| | | | £867 |
| Reversion—as before ...      ...      ... | | | 104 |
| | | | £971 |

### 7. Allowance for Income Tax

A matter requiring very careful consideration in the valuation of terminable incomes on a dual rate basis, such as those from leasehold properties, is the effect of a high rate of income tax.

Income from landed property, like income from any other source, is subject to income tax; its assessment in this case being governed by the rules of the Income and Corporation Taxes Act, 1970. The maximum rate of tax is fixed yearly by the Finance Act for the current year.

Income tax is not deducted as an outgoing in finding the net income of a freehold property for valuation purposes, because it is usually taken for granted that the income from every type of security is subject to this charge, i.e., comparisons between securities are usually made on a " gross " basis as regards income tax. In the event of an investment being tax free, for example, building society interest, the tax free rate is usually " grossed up " at the standard rate of income tax, i.e., the tax free rate of interest is converted to that rate of interest which after deduction of income tax at the standard rate shows a return equal to the tax free rate quoted.

When the effective return on, say, Government securities is stated to be, say, 6 per cent, it is understood that this return is subject to income tax at the standard rate. It is not usual with this class of security to deduct the tax first and quote a rate of interest free of tax. Since the rates per cent on which valuations of different types of property must be directly comparable with rates of interest yielded by other types of investment, no deduction for income tax is made from net income before applying the appropriate figure of Years' Purchase. In the case of leasehold properties, however, a part of the so-called " net income " from the property is not really income at all, but represents a sinking fund for the replacement of capital. The rules of assessment to income tax make no allowance for this fact, so that income tax is charged not only on that part of the income which represents interest on capital, but also on that part which represents sinking fund. In principle, therefore, some deduction should be made for the latter part of the tax in every leasehold valuation.

Where the lease has still a considerable number of years to run, that part of the net income which represents sinking fund is comparatively small and the incidence of tax on it is sometimes ignored, because it has little effect on the valuation where the term has over seventy years to run.

But where the term of the lease is comparatively short, the sinking fund to replace capital will absorb a considerable part of the whole income from the property and income tax on it at the standard rate becomes a considerable item. This is reflected in the prices realised for such interests, and it is found necessary, both in analysis of transactions and in subsequent synthesis to find values of properties under consideration, to take direct account of the fact that the income from the property will have to cover not only interest on capital and the necessary sinking fund, but also tax on that sinking fund element of the income. If this is not done, one of two things results—either tax on the sinking fund has to be paid out of the sinking fund itself, so that insufficient is set aside for replacement of capital, or the tax is paid out of the true income from the property, with the result that the effective rate of interest on the purchase price is reduced.

The most accurate method of effecting the necessary adjustment is by increasing the sinking fund factor in the formula for Years' Purchase so that it will cover both the sinking fund and the tax on it. This may be done by multiplying it by a fraction representing the ratio of untaxed income to taxed income. Thus, if the standard rate for the year is 50% the ratio of untaxed income to taxed income can be expressed as $\frac{100}{50}$ or 2. In other words, the figure representing sinking fund in the Years' Purchase formula must be doubled.

We have already seen that the normal formula for finding the Years' Purchase of a terminable income is—Y.P. $= \dfrac{1}{i+s}$

The following statement shows the effect of three different rates of income tax on this formula:—

(i) Income tax at 35%.

$$\text{Years' Purchase} = \frac{1}{i+s \times \dfrac{100}{100-35}} = \frac{1}{i+s \times \dfrac{100}{65}} \text{ or } \frac{1}{i+1\cdot538s}$$

(ii) Income tax at 37·5%.

$$\text{Years' Purchase} = \frac{1}{i+s \times \dfrac{100}{100-37\cdot5}} = \frac{1}{i+s \times \dfrac{100}{62\cdot5}} \text{ or } \frac{1}{i+1\cdot6s}$$

(iii) Income tax at 38·75%.

$$\text{Years' Purchase} = \frac{1}{i+s \times \dfrac{100}{100-38\cdot75}} = \frac{1}{i+s \times \dfrac{100}{61\cdot25}} \text{ or } \frac{1}{i+1\cdot633s}$$

The tax adjustment factor applied to the sinking fund can be found as TG on P. 437 of the Tables.

*Example.*—A property held for a term of five years unexpired at a rent of £20 per annum and subleased for the full term, less three days, at £420 per annum, has been purchased on the following basis:—

| | |
|---|---:|
| Net income per annum ... ... ... ... | £420 |
| Deduct Ground Rent ... ... ... ... | 20 |
| | |
| Net income (including sinking fund) ... ... | £400 |
| Y.P. 5 years on dual rate table @ 7 and 2½% | 3·843 |
| | |
| | £1,537 |

The purchaser now discovers that owing to the deduction of income tax, the income is insufficient to enable a sinking fund to be set aside to recoup the capital. What allowance should have been made in the valuation for this factor taking 40% as the rate of tax?

*Answer.*—The error involved is that no allowance has been made for the incidence of income tax on that part of the £400 income which must be set aside as sinking fund. The error could have been avoided by first adjusting the figure of Years' Purchase to allow for this factor.

Years' Purchase for 5 years @ 7 and 2½% (allowing for tax on S.F. element of income).

$$= \frac{1}{i + s \times \dfrac{100}{100 - 40}}$$

$$= \frac{1}{\cdot07 + (\cdot1902469 \times 1\cdot67)}$$

$$= \frac{1}{\cdot07 + \cdot317} = \frac{1}{\cdot387}$$

$$= 2\cdot58$$

*Amended Valuation*—

| | |
|---|---:|
| Net income ... ... ... ... ... ... | £400 |
| Years' Purchase for 5 years @ 7 and 2½% (allowing for tax on S.F.) ... ... ... | 2·58 |
| *Purchase price* ... | £1,032 |

*Note.*—In practice the valuation of such a short-term lease might present a number of awkward problems. The valuer would be concerned with the state of repair of the premises, with the nature and extent of the repairing covenants in the head-lease, and with the risk of the head-lessee being liable to a heavy claim for dilapidations from the freeholder which may only partially be covered by his own claim against the sub-lessee.

In answering the question these points have been ignored in order to focus attention on the mathematical problem of adjusting the Years' Purchase to provide for income tax on sinking fund.

To avoid the labour of direct calculation tables have been prepared which give directly numbers of Years' Purchase at varying rates of interest, both remunerative and accumulative, for different terms of years, allowing for the incidence of income tax on the sinking fund at various rates of tax. These tables will be found in the coloured sections of Parry's Tables. The Years' Purchase used in the last example can thus be found direct.

In considering this problem of tax on sinking fund, it must be remembered that, while the standard rate of income tax is the maximum rate at any given date, the effect of the various reliefs and allowances permitted by the income tax system is that the effective average rate for many persons is below this figure. On the other hand, when the size of the particular income makes it liable to the additional charge of surtax, the party's effective rate of tax may exceed the standard rate.

A valuer cannot know the circumstances of all prospective purchasers, so that an allowance based on the standard rate may be the best estimate he can make of the probable effect of tax on sinking fund on the market price. But in advising a purchaser as to the price he can afford to pay for a short leasehold interest the valuer is bound to consider the circumstances of the particular client. It could be argued that the valuer is concerned with finding the market value of the interest he is valuing and that an impersonal rate should therefore be employed. The adviser must, however, bear in mind that a short leasehold interest is one which appeals much more to those in the lower income groups than to those in the higher income groups, due to the different rates of tax which each group pays.

There is also the principle to be observed that analysis of transactions and valuations based on the results of such analyses must be on the same footing and it can be argued that to a certain extent the rate of tax employed by a valuer is immaterial provided that this is so. The rate of income tax used is interdependent with the remunerative rate employed as indeed is the accumulative rate.

# Chapter 6

## Nature and Use of Valuation Tables (contd.)

### 1. DEFERRED INCOMES

THE VALUER frequently has to deal in practice with cases where the whole or part of the income from a property will not commence until after the lapse of a certain number of years. In other words, he has to find the capital value of a deferred income.

One method of making such a valuation is first to estimate the capital value of the income as though it were commencing at once and then to find the present value of that capital sum by multiplying it by the P.V. of £1 receivable at the end of the term for which the income is deferred.

This method illustrates perhaps more clearly than any other the principle underlying all valuations of deferred incomes, but for convenience in working certain variations of the method are usually adopted in practice.

*Example.*—Freehold shop property worth a net income of £1,000 per annum has been leased for a term having 20 years unexpired at a peppercorn. What is the value of the freeholder's interest on a $7\frac{1}{2}$ per cent basis?

| *Valuation*— | Future Net Income | £1,000 |
|---|---|---|
| Years' Purchase perp. @ $7\frac{1}{2}\%$ ... ... ... | | 13·33 |
| Value if income were receivable at once ... ... | | £13,330 |
| P.V. £1 in 20 years @ $7\frac{1}{2}\%$ ... ... ... | | ·235 |
| *Value of freeholder's deferred income, say* | | £3,130 |

The above calculation may be expressed in a slightly different form by first deferring the figure of Years' Purchase and then applying it to the income thus:—

| | Future Net Income | £1,000 |
|---|---|---|
| Y.P. perpetuity @ $7\frac{1}{2}\%$ ... ... | = | 13·33 |
| P.V. £1 in 20 years @ $7\frac{1}{2}\%$ ... | | ·235 |
| Y.P. perp. deferred 20 years @ $7\frac{1}{2}\%$ ... ... | | 3·13 |
| | *Value* | £3,130 |

Or an alternative method is to subtract from the figure of Years' Purchase for perpetuity the Years' Purchase for the number of years which must elapse before the perpetual income commences. as follows:—

|  | | | Future Net Income | £1,000 |
|---|---|---|---|---|
| Y.P. perp. @ 7½ %... | ... | ... | = 13·33 | |
| Y.P. 20 years @ 7½% | ... | ... | = 10·19 | |
| Y.P. perp. deferred 20 years @ 7½% | ... | ... | 3·14 | |
| | | | *Value* | £3,140 |

Where the income to be valued will ultimately be receivable in perpetuity, as in the above example, the same result may be obtained direct by the use of the table of " P.V. of £1 p.a. receivable in Perpetuity after the expiration of a given number of years " on pp. 41–56 of Parry's Tables.[1] Thus the figure of Y.P. for perpetuity deferred 20 years at 7½ per cent is given as 3·14.

The advantage as regards capital appreciation free of income tax which is possessed by this type of investment was commented on in Chapter 5, Section 3. In cases of deferred incomes where a valuer (probably with capital appreciation in mind) decides to use the Present Value of £1 adjusted for the incidence of income tax, it is quicker to refer to the tables of Years' Purchase of a reversion to a perpetuity in the coloured pages of Parry's Tables.)

Where the deferred income will be receivable for a limited number of years only, the appropriate figure of Years' Purchase must be found by one of the following alternative rules:—

(i) Multiply the Years' Purchase for the period for which the income will be received by the P.V. of £1 receivable at the end of the period which must elapse before the income starts; or

(ii) Subtract the Years' Purchase for the period which must elapse before the income starts from the Years' Purchase for a period extending from the present day up to the time when the income ceases.

The second rule must only be used when single rate tables are employed in the calculation. Its application to dual rate figures involves a mathematical error which will be explained in a later example.

*Example.*—What is the capital value of an income of £500 receivable for a period of 20 years commencing in 10 years' time? Assume 5 per cent to be the rate of interest on capital and also the rate at which a sinking fund can be accumulated.

---

[1] 9th Edition.

*Valuation—*

*Applying Rule* (i).

| | | | |
|---|---|---:|---:|
| | Future Net Income | | £500 |
| Y.P. 20 years @ 5% ... ... ... | | 12·462 | |
| P.V. of £1 in 10 years @ 5% ... | ... | ·614 | |
| | | | |
| Y.P. 20 years deferred 10 years @ 5% | ... | | 7·65 |
| | | | |
| | *Value of deferred income* | | £3,825 |

*Or, applying Rule* (ii).

| | | | |
|---|---|---:|---:|
| | Future Net Income | | £500 |
| Y.P. 30 years @ 5% ... ... | | = 15·372 | |
| Y.P. 10 years @ 5% ... ... | | = 7·722 | |
| | | | |
| Y.P. 20 years deferred 10 years @ 5% | ... | | 7·65 |
| | | | |
| | *Value of deferred income* | | £3,825 |

2. VARYING INCOMES

More often than not the valuation of a deferred income forms part of the calculation involved in finding the capital value of some property, the income from which may be expected to increase or decrease in the future.

The following are typical examples of such cases:—

(i) Freehold property at present let for the remainder of a building lease at a ground rent. When the ground lease expires the freeholder will be in possession of the full rack rental value of land and buildings.

(ii) Land and buildings at present let on lease at a low rent. When the present lease expires, the owner will be able to re-let at the full rental value of the premises. Or the reverse case of a property let on lease at a rent greater than its present rental value, with the prospect of a reversion to a lower rent when the lease runs out.

(iii) Property let on lease at a rising rent—e.g., for a term of twenty-one years, at a rent of £100 for the first seven years, £125 for the next seven, and £150 for the balance of the term.

In all such cases the mathematical problem involved is that of valuing the present income for the period for which it is likely to endure and then estimating the present capital value of the reversion to a greater or less income in the future. The second part of the calculation will involve the use of those rules referred to in Section 1 of this Chapter.

Besides the mere mathematics of the question, however, the valuer must exercise his judgment and experience as to the security of the income at the different stages of his calculation.

In case (i) above, the present income is probably derived from a well secured freehold ground rent which may fairly be capitalised on a 5 per cent to 7 per cent basis. But the future income will be derived from the full rack rental of land and buildings combined and will not afford the same security; in valuing it a higher rate per cent must be adopted appropriate to the type of property from which the income will be derived—houses, shops, offices, etc.

In case (ii), if the property is leased at less than its true rental value the security of the present income will be greater than that of the estimated income obtainable when the property is re-let, and a somewhat lower rate per cent should be adopted than that used for the reversion. On the other hand, if property is over-rented the security will be reduced and the income under the present lease may have to be valued at a higher rate per cent than would be appropriate for the true rack rental value, unless the apparent lack of security is offset by the fact that the present lessees are a substantial undertaking whose personal covenant to pay the rent is a guarantee of the income.

These considerations have already been discussed in some detail in Section 4 of Chapter 3.

The following examples illustrate the above points as well as the mathematical process of valuing varying incomes.

*Example.*—Freehold ground rents of £600 per annum (£120 per annum each) are secured on five shop properties of an estimated rental value of £1,000 per annum each on full repairing lease. The ground leases are for 80 years, having 19 years unexpired and the buildings have been kept in good condition by the lessees under their repairing covenants. Value the freeholder's interest.

*Valuation—*

| | | | |
|---|---|---|---|
| *Income for next* 19 *years*...... | | £600 | |
| Y.P. 19 years @ 6% (well secured freehold G.R's) ... ... ... ... | | 11·16 | |
| | | | £6,696 |
| *Reversion to rack rents* (net) | | £5,000 | |
| Y.P. perp. @ 8% ... ... = | 12·5 | | |
| Y.P. 19 years @ 8% ... = | 9·6 | | |
| Y.P. perp. deferred 19 years @ 8% | | 2·90 | |
| | | | £14,500 |
| | | | £21,196 |
| | | *But, say,* | £21,200 |

*Note.*—(i) The figure of 2·90 could also have been obtained direct from the table of " P.V. of a Reversion to a Perpetuity " or by multiplying 12·50 by P.V. of £1 in 19 years at 8 per cent.

(ii) The rate of interest received during the term, i.e., for the next 19 years is $\dfrac{£600 \times 100}{£21,200} = 2·8\%$—i.e., *less* than the rate of interest used to find the multiplier of 11·16. Conversely when the income of £5,000 per annum in reversion is received the rate of interest will be $\dfrac{£5,000 \times 100}{£21,200} = 23·6\%$—i.e., *more* than the rate of interest used to find the capital value of the reversion.

*Example.*—A freehold shop and upper part in a first-class trading position let to a multiple firm on lease having four years unexpired at £1,450 per annum. The property is worth £2,800 per annum at the present time. Value the freeholder's interest.

*Valuation*—

| | | |
|---|---:|---:|
| *Income for next 4 years* (net) | £1,450 | |
| Y.P. 4 years @ 5½%   ...   ...   ... | 3·5 | |
| | | £5,075 |
| *Reversion to full rack rent* (net) | £2,800 | |
| Y.P. perp. @ 7% ...   ...   = | 14·3 | |
| Y.P. 4 years @ 7%   ...   = | 3·4 | |
| Y.P. perp. deferred 4 years @ 7%   ... | 10·9 | |
| | | £30,520 |
| | *Say* | £35,600 |

*Example.*—Freehold shop property in a newly developing area has just been let on a 21 years' full repairing lease to a substantial firm at a rent of £800 for the first 7 years, £1,000 for the next 7 years and £1,200 for the balance of the term. These rising rents are intended to keep pace with probable increases in rental value in the district, and it is for this reason that the same rate of interest is used to capitalise each rent. It is expected that at the end of the lease the premises will readily re-let at £1,200.

Value the freeholder's interest.

*Valuation*—

*Method* (1)

| | | |
|---|---:|---:|
| *First seven years*    Rent reserved | £800 | |
| Y.P. 7 years @ 8%   ...   ...   ... | 5·21 | |
| | | £4,168 |

| | | | |
|---|---|---|---|
| *Next seven years* | Rent reserved | £1,000 | |
| Y.P. 7 years @ 8% ... ... | 5·21 | | |
| P.V. £1 in 7 years @ 8% ... | ·58 | | |
| | | 3·03 | |
| | | | £3,030 |
| *Last seven years and Reversion to* ...£1,200 | | | |
| Y.P. perp. deferred 14 years @ 8% ... | 4·26 | | |
| | | | £5,112 |
| | | *Value, say* | £12,300 |

*Method* (2)

| | | | |
|---|---|---|---|
| *First seven years* | Value as above | | £4,168 |
| *Next seven years* | Rent reserved | £1,000 | |
| Y.P. 14 years @ 8% ... ... | 8·24 | | |
| *Deduct* Y.P. 7 years @ 8% ... | 5·21 | | |
| | | 3·03 | |
| | | | £3,030 |
| *Last seven years and* | | | |
| *Reversion to* | Rent reserved | £1,200 | |
| Y.P. perp. @ 8% ... ... | 12·50 | | |
| *Deduct* Y.P. 14 years @ 8% ... | 8·24 | | |
| | | 4·26 | |
| | | | £5,112 |
| | | *Value, say* | £12,300 |

*Example.*—It is required to value a leasehold shop held for a term of 99 years having 60 years still to run at a ground rent of £30 per annum. The shop is sub-let on repairing lease expiring in 15 years' time at £600. The present estimated rental value on lease is £1,000.

*Valuation*—

| | | | |
|---|---|---|---|
| *Next* 15 *years* | Rent reserved | £600 | |
| *Deduct* ground rent ... ... ... | 30 | | |
| | Net Income | £570 | |
| Y.P. 15 years at 8% and 2½% ... ... | 7·37 | | |
| | | | £4,200 |
| *Last* 45 *years* Estimated rental value ... | £1,000 | | |
| *Deduct* ground rent ... ... ... | 30 | | |
| | Net Income | £970 | |
| Y.P. 45 years @ 9% and 2½% ... | 9·78 | | |
| P.V. of £1 in 15 years @ 9% ... | ·27 | | |
| | | 2·64 | |
| | | | £2,561 |
| | | *Value, say* | £6,750 |

In this case, which involves the use of *Dual Rate* figures, Method (2), shown in the previous example, would give a different result. Thus:—

| | | | |
|---|---|---|---|
| (*a*) Y.P. 60 years @ 9 and 2½% | ... | ... | 10·272 |
| *Less* (*b*) Y.P. 15 years @ 9 and 2½% | ... | ... | 6·860 |
| | | | 3·412 |

The reason for this difference is that in (*a*) the figure of Years' Purchase used allows for sinking fund at 2½ per cent for a longer period than that actually required (i.e., 60 years instead of 45 years); and in (*b*) for sinking fund for a shorter period than that actually required (i.e., 15 years instead of 45 years). Subtraction of the one figure from the other does not correct these errors.

In most cases the effect on the figure of Years' Purchase for the deferred term is comparatively slight, but in some cases the ultimate effect may be substantial. The point does not arise in connection with the use of single rate figures since, as explained in Section 6 of Chapter 5, these are made up of the totals of the separate present values of each instalment of income receivable in the future.

The calculation as set out in the last example envisages the taking out of two sinking funds. In practice one sinking fund only would in all probability be taken out. This might be on the basis that the annual sinking fund remains equal throughout the whole term of 60 years or on the basis that the premium for the last 45 years was greater (possibly in proportion to the net income) than that to be paid in the first 15 years of the term. In either case, the mathematical result would not be the same as that arrived at above.

A calculation based on a single sinking fund involves the use of an equation. The method shown on the lower half of p. 72 is sufficiently accurate for most cases in practice and this method is used in examples included later in the book. Nevertheless its inherent inaccuracy and the difficulty involved in its use when allowance is made for the incidence of income tax on the sinking fund element in the net income, should be recognised. These matters are considered in some detail in Appendix A.

### 3. VIRTUAL RENT AND COSTS IN USE

"Virtual" or "sitting" rent is the term applied to the true annual cost of premises to a lessee. It is the rent paid plus the annual equivalent of any capital sums he may have expended on the premises from time to time.

When a person expends capital on property in which he has only a terminable interest, it must be remembered that not only might this capital invested elsewhere have borne interest at a fair rate per cent, but also that an annual sinking fund ought to be provided to replace this capital by the time the party's interest in the property expires.

For instance, if a lessee whose term has thirty years still to run spends £500 on improvements to the property, not only will the expenditure cost him interest on the £500 throughout the term, but he ought also to provide for the replacement of the £500 by the time his lease runs out thirty years hence.

The annual amount of interest and sinking fund on the sum in question is known as its " annual equivalent " and can be found either by multiplying the capital sum by " the annuity which £1 will purchase," or by dividing it by the appropriate figure of Years' Purchase for the period which the lease still has to run when the expenditure is made. The effect of either method is to spread the expenditure over the term and show its true annual cost to the lessee.

The rate per cent at which interest on capital is allowed will be that which might reasonably be expected from a security of similar type to the property in question.

*Example.*—What is the annual equivalent of a capital sum of £500 expended on property by a lessee whose term has still thirty years to run, assuming interest on capital at 7 per cent?

*Answer*—

$$\frac{\text{Capital Expenditure £500}}{\text{Y.P. 30 years @ 7 and 2}\frac{1}{2}\% \text{ (Tax @ 38·75\%)}}$$
$$= \frac{£500}{9\cdot33}$$
$$= \textit{Equivalent annual cost} \qquad £54$$

Capital expenditure by a lessee may be of two principal types— (i) a premium paid on the taking up of a lease; (ii) alterations, improvements and other capital works to the property itself.

In either case the annual equivalent of the capital sum or sums expended must be added to the rent actually paid in order to find the lessee's " virtual " or " sitting " rent. But in regard to (ii) it should be noted that the capital sum must be spread over the number of years still remaining to the lease at the time when the expenditure was made, since this is the period over which the lessee should be providing a sinking fund for the replacement of the sum in question.

Additions or improvements to a property—the building of a garage or the putting in of a new shop front—are clearly capital expenditure. But a large sum spent on internal and external decorations and repairs after a lessee has been in possession for a number of years may properly be regarded as merely accrued annual repairs. On the other hand, if a lessee spends a considerable sum on repairs immediately upon taking up a lease, it may fairly be assumed that the rent reserved was lower on account of the condition of the premises and that the expenditure is really in the nature of a premium, which should be spread over the term of the lease in calculating the sitting rent.

When a lessee carries out alterations to a property, he may have to enter into a covenant with his landlord that he will restore the premises to their original form at the end of the lease. The estimated cost of this work must then be considered in calculating virtual rent. The lessee will not only lose interest on this sum during the term, but he should be setting aside a sinking fund to provide for it, and this will form part of the annual equivalent cost of the premises to him.

Where premises are used for a trade, business or profession, a tenant who makes an improvement to the property may be entitled to compensation for it at the end of his tenancy under the terms of the Landlord and Tenant Act, 1927, or he may be entitled to a new lease on the expiration of the present term under the Landlord and Tenant Act, 1954 (Part II) at a rent which excludes the value of the improvement. Where either is the case, it is not necessary to provide for the setting aside of a sinking fund for part or whole of the cost of the work. In practice, the compensation payable under the 1927 Act is often a somewhat speculative matter, and the claim to a new term under the 1954 Act may be defeated.

The provisions of these Acts are dealt with in a later Chapter.

Repairs, rates and other outgoings which the lessee pays are not usually taken into account in finding the virtual rent or annual equivalent cost of the premises to him, i.e., virtual rent is usually on the same basis as net rent.

Two main reasons are usually given as a justification for the calculation of virtual rent:—

(a) So that an actual occupier may know the annual cost to him of his occupation.

(b) So that a prospective occupier can decide between alternatives—for example, buying one set of premises freehold or taking a lease of similar premises and paying a premium plus an annual rent. In the circumstances cited where the premises are similar, the practice of ignoring repairs, rates and other outgoings will do no harm but clearly prospective occupiers may wish to examine other alternatives—for example, the alternative of taking new premises with a high rent but low annual repair costs against old premises with a low rent and high annual repair costs. In such a case, ignoring repair costs would be fatal to the exercise.

A method which allows a full comparison of alternatives to be made is that of " Costs in Use." The principles involved are similar to those applied to virtual rent and the method of dealing with capital costs is the same, although less complex mathematical devices than those discussed are frequently used. The main difference arises over annual costs and for costs in use purposes all annual costs are brought into consideration. Thus costs of lighting and heating would be brought in and such things as additional labour costs which might be incurred if a poorly laid-out factory were preferred to a well laid-out factory, additional handling costs which might be incurred if a multi-storey warehouse were preferred to a single-storey warehouse.

### 4. Premiums and Extensions and Renewals of Leases

A premium usually takes the form of a sum of money paid by a lessee to a lessor for the grant or renewal of a lease on favourable terms or for some other benefit.

Where a premium is paid at the commencement of a lease, it is usually in consideration of the rent reserved being fixed at a figure less than the true rental value of the premises.

From the lessor's point of view this arrangement has the advantage of giving additional security to the rent reserved under the lease, since the lessee, having paid a capital sum on entry, has a definite financial interest in the property, which ensures that he will do his utmost throughout the term to pay the rent reserved and otherwise observe the covenants of the lease. Premiums are only likely to be paid where there is a strong demand for premises on the part of prospective tenants.

The parties may agree first on the proposed reduction in rent and then fix an appropriate sum as premium, or they may decide the capital sum to be paid as premium and then agree on the reduction in rent which should be allowed in consideration of it.

In either case, since it is the lessor who stands to gain most from the arrangement, the calculation is usually made from the lessee's point of view, which tends to give a slightly lower figure.

Where the reduction in rent is agreed, the appropriate premium will be found by treating this reduction as a profit rent to be enjoyed by the lessee and capitalising it by the Years' Purchase for the term of the lease.

Where the premium is fixed first, in order to arrive at the reduction to be made in the rent it will be necessary to spread it over the term either by multiplying the agreed figure by the annuity which £1 will purchase, or by dividing by the Years' Purchase for the term of the lease.

*Example.*—(*a*) Estimate the premium that should be paid by a lessee who is to be granted a 30-years lease of shop premises at a rent of £1,000 p.a. The full rental value of the premises is £1,500 p.a.

(*b*) A shop worth £250 p.a. is about to be let on full repairing lease for 35 years. It is agreed between the parties that the lessee shall pay a premium of £700 on the grant of the lease. What should the rent be throughout the term?

*Note.*—In both cases the parties have agreed that the calculation shall be based on the dual rate table of Years' Purchase at 8 and $2\frac{1}{2}$ per cent (Tax @ 40%).

*Answer—*

(*a*)

| | | |
|---|---|---|
| Present rental value ... ... ... ... | £1,500 | |
| Rent to be paid under lease ... ... ... | £1,000 | |
| | | |
| Future profit rent ... ... ... ... | £500 | |
| Years' Purchase for 30 years @ 8 and $2\frac{1}{2}$% (Tax @ 40%) ... ... ... ... ... | 8·48 | |
| | | |
| *Premium, say* | £4,240 | |

(*b*)

Present rental value ... ... ... ... £250

*Deduct:* Annual equivalent of proposed premium of £700:

$$\frac{£700}{\text{Y.P. 35 yrs. @ 8 and } 2\frac{1}{2}\% \text{ (Tax @ 40\%)}} = \frac{700}{9\cdot06} = £77$$

*Rent to be reserved, say* £175

Where the term of a lease is drawing to a close, lessees frequently approach their lessors with a view to an extension or renewal of the term so as to be able to sell the goodwill of the businesses which they have built up.

The usual arrangement is for the lessee to surrender the balance of his present term in exchange for the grant of a new lease, probably for the term on which he originally held, or for some other agreed period.

The Landlord and Tenant Act, 1954, which gives tenants of business premises security of tenure has not seriously affected this practice. It has undoubtedly strengthened the hand of the lessee in negotiations; but tenants prefer to hold their premises under a definite lease rather than to rely merely on their rights under the Act which in the end depend upon litigation and an intending purchaser of a business held on a short lease will not as a rule go ahead relying merely on rights under this Act.

If the true rental value of the premises exceeds the rent reserved under the present lease, it is obvious that the lessee will have to compensate the lessor for the proposed extension. The form which this compensation shall take is a matter of arrangement between the parties. It may be agreed that the fresh lease shall be granted at the same rent and on the same terms as at present, the lessee paying a premium to the lessor; or the payment of a capital sum may be dispensed with in consideration of the lessee paying an increased rent throughout the proposed new term. Again, the parties may agree on the payment of a certain sum as premium and also on an increased rent throughout the term, with the possible additional obligation on the lessee of making some capital improvement to the premises when the new lease is granted.

The valuer usually acts for one side or the other and in rare cases may be called upon to decide as between the parties the appropriate figure of increased rent or premium.

The calculation may be made either from the lessee's or the lessor's point of view, but in any case the lessee must be credited with the improved value of the property for the unexpired term of the existing lease. For example, suppose the balance of the lessee's term is seven years and he is occupying the premises at a profit rent of £500 a year, it is clear that he has a valuable interest in the property which he will be giving up in exchange for the new lease. He is therefore entitled to have the value of the surrendered portion of his term set off against any benefits which he may derive from the proposed extension.

Whether the calculation is made from the lessor's or the lessee's point of view the principle involved is that of—(i) estimating the value of the party's interest in the property, assuming no alteration in the present term was made; and (ii) estimating the value of the party's interest, assuming that the proposed renewal or extension were granted. The difference between these two figures should indicate the extent to which the lessee will gain or the lessor lose by the proposed extension.

If a premium is to be paid, the above method will suggest the appropriate figure. If, instead of a premium, the parties agree on the payment of an increased rent, the required figure may be found by adding to the present rent the annual equivalent of the capital sum arrived at above, although the method used in the examples below is to be preferred.

The terms for the extension or renewal of a lease are seldom a matter of precise mathematical calculation. An estimate of rent or premium made from the freeholder's standpoint usually differs from one made from the lessee's, and the figure finally agreed is a matter for negotiation. A valuer acting for either lessor or lessee will carefully consider all the circumstances of the particular case, not only as they affect his own client but also as they affect the opposite party. Probably he will make valuations from both points of view as a guide to the figure which the other side might be prepared to agree in the course of bargaining.

Since the balance of the lessee's term is usually a short one, the incidence of income tax on sinking fund should be considered in valuing his interest under the existing lease. It will be borne in mind, however, that the lessee is not, as a matter of fact, placing his short leasehold interest on the market. On the contrary, the fact that negotiations for renewal have been opened suggests that both lessor and lessee are provisionally agreed on the lessee continuing in possession. While, therefore, the question of income tax on sinking fund cannot be ignored, and while since the last war it has become more usual in practice to calculate its precise mathematical significance in any particular case under consideration, it may in some cases affect the negotiations indirectly rather than be raised as a direct issue by either party.

If the effect of income tax is taken directly into account in calculating the value of the lessee's present interest, the calculation of the proposed interest should be on the same basis.

In the three examples which follow, the calculation of premium or rent has been made from both the freeholder's and the lessee's points of view. The effect of income tax at 40% on the open market value of the lessee's present and future interests has been taken into account.

*Example.*—A lessee holding a shop on a repairing lease for 40 years, of which six years are unexpired, desires to surrender his lease and to obtain a fresh lease for 40 years at the same rent. The rent reserved under the present lease is £1,000. The true rental value is £2,500 per annum.

What premium can reasonably be agreed between the parties?

(1) *Lessee's point of view:*

*Proposed Interest—*

|  |  |  |
|---|---|---|
| Profit rent ... ... | £1,500 p.a. | |
| Y.P. 40 years @ 8 and 2½% | | |
| (Tax @ 40%) ... ... ... | 9·55 | |
| | | £14,340 |

*Present Interest—*

|  |  |  |
|---|---|---|
| Profit rent ... ... | £1,500 p.a. | |
| Y.P. 6 years @ 8 and 2½% | | |
| (Tax @ 40%) ... ... ... ... | 2·93 | |
| | | £4,395 |

On this basis *Gain to Lessee* £9,945

(2) *Freeholder's point of view:*

*Present Interest—*

| | | | |
|---|---|---|---|
| *Next* 6 *years* | Rent reserved | £1,000 | |
| Y.P. 6 years @ 6% (well secured) | | 4·92 | |
| | | | £4,920 |
| *Reversion to* | True rental value | £2,500 | |
| Y.P. perp. deferred 6 yrs. @ 7% | | 9·52 | |
| | | | £23,800 |
| | | | £28,720 |

*Proposed Interest—*

| | | | |
|---|---|---|---|
| *Next* 40 *years* | Proposed rent | £1,000 | |
| Y.P. 40 years @ 6% ... ... | | 15·046 | |
| | | | £15,046 |
| *Reversion to* | True rental value | £2,500 | |
| Y.P. perp. deferred 40 years @ 7% ... ... ... ... | | ·954 | |
| | | | £2,385 |
| | | | £17,431 |

| | |
|---|---|
| *Loss to Freeholder* | £11,289 |

The premium will probably be fixed at, say, £10,500.

*Example.*—Assume that in the previous example it was agreed that the lessee should pay an increased rent throughout the new term in lieu of a premium; what should that rent be?

(1) *Lessee's point of view:*

| | | |
|---|---|---|
| Full rental value ... ... ... ... | | £2,500 |
| *Deduct* annual equivalent of value of present interest:—(see above) ... ... | £4,395 | |
| | | = £460 |
| ÷ Y.P. 40 years @ 8 and 2½% (adjusted for tax @ 40%) ... ... ... ... | 9·55 | |
| *Fair rent for new lease, say* | | £2,040 |

(2) *Freeholder's point of view:*

| | |
|---|---|
| Value of present interest (as above) ... | £28,720 |
| *Deduct* value of proposed reversion to £2,500 (as above) ... ... ... | £2,385 |
| Value of proposed term ... ... ... | £26,335 |
| ÷ Y.P. 40 years @ 6½% ... ... ... | 14·15 |
| *Fair rent for new lease, say* | £1,850 |

The rent will probably be fixed at £1,950 p.a.

The above approach from the freeholder's point of view rests upon the assumption that so long as the capital value of his interest is not lowered, he will be satisfied with the arrangement.

Where, as part of a bargain for a renewal or extension of a lease, the lessee is to make an expenditure upon the property which will benefit the value of the lessor's reversion, the lessee must be given credit for the value due to his expenditure which will enure to the lessor at the end of the term, and the sum must be taken into account when considering the cost of the new lease to the lessee.

*Example.*—A warehouse in a city centre is held on a lease having 8 years unexpired at £2,700 a year. The present rental value is £4,000 per annum. The lessee is willing to spend £10,000 upon improvements and alterations affecting only the interior of the building, which will increase the rental value by £1,600 per annum, provided the lessor will accept a surrender of the present lease and grant a new lease for a term of 30 years. The lessee is willing to pay a fair rent under the new lease or a premium. The lessor is agreeable to grant the new lease provided that the rent is fixed at £2,500 per annum, that a proper premium is paid and that the new lease contains a covenant that the lessee will carry out the improvements. What premium, if any, should you advise the lessee to offer if the new rent is £2,500 p.a.?

*Answer—*
(1) *Lessee's point of view* :
Proposed Interest—

| | | | | | |
|---|---|---|---|---|---|
| Rental value ... ... ... | £4,000 | | | |
| *Add* value due to outlay ... | £1,600 | | | |
| | | £5,600 | | |
| Head rent | | £2,500 | | |
| Profit rent | | £3,100 | | |
| Y.P. 30 years @ 11 & 2½% (adjusted for tax @ 40%) | | 6·76 | | |
| | | | £20,956 | |
| *Deduct* expenditure on improvement | | | £10,000 | |
| | | | £10,956 | |

Present Interest—

| | | | |
|---|---|---|---|
| Rental value | £4,000 | | |
| Rent paid | £2,700 | | |
| Profit rent | £3,100 ·300 | | |
| Y.P. 8 years @ 11 & 2½% (adjusted for tax @ 40%) | 3·32 | | |
| | | £4,316 | |
| *Gain to Lessee* | | £6,640 | |

(2) *Freeholder's point of view :*
   *Present Interest—*

| | | | | | |
|---|---|---|---|---|---|
| First 8 years | ... | ... | ... | ... | £2,700 |
| Y.P. 8 years @ 8% | ... | ... | ... | 5·75 | |
| | | | | | £15,525 |

*Reversion*

   *Note.*—Since the estimated increase in rent due to improvements represents 16 per cent on the sum expended, and since this is greater than the rate of interest which might reasonably be expected from such a property as this when let at its full rack rental, it would be worth the landlord's while, at the end of the present lease, to carry out the improvements at his own expense in order to obtain the increased income. The reversion can therefore be valued as follows : —

| | | | | |
|---|---|---|---|---|
| *Reversion* to rental value after improvements | ... | ... | ... | £5,600 |
| Y.P. in perpetuity | ... | ... | | 10 |
| | | | | £56,000 |
| *Deduct* cost of improvements | ... | | | £10,000 |
| | | | | £46,000 |
| P.V. £1 in 8 years @ 10%... | ... | | | ·47 |
| | | | | £21,620 |

*Value of Present Interest* £37,145

*Proposed Interest—*

| | | | | | |
|---|---|---|---|---|---|
| First 30 years | ... | ... | ... | £2,500 | |
| Y.P. 8% for 30 years | ... | ... | | 11·26 | |
| | | | | | £28,150 |
| *Reversion* to full rental value | ... | | £5,600 | | |
| Y.P. perp. deferred 30 years @ 10% | | | ·57 | | |
| | | | | £3,192 | |
| | | | | | £31.342 |

*Loss to Freeholder, say* £5,800

Suppose that it had been decided between the parties that no premium should be paid and that the rent under the new lease should be adjusted accordingly. What would be a fair rent in these circumstances?

(1) *Lessee's point of view :*

| | | |
|---|---|---|
| Rental value after improvements have been carried out ...     ... | | £5,600 |
| *Deduct* annual equivalent of— cost of improvements ...     ... | £10,000 | |

*Present Interest—*

| | | | |
|---|---|---|---|
| Profit rent     ...     ...     ... | £1,300 | | |
| Y.P. 8 years @ 11 and 2½% (Tax @ 40%)     ...     ... | 3·32 | | |
| | | £4,316 | |
| | | £14,316 | |
| ÷ Y.P. 30 years @ 11 and 2½% (Tax at 40%)     ...     ... | | 6·76 | £2,120 |

*Fair rent for new lease*     £3,480 p.a.

(2) *Freeholder's point of view :*

| | | |
|---|---|---|
| Value of present interest, as above   ... | | £37,145 |
| *Deduct* value of proposed reversion to full rental value after improvements have been carried out     ...     ... | £5,600 | |
| Y.P. perp. deferred 30 years @ 10% | ·57 | |
| | | £3,192 |
| Value of proposed term     ...     ... | | £33,953 |
| ÷Y.P. 30 years @ 8% ...     ...     ... | | 11·26 |
| *Fair rent for new lease* | | £3,000 p.a. |

*Note.*—In the above case the calculation shows that the lessee can afford to pay either by way of rent or premium a larger sum than that which the landlord requires: this is frequently the case where the property has latent value.

# Chapter 7

## Outgoings

### 1. Generally

MOST TYPES of property are subject to outgoings of various kinds. Where the owner is also the occupier, he will be liable for all outgoings. In the case of leases it is usual to transfer most of the burden to the lessee. Nevertheless some outgoings in some cases will be borne by the landlord and in a few rare cases the whole may be paid by the landlord. Outgoings paid by the landlord must be deducted from the rent in order to find the net income derived from his interest in the property.

Where it is required to find the rental value of a property which is owner-occupied, the usual practice is to estimate the rent at which it might be expected to let on such a type of tenancy as is usual for that class of property and deduct the outgoings to which the owner would be liable under the terms of such a tenancy.

Outgoings may be fixed at ascertainable amounts, or may be wholly or partly variable in character and require to be estimated. For example, a house may be let on lease at an exclusive rent, the landlord being responsible for fire insurance only; in this case, the insurance premium can easily be ascertained and deducted from the rent paid. A similar house may be let on terms that the landlord shall be responsible for repairs; in this case, the cost will vary from year to year, and an estimate must be made of the equivalent average annual cost of repairs to be deducted from the rent.

It is proposed in this Chapter to discuss the principal outgoings to which land and buildings may be subject, but before doing so it may be pointed out that outgoings, besides affecting the net income from a property, may also influence the figure of Years' Purchase by which that income is capitalised.

Thus, in the case of properties let at inclusive rents, where the outgoings form a substantial proportion of the income, the possibility of future variations in outgoings, and consequently in net income, may affect the rate per cent at which the net income is valued, since the risk of such variations reflects upon the security of the income. For example, the present net income receivable from a block of flats may be accurately estimated, but the income in the future will vary from year to year according to the amount it is found necessary to expend on repairs.

In the case of properties to be let at an exclusive rent, the influence of outgoings is indirect, but the tenant will have regard to the outgoings to be paid by him in determining the rent he can afford to pay. For example, a prospective tenant may be offered two similar factory premises which, on other considerations, are of equal value; one of them he finds to be of indifferent construction and to have a considerable extent of external painting, with a consequent heavier liability to repair. In such a case he will be willing to offer a higher rent for the premises where the cost of repairs is likely to be less.

## 2. REPAIRS

(a) *Generally.*—The condition of repair of a property is an important factor to be taken into account when arriving at the capital value.

Regard must be had to the need for immediate repairs, if any, to the probable annual cost, and to the possibility of extensive works of repair, rebuilding or modernisation in the future.

The age, nature and construction of the buildings will affect the allowance to be made for repairs. Thus, a modern house, substantially built, with a minimum of external paintwork, will cost less to keep in repair than a house of some age, of indifferent construction and with extensive external woodwork. Again, by way of example, the stone houses found in Lincolnshire and other parts of the country need very little repair compared with the plaster and weather-boarded houses found in parts of the Eastern Counties.

(b) *Immediate Repairs.*—If such repairs are necessary, the usual practice is to calculate the capital value of the premises in good condition and then to deduct the estimated cost of putting them into that condition.

(c) *Annual Repairs Allowance.*—It is obvious that the cost of repair of premises will vary from year to year.

For the purpose of arriving at the net income of a property where the cost of repairs has to be deducted, it is necessary to reduce the periodic and variable cost to an average annual equivalent. This may be done by reference to past records, if available; by an estimate based on experience possibly, in some cases, expressed as a percentage of the rental value; or by examining in detail the cost of the various items of expenditure and their periods of recurrence.

Where reference is made to past records, it is essential to check the average cost thus shown by an independent estimate of what the same item of work would cost at the present day.

One of the dangers of using a percentage on rental value can be illustrated by the following example. Two houses are very similar physically, but one of them is so situated as to command a rent considerably in excess of the other; the cost of repair is likely to be similar, but different percentages would have to be taken to arrive at the correct answer. While the percentage basis may be of some use, it is suggested that the only wise course is to judge each case on its merits and to make an estimate of the cost of the work required to put and keep the premises in good condition.

The third method of estimating the probable average annual cost of repairs is illustrated in the following example.

*Example.*—A small and well-built house of recent construction, comprising 3 bedrooms, 2 reception rooms, kitchen and bathroom, is let on an annual tenancy, the landlord being responsible for all repairs, at a fair rental of £350 per annum. From inspection it is found that the house is brick built, in good structural condition, with a minimum of external paintwork. It is required to estimate the average annual cost of repairs.

(a) Experience might suggest an allowance of 25 per cent of the rent.

(b) This estimate might be checked by considering the various items of expenditure and how often they are likely to be incurred, as follows:—

| | |
|---|---|
| (1) External decorations every 4th year £160      ...      ...      ...      ...      = | £40 p.a. |
| (2) Internal decorations every 7th year £210      ...      ...      ...      ...      = | £30 p.a. |
| (3) Pointing, every 25th year, £200      = | £8 p.a. |
| (4) Sundry repairs, say  ...      ...      ... | £12 p.a. |
| | £90 p.a. |

The method used in the example can be equally well applied to other types of property, regard being had in each case to the mode of construction, the age of the premises, the extent of the external paintwork and all other relevant factors which will affect the annual cost.

(*d*) *Conditions of tenancy.*—Regard must be had to the conditions of tenancy in estimating the annual cost. Where premises are let on lease the tenant is usually liable for all repairs and no deduction has to be made.

In many cases where houses are let for terms of three or five years there is some liability on the tenant for repairs. In the case of annual tenancies, or tenancies for a shorter period, the tenant usually undertakes a less stringent liability for repairs than in the case of a letting on an agreement for three or five years.

Reference should be made wherever possible to the actual lease or tenancy agreement to verify the exact liability to repair of the parties. In the case of short lettings, it must also be remembered that on the conclusion of the tenancy, the premises will need redecoration before re-letting or sale even if in a fair state of repair at the date of valuation.

If the cost of repairs is expressed as a percentage of the rental value it must not be forgotten that this may have been estimated upon the basis that the landlord may also have undertaken to pay other outgoings besides repairs. The percentage to be adopted in such cases where applied to the inclusive rent will be somewhat less.

(*e*) *Future Repairs.*—In considering the value of property it may be necessary to make allowance for the possibility of extensive works of repair, improvement, or even ultimate rebuilding in the future. Where the possibility of such works is long deferred it is not usual in practice to make a specific allowance therefor.

In some cases it may be necessary to make allowance for a contingent liability in the future. For example, at his inspection of a house a valuer finds that the flank wall is bulged. It is not in such a condition as to warrant any immediate expenditure, but there is the risk of expenditure in the future.

Where a number of similar properties are purchased for investment, it is suggested that it would be proper to make an allowance for such risks by a deduction of a proportion instead of the whole of the estimated cost in each case, it being reasonable to assume that in a number of cases the expenditure may not prove necessary.

### 3. Sinking Funds

The allocation of a proportion of a terminable income for reinstatement of capital has already been referred to.[1]

It is sometimes suggested that provision should be made, in addition to the cost of repairs, for a sinking fund for the reinstatement of buildings over the period of their useful life. In some countries it is standard practice to do so.

[1] See Chapter 5.

In the case of properties where the buildings are estimated to be nearing the end of their useful life this provision may have to be made, but in most valuations the risk of diminution in the value of buildings in the future is reflected in the percentage yield to be derived from the property.

### 4. GENERAL RATES

Rates are normally the personal liability of a tenant, but in some cases, such as lettings on weekly tenancies, the landlord undertakes to pay rates.

Rates are levied on the rateable value at a poundage which varies considerably in various districts.

To arrive at a fair amount to be deducted, regard must be had not only to the actual amount paid at the present time but also to possible changes in rate poundage and assessment in the future, if the rent cannot be increased on account of the increase in rates.

As regards changes of assessment, the present rateable value of a property must not necessarily be taken to be correct.

All assessments are due to be revised every few years.[2] An individual assessment may, however, be revised at any time.

If an assessment appears too high, regard should be had to the possibility of its amendment at the earliest possible moment. If too low, it is to be anticipated that it will be revised at least at the next revaluation.

It would obviously be incorrect, where no provision exists to adjust the rent paid in respect of alterations in rates, to base a valuation on the assumption that rates will continue at their present level, when there is every possibility of an increase in assessment.

With regard to possible variation in rate poundage, unless there is some clear indication of a substantial change in the future it is usual to assume continuance at the present amount.

It should be borne in mind that any alterations in rates due to changes in assessment and for rate poundage are passed on to the tenant in cases of tenancies under the Rent Acts where the rent is inclusive.

In the case of other tenancies at inclusive rentals the provisions of the lease or tenancy agreement must be examined to see if a similar provision is made. Where such " excess rates " clauses are present no account need be taken of possible changes in the future for the term of the lease or agreement.

### 5. RATES NOT INCLUDED IN THE GENERAL RATES

Water rate is usually chargeable at a percentage of the net annual value, and is payable by tenants. Where the landlord has undertaken to pay water rate this must be deducted.

---

[2] For further details see Chapter 16.

In certain districts there are special rates for certain purposes, and enquiries should always be made to ascertain if there are any such charges as sewer rate, drainage rate, betterment rate, and the like.

### 6. INCOME TAX, SCHEDULE A

The income from landed property, equally with that from other sources, is subject to income tax, which is assessed in accordance with the rules of the Income and Corporation Taxes Act, 1970.

As was explained in Chapter 5, it is customary to disregard income tax as an outgoing since it is a form of taxation to which all types of income are equally liable.

Allowance may have to be made for the tax, however, when valuing leaseholds and other assets of a wasting nature, such as sand and gravel pits. The reason for this is that the tax is levied on the full estimated net annual value of the property without regard to the necessity, in such cases, of a substantial proportion of the income having to be set aside as a sinking fund to replace capital.

### 7. TITHE REDEMPTION ANNUITY

This charge has now replaced " tithe rentcharge " which, in its turn, was derived from the old payment of " tithe."

" Tithe " consisted of a tenth part of the produce of the soil and of things nourished on the soil, but in 1836 tithe was commuted into a money payment known as tithe rentcharge.

The Tithe Act, 1936, abolished tithe rentcharge as from 2 October, 1936.

Tithe Redemption Annuity is payable half-yearly, 1 April and 1 October, and was formerly collected by a body known as the Tithe Redemption Commission; this has now been abolished and all of its functions have been transferred to the Inland Revenue.

The charge is usually payable by the freeholder, but if the land is leased for over fourteen years at a rent less than two-thirds the full net annual value the lessee will be liable.

Tithe redemption annuity may be redeemed in whole or in part at any time on the application of the land owner. In certain specified circumstances it is compulsorily redeemable. The cost of redemption will be the present value of the annuity calculated by the Treasury at a rate of interest fixed by reference to some appropriate Government security or securities.

### 8. INSURANCES

(a) *Fire Insurance.*—This outgoing is commonly borne by the landlord and will be deducted in finding the net income, unless the premises are let on lease, when the lessee usually undertakes to pay, or unless the tenant's occupation is for some hazardous purpose such as a wood-working factory, oil merchant, etc., when the tenant may have to pay the whole or a portion of the premium.

Where the premium is likely to be large, it may be desirable to check the amount for which the premises are insured to ensure that a proper allowance is made for fire insurance in arriving at the net income.

Usually the cost of fire insurance is comparatively small—from $7\frac{1}{2}$–$12\frac{1}{2}$p per cent on the sum insured—and it has often in the past been included in a general allowance for " repairs, insurance and management " based on a percentage of the rent.

(b) *Other Insurances.*—In many cases of inclusive lettings, e.g., where blocks of flats or offices are let in suites to numerous tenants, allowance must be made for special insurance, including insurance of lifts, employers' liability, third party insurance, and social security. These cases will be dealt with in greater detail in the Chapters relating to those types of property.

9. MANAGEMENT

Agency charges on lettings and management must be allowed for as a separate outgoing in certain cases.

An allowance should be made even where the investor will manage the property himself.

In cases where the amount of management is minimal, as with ground rents and property let on full repairing lease, the allowance would be so small that it can be ignored.

In yet other cases, such as agricultural lettings and houses let on yearly tenancies or short agreements, the item is often included in a general percentage allowance for " repairs, insurance and management ".

Where appropriate to make a separate deduction for " management," it can usually be estimated at from 5 per cent to 10 per cent of the gross rents.

It may be mentioned in this connection that the allowance to be made for this type of outgoing, and for voids and losses of rent referred to below, cannot be entirely dissociated from the Years' Purchase to be used. In making analysis of sales of properties let at inclusive rents the outgoings have to be deducted before a comparison can be made between net income and sale price to arrive at a Years' Purchase. If management is allowed for in analysis, the net income is reduced and a higher Years' Purchase is shown to have been paid than would have been the case if management was not allowed for.

Accordingly when, in making a valuation, a figure of Years' Purchase is used derived from analysis of previous sales, it is important that similar allowances are made for outgoings as were made in the cases analysed.

# Chapter 8

## Valuation of Life Interests

### 1. GENERALLY

IN THIS CHAPTER it is proposed to give a brief outline of the principles of determining the values of life interests in property and of the methods used in applying them.

In the case of freehold or leasehold property, the property passes on the death of the freeholder or lessee to his heirs or to whom he may specify and the income is therefore considered to continue in perpetuity or for the length of the lease as the case may be. With lifehold property, on the other hand, the interest ceases on death and the lifeholder has no control over who obtains the property on his death.

A life interest may exist in either freehold or leasehold property. A life interest in leasehold property ceases on the death of the tenant for life or the expiration of the lease, whichever is the earlier.

On the death of a tenant for life, the property passes either to a reversioner or a remainderman. A remainderman is a man other than the original grantor and his heirs who succeeds to the property while the original grantor or his heirs would be reversioners. A "contingent remainder" is a remainder depending upon a certain event before it takes effect, such as, for example, a remainderman outliving a tenant for life.

A tenant for life of a freehold interest is a person who is, in effect, the owner of the freehold for his life, although he has power to sell the freehold absolute in the settled land subject to devotion of the proceeds of sale to specified purposes protecting the reversioner. He may wish to sell his own life interest, an interest entitling the purchaser to the property for the life of the tenant for life only and it is with the valuation of such interests and associated interests that this chapter is concerned.

Leases for life can be made by a landlord granting a fixed term of years, terminable by himself or the lessee and his heirs on the death of a person named, usually the lessee. As one such party would gain by terminating the lease on the death, these interests are leases for life for all practical purposes.

The valuation problems which may arise when an interest in land is held for, or subject to, the life or lives of one or more persons, are various. Thus the valuer may have to determine:

(1) The value of a life interest in a freehold property.
(2) The value of the reversion to a freehold property after the death of a life tenant.
(3) The value of a life interest in a leasehold property.
(4) The value of the reversion to a leasehold interest after the death of a life tenant.
(5) The value of a life interest which will begin at the expiration of a certain period if the life is then in being (a contingent remainder).
(6) In any of the above cases the life interest may last only so long as two or more persons are alive, or it may last only so long as any one of two or more persons is still alive.

No new problems arise in the determination of the net income to be valued, nor in the choice of the appropriate remunerative rate per cent, except that, since the life of a particular individual is extremely uncertain, the purchase of any interest involving a life tenant must be speculative in nature and the demand for such interests is restricted. A rather higher rate would therefore be appropriate than that used for valuing incomes for terms certain. The new factor to be considered is the chance of life or death.

These chances are fairly well known, for although, to take an example, we have not the least idea how long a particular person now aged 50 will live, statistics show that, on the average, the mean expectation of life of men aged 50 is 22·68 years and of women of that age 27·57 years (see pages 484 and 485 of *Parry's Valuation Tables*—column $e_x$).

The Years Purchase for life tables, however, are not based upon the "mean expectation" figures but upon the basic information from which the mean expectation figures were derived. This is the English Life Table No. 12 based on population enumerated in the 1961 census and mortality experience of the population during 1960, 1961 and 1962.

A "Life Table" (see pages 484 and 485 of *Parry's Valuation Tables*, column $l_x$) shows how many, of some convenient number of infants born, may be expected to be alive at each year of life within the possible span of human existence. The number born in the English Life Table No. 12 is taken as 100,000. From this information, the table shows in column $p_x$ the "probability factor", that is the probability that a person of a given age will survive at least one year. Other probabilities can easily be determined. Thus the table shows that of 90,085 males alive at 50, 68,490 will attain the age of 65. The probability of a man aged 50 living to enjoy his pension at 65 is therefore, $\dfrac{68,490}{90,085}$.

## 2. SINGLE AND DUAL RATE SYSTEMS

A lifehold interest is a depreciating asset and provision can be made for the replacement of the capital invested in purchasing such an interest by taking out an insurance policy insuring the life for the purchase price as soon as the interest is bought. Interest allowed on the insurance premiums payable is unlikely to be obtained at as high a rate as the remunerative rate required from the investment and there is therefore a case for the use of dual rate tables.

Dual Rate Life Tables are not included in the ninth edition of *Parry's Valuation Tables* (they are available in the eighth edition) but Section 4 of this Chapter shows how the Years Purchase at a dual rate can be determined, if required.

Alternatively, the Years Purchase for a Single Life tables on pages 439 to 447 of *Parry's Valuation Tables* (which are based on the Single Rate principle) can be used, with an upwards adjustment of the remunerative rate, if considered necessary.

## 3. YEARS PURCHASE FOR A SINGLE LIFE— SINGLE RATE PER CENT

This problem can be worked from general principles as in the following example but it will be obvious that the amount of arithmetic involved will be very great unless the life tenant is of advanced age. The figures of Years Purchase for ages from 1–100 years, both male and female, are shown on pages 439 to 447 of *Parry's Valuation Tables*.

*Example*

What is the present value of an income of £1 per annum receivable for the life of a man now aged 102, interest being allowed at 5 per cent per annum.

The English Life Table No. 12 shows that of 100,000 males born, 25 will attain the age of 102. The table further shows that of these 25 persons, 15 will live to be 103. Thus the probability of a person who is just 102 living to receive an income payable if he lives to be 103 is $\frac{15}{25}$ or ·6 and this figure, the probability that a person of a given age will survive at least one year, is given in the English Life Table No. 12 (column $p_x$). The "contingent present value" of the first year's income is therefore, the present value of £1 in 1 year at 5 per cent multiplied by the probability of living to receive it:
$$£·952 \times ·6 = £·571$$

Similarly, with the second year's income, the Life Table shows

that only 9 persons will live two years more to be 104. The probability factor is, therefore, $\dfrac{9}{25}$ or ·36, and the contingent present value
of the second year's income:

$$£·907 \text{ (P.V. of £1 in 2 yrs. at 5\%)} \times ·36 = £·327$$

Each years contingent income is valued in this way. The tables
show, however, that no male will reach the age of 108. Thus the
sixth and subsequent years incomes will not be received by the tenant
for life. The years purchase (or present value of £1 per annum) is
the sum total of these contingent present values as follows:

| Age | Males alive | Probability factor (a) | P.V. (b) | Contingent P.V. (a)×(b) |
|-----|-------------|-------------------------|----------|--------------------------|
| 102 | 25 | | | |
| 103 | 15 | ·60 | ·952 | ·571 |
| 104 | 9 | ·36 | ·907 | ·327 |
| 105 | 5 | ·20 | ·864 | ·173 |
| 106 | 3 | ·12 | ·823 | ·099 |
| 107 | 2 | ·08 | ·784 | ·063 |
| 108 | 0 | Nil | ·746 | Nil |

Years Purchase (male) aged 102 @ 5%      1·233

## 4. YEARS PURCHASE FOR A SINGLE LIFE— DUAL RATE PER CENT

The problem here is to find the present value of an income of £1
per annum, receivable for a life, when interest on the capital value
is expected at a higher rate than the interest allowed in estimating
the premiums paid to insure that life.

For this purpose we must ascertain the annual premium payable
to insure the life. This could be obtained by enquiry from a prospective insurance company but a table of premiums required to
insure £1 at the end of the year in which a person may die for ages
from 1 to 100 years, based on the English Life Table No. 12 and at
premium interest rates from 3 to 5 per cent is given on pages 478–481
of *Parry's Valuation Tables*.

The table also contains typical premium rates which may be
offered by a Life Assurance Company for non-profit whole life
assurance for ages from 21–80 years.

Once the premium is known, the years purchase can be obtained
by an adaptation of the formula $Y.P. = \dfrac{1}{i + \text{s.f.}}$ which relates to leasehold interests.

The premium required to insure £1, can be substituted for "s.f." but in addition, allowance must be made for the fact that, unlike a sinking fund which is provided at the end of the year out of the year's income, the premium to insure the life must be paid as soon as the interest is purchased. The formula is therefore adapted to allow for this and becomes:

$$\text{Y.P.} = \frac{1 - P(1 + j)}{i + P(1 + j)}$$

where P = annual premium to secure £1
 i = remunerative rate required
 j = insurance premium interest rate.

*Example*

Calculate the Years Purchase in respect of the life of a man aged 40. The investor requires an 8 per cent return on capital he invests. The life can be insured for an annual premium of 1·54 per cent which is based on an insurance premium interest rate of 5 per cent.

$$\text{Y.P.} = \frac{1 - \cdot 0154 (1 + \cdot 05)}{\cdot 08 + \cdot 0154 (1 + \cdot 05)} = \frac{\cdot 98383}{\cdot 09617}$$
$$= 10 \cdot 23$$

This compares with a Y.P. (Single Rate) male aged 40 @ 8 per cent of 10·808.

It will be appreciated that the insurance premium has to be found out of taxable income, similar to the case of leaseholds where the sinking fund to replace capital must be found out of taxable income. With leaseholds, the coloured Y.P. tables allow for this by increasing the sinking fund element to $\frac{100}{100-t}$ s.f., where t is the tax rate expressed as a percentage. There are no coloured life tables but allowance can be made for this factor, if considered necessary, particularly where the life expectation is short and the premium to insure the life would be high, by an upwards adjustment of the remunerative rate.

## 5. REVERSION AFTER A DEATH TO A FREEHOLD INTEREST

The method used is that, from the present value of a perpetual income beginning at once, is subtracted the present value of the life interest.

*Example*

To find the Y.P. for a freehold reversion after the death of a man now aged 45, interest being reckoned at 8 per cent.

| Y.P. perpetuity @ 8% | 12·500 |
|---|---|
| Y.P. (male) aged 45 @ 8% | 10·206 |
| Y.P. for reversion | 2·294 |

This problem is one of the most important occurring in practice. The method used above may be compared with that employed in the valuation of perpetual incomes deferred for a term certain.

## 6.   LIFE INTERESTS IN LEASEHOLDS

An interest of this nature can arise where a person inherits a life interest in a leasehold property or where a leaseholder grants a life interest in his lease.   In either case, the maximum period the interest can last is the term of the lease, but the interest will cease beforehand if the life tenant dies.   The problem, therefore, is to find the present value of £1 p.a. receivable for the life of the tenant or the length of the lease, whichever is the shorter.

This could be worked from the general principles used in the calculation of the Y.P. for life (Single Rate) detailed in Section 3 of this Chapter.

*Example*

To find the present value at 6 per cent interest of an income of £1 p.a. receivable for a maximum period of three years, provided a woman, now aged 55, lives so long, or otherwise for as long as she lives.

The English Life Table No. 12 shows 90,652 women living at age 55.   Of this number, 90,034 will live to be 56

> 89,362 will attain the age of 57, and
>
> 88,631 will reach 58 in 3 years time when the lease expires.

Thus the contingent present value of the first years income is

$$\frac{90,034}{90,652} \times \text{P.V. of £1 in 1 yr. @ 6% (·943)} = ·937$$

and of the second year's income $\dfrac{89,362}{90,652} \times$ P.V. of £1 in 2 yrs. @ 6% (·890) $= ·877$

and of the third year's income $\dfrac{88,631}{90,652} \times$ P.V. of £1 in 3 yrs. @ 6% (·840) $= ·821$

The Years Purchase in respect of a life interest (female) aged 55 in a 3-year lease is the sum total of these contingent present values   ...      ...      ...      ...      ...   $= 2·635$

It is obvious that if the term is a long one and the life not very advanced, the calculation becomes very lengthy and laborious or alternatively a very large book of tables would be required. In practice therefore, a method of comparing the Y.P. for the lease with the Y.P. for life may be used. If the Y.P. for the life is the lower, this may be taken as the lease will probably last longer than the life. This Y.P. may be too high mathematically as it will consist of contingent present values for the whole possible life span whereas it should be limited as above to the years of the lease. An adjustment might be made, if considered appropriate. If the lease Y.P. is lower, that Y.P. may be taken with an appropriate reduction to allow for the possibility of the tenant dying before the end of the lease. Thus, in the above example the exact Y.P. has been calculated at 2·635 whereas the Y.P. for the lease period of 3 years at 6 per cent (Single Rate) is 2·673.

*Example*

What is the value of a life interest in a profit rent of £1,000 per annum held by a female aged 35 in a leasehold property having 55 years unexpired.

*Valuation—*

As it is necessary to compare two Y.P.s but there are no dual rate life tables, the single rate table has been used in both cases to be consistent, the remunerative rate being adjusted upwards accordingly.

| | |
|---|---:|
| Profit Rent ... ... ... ... ... ... | £1,000 |
| *Compare* Y.P. 55 yrs. @ 10% = 9·947 | |
| *with* Y.P. female aged 35 @ 10% = 9·540 | |
| The Y.P. for the life interest is less and that figure, 9·54 Y.P. is therefore taken. It is slightly too high, as it consists of more than 55 contingent present values. However, the error is only very small in this case, therefore say 9·5 Y.P. ... ... ... | 9·5 |
| | £9,500 |

*Example*

As above, but the lease has only 10 years unexpired.

| | |
|---|---:|
| Profit Rent ... ... ... ... ... ... | £1,000 |
| *Compare* Y.P. 10 yrs. @ 10% = 6·145 | |
| *with* Y.P. female aged 35 @ 10% = 9·540 | |
| The lease Y.P. is less. That figure, 6·145 Y.P., is taken and adjusted downwards to allow for the possible death of the tenant for life before the lease expires ... ... ... ... *Years Purchase, say,* | 6 |
| | £6,000 |

### 7.  VALUE OF A LEASEHOLD REVERSION AFTER A LIFE INTEREST

*Example*

What is the value of the reversion to a net income of £2,500 per annum from a good class shop property after the death of a tenant for life (female) aged 83.  The reversion is to a leasehold interest which has at present 63 years to run at a ground rent of £100 per annum.

*Valuation—*

The method involves a comparison between the Y.P. for the lease and the Y.P. for the existing life.

| | | |
|---|---|---:|
| Net Rent ... ... ... ... ... ... | | £2,500 |
| *Less* Ground Rent ... ... ... ... | | 100 |
| **Profit Rent** ... ... ... ... ... | | £2,400 |
| *Compare* Y.P. for the lease—Y.P. 63 yrs. @ 8% (single rate table used as we are comparing two Y.P.s and there are no dual rate life tables—the remunerative rate has, therefore, been increased to allow for this) | 12·402 | |
| *with* Y.P. for life aged 83 (female) @ 8% ... The tenant for life is likely to die before the lease expires and the difference between the two Y.P.s is taken as the Y.P. for the leasehold reversion ... ... ... ... ... | 3·456 | |
| | 8·946 | 8·946 |
| Value of leasehold reversion ... ... ... | | £21,470 |

*Example*

What is the value of a reversion to a net income of £1,000 per annum from statutory tenancies of small houses after the death of a tenant for life (male) aged 40.  The reversion is to a leasehold interest which has at present 10 years to run at a Ground Rent of £50 p.a.

*Valuation—*

| | | |
|---|---|---:|
| Net Rents from houses ... ... ... | | £1,000 |
| *Less* Ground Rent ... ... ... ... | | 50 |
| **Profit Rent** ... ... ... ... ... | | 950 |
| *Compare* Y.P. for 10 yrs. @ 10% ... ... (single rate taken and remunerative rate increased for the reason given in the previous example) | 6·145 | |
| *with* Y.P. for life aged 40 (male) @ 10% ... | 9·053 | |

Thus in this case, the chances are that the life tenant will outlive the lease, in which case the reversioner will never enjoy the profit rent. On the other hand, there is a possibility that the tenant for life may die before the lease ends so that the reversion must have some value, possibly only nominal.

The method may be criticised because the Y.P. for life is the present value of the chances of receiving an annual income for the whole possible life span of a male aged 40, whereas it should represent the present value of his receiving an income for 10 years only. The life Y.P. considered is, therefore, too large, the degree of inaccuracy depending upon the length of the lease and the age of the life tenant. However, the amount of labour involved in calculating an exact years purchase based upon the probability of receiving each years income would be tremendous except where the lease is very short or the life tenant very old.

### 8. VALUE OF A REMAINDERMANS' LIFE INTEREST COMMENCING ON THE DEATH OF THE EXISTING LIFE TENANT, IF THE REMAINDERMAN IS STILL ALIVE

This is a "contingent remainder" as the remainderman's interest is contingent upon his outliving the tenant for life. The value of the remainder is obtained by deducting the Y.P. for the existing life interest from the Y.P. for the remainderman's present age.

*Example*

Value the interest of a woman aged 24 who is a tenant for life of a freehold shop producing a net income of £2,000 per annum after the death of her father, aged 61.

| | | | | | |
|---|---|---|---|---|---:|
| Net Income | ... | ... | ... | ... | £2,000 |
| Y.P. for life (female) aged 24 @ 8% ... | | | ... | 12·054 | |
| Y.P. for life (male) aged 61 @ 8% | | | ... | 7·365 | |
| | | | | | 4·689 |
| | | | | | £9,378 |

### 9. YEARS PURCHASE FOR THE JOINT CONTINUATION OF TWO LIVES

Where an interest is dependent upon the continuation of both of two lives so that the interest terminates as soon as one of them ceases, the possibility of receipt of each year's income is reduced and the Present Value of each year's income will need to be multiplied by the probability of survival of each of the two persons. Otherwise the same method of computation is used as for the Y.P. for Single Life (Single Rate). The Y.P. for the joint continuation of two lives will thus be less than the Y.P. for either life. The tables are shown on pages 450 to 465 of *Parry's Valuation Tables*.

The same principle is used if the income is dependent on the joint continuation of three or more lives, the fractions of probability of each separate life being multiplied together to obtain the fraction of probability of their joint continuation.

*Example*

What is the value of a Net Income of £1,000 per annum secured upon a freehold shop property, held for the joint continuation of the lives of a man aged 60 and a woman aged 45?

| | | | | | | |
|---|---|---|---|---|---|---|
| Net Income ... | ... | ... | ... | ... | ... | £1,000 |
| Y.P. Joint continuation of two lives aged 45 (female) and 60 (male) @ 8% ... | | ... | ... | ... | ... | 7·306 |
| Capital Value | ... | ... | ... | ... | | £7,306 |

## 10. Years Purchase for the longer of Two Lives

The problem here is to find the Years Purchase of an income which is receivable as long as one or other of two persons is still alive. Thus the probability of the receipt of the income is increased beyond that of either single life.

The rule to be used is to add together the Years Purchase for each single life and to subtract from the total the Years Purchase for their joint continuation.

The reason for this rule is easy to see. The income lasts throughout both lives but if we add together the Y.P.s for each of the two lives we are double counting the period when they are both alive. We must, therefore, subtract the Y.P. for the joint continuation of their two lives.

*Example*

To find the Y.P. at 7 per cent of an income receivable for the longer of two lives of two women, now aged 60 and 75.

The Y.P. for the single lives is obtainable from page 445 of *Parrys' Valuation Tables* whilst that for their joint continuation is obtainable from page 465 of the same book.

| | | | | |
|---|---|---|---|---|
| Y.P. for life (female) aged 60 @ 7% ... | ... | ... | 9·477 |
| Y.P. for life (female) aged 75 @ 7% ... | ... | ... | 5·583 |
| | | | | 15·060 |
| Y.P. for Joint Continuation of two lives aged 60 and 75 (females) @ 7% ... | ... | ... | ... | 5·121 |
| Y.P. for longer of two lives aged 60 and 75 (females) @ 7% ... | ... | ... | ... | 9·939 |

A further example is given on page 469 of *Parry's Valuation Tables*.

# Chapter 9

## The Valuer—His Functions and Methods

### 1. GENERALLY

IT HAS already been emphasised that the primary problem of valuation is the ascertainment of present market value—that is, the price at which an interest in a property can be expected to sell as between a willing vendor and a willing purchaser, both of whom are fully informed regarding the interest in question, who are neither forced to buy nor to sell and who are free to deal elsewhere if they choose.

But although most of the valuer's problems involve consideration of present market value, there are often other factors in the problem to which his attention must also be directed.

It is often necessary to have regard to future trends of value, to consider if prices at which interests in properties have been sold are reasonable or likely to be maintained, and to examine the possibilities of changes in rental value.

When valuations are made for certain special purposes, e.g., for probate or in connection with compulsory purchase for public undertakings, the valuation, although based on market value, may be regulated by statutory provisions as to the date at which the valuation is to be assumed to be made and as to the factors which may or may not be taken into account in making it.

Again, where properties are purchased for investment, the valuer may be asked to advise on policy, to suggest what reserves should be created for future repairs or in respect of leasehold redemption, and to advise generally on the many problems involved in good estate management.

The knowledge required to deal with all these matters can only be gained by experience but the student will find it of great advantage to keep abreast of current affairs, international, national and local, and in the light of them to make a careful study of sale prices and rental values, particularly in areas with which he is acquainted and where he may have the opportunity of seeing the properties which are the subject of recorded transactions.

### 2. THE ANALYSIS OF RENTS AND SALES

In estimating the market value of an interest in property the valuer must consider all the evidence available.

The property may be let at a rent, in which event its reasonableness or otherwise must be considered in relation to the rents of other similar properties.

The rate per cent at which the net income is to be capitalised will be determined by reference to the rate shown by analysis of the sale price of other similar properties.

The keeping of accurate records of rents and sales prices, and of analyses of the latter to show investment yields is therefore of very great assistance to the work of the valuer.

An example is given in Chapter 3 of an analysis of rents made to determine the rental value of offices.

Similar methods, usually related to the superficial area of premises, can be used for the making and keeping of records in connection with a variety of properties.

In analysing sale prices the usual steps in making a valuation are reversed. The purchase price is divided by the estimated net income to find the figure of Years' Purchase, from which can be determined the rate per cent yield which the purchase price represents.

In the case of perpetual incomes the " yield," or rate per cent, at which the purchaser will receive interest on his money, can be found by dividing 100 by the figure of Years' Purchase. In the case of incomes receivable for a limited term, it must be found by reference to the Valuation Tables.

*Example.*—Freehold property producing a net income of £100 per annum has recently been sold for £2,000.

Analyse the result of this sale for future reference.

*Analysis.*— $\dfrac{\text{Purchase Price £2,000}}{\text{Net Income £100}}$ represents 20 Y.P.

$$\left.\begin{array}{l}\text{Rate at which purchaser will}\\ \text{receive interest on his money}\end{array}\right\} = \dfrac{100}{20\ \text{Y.P.}} = 5\%.$$

*Example.*—Shop premises held on lease for an unexpired term of 52 years at a rent of £150 have been sold for £1,300; the rental value is estimated to be £275.

*Analysis.*—The profit rental is £125. The purchase price is £1,300 which divided by £125 represents 10·4 Years' Purchase. On reference to the dual rate tables for a term of 52 years this is seen to be very nearly equal to 8 per cent and $2\frac{1}{2}$ per cent with tax at 38·75%.

*Example.*—Similar, but somewhat smaller, premises nearby are held on lease for an unexpired term of 45 years at £75; the lease was recently sold for £1,250. On the evidence of the previous example, at what do you estimate the rental value?

*Answer.*—It would seem proper to apply the rate per cent derived from the previous analysis.

$$\frac{\text{Sale Price}}{\text{Y.P. for 45 yrs. @ 8\% \& 2}\tfrac{1}{2}\% } = \frac{\text{£1,000}}{10\cdot0} = \text{£100 Profit rent}$$
(tax @ 38·75%)

Add lease rent     75 p.a.

Rental Value   £175 p.a.

Although this means of ascertaining rental value must be resorted to where other evidence is not available, if possible rental values should be estimated by analysing the results of recent lettings of comparable properties and an estimate based on the analysis of a capital transaction should be avoided if at all possible. The object of analysing a capital transaction is usually to find the remunerative rate of interest.

In many instances comparisons of rental value will only be of value if restricted to a particular locality; this is obviously so in the case of shops, where wide variations in rent can occur within a distance of a few hundred yards.

In the case of residential properties the area for comparison purposes may be more extended; although evidence of value of a particular type of property in one town may have little significance in relation to another town, say 30 miles away, even in respect of identical property.

In estimating the yield likely to be required from a particular type of investment, evidence over a much larger area can usefully be employed.

For instance, the yield from ground rents or good class shop properties is likely to be found similar on analysis over a large area.

The following example shows a convenient form of office record for sales of both leaseholds and freeholds.

*Example.*—In a well-established suburban shopping centre particulars are available of transactions in shop properties during the past year.

It is necessary to prepare records of these transactions, including an analysis of the sale prices, to indicate the investment yield in each case, from the following particulars:

(1) Substantial shop premises held for an unexpired term of 58 years at a ground rent of £50 per annum and let for 10 years unexpired to a good tenant at £400 on a full repairing lease. The full rental value is estimated at £700. Sold for £4,100.

(2) Freehold premises recently let at a fair rent of £650 per annum on a full repairing lease for 21 years. Sold for £8,125.

(3) Freehold premises worth £1,000 per annum but let for 7 years at £300 per annum. Sold for £9,000.

(4) Leasehold premises held for a term of 26 years at £400 per annum ground rent. The premises are sublet for 10 years at £700 per annum net and are worth £900 per annum. Sold for £2,300.

| 1 | 2 | | 3 | 4 | 5 | 6 | 7 | 8 | 9 | | 10 |
|---|---|---|---|---|---|---|---|---|---|---|---|
| Property | Map Ref. | | Interest Valued | Date of Sale | Sale Price | Present Net Income | Lease or Sub-lease | Estimated Net Rental Value | Rate of Interest | | Remarks |
| | Sheet | No. | | | | | | | Term | Reversion | |
| 1 | | | Leasehold 58 years @ £50 | | £ 4.100 | £ 350 | 10 years | £ 700 | 7 | 9 | S.F. 2½% Tax @ 38·75% |
| 2 | | | F | | 8,125 | 650 | 21 years | 650 | 8 | 8 | |
| 3 | | | F | | 9,000 | 300 | 7 years | 1,000 | 5 | 8 | |
| 4 | | | Leasehold 26 years @ £400 p.a. | | 2,300 | 300 | 10 years | 900 | 8 | 10 | S.F. 2½% Tax @ 38·75% High ground rer |

Notes.—

1. *In column 1 the address of the property would be inserted. A full description of the property is unnecessary as the data obtained from the records would probably relate largely to properties with which the valuer is acquainted and which, if in doubt on any point, he would inspect when making comparison.*

2. *In connection with records of this type it is useful to mark and number the properties on a set of 1/2500 or 1250 if available, ordnance plans or special street plans for each shopping centre are prepared in some cases.*

3. *The rates of interest in column 9 are found by making a calculation capitalising the rent reserved and the net income in reversion and finding by trial and error the rates of interest which give the closest figure to the sale price.*

It is in the analysis of past sales and the application of the evidence derived therefrom to a particular case that the skill and experience of the valuer is called into play. He must consider carefully the extent to which the property to be valued is similar to those that have been sold. The correctness or otherwise of the rent must be determined; trends of value since the evidence was accumulated must be considered.

In some cases the prices at which properties have changed hands may be above or below " market value ". The vendor may have been anxious to dispose of a property quickly and have taken a rather lower price than might have been expected; or a high price may have been given by a buyer in urgent need of a certain type of accommodation.

It follows that sales records cannot be used blindly. Sales transactions and lettings must be examined critically and allowances made for cases which depart from the general trend.

In some cases the general trend of sale prices or rents may be higher or lower than the valuer considers justified by the facts. In these circumstances, when advising on market value, he will no doubt point out that the present value is likely to change in the future by reason of factors that in his opinion have not received due consideration.

### 3. METHODS OF VALUATION

The investment method of valuation was introduced in Section 5 of Chapter 1. When valuing by this method the valuer will proceed on the following lines:—

1. He will determine the net income of the property.

2. He will determine the rate per cent at which it should be valued.

3. He will multiply the net income by a figure of Years' Purchase based, by reference to tables, on his estimate of the appropriate rate per cent.

It may happen that there is little or no evidence of other transactions upon which the valuer may base his estimates of rental value, or of the appropriate rate per cent. For example, in estimating the rental value of a shop it may be found that there have been no recent lettings of similar shops in the area. Or in dealing with a large industrial property, only suitable for a limited number of trades, similar properties are not likely to be numerous and may come into the market only on rare occasions.

Other methods of valuation are: —

(a) Direct comparisons of capital value.
(b) Valuations based on cost.
(c) Valuations by reference to profits.
(d) The residual or development method.

These methods may also be used as a check on a valuation made by the ordinary procedure; they may, however, introduce a larger margin of error and need considerable experience to be used to the best advantage.

In the case of properties for which the market is primarily for investment, it is usually preferable and more accurate to use rates of interest and rental value as the bases of comparison.

(a) *Direct Comparison of Capital Values.*—In some cases there may be very little evidence of rental value upon which the analysis of sales can be based to arrive at a rate per cent appropriate to the type of property in question; but there may be extensive evidence of sale prices. For instance, in many areas residential properties change hands frequently for occupation by the purchaser, but evidence of lettings is, today, very scanty. In such cases the direct comparison of one capital value with another can properly be made and is almost invariably the method used to value such properties with vacant possession.

Unless, however, the properties are very similar in size and character, it is necessary to weigh very carefully all the respective advantages and disadvantages of each property to arrive at a fair comparison.[1]

The application of the direct comparison method to land with present or prospective building value will be considered later in the book in connection with the valuation of "development properties".

Direct comparisons are seldom practicable in regard to properties held on lease, unless one is dealing with a number of properties where the length of term, the conditions of the lease and all the other circumstances of the tenure are very similar. As a general rule, comparison of properties held for limited terms has to be made through the method of analysis of sales already referred to.

(b) *Valuation by reference to cost.*—In certain instances recourse may be had to cost as evidence of value, particularly in cases where properties of the type under consideration seldom change hands in the market.

---

[1] See also Chapter 13 for an indication of methods used in respect of residential property.

The value of the land, estimated by comparison with the value of similar land in the neighbourhood, together with what may be called the replacement cost of the buildings, may be useful, if by no means conclusive, evidence of value.

The cost of building certain premises, however, is not necessarily a reliable guide to their value. For example, an ordinary residential property may have been built without regard to expense to suit the whim of a particular occupier. It is not to be expected that on sale the cost to him can be recovered as the price.

When considering cost, what is required is not necessarily the cost of exact duplication of the present structure, but the cost of providing the same accommodation in substantially the same form, omitting any unnecessary features which do not add to value.

For example, it may be required to value factory premises erected at some considerable cost and provided with architectural features and ornamentation which are not required today. The cost of these should be excluded when considering replacement cost.

The present cost basis involves the assumption that a prospective purchaser would be prepared to pay, for the accommodation provided by the premises, what it would cost him to provide similar accommodation elsewhere. In the absence of any similar properties on the market for sale, this may be a reasonable assumption.[2]

(c) *Valuation by reference to Profits.*—In the case of certain types of property, capital value is usually estimated by reference to the volume of the trade or business carried on. In the case of hotels, public houses, and sometimes in the case of cinemas and theatres, comparisons with other properties are difficult, as the value depends primarily upon the earning capacity of the property. In such cases the method of approach is to make an estimate of the gross earnings or receipts, to deduct therefrom the working expenses incidental to the earnings, to deduct further an amount to represent interest upon the capital which would have to be provided by a tenant and an amount for remuneration to the tenant for his risk and enterprise. The balance which is left is the amount which can reasonably be expected to be paid in rent. Where past records of the business done are available, this will facilitate the preparation of reliable estimates of turnover and expenses for the future.

The estimated rental value will then be capitalised at a Years' Purchase arrived at by the analysis of sales of other similar properties.

This method, sometimes called the " Accounts " method, is obviously a very indirect one and is sometimes checked by other methods, as, for example, in the case of hotels, by a value per

---

[2] For a more detailed consideration of the application of this method to rental valuations for rating purposes see Chapter 16.

bedroom. It is a method ordinarily only used for certain special types of property and is usually used in valuation for rating.[3]

(*d*)  *The Residual or Development Method.*—In the case of certain types of property capable of yielding a higher income if capital is expended in their improvement, alteration or development, the valuer must have regard both to the capital value of such increased income and also to the expenditure which must be incurred in order to produce it.

Valuations of this type are considered in detail in Chapter 12, in connection with the valuation of "development properties". But in principle the method of approach is to ascertain the present capital value of the estimated future income and to deduct therefrom the cost of all the works and other expenses necessary to put the property into the state to command such income and also, in most cases, an allowance for " risks ".

The allowance for " risks " is made because the prospect of deriving an increased income from the development of land is a speculative one and the prospective developer is unlikely to purchase except at a price which allows some margin for this element of risk.

In this type of valuation it is necessary to make certain assumptions with regard to the way in which the property can best be developed in the future. For the method can only be considered a satisfactory one if it is based on the best utilisation of the property—that is to say, the one likely to yield the largest margin of profit but account must be taken of any limitation imposed by planning consent.

It is obvious that a method such as this, in which a number of different factors are employed, each dependent on the judgment of the individual valuer, is likely to involve a wide margin of error. In practice, a valuation by comparison based on prices realised on actual sales of comparable properties is to be preferred to a valuation made by the residual or development method.

### 4.  THE COST OF BUILDING WORKS

(*a*)  *Purposes for which required.*—It is often necessary, in connection with the valuation of land or buildings for various purposes, to estimate the cost of development works, of erecting new buildings, or of making alterations to buildings.

The following are examples of such cases : —

    (i) In valuation of land likely to be developed in the future it is usually necessary to form some estimate of the cost of the necessary development works, including roads, sewers, public services, and the provision of amenities such as tree planting, open spaces and the like.

---

[3] See Chapter 16.

(ii) In connection with the development or redevelopment of town sites for various purposes, estimates of the cost of building works are required.

(iii) Similar estimates are necessary where a valuer is called on to advise as to the sum for which existing premises should be insured against fire.

The principal methods used in preparing estimates of this character are outlined below.

(b) *Accuracy of estimate.*—The method to be adopted in arriving at approximate costs of buildings and development works will depend upon the accuracy desired and the information available.

In estimating the development value of large areas of land, it is necessary to make assumptions as to the value which the land, or various parts of it, will command in the future. These estimates will be based on the evidence available at the time when the valuation is made, but will necessarily depend on factors which may vary considerably in the future. Any greater degree of accuracy in estimating the cost of necessary development works will therefore be out of place.

In many cases estimates have to be made of the cost of works to be carried out in the future. In view of the fluctuations in cost that may occur before the works are carried out, undue refinement or accuracy in the methods used would again be out of place.

In many instances, both in connection with building estates and with the development of individual sites, the particulars available of the type of building proposed to be erected, or which in fact can be erected, on a particular site may be very scanty. In the absence of detailed plans and specifications, any estimate of cost can only be arrived at by means of an approximation.

It is not possible to formulate any general rule in this connection. The circumstances of each case must dictate the degree of accuracy to be attempted, and the usefulness of the result achieved will depend largely upon the experience of the valuer in applying his knowledge, derived from other similar cases, to the one under review.

(c) *Bills of quantities.*—Where detailed drawings and a specification are available, it is possible for a bill of quantities to be prepared and for this bill to be priced by a quantity surveyor or contractor. This is the most accurate method of arriving at cost of works, but is not often practicable.

An approximate bill of quantities may be prepared whereby only the principal quantities in various trades are taken off, the prices to be applied being increased beyond what is customary, to include for various labours which normally would be measured and valued separately.

In the case of works of alteration, approximate quantities may be the only way of arriving at a reasonably accurate estimate where the works are extensive or present unusual difficulties.

(d) *Unit comparisons.*—The most common approximate method of comparing building costs is per square metre of gross floor area.

The gross floor area of a proposed building can be arrived at with an acceptable degree of accuracy from sketch plans or from a study of the site on which the building is to be erected, taking into account the likely requirements of the local planning authority, the restrictions imposed by building regulations and any rights of light or other easements.

The gross floor area having been determined the total cost can be estimated by applying a price per square metre derived from experience of the cost of similar buildings or from a publication such as Spon's Architects' and Builders' Price Book which is revised annually. Costs per square metre are based on typical buildings and do not include external works. Adjustments will, therefore, be required if the building is not typical, if site conditions are abnormal and for external works.

Gross floor area is determined by taking the total floor area of all storeys of the building measured between external walls and without deduction for internal walls. This is the basis adopted by "Spon" but the area covered by external walls is not infrequently included, i.e., gross external measurements are used. The price per unit will of course vary slightly according to the method used.

It should be noted, however, that in the majority of cases gross floor area will differ from net lettable area.

(e) *Other methods of comparison.*—In the case of building estates, the cost of road and sewer works is often estimated on a linear basis, the inclusive cost of construction of various types of road being worked out at per metre run. This price almost always provides for the roads to be completed to the standard required by the local authority.

In the absence of a detailed development scheme, it is usually desirable to prepare a sketch plan of the proposed development in order to estimate the cost of the development works required. It may sometimes be possible, however, to make a comparison between one estate and another, whereby the total development cost per unit may be estimated by reference to the development costs of other land of a similar character in the neighbourhood.

The usefulness of these methods necessarily depends upon the extent of the information available and upon the experience of the valuer, who must make full allowance for any differences between the properties from which his experience is derived and the particular property to which such figures are to be applied.

(f) *Alterations and repairs.*—The use of an approximate bill of quantities in the case of alterations has already been referred to. A similar degree of accuracy may often be arrived at by preparing a brief specification of the works required to be done and placing a " spot " amount against each item.

Similar methods may be used in regard to repairs.


### 5. The Problem of Continuance of Income

In considering the question of rental value in Chapter 3 it was stated that, as a general rule, the present rental value of a property is assumed, for the purpose of valuation, to continue unchanged in the future.

*Example.*—Freehold shop premises built about 60 years ago are let on lease for an unexpired term of 30 years to a good tenant at £800.

The present annual rental value is estimated to be £800. It is estimated that at the end of the term the buildings will be out of date and that rebuilding will be required. The present cost of rebuilding is estimated to be £5,000 and the value of the site at £220 per annum.

The analysis of sales of properties similar in nature in the same district but more modern and whose structural life is estimated to be 75 years or more sell at 12·5 Years' Purchase of the present rental value.

What is the present market value of the property?

*Valuation.*—

Method 1.

Applying the evidence of other sales it would appear that the property in question could properly be valued at a higher rate of interest than 8 per cent to allow for the work involved because the buildings have only a 30 year life.

| | | | | | |
|---|---|---|---|---|---|
| Rent on lease ... | ... | ... | ... | ... | £800 |
| Y.P. in perp., say | ... | ... | ... | ... | 10 |
| | | | | | £8,000 |

*Method* 2.

Assuming a reversion to site value at the end of the lease.

| That portion of present rent which will continue | | | | £220 p.a. | |
|---|---|---|---|---|---|
| Y.P. for 30 years @ 8% | ... | ... | | 11·3 | |
| | | | | | £2,486 |
| Remainder of rent | ... | ... | ... | £580 p.a. | |
| Y.P. for 30 years @ 8% and 2½% (tax @ 38·75%) | ... | ... | | 8·5 | |
| | | | | | £4,930 |
| Reversion to site value | ... | ... | | £220 p.a. | |
| Y.P. in perp. @ 7% deferred 30 years | | | | 1·88 | |
| | | | | | £414 |
| | | | *Value, say* | | £7,830 |

*Method* 3.

Assuming continuance of rental value and making provision for rebuilding.

| Rent on lease ... | ... | ... | ... | £800 p.a. | |
|---|---|---|---|---|---|
| Y.P. in perp. @ 8% ... | ... | ... | | 12·5 | |
| | | | | £10,000 | |
| *Less* cost of rebuilding | ... £5,000 | | | | |
| P.V. £1 in 30 years @ 8% | ... | ·1 | | 500 | |
| | | | *Value* | £9,500 | |

Method 1 has the merit of simplicity but the increase in the rate of interest is very much a matter of opinion.

Methods 2 and 3 are open to objection on a number of grounds.

In Method 2 it may be argued that it is difficult to know what will be the value of the site upon reversion after the useful life of the building, 30 years hence. The only evidence of the value of the site is present-day selling prices, which suggest the figure of £220 used in the example, but this value may be considerably modified in the future. A similar objection applies to the figure of £5,000 for cost of rebuilding in Method 3, which, of necessity, has been based on present-day prices, although these may be very different 50 years hence.

Another serious objection is the difficulty of predicting the life of a building with any degree of accuracy, particularly over a long period of years. Such an estimate of the life of the building as is made in the example must necessarily be in the nature of a guess unless considerable data is accumulated over a long period showing the useful life in the past of similar buildings. Even such evidence, over perhaps 40 or 50 years in the past, is not conclusive of what the useful life of buildings will be in the future.

On balance it would appear that in many cases there is probably less inaccuracy involved in assuming the present income to be perpetual and using a higher rate to cover risks, than would be involved in the more elaborate methods of allowing for possible variation in income.

On the other hand, Method 2 is commonly used in practice in America and has the advantage of giving to an investor a more direct indication of the actual rate per cent he is likely to derive from an investment than does Method 1, provided it is used in conjunction with analysis of sales made on similar lines.

In cases where it can confidently be assumed that existing buildings will be worn out in a few years' time, Method 2 may be obviously the soundest.

In some cases of isolated properties on small sites it may be impracticable to have regard to future site value where the life of the buildings is considered to be limited.

*Example.*—Two tenement houses occupying a site with a frontage of 42 feet and a depth of 90 feet produce a net income of £100. The buildings are 70 years old and are likely to require rebuilding within 50 years. Similar properties in the vicinity have sold recently for eight Years' Purchase of the net income. There are a number of similar small sites in the neighbourhood that have been vacant for several years for which no offers have been made.

*Valuation.*—In this case the value of the site when the buildings have to be pulled down is problematical. There is, however, direct evidence that, in view of the risks, such properties are sold for eight Years' Purchase, that is to say, to show $12\frac{1}{2}$ per cent. The valuation is therefore based on this figure.

| | | |
|---|---|---|
| Net income ... ... ... ... | £100 | |
| Y.P. in perp. @ $12\frac{1}{2}$% ... ... | 8 | |
| | —— | £800 |

If it were possible to predict accurately the life of the buildings both the analysis of sales and the valuation might take into account the terminable nature of the income.

| | | |
|---|---|---|
| Net income ... ... ... ... | £100 | |
| Estimated duration 50 years | | |
| Y.P. 50 years @ 11% and $2\frac{1}{2}$% ... | 7·9 | |
| (Tax @ 38·75%) | —— | £790 |

In view of the vacant sites remaining unsold no account has been taken of the reversion to site value.

A purchaser acquiring such an investment as this would be imprudent if he regarded it as showing a net return of 12½ per cent. If he wished to maintain his capital intact he would set aside a proportion of the income yearly for this purpose.

## 6. MANAGEMENT OF INVESTMENTS

The valuer is often required to advise on the policy to be adopted in the management of investment properties.

To deal adequately with all the types of problem likely to be encountered would be beyond the scope of this book, but reference is made below to a number which involve considerations of value.

Speaking very generally it may be said that good estate management should aim at securing the maintenance, and if possible the increase, of income and capital value.

To advise on a group of investment properties of varying types involves consideration of a number of factors, including—

(a) The possibilities of increase or decrease in future capital value.

(b) An examination of present rents with a view to possible increases or reductions.

(c) Consideration of outgoings.

(d) The provision of reserves for future repairs or other capital expenditure, to enable the cost of repairs to be spread evenly over a period, and to provide sinking funds for wasting assets such as leasehold properties.

(a) *Maintenance of capital values.*—From time to time it will be desirable to review the properties comprised in a landed estate to decide if some should be sold or otherwise dealt with and to consider whether or not they are likely to increase or decrease in value.

As an obvious and desirable objective is to maintain or enhance the capital value of the estate, properties likely to depreciate should be sold and other properties sought to replace them of a character which may enhance in value or at least not depreciate.

For example, assume that a large estate includes three streets of freehold three-storey houses about 80 years old, let out in tenements. The houses are in poor repair and of indifferent construction. The neighbourhood is likely to depreciate, and there is some risk that the whole of the properties will be included in the area of a Clearance Scheme under the Housing Acts. An offer to purchase has been received based on nine Years' Purchase of the net income.

In the circumstances, as assumed, it is probable that the offer made is close to the present market value and, having regard to the prospects of future diminution in value, a sale now would appear to be desirable.

Since the passing of the Town and Country Planning Act, 1947,[4] the possibilities of enhancement of capital value are considerably more restricted and dependent upon the grant of planning permission.

There will still remain, however, the possibility of investment in properties of a type where increases in value may be expected and which are not dependent upon the grant of planning permission.

For example, a block of shops offered for sale may be the subject of leases granted some time ago at rents which at the end of the lease may be expected to be substantially increased.

An investment in property of this type offers possibilities of an increase in capital value in the future.

(b) *Examination of rents.*—A periodic examination of rentals should be made to ensure that when a property comes into hand the rent is increased to the market value. In a few cases it may be found that, owing to a fall in values in the district, or for other reasons, a property is over-rented. It will probably be wise to treat the excess over market value with caution; in making provision for the future it must be remembered that the only security for the enhanced rent is the tenant's covenant to pay, and in the event of his failure the rent will need to be reduced.

Since the last war, there has been a general tendency for rental values to increase. In order that landlords can secure the benefit of such increases, it is usual in the case of occupation leases at rack rents, for the term to be kept as short as possible. Advisers acting for tenants, however, usually endeavour to secure as long a term as possible. Frequently leases contain " break clauses ". Before 1939 these were often unilateral but it is more normal now to make such clauses mutual. The comparatively recent innovation of " rent revision clauses " in long leases has already been noted.[5]

(c) *Outgoings.*—The present outgoings, particularly those liable to variation such as repairs and rates, need to be scrutinised. Where the landlord is responsible for outgoings it should be seen that rating assessments are correct (in the absence of " excess rates clauses ")[6] and that adequate provision is made for repairs.

---

[4] Now incorporated in the T. & C.P. Act, 1962.
[5] See Chapter 4, Section 3 (ii).
[6] See Chapter 6, 4.

(*d*) *Reserves.*—Certain outgoings, in particular repairs, will vary in amount from year to year. For instance, external painting may be required perhaps every five years.

It is usually desirable that the available income from an estate should be reasonably constant, and in the years when such expenditure is not actually incurred an amount should be set aside for future use. So that if the cost of external painting every fifth year is estimated at £500, a sum of £100 should be set aside each year to meet it.

Where property is held on lease with full repairing covenants, or where there is a covenant to reinstate after alterations, provision should be made for future expenditure either by setting aside a certain amount of income each year or on the lines indicated below.

Where income is derived from leasehold properties proper provision should be made for the replacement of capital at the end of the term. This may be done by means of a sinking fund policy or it may be possible to find a suitable investment—for example, ground rents with a reversion to rack rents which will come into hand at about the time when the leasehold interests run out.

The latter arrangement has certain advantages over the sinking fund method. The value of the reversion accumulates at a higher rate of interest in most cases; also a sinking fund, if established, has to be paid out of taxed income, and reduces the net available revenue. It may well be, however, that the capital resources of an estate do not permit of the purchase of suitable investments and provision for the future has to be made out of income.

A valuer may have to advise a particular investor in landed property on the types of investment best suited to him. In such a case, the valuer would have to take account of such a factor as the investor's liability to income tax.

### 7. CONCLUSION

The following example illustrates a number of the points referred to in this Chapter.

> *Example.*—Trustees have asked you to report on an estate, details of which are set out below. You are particularly asked to advise on (*a*) the sale of any of the properties which in your opinion should be disposed of; (*b*) what steps, if any, are necessary to maintain a steady annual income and to utilise resources available to the best advantage; (*c*) what net income you consider should be available after the payment of all outgoings and after making adequate provision for the future.
>
> The particulars of the properties given below include additional information which would be revealed by an inspection.

*Particulars of Estate*

1. A range of freehold lock-up garages let on weekly tenancies at rents totalling £800 per annum inclusive. Rates payable for the current year total £300. The landlord does all repairs. The average expenditure for repairs, etc., for the last five years has been £150 per annum. The buildings are of asbestos on light steel frames and are 40 years old. The steel frames are badly rusted.

   The site area is 1,200 m² and is in an industrial district. It is allocated for this purpose in the relevant Development Plan.

2. A terrace of 12 shops, each with a frontage of 18 feet, with two storeys over, built 35 years ago and let on leases now having 7 years to run with full repairing covenants. The shops produce a total rental of £3,600. The market value today of each shop is estimated at an average of £500 per annum.

3. A freehold public house let on lease to a firm of brewers at £400 per annum; the lease has an unexpired term of 45 years; the lessees have recently offered £27,000 for the freehold.

4. Ground rents secured on 25 tenement houses at £4 each, let on lease for 99 years with 20 years unexpired; the buildings are old and may be included in a clearance area; the site has a total area of 1,500 m² and is zoned for residential purposes in the development plan of the Planning Authority. Similar sites have been sold at £1 per square metre recently.

*Notes for Report to Clients*

**A.  Present income from Estate**

1. *Lock-up Garages*

| | | | |
|---|---|---:|---:|
| Gross Income ...   ...   ... | | | £800 |
| Outgoings: | | | |
| Rates   ...   ...   ... | £300 | | |
| Repairs, etc.   ...   ... | £150 | | |
| Management   ...   ... | £100 | | |
| | | £550 | |
| | | | £250 |

2. 12 *Shops*
   Rentals ...   ...   ...   ...   ...   ...   £3,600

3. *Public House*   ...   ...   ...   ...   ...   400

4. *Ground Rents*   ...   ...
   25 houses at £4   ...   ...   ...   ...   100

                                           £4,350

### B. Lock-up Garages

The buildings are at the end of their physical life; the out-goings are high relative to the gross income.

Enquiries of the local planning authority indicate that planning consent for the erection on the site of two factories each of 300 m² would be forthcoming.

There is a very keen demand for such accommodation and lettings of comparable buildings indicate rents of £6 per m² net.

The Trustees should be advised to apply for consent and on receipt to terminate the existing tenancies. The site should then be cleared and two such buildings should be erected and let.

The estimated net income would be £3,600 per annum.

The costs of development would comprise:—

| | | | | |
|---|---|---|---|---|
| Cost of demolition | ... | ... | ... | £200 |
| Cost of buildings | ... | ... | ... | £20,000 |
| Professional fees and commissions | | ... | | £750 |
| | | *Total, say,* | | £21,000 |

*Note.*—The above makes no provision for finance costs, loss of income during the development period and the value of the site but excluding these items the estimated income represents a return of almost 17 per cent on the total expenditure.

### C. Public House

It is advised that the public house be sold at £27,000, which is considered an advantageous figure. Of this amount £21,000 is to be spent on the factories mentioned above, leaving £6,000 available for other purposes.

### D. Shops

The estimated future income seven years hence is:—12 shops at £500 = £6,000, an increase of £2,400.

Several tenants are desirous of negotiating new leases; eight of the shops are in poor repair.

It is advised that negotiations be pursued and the repairing covenants of the leases enforced where necessary.

### E. Ground Rents

The reversionary value is small in view of the allocation on the development plan.

It is considered that the interest should be sold and it will probably not fetch more than £1,000.

### F. Future Income

(i) The net income from the garage site will increase shortly by some £3,350 (£3,600—£250).

(ii) In seven years' time the rents from the shops will increase by £2,400. There is some possibility that, by accepting surrender of the present leases now in return for the grant of new leases immediately, there will be an immediate increase in income.

(iii) The sale of the public house will mean a decrease in income of £400 p.a.

(iv) The sale of the ground rent will mean a decrease in income of £100 p.a.

## G. *Summary*

1. Estimated available income—

| | |
|---|---|
| (i) Factories    ...    ...    ...    ...    ... | £3,600 |
| (ii) Public House ...    ...    ...    ...    ... | — |
| (iii) Shops ...    ...    ...    ...    ...    ...<br>(to rise to £6,000 p.a. in seven years with the possibility of an immediate increase) | £3,600 |
| (iv) Ground Rents ...    ...    ...    ...    ... | — |
| *Total* ...    ... | £7,200 |

plus the income from £6,000

2. The public house and ground rent to be sold at a total estimated at £28,000 but allowance should be made for capital gains tax and costs of sale.

3. The lock-up garages to be demolished and the site re-developed at an estimated cost of about £21,000.

4. A suitable investment to be found for a sum of £6,000 less amounts to be paid for costs and capital gains tax.

5. The possibility of obtaining an immediate increase in income from the shops by negotiating with the tenants for new leases now should be explored.

6. The trustees be advised that the total available income from the estate will be at least £7,200.

# PART 2

# Chapter 10

## Part 1—Principles of the Town and Country Planning Acts, 1947-59

### 1. GENERALLY

THE PROVISIONS of these Acts will be considered again later—

(i) in relation to the incidence of planning control (Chapters 18 and 19), and

(ii) in relation to compensation for compulsory purchase (Chapter 23).

A brief outline of the principles underlying them may, however, be useful at this stage since these basic principles had a considerable influence on general valuation practice for a period of over ten years (1947-1958) and still have a bearing on certain types of case at the present day.

It will be convenient to begin with a brief outline of the Town and Country Planning Act, 1947, and then to examine the extent to which its provisions were modified and amended first by those of the Town and Country Planning Acts of 1953 and 1954, and later by those of the Town and Country Planning Act, 1959.[1]

The term "development value", here and elsewhere in the book, refers to that additional value—over and above what is referred to later as "existing use value"—which a property may have in the open market because of the prospect—immediate or future—of its being put to some more profitable purpose, e.g., by the erection or extension of buildings or by a change of use.

### 2. THE TOWN AND COUNTRY PLANNING ACT, 1947

The following is a summary of those provisions of the Act which have a direct bearing on the subject of valuations. They are expressed in the past tense in order to give a complete picture of the Act as originally enacted, but only those which are printed in italics have been substantially affected by later legislation.

(i) Within three years from 1 July, 1948, every local planning authority had to submit a "development plan" showing the way in which they proposed that land in their area should be used. Amongst other things, this "development plan" might define the sites of proposed roads, public and other buildings and works, airfields, parks, pleasure

---

[1] See now the Land Compensation Act, 1961, and the Town and Country Planning Act, 1962.

grounds, nature reserves and other open spaces; or allocate areas of land for use for agricultural, residential, industrial or other purposes. *It might also designate land which it was proposed to acquire in the future for public purposes.* These development plans were to be subject to amendment at least once in every five years.

(ii) As from 1 July, 1948, no owner might develop his property—e.g., carry out building operations, or mine it, or substantially change its existing use—unless permission for development was given under the Act, in most cases by the local planning authority. Subject to a right of appeal to the Minister, the local planning authority might refuse permission or grant it subject to conditions.

(iii) The fact that permission was refused, or restrictions on development imposed, did not, as a general rule, entitle the owner to compensation unless the proposed development was of a type specified in Part II of the Third Schedule to the Act which enumerated certain strictly limited forms of development—for example, an improvement or alteration to a building involving an increase of not more than one-tenth of the existing cubic content.

(iv) *Where permission was given for any development other than "existing use" development (i.e., development of the kind specified in the Third Schedule to the Act), the owner was required to pay a "development charge" based on the difference between (a) the value of the land with the benefit of the permission, and (b) its value with permission refused.*

(v) *Where land was acquired compulsorily for public purposes, the basis of compensation was its "existing use value"— i.e., its value assuming that any future development was restricted to those forms of development specified in the Third Schedule to the Act.*

(vi) *The effect of (ii) to (v) above was that owners were no longer entitled, as of right, to the development value of their land— i.e., that part of the market value in excess of the value the land would have if restricted to its existing use. For all practical purposes development values were under the control of—although not formally vested in—the Crown.*

(vii) Any owner who could prove that his land was depreciated in value in consequence of the above provisions of the Act might submit a claim—under Part VI of the Act—based on the difference between (a) the value of his property if restricted to "existing use" development only, and (b) the value it would have had if the Act had not been passed.

(viii) *A fixed sum of £300 million—known in practice as "the £300 million fund" or "the Global Fund"—was allocated to meet such claims so far as it would extend and this was to have been distributed in the form of Government stock by July, 1953, in accordance with a scheme to be prepared by the Treasury and approved by Parliament.*

(ix) *The consideration of claims for loss of development value, and the levying of development charges, was the duty of the Central Land Board established under the Act.*

To summarise the principles underlying the above provisions—the 1947 Act recognised an owner's right to some compensation in respect of development value existing at 1 July, 1948, but not in respect of development value accruing after that date. In theory, at any rate, the recognised basis for all dealings in land after 1 July, 1948, was "existing use value".

### 3. EXISTING USE VALUE

"Existing use value" is a term which was first introduced into valuation practice by the provisions of the 1947 Act. It indicates the value which can be assigned to a property if it be assumed that no "development", within the meaning of the Town Planning Acts, will take place in the future except such forms of development as were formerly specified in the Third Schedule to the Town and Country Planning Act, 1947, which has now been replaced by the Third Schedule to the Town and Country Planning Act, 1962.

"Development" is defined in Section 12 (1) of the Town and Country Planning Act, 1962,[2] as "the carrying out of building, engineering, mining or other operations in, on, over or under land, or the making of any material change in the use of any buildings or other land". But the section goes on to specify a number of works and uses which are not deemed to involve "development" within the meaning of the Act and which consequently do not require town planning permission. Among such exceptions may be mentioned works for the maintenance, improvement or other alteration of any building which affect only the interior of the building and which do not materially affect its external appearance.[3] Also, in the case of buildings used for any specified class of purpose, their use for a different purpose falling within the same class.

In so far, then, as the value of a property may be affected by the possibility of carrying out some work or effecting some change of use which either does not amount to "development" or is "development" of a type specified in the Third Schedule, that factor may be taken into account in considering the "existing use value".

---

[2] Replacing Sec. 12 (2) of the 1947 Act.

[3] But this exception does not extend to the alteration of a building by the provision of additional space below ground if the work was begun after 6 December, 1968.—T. & C.P. Act, 1968, Sec. 74 and T. & C.P. Act, 1968 (Commencement No. 1 Order).

Any value due to the possibility of "development" falling outside the scope of the Third Schedule may be conveniently described as "development value".

The Third Schedule, as now amended by the Town and Country Planning Acts, 1962 and 1963, is printed in Appendix B (1) and (2). It may be noted here that the Schedule includes the following types of work or use which are particularly likely in practice to have a bearing on value:—

*Rebuilding.*—Necessary rebuilding, provided that the cubic content of the original building is not exceeded by more than one-tenth (or an alternative figure of 1,750 cubic feet in the case of dwelling-houses).

*Use of dwelling-houses.*—The use as two or more separate dwelling-houses of any building used as a single dwelling-house.

*Alterations to buildings.*—Enlargements, improvements or other alterations to buildings which do not increase the cubic content by more than one-tenth (or 1,750 cubic feet in the case of dwelling-houses).

*Change of user.*—Where a building or land is used for a specified class of purpose, its use for some different purpose falling within the same "use class", e.g., where the use of a shop is changed from one form of retail trade to another.

From this very brief note on "existing use value" it will be apparent that the 1947 Act did not directly affect the valuation of properties whose value is derived solely from their present use as agricultural land, houses, flats, offices, shops, factories, etc., and is not dependent to any appreciable extent on the prospect of future development either in the form of building or other works or a substantial change in user.

The valuation of such types of property is considered in Chapters 11, 13 and 14.

### 4. THE TOWN AND COUNTRY PLANNING ACT, 1953

This Act abolished the levying of development charge as from 18 November, 1952. From that date until the introduction of Betterment Levy under the Land Commission Act, 1967, where planning permission was given for the development of land the owner was entitled to the benefit of any development value which might be released in consequence, without being subject to any charge in respect of the increased value of his property.

The Act also suspended the making of any payments from the "£300 million fund" pending the coming into force of new legislation—i.e., the Town and Country Planning Act, 1954.

### 5. THE TOWN AND COUNTRY PLANNING ACT, 1954

This Act came into operation on 1 January, 1955.

Under its provisions no general distribution of compensation was made from what was formerly known as the "£300 million fund", but owners who had established claims on that fund under Part VI of the 1947 Act were entitled to claim additional compensation —over and above any loss of "existing use value"—in certain circumstances defined in the Act.

The Act confirmed the guiding principle of the 1947 Act—that, in general, no compensation should be paid for development value which had accrued since 1 July, 1948, and which was lost to an owner because planning permission was refused, or was granted subject to conditions, or because his land was acquired for public purposes on a basis of existing use value.

As regards development value the existence of which at 1 July, 1948, was evidenced by an established "Part VI claim" the Act made the following provisions:—

> (i) Where transactions in land before 1 January, 1955, had been based on the 1947 Act principles that development values were vested in the State, subject to owners' claims on the £300 million fund—owners were entitled to a payment not exceeding the amount of this established "Part VI claim".
>
> Typical cases were those where, under the 1947 Act, development charge was levied, or land was acquired compulsorily at "existing use value", or an adverse planning decision was given without compensation. But such claims had to be made on or before 30 June, 1955.
>
> (ii) Where on or after 1 January, 1955, land was acquired for public purposes, additional compensation for loss of development value might be payable, but only up to the limit of what remained of the original "Part VI claim"—known at this stage as the "unexpended balance of established development value". Similarly, where land was the subject of an adverse planning decision made on or after that date, compensation might be payable in respect of any consequent depreciation in development value, subject to the same limitation as to amount and subject also to a considerable number of exceptions.

As a general rule, therefore, the right to receive a payment under the 1954 Act in respect of loss of development value was dependent on a "Part VI claim" having been established under the 1947 Act.

The above provisions, coupled with the repeal of development charge by the 1953 Act, had the effect of creating two distinct levels of value:—

> (i) where land changed hands in the open market—in which case the owner might demand the full value of his land taking into account all the possibilities of future development.

(ii) where land was acquired for public purposes under compulsory powers—in which case the owner was only entitled
to its existing use value plus an additional payment which
was limited by the amount of development value existing
at 1 July, 1948, calculated by reference to 1947 values.

Such a gap, which naturally tended to widen with the passage of
time, considerably increased the dissatisfaction normally felt by an
owner whose land is compulsorily acquired.

### 6. THE TOWN AND COUNTRY PLANNING ACT, 1959

The compensation provisions of this Act, as now incorporated
and re-enacted in the Land Compensation Act, 1961, are considered
in detail in later Chapters.

For the purpose of this brief summary it is sufficient to note
that in the case of compulsory acquisitions after 28 October,
1958, it abolished the limitations on value prescribed by the 1947
and 1954 Acts and provided, as the basis of compensation, the
open market value of the land acquired having due regard, in
appropriate cases, to the reasonable prospects of obtaining planning permission for development.

This had the effect of abolishing the two levels of value referred
to above, so far as compensation for compulsory acquisitions is
concerned.

But neither the 1959 Act nor the Land Compensation Act, 1961,
affected the provisions of the earlier Acts regarding compensation
for refusal of planning permission. So that while the owner who
obtained planning permission was free to realise the full development value of his land, the compensation (if any) for loss of such
value payable to the owner who was refused planning permission
for new development was still related to such development value
as existed at 1 July, 1948.

## Part 2—The Land Commission Act, 1967

This Act had two primary purposes, to impose a charge for betterment, and to stimulate the development of land. Its main impact was
in respect of betterment.

As has been seen the 1947 Act sought to make a charge for betterment by means of a development charge payable before the realisation
of development value. This scheme was abandoned following the
1953 Act. The Land Commission Act 1967 re-introduced such a
scheme whereby, upon the realisation of development value,
betterment levy became payable.

The betterment levy scheme has several parallels with the 1947 Act
approach while at the same time incorporating various features

aimed at avoiding the disabilities that emerged from the operation of the 1947 Act. Betterment Levy was payable upon the occurrence of specific acts grouped in 6 Cases. These Cases covered:—

Case A, sale of an interest (including compulsory purchase);
Case B, grant of a lease;
Case C, development of land;
Case D, payment of certain planning compensation;
Case E, purchase or release of easements and restrictive rights;
Case F, payment of certain compensation; and variations in leases.

The details of the Cases and the assessment of levy is dealt with in Chapter 29. Nonetheless it can be seen that betterment levy liability arose on the full spectrum of property activities. If in any of the Cases development value were realised the levy became payable.

It is clear from this that the meaning of development value lies at the heart of the matter. In the 1967 Act this value was defined as any value in excess of current use value. Current use value is the value of an interest assuming permission would be granted for any development specified in the Third Schedule of the 1962 Act plus any development contained in the General Development Order 1963 and in further Regulations made under the 1967 Act.

The test as to whether development value had been realised was broadly to deduct from the consideration received (the value when development was begun in Case C) the current use value of the interest. Any positive sums that emerged were regarded as representing development value.

A comparison of the 1967 Act scheme with that of the 1947 Act shows various differences which went some way to overcome the earlier Act's criticisms. These included the fact that current use value was wider in scope than existing use value: further, an allowance of 10 per cent of the current use value was added and, perhaps most important of all, betterment levy was fixed at 40 per cent compared with the 100 per cent development charge. In these ways the disincentive effects of development charges were considerably mitigated.

The 1967 Act came into effect on the 6 April, 1967, the "first appointed day" of the Act, and applied to all events falling within the Cases from that day up to and including the 22 July, 1970. On the latter date the government announced that legislation would be introduced to abolish betterment levy in respect of future transactions. As a result the current position is that betterment is not subject to any special legislative provisions. Any profits that now accrue due to betterment are subject to the general taxation provisions relating to other profits in the form of capital gains tax or income/corporation tax.

As part of the 1967 Act scheme a central agency was established to administer the betterment levy scheme, similar to the Central Land

Board established by the 1947 Act. This agency was called the Land Commission. The Commission had headquarters in Newcastle and regional offices around the country. The Commission operated the scheme by supervising the assessment and collection of the levy, although the Valuation Offices of the Inland Revenue in fact dealt with the preparation and agreement of the valuations required for the assessment of levy. All levy collected by the Commission was payable to the Treasury where it was incorporated with other sources of government income.

The 1967 Act did however give the Commission a further role of equal importance with that of collection of levy. Under Part II of the Act the Commission was given wide powers to acquire, manage and dispose of land. The purpose of this was to allow the Commission to take an active role in the bringing forward of land for development. In its years of operation between 1967 and 1970 it did acquire and dispose of a certain amount of land but its more ambitious projects failed to reach fruition before its activities were halted in September 1970. It is therefore almost impossible to gauge how effective this aspect of its powers might have proved.

The history of legislation in relation to the compensation/ betterment problem has shown many fluctuations since 1947. In relation to betterment, efforts to recoup betterment have fluctuated between the fully comprehensive to the comparative inattention of the present day. As for compensation, this has developed over the years to the current scheme which is the residue of the 1947 Act scheme with the 1954 Act modifications.

# Chapter 11

## Agricultural Property

### 1. FARMS

**Valuation for Rent**

THE VALUATION of farms, whether for rent or for sale, is often a humiliating exercise. All the theoretical approaches may have been blended with thirty years' skill and experience to deduce that the annual value of Coldharbour Farm is fifteen pounds a hectare. It is put out to tender, and a genuine farmer—no speculator, that is, but the current edition of ten generations never greater than " reasonably skilled in husbandry "—takes it on at twenty-two pounds fifty.

This introduction is intended to disenchant the reader who meant, after learning Chapter 3 by heart, to specialise in farm valuations. Granted, it is necessary to understand the theoretical calculation of rent, for each method is based on a proven element of practice. At the same time the would-be valuer needs rather more than both theory and experience to estimate the " true worth " of a farm. There is no standard phrase to define that extra something. Outside these four walls or the confessional, even the loosest-tongued practitioner uses some euphemism for " guesswork ".

Farm rents are subject to the same laws of supply and demand as rents for other forms of property, but in many ways they seem to make their own rules. One well-established phenomenon is that although they fluctuate with farming prosperity, they tend to lag behind to the landlord's disadvantage. From time to time, notably during and after a war, there is a boom in farming, but it will be some years before that upward trend is reflected in rents. Meanwhile the first edge of the boom may have been dulled, by which time many a landlord is reluctant to propose that a share of the farmer's increased income might equitably come his way. In times of agricultural depression, on the other hand, rents are correspondingly much quicker to fall. Either the landlord may grant a temporary remission, which next audit day becomes taken for granted, or the tenant will quit and the farm yield a diminished rent on reletting.

Of the factors which shackle farm rents, most notable is the security of tenure introduced by statute in 1948 and only slightly modified since. In effect, once a tenant has taken a farm and is farming it tolerably, the landlord cannot get rid of him except for a limited number of reasons. These reasons will be found in section 24 (2) of the Agricultural Holdings Act, 1948. Briefly, they are:

(a)   that the Minister has given advance consent to the notice to quit;

(b)   that the land is required for a use other than agriculture;

(c)   that the tenant has not farmed in accordance with the statutory rules of good husbandry;

(d)   that the tenant has not paid his rent, or has failed to remedy previously specified breaches of contract;

(e)   that the tenant has caused damage to the reversion by some irremediable breach of contract;

(f)   that the tenant has gone bankrupt;

(g)   that the tenant has died.

A tenancy for two years or more, however clearly specified the term, does not expire by effluxion of time but continues from year to year subject to a minimum of twelve months' notice to quit. If notice to quit emanates from the landlord, the tenant can challenge it and, unless one or more of the limited exceptions apply, put the landlord to a non-plus. Furthermore, section 2 of the 1948 Act provides that most short-term tenancies are deemed for this purpose to be tenancies from year to year, and thus to confer security of tenure upon the tenant.

There are statutory means of raising the rent through arbitration, which will be discussed presently; landlords have lately become less reluctant to resort to this procedure, and the triennial rent increase is now almost as familiar as the annual wage demand. Arbitrators still tend to be cautious in their awards, which often contrast sharply with rents of comparable farms which have been re-let by tender. The present situation is both artificial and confused, and all statistics should be treated with caution unless the valuer has knowledge of the attendant circumstances.

### Current rents and trends

Among the plethora of farm facts and figures published by such authorities as the Ministry of Agriculture, rents too frequently receive no more than footnote status. However, in 1959 the results of an extensive survey undertaken by the Department of Estate Management of Cambridge University were published in book form[1] and are unlikely to be rivalled for some time to come for fullness and factuality.

The Agricultural Land Service of the Ministry of Agriculture now publishes annually the results of a Rent Enquiry. The latest report[2] indicates a continuing rise in average rents. While these figures, which are average rents, may be of general interest, the valuer is almost always concerned with the rental value of a particular

---

[1] *Farm Rents*, by D. R. Denman and V. F. Stewart. George Allen & Unwin.

[2] Technical Report 19, Agricultural Land Service, July 1969.

holding. The figures contained in these two reports may also be of assistance to the reader who has no conception whatever of the rent a farm will command. For such a reader the figures employed in the examples later in this chapter may provide some indication.

### Factors affecting rent

Kipling wrote that there were nine and sixty ways of constructing tribal lays, " and every single one of them is right!" The same may be said of the alternative methods of valuing for rent. However different their approach, theoretically they should approximate to the same result. But since even those based on the most authentic accounts and records are suspect unless coupled with a look at the land, something must first be said of the visual side of farm surveys; then of the less tangible factors that affect the valuation.

The main points to be considered in viewing a farm are:

*The general situation.*—The position on the map, both large and small scale, has an overall bearing on the value. The point need not be laboured but, other things being equal, a farm close to a town with its twice-weekly cattle market and its six-day Supermarket is more esteemed than one situated among untrodden ways. " Twenty minutes by bus " will influence both the farmer with his produce to sell and the availability of farm labour, whether regular or part-time.

*The lie of the land.*—The height, aspect, contours and exposure of the farm are features which the practised valuer instinctively takes into account. All have a bearing on the cropping and livestock policy. For instance, steep slopes will inhibit or prohibit arable cultivations and limit the enterprises to sheep or cattle. High, exposed land will rule out dairying and limit the livestock to the raising, not the fattening, of livestock; and so on.

*Climate and rainfall* also are bound up with the farm's potentialities. Most crops of any value have their special requirements. The better grasslands, for example, lie in the wetter districts, while barley and wheat would sooner be deprived of moisture than sunshine.

*The size of the farm.*—The Cambridge Survey of Farm Rents revealed that small farms have consistently higher rents per acre than large ones. At the two extremes of the farms sampled in 1957, those below 50 acres averaged £2·62 per acre (£6·29 per hectare), while those over 500 averaged £1·17 (£2·80 per hectare). Rent increases, however, have been higher on the large farms, which is to be expected with the expansion of mechanised farming that needs broader acres to make the most use of powered equipment.

*The land itself*—that is to say, the quality, the composition and the texture of the soil. Fertilising and manuring will do much to raise the productive capacity of any soil, but with naturally infertile soils the law of diminishing returns—the point at which the extra few units of nitrogen cost more than the extra yield is worth—operates early. For this reason a smallholding of good black fen is more valuable than a parish of light sand. Whereas an unfamiliar soil needs a chemical analysis to suggest its full potentialities, much can be learnt by physical inspection. To this end a soil auger, or at second best a spade, is an invaluable aid towards assessing quality, depth and the height of the water table. At the same time the valuer will note which fields have been tile or mole drained, and whether the drainage system is being maintained, particularly by attention to the outfalls.

*Water Supply to Fields.*—While much of the value of a farm may depend on measures taken to get water off, it may cost a good deal in labour and materials to get it on. Cattle are avid water bibbers, and on a grass farm where the beasts do the round of the pastures a system of field troughs with a piped supply is essential. Few livestock farms lack this equipment today, but any that do will command a very low rent, until the deficiency is supplied.

*Roads and Approaches.*—Apart from the desirability of concrete contact with the outside world, all-weather access is necessary within the farm itself, from yard to field and from one field to another. Many farm roads are of adequate strength for the horse-drawn traffic they were built to sustain, but fail to stand up to tractors and machinery.

*Fences and Gates.*—Their maintenance is normally the tenant's job, legally so in the absence of written agreement to the contrary. Good fences, it is said, make good neighbours. With livestock farming they also make good bargaining points when negotiating rents.

*Main Water and Electricity* are virtually essential. If the installations are out of date or absent, and the landlord does not undertake to provide them, the tenant will reckon on providing them himself probably on borrowed money. The rent will suffer accordingly.

*The Cottages.*—The tradition of Hodge contentedly supping his humble pottage in a humble cottage begot from wattle, daub and thatch disappeared with Thomas Hardy. Today any farm labour worth its overtime reasonably demands as a minimum a bath, indoor sanitation and a shed for at least one car. Where the farm cottages fall appreciably short of this minimum, labour is hard to attract and the farm is correspondingly less valuable. In addition to the quality of the cottages, their quantity must be considered in relation to the farming system. There are no hard and fast rules, for an arable farm will need proportionately more workers than a hill sheep farm, but one service cottage per 50 hectares is some sort of guide. Incidentally, the invaluable Cambridge survey found that the number of cottages per holding appeared to have a direct bearing on rent: the greater the number the higher the rent per hectare.

*The Buildings* are of paramount importance. At the least they should be adequate to house the livestock, machinery and produce which the farm requires and yields. Those to do with dairying should conform to the provisions of the Milk and Dairies Regulations, while the growing demand for multi-purpose buildings adds a cachet to those adaptable for a variety of enterprises. Strictly specialist buildings, e.g., pig fattening or deep litter houses, should be regarded with some reserve, for it is not every farmer who aims to grow rich on the profits from bacon and eggs. They may be a liability, adding nothing to the rental value.

*Other Factors* which influence rent include the responsibility for repairs and maintenance. If a tenant accepted a full repairing lease, he would naturally expect to pay a lower rent than if the landlord shared the burden. This factor, and the responsibility for outgoings, are discussed later on in connection with capital valuations.

## " *Rent Properly Payable* "

Because many rental valuations today arise in relation to sitting tenants, something should be said about their statutory aspect, particularly the interpretation of the " rent properly payable " which the valuer is seeking.

Under section 8 of the Agricultural Holdings Act, 1948, either landlord or tenant of a farm held from year to year may get the rent adjusted in the light of new circumstances. At any time after three years from the commencement of the tenancy they may appoint an arbitrator to determine " what rent should be properly payable " for the holding. For ten years there was doubt as to what that expression meant. Did it take into account, for example, the presence of a sitting tenant, whose virtually impregnable position would depress the valuation? Light was shed by section 2 of the Agriculture Act, 1958, which laid down that

> . . . the rent properly payable in respect of a holding shall be the rent at which, having regard to the terms of the tenancy (other than those relating to rent), the holding might reasonably be expected to be let in the open market by a willing landlord to a willing tenant, there being disregarded . . . any effect on rent of the fact that the tenant who is a party to the arbitration is in occupation of the holding.

Reverting to section 8 of the 1948 Act, further instructions to the arbitrator are equally applicable to the valuer at large. In determining the rent properly payable, the arbitrator

> (a) shall not take into account any increase in the rental value of the holding which is due to:—
>
> > (i) improvements which have been executed thereon, in so far as they were executed wholly or partly at the expense of the tenant (whether or not that expense has been or will be reimbursed by a grant out of moneys provided by Parliament) without any equivalent allowance or benefit made or given by the landlord in consideration of their execution and have not been executed under an obligation imposed on the tenant by the terms of his contract of tenancy, or

    (ii) improvements which have been executed thereon by the landlord, in so far as the landlord has received or will receive grants out of moneys provided by Parliament in respect of the execution thereof; and

   (b) shall not take into account the relief from payment of rates granted by Part V of the Local Government Act, 1929, to occupiers of agricultural hereditaments; and

   (c) shall not fix the rent at a lower amount by reason of any dilapidation or deterioration of, or damage to, buildings or land caused or permitted by the tenant.

To summarise: it is the duty of an arbitrator—and, one might imply, the normal aim of the valuer—to value a farm at a rent at which it might *reasonably* be let in the open market by a *willing* landlord. " Reasonably " will prohibit his using as yardstick the freak bids which secured Mr. Throgmorton Moneybags the two farms adjoining a year before the Exchequer clapped down on hobby farmers. The presence of a sitting tenant—whose intent may be to adhere to his statutory rights for the rest of his life—is to be ignored, as are improvements made by him. Where the landlord has embellished the farm with grant-aided improvements—such as those which attract 40 per cent of their cost under the Farm Improvements scheme—account must be taken only of his share of the cost. On the other hand, the fact that agricultural land and buildings are de-rated —and are therefore presumably worth more to a tenant who does not have to pay local rates on them than they would be if he did— must be banished from the mind (an achievement engagingly easy). Finally, to the extent that its world-weary air is due to the tenant's neglect, no diminution in rent is to be made where the farm has been wantonly pledged as a hostage to Nature.

## Methods of Approach

There are three generally accepted methods of valuing for rent:

   (1) The field-to-field valuation;
   (2) Rent as a proportion of estimated profits from the farm;
   (3) Rent as a proportion of turnover (or gross income).

To illustrate these methods, we will apply each to the same farm,[3] namely:

    A farm of 180 hectares in the south-east of England. The soil is brick earth of high fertility and the fields are large and easily worked. There is a fair range of buildings with yard and parlour suitable for a dairy herd of 60 cows with followers. A pleasant farmhouse is in a very good state of repair. The farm is in a good situation and there is an adequate labour supply locally.

    A prospective tenant has had twenty years' experience of farming, much of it in dairying and cash cropping. He has sufficient capital to run a farm of the size. After careful inspection of the land and buildings he envisages the following farm plan:—

---

[3] Adapted from a case study in *Farm Rents and Tenure* by J. T. Ward. Estates Gazette Ltd., 1959.

*Cropping.*—140 ha. of tillage under a four-course rotation of corn, corn, roots, leys. This will give each year 70 ha. of corn, mainly wheat and barley with some oats for feeding (Feed acreage 10 ha.) Previous experience on the farm indicates high yields with an average of 40 quintals. 35 ha. of sugar beet with an estimated yield of 320 quintals, 35 ha. one-year leys and 40 ha. of permanent grassland complete the cropping. The leys and permanent grass will be used for grazing, silage and hay and this, together with the sugar beet tops, should provide sufficient forage for the dairy herd, followers and sheep. The wheat will all be sold off but some of the barley and oats will be kept back for the stock. There should be a surplus of straw and at least 100 tonnes should be available for sale.

*Stocking.*—60 Ayrshire dairy cows averaging 3,500 kg. with 45 heifers in a self-contained dairy herd. The best twenty cows and heifers will be put to a dairy bull for replacements. The others will be crossed with a beef bull and the calves sold off at a week old. A flock of 100 Clun ewes will follow the dairy herd.

The farm will be run with a labour force of five regular workers consisting of a foreman, 2 cowmen who will also look after the young stock and sheep and 2 tractor drivers. Most of the arable work, including the sugar beet harvesting, will be highly mechanised, but a considerable amount of casual labour will be required for thinning the sugar beet.

## The Field-to-field Valuation

This is the skill-and-experience method, astounding to client and pupil alike. Each field on the farm is inspected, and spot-figured at so much a hectare. If the farm is much of a muchness throughout, one figure per hectare may be applied to the whole. More likely the valuer will differentiate between the best arable, the medium and the poor. Traditionally he will put a higher figure on the permanent pasture than on the arable, although in these days of ley farming, when many farmers maintain that grassland should be ploughed up and resown at most every seven years, the disparity may shrink to nil.

A spot valuation requires a sound knowledge of rental values in the neighbourhood, since it is a comparative method. Because of the slow turnover in farm tenancies since the war, and the relative paucity of rental arbitrations, such knowledge is not always to be garnered. Where a farm has recently been let by agreement, or the rent adjusted by agreement or arbitration, the amount agreed upon or awarded does, however, have a habit of making itself known, either brazenly or through the grapevine.

In the course of his field-to-field assessment, the valuer will have in mind those factors outlined above: the physical features, the soil quality, the provision and state of cottages, fences, roads and other fixed equipment. It is not usual to value the farmhouse and cottages separately; their adequacy is taken into account in assessing the thing as a whole. Thus if there were two farms otherwise indistinguishable, but one was better equipped than the other, there would be a case for rentally valuing A at say a pound a hectare more than B.

A field-to-field valuation of our example farm might work out thus:

| | | | | | | |
|---|---|---|---|---|---|---|
| Arable land: | | | | | | |
| First class | ... | 120 ha. | @ | £20 | = | £2,400 |
| Second class | ... | 12 ha. | @ | £15 | = | 180 |
| Permanent pasture: | | | | | | |
| First class | ... | 30 ha. | @ | £18 | = | 540 |
| Second class | ... | 10 ha. | @ | £10 | = | 100 |
| Coppices, roads, buildings, etc. | ... | 8 ha. | @ | £4 | = | 32 |
| | | 180 ha. | | | | £3,252 |

The figure for " coppices, roads, etc." is to some extent arbitrary: the total can be satisfactorily rounded to £3,250. This represents an average of £18·06 per hectare.

### Rent as a proportion of profit

With this method one tends to examine the matter from the tenant's point of view. It entails, drawing up a budget of estimated annual returns and expenditure based on what an average sort of farmer would consider a suitable system for the farm in question, be it milk production, beef fattening arable cropping, or a bit of every-thing. The balance between outgoings and incomings represents a combination of the farmer's personal income and what he would be prepared to pay for rent.

On our example farm the annual budget[4] might be estimated thus:

*Estimated Output*

| | | |
|---|---|---|
| 60 ha. corn × 40 quintals @ £2·75 ... ... ... | £6,600 |
| 35 ha. sugar beet × 320 quintals @ 65p ... ... | 7,280 |
| 60 cows × 3,500 kg. milk @ 3·2p ... ... ... | 6,720 |
| 12 cull cows @ £60 ... ... ... ... | 720 |
| 40 beef-cross calves @ £20 ... ... ... ... | 800 |
| 100 ewes (net output of lambs, wool and draft ewes @ £11 per ewe) ... ... ... ... ... | 1,100 |
| | £23,220 |

In addition there may be a number of miscellaneous items, including sales of straw.

[4] The student seeking statistics from which he can make calculations similar to these is referred to the Ministry of Agriculture's *The Farm as a Business*, published by H.M. Stationery Office. Most farm products are the subject of guaranteed prices, which are announced every April in a White Paper *Annual Review and Determination of Guarantees* (H.M.S.O.) and extensively publicised in the national and the farming press. The prices of fertilisers, feedingstuffs, etc., are quoted weekly in the farming papers.

*Estimated Expenditure*

| | | | | | | |
|---|---|---|---|---|---|---|
| Feedingstuffs: 1,800 kg. @ 60p | ... | ... | ... | £1,080 |
| Seeds: | 140 ha. @ £7·50 | ... | ... | ... | 1,050 |
| Fertiliser: | 175 ha. @ £10 | ... | ... | ... | 1,750 |
| Labour—Regular, 5 men including overtime, insurance, perquisites, etc. | ... | ... | 5,000 |
| Casual | ... | ... | ... | ... | 500 |
| Power and machinery (fuel, oil, repairs and depreciation @ £25 per ha.) | ... | ... | ... | ... | 4,375 |
| Miscellaneous, 10 per cent of total expenditure | ... | 1,375 |
| | | | | | | £15,130 |

This produces a margin of £8,090 and poses the controversial question: What proportion of it might be earmarked for rent? Looking at it through the tenant's eyes, the more rent he pays the less he will have for spending. A younger farmer, eager to progress, would probably be content with a lower income for the sake of getting hold of such a desirable farm; indeed, if he hasn't been long at the game he may have to borrow capital to stock and equip the farm, so that a further slice of this margin must be set aside for interest charges. By contrast, an established farmer with family responsibilities and accustomed to high living may have firmer ideas about the income he requires.

In the witness box one might quite properly evade a categorical answer by submitting that, factually speaking, the collation of rents with profits on farms newly let within the past few years has shown a variation between 25 and 50 per cent. If we take 40 per cent as an acceptable proportion, our example farm is worth £3,236 a year, or, say, £18 per hectare.

### Rent as a proportion of turnover

This method requires similar data to the last, but less of it. In other words, it is based on the estimated potential cash output of the farm, expenditure being ignored. Calculations should be based on a reasonable average system of farming the holding in question. This means that although the present tenant may be making a subsidiary fortune out of growing mushrooms as a hobby, the receipts from this essentially sideline enterprise should be disregarded.

Today's rapidly escalating expenses make this method uncertain: it would be difficult to quote generally accepted percentages of gross output for valuation purposes, but 15 per cent is suggested. On a farm more than usually economical to run 12½ per cent might be acceptable.

Applying this method to our example farm, 15 per cent of the gross turnover of £23,220 represents £3,483 a year, or £19·35 per hectare.

The "turnover" method has been used by many generations of valuers, but rarely if ever exclusively. As a check it can be useful; but even on the most primitive farm, whose income is derived from the sale of goat-cheese and heather, there are factors—evasively known as "variables"—which may or may not have a bearing; but none more compelling than the labour requirement.

## Valuation for sale or purchase

As with other forms of real property, the capital value of a farm is ascertained by estimating the rental value, deducting various out-goings, and multiplying the result by so many years' purchase.

Unless the farm has been recently let at its full fair rent, it will be necessary to assess the rental value on one, or preferably more, of the bases already described.

### Outgoings

This subject is dealt with in Chapter 7; the following summary includes a number of outgoings which are peculiar to agricultural property.

*Tithe Redemption Annuities.*—These are fixed payments, under the Tithe Act, 1936, in lieu of tithe rentcharge, payable for a period of 60 years from 2 October, 1936. T.R.A. is essentially an owner's burden which he cannot transfer to a tenant, so that it must be deducted from the capital value of the land from which it arises. It is therefore reasonable to capitalise it separately at the appropriate years' purchase for the unexpired term at the current rate of interest, and deduct it as a lump sum, rather than subtract it from the rental value prior to capitalising the net annual value.

In some circumstances it must be redeemed in which case the cost of redemption which is based on the unexpired term and a rate of interest fixed by the Treasury from time to time. Where the rate of interest used to capitalise the net income from the property is below the rate fixed for redemption it is probably preferable to deduct the cost of redemption rather than the capitalised cost of paying the annuity.

Particulars about tithe redemption annuities, including the current redemption rate, may be obtained from the Board of Inland Revenue, who on 1 April, 1960 took over all the functions of the *ci-devant* Tithe Redemption Commission.

*Drainage Rates* are levied by Drainage Boards towards the cost of keeping rivers in order. There are two types:

  (i) Owners' drainage rates, which are applied to new works or the improvement of existing works, and help to meet the expenses of the River Authorities which look after "main rivers";

  (ii) Occupiers' drainage rates, for the maintenance of existing works.

Both rates in the first instance are payable by the occupier, but if he is a tenant he can recover the owner's rate from his landlord. He may, however, covenant to be responsible for both.[5]

Under the Land Drainage Act, 1961, a River Authority may meet the expenses of drainage works through "drainage charges". These are levied on the occupier, but a landlord may contract to pay them.

*Repairs* are likely to be the highest of all outgoings. What proportion of the gross rent should be deducted will depend on the general condition of the fixed equipment and, where a farm is let, the respective liabilities of landlord and tenant.

Repairing covenants and customs used to be diverse and incomplete, until a generally welcome uniformity was introduced in 1948 through The Agriculture (Maintenance, Repair and Insurance of Fixed Equipment) Regulations (S.I. 1948 No. 184). Familiarly known as the Repairs Regs., or the Model Clauses or, in the tradition of espionage and the tenants of H.M. prisons, plain S.I. One-eight-four, these regulations divide between the landlord and tenant of an agricultural holding the responsibility of maintaining, repairing and insuring the fixed equipment on it—and "fixed equipment" embraces not only buildings but fences, hedges, ditches, practically every immovable short of the land itself. Specific liabilities, from replacing the burnt-out farmhouse to cleansing the duckpond, occupy two closely printed pages.

The regulations apply to all farms which are let on an oral agreement; previously responsibility depended on local custom, an authority often so vague that the parties would drown in the Glebe Brook whilst arguing whose was the liability to renew the blocked culvert thanks to which the said brook was about to burst its banks.

Written agreement will still override the model clause, although if it deals with the liabilities in a manner substantially different, either party may request an adjustment to conform with the regulations, and if need be refer the matter to arbitration.

In determining the landlord's liability for repairs, therefore, the terms of any existing agreement must be reviewed in the light of the regulations and their trend towards universality.

The amount to be deducted for annual repairs will further depend on:

  (a) the class, situation and character of the buildings and other fixed equipment;

---

[5] The Agriculture (Miscellaneous Provisions) Act, 1968, s. 21 provides that drainage charges shall be charged per acre on chargeable land instead of on the annual value of hereditaments.

   (b)  their construction, age, size and condition;

   (c)  the use to which they are put;

   (d)  their suitability to alternative systems of farming;

   (e)  any excess of buildings over the normal requirements of the holding.

An old-established standard of deduction for repairs is one-eighth of the gross rent or rental value. This was the statutory allowance for land and buildings in assessing a farm for income tax under Schedule A. In current practice, $12\frac{1}{2}$ per cent is too low for most **farms.**

Valuers very often base their repairs allowance on so much a hectare rather than $x$ per cent of the rent. This may vary from £1·25 to £4·50 a hectare.

*Insurance and management* are not always separately deducted. Where the model repair clause applies to a farm, the landlord is under an obligation " to keep the farmhouse, cottages and farm buildings insured to their full value against loss or fire". The response to that may well be to take it automatically into account when estimating a figure for repairs. Frequently no allowance is made for management, especially when an individual farm, as distinct from an estate, is being valued. Where these two outgoings are separately assessed, 5 to 10 per cent is a reasonable range for insurance-and-management.

### Years' Purchase

A study of farm sales over the past decade or so shows a variation in Y.P. from 14 to 89 times the rent being paid for them. The average remained remarkably constant at 25 Y.P. Admittedly these figures are based on gross rents and on farms sold without vacant possession; nevertheless, they serve to illustrate the vanity of dogmatising and give the valuer a choice between, say, 15 and 35.

### Example capital valuation

For this we again exhibit the farm lately valued for rent at £3,250 per annum. The outgoings comprise a Tithe Redemption Annuity of £65. Owner's Drainage Rate £35.

| | | | |
|---|---:|---:|---:|
| Rental value  ...    ...    ...    ...    ...    ...    ... | | | £3,250 |
| *Less*—Repairs and insurance @ £2·70 per ha., say | 480 | | |
| Owner's drainage rate ...    ...    ... | 35 | | |
| Management, 5%    ...    ...    ... | 160 | | |
| | —— | | 675 |
| Net income    ...    ...    ...    ... | | | £2,575 |
| Years' purchase...    ...    ...    ... | | | 25 |
| | | | £64,375 |
| *Deduct* redemption costs, £65 × 11 Y.P.  ...    ...    ... | | | 715 |
| *Capital value, say*    ...    ...    ... | | | £63,660 |

£350 per hectare is a realistic figure for this kind of tenanted farm. For various reasons not unconnected with taxation and inflation, there is an increasing demand for such farms, and values are likely to rise.

The valuation of farms with vacant possession is a very different matter, and is largely one of collecting and comparing recent market prices of similar farms. The factors to be considered are broadly similar to those set out above; current values run between £650 and £825 per hectare.

### Low rents and contingencies

The above example is based on the full rental value of a farm assumed to be well equipped and in good tenantable repair. These conditions do not always obtain. First, there may be a sitting tenant getting away with rental murder; secondly, the farm may cry out for immediate, specific repairs; thirdly, the current rent may have been estimated subject to the provision of, say, piped water or a couple of extra cottages; and so on.

To illustrate one mode of taking contingencies into account we display—for positively its final appearance—our exhibition-soiled demonstration farm, with new liabilities added.

> Although its rental value has been estimated at £3,250, the farm is occupied by a tenant sitting on the 8-year remainder of a 21-year lease at a rent of £1,800 a year. The landlord's share of repairs has been somewhat neglected, and the tenant insists on their being put right, at an estimated £700, before he will come to speaking terms with a new owner.

Since the tenant is on a long lease at a fixed rent, the landlord has no immediate powers to have the rent raised by arbitration: he must wait until the lease expires and the tenancy resolves itself into an annual one under the protection of the Agricultural Holdings Act. Nor can the landlord charge interest on the cost of immediate repairs. They represent an expenditure for which there is no direct return and a liability from which there is usually no escape; for the repairs clause in the lease will likely contain some provision similar to that in the statutory repairs regulations (S.I. 1948/184): "if the landlord fails to execute repairs which are his liability within three months of receiving from the tenant a written request specifying the necessary repairs and calling on him to execute them, the tenant may execute such repairs and . . . recover the reasonable cost from the landlord forthwith."

| | | | | |
|---|---|---:|---:|---:|
| Present rent reserved ... ... ... ... ... | | | | £1,800 |
| *Less*—Repairs and insurance @ £2·70 per ha. ... ... ... ... say, | | £480 | | |
| Drainage rate ... ... ... ... | | 35 | | |
| Management 5% ... ... ... | | 90 | | |
| | | | 605 | |
| | | | £1,195 | |
| Y.P. for 8 years @ 3½% ... ... ... | | | 6·87 | |
| | | | | £8,209 |
| Reversion to full rental value ... ... ... ... | | | | £3,250 |
| *Less*—deductions as above but management 5% of £3,250 ... ... ... ... | | | | 675 |
| | | | | £2,575 |
| Y.P. in perpetuity @ 4% deferred 8 years ... | | | | 18·25 |
| | | | | £47,393 |
| | | | | £55,602 |
| *Deduct* | | | | |
| Redemption of T.R.A. (as above) ... ... | | | | 715 |
| Immediate repairs ... ... ... ... | | | | 700 |
| | | | | 1,415 |
| *Capital value, say* ... ... ... | | | | £54,200 |

The difference in rates per cent employed is due to the first 8 years' income being well secured, i.e., the tenant is paying considerably below the rental value and is therefore likely to anticipate each rent day with something approaching goodwill. After that the position is more speculative and so, as is the custom, a higher rate of interest, equivalent to a lower years' purchase, is applied.


## 2. WOODLANDS

Woodlands comprise two forms of assets which are generally separately valued: the site and the trees growing upon it. The value of woodland as land is based on what it might fetch if let or sold in its natural, unimproved state, i.e., its site or prairie value. Sales are less uncommon than lettings, and neither is an everyday occurrence. Fortunately for the valuer who seeks information on present-day figures, the Forestry Commission is a customer commendably willing to talk money. As an indication of woodland worth, the *Fiftieth Annual Report and Accounts* 1969–70 *by the Forestry Commission* (H.M.S.O. 1970) gives the average cost of plantable land during the year as £19 3s. 1d. per acre (about £46 per hectare), about £18 per hectare more than in the previous period.

*Timber valuation*

This is a specialised subject whose details fall outside the scope of this book. Very briefly, the timber and other trees are measured with the aid of a timber tape, a pole graduated in metres (or some more portable instrument for estimating height) and a book of timber tables. The volume of standing timber is calculated, and a price is applied from, say, £4 to £17 per cubic metre, depending on species, age, quality, access, etc.

On the sale of a farm the trees in the hedgerows or standing alone or in clumps may be treated as a separate item, in which event they must be separately measured and priced as they stand. Otherwise their mere presence, not their value as timber, is noted as an added amenity to enhance the value per hectare of the land, on the grounds that they afford shelter for livestock, wind protection, or constitute an integral part of a hedge or (deplorably) a barbed wire fence.

*Coppice and underwood*

Coppice consists of trees cut to within a foot or two from the ground to encourage the "stools" to produce several shoots at a time. Every few years the crop is harvested and the stools left to shoot again. Several species are grown as coppice, notably hazel and sweet chestnut. Where a farm includes coppices, by custom the then privilege of taking the crop belonged to the tenant, although then, as now, they might be reserved to the landlord.

In other days coppice shoots would steadily find a use—for fencing, hurdles, crates, peasticks and such rustic purposes. Today many thousands of acres are practically worthless. In certain localities there is still a demand: much chestnut coppice in Kent, for example, is needed for hop poles, when it is grown on a 12-to-17 year rotation and the cutting rights are put up for auction in parcels of so many acres or parts of an acre called "cants". In the past few years such sales have attracted as much as £400 per hectare, although £225 is nearer the average. Hazel coppice is nowadays hardly saleable: specialist demand, for example for charcoal burning, may keep the trade alive in a few places, but no general guide to values can be given. Mixed coppice, again, may contain pitwood samples, or a stem here and there that would make a passable fencing stake; otherwise the whole area may be written off as valueless scrub. Occasionally it is possible to sell oversize coppice for pulpwood: prices of the order of £50 per hectare can be expected.

In those rare cases where a valuer has convictions about a continuing market, and the courage of them, the coppice as coppice may be valued by estimating the net return at the next cutting and making a pro rata deduction according to length of rotation. For instance, if a 10-year-old stand of chestnut is being cut every 15 years and has locally been yielding £200 per hectare net, in today's immature state it might be worth 10/15ths, or say £130 per hectare. Theory may protest that this disregards compound interest and the fact that after cutting the stools will provide another crop with another potential £200 two decades from now. Practice deigns not to answer, save by heeling both feet in the ground.

## 3.  COTTAGES

We have seen that in valuing a farm the house and cottages that go with it are not as a rule separately treated; the valuer takes into account their presence, condition or, indeed, absence as just one of those factors which influence overall rental-per-acre. Nevertheless, far from all rural cottages are part and parcel of somebody's farm on the woodlands.

Where they are separately valued, country cottages are treated basically as other residential property: for rent, either at what they are let or at what they are worth to be let; for sale, at so many years' purchase of the net rent or annual value.

Standing as they do in the realm of the modestly rented, two special points need to be watched:

(1) Whether any statutory notices, requiring execution of works, demolition or closing, etc., are outstanding under the Housing or Public Health Acts.

(2) Whether the rent is limited under the Rent Acts.

A cottage of the rural workers' type, subject to letting restrictions and with no ideas above its station, may be capitalised at about 12 Y.P. of the net rent. But where one is available with vacant possession its value generally bears no relation to the few pence a week Granny Pippin was paying for it, regular as clockwork, up to the minute she died. Such cottages—and they are legion—most often cost more to maintain than the statutory or sentimental rent reserved. In fact, they may financially represent a dead loss, and a minus figure multiplied by even a nominal Y.P. hardly represents a saleable proposition.

To redress the balance there is frequently a demand for country cottages at a figure that bears no relation to rental value, years' purchase or the cost of bricks. The magic labels "weekend retreat" or "little country place" coupled with a "wealth of old oak" are touchstones which will promote a cottage from £500-worth to a selling price derived from no established principles of valuation. With such the valuer can do no more than hazard a guess based on what weekend colonists or away-from-it-allers have been paying for similar gold mines in the neighbourhood.

## 4. OTHER HOUSES

Country houses in general are valued no differently from their urban or suburban counterparts. The exception, fortunately a rare one, is the mansion house: the Big House, the pivot of the landed estate. It will probably have a large garden attached and a few hectares of parkland, which can be regarded either as an additional attraction or merely paddock space for the white elephant.

In making a cockshy at the rental value of a country mansion, the time-tested factors, *faute de mieux*, may be provisionally applied. With the statelier homes the rent at which they are worth to be let proportionally diminishes according to magnitude and the lack of modern comforts or, where these are installed, the expense of running them. The cost of maintaining the gardens and the wages of the indoor servants are expenses reduced only by the impossibility of getting domestic help. The incidence of dry rot and death watch beetle, whose tastes are lucullan and whose preference for the more ducal houses is a proven phenomenon, is another factor to explain why the "hypothetical tenant" so often fails to hypothesise.

In short, unless some public body or private company makes a bid for the place with a view to its use as a school, country club, sanatorium or conversion to flats—in which event valuation is more a matter of haggling than of applied principles—the vast country house may have only a demolition value, ranging from nil to a couple of hundred pounds for the lead. There are no Modern Methods of valuing mansions.

## 5. SPORTING RIGHTS

On the sale of an individual farm, such sporting as it may afford is thrown in, as it were, as yet another justification for the adjective "desirable". On a country estate, however, shooting and fishing are customarily treated as separate assets, for which there is nowadays keen demand.

*Shooting rights* are commonly let on a 3- or a 7-year lease. The rent will depend not the least on the prevalent species and plenitude of game (the Agricultural Holdings Act, 1948, defines game as meaning deer, pheasants, partridges, grouse and black game, but the trigger-happy will punctually pay for the right to perforate other fowl, e.g., snipe, woodcock, wild duck). For the rest it will vary according to the provisions for payment of keepers' wages, local rates (where applicable), keepers' cottages and so on. Recent lettings have varied from 15p to £1 per hectare, 60p being a rule-of-thumb figure, given a thumb neither rigid nor narrow. Some grouse moors are valued for rent on an estimate of the potential bag, perhaps £1·50 a brace.

*Fishing rights.*—The most esteemed subjects of exaggeration are the "game" fish, e.g., salmon, trout and grayling, but there is lively competition for the less lordly coarse fish, from the cannibal pike to the wily one under the bridge which defies identification.

Leases of salmon rivers may yield an annual rent of £100 a mile, where riparian rights cover both banks. Trout fishing is about half as valuable. Coarse fishing will let for a lot less, but where lettable to the angling fraternity at large on a system of daily permits or season tickets, the owner may look to retire that much earlier.

In capitalising sporting rights, 10 to 12 years' purchase of the net rent is both traditional and, by present day demands, cautious. On estates well endowed for piscation or venery, far removed from New Towns and the knavish attentions of mechanised poachers, up to 25 Y.P. can be applied.


## 6.  SUMMARY—THE COUNTRY ESTATE

For some generations past discussions on landed estates have been largely concerned with their break-up. There is life in them yet, each a self-contained entity with its large house and parkland, its dozen or more farms, its woodlands and sawmill, its houses and cottages, almshouses, watermill, minerals,[6] wayleaves and easements,[7] and its fear of death *vis-a-vis* duty.[8]

An agricultural estate which comes into the market is more often sold in parts than as one; its value therefore depends upon the nature of the individual properties of which it is composed rather than on its worth as a whole. Even when valuing the smaller estate for sale as a whole its components are more surely treated separately, particularly since some assets are better secured than others and so merit a higher years' purchase.

The demand for agricultural property is unlikely to fall below the supply in any predictable future. Apart from the conception (latterly open to doubt) of agricultural land as an indestructible investment, purchasers are attracted by the concessions and advantages it enjoys in connection with income tax. There is, furthermore, the added attraction—particularly to the next in succession—of the 45 per cent rebate in estate duty which this type of property attracts.

Investors are also influenced by the possibility of farmland in some situations being required later on, at enhanced values, for non-agricultural purposes. Finally, there is that "pride of ownership", an intangible attribute transcending even the pleasures of dining off the home-bred Hereford or running the Rolls on the farm accounts.

---

[6] See Chapter 28.
[7] See Chapter 26.
[8] See Chapter 15.

# Chapter 12

## Development Properties

### 1. GENERALLY

THE TERM " Development Properties " is used here to indicate the type of property the value of which can be increased by capital expenditure, by a change in the use to which the property is put, or possibly by a combination of capital expenditure and change of use. It has commonly been applied to areas of undeveloped land close to existing development and likely to be in future demand for building purposes; to individual sites in towns, at present unbuilt on; and to other urban sites occupied by buildings which have become obsolescent or which do not utilise the site to the best advantage. The value, which in these cases is latent in the property, can only be released by development and in all cases is subject to the necessary planning permission being granted.

In valuing a development property it may be necessary (i) to determine the best uses to which a piece of land or property can be put in the future having regard to the planning permission likely to be granted; this may involve assuming a planning consent, in which case the probable conditions of the assumed consent should be clearly stated: (ii) to estimate the market value of the land when put to this use: (iii) to consider the time which will elapse before the land can be so used: and (iv) to estimate the cost of carrying out the works required to put the land to the proposed use together with such other items involved as legal costs and agent's commission on sales and purchase and the cost of financing the project.

Where data of recent similar transactions enable the valuer to use the comparison method of valuation he will do so even if he has to look outside the area in which the land is situated, for example sales in other towns in the same part of the country having a similar population. The above factors will then bear on his consideration somewhat indirectly. Where no comparables are available he may have to employ the "Residual Method" of valuation described in section 3 (*d*) of Chapter 9 and even when he can value by comparison he would be wise to make an alternative valuation by the Residual Method. As indicated above this is essentially a forecast of sales and expenditure and it is more convenient to set out the figures in a different form. Such statement is known as a Viability or Feasibility Report or Statement. Examples are given below but such a Report or Statement contains the same figures as are employed in a Residual Valuation.

Where the residual method is employed the market value of the property when developed to the best advantage is ascertained and allowance made for the period of deferment; the cost of the necessary works and an allowance for profit and risk is then deducted; on this basis the result should represent the present value of the property in its existing condition.

When the residual method is employed it is obvious that any errors made in the estimates of value, cost of development, etc., will be reflected in the valuation arrived at, so that considerable skill is required when applying this method if consistent and accurate results are to be obtained. Moreover, it frequently happens that the amount of the estimates of value and cost are very large compared to the value of the property in its present state: a small error in the estimates will entail a large error in the residue in such cases.

Although before the last war the residual method was frequently used as the only method of valuation applied in any particular case, direct comparison of the property being valued with other similar properties is a more reliable method and is preferred by the Lands Tribunal[1] although the residual method has been accepted by the Tribunal in some cases.[2] The Tribunal's criticism of the residual method is essentially that of the inherent weakness referred to in the preceding paragraph.[3]

When the residual method is used the value when developed, can be substantiated by comparison with that of properties that have been similarly developed and sold after the works have been completed.

Also, in some instances a comparison may be available of the cost of the work proposed to be done. For example, in the case of industrial development comprising the erection of ground floor

---

[1] See *Johnson v. East Barnet U.D.C.*, [1962] R.V.R. 750. Seven cases reported together including *Eley v. Derby*, [1964] R.V.R. 278; *Budgen v. Birmingham*, [1964] R.V.R. 232; *Colclough v. Store*, [1966] R.V.R. 777; *Georgallides v. Camden*, [1967] R.V.R. 61; *Boorman v. Chatham*, [1967] R.V.R. 301; *Clayland Securities Ltd. v. Store*, [1968] R.V.R. 683. There is a reference to the method in *Kaye and Ors. v. Basingstoke*, [1968] R.V.R. 744.

[2] See *Baylis's Trustees v. Droitwich Borough Council*, [1966] R.V.R. 158; *St. Clement's Danes Holborn Estate Charity v. Greater London Council*, [1966] R.V.R. 333; *Clinker & Ash Ltd. v. Southern Gas Board*, [1967] R.V.R. 477.

[3] See *Liverpool and Birkenhead House Property Investment Co. Ltd. v. Liverpool City Council*, [1962] R.V.R. 162.

In *Wood Investments Ltd. v. Birkenhead Corporation*, [1969] R.V.R. 137, Mr. John Watson, a member of the Lands Tribunal said, with regard to a witness' residual valuation, that it "provides a telling illustration of its (the residual methods) uncertainties. The key figures are (a) the value of the completed buildings estimated at £265,537 and (b) the cost of providing it estimated at £230,210. £35,327 which is (a) less (b) is the land but (a) and (b) are necessarily rough estimates and there must be some margin for error. If (a) turned out to be only 5 per cent too high and (b) 5 per cent too low the residual value of the land would be approximately £10,500 instead of approximately £30,000 and if the 5 per cent errors happen to be the other way round it would be over £60,000."

factories, the probable cost of erecting a proposed building may be found by reference to the actual cost of building similar premises in the same area. It is usual to break down the cost to a convenient unit, e.g., per square metre,[4] to allow for differences in sizes but allowance must also be made in the unit cost for differences in standard of finish and accommodation, for differing site conditions and rises in costs of building.

In considering the value of a piece of land thought to be suitable for building purposes, or a piece of land already built on but which it is thought profitable to redevelop, it is first necessary to decide the type of development or redevelopment for which the land is best suited, due regard being had to the planning permission likely to be granted. It is frequently necessary to work on an assumption as regards what consent will be forthcoming and the conditions attached to it, particularly in relation to density. As mentioned above where this is done, the valuer must state clearly what consent is assumed and what the conditions are.

The type of development or redevelopment can be considered under three main headings:—(i) dwelling-houses or flats; (ii) shops and commercial premises; (iii) industrial buildings. But whichever type of development is considered most suitable, there are certain general considerations which apply to all.

It can be said that there is at any given time a general demand for land for building purposes dependent upon factors applicable to the country as a whole, and that the extent to which this demand is localised in certain areas or in the neighbourhood of certain towns will depend upon local factors.

General factors affecting the demand for land include the state of prosperity of the country and population trends.

It is obvious that in prosperous times there will be a demand for sites for such buildings as offices, shops and the like. When the population is increasing there will be a larger demand for houses and for an improved standard of housing, both in quality and quantity, as family incomes increase.

It does not, of course, follow that because a certain type of development is provided for in the development plan for the area that the land can profitably be developed for such a use immediately or even within a reasonable period in the future. For instance, with a view to controlling the number of persons employed in the centre of cities, large areas in the centre of cities have been allocated for " commercial " use, i.e., primarily storage purposes, warehousing, but at the present time the development of the land for this purpose is, in some cases, unprofitable.

The prospect of profitable development of any particular piece of land within the conditions imposed, or likely to be imposed,

---

[4] See Chapter 9, Section 4.

by the planning authority will depend largely on local circumstances, and past evidence of trends of development in the neighbourhood will have to be taken into account. The valuer has also
to consider general trends affecting development in the country as
a whole.

In some cases of doubt or complexity it may be necessary to
obtain an indication of the sort of planning consent likely to be
forthcoming by informal discussion with the local planning authority
before putting forward even a tentative valuation.

The nature of the development likely to be permitted having
been ascertained  or assumed, it is also necessary to assess its commercial possibilities.  It does not follow that, because planning
consent is likely to be obtained, there is necessarily a market for that
particular form of development.

For some years, the developer of the land, i.e., the person who
purchases the land has been almost always the person who builds
the houses (in the case of residential development) and such a person
is often referred to as a "builder/developer".  Until 1939 this was
not so often the case.  Purchasers or owners of land then frequently
developed it by employing a building contractor to construct the
buildings on the land developed.  The developer would expect to
receive a profit from the development of the land and the contractor
from the construction of the buildings.

To distinguish between a "builder/developer" from a person
undertaking the last form of operation the latter is often referred to
as a "developer".


## 2.   VIABILITY STATEMENTS

As explained above this is a statement of forecast of sales and
costs of development.  It can be presented in a number of different
forms including that of a profit and loss account.  The form used
herein is one frequently employed.

   *Example.*—A developer has been negotiating for the purchase of a
   freehold site which could accommodate a small block of four
   self-contained flats each with garage.  He can buy it for £5,000
   subject to contract and to outline planning consent for the above
   development.

   Sketch plans indicate that the flats will have floor areas of
   100 m² each and investigation of sales of flats in the same
   area indicate that selling prices will be £5,250 including garage
   on a leasehold basis—99 years at a ground rent of £20 per annum
   per flat.

   You are instructed to advise a finance house on the proposal
   generally and your report is to include a Viability Statement.

*Viability Statement*
*Sales*

| | | |
|---|---|---|
| 4 flats @ £5,250 each ...   ... | | £21,000 |
| Ground Rents: 4 × £20 p.a. @ | | |
| 7 Y.P.   ...   ...   ... | | 560 |
| | | £21,560 |

| | | | |
|---|---|---|---|
| *Costs—Land*   ...   ...   ... | | £5,000 | |
| Cost of building: | | | |
| 400 m² @ £24 per m²   ... | £9,600 | | |
| 4 garages @ £150 each   ... | 600 | | |
| Site preparation, approach road | | | |
| and gardens ...   ...   ... | 300 | | |
| | | £10,500 | |
| *Architect's fee* for plans (agreed fee) | | £100 | |
| *Legal Costs:* | | | |
| On purchase of site   ...   ... | £100 | | |
| On sale of flats ...   ...   ... | £275 | | |
| | | £375 | |
| *Agents Commission* on sale of flats | | | |
| (agreed)   ...   ...   ... | | £500 | |
| *Finance Costs*—on say £15,000 | | | |
| for say 6 months @ 12 per cent | | £900 | |
| | | | £17,375 |
| *Estimated profit*   ... | | | £4,185 |

It is thought that many developers judge whether the profit level is sufficiently worth while to warrant undertaking the development, by expressing the estimated profit as a percentage of the total costs of development. In the above case the return is 24 per cent since £4,185 represents 24 per cent of £17,375. This percentage can be used as a basis for comparison between one development and another of the same type. Alternatively the estimated profit can be expressed as a percentage of the total sales (£21,560 in the above example) or the amount of profit per unit estimated (£1,050 per flat in the above).

### 3.  FACTORS AFFECTING VALUE

In dealing with a particular area of land the local circumstances must be carefully considered, e.g., the growth of prosperity of the town, the existing supply of houses, factories or other buildings, and the amenities of the particular property under consideration.

It is, of course, essential that proper access to the land is available. The proximity of public services is, also, of considerable importance, such as public sewers, gas, electricity and water supplies. The existence of restrictions and easements must be checked.

The factors vary according to the type of development for which it is considered the land is most suitable due regard being had to town planning consent likely to be forthcoming or assumed.

In the case of land to be used for houses or flats, these will include the proximity of good travel facilities, the existence of shops, schools, churches and the like or the possibility of the provision thereof in the future. Local employment conditions also affect demand. Regard must also be had to the presence of open spaces, parks and golf courses and the reservation of land under planning control for similar purposes. The character of the neighbourhood must be considered to determine the most suitable type or types of development; also whether the character is changing.

Local shops or " multiple " positions depend on population " catchment area." The demand for land for shops will largely be dependent on the present or future number of houses. The valuer will have to decide whether the shops to be built will be of the " multiple " class or " local " shops. The former depend upon large numbers of shoppers often drawn from a wide area, while the latter find their customers from houses within a comparatively short distance.

The most important factors in the case of warehouse and industrial developments are access by road and an adequate supply of suitable labour. Proximity to ports and markets and to sources of power and materials, are now less important than they were due to the increase in road transport facilities.

With regard to the development of land for industrial purposes, the necessity for obtaining an Industrial Development Certificate from the Department of Trade and Industry must not be overlooked. Such a certificate is necessary where the floor space of the proposed building will exceed 5,000 sq. ft.[5] No application for consent can be considered without such a certificate.

Whether development is likely to be profitable or not is dependent upon the demand for the property when it has been completed. The physical state of the land, availability of services, etc., are also important factors to be taken into account. Until 1947 these were the only factors to be considered but since then the town planning provisions affecting the land are the overriding factor which the valuer has to consider.

## 4. DEVELOPMENT SCHEMES

(a) *Generally*.—In relation to small areas of land it may be a comparatively simple problem to determine the best use to which the land can be put, having regard to general trends of development in the neighbourhood, the factors affecting the particular piece of

---

[5] Town and Country Planning Act, 1962, Secs. 38 and 39, as amended.

land under consideration and the provisions of the relevant Development Plan.

> *Example.*—You are asked to advise on the value of some plots of land fronting a residential road which has been made up and taken over by the local authority. There are soil and surface water sewers in the road and gas and electric services are available. The property comprises sixteen plots, with a total frontage of 180 m and a depth of 40 m. These are the remaining plots in this road; the rest of the frontage has been developed for houses selling at about £5,500 with frontages of about 12 m each. From the enquiries you have made you find that similar plots in the area have sold at prices ranging from £1,100–£1,250 each. There is a demand for houses of the character already erected, and it is expected that all of the plots could be built on and the houses disposed of within one year.

You have ascertained from the local planning authority that they would permit the development of this land for residential purposes. The land is in an area allocated for residential development.

> *Valuation.*—In this instance there cannot be very much doubt as to the type of development that should take place.
>
> After inspecting the land and the area and taking into account the prices realised and the upward trend in values, it might be considered that a fair value per plot would be £1,325, giving a total valuation of £20,000 on the assumption that planning consent for this form of development would be granted subject to only usual conditions.

> *Note.*—In this instance the procedure has been a direct comparison with the sale prices of other similar properties in the vicinity. A speculating builder, before buying, even at a figure which he feels satisfied is a fair market value, would be wise to prepare a viability report on the following lines to forecast the probable rate of profit. A valuer advising on the sale price of the land would be wise to do the same since the forecast may bring to light some factor which might otherwise be overlooked or given too little weight.

### Viability Statement

| | | |
|---|---|---|
| *Selling prices* 15 × £5,600 ... ... | | £84,000 |
| *Costs of development:* | | |
| Land ... ... ... ... ... | £20,000 | |
| Building Costs—15 houses of 90 m² each @ £32·50 per m² including garages, say ... ... ... | £44,000 | |
| | c/f. £64,000 | £84,000 |

|  |  | b/f. | £64,000 | £84,000 |
|---|---|---|---|---|
| Plans ...  ...  ...  ...  ... |  |  | £100 |  |
| Legal Costs: |  |  |  |  |
|    On purchase of land  ...  ... |  | £355 |  |  |
|    On sale of houses  ...  ... |  | £1,120 |  |  |
|  |  |  | £1,475 |  |
| Sale Commission @ £100 per house |  |  | £1,500 |  |
| Finance @ 12 per cent on say £30,000 for 8 months, say  .. |  |  | £2,500 |  |
|  |  |  |  | £69,575 |
| *Estimated profit*  ... |  |  |  | £14,425 |

£14,425 represents 21 per cent of £69,575 or £900 per house.

*Notes.*—1. The sale price of £5,600 could be substantiated by reference to sales of similar houses in the same area. If as has been the case since the last war there has been a rise in prices of such houses in the area the developer may deliberately increase his estimate to allow for a continuation of increase. If he adhered to prices current at the date of the purchase of the land he would find that he was constantly losing opportunities of purchase due to higher bids from others, if he worked on the same level of profit as others. The developer would probably do a number of such calculations within a price bracket. It is preferable to work on prices current at the date of purchase and a lower profit margin and to regard any increase in prices obtained in the event as " super-profits." To be too optimistic is likely to bring disaster.

2. There is an obvious interdependence between the figures of selling prices (£5,600 above) and building costs (£32·50 per m² above). The better the quality of the house offered the higher will be the price realised and the higher the cost of building. The object of the developer is to maximise the difference between the two figures by use of his experience, expertise and skill in design and efficiency in sales organisation and building costs.

3. Most developers use stock plans or adapt plans they have used before and a full scale architects fee would not be payable in most cases. Where fresh plans have to be prepared a much larger figure would have to be allowed: if the developer offers the designer too small a fee, the design and hence the saleability of the houses is likely to suffer.

4. There is a similar interdependence between the amount of the selling agents commission and the prices obtained and moreover the speed of sales. If selling agents are paid too little they will not use maximum efforts to sell.

5. Since proceeds of sales will start to be received in say 6 months it will not be necessary for the developer to borrow the

*Month*

| Items | 1 | 2 | 3 | 4 | 5 | 6 | 7 | 8 | 9 | 10 | 11 | 12 |
|---|---|---|---|---|---|---|---|---|---|---|---|---|
| | £ | £ | £ | £ | £ | £ | £ | £ | £ | £ | £ | £ |
| Land ... ... ... ... | 20,000 | | | | | | | | | | | |
| Building costs ... ... | | 4,000 | 4,000 | 4,000 | 4,000 | 4,000 | 4,000 | 4,000 | 4,000 | 4,000 | 4,000 | 4,000 |
| Plans ... ... ... ... | | | 100 | | | | | | | | | |
| Legal fees ... ... ... | 355 | | | | | | | | | | | |
| Interest at 1 per cent per month ... ... ... | | 204 | 245 | 289 | 332 | 375 | 317 | 259 | 200 | 140 | 80 | 19 |
| | 20,355 | 24,559 | 28,904 | 33,193 | 37,525 | 41,900 | 36,057 | 30,156 | 24,196 | 18,176 | 12,096 | 5,955 |
| Net proceeds of sales, i.e., 2 houses at £5,250 each less £170 per house (legal costs and sale commission) ... | — | — | — | — | — | 10,160 | 10,160 | 10,160 | 10,160 | 10,160 | 10,160 | 10,160 |
| Net balance of drawings ... | 20,355 | 24,559 | 28,904 | 33,193 | 37,525 | 31,740 | 25,897 | 19,996 | 14,036 | 8,016 | 1,936 | — |

Total interest = £2,460

Note how the amount drawn builds up from the initial payment for the land to the point in time when the first sales are made from when it decreases until it is all repaid. The profit in cash all accrues to the developer in the last two or three months.

In the above table it is assumed that the interest is added to the loan, i.e., it is "rolled up", as distinct from being paid regularly by the borrower from his own resources.

whole of the estimated land and building costs (£64,000) for the whole period of the development (12 months). About half the total figure for something over half the total period will give the cost of finance in this case.

If it is required to substantiate this figure, a " cash flow " forecast should be prepared. The Table on page 159 assumes the sale of two houses per month starting in the seventh month. Such a forecast would be useful to (and probably required) by any finance house providing the money for the development.

It may be necessary in the case of larger areas to prepare sketch plans of a suitable development, making provision, for instance, for certain portions of the estate to be developed for shops, others for flats, and others for houses, probably with varying densities. In such cases the problem is more complicated but the principle is the same.

It is of course simple to set out the above figures in the form of a residual valuation:—

| | | | |
|---|---|---:|---:|
| *Selling prices:* ...  ...  ...  ... | | | £84,000 |
| Less Building costs—15 houses of 90 m² | | | |
| each @ £32·50 per m² ...  ... | £44,000 | | |
| Plans ...  ...  ...  ...  ... | £100 | | |
| Legal costs  ...  ...  ...  ... | £1,475 | | |
| Sale commissions  ...  ...  ... | £1,500 | | |
| Finance  ...  ...  ...  ... | £2,500 | | |
| | £49,575 | | |
| Developer's profit—say 29 per cent (or alternatively 17 per cent of £84,000) ...  ...  ...  ... | £14,425 | | |
| | | £64,000 | |
| *Value of land*  ... | | | £20,000 |

*Note.*—If the cost of building were taken at only £1·25 per m² different, the total cost would vary by £1,680 but this would make a difference of over 8 per cent to the value of the land.

(*b*) *User of land.*—When preparing a scheme in outline, the extent of the various uses to which the land is to be put must be determined, and a lay-out prepared to indicate the plots that will be provided and the roads and sewers that will have to be constructed; regard must be had to the provision of suitable size plots and to any restrictions in force relating to the density of buildings and to the proportion of sites that may be covered. For average-sized shops with upper storeys, frontages of 5 m–7 m and depths of 24 m–40 m may be considered to be suitable. For houses, even greater latitude will be required, according to the density, from as low as 6 m frontages for the smaller classes of houses, at densities of 37 or more per hectare, to 30 m or more frontages for larger houses built to a density of 10 to 15 houses per hectare.

In the case of large estates, it may be necessary to make reservations for special plots for open spaces, tennis courts, for a church or community centre.

In relation to those parts allocated for commercial purposes, it may be considered that a site should be set aside for a petrol-filling station, public-house or the like.

Even though a scheme is prepared only for the purpose of arriving at the value of the land it might be worth while to discuss the scheme informally with the local planning authority. It would be found in many instances that different densities should be allowed for in different parts of the land and provision made for roads, open spaces, etc.

(c) *Roads.*—The road lay-out should be such as to provide good and easy access to all parts of the estate. If there are any changes of level, regard must be had to the provision of easy gradients. So far as is practicable, plots of regular shape and of suitable size must be produced by the road lay-out, at the same time avoiding undue monotony and lack of amenity. The lay-out of soil and surface water sewers must be determined in relation to the available outfall and will need to be constructed to the requirements of the local authorities. The current specification of the local authority for roadwork must also be considered.

Until recent years it was possible for the developer to construct only " builders' roads ", leaving the local authority to take over the roads after they had been made up. The relevant statutes were originally the Public Health Act, 1875, or the Private Street Works Act, 1892. These Acts were consolidated in the Highways Act, 1959, which refers to the Acts as the " codes " of 1875 and 1892 respectively.

Under the 1875 code the local authority may request the " owners " to make up the road within a specified time, and if this request is not complied with the local authority may execute the work and charge the cost to the " owners " in proportion to the frontage of their land on the road in question. Under the 1892 code, which is applicable only where adopted, the local authority may execute the work without giving the "owners " the option of doing it; the cost will be apportioned having regard to benefits derived, and not necessarily on a frontage basis. The provisions of these codes may be important when valuing land on which there are incomplete roads. But it is now normal practice to construct roads fully so that no road charges fall on the frontagers.

The New Streets Act, 1951, provided that, with certain exceptions, no work for erecting buildings could be begun unless the owner of the land or his predecessor had paid to the local authority or secured the payment to their satisfaction such sum as may be required to meet the ultimate liability for private street works in respect of the building. These provisions have now been consolidated in the Highways Act, 1959.[6] Thus the position with regard to " builders' roads " which in the past have often remained in their original rough state for long periods is modified. The Act applies in Boroughs (other than Metropolitan Boroughs) and in Urban Districts in England and Wales and in any Rural District where it is applied by order of the Minister of Housing and Local Government on the application of the County Council after consulting with the Rural District Council. Where the Act applies, no work for the erection of a building which will front on to a private street may be done unless the cost of the street works which would be recoverable in respect of the frontage by the local authority has been paid or secured. Among the exceptions are (i) where an agreement has been made under the Highways Act, 1959,[7] where the estate developer agrees to construct roads, etc., to an agreed specification and the authority agrees to take over the roads when the frontages are fully built up and after the developer has maintained the roads for 6 months, and (ii) where the street was already built up on 1 October, 1951.

This Act also enables the majority of the frontagers in a street to compel the local authority to make up the street and to take it over as a highway.

(d) *Special Factors.*—It may be found that the land is so situated that it would not be possible to connect to a public sewer by gravity and allowance would have to be made for the cost of constructing a pumping station. In other cases it may be practicable, in the case of low-density houses, to adopt cesspool drainage, subject to the requirements of the Public Health Acts, although, except in rural areas, cesspool drainage for the development of estates is unlikely to be permitted. It may be worth while to duplicate water services on each side of the road. Enquiries must also be made as to the terms upon which supplies of gas and electricity and the installation of telephone cables can be obtained, as the nearest mains or cables may be at some considerable distance and supplies inadequate.

## 5. Plot Values

An indication of the method of approach that might be adopted by a speculative builder considering the purchase of plots has already been given. But instead of plots being sold for a lump sum they may be sold subject to a rentcharge or let on building lease at a ground rent per m² or per metre frontage. Letting on ground leases and selling subject to rentcharges are far less common today than before 1939, probably due to the effect of inflation and the heavy demand for land.

---

[6] Secs. 192-199.
[7] Sec. 40.

In the case of plots for dwelling-houses, the usual practice in the South of England has always been for plots to be sold outright; prior to 1939 some plots were let on 99 years' building lease at a ground rent of so much per foot frontage. In the North and Midlands the rental value or capital value of plots has usually been expressed at so much per square yard. For instance, take the case of a house plot with 30 ft. frontage and 150 ft. depth. In the South a possible ground rental value might have been 8s. per foot frontage p.a. (£12 p.a. in all) or the capital value might be quoted at £8 per foot frontage (£240 in all). In the North or Midlands the corresponding figures would be approximately 6d. per square yard p.a. rental or 10s. per square yard capital value.

The methods adopted and the rates applied depended upon local circumstances and the appropriate figures were arrived at by comparison.

In the case of shops and offices, it may be possible to estimate the ground rent as a fraction of the estimated rack rental of the type of building likely to be erected on it but this approach is open to similar criticisms as the residual method, i.e., the degree of cover applied makes a very large difference to the result. This is so to such an extent that the method is only useful in practice as a rough check and it is to be avoided if possible. For example, if the rack rental value of a notional block of offices considered suitable for a site is £10,000 p.a. and the valuer is of the opinion that a ground rent for the site should be 4 times covered, the ground rental value would be £2,500 p.a. If a cover of 5 times is taken, the result will be £2,000 p.a., a difference of 20 per cent of £2,500 p.a. Alternatively and preferably, the valuer should estimate the capital value of the land by comparison and then, if required, arrive at a ground rent by decapitalising the amount on a 8–10 per cent basis.

In any case, such estimates will be checked, whenever possible, by the evidence of actual lettings of comparable pieces of land.

## 6. PERIOD OF DEVELOPMENT

In the case of an extensive estate, the development works necessary to provide suitable plots will take some time and prior to 1939 not all the plots were sold or let immediately. It was therefore necessary to estimate the time over which the sales were likely to spread.

The period to be allowed was necessarily somewhat speculative, but in an area where there was a large demand for land for development purposes, and where similar land was being or had recently been developed, it was possible to determine it with some accuracy. The most difficult problems arose where the land being dealt with was not likely to become ripe for development for some time in the future, and any estimate in this case of the period of development was necessarily approximate.

In recent years, the speed of development has been determined by the speed of building, at least in South-East England, where demand has been at a high level for some years and where this is the case it is not necessary to defer sales or development works except in special cases.

Where the area of land being considered is large and the value per hectare or per unit high and where the land has to be purchased outright (i.e., where deferred payment is not possible) the cost of financing the development will be found to be disproportionately high because the whole of the land value has to be carried for a considerable period before sales returns balance costs. In the case of such large areas where a considerable period of time is involved the valuer has great difficulty in deciding by how much he should increase sale prices of the last houses to be sold, assuming a rise in price is to be expected.

## 7. INCIDENTAL COSTS

In most cases certain additional expenses will be incurred beyond the bare constructional costs of roads and sewers.

If open spaces or other amenities such as belts of trees are provided by the developer the cost must be taken into account.

Professional services are likely to be required for the preparation of detailed lay-out schemes and the drawings and specifications for constructional works; fees for this may be taken from 5 per cent to 8 per cent on the cost of the works.

Legal charges may be incurred both in respect of the purchase of the land (and stamp duty) and of the sales. The amount to be allowed has to be worked out from a scale of solicitors charges regard being had as to whether the land is registered or unregistered.

A detailed estimate of the cost of advertisements and commission on sales payable to agents must also be made.

## 8. DEVELOPER'S PROFIT

As indicated in Section 1 of this Chapter, prior to 1939 residential development was frequently carried out by a developer (in contrast to the more usual post war builder/developer) and it was then necessary to consider the margin to be allowed to such a purchaser. It is obvious that, if he had to invest a considerable sum, a return of say, 5 per cent or 6 per cent of the capital invested was not adequate having regard to the risks that are run. However carefully estimates were prepared, circumstances changed, costs rose or the prices expected were not attained.

The margin allowed depended largely on the risk involved and the amount spent on development works. With land ripe for development in ready demand and likely to be sold within one or two years without extensive works having to be done, an allowance of 10 per cent of the total of the estimated plot sales was usually made prior to 1939. For more speculative developments a margin of 20 per cent or 25 per cent might have been used.

An indication of the assessment of a builder/developer's profit has been given in Section 2. In contrast to a developer who would expect to receive a profit from the development only (and none from the construction) a builder/developer would look for both elements. It is for this reason that a builder/developer can usually outbid a developer in the case of residential development.

In nearly all cases of residential land today purchasers are builder/developers and no attempt is now made, as was often previously done, to divide profit between development of the land on the one hand and the profit to be made on building houses on the other. Profit is now considered as a whole as is illustrated in previous examples.

## 9. URBAN SITES

The previous sections of this Chapter have been concerned mainly with land, not built upon, in the vicinity of existing development.

In the centre of towns, in built-up areas, it is often necessary to consider the value of a site which has become vacant through buildings having been pulled down, or which is occupied by buildings which are obsolescent or do not utilise the site to the full.

The general method of approach suggested in Section 1 can be used, i.e., to value by comparison with sales of other sites by reference to an appropriate unit, e.g., per square metre or metre frontage and to check the result by drawing up a viability statement or by a valuation by the Residual Method.

As in the case of building estates, the type of property to be erected and the use to which it can be put when completed is entirely dependent upon the planning permission which will be granted. An indication will probably be obtained by an inspection of the development plan.

Sites are often restricted as to user, height of buildings, the percentage of the site area that may be covered at ground floor and above, by conditions imposed when planning permission is granted.

There may be further restrictions on user owing to the existence of easements of light and air or rights of way.

A site may be bare, but may contain old foundations and the cost of clearing may be considerable, on the other hand advantage may be taken of existing runs of drains.

In many areas the cost of development may be seriously increased by the presence of underground water or the difficulty of access with building materials in a crowded and busy thoroughfare.

Factors of this kind must be carefully considered both in relation to any suggested scheme of development and also when comparing two sites which apparently are very similar but which are subject to different restrictions or conditions.

The existence of restrictive covenants may reduce the value of a site although the possibility of an application for their modification or removal under Section 84[8] of the Law of Property Act, 1925, must not be lost sight of. It is frequently possible to insure against restrictions being enforced where these are contained in old documents and where there is considerable doubt as to whether they are any longer extant. Where applications are made to the Tribunal it must be remembered that the Tribunal can award compensation to the person having the benefit of the covenant. In the case of restrictions preventing the conversion of houses it may be possible to take similar action to that under Section 84[8] of the Law of Property Act, 1925, under the Housing Act, 1957.[9]

Where possession of business premises is obtained against tenants in occupation at the termination of their leases for purposes of redevelopment under Section 30 of the Landlord and Tenant Act, 1954,[10] the amount of compensation to be paid must be deducted as part of the costs of development.

As in the case of a building estate, the value of urban sites is best found by direct comparison using an appropriate unit. When using the residual method in the case of urban sites it is necessary to consider first the extent and type of the most suitable buildings which can be erected on the site and then, by comparison with other similar properties, to estimate the value of the accommodation they will provide when erected.

An approximate estimate of the cost will then be made, based on the cube of the proposed building or by some other suitable method of comparison.

An allowance for developer's profit will usually have to be made and the considerations already outlined in Section 8 of this Chapter apply in principle; but where there is a strong demand for sites—for instance, in important shopping streets—prospective purchasers will be content with a reasonable return on their investment without any large margin for risk or profit.

In some cases it may be difficult to decide if a site with old buildings on it has a development value as a site suitable for rebuilding. Which view is adopted will depend largely on the estimated useful life of the existing buildings and the rate per cent at which they should be valued.

> *Example.*—Freehold shop premises comprise ground floor and basement and three floors over. The site has a frontage of 6 m and a depth of 25 m.

---

[8] As amended by the Landlord and Tenant Act, 1954, Sec. 52 and by the Law of Property Act, 1969.

[9] Sec. 165.

[10] See Chapter 14.

The building is 120 years old and the upper part is very dilapidated, the floors are unsafe for any loading, and access is by an outside staircase from a yard at rear. This upper part has been empty for several years.

The ground floor and basement are let on a 7 years' lease expiring 2 years hence producing a net income of £700 p.a., which is considered to be fair. The shop front is in good repair and was installed 12 years ago. The present assessment is G.V. £650; R.V. £513; and the tenants have been in occupation for 30 years.

If the buildings were pulled down and replaced with modern premises, extending the shop to the rear and with a good upper part, it is estimated they would let on lease at £1,350 p.a.

The cost of rebuilding is estimated at £9,000 inclusive of fees, etc., and developer's profit.

What is the value of the freehold?

*Valuation—*

(a) *Based on present letting:*

| | | |
|---|---|---|
| Rent on lease ... ... ... ... | £700 | |
| Y.P. perp. @ 8½ per cent ... ... | 11·765 | |
| *Value, say* ... | | £8,235 |

(b) *Based on redevelopment:*

| | | |
|---|---|---|
| Rent on lease ... ... ... ... | £700 | |
| Y.P. 2 years @ 8½ per cent ... ... | 1·77 | |
| | | £1,239 |
| Reversion to improved rental value... | £1,350 | |
| Y.P. perp. @ 7½ per cent ... ... | 13·33 | |
| | £18,000 | |
| Cost of rebuilding, fees, etc., and developer's profit .. £9,000 | | |
| Compensation to tenant[11]—twice N.A.V. £513 ... ... 1,026 | | |
| | £10,026 | |
| | £7,974 | |
| P.V. of £1 in 3 years @ 7½ per cent ... | 0·80 | |
| | | £7,179 |
| *Value, say* ... | | £8,400 |

*Note.*—The value of the reversion has been deferred three years to allow for rebuilding during the year following the expiration of the lease.

[11] Under Sec. 37 of the Landlord and Tenant Act, 1954.

## 10.  GROUND RENTS

The rent reserved on the lease of a plot of land for building purposes is termed a " ground rent."

At the date of the lease it will, as a rule, represent the fair rental value of the land in the open market.  But during the course of a long-term building lease, probably 99 years or longer, considerable changes may occur.  As the surrounding district develops, land will become more valuable.  After the lapse of even a few years there may be an appreciable difference between the ground rent reserved under a building lease and the rent which the land would then command if cleared of existing buildings and freed from the terms of the lease.

Until buildings are actually erected on a building plot, the ground rent reserved on it is regarded as " unsecured."

Until the early 1950s the rate per cent at which the income or estimated income from " unsecured " ground rents should be capitalised usually varied between $5\frac{1}{2}$ per cent and $6\frac{1}{2}$ per cent, according to the circumstances of the case.  At that time the estimated income from a large area of building land, where there was consider-able uncertainty as to the time which must elapse before all the plots were covered with buildings, might well have been regarded as representing a 6 per cent security.  On the other hand, a similar income from a smaller area which could probably have been fully developed in a year or two's time, or from a well-situated site towards the centre of a town, might fairly have justified the adoption of a $5\frac{1}{2}$ per cent basis.  The valuer had to be governed by the particular circumstances of each case and his experience of the selling prices of similar areas in the district.  Because of the pressure of inflation since the 1950s, such low rates no longer apply and returns are in the order of 10 per cent.

When buildings are erected on land on which a ground rent is reserved, the ground rent is spoken of as being " secured " and if offered for sale as an investment will probably fetch a higher figure of years' purchase, representing a lower yield to the purchaser.  In the case of secured ground rents the lessee can frequently afford to pay more than 10 years' purchase to secure the freehold, and often does so.  He may have the right to enfranchise.

The " security " lies in the fact that the lessee, having gone to the expense of erecting buildings on the land and probably being in receipt of a substantial rack rental from them, is not likely to risk forfeiture of his land by failure to pay his ground rent.  Even if he did so, the owner of the ground rent would then become entitled to the income from both land and buildings.

The extent to which a ground rent is secured depends upon the suitability of the building which has been erected on the land and the margin between the ground rent and the net rack rental value of land and buildings.

In the case of suburban shop plots the land is likely to represent a fairly high proportion of the value of the whole and the ground rent may be expected to represent a higher proportion of the net rack rental, possibly a quarter or more, than in the case of houses.

In the case of still more valuable sites, the full annual value of the land may easily constitute a very considerable proportion of the annual value of land and buildings combined and it is impossible to lay down any hard and fast rule as to the extent to which the ground rent should be " covered ". Provided the margin between ground rent and net rack rent is sufficient to allow for a reasonable return on capital expended in the erection of suitable buildings, the ground rent will probably be regarded as " well-secured ".

*Example.*—Two shops, A and B, both comprise ground, first and second floors and each occupy a site 6 m by 25 m. One is in the suburbs and is worth £600 per annum on lease. The other is more centrally situated and is worth £1,000 per annum on the same terms.

Both are held on 99-year leases granted five years ago; A at a ground rent of £60 and B at a ground rent of £400.

Can these ground rents be regarded as well secured?

*Valuation—*

*Note.*—Although these two shops are very differently situated, the cost of erecting a similar building on the site in each case will not differ substantially. The difference in rack rental between the two is due not to superior buildings in the case of B but to a superior trading position and the prospect of greater profits. Assume the cost of building to be £6,000 in each case and that 9 per cent might represent an appropriate return on this expenditure.

*Shop A—*

| | |
|---|---:|
| Net rack rent ... ... ... ... ... | £600 |
| Cost of buildings, £6,000: Allow 9 per cent ... | £540 |
| Margin for ground rent | £60 |

The ground rent of £60, representing one-tenth of the net rack rent, may be considered well secured.

*Shop B—*

| | |
|---|---:|
| Net rack rent ... ... ... ... ... | £1,000 |
| Cost of buildings, £6,000: Allow 9 per cent ... | £540 |
| Margin for ground rent | £460 |

The ground rent of £400, although it represents 40 per cent of the net rack rent, may still be regarded as reasonably covered.

It will be apparent from the above example that the fact that a ground rent secured on premises in an important position is high in relation to annual value does not necessarily mean that it is poorly secured. If the type of premises is in good demand and let to a tenant of substance and the margin between ground rent and rack rent allows a fair return on capital expended on buildings, the ground rent sold as an investment may well fetch as high a figure of years' purchase as one secured ten times on less satisfactory property.

In valuing freehold ground rents from an investment point of view where the term of the ground lease has still a considerable number of years to run, say round about 60 years or more, it will usually be found that the value of the reversion to the full rack rental at the end of the term is comparatively slight. In such cases it is usual to value the existing ground rent as receivable in perpetuity and to ignore the possibility of an increased income from land and buildings in the distant future.

If, however, the amount of the ground rent represents only a small fraction of the rack rental value of the land and buildings this approach may result in too low a figure and in such cases the calculation should be made by finding the total of the values of the term and reversion separately.

In some cases terminable securities known as leasehold or improved ground rents may be created. For instance, a freeholder may grant a building lease of a fairly substantial area of land to a lessee at a ground rent of £250. The lessee, by dividing the land into, say, ten plots, which he sub-leases for the whole of his term, less a few days, at a ground rent of £30 each, may create leasehold ground rents of £300 per annum, representing a net income or profit rent of £50 per annum for the term of his lease. Or a lessee, holding a number of building plots at a ground rent of £30 each and having erected houses upon them, may sell the leasehold interest in the houses, reserving to himself a ground rent of £40 per annum on each for the term of his lease less a few days. In this way an " improved " leasehold ground rent of £10 is created on each house.

From an investment point of view, leasehold or " improved " ground rents with a substantial number of years of the lease still to run can usually be sold to show a return about 1–2 per cent higher than that required from comparable freehold ground rents.

Even when the term exceeds 60 years the income from leasehold ground rents should be valued as a terminable income and not in perpetuity.

Since about 1950, it has become customary to include a provision whereby the amount of a ground rent in a large lease can be increased at intervals. Bases for variation differ as do intervals: some revisions can only be made upwards. For example a building lease for 99 years may reserve a ground rent of £500 per annum for the first 14 years of the lease and thereafter the ground rent is to be not less than £500 per annum and is to represent a quarter of the net rack rental value of the accommodation erected on the site, this amount to be agreed between the parties or settled by arbitration in default. Such a clause is known as a rent revision clause and such a lease might contain similar provisions at the end of each 14-year period. There is a tendency for review periods to become shorter.

The object of this is to provide a hedge against inflation and a freehold ground rent would sell at a higher figure of years purchase if the ground lease reserving it contained such a clause, than it would if no such provision had been made.

# Chapter 13

## Residential Properties

### 1. GENERALLY

THE RANGE of properties to be considered in this Chapter is a wide one, including tenements, cottages and small houses let at weekly or monthly rents, moderate-sized houses, large houses and flats.

At the outset it is necessary to distinguish between properties let at rents under existing tenancies and bought for investment and properties offered on the market with vacant possession.

The former can, as a rule, be valued by the method of multiplying the net income by an appropriate figure of Years' Purchase. But in the case of the latter, the only practicable method of valuation would seem to be that of direct comparison of capital values based on records of recent sales in the same or comparable districts.

Whatever the method of approach to a particular problem, however, the two principal factors which influence the value of residential properties are (i) accommodation, and (ii) situation. The prospective tenant or purchaser will consider the nature and extent of the accommodation offered, and will at the same time have regard to the situation of the property as it affects the general amenities of life, time of travel to work, proximity to schools and like matters.

For example, a prospective occupier viewing an ordinary three-bedroomed, semi-detached, suburban house, will probably already have in his mind some idea of the number of rooms he requires and their approximate size. He will consider the arrangement of the rooms for convenience in use, the adequacy of the domestic offices—kitchen, scullery, bathroom, etc.—the presence of central heating and the type of fuel used, the aspect of the rooms, the presence of a garage or parking space, the size of the garden, the state of repair, and all the other details which make the property attractive to him or otherwise.

It is true that in some cases all such proper considerations may be swamped by the urgent desire to secure a house of any kind. But, even allowing for this factor, it is not difficult to imagine two houses of the above type identical in construction, size, accommodation and state of repair, and yet so different in their situation that one may readily fetch £4,500 in the open market, while the other may only be worth £3,000.

The effect of position on value is influenced not only by such concrete considerations as have already been referred to, but also by such uncertain factors as changing fashions and the value of a good address. In valuing residential property it is often important to have regard not only to the present character of the neighbourhood but also to the possibility of changes in the future, dependent on an increase or decline in its popularity.

To summarise the effect of position and accommodation, it can be said that the general level of values in a neighbourhood is determined by situation factors, while differences in value between individual properties are determined by the nature and extent of the accommodation they offer.

## 2. STATUTORY PROVISIONS

Although it is beyond the scope of this book to examine legislation directly affecting the valuation of residential property in detail, a brief summary of this legislation is necessary as a background.

### (i) THE RENT ACTS

With minor exceptions and subject to subsequent amendments, all legislation concerned with rent control of dwelling-houses is now contained in the Rent Act, 1968.

*Previous Legislation—Historical.*—The first Act restricting rents and mortgage interest was passed in 1915 to prevent profiteering by landlords during the 1914-18 War. The Act limited the rent which could be charged for a house coming within its provisions and restricted the landlords' right to recover possession of such houses.

The provisions of the original Act were amended by a number of Acts passed between 1915 and 1939 and the scope of the properties falling within the Rent Acts was reduced. The scope was determined mainly be reference to rateable value and by 1939 all but comparatively small dwellings had been freed. In 1939, a new Act was passed at the outbreak of war and brought into control all but comparatively large houses. From 1939 onwards there were therefore two categories of controlled houses, those under legislation prior to 1939 and those brought into control in 1939, known respectively as " old " and " new " controlled houses. In each case the rent recoverable was determined by reference to the rent at which the house concerned was first let and additions could only be made for increases in rates and for improvements. In addition, in the case of old controlled houses overall percentage additions were possible as well as certain increases in the case of properties sub-let.

Until 1949, there was no control of the rent which could be

charged for a newly-erected house, except under the Building Materials and Housing Act, 1945. The Landlord and Tenant (Rent Control) Act, 1949, enabled either the landlord or the tenant to apply to the tribunal appointed under the Furnished Houses (Rent Control) Act, 1946, to determine the reasonable rent in the case of dwelling-houses let for the first time since 1 September, 1939. New properties completed after 29 August, 1954, were free from such control.

The Housing Repairs and Rents Act, 1954, provided for increases to be made in the case of properties in good condition, the amount of the increase being based on the statutory allowance for repairs for rating purposes, provided that the landlord had spent certain specified sums on repairs to the house. This Act also provided for increases in respect of services.

The Rent Act, 1957, de-controlled dwelling-houses with rateable values on 7 November, 1956, of over £40 in London or £30 elsewhere. It also provided that the Rent Acts should not apply to tenancies created after the commencement of the Act—creeping de-control. For properties below the limits of rateable values specified which remained controlled, the maximum recoverable rent was determined on the basis of applying a multiplier to the 1956 gross value of the property. This method of determining controlled rents is still in force under the Rent Act, 1968, and is considered in more detail later.

The Rent Act, 1965, left unaffected tenancies controlled under the Rent Act, 1957, but re-imposed control on the majority of houses de-controlled under the 1957 Act. The 1965 Act applied to dwelling-houses with rateable values on 23 March, 1965, not exceeding £400 in London or £200 elsewhere. The 1965 Act super-imposed on the 1957 Act system of determining controlled rents, a system of determining rents known as regulated rents, although it was intended, in the long run, that regulated rents would replace controlled rents. Regulated rents are retained under the Rent Act, 1968.

*The Rent Act,* 1968—This Act consolidated the enormous and complex body of legislation known as the Rent Acts, including the unrepealed provisions of the 1957 and 1965 Acts. Thus the present position is that tenancies within the Act are either controlled or regulated.

Controlled rents are based on the 1956 gross value of the property for rating purposes. The basic amount of the rent is as follows:

(*a*) If the tenant is not responsible for repairs it is twice the gross value.

(*b*) If the tenant is responsible for all repairs, it is one and a third times the gross value.

(c) If the tenant is responsible for some but not for all repairs, the rent limit is between the amounts in (a) and (b) above, the exact amount is to be settled by written agreement between the landlord and the tenant or, failing agreement, by the County Court.

In (a), (b) and (c) above, the expression repairs does not include internal decorative repairs.  If the landlord is responsible for internal decorative repairs (or has elected to be so), the amounts specified in (a), (b) and (c) are increased to:

(a) two and one-third, (b) one and two-thirds, (c) between two and one-third and one and two-thirds.

If neither the landlord nor the tenant is responsible for repairs the landlord is treated as being responsible for repairs other than internal decorations.  There are special provisions if business premises are let together with living accommodation.

In addition to the amount based on the gross value the landlord may add to the rent the amount of any rates which he pays and also the reasonable charges as agreed in writing with his tenant for any services which he provides. The landlord may also increase the rent by twelve and a half[1] per cent of his expenditure on improvements.

If a house is in a bad state of repair the tenant can apply to the local authority for a certificate of disrepair.  So long as the certificate is in force the rent recoverable is limited to four-thirds of the gross value.

Under the regulated tenancy system, the landlord or tenant or both can apply to the rent officer for the registration of a fair rent.  Once such a rent has been determined and registered it is the maximum rent which can be charged for the property.  A fair rent is an open market rent subject to certain special rules laid down in section 46.  This section states that in determining a fair rent regard must be had to all the circumstances (other than personal circumstances) and in particular to the age, character and locality of the dwelling-house and to the state of repair.  It must be assumed that the number of persons seeking to become tenants of similar dwelling-houses in the locality on the terms (other than those relating to rent) of the tenancy is not substantially greater than the number of such dwelling-houses in the locality available for letting on such terms.  To be disregarded are disrepair or other defects attributable to the tenant and any improvements carried out, otherwise than in pursuance of the terms of the tenancy, by the tenant or his predecessors.

*The Housing Act*, 1969—The main provision of this Act to be noted here is that whereby on the grant of a qualification certificate, which relates to the standard of repair and amenity of a house, by a local authority, a controlled tenancy can be converted into a regulated tenancy.

---

[1] See the Housing Act, 1961. Prior to this Act the percentage was eight.

## (ii) The Landlord and Tenant Act, 1954, Part I and the Leasehold Reform Act, 1967

The protection of tenants occupying dwelling-houses on ground leases has caused concern for a number of years and these two pieces of legislation represent the two major steps taken to ensure that such tenants are not automatically dispossessed when their contractual right to remain in occupation has expired.

*The Landlord and Tenant Act, 1954—Part I*—This Act came into effect from 1 October, 1954. Part I applies to houses let on "long tenancies" (i.e., for more than 21 years) which, on account of the rent being a "low rent" (i.e., less than two-thirds the rateable value on 23 March, 1965) are outside the protection of the Rent Acts.

The limits of rateable value within which Part I of the 1954 Act applies are £400 in London and £200 elsewhere.

Both the above figures relate to the rateable value in force prior to the 1956 revaluation.

A tenant is not protected if the landlord is the Crown or a local authority, the Development Corporation of a new town or certain housing associations and trusts.

The effect of the Act is to continue the tenancy automatically after the date when it would normally expire, on the same terms as before, until either the landlord or the tenant terminates it by one of the notices prescribed by the Act.

The landlord and the tenant can agree on the terms of a new tenancy to take the place of the long tenancy.

A long tenancy can be terminated by the landlord by giving one of two types of notice, each of which must be in prescribed form. If the landlord wishes the tenant to stay in the house he must serve a landlord's notice proposing a statutory tenancy. If he wishes the tenant to leave he must serve a landlord's notice to resume possession.

Should a tenant wish to terminate a long tenancy he must give not less than one month's notice in writing.

A landlord's notice proposing a statutory tenancy would set out the proposed terms as to rent and repairs, including "initial repairs." The landlord and tenant can negotiate on these terms and come to an agreement in writing. If they cannot do so the landlord can apply to the County Court to decide those items which are in dispute.

The Rent Act, 1968, procedure already referred to for the determination and registration of fair rents applies to tenancies arising from these provisions.

Where a tenant remains in possession after the end of the long tenancy he is relieved of any outstanding liability in respect of repairs arising under that tenancy. The new terms proposed by the landlord may provide for the carrying out of repairs when the new terms come into force. These repairs are known as "initial repairs" and the tenant may have to bear some or all of the cost of them. Where a tenant leaves at the end of the long tenancy his liability under the tenancy is not affected by the Act. "Initial repairs" may be carried out either by the landlord or by the tenant or partly by one and partly by the other; neither need do any unless he wishes. If the landlord carries out the repairs he is entitled to recover from the tenant the reasonable cost of the repairs in so far as they were necessary because the tenant did not meet his obligations under the long tenancy. Payment can be made by the tenant either by a lump sum or by instalments, as agreed between the parties or as determined by the County Court.

Where a landlord serves notice to resume possession the tenant if he wishes to remain in the house should so inform the landlord. If he does not agree to giving up the house, the landlord can apply to the County Court for a possession order. The grounds upon which a landlord can apply for possession include the following: — (i) that the landlord proposes to demolish or reconstruct the premises for purposes of redevelopment, that he will require possession for this purpose at the end of the long tenancy, and that he has made reasonable preparation for the redevelopment; (ii) that suitable alternative accommodation will be available for the tenant; (iii) that the tenant has failed to comply with the terms of his tenancy as to payment of rent or rates or as to insuring or keeping insured the premises; (iv) that the tenant, or a person residing with him, or any sub-tenant of his has caused nuisance or annoyance to adjoining occupiers; (v) that the premises, or any part of them, which the tenant is occupying is reasonably required by the landlord for occupation as a residence for himself or any son or daughter of his over 18 years of age or his father or mother. In the last case the Court must not make an order for possession where the landlord purchased the property after 21 November, 1950, or where it is satisfied that having regard to all the circumstances of the case, including the availability of other accommodation, greater hardship would be caused by making the order than by refusing to make it.

*The Leasehold Reform Act*, 1967—This Act came into force on 27 October, 1967, and represents a very radical departure from previous property law. The White Paper[2] which preceded the legislation stated the Government's view that "the basic principle of a reform which will do justice between the parties should be that the freeholder owns the land and the occupying leaseholder is morally entitled to the ownership of the building which has been put on and maintained on the land". This principle has, however, only been extended to the limited range of properties to which the Act applies.

---

[2] Cmnd. 2916 of 1966 "Leasehold Reform in England and Wales".

The Act enables qualified leasehold owner-occupiers either to purchase the freehold reversion from the ground landlord or to obtain an extension of the term of the lease.

The following requirements must be met before a leaseholder is qualified and entitled to the benefits conferred by the Act:

(a) The term of the existing lease must be more than 21 years and the rent reserved must be less than two-thirds of the rateable value.

(b) The leaseholder must have occupied the house for five of the last ten years as his main residence. Use of part of the premises for another purpose, for example as a shop, does not necessarily disqualify.

(c) The rateable value of the house on 23 March, 1965, must not exceed £400 in London and £200 elsewhere.

## Enfranchisement

Where a leaseholder is qualified under the Act and gives his landlord written notice of his desire to purchase the freehold interest, then except as provided by the Act, the landlord is bound to make to the leaseholder and the leaseholder to accept (at the price and on the conditions provided) a grant of the house and premises for an estate in fee simple absolute, subject to the tenancy and to the leaseholder's incumbrances but otherwise free from incumbrances.

The price payable, as defined in section 9 of the Act as amended by section 82 of the Housing Act, 1969, is the amount which the house and premises might be expected to realise if sold in the open market by a willing seller with the tenant and members of his family who reside in the house not buying or seeking to buy. It must be further assumed that the freehold interest is subject not only to the existing lease but to a further extension of the lease at a modern ground rent.

Within one month of the ascertainment of the price payable the tenant may give written notice to the landlord that he is unable or unwilling to acquire at that price, in which case the notice of his desire to have the freehold ceases to have effect. In such circumstances the tenant must pay just compensation to the landlord.

## Example

The leaseholder of a late 19th century brick-built four-bedroom semi-detached house with garage, in a fairly good residential area, wishes to purchase the freehold interest. The lease is for 99 years from 1 January, 1889, at an annual ground rent of £5.

On 1 January, 1970, the leaseholder, who is qualified under the Act, served the necessary statutory notice under the Leasehold Reform Act, 1967, claiming the right to have the freehold.

The house occupies a site with an area of 301 square metres. Comparable residential building land in the area has recently changed hands at £24,500 per hectare. Similar houses in the area have been sold on the open market with vacant possession at figures ranging from £5,000 to £6,000.

*Valuation—*

In order to value the reversion after the existing lease it is necessary to estimate a modern ground rent:

| | | |
|---|---|---|
| 301 m² @ £2·45/m², *say* ... ... | £740 | |
| *Add* Costs of redevelopment, *say* ... | 260 | |
| Capital value of site with all services ... | £1,000 | |
| Modern ground rent @ 8% ... ... | £80 p.a. | |
| *Term*—present ground rent ... ... | £5 p.a. | |
| Y.P. 18 years @ 7% ... ... ... | 10·05 | |
| | | £50 |
| *Reversion*—after 31 December, 1988, to modern ground rent based on 1970 site value ... ... ... ... ... | £80 p.a. | |
| Y.P. perpetuity @ 8% deferred 18 yrs. | 3·12 | |
| | | £250 |
| Price payable for enfranchisement ... | | £300 |

## Extension of the Existing Lease

Where a leaseholder is qualified under the Act and gives the landlord written notice of his desire to extend his lease then except as provided by the Act the landlord must grant and the leaseholder must accept a new tenancy for a term expiring fifty years after the term date of the existing tenancy.

With the exception of the rent the terms of the new tenancy will be the same as the term of the existing tenancy. Rules for the ascertainment of the new rent are laid down in section 15 of the Act but the main point to be noted is that the rent must be a ground rent in the sense that it represents the letting value of the site without including anything for the value of the buildings on the site. This modern ground rent which is payable as from the original term date can be revised if the landlord so requires after the expiration of twenty-five years.

Where a leaseholder exercises his right to have an extension of his lease, he cannot exercise his right to acquire the freehold interest unless notice is given before the original term date.

*Landlord's Over-Riding Rights*

In certain circumstances the leaseholder's right to purchase the freehold or extend the lease may be defeated. If the landlord can satisfy the Court that he requires possession of the house for re-development or for his own occupation or occupation by an adult member of his family, the Court may grant an order for possession. The tenart is entitled to receive compensation for the loss of the buildings.

*Retention of Management Powers*

In circumstances specified in section 19 of the Act, landlords could retain certain powers of management on enfranchisement in order to maintain adequate standards of appearance and regulate redevelopment in an area.

*Appeals*

In the event of a dispute between the parties as to amounts payable, an appeal can be made to the Lands Tribunal who have given a number of decisions which refer to amounts to be paid for freeholds.[3]

### (iii) The Housing Acts

The provisions of the Housing Acts give local authorities wide powers to prevent overcrowding of working class houses, to ensure that they are kept in reasonable repair and condition and to have them improved. The main Act is the Housing Act, 1957.

Individual houses unfit for habitation can be dealt with by closing and demolition orders, or by calling upon the owner to carry out the necessary repairs. Obstructive buildings may be ordered to be demolished. Large unhealthy areas may be cleared or redeveloped, the compensation payable to owners of unfit houses being limited to the value of the bare site.

The compensation provisions of the Act are dealt with at length in Chapter 25.

### (iv) Local Authority Participation in Private Housing Finance

There are two codes under which local authorities are empowered to play some part in the finance of private housing. The first is the Small Dwellings Acquisition Acts, 1899–1923, and the second in the Housing (Financial Provisions) Act, 1958, as subsequently amended. The former is less comprehensive and flexible than the latter and, consequently, is less widely used.

The increase of local authority activities in this field in recent years is becoming significant in some local house property markets as, although in some cases they compete with normal sources of

---

[3] See *Custins v. Hearts of Oak Benefit Society*, THE ESTATES GAZETTE, January 18, 1969 p. 239, also *Farr v. Millersons Investments Ltd.*, 1971, J.P.L., 523 — the general principles applicable.

house finance such as building societies, in many cases they provide money which is difficult or impossible to obtain from any
other source.

### The Small Dwellings Acquisition Acts, 1899–1923

Under this code certain types of local authority are empowered
to make advances for the purchase or construction of houses.
There are conditions attached to these loans relating to residence
in the house by the borrower and the rate of interest to be charged
is laid down.

### The Housing (Financial Provisions) Act, 1958, and the House Purchase and Housing Act, 1959.[4]

These Acts make provision, *inter alia,* for local authorities to
make advances on mortgage, to guarantee advances made by building societies and to make grants for conversion and improvement.

Mortgage advances may be made for acquiring existing houses,
erecting new houses, converting buildings into houses and altering,
enlarging, repairing or improving houses. The authority must be
satisfied that the house is, or will be made, in all respects fit for
human habitation and no advance may be made unless the interest
to be mortgaged is the freehold or a term of years with an
unexpired term at least 10 years longer than the period for
repayment of the loan.

Grants for conversion and improvement of houses are of three
types.[5]

*Standard Grants.*—Under the 1959 Act local authorities are
obliged to make grants of half the cost of providing " standard
amenities " up to a maximum grant of £155. Standard amenities
include a fixed bath or shower, a wash-hand basin, a sink and a
water closet. Certain conditions including one which relates to the
person receiving the grant or a member of his family occupying the
house or the house being let or kept available for letting, must be
complied with and failure to comply may involve repayment of a
proportion of the grant.

*Improvement Grants.*—These grants may be made at the discretion
of the local authority for the repair and improvement of houses to
bring them up to a defined standard of comfort and convenience,
for the conversion of houses into two or more self-contained
dwellings and for converting a building into a house or flats. The
normal maximum grant is £1,000 for a building of not more than
two storeys and £1,200 for a building of three or more storeys.

*Special Grants.*—These grants were introduced by the Housing
Act, 1969, and are intended to encourage the provision of standard

---

[4] Amendments and additions to this code are made in the Housing Acts, 1961,
1964 and 1969. In Intermediate and Development Areas higher grants are payable
(Housing Act, 1971).

[5] A useful booklet "*House Improvement and Rents—A Guide for Landlords and
Tenants*" has been prepared by the Ministry of Housing and Local Government
and the Central Office of Information, H.M.S.O. Dd. 715675 10/69.

amenities in houses in multiple occupation where more than one set of such amenities is required.

Where improvements are carried out to tenanted houses, if the tenancy is to remain controlled the rent limit under the Rent Act, 1968, will be increased by 12½ per cent of the cost, excluding grant, of the improvements. If the improvements satisfy the requirements for a qualification certificate a controlled tenancy may be converted into a regulated tenancy and a fair rent can be determined and registered. If the tenancy is already regulated the fair rent can be adjusted to take account of the improvements.

The increase from a controlled rent to a fair rent has to be phased over a period of two to three years[6] and this is a major deterrent to landlords who would otherwise carry out the necessary works.

## 3. COTTAGES, SMALL HOUSES AND TENEMENTS

(a) *General Method of Valuation.*—The rents of small houses, cottages and tenements are usually payable weekly or monthly, the landlord being responsible for all outgoings, including repairs, rates and water rate.

In free market conditions slight differences in style and accommodation—for instance, a few metres of front garden with a dwarf brick wall and railings, or the fact that the front living room opens out of a small hall-passage, instead of direct on to the street—may cause a considerable difference in rental between houses within a few hundred metres of each other.

The gross yearly income is estimated by taking 48 to 52 weeks' rent, according to whether or not it is thought necessary in the circumstances to make allowance for loss by irrecoverables. The effect of control is greatly to reduce the risk of loss of rent by bad debts.

If, owing to overcrowding, a house is let at what may be regarded as an excessive rent the excess should be disregarded, since it will certainly be lost should the local authority exercise its powers under the Housing Act, 1957.[7]

In the case of tenancies controlled under the Rent Act, 1968, rents will usually be found to be well below the level of the regulated rents and the true rental value of the premises and provided that the property is in good repair and unlikely to be the subject of an Order under the Housing Act, 1957, now or in the future, the income can be regarded as fairly secure. The conversion of a controlled to a regulated tenancy would normally be expected to cause a substantial increase in rent.

Since the landlord pays all outgoings, including rates, the deduction from gross rent to arrive at estimated net income is

---

[6] Rent (Control of Increases) Act, 1969, a useful booklet "*Phasing of Rent Increases— A Guide for Private Landlords and Tenants*" has been prepared by the Ministry cf Housing and Local Government, H.M.S.O. Dd. 716122 5/70.

[7] Part IV and the 6th Schedule; see also Sec. 59 relating to compensation for compulsory purchase.

considerable. Average expenditure on repairs over the last few years, checked where necessary by comparison with other similar properties, is the most reliable guide to this figure.

The rate per cent at which the net income should be capitalised varies widely according to the circumstances of the particular case and the state of the local market. In the case of freeholds it may range from as low as 7 per cent where the security is good to figures of 12 per cent or more where property is old, in poor repair and occupied by an unsatisfactory type of tenant. The rate of interest is lower than it would probably otherwise be because of the large increase in capital value which occurs if vacant possession is obtained.

In this connection it may be noted that the market for what may be described as " tenements " i.e., large buildings let out to a number of tenants—is usually poor and uncertain compared with that for small, fairly modern houses let to single families. This is particularly so at the present time owing to the high cost of repairs in the case of the " tenement " type and to the large increase in capital value if vacant possession is obtained of a house let to a single family.

(b) *Outgoings*.—The principal outgoings are rates, water rate, repairs, insurance and management.

If the amount at which the property is assessed to rates appears to be below the general level of assessments, regard must be had to the possibility of an increase in the assessment. The chances of an increase in the poundage of the rates must also be borne in mind. It is essential in such cases to ascertain whether under the lease or agreement such increases may be passed on to the tenant. In the case of lettings in recent years there has been a marked tendency to make the rent exclusive.

Under the Rent Act, 1968, any increase in rates due either to changes in assessment or poundage can be passed on to the tenant.

It is generally preferable to make the allowance for repairs by deducting a lump sum per property which should be checked by reference to past records and to the age, extent and construction of the premises.[8] For example, the allowance in the case of a house stuccoed externally and requiring periodic painting will naturally be higher than in the case of a similar house with brick facings in good condition. It has been customary in the past to estimate the amount to be allowed for repairs as a percentage of the rent but this method is unreliable.

Where in the past the work of repair has been left undone it may be necessary to include in the valuation a capital deduction for immediate expenditure to allow for the cost of putting the property into a reasonable (but not necessarily a first-class) state of repair.

---

[8] See Chapter 7, Sec. 1 (c).

The annual cost of insurance can usually be determined with sufficient accuracy. The premium on a small house will not be great, the rate being 10p per cent or a little higher on the cost of rebuilding the premises.

Management may cost from 5 per cent to 10 per cent according to the circumstances and the services rendered.

Reference so far has been made to the estimation of net income by calculating each outgoing separately. It is useful as a check to determine the percentage which they represent of the gross rents. This is found to vary from 45 to 75 per cent, or even higher. The percentage will largely depend on rates and level of assessments, either of which may vary widely as between one district and another.

(c) *State of Repair.*—Careful consideration must be given to the condition of repair as affecting the annual cost of repairs, the life of the building and the possibility of heavy expenditure in the future. Particular attention should be paid to the structural condition, the presence or absence of dampness in walls or ceilings, the proper provision of sanitary accommodation and of cooking and washing facilities.

Regard should be had to the possibility of the service of a dangerous structure notice in respect of such defects as a bulged wall.

Where premises are in such a condition as to be a nuisance or injurious to health, the local authority may require necessary works to be done.[9] They may also serve a notice to repair a house, which is in any respect unfit for human habitation.[10] The standard for deciding whether a house is " unfit for human habitation " is that laid down by Section 4 of the Housing Act, 1957.

Where a house cannot be made fit for human habitation at a reasonable cost, the local authority may serve a demolition order, or in respect of any part of a building unfit for habitation including any underground room, they may serve a closing order.[11]

In lieu of making a demolition order a local authority may purchase a house which is unfit if they consider that it can be rendered capable of providing accommodation of a standard which is adequate for the time being.[12]

Power is given by the Housing Act, 1957, to make and enforce building regulations in respect of working-class houses. Where in force, they require generally the proper provision of sanitary and washing accommodation and food storage facilities for each family and also adequate lighting and ventilation. Special provision is made in the Housing Acts, 1961, 1964 and 1969, as regards houses in multiple occupation.

---

[9] Public Health Act, 1961, Sec. 26.
[10] Housing Act, 1957, Sec. 9.
[11] *Ibid.*, Sec. 27.
[12] *Ibid.*, Sec. 29.

Where, on inspection, a property is considered not to comply with statutory enactments or by-laws in force, allowance should be made in the valuation for the cost of compliance.

The allowance for annual repairs included in the outgoings is usually based on the assumption that the property is in a reasonable state of repair, at least sufficient to justify the rent at which it is let. If it is not, a deduction should be made from the valuation for the cost of putting it into reasonable repair.

(*d*) *Clearance Areas*.—There are many houses, let either as a whole or in parts, which are of considerable age, indifferent construction, or so situated as likely to be included in a Clearance Area under the Housing Act, 1957.

A local authority may either require the houses therein to be demolished or may acquire houses and buildings for the purpose of demolishing them and re-planning the area.[13]

Particular regard must be had to the possible application of this procedure, and to the statutory provisions applying to individual houses in a clearance area, when valuing old or defective property.

It must be remembered that a house, although not unfit in itself, may be included in consequence of its being in, or adjoining a congested or overcrowded area.

For a detailed consideration of the provisions of the Housing Acts see Chapter 25.

(*e*) *Duration of Income*.—In addition to the factors already considered, regard must also be had to the length of time during which it is expected that the net income will continue.

In the case of houses of some age, it is sometimes suggested that an estimate should be made of the length of life of the property. and the net income valued for that period with a reversion to site value. But, as explained in Chapter 8, it is more useful for the factor of uncertainty of continuance of income to be reflected in the rate per cent adopted.

In such cases a net yield of 10 per cent or $12\frac{1}{2}$ per cent may well be expected, whereas in the case of more modern properties, the yield may be as low as 7 per cent.

Where, however, there are strong reasons for assuming that the life of the property will be limited, allowance should be made for that factor in the valuation.

If demolition of existing buildings is likely in the future under the provisions of the Housing Act, 1957, the income may properly be valued as receivable for a limited term with reversion to site value. Similarly, if unfit property is likely to be acquired compulsorily as part of a " clearance area " compensation may be restricted to bare site value, so that again it may be proper to treat the present income as of limited duration only.

---

[13] Housing Act, 1957, Secs. 42–52.

In each of the above cases bare site value will be affected by the provisions of the Land Compensation Act, 1961.

*Example.*—A terrace house in a suburban area built about 40 years ago comprises ground, first and second floors, with two large and one small room on each floor. There is one W.C. on the ground floor and one on the second floor. Each of the small rooms has been adapted for use as a kitchen, and a sink and ventilated food storage provided. The house is situated in a neighbourhood where the development is open in character. The general structural condition is good, with the exception of the flank wall of the back addition, which is badly bulged, and extensive signs of rising damp in the front wall.

There are three tenants: the ground floor producing 77½p per week, the first floor 90p, and the second floor 77½p. These rents are the maximum rents permitted under the Rent Act, 1968.

The total rateable value is £66. Rates and water rate are 50p in the £.

What is the present market value?

*Valuation—*

| Gross Income— | | | | Per Week | Per Ann. |
|---|---|---|---|---|---|
| Ground Floor | ... | ... | ... | 77½p | |
| First Floor | ... | ... | ... | 90p | |
| Second Floor | ... | ... | ... | 77½p | |
| | | | | —— £2·45 | |
| | | | | | £127 |

| Outgoings— | | | | £ | |
|---|---|---|---|---|---|
| Rates, £66 @ 50p | ... | ... | ... | 33 | |
| Repairs and Insurance | ... | ... | 27 | |
| Management, say | ... | ... | ... | 7 | |
| | | | | — | 67 |
| | | | Net Income ... | 60 | |
| | | | Y.P. perpetuity, *say* | 10 | |
| | | | | | £600 |

| Estimated cost of repair of flank wall and damp in front wall | ... | ... | ... | ... | ... | ... | 200 |
|---|---|---|---|---|---|---|---|
| | | | | | *Value, say* | £400 |

*Example.*—A terrace of twenty cottages about 70 years old, each comprising ground and first floors, with two rooms on each floor, and back addition scullery with outside W.C., are let at weekly rents of 50p each. The R.V.s are each £15, rates and water rate amount to 40p. The 1956 Gross Value of each was £15. The neighbourhood is a poor one and arrears amount to £48 in respect of six of the cottages. The external paintwork is poor, there are outstanding sanitary notices in respect of four cottages requiring the interior to be cleansed of vermin. The cottages have an average frontage of 5 m and long gardens, the depth of the site being 60 m.

The value of the site for the erection of 12 dwelling-houses is considered to be approximately £650 per unit.

*Valuation.*—An examination shows that the rents are equal to $\frac{4}{3} \times$ 1956 G.V. plus rates, i.e., $\frac{4}{3} \times$ £15 + £6 = £26. The arrears for the greater part appear due to the poor state of repair.

The premises are nearing the end of their useful life, but if put in repair will be good for thirty years.

On the basis of the present rents the value would be:—

| *Site and Building* | | | £ |
|---|---|---|---|
| Gross Rents, 20 @ 50p ... ... | | | 520 |
| Outgoings— | £ | | |
|    Rates, £15 @ 40p ... | 6 | | |
|    Repairs and Insurance ... | 7 | | |
|    Management ... ... | 5 | | |
| | — | £18 | |
| No. of Houses ... ... ... | | 20 | |
| | | — | 360 |
| | | | 160 |
| Y.P. 30 years @ 12 and 2½% (tax @ 37·75%) | | | 6·4 |
| | | *Say* ... | £1,000 |
| Less cost of complying with Sanitary Notices, say | | ... | 100 |
| | | | £900 |
| Reversion to site for 12 houses @ £650 per unit ... ... ... ... ... | | £8,000 | |
| P.V. £1 in 30 years @ 7% ... ... | | 0·13 | |
| | | | 1,040 |
| | | *Value, say* | £1,950 |

The position must be examined to ascertain if it would be worth while to put the houses into proper repair in which case the rents could be increased to twice the 1956 Gross Value. The cost would be, say, £800, and the annual allowance for repairs and insurance would have to be increased from £7 to say £10 per annum for each cottage.

On this basis the value is:—

*Site and Building*

| | | | |
|---|---|---:|---:|
| Gross Rents, 20 × 2 × £15 + £6 ... ... | | | £720 |
| Outgoings:— | | £ | |
|     Rates £15 @ 40p ... ... | | 6 | |
|     Repairs and Insurance ... | | 10 | |
|     Management ... ... ... | | 7 | |
| | | £23 | |
| No. of Houses ... ... ... | | 20 | |
| | | | £460 |
| Net Income ... | | | £260 |
| Y.P. 30 years @ 9 and 2½% (tax @ 37·75%) ... | | | 7·9 |
| | | | £2,054 |
| Less cost of repairs ... ... ... ... | | | 800 |
| | | | £1,254 |
| Add value of reversion, as above ... ... | | | 1,040 |
| Value, to allow for deferment of increased rents, *say* ... ... ... ... ... ... | | | £2,300 |

It would therefore be profitable to spend the £800 capital on repairs and thus to obtain the increased income.

## 4. MIDDLE-CLASS AND LARGER RESIDENTIAL PROPERTIES

(*a*) *Generally.*—For many years after the 1914-18 war the shortage of housing accommodation led to very much higher prices being paid for properties with vacant possession than for those let to tenants and purchased as an investment.

At the outbreak of the last war in 1939 the shortage had been largely overcome. The disparity in value between houses with or without vacant possession had disappeared except in the case of properties which had not been freed from rent control; in some areas, new houses were more easily let than sold and houses let at good rents to reliable tenants sometimes commanded a higher value than the same house with vacant possession.

At the present time there are still large differences between the values of controlled houses (a) for investment, and (b) for occupation. At the time of writing there is an upward tendency in the value of all types of houses with vacant possession.

When valuing with vacant possession, as already pointed out in Section 1 of this Chapter, the capital value must be fixed by direct comparison with prices actually realised on sale.

In the case of houses which are let the usual method of capitalising the net income by a figure of Years' Purchase must be used.

Whichever method of valuation is adopted, however, the same factors are likely to influence the valuer in deciding whether the rent at which a property is let is a reasonable one, or what price it is likely to realise on sale with possession.

(*b*) *Factors affecting Value.*—The factors in question may be very briefly summarised as follows:—

(*i*) *Size and number of rooms.*—A prospective occupier is primarily in search of a certain amount of accommodation. He is likely, in the first instance, to restrict his enquiries to properties having the number of rooms of the size he requires.

(*ii*) *Position.*—The prices he is prepared to pay for this accommodation will be influenced by all the factors associated with position.

Proximity to shops, travelling facilities, open spaces, golf courses and schools; the character of surrounding property, building development in the neighbourhood, the presence and cost of public services, the rate in the £ for the district and the level of assessments, are all matters to be taken into account.

(*iii*) *Planning, etc.*—In viewing the property itself the prospective occupier will also consider such points as the arrangement, aspect and lighting of the rooms, the adequacy of the domestic and sanitary offices, the method of heating, the presence or absence of a garage, the size and condition of the garden.

The value of the accommodation provided by a house will be increased or diminished according to the way in which, in the details enumerated, it compares with other properties of a similar size.

(*iv*) *Age and condition of repair.*—Changes in taste and fashion and the greater amenities provided in modern houses tend to reduce the value of older houses.

The condition of repair must be considered both as regards the cost of putting the premises into a satisfactory state of repair now and the cost of maintenance in the future.

A number of the points already mentioned in connection with working-class property must be considered.

The principal points include the condition of the main structure and roof; the penetration of damp, either by reason of a defective damp-proof course or insufficient insulation against wet of the external walls; the presence of conditions favourable to dry rot; the presence or absence of such rot or of wet rot or attack by woodworm or beetle; the arrangement and condition of the drainage system; the condition of external paintwork; internal decorations.

Houses with a large expanse of external paintwork or complicated roofs with turrets and domes will cost more in annual upkeep than houses of plainer design. The annual cost of repairs will also be influenced by the age of the premises.

When houses are let, the incidence of the liability for repair as between landlord and tenant is an important factor in their valuation. In the case of the larger houses let on long lease the tenant usually undertakes to do all repairs; but in the case of short term lettings of small or moderate sized houses, the bulk of the burden has usually fallen on the landlord. In this connection the provisions of the Housing Act, 1961, should be noted as regards leases granted after 24 October, 1961.[14]

(c) *Methods of Valuation.*—Under pre-war conditions, when a house was not let, or it was desired to check the fairness of the existing rent, the method of direct comparison of rental value with other properties was often used.

As an alternative to this direct method, a room to room valuation based on analysis of lettings was sometimes used in the case of large houses, although considerable experience was necessary in applying this method in practice.

An alternative method of indirect comparison was the analysis of actual lettings to show the rental value per square foot, and the application of a similar figure to the floor area of the property under consideration. In applying this method it was usual to measure only the floor areas of the living rooms and bedrooms and kitchen, the size and character of such other accommodation as bathroom, etc., being taken into account in the figure per square foot employed.

In dealing with ordinary residential properties the direct comparison method of estimating rental value was usually the most practical approach. The refinements introduced by the alternative methods shown above depended entirely for their accuracy on the judgement of the valuer in applying the correct price per room or per foot, as the case might be.

---

[14] Sec. 32.

At the present day estimates of open market rental value for house property are seldom made. If a house is vacant, it will almost certainly be put on the market with vacant possession, and its capital value arrived at by direct comparison with recent sales, without reference to rental value. Comparisons are made between houses (or flats) to find fair rents on the basis of so much per square metre of net floor space.

> *Example.*—A small, semi-detached, brick-built modern house in good repair, on a plot with 9 m frontage, contains two reception rooms and W.C. on ground floor, two large and one small bedroom, bathroom and W.C. on the first floor.
>
> What is its market value ?
>
> *Valuation.—Direct comparison of capital value.*—Similar houses in the neighbourhood sell for prices ranging from £4,000 to £4,500; by direct comparison of position, size of rooms, condition of repair and the amenities provided, the value is estimated to be £4,250.

In the case of tenant-occupied houses where the tenant is protected by the Rent Acts or where he holds the house under a lease or agreement with a reasonable term to run at a low rent, the tenant himself may be anxious to purchase the property and so obtain the chance of re-selling with vacant possession at a profit. In these circumstances the price he will pay is likely to be the result of bargaining between the parties. The tenant is obviously not going to pay full vacant possession value. The landlord is not likely to be content with investment value only. The result will usually be a purchase price between these two extremes.

(*d*) *Sales Records.*—The systematic recording of the results of sales will be of great help to the valuer. The form such records can take can vary widely.

## 5. Blocks of Flats

(*a*) *Generally.*—The valuation of a block of flats does not differ in principle from the valuation of properties already considered.

The problem is only complicated by the greater difficulty in forming a correct estimate of gross income and of outgoings.

(*b*) *Gross Income.*—In a few cases flats are let at inclusive rents, the tenants not being liable for any outgoings, although extra charges for special services are usually encountered.

In estimating gross income the dates of existing agreements must be regarded, for some rents may have been fixed some time ago and be below rental value.

If the flats are within the scope of the Rent Act, 1968, the income can be considered as additionally secured; if not there may be the possibility of increase in the future. At the present time flats generally are in keen demand.

Among the many factors affecting the present rental value are the presence of lifts, central heating, constant hot water, refrigerators, the adequacy of natural lighting, the degree of sound insulation between flats, convenience of proximity to main traffic routes offset by possible nuisance from noise.

Before 1939 it was quite usual to make an allowance of from 5 per cent to 15 per cent in respect of " voids ", on the assumption that it was unlikely that all the flats in a block would be occupied throughout the whole year. Under present conditions such an allowance is almost invariably considered unnecessary.

(c) *Outgoings.*—In estimating the allowance to be made for outgoings on an existing block of flats it is necessary to study the tenancy agreements carefully in order to determine the extent of the landlord's liabilities. In recent years there has been a marked tendency to make tenants responsible for all possible repairs but the provisions of the Housing Act, 1961[15] must be kept in mind.

In estimating the income and expenditure for a proposed block of flats, regard will be had to the rents and terms of tenancy usual for the type of building in the neighbourhood. So that if flats of the type under consideration are normally let on terms which throw the cost of internal repairs on the tenants, the outgoings will be estimated on that basis.

*Rates.*—When rateable values are known, the present cost of rates and water rate can easily be ascertained. But the assessments must be carefully considered, as they may appear to be too high or too low in relation to the rents obtained. In either case regard must be had to the possibility of future adjustment.

Where the individual flats are subject to the Rent Act, 1968, increases or decreases in rates are passed on to the tenant. Where the Act does not apply, enquiry must be made as to whether the tenancy agreements allow for the burden or benefit to be passed on. The general tendency of recent years has been to let flats on an exclusive basis.

*Repairs.*—It is difficult to give any general guide to the allowance to be made for repairs, since the cost will depend upon many factors.

An exterior of stucco work, needing to be painted approximately every five years, will cost much more than one of plain brickwork, which is only likely to involve expenditure on repointing every 25 or 30 years. Regard must also be had to the entrance hall, main staircase and corridors, those having marble or other permanent wall coverings will have a low maintenance cost; other types of decoration requiring considerable expenditure to keep in a satisfactory condition will have a much higher maintenance cost.

[15] Sec. 32.

About 10 per cent of the gross rents is likely to be absorbed by external repairs and the repair of entrance hall, main staircase, etc. Where the landlord is responsible for internal repairs a further allowance of 7½ per cent to 10 per cent of the gross rents will be necessary.

*Services.*—Until the Rent Act, 1957, rents were frequently inclusive of services. The tendency is now for these to be covered by a separate service charge payable in addition to the rent in the case of decontrolled tenancies. Such service charges are usually variable according to cost. It is necessary for the valuer to check that the charge is sufficient to cover costs and depreciation and the following figures will give some indication of costs. Where services are included in rents paid, the cost must be deducted from the gross rents together with other outgoings to find the net income.

If it is possible, the valuer should endeavour to obtain a sight of the accounts of the buildings to be valued for the last few years to see what the actual outgoings have been. This should enable him to make a forecast for the future but he must be prepared to have regard to trends of increase or decrease and to adjust his estimate of future figures in the light of his practical experience.

Frequently it is found that landlords make a profit on their services, i.e., the total service charge exceeds the cost of the services plus depreciation on installations, etc. Some valuers add this profit to the net income, others ignore it, while others capitalise it separately at a low figure of Years' Purchase. It is submitted that no one of these different approaches is preferable to the others but it is essential to keep in mind that the valuer who adds the profit on services to the net income before capitalising the total will use a lower figure of Years' Purchase (i.e., he will employ a higher rate of interest) than a valuer who omits the profit on services altogether.

*Hot Water and Central Heating.*—At the present day the figure in the case of a coke-operated boiler is likely to be, say, £75 per annum for a medium-sized flat in a modern block. Much depends, however, on the age of the installation, the degree of heat loss, and the type of fuel. Solid fuel is generally the cheapest, followed by oil, gas and electricity in that order.

*Lifts.*—Maintenance and insurance costs will depend upon the size and age of the lift. At the present day the overall figure for electricity, maintenance, etc., for a small passenger-operated electric lift might be £30–£35 p.a.

*Electric Lighting.*—An allowance of £3 p.a. per lighting point should be sufficient.

*Gardens.*—The cost will depend upon the circumstances of each case. Extensive gardens or the presence of flower boxes may involve considerable annual expenditure.

*Insurance.*—Allowance has to be made for fire, employers' liability, third party, public liability and boiler insurance, also for national health insurances for employees.

*Management.*—An allowance of 5 per cent on the total rents collected is usual, although in special circumstances a smaller fee may be paid. The suggestion is sometimes made that, in preparing a valuation, no allowance should be made for management as an outgoing. But it is submitted that the expense is one to which a prospective purchaser is bound to have regard even if he intends to manage the property himself in which case allowance should be made for the trouble involved.

The point directly affects the estimated yield from the property. In applying a Years' Purchase to the net income, the rate per cent upon which it is based will have been fixed by reference to the results of analyses of other sales. Consequently, if cost of management was allowed for in estimating the net income of those properties with which comparison is made, a similar allowance must be made in the valuation in question.

(*d*) *Net Income and Yield.*—A reasonable deduction from gross income having been made in respect of estimated outgoings, a figure will be arrived at representing prospective net income.

However carefully this figure may have been estimated, it is likely to vary from time to time, particularly in relation to expenditure on repairs. The valuer will have regard to this fact in selecting the rate per cent of Years' Purchase on which his valuation will be based.

The rate per cent yield on the purchase prices of blocks of flats varies considerably. At the time of writing first-class flats are showing about 8 per cent. A considerably higher return is likely to be expected from " converted " houses, probably 10 to 12 (or even more) per cent.

*Example.*—You are requested by a prospective purchaser to value for investment a large freehold property comprising eight blocks of flats, some of three storeys and some of two, erected about six years ago. The Vendor's agents inform you that the flats are all let, at rents from £350–£400. The standard form of tenancy agreement provides that the tenants are liable for internal decorative repairs.

The following particulars are also supplied. Total rent roll, £31,085, including 18 garages, £720. Outgoings last year: Repairs, £150; lighting, £160; upkeep, £270; insurances, £350.

As a result of your inspection the following additional facts are established:

The tenants pay the rates on both flats and garages, the rents for the latter averaging 75p per week. The rents of the flats are fair. The agreements are for three years.

The gardens are extensive. The general condition of repair is satisfactory.

The flats are brick-built with tiled roofs, concrete floor, and a modern hot water system: there is no lift.

There is a large waiting list for flats.

The landlord provides no services other than lighting of common parts and upkeep of the gardens.

The outgoings seem to be reasonable except for the amount for repairs and maintenance which is obviously too low.

|  |  |  |  |  |  |  |
|---|---|---|---|---|---|---|
| Total Rent Roll | ... | ... | ... |  |  | £31,085 |
| *Less* Garages | ... | ... | ... | ... |  | 720 |
|  |  |  |  |  |  | £30,365 |
| Outgoings— |  |  |  |  |  |  |
| Lighting | ... | ... | ... | ... | £160 |  |
| Garden ... | ... | ... | ... | ... | 270 |  |
| Insurances | ... | ... | ... | ... | 350 |  |
| Repairs— |  |  |  |  |  |  |
| 72 flats @ £50 | ... | ... | ... | 3,600 |  |  |
| Management, *say* | ... | ... | ... | 1,500 |  |  |
|  |  |  |  |  |  | 5,880 |
|  | Net Income, *say* | ... |  |  |  | £24,485 |
|  | Y.P. @ 8%, | ... |  |  |  | 12½ |
|  |  |  |  |  |  | £306,062 |
| 18 garages, gross | ... | ... | ... | ... | £720 |  |
| *Less*— |  |  |  |  |  |  |
| Repairs and insurance | ... | £50 |  |  |  |  |
| Management, *say* | ... | ... | 70 |  |  |  |
|  |  |  |  | 120 |  |  |
|  | Net Income | ... | ... | £600 |  |  |
|  | Y.P., *say* | ... | ... | 8 |  |  |
|  |  |  |  | 4,800 |  |  |
|  | *Value, say* | ... | ... |  |  | £310,850 |

## 6. RECENT GOVERNMENT PROPOSALS

In July 1971, the Government published a White Paper (Cmnd. 4728) " Fair Deal for Housing " which proposes very substantial changes in housing legislation. The main proposals are to speed the change from controlled to fair rents, to apply fair rents to the public housing sector and to grant rent rebates in case of need in both the public and private sectors.

# Chapter 14

## Commercial Properties

### 1. GENERALLY

THE TYPES of property dealt with in this Chapter can conveniently be grouped as follows: —

(a) Shops.

(b) Industrial Premises.

(c) Offices.

The dividing line between the different types cannot, of course, be drawn too rigidly. Premises may be so situated and constructed as to be of value for a number of alternative purposes. For example, premises in a second rate position originally constructed for use as a wholesale distributive depot may now let more readily and at a higher rent for the purposes of a shop.

At one time market value would have been governed by the most profitable use to which such premises might be put. Now, any greater value which is dependent upon a material change in use should only be taken into account if town planning permission for such development will be granted by the local planning authority.

One feature common to all the above three classes of property is that, generally speaking, they are occupied for the purpose of carrying on an industry, trade or profession in the expectation of profit: and it is the profit which can reasonably be expected to be made in the premises which in the long run will determine the rent a tenant can afford to pay for them.

The principal factors affecting each class are considered in detail later and they fall under three broad categories, viz: quality and quantity of the accommodation and the situation of the premises.

In the case of shops, the chief consideration affecting rent is likely to be the number of persons passing the premises in the course of the year and the type of goods they are likely to be able to afford to buy. In the case of offices, the prestige which fashion may give to a particular district, and convenience of situation and access for business purposes generally, will largely determine rent. In respect of industrial premises, accessibility and a ready supply of labour will probably be decisive factors.

There are some types of property which, although capable of inclusion in one or other of the above classes, are seldom let to a tenant for trading purposes and in respect of which there may be little or no evidence of rental value transactions to guide the valuer in arriving at a proper valuation. Typical examples are premises occupied by a statutory undertaking, such as a gas or electricity works, premises occupied for charitable purposes, premises occupied by a school and unsuitable for any other purpose.

In many cases such properties are only likely to come upon the market if the use for which they were built has ceased. In these circumstances it will be necessary to consider the alternative use to which they can be put—if town planning permission is likely to be forthcoming to enable such a change of use to be made—the cost of converting them to such use and the value they will have when converted.

Where any have to be valued for the particular purpose for which they are used resort may be had to the Structural Value Basis, or to Value as a Going Concern: both these methods are described in other Chapters.

Another feature common to all these types of property is that the provisions of the Landlord and Tenant Act, 1927 (Part I), as to compensation for improvements apply. The security of tenure afforded by Part II of the Landlord and Tenant Act, 1954, as amended by the Law of Property Act, 1969, also extends to all three classes of property. The provisions of the Offices, Shops and Railway Premises Act, 1963, apply to offices and shops. Before considering each type of property in detail, it has been thought desirable to outline these provisions.

## 2. LANDLORD AND TENANT ACTS, 1927 (PART I) AND 1954 (PART II)

(a) *Landlord and Tenant Act, 1927 (Part I)*.—This Act gives tenants of premises let for trade, business or professional purposes the right to compensation for improvements made during the tenancy. It also gave a right to compensation for " goodwill " in the case of premises let for trade or business purposes.

The provisions in regard to " goodwill " are made unnecessary by the security of tenure given by Part II of the Landlord and Tenant Act, 1954, and are repealed. The provisions as to compensation for improvements remain, subject to certain amendments made by Part III of the 1954 Act, and are comparatively unimportant in practice and in their effect on values.

The tribunal for the settlement of questions of compensation for improvements under the Act is the County Court, but claims are referred by the Court to a referee, who is selected from a special panel.

The notes which follow do not attempt to give details of procedure under the Act. but merely to indicate the possible effect on value of the tenant's right of claim.

*A tenant's claim for compensation for improvements*[1] is limited to (*a*) the net addition to the value of the holding as a whole which is the direct result of the improvement, or (*b*) the reasonable cost of carrying out the improvement at the termination of the tenancy, whichever is the smaller. In determining the compensation, regard must be had to the purpose to which the premises will be put at the end of the tenancy and to the effect that any proposed alterations or demolition or change of user may have on the value of the improvement to the holding.

It may be said, therefore, that in principle the basis for determining the compensation payable to the tenant is the benefit which the landlord will derive from the improvement.

In order that an improvement may carry a right to compensation under the Act, the tenant must first have served notice on the landlord of his intention to make the improvement, together with full particulars of the works and a plan. If the landlord does not object, or, in the event of objection, if the tribunal certifies that the improvement is a " proper " one, the tenant may carry out the works. Alternatively, the landlord may offer to carry out the improvement himself in consideration of a reasonable increase in rent.

In practice it is found that the tenant's right to compensation for improvements results in the service on landlords of very few notices under the Act. It does strengthen the tenant's hand a little in negotiating reasonable terms for a renewal of the tenancy, or for some modification in the terms of it, when he has it in mind to carry out improvements to the property.

In valuing any given property it is desirable to ascertain whether in fact improvements have been made by the tenant within the terms of the Act which may give rise to a claim for compensation at the end of the tenancy. The way in which a potential claim for compensation should be taken into account when preparing a valuation must depend on the circumstances. An example is given later in this Chapter.

(*b*) *Landlord and Tenant Act*, 1954 (*Part II*) and *Law of Property Act*, 1969 (*Part I*).—Subject to certain exceptions and qualifications, this Part of the Act ensures security of tenure where any part of a property is occupied by a tenant for the purposes of a business carried on by him—provided it is not carried on in breach of a general prohibition in the lease.

The term " business " in the Act means any trade, profession or employment and also any activity carried on by a body of persons corporate or unincorporate. The Act therefore covers not only ordinary shops, factories and commercial and professional offices,

---

[1] Landlord and Tenant Act, 1927, Secs. 1-3.

but also premises occupied by voluntary societies, doctors' and dentists' surgeries, clubs, institutions, etc.[2]  The scope of premises to which the 1954 Act applies is wider than that of the 1927 Act which applies to premises let for trade, business or professional purposes.

The Act extends not only to lettings for fixed terms, e.g., twenty-one or ninety-nine year leases, but also to periodic tenancies, e.g., quarterly, monthly or weekly tenancies.  But the following types of tenancy are excluded:—

   (i) tenancies of agricultural holdings;
  (ii) mining leases;
 (iii) tenancies within the Rent Act, 1968, or which would be but for the tenancy being a tenancy at a low rent.
  (iv) tenancies of on-licensed premises, with some exceptions;
   (v) " service " tenancies, i.e., tenancies granted by an employer only so long as his employee holds a certain office, appointment or employment;
  (vi) tenancies for a fixed term of six months or less, with no right to extend or renew, unless the tenant and his predecessor (if any) have been in occupation for more than twelve months.

The general principle upon which this Part of the Act is based is that a tenancy to which it applies continues until it is terminated in one of the ways prescribed by the Act.  Thus, if it is a periodic tenancy, the landlord cannot terminate it by the usual notice to quit.  If it is for a fixed term, it will continue automatically after that term has expired, on the same terms as before, unless and until steps are taken under the Act to put an end to it.

One way in which a tenancy can be determined is by the parties agreeing on the terms of a new tenancy to take effect from a specified date.  A tenancy may also be terminated by normal notice to quit given by the tenant, or by surrender or forfeiture.  In the case of a tenancy for a fixed term, the tenant may terminate it by three months' notice, either on the date of its normal expiration or on any subsequent quarter day.

Apart from the above cases, the methods available to landlord or tenant to terminate a tenancy to which Part II of the Act applies are as follows:

The landlord may give notice, in the form prescribed by the Act, to terminate the tenancy at a specified date not earlier than that at which it would expire by effluxion of time or could have been terminated by notice to quit.  Not less than six months' notice must

---

[2] A tennis club registered under the Industrial and Provident Societies Act, 1893 was held to be within the Act in *Addiscombe Garden Estates Ltd. and Another v. Crabbe and Others*, Q.B.D., 1957, but the business of sub-letting part of the premises as flats with a view to making a profit out of the rentals is not a business within Part II of the Act—see *Bagettes Ltd. v. G.P. Estates Co. Ltd.*, C. of A., 1955.

be given. It is to be noted that a landlord must give six months' notice to terminate a quarterly, monthly or weekly tenancy. The notice must require the tenant to specify whether he is willing to give up possession and must state whether, and if so on what grounds, the landlord would oppose an application for a new tenancy.

After notice has been served the parties may negotiate on the terms of a new tenancy or may continue negotiations begun before the notice was served. If they cannot agree on the terms, or if the tenant wishes to remain in the premises but the landlord is unwilling to grant him a new tenancy, the *tenant* can apply to the County Court for a new tenancy and the Court is bound to grant it unless the landlord can establish a case for possession on certain grounds specified in the Act.

A tenant holding for a fixed term of more than one year can initiate proceedings by serving a notice on his landlord in prescribed form requesting a new tenancy to take effect not earlier than the date on which the current tenancy would come to an end by effluxion of time or could be terminated by notice to quit. This notice must state the terms which the tenant has in mind. If the landlord opposes the proposed new tenancy, the tenant can apply to the Court for the grant of a new tenancy, the terms of which can be agreed between the parties or, in default of agreement, will be determined by the Court.

The Court must have regard to the following points in fixing the terms of a new tenancy[3]:—

   (i) The tenancy itself may be either a periodic tenancy or for a fixed term of years not exceeding fourteen;

  (ii) The rent is to be fixed in relation to current market value and the following are to be disregarded in determining it:

    (a) the fact that the tenant is a sitting tenant;

    (b) any goodwill attached to the premises by reason of the carrying on of the tenant's business on the premises;

    (c) any improvement carried out by a person who was the tenant at the time of improvement but only if the improvement was made otherwise than in pursuance of an obligation to the immediate landlord and if the improvement was not carried out during the current tenancy, that it was completed not more than 21 years before the application for the new tenancy.

    (d) in the case of licensed premises, any additional value attributable to the licence.

 (iii) The terms may include provision for varying the rent.

 (iv) Other terms of the tenancy must be determined having regard to the terms of the current tenancy and to all relevant circumstances.

---

[3] Landlord and Tenant Act, 1954, Sections 34 and 35, as amended by Law of Property Act, 1969, Sections 1 and 2.

Subject to certain safeguards, the Court will revoke an order for the new tenancy if the tenant applies within fourteen days of the making of the order, thus a tenant is not bound to accept the terms awarded by the Court.

During the period while an existing tenancy is continuing only by virtue of the Act and provided the landlord has given notice to determine the tenancy or the tenant has requested a new tenancy, the landlord may apply to the Court for the determination of a " reasonable " rent.[4] The reasonable rent is determined in accordance with the same rules which apply to a rent for a new tenancy but is on a year to year basis.

A landlord can successfully oppose an application for a new tenancy on the following grounds:—(i) That the tenant has not complied with the terms of his tenancy. (ii) That the tenant has persistently delayed paying rent. (iii) That the landlord can secure or provide suitable alternative accommodation for the tenant, having regard to the nature and class of the business and to the situation and extent of, and facilities afforded by, his present premises. (iv) That the landlord will suffer substantial loss if new tenancies are granted of parts of the premises where the landlord is in a position to let or sell as a whole. This applies only where such tenancies were granted by an intermediate landlord or landlords. (v) That the landlord intends to demolish or reconstruct the premises.[5] (vi) That the landlord requires the premises for his own occupation—but landlord is debarred from using this ground if he acquired the premises less than five years before the end of the tenancy. This five-year limitation gives rise to difficulty when purchasers wish to reconstruct premises for their own occupation.[6]

A tenant who is refused a new tenancy, is entitled to compensation from his landlord if either the landlord or the Court refused on grounds (iv), (v) or (vi) above, and there is no agreement which excludes compensation effectively. Such compensation is in addition to any the tenant may be entitled to under the Landlord and Tenant Act, 1927, in respect of improvements.

If the business has been carried on on the premises for less than fourteen years, the compensation is equal to the rateable value of the premises. If it has been carried on for fourteen years or more,

---

[4] Law of Property Act, 1969, Section 3.
[5] The following cases relate to this ground:—
  *Gilmour Caterers Ltd. v. Governors of St. Bartholomew's Hospital*, C. of A., 1956.
  *Betty's Cafés Ltd. v. Phillips Furnishing Stores, Ltd.*, H. of L., 1958.
  *Biles v. Caesar and Others*, C. of A., 1956.
  *Percy E. Cadle & Co., Ltd. v. Jacmarch Props, Ltd.*, C. of A., 1956.
  *Joel v. Swaddle and Another*, C. of A., 1957.
  See also Law of Property Act, 1969, Section 7.
[6] See *Atkinson v. Bettison*, C. of A., 1955; *Fisher v. Taylor's Furnishing Stores, Ltd.*, C. of A., 1956.

the compensation is twice the rateable value. Where net annual value differs from rateable value, net annual value is to be taken as the basis for compensation.

In general it is not possible to contract out of Part II of the Act but Section 5 of the Law of Property Act, 1969, introduces an important exception whereby the Court may, on the joint application of landlord and tenant, authorise an agreement which excludes the Act or for the surrender of a tenancy. Again in general it is not possible to exclude or modify the right to compensation under the Act but this is permitted by agreement where the tenant or his predecessors in business have occupied the premises for less than five years.

The effect of these provisions on the value of business premises falling within Part II of this Act has, generally speaking, been slightly to lower rents obtainable from sitting tenants when leases fall in. There is no doubt at all that it strengthens the hand of a tenant very considerably indeed in negotiations for new leases or in negotiations for the surrender of an existing lease in return for a new lease. Nevertheless, lessees still prefer to have a lease for a definite term of years rather than to rely solely on their rights to a new lease under the Act. Tenants who have only a few years of their lease unexpired and who wish to sell the goodwill of their businesses nearly always have to surrender their existing short leases to secure a sufficiently long term to obtain the full value of their business. In practice purchasers require the security of a term of years rather than the rights under this Act.

With few exceptions, it would seem that reversions after an existing lease should be valued on a capitalised rental value based on the terms—referred to above—to which a court must have regard when settling disputes between the parties for new tenancies. If a landlord's interest is valued on the assumption that a new tenancy will not be granted, allowance should be made for compensation which may have to be paid to the tenant.

There is little doubt that the security of tenure afforded by Part II of the Act increases the value of a tenant's interest. If his interest is valued upon the basis that he will have to give up possession at the end of the lease for one of the reasons set out above which attract the payment of compensation, an appropriate addition should be made. Conversely the effect is to decrease the value of a landlord's interest. Only in a comparatively few cases can reversions be valued on the basis of vacant possession.

In general, the 1954 Act has had a much greater effect in practice than the 1927 Act.

The following example illustrates the possible effect of both the 1927 and the 1954 Acts in various circumstances:—

*Example.*—Shop premises are let on a lease at £500 per annum for a term with three years unexpired. Improvements were carried out two years ago at a cost of £3,000 by the tenant, who served notice of his intention on the landlord under the Landlord and Tenant Act, 1927, and received the landlord's consent thereto.

It is considered that without these improvements the rental value is fairly represented by the lease rent, but that in consequence of the work done the annual rental value has been increased to £750 per annum. The present Rateable Value is £250. Prepare a valuation of the freehold interest.

*Valuation—*

As the tenant has a right to a new lease at a rent which excludes the value of the improvements made by him, the rental value of £750 per annum should be ignored for the probable period of the new lease, a maximum of 14 years, although the present rent is well secured.

| | | | |
|---|---|---|---|
| Rent payable under lease ... ... | £500 | | |
| Y.P. for say 17 years @ 7% ... ... | 9·76 | | |
| | | | £4,880 |
| Reversion to ... ... ... ... | £750 | | |
| Y.P. perp. @ 8% deferred 17 yrs. ... | 3·38 | £2,535 | |
| | | *Value, say* | £7,415 |

If it is known that the landlord wishes to occupy the premises himself when the present lease terminates, the value would be:—

| | | | |
|---|---|---|---|
| Rent reserved under lease ... ... | £500 | | |
| Y.P. for 3 yrs. @ 7% ... ... ... | 2·62 | | |
| | | | £1,310 |
| Reversion to ... ... ... ... | £750 | | |
| Y.P. in perpetuity @ 8% deferred 3 yrs. | 9·92 | £7,440 | |
| | | | £8,750 |

*Deduct—*

| | | | |
|---|---|---|---|
| Compensation under the Landlord and Tenant Act, 1954 ... ... ... | £500 | | |
| Compensation under the Landlord and Tenant Act, 1927 ... ... ... | £3,000 | | |
| | £3,500 | | |
| P.V. £1 in 3 years @ 2½% ... ... | ·93 | | |
| | | | £3,255 |
| | | *Value, say* | £5,500 |

It is assumed for the purposes of the above that the landlord is not debarred by the five-year restriction and that compensation under the Landlord and Tenant Act, 1927, may fairly be represented by the cost of the improvement—£3,000. It is also assumed that the tenant has been in occupation for over fourteen years and thus the amount of compensation under the Landlord and Tenant Act, 1954, is twice the R.V.

If the landlord intended to demolish the premises, the valuation would be:—

| | | | |
|---|---|---:|---:|
| Rent reserved under lease ... ... | | £500 | |
| Y.P. for 3 years @ 7% ... ... ... | | 2·62 | £1,310 |
| | | | |
| Reversion to site value, say ... ... | | £12,000 | |
| P.V. £1 in 3 years @ 7% ... ... | | ·82 | £9,840 |
| | | | £11,150 |

*Deduct—*

| | | | |
|---|---|---:|---:|
| Compensation under the Landlord and | | | |
| Tenant Act, 1954 ... ... ... | | £500 | |
| P.V. £1 in 3 years @ 2½% ... ... | | ·93 | |
| | | | £465 |

*Value, say*  £10,685

In this case no compensation would be payable under the 1927 Act as the demolition would entirely negative the effect which the improvement would have on the value of the holding.

### 3.  OFFICES, SHOPS AND RAILWAY PREMISES ACT, 1963

This Act applies not only to offices, shops and railway premises but includes canteens for those employed in such premises, catering establishments open to the public, wholesale establishments and fuel storage premises.  It covers such parts of the premises as stairs, passages, landings, storerooms, entrances, exits, and yards, as well as the actual rooms or places where people work.  It does not apply to premises where self-employed persons work or where only certain relatives are employed nor to mines below ground, outworkers dwellings, premises occupied solely by members of the armed forces or premises used for employment for not more than 21 hours a week. Factories are covered by the Factory Acts (See Section 6 of this Chapter).

The Act and Regulations made under it lay down requirements covering the following matters: Cleanliness, Overcrowding, Temperature, Ventilation, Lighting, Sanitary Conveniences, Washing Facilities, Drinking Water, Cloakrooms, Seating and Eating Facilities, Floors, Passages and Stairs (construction, obstruction and maintenance), Fencing of exposed parts of Machinery, Cleaning of Machinery, Heavy Work, First Aid and Fire Precautions.

Local Authorities, Fire Authorities and H.M. Factory Inspectors and H.M. Inspectors of Mines and Quarries are variously responsible for enforcing the provisions of the Act. Penalties can be imposed for non-compliance.

Generally speaking the occupier of premises is responsible for complying with the provisions of the Act but owners are responsible where the occupier's premises covered by the Act are held on lease and do not take up a whole building or where the premises are contained in a building of which different parts are owned by different persons.

The obligations must be kept in mind when leases are being granted or freehold or leasehold interests are being valued. A deduction should be made for the cost of complying with any matters required to be done or likely to be required.

### 4. SHOPS

(a) *Generally.*—These may vary from small shops, with upper floors, in secondary positions likely to let from rents as low as £200 per annum, to large modern premises with extensive floor space on upper floors used as showrooms, workrooms, or offices, the whole commanding rents measured in terms of many thousands of pounds per annum.

As already indicated, the chief factor affecting values is that of position and its effect on trade. The prospective purchaser or tenant is likely, in nearly every case, to attempt some estimate of the trade in those premises in that position. The degree of accuracy that he will attempt to achieve will depend largely on circumstances. It is well known that many of the bigger concerns, with a large number of branches, have arrived from experience at certain methods of assessing with a fair degree of accuracy, the turnover they are likely to be able to achieve in a given shopping position. From such an estimated turnover it is necessary to deduct the cost of the goods to be sold; from the gross profit remaining will fall to be deducted wages, overhead charges and a margin for profit and interest on capital. There remains a balance or residue which the tenant can afford to pay in rent, rates and repairs.

The use of shop premises for one particular retail trade can, with some exceptions, be changed to its use for another retail trade without the necessity for obtaining town planning permission. If, therefore, premises are capable of occupation for a number of different purposes, and are likely to appeal to a number of different tenants, there will be competition between the latter, and the prospective occupier whose estimate of the margin available for rent, etc., is largest, is likely to secure the premises by tenancy or purchase.

It is not suggested that a valuation of shop premises should be based on an analysis of the probable profits of any particular trade in order to arrive at the rent a tenant can afford to pay for them, largely because the probable profits are based on amounts which in practice are very difficult to assess with any reliable degree of accuracy. But the general factors likely to influence prospective occupiers in their estimate of turnover and margin available for rent will certainly have to be taken into account by the valuer.

It is a commonplace that shops in the main thoroughfare of an important town with large numbers of passers-by will command a much higher rent than those in subsidiary positions. Again, the potential purchasing power of the passers-by must be considered: for instance, the amount of money they have available to spend in the shops is likely to be greater in Bond Street, London, than in the main shopping street of a small provincial town.

In some instances large variations in value may be found within a comparatively short distance. A position at the corner of a main thoroughfare in a side street may be of considerable value, whereas twenty or forty yards down the side street the shops will be of comparatively small value. Position is therefore a factor to which most careful consideration must be given.

Some of the most important points in regard to position are: In what class of district is the shop situated? What is the type of street and what sort of persons use it? What is the position of the shop in the street? Is it at a focal point such as the corner of an important road junction? Are there any multiple shop branches nearby or any " magnet " such as a big store? Is the property close to premises which break the continuity of shopping, such as a town hall, bank or cinema? How does its position compare with the best position in the street and the best position in the town?

(b) *Type of Premises.*—The next most important factor is the type of premises and their suitability for the display and sale of goods. The available frontage for the display of goods needs first consideration, together with the condition and character of the shop front. The suitability of the interior must then be considered; the adequacy of its lighting; the presence or absence of access at the rear for receipt or delivery of goods (this is becoming increasingly important as parking, waiting and loading restrictions become imposed over more and more roads in the centres of towns); the character of the upper floors, whether separately occupied or only usable with the shop; the general condition of repair and the sanitary accommodation.

In the case of newly erected premises, shops are often offered to let on the basis that the tenant fits out the shop and installs his own shop front at his own expense; what is offered is a "shell" often with the walls and ceiling to be plastered and the floor in rough concrete. In more established districts premises will be offered to let complete with shop front. If the latter is modern and likely to be suitable for a number of different trades, the value of the premises may be enhanced thereby. If, however, the shop front is old-fashioned, or only suitable for a limited number of types of business, it will be necessary to have regard to the fact that any prospective occupier will need to renew the shop front.

Sometimes a factor of importance is the right of a tenant to display goods on a forecourt. There are many shops where the enforcement of a building line or the like, has created a forecourt of considerable extent and of value to a number of trades, such as ironmongers, greengrocers and others, for the display of goods.

In considering particular premises it may be necessary to have regard to the possibility of structural alterations in the future for the purpose of improving the premises.

In valuing premises of some age, regard may have to be had not only to their probable useful life but also to the possibility of their being redeveloped in whole or in part or of additions being made, for example to extend the selling space to a greater depth, subject to the necessary town planning consent.

As regards accommodation on upper floors, it is necessary to consider the best purpose to which they can be put. In the more important positions it is frequently found that such floor space can be used for the display and sale of goods. In less prominent positions it may be more profitable for the upper part to be let off separately for use as offices or dwelling purposes. But in such cases it must be borne in mind that town planning permission for a change in use may not be forthcoming.

The extent to which large basement areas are of value will again depend largely upon position. In valuable situations where rents are high any prospective tenant is likely to wish to use the whole of the ground floor area for the display of goods and an extensive and dry place for storage will enhance the rental value of the premises considerably. In less important positions the use of the rear portion of the ground floor for storage purposes may be more practicable, and the enhancement of value due to the presence of a basement may be quite small.

(c) *Type of tenant.*—This is of considerable importance to the value of property from an investment point of view. For instance, certain types of trade, including chemists, grocers and butchers, are regarded as particularly stable, while others, such as cafés, are regarded as less satisfactory as a rule.

The tenancy of a large multiple concern is considered to give exceptional security to the income, since the mere covenant to pay rent by such an undertaking can be relied on for the duration of the lease even if the profits from the particular branch are less than was expected.

(d) *Terms of the lease.*—Shop property may be let on various repairing terms; on the one hand the tenant may be responsible for all repairs and insurance and at the other extreme the landlord may be responsible for all repairs. In between these extremes a variety of different responsibilities is found. The tendency in the last twenty years or so is for the responsibility to be put on to the tenant. Where the landlord has any responsibility for outgoings an appropriate allowance must be made in the valuations.

The length of the lease is often an important point. A lease to a sound tenant for a long term without a break was, before 1939, attractive from an investment point of view. At the present time, however, it is usually considered to be a disadvantage due to the effect of inflation, since it does not enable the rent to be revised to reflect the current value of the £. Where terms of more than 7 years are granted it is important to ascertain if there is a rent revision clause which would enable the lessor to re-assess the rent.

The terms of letting of the upper portion (if separate from the shop) must also be noted and the presence of any tenancies under the Rent Act, 1968.

(e) *Rental Value.*—When making comparisons of rental value between shops in very similar positions, regard must be had to size. Lock-up and small shops may provide sufficient floor space to enable a large variety of businesses to be carried on profitably and may be in great demand; whereas, in the case of larger shops for which there is less demand it may be found that the rent is not increased in proportion to the additional floor space available.

For example, in a given position, a lock-up shop with a frontage of 6 metres and a floor space of 90 square metres may command a rent of £900 per annum, equivalent to £10 per square metre; whereas, nearby, in a very similar position, a larger shop with a frontage of 9 metres and a depth of 20 metres may only command a rent of £1,250 per annum, equivalent to a rent of £7 per square metre.

An experienced valuer can usually estimate rental values by direct comparison with rents actually paid, using his own judgment and knowledge of the locality to guide him as to the variations in rent per square metre which should be made according to size, position, etc. Some valuers compare shops solely by reference to the frontage while rental values are sometimes expressed in terms of £'s per annum by reference to "standard units" of say 5·5 m × 12 m or 6 m × 15 m. The rental values of shops of different sizes are found by comparison with the rental value of a given standard unit in that area.

In valuing extensive premises comprising basement, ground, and a number of upper floors, there may be some difficulty in deciding upon the comparable rental values of the different floors. Generally speaking, the ground floor is obviously the most valuable and will require the greatest care in fixing the figure per square metre of floor space. The value of accommodation in basements or on upper floors is usually much lower and may sometimes be very much a matter of opinion. It will usually be found however, that by comparing the rents of shops with basement and upper floors with those of shops without this accommodation, one can get a reasonably accurate guide to the value of the various floors. For instance, if a shop without upper floors is let at £400 per annum and another comparable shop of the same size but with 1st and 2nd floors above is let at £600, it may be reasonable to assume that the rent of the upper portion is, say, £200. Comparison, where possible, with one or two cases where upper floors are let separately will enable the valuer to check this figure and probably to decide a reasonable rental per square metre for the 1st and 2nd floors of the building he is valuing.

The method of approach to problems of this type is illustrated by the following example :—

*Example.*—You are asked to advise on the rental value of shop premises comprising basement, ground, 1st and 2nd floors, in a large town. The premises are old but in a fair state of repair; the basement is dry, but has no natural light; the upper part is only capable of occupation with the shop. The net floor space is as follows:—Basement, 110 square metres; Ground Floor, 90 square metres; First Floor, 80 square metres; Second Floor, 70 square metres. The shop has a frontage of 6 metres.

The following particulars are available of lettings of shops in comparable positions, but all of them are more modern premises:—

(1) Premises similar in size let at £2,450: areas—Basement, 100 square metres; Ground Floor, 90 square metres; First Floor, 70 square metres; Second Floor, 60 square metres.

(2) A lock-up shop, 4 metres frontage and 5 metres depth, let at £600.

(3) A shop and basement, frontage 15 metres, ground floor area, 280 square metres, basement, 100 square metres let at £3,000. The upper part is separately let in floors as follows:—First Floor, 140 square metres at £700; Second Floor, 130 square metres at £520.

(4) The basement under lock-up shop No. 2 and three more shops, is dry and well lit with direct street access; floor space is 50 square metres and it is let at £125.

*Note.*—In practice these lettings might be on different terms and adjustments would be required to the rents to reduce them to net figures. The lettings might also have been made over a considerable period of time during which there might have been fluctuations in the level of rents.

*Analysis*—

Analysis of the first letting is best deferred until the other lettings of various parts of premises have been dealt with:—

| Letting | Floor | Area in m² | Rent | Rent per m² |
|---|---|---|---|---|
| 2 ... | Ground ... ... | 20 ... | £600 ... | £30 |
| 4 ... | Basement ... | 50 ... | £125 ... | £2·50 |
| 3 ... | First ... ... | 140 ... | £700 ... | £5 |
| 3 ... | Second ... ... | 130 ... | £520 ... | £4 |

The evidence from these lettings can be used to analyse the letting of shop No. 3 as follows:—

| | |
|---|---|
| Rent ... ... ... ... ... ... ... | £3,000 |
| Value of basement: | |
| 100 square metres @ say £2 ... ... ... | 200 |
| Rent for shop ... ... ... ... ... | £2,800 |
| Area of shop 280 square metres @ £10 ... ... | £2,800 |

This evidence can then be used to check the letting of shop No. 1, as follows:—

| | | | | |
|---|---|---|---|---|
| Basement | —100 square metres @ £2... | £200 | |
| Ground Floor— 90 | „ „ @ £20... | 1,800 | |
| First Floor — 70 | „ „ @ £4... | 280 | |
| Second Floor — 60 | „ „ @ £3... | 180 | |
| | | | £2,460 |
| | | *Actual Rent* | £2,450 |

*Valuation*—

Bearing in mind age, position and all other relevant factors, the valuation might be as follows:—

| | | | | |
|---|---|---|---|---|
| Basement | —110 square metres @ £1·75 ... | £192 | |
| Ground Floor— 90 | „ „ @ £17·50 ... | 1,575 | |
| First Floor — 80 | „ „ @ £3·50 ... | 280 | |
| Second Floor — 70 | „ „ @ £2·75 ... | 192 | |
| | | | £2,239 |
| | | *Rental Value, say* | £2,250 |

There has been a very considerable rise in rental values since 1939 and in the case of shops in first-class positions there seems little likelihood of any decline in the near future. The rise has not always been at the same rate. At certain times rents have "levelled off" only to climb again after a time.

(f) *Capital Value.*—Similar methods of analysis and comparison can be used in determining the appropriate rate per cent to use in capitalising rental value.

Shops let to good tenants can generally be regarded as a sound security since rent ranks before many other liabilities, including debenture interest and preference dividends in the case of limited liability companies.

Before 1939, an appropriate rate for the valuation of shop premises in a good position and let at a fair rent to a substantial tenant might have been as low as 5 per cent. On the other hand, in the case of the smaller types of shop in secondary positions, it might have been difficult to find a purchaser even on a 10 per cent basis.

At the present day rates per cent may vary from 7 to 11 per cent in the case of premises let at their full rental value.

In some cases, particularly in new districts, shops may be let on lease at " rising rents " e.g., £900 for the first 7 years, £1,000 for the next 7 years, and £1,100 for the balance of a 21-year term. If the valuer is satisfied that these increases are justified by the probable growth and development of the district, or that rent has purposely been kept low in the early years to encourage the establishment of business, the income may be valued at a normal rate per cent. But, if there is any doubt about the tenant's ability to meet these increases, the excess over what is considered a fair average rent should be valued at a much higher rate, as it is secured only on the tenant's covenant.

Where the upper part of freehold shop premises is let separately e.g., for residential purposes, it is probably desirable to value it separately at a different rate to that used for the income from the shop. In the case of leaseholds, however, this would involve an apportionment of the ground rent, and a more practical method may be to deduct the ground rent capitalised at a fair average rate per cent for the whole premises.

In any particular case, evidence of actual transactions is usually the best basis for capitalising rental values and the method of approach is indicated in the following example:

*Example.*—You are required to value certain shop premises situated in St. Ann's Road in a provincial town. St. Ann's Road is about a mile from the High Street of the same town, which is the main shopping centre, but it has been growing in importance owing to housing development on this side of the town and to the fact that the High Street is now almost fully developed. Nevertheless, the shops in St. Ann's Road are definitely in a " secondary " position.

These premises were built in 1930 and are in a good state of repair. The upper part has a separate entrance. The net floor space is as follows:—Ground Floor, 122·63 m²: First Floor, 74·32 m²; Second Floor, 65·03 m². The frontage is 6·71 m. It is let at £375 p.a. on lease now having 5 years unexpired.

The following particulars of lettings and sales have been extracted from a local agent's records. They relate only to very recent transactions in premises which are most nearly comparable to those under review as regards position and tenants.

*Lettings.*

(1) A lock-up shop, frontage 5·49 m, depth 15·24 m, let for 10 years at £600 p.a.

(2) An upper part on two floors of 117·00 m² in all let on 7 years' lease at £450 p.a.

(3) A shop, basement and upper part on two floors, let as one unit for 7 years at £1,900 p.a. It has a frontage of 9·75 m and the net floor areas are:—Ground Floor, 178·37 m²; Upper Part, 232·26 m²; Basement, 37·16 m².

(4) The lease of a lock-up shop having 10 years to run at £170 p.a. was sold for £2,500. Frontage 6·10 m, depth 12·19 m.

*Sales.*

(*a*) Shop No. (3) above has just been sold for £25,000.

(*b*) A shop and upper part let at £150 p.a. on lease having 7 years to run, changed hands at £6,050. It is now worth £650 p.a. on lease.

(*c*) A shop and upper part let at £400 p.a. on lease having 9 years to run was sold for £8,950. It is worth £800 p.a. on lease.

*Analysis.*

Analysis of the available data will provide useful evidence of comparable rents on a floor space basis and of the rate per cent at which properties in the vicinity are selling.

*A.—Lettings—*

| | Rent £/p.a. | Frontage | Depth | Area in in m² | Rent per £/m² |
|---|---|---|---|---|---|
| (1) | 600 | 5·49 m | 15·24 m | 83·67 | 7·17 |
| (2) | 450 (upper part) | | | 117·00 | 3·84 |
| (3) | 1,900 | 9·75 m | 18·29 m | 178·37 | 6·00 (shop) |
| | | | | 232·26 | 3·50 (upper part) |
| | | | | 37·16 | 1·50 (basement) |
| (4) | 725 | 6·10 m | 12·19 m | 74·36 | 9·75 |

*Note:*—(*i*) The rent of £725 p.a. for shop (4) is obtained:—

| | | | | |
|---|---|---|---|---|
| Rent reserved | ... | ... | ... | £170 p.a. |
| Premium paid ... | ... | ... £2,500 | | |

$\div$Y.P. @ 8 and 2½% for
    10 years (Tax @ 37·75%)     4·5

| | | | | |
|---|---|---|---|---|
| Annual Equivalent | ... | ... | ... | £555 p.a. |
| Full Rental Value | ... | ... | ... | £725 p.a. |

(*ii*) The rents of £6·00 and £3·50/m² for (3) are lower than the others probably because the competition for these larger areas of floor space would be slightly less. The rent of £9·75/m² for shop (4) is higher than the others probably because the tenant particularly wanted to obtain premises in this centre, hence his payment of a premium.

From a knowledge of the district and after considering the available evidence, it is thought that a valuer would decide that a fair rental value for the shop to be valued is £6·50/m² for the ground floor and £3·75/m² for the upper part.

*B.—Sales—*

(a) £25,000 represents about 13 years' purchase of the rent of £1,900 p.a., i.e., **a little over 7½ per cent.**

| | | | | |
|---|---|---|---|---|
| (b) Purchase price | ... | ... | ... | £6,050 |
| *Deduct* Value of rent reserved for 7 years £150 p.a. | | | | |
|     Y.P. @ 5½% for 7 years ... | | ... | 5·68 | |
| | | | *Say* | 850 |
| | | | | £5,200 |

£5,200 represents 8 Y.P. of the full rental value of £650, i.e., a return of **7½ per cent** (deferred 7 years).

| | | | | |
|---|---|---|---|---|
| (c) Purchase price | ... | ... | ... | £8,950 |
| *Deduct* Value of rent reserved for 9 years £400 p.a. | | | | |
|     Y.P. @ 6% for 9 years ... | | ... | 6·80 | |
| | | | | £2,720 |
| | | | | £6,230 |

£6,230 represents 7·8 Y.P. of the full rental value of £800 p.a. i.e., a return of **7 per cent** (deferred 9 years).

It would be unwise to rely only upon three transactions but, after considering all the evidence available as well as the above, it might be decided that the yield to be expected from this type of property would be 7½ per cent, if let at its full rental value, and 5 per cent if let at £375 p.a., this being a very secure rent.

*Valuation—*

| | | | | | |
|---|---|---|---|---|---|
| Rent reserved | ... | ... | ... | ... | £375 p.a. |
| Y.P. @ 5% for 5 years | ... | ... | ... | 4.33 | |
| | | | | | £1,625 |
| Reversion in 5 years to full rental value of— | | | | | |
| Ground Floor 122·63 m² @ £6·50 | ... | | £797 | | |
| Upper Parts 139·35 m² @ £3·75 | ... | | 523 | | |
| | | | | £1,320 p.a. | |
| Y.P. in perpetuity @ 7½% deferred 5 years | ... | | 9·29 | | |
| | | | | | £12,263 |

*Value, say* £14,000

## 5. INDUSTRIAL PREMISES

(*a*) *Generally.*—Reference was made in Chapter 3, Section 4 (*c*), to the method of ascertaining the rental values of this type of property on a floor space basis in terms of square metres.

In many areas there may be more evidence of sales and thus it may be preferable to value by direct comparison of capital values.

The range of properties to be considered is extensive and varies from shop or residential property, converted for use as storage or for factory purposes, to well-constructed, well-lighted, up-to-date premises with many amenities.

Situation is one of the chief factors affecting value, including such points as access to main roads, railways or canals (of recent years the importance of these two factors has diminished), also proximity to markets and, in particular, to the supply of suitable labour.

In making comparison between premises otherwise similar, the influence of these matters must be carefully considered.

(*b*) *Construction.*—Good natural lighting is essential in many trades; and premises in which the use of artificial light during daylight hours can be kept to a minimum will obviously command a higher rent than those where a good deal of work has to be done under artificial light.

The rates of insurance for many trades are comparatively high. The risk of fire will be minimised by fireproof construction and by the presence of sprinklers. For the purpose of insurance, premises are graded by Insurance Companies in accordance with the rules of the Fire Offices Committee.

The means of escape from fire will need to be considered, also the provision of adequate sanitary accommodation and adequate ventilation. It must be ascertained that the premises under consideration comply with the requirements of the Factory Acts and the Statutory Rules and Orders made thereunder in respect of these matters. The mode of construction may also be important in relation to the annual cost of repair. The rental value on lease will be diminished, for example, where the roof is old and by reason of age or construction is likely to leak.

Consideration should also be given to the means of heating. A modern system of central heating, whether hot water or steam, will reduce maintenance costs, particularly with modern boiler installations with automatic firing.

The lay-out of the premises should be such as to facilitate dealing with the delivery and despatch of goods, and the handling of goods within the premises without undue labour.

For many trades the floor space on the ground floor is of considerably greater value than that on upper floors, although this may be offset in the case of valuable sites, particularly in central districts, by adequate provision for handling goods by lifts or conveyors between floors. Particularly in the case of ground floors is it a disadvantage if the whole of each floor of each building is not at the same level, i.e., if there are steps or breaks in the floor.

The artificial lighting system should be considered, to see that there is an adequate standard of illumination to enable work to be done satisfactorily.

In large factories the provision of adequate canteen, welfare and car parking facilities is an essential point.

In some cases it may be found that premises, by reason of age or construction, are suitable only for warehouse purposes, for which there is a limited demand, unless further expenditure is incurred in the provision of adequate sanitary accommodation and means of escape. Even when this can be provided at an economical cost it may not be possible to take into account the higher (factory) value because no planning consent is forthcoming for the change of use. In other cases premises may have been constructed for the purpose of a particular trade or industry, and are not suitable for general use without some modification. For example, for a particular trade buildings may be erected with a ground storey 8 m high, expensive to heat and light and of a height excessive for most purposes. Unless an occupier can be found who requires the additional height, it is likely that a lower rent would be paid for the higher floor because of the additional cost of heating the unwanted space.

(c) *Rental and Capital Values.*—In some cases it may be found that land is sold and factories erected to the requirements of an occupier who purchases the freehold, and there may be little evidence of rental values. In such cases regard must be had to the selling price rather than the rental value of the accommodation when making a valuation. Wherever possible, values arrived at on this basis should be checked by consideration of rental value.

In the centres of towns a large building is often let off in floors, the tenants paying exclusive rentals, the landlord being responsible for the maintenance of common staircases, lift, and sometimes the provision of heating or the supply of power. The method of valuation in such cases will be on the lines indicated in this Chapter in respect of office premises, an estimate of the net income being made by deducting the outgoings from the gross rentals and, where necessary, the actual rentals being checked against comparable values for other similar properties.

Factory and warehouse premises are less commonly bought or sold for investment purposes than shops and offices, although this practice is more prevalent than, say, ten or more years ago, in the case of modern ground floor premises suitable for a variety of industrial trades. Probably 8-12 Years' Purchase, according to the special circumstances of each case, is a fair indication of the range which can be supported by analysis of transaction.

Before a new factory over a certain size can be erected or a non-industrial building can be used for industrial purposes, under provisions contained in the Town and Country Planning Act, 1962, the Control of Office and Industrial Development Act, 1965, and the Industrial Development Act, 1966, an industrial development certificate must be obtained from the Department of Trade and Industry. This is one of the ways in which the Department is expected to ensure a proper distribution of industry over the country as a whole and the Department is particularly required to have regard to the need for providing appropriate employment in development areas.

It follows that a high vacant possession value will attach to existing buildings in areas where the policy of the Board in regard to the distribution of industry makes it very unlikely that certificates for the erection of new industrial buildings or for the change of use of buildings from some non-industrial use to an industrial use will be obtainable. In these, and in other cases where the supply of factory accommodation falls far short of the demand, direct comparison of capital values by analysis of sales on the basis of a square metre of floor space is likely to be the most practical method of valuation.

Under provisions contained in the Local Employment Acts, 1960, 1963 and 1970 and the Industrial Development Act, 1966, grants may be made towards the cost of erecting or extending industrial buildings and of adapting existing buildings for industrial use in development areas and intermediate areas. In addition, under provisions contained in the Capital Allowances Act, 1968, certain capital allowances for industrial buildings can be deducted in the charging of the profits of a company to corporation tax.

In making comparisons between one property and another careful note must be made of the factors already mentioned. It may be found that one factory in a similar position and of a similar area and construction has a modern central heating system, sprinklers, road and rail access, whereas the other lacks these amenities. Such differences are usually taken into account by modifying the price per unit of floor area. But it must not be overlooked that the provision of additional facilities of this kind may be possible at a comparatively small cost and it may be more realistic to value the property as if the improvement had been carried out and to deduct the cost.

It may sometimes be found that extensive factory premises comprise new and old buildings, some of which may be of little value in the open market. They may, for instance, have been erected for the purposes of a particular trade and although the covered floor space area may be extensive, they may have a comparatively low market value.

The following example is typical of fairly modern factory premises: —

> *Example.*—You are instructed to prepare a valuation for mortgage purposes of a large factory on the outskirts of an important town.
>
> The premises are in the occupation of the owners, by whom they were acquired in 1938; the premises are of one storey only for the greater part, with offices, canteen and kitchens on the 1st floor at the front of the building. The factory is brick built with steel span roof trusses covered externally with corrugated asbestos and lined internally. There is good top light. The floor is of concrete finished with granolithic paving. There is an efficient central heating system. Gas, electricity and main water supplies are connected. The site has a frontage of 91·44 metres to a main road and has a private drive-in with two loading docks. There is adequate lavatory and cloakroom accommodation. The site area is 1 hectare.
>
> Temporary buildings for storage purposes with breeze-slab walls and steel-truss roofs carried on steel stanchions have been erected since the property was purchased.
>
> The available net areas, exclusive of passages and staircases in terms of square metres, are as follows:—Main factory, 2,800; boiler house 65; men's and women's lavatories and cloakrooms, 84; loading docks, 110; outside temporary stores, 280; 1st floor offices 110; 1st floor lavatories, 28.
>
> There are a number of similar factories in the vicinity, of areas from 900 to 2,500 square metres, let within the last five years at rents of from £3 to £4 per square metre, the area being exclusive of lavatories, canteens, etc. The rents show a tendency to increase.

*Valuation*—

> It is usual for valuations of industrial premises to be based on the net area available for use for the purposes of the business carried on.
>
> As a result of an inspection, it will be possible to decide a fair basis of valuation in comparison with those factories where there is evidence of rental value.

A reasonable basis for a valuation might be as follows:—

| | | m² | £ |
|---|---|---|---|
| Ground Floor: | Main factory floor | 2,800 @ £3·50 ... | 9,800 |
| | Loading bays ... | 110 @ £3·50 ... | 385 |
| | Outside stores ... | 280 @ £2 ... | 560 |
| First Floor: | Offices ... ... | 110 @ £4 ... | 440 |
| | | Rental Value ... | 11,185 |
| | | Y.P. perpetuity, say ... | 10 |
| | | *Value,* say | £110,000 |

*Notes—*
  (1) The increased value placed on floor space used as offices reflects the higher standard of finish and amenity compared with the main factory.
  (2) It will be observed that the total area covered by buildings, allowing for outside walls, etc., is probably about 4,000 square metres, so that on a site of 1 hectare there is room for extension. This might be dealt with by valuing any " excess " land separately; but for the purpose for which the valuation is required (mortgage) it has been disregarded.

### 6. OFFICE PROPERTIES

(a) *Generally.*—In many ways the methods to be used in the valuation of office properties are analogous to those already described in Chapter 13, Section 5, in relation to residential flats.

The range of properties to be considered is again extensive. At the one extreme there are converted dwelling-houses, perhaps in a small provincial town where the demand for office accommodation is limited; at the other, there are modern buildings in large towns constructed specifically for offices, containing considerable floor space and providing within one building many amenities, which may include restaurants, club rooms, shops, post office, etc., and equipped with central heating and lifts. In the latter case the services provided by the landlord may be considerable, and may include not only lighting and cleaning of the common parts of the building but also the cleaning of offices occupied by tenants. The cost of such services is usually covered by a service charge payable in addition to the rent.

There is control over the provision of new offices, whether by new building or extension or conversion of existing buildings, similar to that already referred to on industrial buildings. Under provisions in the Control of Office and Industrial Development Act, 1965, before an application for planning permission for office development over a certain size can be effective, an office development permit must be obtained from the Department of Trade and Industry. This control applies in the metropolitan region and in any other area designated by order.

The method of valuation usually employed will be to arrive at a fair estimate of the gross income, deduct therefrom the outgoings borne by the landlord, and apply to the net income so arrived at an appropriate figure of Years' Purchase.

(b) *The Income.*—The annual value is usually considered in relation to area, and in advertisements of floor space to let in office buildings the rent is often quoted at so much per unit of floor area. Before buildings are erected this practice is difficult to avoid but it gives rise to disputes as to the actual area involved. Once buildings are erected, rentals should be quoted in terms of pounds per annum; this will avoid disputes as to the actual floor area.

Actual lettings will require careful consideration and analysis and may often appear to be inconsistent. This may be accounted for by the fact that the tenancies were entered into at various dates and that the landlord will have sought to make the best bargain he could with each tenant. A further factor is connected with the question of varying areas of floor space. It may be, for example, that the whole of the fifth floor of a building is let to one tenant, whereas the sixth floor is let to seven or eight different tenants, so that the total net income derived from the higher floor may be greater than that from the one below.

The valuer's estimate of a fair and proper rental will depend upon the circumstances of each case and upon his judgment of the way in which the building can best be let. He will be guided primarily by the level of rental value obtaining in the district, found by analysing recent lettings of similar accommodation in comparable buildings in the area.

Since 1939 there has been a very heavy increase in the rents of office premises, and in most central districts there are few signs of a falling off.

When dealing with office premises which are empty, or when estimating the rents at which a proposed new building will let, it is usual to make comparison with other properties on the basis of the terms at which such accommodation is usually let. For instance, if it is expected that the offices will be let at a rent exclusive of rates, a fair rent on this basis will be estimated by comparison with the lettings of other similar premises on similar terms as regards rates and also as regards such other items as repairs and service charges. It is equally important that the same basis of area is used in analysis as is employed in the subsequent calculation, i.e., if a net floor area is used to divide into a certain rent, net floor area must be applied to the offices under consideration.

(c) *Terms of Tenancy.*—These, as has been stated, will vary considerably. Lettings are today almost always exclusive of rates, and the landlord will normally be responsible for external repairs, maintenance of staircases, lifts and other parts in common use, in the case of buildings let in suites. The tenants may be liable for all repairs to the interior of the offices under full repairing leases, or the covenants may be subject to exceptions in respect of structural repairs. Where whole buildings are let to single tenants, the lease is normally a full repairing and insuring one.

Where accommodation is let in suites it is quite likely that individual variations will be found in the tenancies within the same building, and careful examination of the terms of tenancy for each letting is necessary to determine what is a fair allowance to make for the outgoings to be borne by the landlord.

(d) *Outgoings.*—The use of a percentage deduction from gross rentals to arrive at a net income, or even to give any accurate indication of costs in regard to the principal outgoings likely to be found is in most cases very unreliable. Where available it will usually be found desirable to examine the actual cost of the outgoings for the property under consideration, and to consider them critically in the light of experience and by comparison with other similar properties.

Repairs.—The average annual cost of repairs will depend upon the type of construction, the planning and age of the building, and the extent of the tenants' liabilities under their covenants. Where tenants are only liable for internal decorative repairs (fair wear and tear excepted) the landlord must expect to bear practically the whole of the cost and a comparatively large allowance must be made.

Probably the soundest method is to make an estimate of the periodic cost of external and internal repairs by reference to the actual building and reduce this to a yearly allowance, checking the result by comparison with a similar building.

Rates.—In the case of existing buildings in assessment the present rates can be easily ascertained.

In the comparatively few cases found today where the landlord pays the rates a most important point is whether the terms of the tenancy permit of any increase being passed on to the tenant.

In regard to water rates, in some instances it will be found that a private well has been sunk, particularly in the case of highly rented properties where the cost of water rates is substantial.

Services.—There is no hard and fast rule as to the items covered by this term. The general tendency is to increase the scope and to recover from tenants not only the actual cost but also an amount for supervision of services and repairs to buildings let in suites. As stated above the items are usually covered by a separate service charge payable as additional rent. Where this is the case the valuer concerned should satisfy himself as to the conditions of the charges, in particular he should ascertain if increases in costs can be passed on to tenants. He should also ascertain if the amount of the charge is sufficient to cover the cost of the services, allowing for depreciation to installations. In many cases, it may be found that the landlord makes a considerable profit on the services he supplies.[7]

The following items usually fall under the heading of services. The remarks given against each item give the considerations to be kept in mind when examining the cost of individual services to ascertain if the service charge covers the cost of provision adequately.

*Heating and Domestic Hot Water.* — The annual cost of central heating will depend largely on the type and age of the system and the type and amount of fuel used. In the case of modern buildings at the present day a figure of £1 to £1·50 per square metre is probably not an unreasonable one to cover the cost of central heating and hot water supplies to lavatory basins.

*Lighting.*—Tenants are usually responsible for the cost of lighting the offices, but the landlord will be responsible for lighting staircases and other parts of the building in common use. The amount to be borne by the landlord will depend upon the extent of the lighting which he provides, including the replacement of bulbs.

*Lifts.*—The annual cost of the maintenance of lifts will vary considerably. Much will depend upon the age and type of lift, and the amount of traffic carried.

The cost of an electric passenger-operated lift is likely to be £30–£35 per floor per annum.

*Cleaning.*—When provided, this will depend on the number of staff employed. A charge of up to £1 per square metre per annum is not unusual where the landlord provides cleaning to the offices.

Where tenants are responsible for providing their own services e.g. heating, no account need be taken of the cost except in so far as it will affect the rental value of the accommodation.

*Staff.*—The cost of staff again must be ascertained in respect of each particular case, and consideration should be given as to whether or not the actual number of staff employed is adequate for the building.

Insurance.—There will be a number of insurances to be borne by the landlord. The ordinary rate for fire insurance of 10p per cent will usually be found, and in addition there are insurances for third party risks, lifts (if any), boilers and heating, and National Insurance.

---

[7] Whether this profit should be taken into account or not has already been considered—see Chapter 13, Section 5.

Management.—An allowance for management is usually considered to be necessary, and this is likely to vary between 3 per cent and 5 per cent on the gross rents.

Before 1939 voids often represented a substantial proportion of the gross income in the case of older buildings. At the time of writing this factor may generally be ignored.

(e) *Net Income and Capital Value.*—The estimate of net income made on the lines indicated above will not necessarily accord with the actual net income of any recent year. It should, however, represent what can be taken to be a fair expectation over a considerable period.

The basis upon which it is to be capitalised will depend on the type of property, its situation and neighbourhood, the competition of other properties in the vicinity, and the valuer's estimate of the general trend of values for the type of investment under consideration. The rate of return may vary from as low as 7 per cent for the higher class of modern building let to first-class tenants, to 10 per cent for poor properties let to indifferent tenants.

Care should be taken, in analysing sale prices to arrive at rates per cent, to ensure that the methods used are similar to those it is intended to apply to the valuation. For example, reliable evidence of years' purchase and rate per cent can only be deduced from the result of a sale where an accurate estimate of net income is first made to compare with the sale price.

In some cases an investment that has to be valued may comprise different types of property, which in themselves might be valued at differing rates per cent. For example, a property might comprise shops on the ground floor, basement restaurant, and offices in the upper parts. The rates per cent applicable separately might be 7½ per cent for the shops, 9 per cent for the restaurant and 8 per cent for the offices. Where the property is held on lease at a ground rent considerable difficulty may arise in determining how this should be apportioned so as to arrive at a fair net income in respect of each of the different types of letting. It is probably best in practice for the valuer to deduct the ground rent capitalised at the average rate per cent applied to the various net incomes derived from the property.

*Example.*—You are required to make a valuation for sale in the open market as an investment of a block of offices on ground and five floors over. You are furnished on receiving your instructions with the following details:—

The block is leasehold having 80 years to run at a ground rent of £600 p.a.

The landlord supplies services consisting of a lift (with attendant), central heating to the offices (but not hot water to lavatory basins for which the tenants are responsible), and lighting and cleaning those parts of the building not let to tenants. The cost of these services is recoverable from the tenants by a service charge which you investigate and find is reasonable. The provisions in the lease as regards the service charge have the normal escalator clauses which cover rises in costs. The tenants arrange for their own office cleaning and pay for their own lighting.

You are provided with the following schedule of tenancies:—

*Ground Floor.*

Let to an Insurance Company for offices at £3,500 per annum exclusive for forty-two years from this year.

*First Floor.*

Let at £1,000 p.a. exclusive, on lease for twenty-one years, expiring in 3 years.

*Second Floor.*

Let at £450 p.a. exclusive, for 14 years, now having 3 years to run.

*Third Floor.*

Let at £1,775 p.a. exclusive, on seven years lease now having 5 years to run.

*Fourth Floor.*

Let at £1,500 p.a. exclusive, for ten years, now having 3 years to run.

*Top Floor.*

Let at £275 p.a. exclusive, for twenty-one years, now having 3 years to run.

All tenants do internal repairs.

On inspecting the premises it is found that they are well constructed in brick and stone with slate roof. The condition is good and much of the interior is finished in tiles: you estimate that they were built in 1930. You have been given a plan of the building from which you ascertain the following to be the net floor areas:—

| Floor | Area in square metres |
|---|---|
| Ground | 325 |
| First | 288 |
| Second | 275 |
| Third | 265 |
| Fourth | 265 |
| Top | 93 |

*Valuation—*

The first stage in the valuation is to draw up a schedule collating the information to hand. This is best done in columnar form and, in this instance, would be as follows:—

See Schedule I (page 229).

Columns 1, 2, 3, 5 and 8 present no difficulty. Column 4 is completed from Columns 2 and 3. Column 6 is completed by a careful scrutiny of the whole schedule: those floors marked * are the most recently let and form the basis for the other figures. The valuer would rely, not only on the rents obtained for this building, but also on his local knowledge of similar recent lettings of comparable accommodation. Column 7 is obtained from 3 and 6.

The actual and estimated gross income is now apparent as:—

| | | | |
|---|---|---|---|
| For the next three years | ... | £8,500 p.a. | |
| Then onwards ... | ... | ... | £11,900 p.a. |

*Outgoings—*

After consideration of all the factors concerned and checking the information gained on inspection, the valuer might decide on the following—

| Item | £ | Remarks |
|---|---|---|
| Repairs, say ... ... | 1,200 | About 10% of the gross rental value; this could be checked by an estimate of cost based on the actual building. |
| *Insurances:—* | | |
| Fire ... ... ... | 240 | |
| Insurances other than fire ... ... ... | 75 | Third party, National Insurance for caretaker, boiler insurances, etc. |
| Management, say ... | 500 | 4% of rental value. |
| Ground rent ... ... | 600 | |
| Total ... ... ... | £2,615 | Excluding Ground Rent, 24% of present rents or 17% of full rental value. |

| | | | | | |
|---|---|---|---|---|---|
| Gross Rents for next three years... | ... | £8,500 | | |
| *Less* outgoings as above ... | ... | ... | 2,615 | |
| | Net Income ... | 5,885 | | |
| Y.P. for 4 yrs. @ 6½ & 2½% ... | ... | 3·27 | £19,244 |

| | | | | |
|---|---|---|---|---|
| Gross Rents after 3 years ... | ... | ... | £11,900 | |
| *Less* outgoings as above ... | ... | ... | 2,615 | |
| | Net Income ... | £9,285 | |
| Y.P. for 76 yrs. @ 7½ and 2½% | 12·58 | | |
| P.V. £1 in 4 yrs. @ 7½% ... | ·75 | 9·44 | £87,650 |

*Value, say* £106,000

*Note.*—The above calculation should be adjusted for income tax on the sinking fund element and the double sinking fund method is to be preferred (see Appendix A, 15).

## SCHEDULE I

| 1 | 2 | 3 | 4 | 5 | | 6 | 7 | 8 |
|---|---|---|---|---|---|---|---|---|
| Floor | Present Rent £ | Area m² | Present Rent £/m² | Tenancy Details | | Estimated Rental Value £/m² | Estimated Rental Value £ | Remarks |
| | | | | (a) Term in years | (b) Unexpired term in years | | | |
| Ground* | 3,500 | 325 | 10·77 | 42 | 42 years | 10·77 | 3,500 | Recent letting |
| First … | 1,000 | 288 | 3·47 | 21 | 3 ,, | 8·00 | 2,304 | |
| Second | 450 | 275 | 1·64 | 14 | 3 ,, | 6·70 | 1,842 | |
| Third* | 1,775 | 265 | 6·70 | 7 | 5 ,, | 6·70 | 1,775 | Recent letting |
| Fourth | 1,500 | 265 | 5·66 | 10 | 3 ,, | 6·70 | 1,775 | |
| Top … | 275 | 93 | 2·96 | 21 | 3 ,, | 7·25 | 674 | |
| TOTAL | £8,500 | 1,511 | m² | | | say, | £11,900 | |

# Chapter 15

## Valuations for Mortgage and Probate

### 1. VALUATIONS FOR MORTGAGE

(*a*) *Nature of a Mortgage.*—A mortgage of freehold or leasehold property is a transaction whereby one party—the mortgagor—grants an interest in his property to another party—the mortgagee—as security for a loan.

The transaction is effected by means of a mortgage deed in which the mortgagor usually agrees to pay interest on the loan at a given rate per cent, and may also enter into express covenants as to the repair and insurance of the property. In some cases the mortgage deed provides for periodical repayments of capital as well as interest (as in the case of a Building Society mortgage).

The mortgagor retains the right to recover his property freed from the charge created by the mortgage deed on repayment of the amount due to the mortgagee. This is known as his " equity of redemption ".

Since 1925 a legal mortgage of freeholds can only be made either (i) by the grant of a lease to the mortgagee for a long term of years, usually 3,000, with a provision for cesser on redemption, or (ii) by a charge expressed to be by way of legal mortgage.[1]

A legal mortgage of leaseholds can only be made either (i) by a sublease to the mortgagee of the whole term, less the last day or days, with a provision for cesser on redemption, or (ii) by a charge by way of legal mortgage.[2]

What is known as an " equitable mortgage " may be effected without a mortgage deed either (i) by a written agreement acknowledging the loan and promising to execute a legal mortgage if required, or (ii) by a verbal agreement accompanied by deposit of the title deeds of the property. This type of mortgage does not transfer any interest in the property to the mortgagee.

As a general rule, a mortgage is a sound form of investment offering reasonable security and a fair rate of interest, and although the mortgage deed probably stipulates for repayment at the end of six months it is usual for the loan to continue for a very much longer period.

---

[1] Law of Property Act, 1925, Secs. 85 and 87.
[2] *Ibid.*, Sec. 86. A charge by way of legal mortgage places the mortgagee in the same position as though he had been granted a lease or sublease.

So long as the mortgagor pays the interest regularly and observes the covenants of the mortgage deed, the mortgagee will usually be content to leave him in possession and control of the property. But if the interest is falling into arrears or the mortgagor is unable to meet a demand for repayment of the loan, the mortgagee must take steps to protect his security.

(b) *The Mortgagee's Security.*—The mortgagee's security for the money he has lent depends primarily upon the property and upon the sum it might be expected to realise if brought to sale at any time. His security for payment of interest on the loan at the agreed rate depends upon the net income the property is capable of producing.

The usual advance by way of mortgage is two-thirds the estimated fair market value of the property, thus leaving the mortgagee a one-third margin of safety. Trustees may not in any case advance more than two-thirds of a valuation of the property made by a skilled valuer. Other investors, such as building societies, often make larger advances, particularly if some form of collateral security is offered or where provision is made for repayment of capital by instalments over a certain period. On the other hand, when there is a risk of future depreciation in value, an advance of three-fifths or even one-half may be more satisfactory than the usual two-thirds. In all cases the mortgagee, or his adviser, should consider not only the value of the property in relation to the proposed loan, but also whether the net income from the property is sufficient to provide interest at the agreed rate.

If the mortgagor defaults in payment of interest, observance of the covenants of the mortgage deed or repayment of the loan when legally demanded, the mortgagee has the following remedies against the property—

(i) Under certain conditions[3] he may sell the mortgaged property and apply the proceeds to repayment of the loan and any arrears of interest together with the expenses of sale. Any surplus must be paid to the mortgagor.

(ii) He may apply to the Court for a foreclosure order which will have the effect of extinguishing the mortgagor's equity of redemption.

(iii) He may at any time take personal possession of the income from the property, and after paying all necessary outgoings may apply the balance to paying interest on the mortgage debt, including any arrears. The surplus, if any, must be paid to the mortgagor or applied to reducing the mortgage debt.

---

[3] Law of Property Act, 1925, Sec. 101.

(iv) Under the same conditions as in (i) he may appoint a receiver to collect the income from the property and apply it to the purposes indicated in (iii), including payment of the receiver's commission.

It is evident that these remedies will only be fully effective where, in cases (i) and (ii), the market value of the property exceeds the amount due to the mortgagee, or where, in cases (iii) and (iv), the net income from the property, after paying all outgoings and annual charges having priority to the mortgage, is sufficient to discharge the annual interest on the loan with a margin to cover possible arrears of interest.

Although the property itself is the mortgagee's principal security, it is usual for the mortgage deed to include a personal covenant by the mortgagor to repay the loan. This may be reinforced by the personal guarantee of some third party. So that, in addition to the remedies mentioned above, there is that of action on the personal covenant.

The character and position of the borrower and his guarantor (if any) is therefore a matter of considerable importance to the mortgagee, both as an additional security for the repayment of the loan and also as a guarantee for the regular payment of interest as it accrues due.

The exercise of the mortgagee's remedies may be restricted where the property is one to which the Rent Acts apply.

(c) *The Valuation.*—In making a valuation for mortgage purposes the ordinary principles of valuation apply, but the valuer must have regard to the mortgagee's position in relation to the property and to the remedies available to him in the event of default by the mortgagor.

He will bear in mind that it may be necessary to realise the security in the future and that unless the sale price then is sufficient to cover the mortgage debt, arrears of interest and costs, the mortgagee will suffer loss.

While market value will be the basis of the valuation, the valuer must consider not only the present market value, but particularly whether that value is likely to be maintained in the future and would be readily realisable on the forced sale of the property.

He will consider very carefully any factors such as probable action by the local authority under the Housing Acts, and other statutes, which may unfavourably affect the value of the property in the future. He should fully consider any possible effects of the development plan for the area. Valuations should be on the basis of existing use value unless planning permission has been granted for development. He may also have to ask himself whether the existing market is unduly influenced by national or local conditions of a temporary nature which may have caused something like an artificial " boom " in prices. Any likely capital expenditure on the property, such as accrued dilapidations or the estimated cost of future development or reconstruction, must be allowed for as a deduction.

The net income from the property must be estimated with the utmost care, not only as a sound basis for the valuation, but to make sure that it will adequately cover the interest on the proposed loan.

Any future element of value which is reasonably certain in its nature, such as reversion to full rental value on the expiration of an existing lease at a low rent, may properly be taken into account. But anything which is purely speculative in its nature should be disregarded. The valuer must be cautious when capitalising " full " rents and must consider whether they will be maintained or are likely to fall; this is particularly important where the property is not of a first-class type. The valuer must beware of including in his valuation elements of potential value which may never eventuate.

In the case of business premises, goodwill should be excluded from the valuation.

The valuer should also exclude anything which can easily be sold or removed by the mortgagor, such as timber, unless there are adequate safeguards against such a happening.

Information is sometimes tendered as to the price paid for the property by the mortgagor. This is apt to be misleading. An excessive price may have been paid for a special reason, or market values may since have changed.

The cost of erection of buildings is usually best disregarded for mortgage purposes. Large sums may have been lavished on the gratification of individual tastes, or considerable changes in building costs may have occurred since the property was erected.

(d) *Advice on Policy.*—In addition to his valuation of the property, the valuer may be required to advise as to the nature of the security afforded and as to the sum which may reasonably be advanced.

In the case of trustees, for example, the loan must be made under the advice of an able, practical surveyor or valuer expressed in the report.

Certain types of property are not desirable securities for mortgage purposes. A vacant site, for instance, may be of considerable value and cost nothing for maintenance: but its value is necessarily of a speculative nature and there is no immediate income forthcoming. If, therefore, the mortgage interest falls into arrear, the taking of possession of the land by the mortgagee will not prevent the accumulation of further arrears of interest pending the time when a purchaser can be found.

Factory premises again are a doubtful security, particularly if only suited to the needs of a particular trade which may be dependent on local industrial conditions.

In these and similar cases the valuer will no doubt feel it his duty to accompany his valuation by a clear indication of the risks inherent in the nature of the security, and may advise that, if any advance is made at all, it should certainly be less than the normal two-thirds.

Leaseholds, being in the nature of a wasting security, require careful treatment, particularly where the term is comparatively short. In some cases provision is made in the mortgage deed for repayment of a portion of the principal from time to time, or for periodical revaluations to check the security. In any case care should be taken to see that the property is kept in reasonable repair by the mortgagor while in his possession, so as to avoid any risk of forfeiture.

Buildings which are the subject of a mortgage advance should be insured in the names of both mortgagor and mortgagee. A covenant to this effect is usually included in the mortgage deed, and the mortgagor should be required to hand the policy to the mortgagee and to produce to him from time to time the last receipt for premium. The valuer is often asked to name the sum for which the buildings should be insured. This may be done by an estimate based on the cost of reconstruction as described in Chapter 9.

Very considerable sums of money are lent on mortgage by building societies, mainly to owner-occupiers of small house and shop property. The practice of such societies is to lend money upon the basis of repayment by instalments, usually monthly, which include both interest and principal, fixed according to the term for which the loan is granted, which varies between 10 and 30 years. If the instalments are duly paid the money cannot usually be called in during the term, nor can the instalments be increased, although the rate of interest may be increased except in those few cases where the advance was made at a guaranteed rate of interest. The fact that the principal begins to be reduced so soon as the first instalment is paid, and that repayment continues with each instalment, makes it practicable for the two-thirds limit of advance to be exceeded. In the case of small properties 70% or 80% would be a normal rate for a building society advance, while as much as 90% may be advanced if the society is given collateral security such as the deposit of a sum of money or stock, together with a guarantee by a third party or by an insurance company. Where the proposed mortgagor is a " sitting tenant " (protected by the Rent Acts), who is purchasing the house he occupies, advances are frequently made to cover, not only the whole of the purchase price, but the legal fees as well.

In acting for a building society the valuer is usually only concerned with submitting a valuation and report, the amount of the advance being a question of policy for the society to decide.

Advances are frequently made by insurance companies, the advance being repaid at the end of the term on the maturing of a life assurance policy for the amount of the loan. This gives the borrower the additional advantage that in the event of his death, the property is freed from the mortgage debt. A greater percentage advance can often be obtained by this method which is more expensive than the usual building society mortgage, although income-tax relief is obtainable on both the interest and the life assurance premium.

(e) *Second or Subsequent Mortgages.*—It is possible for there to be more than one mortgage on a property, the second or subsequent mortgages being mortgages of the mortgagor's equity of redemption. Provided they are all registered, the second and subsequent mortgagees will each have a claim on the property in their regular order after the first mortgagee's claim has been satisfied.

It is evident that there will be little security for such an advance unless care is taken to ensure that the total amount advanced, including the first mortgage, does not exceed what may reasonably be lent on the security of the property—normally, two-thirds its fair market value.

## 2. VALUATIONS FOR PROBATE

(a) *Generally.*—When an owner of real or personal property dies, Estate Duty becomes payable to the State on the capital value of all property passing on death and also on certain types of property, such as gifts made within a few years of death, which are " deemed to pass " for the purpose of charging duty.

The amount of Estate Duty payable on the occasion of a death is regulated ·by the total capital value of the various properties comprised in the estate, as shown on a form known as the Inland Revenue Affidavit prepared by the deceased's personal representative. The rate of duty varies according to the size of the estate. The rate of duty is nil where the total capital value does not exceed £12,500. Above that figure duty is calculated in steps at rates from 25 to 85 per cent according to a scale[4] but duty is not to exceed 80 per cent of the total capital value.

For example, suppose a man dies leaving some freehold property worth £10,000, some stocks and shares worth £5,000, also cash at bank, furniture and other personalty worth £3,000 net, reference to the scale of Estate Duty will show that the appropriate rate for an

---

[4] Part I, Schedule 17, Finance Act, 1969, as amended. See Appendix E.

estate whose total capital value is £18,000 is: 25 per cent on (£17,500–£12,500) and 30 per cent on (£18,000–£17,500), a total duty payable of £1,400.

Prior to the Finance Act, 1969, duty was payable at a rate varying from 1 per cent to 80 per cent which varied according to the total size of the estate and duty at the appropriate rate was payable on the capital value of each of the several properties comprised in the estate.

(b) *Basis of Valuation.*—A valuation of freehold or leasehold property for probate does not differ in principle from a valuation for sale or other purposes, but it is regulated by certain statutory provisions.

The basis prescribed for the valuation is the price which the property would fetch if sold in the open market at the date of death, no allowance being made for possible expenses of sale. This is called the " principal value ".[5]

The valuation is usually made by a skilled valuer acting for the estate, whose report should be attached to the Inland Revenue Affidavit.

Estate Duty valuations are dealt with by the Valuation Office of the Commissioners of Inland Revenue and are referred, in the first instance, to the District Valuer in whose district the property is situated, for his opinion.

Frequently, in practice, the personal representative or his solicitor or surveyor, submits the valuation to the District Valuer before the Inland Revenue Affidavit is submitted, and a figure is provisionally agreed—or " prior agreed "—beforehand. Or, where this has not been done, a figure may be agreed with the District Valuer by negotiation after the valuation returned in the Inland Revenue Affidavit has been referred to him for his opinion.

But if, on the advice of the District Valuer, the Commissioners of Inland Revenue insist on a figure of value for freehold or leasehold property which the personal representative is unable to accept, the latter may appeal to the Lands Tribunal, from whose decision there is a right of appeal on a point of law to the Court of Appeal.

The price which the property might be expected to fetch at the date of death—which is the basis of a probate valuation—will include the value of any sporting rights or minerals: but the *commercial* value of any timber, trees, wood or underwood is deducted.

Timber-bearing land is valued as if in its natural and unimproved state—sometimes called its " prairie value "—no duty being charged on the timber until it is actually sold.

In making the valuation it must be assumed that the property is placed on the market in the manner likely to produce the best

---

[5] Finance Act, 1894, Sec. 7 (5).

possible price. · So that if a large estate might be expected to fetch a better price if sold in a number of lots than if offered as a whole, the valuation must assume that it is suitably lotted.

For example, in *Ellesmere v. Inland Revenue Commissioners*[6] an estate of over 2,200 acres, including farms, accommodation land, houses, shops and other premises, was sold shortly after the death of the owner for £68,000. The executors contended that this sum represented the principal value, although the purchaser at the sale had soon afterwards resold a portion only of the estate in lots for £65,000. On the question being referred to one of the special panel of referees (the tribunal for settling disputes at that time) he fixed the principal value at £75,618, the sum which, in his opinion, the estate would have fetched if sold in lots at the date of death. On appeal, the High Court upheld the referee's decision.

It is, of course, a question of fact in any particular case whether a sale in lots is likely to produce the best results or whether the estate is of such a size and nature that its greatest appeal would be to a single purchaser.

In estimating principal value no reduction may be made for the fact that the whole of the property is assumed to be placed on the market at one time.[7] This provision of the Finance Act, 1910, is sometimes called in practice the " flooded market clause ".

For example, assume a person dies on 1 January, 1969, and that his estate includes a large number of weekly cottages in one area. The statutory basis of valuation for probate is the price which the estate would fetch if sold in the open market on 1 January, 1969. But, although in practice the placing of properties of this kind on the market at one time might result in depreciated prices being realised, no allowance may be made for this in the valuation.

Where the personality of the owner was important to the property, so that its value can be proved to have been depreciated by his death, the valuation may be reduced accordingly.[7]

A valuation for probate, like any other estimate of market value, should take into account any statutory provisions, e.g., those of the Town and Country Planning Act, 1962, and any statutory restrictions affecting the value of the property at the date of death—for instance, restrictions imposed on a grant of permission for development or change of user, or the fact that the rents of house property are controlled under the Rent Acts. On the other hand, where property occupied by the deceased at his death is included in the estate, regard must be had to any possible advantages attaching to vacant possession.[8]

---

[6] (1918) 2 K.B. 735. See also *Duke of Buccleuch and Another v. Inland Revenue Commissioners*, R. & V.R. 1965, p. 571, C. of A.

[7] Finance (1909-10) Act, 1910, Sec. 60 (2).

[8] The sitting tenant's bid to be considered—see *Middleton & Bainbridge v. Commissioners of Inland Revenue* (1953), 47 R. & I.T. 639. House let furnished—see *Harris v. Commissioners of Inland Revenue* (1961), 1 R. & V.R. 94.

Where properties having development potential fall to be valued for estate duty purposes, the full value is returned and no deduction is made for capital gains tax for which the estate would be liable if the property were sold.

If under the terms of a settlement, an estate passes on the death of a life tenant subject to an annuity which continues after his death, the value of the property for Estate Duty purposes is reduced by a " slice " of the capital value of the property proportionate to the annuity. For example, suppose that property worth £10,000 and producing an income of £500 (net) per annum is subject to an annuity of £100 per annum. The " slice " of capital value proportionate to the annuity is $£10,000 \times \dfrac{100}{500} = £2,000$. Estate Duty will be payable on £8,000 (£10,000 – £2,000).

On the death of the annuitant the " slice " will be " deemed to pass " and will be liable for duty.

Where property is sold shortly after the date of death at a price above the value agreed for probate, a demand for additional duty may be presented. If the sale price is below the probate value, the estate may claim a refund. To justify either claim the general state of the property market and the local conditions must be the same at both dates.[9] If the valuer acting for an estate knows that the properties are to be sold, it is usual to wait until after the sale and to adopt the sale prices as the value for probate.[10]

Since the basis of valuation for estate duty is the value for sale, a hypothetical liability for capital gains tax on such a sale arises. This hypothetical liability for capital gains tax on death does not affect the valuations for estate duty purposes of the assets in respect of which the hypothetical liability arises. Any real liability for capital gains tax is however treated as a general debt of the estate for example where property was sold before the death and the capital gain liability had not been met at the date of death.

Until 1971 death was an occasion when there was a *deemed* disposal of assets and this gave rise to a liability for capital gains tax. In general, market values were used for valuations for both purposes, the valuation for capital gains tax being adopted for the estate duty valuation. Section 59 of the Finance Act, 1971 (and Schedule 12) abolished this deemed disposal in respect of deaths after 30th March, 1971 but provided that the assets shall be deemed to be acquired on the death by the personal representatives for a consideration equal to their market value at the date of death.

(*c*) *Agricultural Property.*—In addition to the points already dealt with above, there are certain special provisions affecting the valuation of agricultural properties for probate purposes.

---

[9] *Crossley v. Commissioners of Inland Revenue*, reported in " The Estates Gazette " for 17th April, 1954.

[10] Finance Act, 1911, Sec. 18.

Where an estate includes cottages occupied by persons employed solely for agricultural purposes in connection with the property, no account shall be taken of any additional value they might have as residences for persons other than agricultural labourers or work-men on the estate.[11]  For instance, in some districts cottages which are let at very low weekly rents to agricultural labourers would command a much higher rent if let to townspeople for week-end purposes.  In a probate valuation this higher rental value may be ignored.  But the concession only extends to cottages occupied by persons employed for agricultural purposes.  It would not apply, for instance, to a cottage occupied by a chauffeur or a member of the domestic staff of a mansion.

The " agricultural value " of agricultural property is charged with Estate Duty at a rate of 45 per cent less than the current rate known as the " estate rate "[12] applicable to all other types of property. Estate rate is found by ascertaining the proportion which the amount of duty determined in accordance with the scale of estate duty bears to the aggregate principal value of all the property in the estate. Thus, referring to the example on page 236, the estate rate is

$$\frac{1,400 \times 100}{18,000} \text{ per cent, i.e., 7·78 per cent.}$$

In such circumstances duty on the agricultural value of agricul-tural property is payable at 7·78 per cent less 45 per cent of 7·78 per cent, i.e., 7·78 per cent — (45 per cent of 7·78 per cent) = 7·78 per cent — 3·50 per cent = 4·28 per cent.  Where the market value at the date of death exceeds the " agricultural value " the " agricultural value " will be charged on the lower rate and the difference between the two values—known as " excess principal value "—will be charged on the full scale.

For the purpose of this provision the term " agricultural property" means " agricultural land, pasture and woodland, and also includes such cottages, farm buildings, farmhouses and mansion houses (together with the lands occupied threwith) as are of a character appropriate to the property."[13]

" Agricultural value " means the value which the property would have if it were subject to a perpetual covenant prohibiting its use otherwise than as agricultural property decreased by the value of any timber, trees or underwood growing thereon.[14]  It will include the value of any sporting rights which can be exercised without interference with the agricultural user.

[11] Finance Act, 1911, Sec. 18.
[12] Finance Act, 1969, Sec. 35 (2).
[13] Finance Act, 1925, Sec. 23 (2).
[14] *Ibid.*, Sec 23 (4) and Finance Act, 1894, Sec. 22 (1) (g).

Where the value of a property lies solely in its agricultural user it is evident that " principal value " and " agricultural value " will be the same and the whole capital value at date of death will be charged on the lower scale of duty. But where, for instance, certain parts of the property possess potential building value, it will be necessary to make two valuations—(i) an estimate of " principal value " and (ii) an estimate of the price the property might have realised at date of death if it had been subject to the assumed covenant against any but agricultural user. In both valuations the commercial value of timber will be excluded. The importance of this provision largely depends now on the provisions of the Development Plan covering the area in which the property is situated.

*Example.*—The following properties are comprised in the estate of X deceased : —(i) Stocks and shares, cash at bank and other personalty worth (after deducting debts and funeral expenses) £25,000; (ii) a freehold agricultural estate, certain portions of which are suitable for development as a residential estate for which purpose the area is allocated on the Development Plan and which is worth £40,000 in the open market. If the estate were restricted to its present agricultural user its value would be £35,000.

The commercial value of the timber on the estate which is estimated at £500 has been excluded from the above valuations. How will Estate Duty on the freehold property be calculated?

*Answer.*—

The total principal value of the estate is : —

| | | | |
|---|---|---|---|
| Stocks and shares and other assets | ... | ... | £25,000 |
| Freehold agricultural estate | ... | ... | 40,000 |
| *Total principal value* | | ... | £65,000 |

(N.B.—The value of the timber is not aggregated with the rest of the estate.)

On the current scale of Estate Duty (Finance Act, 1969) an estate of £65,000 pays duty of £24,500, i.e., an estate rate of 37·69%.

Estate Duty on the freehold property will therefore be calculated as follows:—

| | | | |
|---|---|---|---|
| Agricultural value ... | ... | ... | £35,000 @ 16·96% |
| Excess principal value | ... | ... | £5,000 @ 37·69% |
| (£40,000 – £35,000) | | | |

No duty will be payable on the timber until it is sold.

In practice the payment of duty is the concern of the estate's legal advisers and the valuer's duty is confined to preparing the valuation. The above example has been inserted merely to illustrate the importance of distinguishing where necessary between " principal value " and " agricultural value ".

In making this distinction it must be remembered that the definition of " agricultural property " includes not only agricultural land and woodlands, but also " such cottages, farm buildings, farmhouses and mansion houses (together with the lands occupied therewith) as are of a character appropriate to the property ". Where an estate consists of a mansion, park, home farm, and a number of other farms, comprising in all a considerable area of agricultural land, the cottages on the estate and the mansion itself with its grounds and park may fairly be regarded as " appropriate to the property " and included in its agricultural value. But in the case of a large house with fair-sized grounds and perhaps only a small area of pasture land attached, it can scarcely be claimed that the house itself is " agricultural property " although the pasture land will be.

The question of what is and what is not " agricultural property " is mainly one of fact, and each case must be judged on its merits.

*Example.*—It is required to value the following for purposes of probate. A country house with a little over 20 ha. of land attached, situated in very attractive surroundings about 30 miles by road from London and within easy reach of a main line railway station with good service of trains.

The accommodation is excellent and includes stables and garages for five cars. All the buildings are in good repair and there is main water and electricity. Drainage is to a septic tank installation. The gardens are attractively planned, and together with the house and outbuildings occupy 2 ha.

The remaining land consists of 2 ha. of woodland and 16 ha. of pasture land. The latter, which is let to a neighbouring farmer, is worth as agricultural land about £400 per ha., but 2 ha. of it have good road frontage, and having been allocated on the Development Plan for development for residential purposes, would realise £40,000 per ha.

There are six cottages on the land, two let to tenants from the village at £2 per week each, two occupied by members of the outdoor staff of the house, and two let at 40p per week each to labourers employed on the grazing land.

The house, together with its gardens and outbuildings, would readily find a purchaser at £40,000.

There is no tithe redemption annuity. The commercial value of the timber is agreed at £400.

*Principal Value*
*Agricultural Property.*

|  | Agricultural Value | Open Market Value |
|---|---|---|
| *Land:* 16 ha. @ £400 per ha. ... ... | £6,400 | |
| 14 ha. @ £400 per ha. ... ... | | £5,600 |
| 2 ha. @ £40,000 per ha. ... ... | | £80,000 |
| *Woodlands:* 2 ha. @ " prairie value " of £20 per ha. ... ... ... ... | 40 | 40 |
| (*Note:* Commercial value of timber is omitted.) | | |
| *Cottages:* 2 occupied by labourers working on the land[15] (say £1,150 each)—additional value to persons other than estate workmen ignored ... ... ... ... | 2,300 | 2,300 |
| | £8,740 | £87,940 |

*Non-Agricultural Property.*

|  | | |
|---|---|---|
| *House:* (assuming that no case can be made for treating this as " agricultural property ") and 2 ha. ... ... ... ... ... | | £40,000 |
| *Cottages:* 4 worth, say, £275 each[16] ... | | £1,100 |
| *Principal Value* | | £129,040 |

The Excess Principal Value is:—£87,940 − £8,740 = £79,200

Duty at the estate rate for the estate will be payable on £120,300 (£129,040 − £8,740) and at the lower rate on £8,740.

(*d*) *Timber.*—It has already been explained that the commercial value of timber, trees, wood and underwood is deducted from the valuation of a property for probate purposes. Nor is the value of timber, etc., aggregated with that of the other assets in finding the total principal value of the estate for the purpose of fixing the rate of Estate Duty. The payment of death duties on timber is governed by the following rules:—[17]

(i) If timber, trees or wood (not including underwood) is felled and sold between the date of death and the next occasion on which the land becomes liable for estate duty, duty at the rate appropriate to the size of the deceased's estate will become payable on the net proceeds of sale, after deducting all necessary outgoings since the death of the deceased. No

---

[15] It is assumed that vacant possession can be obtained but that the cottages not limited to agricultural use would fetch £1,500 each.

[16] It is assumed that vacant possession cannot be obtained.

[17] Finance (1909-10) Act, 1910, Sec. 61 (5); Finance Act, 1912, Sec. 9.

duty is payable on timber, etc., not sold but used for estate repairs.

(ii) If, during the same period, timber is sold standing (with or apart from the land) duty is payable on the value of the timber at the date of death less any duty paid since that date on cuttings and sales.

The rate of duty in either case will be the full estate rate.

It is very desirable in practice to agree the value of the timber with the Inland Revenue as at the date of death. If this be done, an agreed figure is available for the application of rule (ii) above, while in the event of a number of cuttings and sales taking place between one death and the next the total amount of duty payable under rule (i) will be limited to the amount of duty on the agreed valuation. Liability to duty naturally only extends to timber on the land at the date of death. If new areas are planted, or existing woodlands replanted after felling, no liability for duty will arise in respect of sales from these areas until the land again passes on death.

(e) *Land or Buildings forming Part of the Assets of a Company.*—Section 66 of the Finance Act, 1960, provides that in determining the principal value of land or buildings occupied for the purposes of a trade or business carried on by a company, it must be assumed that the land or buildings could be used or occupied only for the purposes of that trade or business. This means that the value must be the going concern value and any higher break-up value of these assets must be ignored. Going concern value is discussed in Section 3 of this Chapter.

(f) *Industrial Property.*—Section 28 of the Finance Act, 1954, provides for a reduction of 45 per cent in the rates of Estate Duty chargeable in respect of industrial hereditaments or plant and machinery used for the purposes of a business, where the business or an interest in the business passes on a death. A business carried on in the exercise of a profession or vocation or carried on otherwise than for gain is excluded from this benefit.

### 3. Valuations on the Basis of a Going Concern

Valuations on the basis of a going concern are required for a number of purposes including Balance Sheet purposes and for an offer for Sales of Shares. A going concern value may be defined as the value of land, buildings and plant in the hands of a purchaser acquiring them as part of a business for which they are designed and used. Such a purchaser will have regard to the amount of profit which he will make out of the business and if the property, the subject of valuation, is not being put to its most profitable use, the going concern value may be lower than the market value.

The method of valuation usually employed is a combination of either a valuation by comparison or by the contractor's method and the profits method.

A ceiling figure is first fixed by comparison or by applying the contractor's theory to the land, buildings and plant. The reason for this is that no proprietor of a business would pay more for his premises than the amount he would have to pay for similar premises or than the amount they cost to construct. When valuing the land, the normal basis of comparison with similar sites would be employed. The value of the buildings would be found by direct capital comparison or by estimating the rental value and capitalising this by a figure of Years' Purchase, or if the contractor's method is employed by cubing the building and applying a suitable figure per unit cube or by reference to the area of floor space. If direct capital comparison is used it is usual to make the figure a full one. If the investment method is employed, both the rental value and the Years' Purchase are kept on the high side for this purpose and the resultant figure is often well above normal vacant possession value. The use of the contractor's method is tending to give way to a valuation by comparison. The value of the plant, equipment and machinery should be ascertained by reference to its replacement cost (as for a fire insurance valuation), allowance being made for its installation and connection to power supply, and for depreciation according to the amount of use it has had and with regard to the amount of maintenance it has received and to its degree of obsolescence. It is evident that the amount will vary in each individual case.

The resultant " ceiling figure " will have to be scaled down if the buildings are of bad lay-out and design and may have to be further reduced when regard is had to a valuation of the concern on a profits basis. Such a valuation would be made by estimating the amount of working capital required to run the concern and the amount of profits which might reasonably be expected from the concern under review. The amount of profits as shown in the accounts may be too high or too low and the valuer must be prepared to alter this figure to what he considers is a reasonable profit. The amount can be ascertained by reference to a rate of return or the amount of real capital employed in the business or by reference to turnover.

The amount of profits should then be expressed as a percentage of the working capital plus the ceiling figure. If the resultant percentage is less than the fair percentage of profit normally associated with the type of business being valued, then the ceiling figure should be reduced to such a figure as will give the normal rate of profit.

If a rental value is required, a valuation on the above lines should first be carried out. The ceiling figure should then be split up again into its component parts, each being reduced by a fraction, represented by the reduced figure over the full ceiling figure, if this latter is reduced when regard is had to the value by reference to profits. A suitable percentage can then be applied to each part to obtain a rental value.

If a leasehold value is required a rental value should first be ascertained and then capitalised by applying a suitable Years' Purchase.

> *Example.*—You are required to value a single-storey freehold factory in a provincial town, your valuation being required for balance sheet purposes on the basis of a going concern. The total floor space is 3,750 m² on a site of 0·5 ha. The buildings are some 10 years old and substantially built. It occupies a good position, all the usual services are connected.

*Valuation.*—Estimated rental value:—

| | |
|---|---|
| 3,750 m² @ £4 ... ... ... ... ... | £15,000 p.a. |
| Y.P. in perpetuity ... ... ... ... | 11 |
| | £165,000 |
| Add value of plant equipment and machinery, *say* ... ... ... ... ... ... | 15,000 |
| Total, | £180,000 |

The valuer would then have to decide on a reasonable amount of trading profits from such a concern, say £14,000, and on the total amount of working capital, say £25,000. £14,000 must then be expressed as a percentage of the ceiling figure plus the amount of working capital:—

$$\frac{14,000 \times 100}{35,000 + 180,000} = 6\tfrac{1}{2}\%$$

If $6\tfrac{1}{2}\%$ is equal to or greater than the fair annual percentage rate of profit, then the valuation can go in at its ceiling figure of £180,000, but if it is less than the real rate, the ceiling figure must be reduced.

Supposing that a fair rate in this instance was 8%, then the amount of working capital plus value of land, buildings, plant and machinery must total—

$$\frac{£14,000 \times 100}{8} = £175,000$$

The amount of working capital must be deducted from this sum, leaving the value of the land, buildings, plant and machinery at £140,000 (£175,000 – £35,000).

# Chapter 16

## Valuations for Rating

### 1. GENERALLY

LOCAL RATES are a charge levied as a general rule upon the occupiers of property in respect of the annual value of their occupation.

In order to ascertain the rate liability of a particular occupier, two things must be known. These are, firstly, the rating assessment of the occupied property expressed in terms of rateable value and secondly, the amount of rate in the pound in force in the rating area in which the property is situated. The rate is fixed periodically, usually annually, by the rating authority and is determined by its own financial needs and those of any precepting authorities. The making of assessments for rating purposes has, since 1950, been the responsibility of the Inland Revenue and it is with these assessments that this chapter is primarily concerned. It is not proposed to deal here with the history and development of the rating system, with the law of rateable occupation, or with procedural details.

### 2. PROCEDURE

The principal statute governing assessment and valuation procedure is the General Rate Act, 1967. It consolidated a number of previous Acts but did not introduce any new principles.

In London the Common Council of the City of London and the various Greater London Borough Councils are the rating authorities for their respective areas. Outside London, the rating authorities are the county and municipal boroughs, urban and rural district councils. Before 1950 the rating authorities were responsible both for making rating assessments and the collection of rates. Since the Inland Revenue became responsible for the making of assessments, the responsibilities of rating authorities have been confined largely to rates collection.

The rating assessments of all rateable hereditaments within a rating area are entered in the Valuation List for that area. The normal procedure is for new valuation lists to come into force every five years. The current list came into force on 1 April, 1963, but the revaluation which should have led to a new 1968 list was postponed and a new list will not now come into force until 1973.

Briefly the procedure for the preparation of a new valuation list is as follows. The Valuation Officer of the Inland Revenue sends out return forms, for completion by owners and occupiers, asking for details of such matters as the rent paid, length and date of grant of lease and repairing covenants. Hereditaments are then inspected and valuations prepared. The new list is drawn up and transmitted to the rating authority at whose offices it is available for inspection before coming into force on 1 April.

The Valuation Officer, the rating authority in certain specified circumstances and any person aggrieved on certain specified grounds may then, or at any time subsequently, make a proposal for the alteration of a current valuation list. Proposals, except where made by the Valuation Officer, must be served on the Valuation Officer and there is a right of objection. Appeal against an objection to a proposal lies normally in the first instance to the Local Valuation Court and thence to the Lands Tribunal. On questions of fact the decision of the Lands Tribunal is final but on matters of law appeal lies to the Court of Appeal and thence to the House of Lords.

## 3. EXEMPTIONS AND RELIEFS

Until 1963 only a very few persons were required to pay rates on the basis of a full net annual value. The occupiers of agricultural land and buildings were (and still are) entirely exempt. Many occupiers, such as those of industrial hereditaments, shops and offices, were relieved by way of a deduction from net annual value to arrive at rateable value. The occupiers of dwelling-houses were relieved because their assessments were related to 1939, instead of 1956 rental values. Charities and similar bodies were relieved on the actual amount of rates payable and may still receive relief although the method of giving it has changed.

The main object of the Rating and Valuation Act, 1961, the provisions of which are now incorporated in the General Rate Act, 1967, was to introduce some order and reason into reliefs and exemptions.

Details of reliefs and exemptions are not appropriate for inclusion in this book except where relief has been, or will be, afforded by way of direct adjustment of Rateable Value. Such reliefs will be referred to again later in this chapter.

## 4. STATUTORY BASIS OF ASSESSMENT

The assessment of the rateable value of a hereditament has to be made in accordance with the statutory provisions in Section 19 of the General Rate Act, 1967. This section uses the terms "Gross Value", "Net Annual Value", and "Rateable Value".

The ascertainment of Gross Value is the first step in the assessment of all properties consisting ". . . of one or more houses or other non-industrial buildings, with or without any garden, yard, court, forecourt, outhouse or other appurtenance belonging thereto, but without other land . . .". Appurtenance includes all land occupied with a house or school. It is thus relevant to houses, shops, offices, warehouses, hotels and public houses.

"Gross value" is defined in Section 19 (6) as "the rent at which a hereditament might reasonably be expected to let from year to year if the tenant undertook to pay all usual tenant's rates and taxes and the landlord undertook to bear the cost of the repairs and insurance and the other expenses, if any, necessary to maintain the hereditament in a state to command that rent".

In the case of the types of property mentioned above, the net annual value is obtained by deducting from the gross value a specific sum in respect of "repairs, insurance and other expenses". The sum to be deducted varies according to the amount of the gross value. These deductions are known as statutory deductions because they are laid down by the Valuation (Statutory Deductions) Order, 1962, and are as follows:

| Gross Value | Deductions from Gross Value |
|---|---|
| Not exceeding £55 ... | 45 per cent of the gross value. |
| Exceeding £55 but not exceeding £430 ... | £25 together with one-fifth of the amount by which the gross value exceeds £55. |
| Exceeding £430 ... | £100 together with one-sixth of the amount by which the gross value exceeds £430. |

In the case of other properties a Gross Value is not required but "Net Annual Value" must be estimated direct. The statutory definition of Net Annual Value in Section 19 (3) is "the rent at which it is estimated the hereditament might reasonably be expected to let from year to year if the tenant undertook to pay all usual tenant's rates and taxes and to bear the cost of the repairs and insurance and the other expenses, if any, necessary to maintain the hereditament in a state to command that rent". Although assessment directly to net annual value applies primarily to industrial properties it also applies to cemeteries, racecourses, caravan sites and similar hereditaments where the land (as distinct from the buildings) is the predominant factor.

Having determined the net annual value, either by deduction from gross value or direct, the rule now is that net annual value equals rateable value. Under the 1956 lists there were some exceptions to this rule when, for example, freight transport and industrial hereditaments were partly "derated" because they were relieved by way of a deduction from net annual value to obtain rateable value. The maximum deduction for the 1956 lists was at first 75 per cent, later reduced to 50 per cent. A smaller deduction, normally 20 per cent, was permitted for shops and offices. Although it does not affect the assessment of houses and flats, the General Rate Act, 1967, contains provisions for granting rate rebates to residential occupiers on grounds of hardship.

There are also provisions for a reduced rate-poundage to be levied in respect of dwelling-houses and for half of such reduction to be levied in respect of "mixed hereditaments". A mixed hereditament is one in respect of which the apportioned rateable value of the private dwelling is greater than the apportioned value of the part used for other purposes.

## 5. PRINCIPLES OF ASSESSMENT

There are certain general principles to be observed in preparing valuations for rating purposes, the most important of which are:

(i) The hereditament being valued must be assumed to be vacant and to let. The statutory definitions assume a tenancy and it is, therefore, necessary to assume that the hereditament is available so that the bid of the hypothetical tenant on the statutory terms can be ascertained.

(ii) The hereditament must be valued "*Rebus sic stantibus*" which means in its actual existing physical state. This rule does not, however, prevent the assumption of minor changes of a non-structural nature. The modernisation of a cottage or the erection of a garage together with access would not be possibilities which could be considered in estimating the rent. Furthermore, the mode or category of occupation by the hypothetical tenant must be conceived as the same mode or category as that of the actual occupier. Thus possible changes of use may be largely irrelevant. A local authority scheme which would involve disturbance at a sufficiently early date might affect the bid of a hypothetical tenant from year to year.

(iii) Prior to *Garton v. Hunter* (1968), if a property was let at what was plainly a rack rent, then that was the only permissible evidence. As a result of that decision, however, other evidence may be examined, and this includes rents passing on comparable properties.

(iv) Assessments on comparable properties may be considered in the absence of better evidence. In the case of dwelling-houses the General Rate Act, 1970, permits the rents of other dwelling houses of the same or a different description as relevant evidence, together with a consideration of the relationship between these rents and Gross Values. The intention seems to be to correct the present imbalance between the assessment of purpose-built flats which are generally fully and properly assessed and other houses, for example, suburban owner-occupied houses which appear to be under-assessed due to lack of rental evidence.

(v) A question of importance is the extent of the rateable here-ditament and whether separate assessments should be made in respect of different parts. The rateable unit will normally be taken as the whole of the land and buildings in the occupation of an occupier within a single curtilage. However, the Court of Appeal in *Gilbert v. Hickinbottom & Sons Ltd.* (1956) 49 R. & I.T. 231, ruled that a bakery and a building used for repairs essential for its efficient operation could constitute a single hereditament although separated by a highway as they were functionally essential to each other. It is not necessary for parts to be *structurally* severed to be capable of separate assessment if the parts are *physically* capable of separate occupation. From the valuation view-point, separate assessments usually, but not necessarily, result in a higher total assessment but this would be partly offset by higher statutory deductions where Gross Value is relevant. If parts are separately assessed and one part ceases to be in rateable occupation then there would normally be no liability for rates on that part.

## 6. METHODS OF ASSESSMENT

There are different methods of assessment but it is vital to bear in mind that whichever method may be used, the end product must be the rent on the basis of the statutory definition of either Gross Value or Net Annual Value. The definitions of these two values are the same except that Gross Value places the liability for repairs, insurance and other expenses necessary to maintain the hereditament on the landlord, whereas Net Annual Value places it on the tenant. Some comment, therefore, on the interpretation of these definitions of value is appropriate before considering actual methods of assessment.

The "rent" is not necessarily the rent actually paid, but the rent which a hypothetical tenant might reasonably be expected to pay. Hypothetical tenants would include all possible occupiers including the actual occupier.

A tenant from "year to year" can occupy the hereditament indefinitely, having a tenancy which will probably continue but which can be determined by notice.

"Usual tenants' rates and taxes" include general rates, water rates and occupiers drainage rate but not Schedule A Income Tax, Tithe Redemption Annuity and owner's drainage rate, which are landlord's taxes.

The question of lack of repair has been before the Courts on a number of occasions in recent years, particularly in relation to dwelling-houses. The general sense of the various decisions is that in assessing Gross Value the rental bid by the hypothetical tenant will be unaffected by lack of repair if the defects are capable of being remedied and might reasonably be expected to be remedied having regard to the age and character of the property. Thus, the landlord's repairing liability would involve putting the premises in a reasonable state of repair initially and thereafter keeping them in that condition and the hypothetical tenant would make his rental bid on this assumption. If, however, the state of the hereditament is such that a landlord would not consider putting it in repair but would accept a lower rent, then the lower rent would form the basis of the assessment.

Thus, generally, the state of repair of the hereditament is not relevant to arrive at Gross Value. The landlord's obligation to repair the hereditament would not extend to an approach road outside the hereditament and the tenant's bid would reflect his own liability to maintain such a road. In the case of a factory where Net Annual Value is obtained directly and the hypothetical tenant would be liable to repair, the state of repair would affect his rental bid.

The principal methods of assessment used are:

(a) by reference to rents paid, which is usually known as the rental method;
(b) the contractor's test;
(c) the profits test; and
(d) by formula.

The choice of method to be used is not necessarily a free one. For some types of hereditament a statutory formula is laid down or a Minister is empowered to make an order laying down the method of determining the assessment.

In cases where there is freedom of choice, the first three methods are appropriate but the general rule is that if the rental method can be used, it must be used in preference to the contractor's test or the profits test.

Their application to particular types of property is dealt with in section 9 of this chapter but a brief description of the first three methods is given here.

(a) *Valuation by reference to rents paid.*—In many cases the rent paid for the property being valued may be the best guide to a rating assessment. But Gross or Net Annual Value can only correspond with rents actually paid provided that (i) the rent represents the fair annual value of the premises at the relevant date and (ii) the terms on which the property is let are the same as those assumed in the statutory definition. The rent paid for any particular property will almost certainly be above or below the true rental value in cases where property has been let for some time and values in the district have since increased or decreased.

Again, properties are often let at a low rent in consideration of the lessee paying a premium on entry, or surrendering the unexpired term of an existing lease, or undertaking improvements or alterations to the premises. In the case of premiums or such equivalent sums, the rent must be adjusted for assessment purposes by adding to it the annual equivalent of the consideration given by the tenant for the lease. Such would not, however, apply if the premium was paid in respect of furniture or goodwill. A rent of business premises may also be low if a tenant's voluntary improvement under an earlier lease has been ignored under Section 34 of the Landlord and Tenant Act, 1954, as amended by the Law of Property Act, 1969.

If the tenant has carried out non-contractual improvements, the rental value of these improvements must also be added to the rent paid.

The rent paid may not be equal to the rental value because there is a relationship between the lessor and the lessee. A typical example is where the property is occupied by a limited liability company on lease from the freeholder who is a director of that company. Rents reserved in respect of lettings between associated companies are often not equal to the proper rental value. Sale-leaseback rents may also differ from rental value.

Adjustments may be necessary in cases where the terms of the tenancy differ from those of the statutory definition of Gross Value. A typical example is that of a shop let on lease, the lessee being responsible for all the repairs. In such a case the rent will certainly be lower than it would have been had the landlord been responsible for the repairs. An addition, in respect of the repairs, must therefore be made to the rent to obtain the Gross Value.

The relationship between rents in accordance with the statutory definitions and lease rents has been a subject of contention. It has been held by the Courts in a number of cases that rents on leases for up to 21 years did not differ materially from rents from year to year. However, these cases were not recent and now it may well be that a rent fixed for 21 years without rent review clauses would be held to differ from a rent from year to year, because the rent reserved over the earlier years of the lease would be high to balance a later expected profit rent.

In *Dawkins v. Ash Brothers* (1969), the House of Lords by a 3–2 majority decision held that the prospect of the demolition of part of the hereditament within a year was a factor which a hypothetical tenant would consider in making his rental bid. This resulted in a lower assessment but involved complex argument as to the point at which actual facts displaced the hypothetical circumstances to be considered in rating law.

Where the rent actually paid is above or below the rental value, or where a property is owner-occupied, a valuation must be made by comparing the property being valued with other comparable properties let at true rental values.

Sometimes a proper rent can be fixed by direct comparison with other similar properties. In other cases it may be necessary to use some convenient unit of comparison, such as the rent per square metre.

With certain special types of property a unit of accommodation rather than of measurement may be used, such as a figure per seat for theatres and cinemas.

When using the rents paid for other similar properties as a basis of assessment regard must be had to the terms on which those properties are let, and to making any necessary adjustments to those rents so that they conform with the applicable statutory definition.

Mention may also be made of the principle of "equation of rents". This is a theory based on the assumption that a tenant would pay only a fixed sum by way of rent and rates. If the rates increase substantially, as they did on industrial property as a result of the 1963 revaluation and the abolition of derating, then the rent should fall. This, however, may be very difficult to prove and in a case concerning the assessment of a large factory for the 1963 list, the Tribunal decided that there was no evidence of industrial rents falling after the 1963 revaluation.

(b) *The contractor's test.*—This method is used in cases where no rental evidence, either direct or indirect, is available. The theory behind the contractor's basis is that the owners, as hypothetical tenants, would in arriving at their bid, have regard to the yearly cost to them of acquiring the ownership of the hereditament. Examples of properties for which the contractor's basis is appropriate are public libraries, town halls, sewage disposal works, schools and crematoria. The method has also been used in the case of a motor racing track where no licence is required and there is no quasi-monopoly. If a quasi-monopoly exists as, for example, with a licensed hotel, then the profits basis would be appropriate.

The contractor's method was described in outline in Chapter 9 and is applied by taking a percentage of the effective capital value of the land and buildings to arrive at the annual value.

There are two possible methods of determining the effective capital value of buildings for this purpose:

(i) by reference to the cost, inclusive of fees, of reconstructing the existing building, known as the replacement cost approach. In the case of a new building the effective capital value might well be the actual cost of construction unless there was some form of surplusage, such as excess capacity or other disability, which would justify a reduction in that cost. With an older building, however, the cost of re-construction would have to be written down to take account of the age and obsolescence of the existing building. Excessive embellishment and ornamentation would normally have to be ignored as it is not something for which the hypothetical tenant would pay more rent.

(ii) by reference to the cost of constructing a simple modern building capable of performing the functions of the existing building, including fees, known as the "simple substitute building" approach. The cost, for example, of a school based on the present day price per student place as certified by the Minister of Education and Science would have to be written down to take account of the extent to which the existing building falls short of the standards of the new substitute building.

In either case the effective capital value which is required is the cost of a modern building less the necessary deductions in respect of disabilities so that the final figure obtained represents as nearly as practicable the value of the old building with all its disadvantages. To this figure must be added the effective capital value of the land, the value being assessed having regard to the existing buildings "*rebus sic stantibus*" and ignoring any prospective development.

The final stage in the valuation is the conversion of effective capital value into a rental value by the application of an appropriate percentage. The figure arrived at should correspond to the annual market value of the capital invested in the land and buildings. In *Coppin (V.O.) v. East Midlands Airport Joint Committee* (1970), concerning the assessment of the East Midlands Airport, Castle Donington, the Lands Tribunal in their decision referred to the fact that both valuers agreed that 5 per cent was the generally accepted rate to be applied to the effective capital value to arrive at Net Annual Value in the normal type of case. It was also mentioned that 3¾ per cent was the rate taken by valuation officers in the de-capitalisation of the effective capital value of non-commercial undertakings of local authorities such as sewage disposal works. In *Shrewsbury School (Governors) v. Hudd*, (1966) R.A. 439, concerning the rating of a public school, 3½ per cent of the cost of a substitute building, fees and site less 70 per cent for age and obsolescence formed the basis of the Lands Tribunal's decision, while in a cemetery and crematoria case, *Gudgion v. Croydon L.B.C.* (1970) R.A. 341, the Lands Tribunal adopted 3¾ per cent on replacement cost less surplusage and disabilities to arrive at Net Annual Value.

The *East Midlands Airport* decision is summarised below:

| | | | |
|---|---|---|---|
| Total Capital Cost of Airport | ... | ... | £1,239,000 |
| *Less* Excess costs | | | |
| (a) excess runway thickness and width. | | | |
| (b) cost of separately assessed hereditaments | ... ... | ... | 248,070 |
| | | | 990,930 |

(Continued overleaf.)

| | |
|---|---:|
| *Less* for "tone of the valuation list"—12½% | 123,866 |
| The reduction was made to convert 1964/65 costs to those appropriate to 1962/63. | |
| | 867,064 |
| *Less* for disabilities at the terminal building | 67,064 |
| | |
| Effective Capital Value ... | 800,000 |
| @ 3¾% ... ... | 30,000 N.A.V. |

("normal" rate of 5% adjusted to 3¾% to reflect the difficulties likely to be met by the hypothetical tenant during the build-up period because the airport was a new venture and did not become operational until April 1965)

It should be emphasised that ability to pay the resultant figure of rent arrived at by a contractors method valuation is a material factor.

(*c*) *The profits test.*—This method is also used only in the absence of rental evidence. The theory is that the hypothetical tenant would relate his rental bid to the profits he would be likely to make from the business he would conduct on the hereditament. It must be emphasised that the profits themselves are not rateable but that they are used as a basis for estimating the rent that a tenant would pay for the premises vacant and to let. Examples of properties to which the profits test may be applied are racecourses, licensed hotels, caravan sites and pleasure piers but the method is particularly applicable where there is a monopoly element and to public utility undertakings.

The method involves the use of the accounts of the actual occupier. From the gross receipts purchases are deducted, after they have been adjusted for variation of stock in hand at the beginning and end of the year, thus leaving the gross profit. Working expenses are then deducted. The residue known as the divisible balance, is divided between the tenant, for his remuneration and interest on his capital invested in the business as a first charge, the rates and the landlord by way of rent.

The tenant's share must be sufficient to induce him to take the tenancy, irrespective of the balance for rent and rates.

The final balance is rent, either on a Gross Value or Net Annual Value basis plus rates. The rates could not be deducted in making the valuation, even though the tenant is liable for their payment, because the amount of the rent and the rates are related to one another.

A profits valuation for the assessment of a licensed hotel to a Gross Value is set out in outline below. The method is similar when Net Annual Value is required directly, as in the case of a racecourse, but with the necessary additions to the working expenses to reflect the tenant's extra liabilities in respect of repairs and insurance of the hereditament.

*Licensed Hotel—Assessment to G.V.*

£

Receipts

*less*       Purchases     (adjusted for stock position)

——————

Gross Profit

*less* Working expenses, from the trading figures, which would be appropriate to a tenant from year to year occupying under the terms of Gross Value. The working expenses deducted may be adjusted, if necessary, to reflect those which the hypothetical tenant would allow and need not necessarily be those actually incurred.

——————

Divisible Balance

*less* Tenant's share consisting of:    (Tenant's share, rent on a
    (i) interest on his capital invested in   Gross Value basis and
        furniture, equipment, stock and   rates)
        working capital at, say, $7\frac{1}{2}\%$.
   (ii) remuneration for running the
        business (an assessed figure)

——————

G.V. and rates

——————

*N.B.*—1. The tenant's share is sometimes arrived at by taking a higher rate, say, $17\frac{1}{2}\%$, on his capital invested in the business to comprise both elements of his share.

2. An alternative method of assessing the tenant's share, which is sometimes used, is to take a percentage of the gross receipts.

3. The divisible balance is sometimes referred to as the amount available after interest on tenant's capital at say, $7\frac{1}{2}\%$, has been deducted.

A shortened version of the profits test is frequently used to value licensed premises, petrol stations, cinemas and theatres.

### 7.  DATE OF VALUATION AND TONE OF THE LIST

Uniformity of assessment is of paramount importance if an equitable distribution of the rate burden is to be ensured.  It is for this reason that periodical revaluations take place over the whole country. These should be made quinquennially but have often been made at less frequent intervals; they take effect from the same date.

Prior to the Local Government Act, 1966, however, proposals to amend, or add to, the valuation list necessitated in law that the valuation should be based on values prevailing at the date of the proposal. After the list had been in force for some time this would often have resulted in assessments being unfairly high because they would not have been in accordance with the "tone of the list", which means they would not have been consistent with assessments already entered in the list. In such cases the Inland Revenue policy was, in fact, to follow the "tone of the list" but such a course of action could not have been upheld successfully if it was an issue at the Local Valuation Court or the Lands Tribunal.

The position has been remedied by Section 20 of the General Rate Act, 1967, re-enacting a provision in the 1966 Act. Section 20 applies the "tone of the list" to all hereditaments except public utility undertakings valued on a profits basis.

The valuation "shall not exceed" the value of the hereditament as if it had been subsisting throughout the year before that in which the valuation list came into force, in which case it would have been valued at the general revaluation date on which the valuation list is based. If there has been a fall in values then the valuation would be made as at the date of the proposal. Regard is to be had to the state of the hereditament, locality, transport services and other local facilities and matters affecting local amenities at the date of the proposal. This necessitates a valuation of the hereditament on its current use and state in the context of the existing locality but based on rent levels of the current list.

The valuation of public houses must be based on the volume of trade carried on at the proposal date. Mineral valuations must be based upon the quantity of minerals extracted at the same date. In both cases the valuation will have regard to values adopted for the current valuation list.

## 8.   RATING OF UNOCCUPIED PROPERTIES

Due to the absence of beneficial occupation unoccupied properties are not normally rateable under general rating law. The General Rate Act, 1967, Section 17 and the 1st Schedule, re-enacting a provision in the Local Government Act, 1966, gives rating authorities a discretionary power to pass a resolution to levy rates on unoccupied properties. Such a resolution must apply to all hereditaments within its area and not, for example, only to offices. Half rates are payable by the owner in respect of the "relevant period of vacancy" which is after six months in the case of newly erected dwelling-houses and three months in the case of all other hereditaments.

## 9. Assessment of Various Types of Property

### (a) Agricultural properties.

Agricultural land and buildings are wholly exempt from rating under Section 26 (3) of the General Rate Act, 1967. "Agricultural land" is defined in Section 26 (3) as "any land used as arable meadow or pasture ground only, land used for a plantation or a wood or for the growth of saleable underwood, land exceeding one quarter of an acre used for the purpose of poultry farming, cottage gardens exceeding one quarter of an acre, market gardens, nursery grounds, orchards or allotments, including allotment gardens within the meaning of the Allotments Act, 1922, but does not include land occupied together with a house as a park, gardens (other than as aforesaid), pleasure grounds, or land kept or preserved mainly or exclusively for purposes of sport or recreation, or land used as a racecourse".

It will be noticed that the definition includes land used for a plantation or a wood or for the growth of saleable underwood but if such land is kept or preserved mainly or exclusively for the purposes of sport or recreation or otherwise excluded from the definition of "agricultural land", the exemption will not apply and the hereditament will be assessed in accordance with Section 27 to its value as if let and occupied in its natural and unimproved state. Where such land is used for the growth of saleable underwood then the rateable value will be the value as if let for that purpose.

"Agricultural buildings" are defined in Section 26 (4) as "buildings (other than dwellings) occupied together with agricultural land or being or forming part of a market garden, and in either case used solely in connection with agricultural operations thereon".

This definition has given rise to some litigation in recent years in connection with buildings used for modern intensive farming practices, particularly broiler houses. In a 1970 House of Lords decision, (*Eastwood v. Herrod (V.O.)*), Lord Reid thought that the test should be whether the buildings are subsidiary and ancillary to agricultural operations. The particular broiler houses, producing 150,000 birds per week, were in no sense ancillary and they were held to be rateable. The Rating Act 1971, however, extends the exemptions by amending the definitions of "agricultural buildings" and "agricultural land" in the General Rate Act so as to include buildings used solely for the keeping and breeding of livestock or for that use together with some agricultural use provided that they are surrounded by or adjoin an area of not less than five acres of agricultural land.

Dwellings are specifically excluded from the definition of agricultural buildings in Section 26 (4), but special provision is made for a house occupied in connection with agricultural land and used by a person primarily in carrying on or directing agricultural operations on the land, or employed in agricultural operations on the land and entitled to occupy the house only while so employed. In such a case, Section 26 (2) provides that the Gross Value must be estimated on the assumption that the house could not be used otherwise than as an agricultural dwelling-house.

There is little or no evidence of the letting of houses within this statutory definition. Assessments are, therefore, arbitrary, often being arrived at by making a deduction (10 per cent is used in some cases) from the estimated rental value of similar houses not occupied in connection with agriculture in order to allow for the statutory restriction.

### (b) Dwelling-houses.

For the purpose of the 1956 lists the Gross Value of dwelling-houses had to be related to the 1939 rents. For the 1963 lists they were valued in accordance with the statutory definition of Gross Value on the basis of the current rents.

The assessments of dwelling-houses in the 1963 lists are considered to be unsatisfactory. This is due to a lack of evidence of rents particularly in suburban areas where the vast majority of houses are owner-occupied. This lack of evidence has led to a disparity between the assessments of houses and purpose-built flats for which the necessary rental evidence existed. The case of *R. v. Paddington Valuation Officer ex parte Peachey Property Corporation Ltd.* (1965) is of interest in this connection because it deals with an attempt to have the 1963 Paddington Valuation List set aside on the grounds of such inconsistencies.

The position is further aggravated by the fact that rents under the Rent Acts are not conclusive evidence of value for rating purposes. (*Poplar A.C. v. Roberts*, 1922.) It may be that the General Rate Act, 1970, referred to in Section 5 (iv) of this chapter will prove helpful in securing more consistency by making better use of available evidence.

One solution, to utilise available evidence, may be to assess certain types of dwelling-houses on the "fair rents" registered under the Rent Act, 1968, adjusted as necessary, to conform to a letting on terms of Gross Value but a revision of law would be necessary so that Gross Value would similarly exclude scarcity. The Lands Tribunal have discouraged the use of evidence of capital values in the assessment of dwelling-houses and flats and there are, indeed, difficulties in establishing a relationship between rental values and capital values of owner-occupied houses due particularly to personal tax advantages in buying rather than renting. Furthermore, the state of repair is relevant to a sale price but may be irrelevant to Gross Value.

With a view to securing uniformity of assessment, valuers usually adopt the method of analysing the rents of houses in a particular area or locality and reducing them to a "datum" figure for Gross Value of so much per square unit of floor space.

This type of analysis of a number of rents might indicate a datum figure for a particular road of, say, £4 per square metre. In assessing the individual houses in the road it may be necessary to vary this figure since one house, for example, may have advantages of central heating or planning which are not reflected in the datum figure. The use of a common datum figure, however, helps to secure some measure of uniformity.

The method of analysis and application varies in practice. Some valuers prefer to utilise outside measurements of the building for quick and easy comparison to arrive at a "reduced covered area" (R.C.A.), while other valuers adopt as a basis the "effective floor area" (E.F.A.).

The danger of these methods is that, if applied too rigorously and without proper discretion, they may result in an old-fashioned badly-planned house being assessed at a higher figure than a modern, conveniently planned house which, although possessing less floor space, is much more attractive to prospective tenants and would therefore command a higher rent.

In any case, the value of the house must be considered in con-junction with the garden, garages, outbuildings and grounds with which it is enjoyed.

The methods used for the assessment of cottages and tenements let on weekly tenancies at inclusive rents do not differ in principle from those applied to dwelling-houses generally except that the amount of the rates and water rate which are paid by the landlord must be deducted from the rent in order to obtain the Gross Value.

*(c) Blocks of Offices and Flats.*

Consideration of the rents actually paid, checked by comparison with rents paid for other similar premises, usually provide a basis of valuation.

With many properties of this type, the landlord is responsible for some or all of the repairs including repairs to the common parts, such as halls and stairways and for the provision of services, such as central heating and hot water, lifts, lighting and cleaning the common parts and for porters and lift attendants. Tenants will pay either rents inclusive of services or separate service charges in addition to the rent.

A normal method of valuation is to find the gross rents from the block, adjust them to bring them to terms of gross value and then deduct the cost of providing the services. The difference is the aggregate gross value of the block and this should be apportioned between the various flats or office suites. The deduction in respect of services would include normal items such as wages and insurance of employees, the running costs of lifts, lighting and cleaning the common parts and a sum for supervision of the services.

Section 23 of the General Rate Act, 1967, applies in all cases where rents are inclusive of services, including the repair, maintenance or insurance of premises not forming part of that hereditament, or where separate service charges are made for such services in addition to the rents. In this latter case, the rent must be treated as increased by the amount of any service charge. The amount deducted from the rent for the cost of services must not include the cost of repairs, maintenance and insurance of the common parts including rateable plant and machinery, or in respect of profit on the services. For this reason it will be understood that repairs to boilers and the cost of a sinking fund to replace the boilers have been held to be costs which may not be deducted because the boilers formed part of the common part of the hereditament. Costs of repairs of a rateable passenger lift have similarly been held not to be deductible. Management costs on services are deductible but rent collection costs are not.

*(d) Shops.*

The assessment of shops is governed mainly by consideration of the rents actually paid. In principle, if a property is let at a market rent, then that rent, adjusted if necessary to conform to the definition of Gross Value, should form the basis of the assessment.

If a shop is let on a full repairing and insuring lease, an addition to the rent of 10 per cent is usually made to convert it into a rent on terms of Gross Value. If the tenant is responsible only for internal repairs, the rent is usually increased by 5 per cent. Such a general practice may be considered too arbitrary and should not be adopted if other figures can be justified. An addition to the rent must also be made for any tenant's expenditure such as the installation of a shop front, particularly in the case of a new shop where the tenant leases and pays rent for only a "shell" and covenants to complete and fit out the shop. It might be thought that the allowance for such expenditure should be obtained by decapitalising at dual rates with allowance for income tax on the sinking fund. The position is by no means clear, however, as in *Caltex Trading and Transport Co. v. Cane (V.O.)* 1962, the Lands Tribunal considered that only simple interest on expenditure was correct while in 1967 they agreed with the use of dual rates but excluded allowing for the effect of income tax on sinking fund as a factor which the tenant would not consider (*F. W. Woolworth & Co. Ltd. v. Peck (V.O.)*, 1967). The use of simple interest only gives the lowest addition to the rent paid while the use of dual rates with allowance for tax gives the highest. The final figure obtained, in any event, should be the rent which the hypothetical tenant would pay for the completed shop on the basis of the statutory definition. Any necessary adjustment for repairs undertaken by the tenant must be applied to the rent after it has been increased by allowing for tenant's expenditure.

Shops only a short distance apart can vary considerably in rental value because of vital differences in their positions. Any factor influencing pedestrian flow past the shop has its effect on value, such as proximity to "multiples", adequate and easy car parking or public transport, the position of shopping "breaks" (for example a brick wall in the middle of an otherwise continuous parade of shops), bus stops and traffic lights and the widths of pavements and streets.

In practice, certain recognised methods of valuation are used with the object of promoting uniformity and facilitating comparison between different properties.

A method in general use for valuing the ground floor of a shop, which is usually a very much more valuable part than the rest of the premises, is the "zoning" method. The front of the shop is the most valuable part and the value per unit of area decreases as the distance away from the front of the shop increases until a point is reached beyond which any further reduction would not be sensible. The zoning method allows for this progressive decrease in value from the front to the rear.

The first step in the analysis of a rent paid for premises including a ground floor shop is to deduct the rent attributable to all ancillary accommodation, leaving that paid for the ground floor selling space only. This rent is then broken down on the assumption that the front part of the shop, back to a certain depth, is worth the maximum figure, say £x per unit of area, the next portion $£\frac{x}{2}$ per unit of area, the next portion $£\frac{x}{4}$ and so on. This process, known as "halving back" is used most extensively but can be varied.

The depth of each zone varies according to circumstances and valuers have different opinions as to the most suitable depths to be used. The choice of the depths of zones should, however, be logical and governed by the depths of the shops under review, as it is pointless to halve back after 7 metres if the minimum depth of any shop under consideration is 10 metres. In the past, for example, some valuers have taken a depth of 15 feet for the first zone and 25 feet for the second while others have divided the shop into zones each 20 feet deep.

The first zone is measured backwards from the front of the shop, which is usually the glass window. This zone may therefore consist entirely of shop front, arcades and show cases. The zoning method is not normally applied to the upper floors, a value per unit applying over the whole area.

The Lands Tribunal have indicated that in their opinion the number and depths of the zones to be adopted is not so important provided that the zoning method is applied correctly and consistently according to the actual depths of the shops whose rents are being devalued and that the same method is applied subsequently when valuing (*Marks & Spencer v. Collier (V.O.)*, 1966, R.A. 107).

When a large shop is being valued on the basis of rental information derived from smaller shops, a "quantity allowance" is sometimes made in the form of a percentage deduction from the resulting valuation of the large shop. This procedure may be justified on the grounds that there is a limited demand for large shops and that therefore a landlord may have to accept a rather lower rent per unit of area than he would for a small shop. This may be valid when a large shop is in what is basically a small shop position but it is probably invalid when it is in that part of a shopping area where large chain stores have established themselves. For this reason, the Lands Tribunal rejected quantity allowances on two shops in Brighton in 1958, in assessments for the 1956 list. (*British Home Stores Ltd. v. Brighton C.B.C. and Burton; Fine Fare Ltd. v. Burton and Brighton C.B.C.* (1958), 51 R. & I.T. 665.) More recently, in a 1963 list reference, concerning a new store built for *Marks & Spencer* in Peterborough and their old store, which they had sold to Boots, the Lands Tribunal refused quantity allowances on the ground that the limited demand and limited supply of large shops was in balance. (*Marks & Spencer Ltd. v. Collier (V.O.)* 1966, R.A. 107.) Furthermore, in *Trevail v. C. & A. Modes Ltd.* and *Trevail v. Marks & Spencer Ltd.* (1967), R.A. 124, the Lands Tribunal expressed doubts as to whether the zoning method was not being stretched beyond its capabilities in the valuation of these large walk-round stores.

Apart from a possible quantity allowance, a disability allowance may be an appropriate deduction in the case of shops with disadvantages such as obsolete lay-out, inconvenient steps, excessive or inadequate height, lack of rear access, inadequacy of toilets or large and obstructive pillars, if their values have been based on those of shops without such disabilities.

In order to be able to check an assessment of a particular shop to see if it is fair by comparison with the assessments of other neighbouring shops, it is essential to be at least reasonably conversant with the neighbouring shops.

The following example illustrates the method of analysing the rent of premises comprising a ground floor shop and two upper floors occupied together with the shop for residential purposes. The analysis is made to ascertain the rental value per unit of area of the front zone of the shop so that it can be compared with the rents of other shops. It is not in this case considered likely that there would be any doubt about the correctness of the figure used for valuing the upper floors.

*Example*

Shop premises comprising a ground floor "shell" and two upper floors situated in a good position in a large town, were let during the year immediately preceding the coming into force of the valuation list at £1,800 per annum on a full repairing and insuring lease for 7 years. The tenant spent £1,000 on a shop front and other finishings. Analyse this rent for the purpose of rating assessments. The shop has a frontage of 6 metres and a depth of 20 metres. The net floor area of the residential first and second floors are 50 square metres each.

*Analysis*

|  |  |  |
|---|---|---|
| Rent reserved ... ... | £1,800 |

*Add*
Annual equivalent of cost of shop front and finishings provided by the tenant— £1,000

Y.P. 7 yrs. @ 8% & 2½% (tax 38·75%)

$$= \frac{£1,000}{3\cdot 38} \qquad ... \quad ... \quad ... \quad ... \quad ... \quad ... \qquad 296$$

2,096

*Add*
10% for tenant's full repairing liability ... ... 210

Full rental value on terms of Gross Value ... ... £2,306

*Deduct*
Rental value of upper floors on terms of Gross Value
100 sq. metres @ £3·50 per sq. metre ... ... 350

Leaving for shop rental value on terms of Gross Value £1,956

Measurement shows that the effective net area of the shop is as follows:

First 7 metres (often referred to as Zone 'A') 42 sq. metres;
Second 7 metres (often referred to as Zone 'B') 40 sq. metres;
Remaining 6 metres (often referred to as Zone 'C') 32 sq. metres.

Let £x per square metre represent the rental value of the first zone and adopting "halving back":

$$\text{then } 42x + \frac{40x}{2} + \frac{32x}{4} = £1,956$$

$$70x = £1,956$$

$$x = £28 \text{ approximately Zone A rental value per sq. metre on terms of Gross Value.}$$

This figure can then be compared with other Zone A rents based on the letting of similar shops in the vicinity to assist in obtaining a rent which represents a fair and consistent basis for the assessment of the shops under consideration.

A more convenient approach is that of reducing areas to "equivalent Zone A" areas. Using the above facts, the total area of 42 + 40 + 32 sq. metres (114 sq. metres) is expressed as:

$$\text{Zone A} \quad 42$$
$$\text{Zone B} \quad 20 \left[\frac{40}{2}\right]$$
$$\text{Zone C} \quad 8 \left[\frac{32}{4}\right]$$

Equivalent Zone A area $= 70$ sq. metres

The analysis then becomes $\dfrac{\pounds1,956}{70}$

$= \pounds28$ approximately as above.

It must be emphasised that the zoning method, although used very commonly in practice, is merely a means to an end in order to find the true rental value. The fixing of zone depths and the allocation of values to the zones are arbitrary processes and strict adherence to an arbitrary pattern may result in absurd answers in particular cases.

On the other hand, the method is based on a sound practical principle, namely, that the front portion of a shop, including the windows, is the part which attracts the most customers and is therefore the most valuable part. Consequently a shop with moderate but adequate depth is likely to have a higher overall-rental per unit of floor space than one with the same frontage but a much greater depth. Similarly, a shop with a frontage of 7 metres and a depth of 15 metres may be worth £2,000 per annum but an adjoining shop with the same frontage of 7 metres and otherwise identical but with double the depth, i.e., 30 metres, will be found to be worth considerably less than £4,000 per annum.

### (e) Factories and Warehouses.

Factories are industrial buildings being "factories, mills and other premises of a similar character used wholly or mainly for industrial purposes"[1]. They are assessed directly to Net Annual Value which is a rent on a full repairing basis. Warehouses, which are non-industrial buildings, require a Gross Value. Both are usually

---

[1] Sec. 19 (6), General Rate Act, 1967.

assessed by reference to effective floor space, the value per square metre being fixed by comparison with other similar properties in the neighbourhood. In some cases a flat rate per unit of floor space may be used throughout the building but in other cases it may be more appropriate to vary the rate applied to each floor.

Properties of this type differ considerably in such matters as construction, accommodation, planning and situation. Any special advantages or disadvantages attaching to the property under consideration must be very carefully examined when applying rents of other similar properties. Particular factors affecting rental values are the proximity of motorways or rail facilities, availability of labour, internal layout, nature of access to upper floors, loading and unloading facilities, natural lighting, heating, ventilation, adequacy of toilets, nature of ancillary offices, canteen facilities, availability of public transport and car parking for staff.

There may be no general demand for factories of highly specialised types in some areas and therefore no evidence of rental values which could be used as a basis for comparison. With such cases it may be necessary to resort to the contractor's test by taking an appropriate percentage of the effective capital value of the land and buildings as a method of obtaining the Net Annual Value.

Plant and machinery is only to be taken into account in the rating assessment if it is deemed to be a part of the hereditament. Section 21 and the 3rd Schedule of the General Rate Act, 1967, specify that five classes of plant and machinery are deemed to be a part of the hereditament and therefore rateable. They are:

*Class* 1.  Machinery and plant used mainly or exclusively for:

    (*a*)  the generation, storage, primary transformation or main transmission of power, or

    (*b*)  the heating, cooling, ventilating, lighting, draining or supplying of water to the hereditament or protecting it from fire.

However, machinery used for manufacturing or trade processes is not included even if used for the purposes specified in (*b*) above.

*Class* 2.  Lifts and elevators mainly or usually used for passengers.

*Class* 3.  Railway and tramway lines and tracks.

*Class* 4.  Plant or machinery, or any part thereof, in the nature of a building or structure including gas holders, blast furnaces, coke ovens, tar distilling plants, cupolas or water towers with tanks.

*Class* 5.  Pipelines, excluding drains, sewers, gas and electricity pipes and pipes forming part of the equipment of and within a factory or petrol storage depot or premises comprised in a mine, quarry or mineral field.

Section 21 (4) gives the Minister power to particularise by means of a Statutory Order the specific items of plant and machinery which fall within any of these five classes. Classes 1 to 4 form the subject of the Plant and Machinery (Rating) Order, 1960.

The effect of these provisions is that the rent to be ascertained is that which a tenant would pay for the land and buildings, including rateable plant and machinery, in accordance with the statutory definition.

There may be no difficulty in assessing the rental value, on a unit of floor space basis, of premises including certain rateable plant and machinery such as sprinkler and heating systems. Other rateable plant and machinery may have to be valued separately from the land and buildings on the contractor's test by adopting as its rental value a percentage of its effective capital value. The percentage of the effective capital value to be taken to obtain the rental value will normally be related to the economic life of the plant and machinery. The shorter the life, the higher the percentage that will be justified.

Three further points hould be noted. They are:

(1) Rateable plant and machinery is not restricted to that found on industrial hereditaments except for Class 5 (pipelines), for example, a passenger lift in a department store is rateable.

(2) The statutory provisions regarding plant and machinery do not apply to a valuation made on a profits basis.

(3) The Valuation Officer, if asked to do so by the occupier, must inform him what plant and machinery he has included in his valuation.

It is still necessary to determine, whether or not hereditaments are "factories, mills and other premises of a similar character used wholly or mainly for industrial purposes", despite the abolition of industrial derating, as these will not require a Gross Value.

## (f) Special Properties.

### 1. Schools

Section 30 of the General Rate Act, 1967, requires the assessment of county and voluntary schools to be made on a formula basis related to a contractor's test. The necessary details regarding the "average cost of providing a place for one pupil" are provided by the Secretary of State for Education and Science. It is from this figure that the Gross Value of the school can be assessed by means of a modified contractor's test valuation. Section 30 also states that regulations may provide that land forming part of, or occupied with, such schools shall be treated as a separate hereditament for rating purposes.

The rating of other schools is not governed by a formula basis and it will probably be necessary to resort to a contractor's test.

Thus, in a 1963 list reference concerning the assessment of Shrewsbury School, a large public school, the Lands Tribunal preferred the contractor's test to a valuation based upon a value per pupil place, although the latter figure can be useful as a comparison between schools. The Gross Value determined by the Lands Tribunal represented £32·50 per equivalent boarding pupil.[2]

## 2. Cinemas and Theatres.

A method of valuation which has been approved by the Lands Tribunal is a quasi-profits or takings method. It involves finding the gross receipts from the sale of seats based upon the estimated number of full houses per week plus, for example, the takings from bingo, advertising and the sale of ice cream, cigarettes and sweets. A percentage of this total figure is then taken to obtain the gross value. An alternative method of making the assessment is to relate it to a price per seat but very wide variations can be found in analysing assessments on this method.

## 3. Licensed Premises.

The method of valuation for rating purposes is a shortened profits method and this is dealt with in detail in Chapter 27.

## 4. Hereditaments occupied by Gas Authorities, Electricity Boards and Statutory Water Undertakings. Railway and Canal Premises.

Premises occupied by Gas and Electricity Boards are excluded from rating by Sections 33 and 34 of the General Rate Act, 1967, respectively, but there are certain exceptions in Sections 33 (2) and 34 (2), such as showrooms and offices not situated on operational land. These properties will need to be assessed in the normal way. Both industries make payments in lieu of rates to rating authorities.

Section 31 and the 4th Schedule of the Act deal with premises occupied for the purposes of Statutory Water Undertakings. These are rateable in accordance with a statutory formula.

Hereditaments occupied for the purposes of the British Railways Board, London Transport Executive or the British Waterways Board are dealt with in Section 32 and the 5th Schedule of the Act. Except for some important exceptions mentioned in Section 32 (2), such as dwelling-houses, hotels, places of public refreshment or premises so let out as to be capable of separate assessment, they are exempt from rating but the owners make payments, in lieu of rates, to the rating authorities.

## 5. Caravan Sites.

A site used for the parking of caravans is normally assessed as a caravan site only. If, however, the caravans remain for a long enough period to constitute the necessary degree of permanence, they may themselves become rateable with the land.

[2] *Shrewsbury School (Governors) v. Hudd* (1966), R.A. 139.

Caravan sites are normally assessed by a profits test. A Lands Tribunal decision on a 1963 list reference,[3] is summarised below:

| | |
|---|---|
| Gross receipts from let outs ... ... ... | £31,050 |
| *Less* Working Expenses ... ... ... ... | 11,050 |
| | |
| Gross Profit ... ... ... ... ... ... | £20,000 |
| *Less* Tenant's share—the Tribunal preferred to assess a figure, £10,000 in this case, rather than adopt a percentage of the gross receipts or of the divisible balance. It is, incidentally, 50% of the Gross Profit or a little over 32% of the gross receipts ... ... ... ... ... | 10,000 |
| | |
| Rent and Rates ... ... ... ... ... | 10,000 |
| *Less* Rates 10s. in the £1 on £6,667 ... ... | 3,333 |
| | |
| | 6,667 |
| *Add* Agreed rateable values of facility buildings | 1,350 |
| | |
| Net Annual Value ... ... ... ... ... | £8,017 |

### 6. *Garage and Service Stations.*

These are normally valued on a direct profits basis. The rental value depends primarily on throughput, being the quantity of petrol sold. A rental value for a certain throughput (per thousand gallons for the 1963 list) is taken to represent the tenant's bid on the terms of Gross Value. The figure varies on a sliding scale which increases with throughput as the tenants overheads would be proportionately less as the trade increases. The Gross Value thus arrived at allows for the petrol sales area only. Additions to this rent would need to be made for such other buildings and land as storerooms, showrooms, lubrication bays and workshops.

For the 1963 valuation lists, the Lands Tribunal in *Petrofina (Great Britian)* v. *Dalby* (1967), R.A. 143, took a tenant's bid of £3·50 per 1,000 gallons based upon a throughout in that case of 135,000 gallons per annum.

---

[3] *Garton v. Hunter (V.O.)*, 1969.

# Chapter 17

## Capital Gains Tax and Income Tax Schedules A & B

### 1. CAPITAL GAINS TAX ON LAND AND BUILDINGS

#### 1. TAXATION OF CAPITAL GAINS—GENERALLY

TRADING GAINS, including capital gains, made in the ordinary course of a business will be assessed under Schedule D, Cases 1 or 2, except that woodlands may be assessed under Schedule B. Individuals will be liable for income tax and, where appropriate, surtax, and companies for corporation tax.

Liability for tax on other gains of a capital nature may arise under capital gains tax legislation.

Short term capital gains tax was introduced by the Finance Act, 1962, and amended by the Finance Act, 1965. Thereafter it related only to gains made within a period of twelve months and such a capital gain made by an individual was subject to income tax and, where appropriate, surtax. A company paid corporation tax on both short term and long term capital gains. The Finance Act, 1971, however, abolished short term capital gains tax and all capital gains are now dealt with under the long term capital gains tax provisions of the Finance Act, 1965.

Long term capital gains tax was introduced under the Finance Act, 1965. It was originally charged on the total amount of long term gains, that is, gains on disposals more than one year from acquisition, which accrue in a year of assessment after deductions have been made for any allowable losses. Long term capital gains tax was generally more favourable to a taxpayer, particularly a surtax payer, as it was charged at a flat rate of 30 per cent, or less (see 2 (*b*) below).

#### 2. LONG TERM CAPITAL GAINS TAX UNDER THE FINANCE ACT, 1965

(*a*) *Exempted Bodies*

Certain bodies are exempt from liability including charities, local authorities, trade unions, friendly societies and scientific research associations and superannuation funds.

(*b*) *Rate of Tax*

Tax is at a flat rate of 30 per cent. The effective rate to a person paying tax at the standard rate, however, is less as there is an alternative basis of charge available—this is that one half of any

271

gain, up to a maximum gain of £5,000 and the whole of any gain over £5,000 is treated as additional unearned income and taxed accordingly. If the total gain in any one year does not exceed £500, no tax is payable.

The profits of companies for corporation tax purposes include any capital gains. Gains are assessed in the same way as they would be for an individual.

### (c) Occasions of Charge

Capital gains tax is payable on all chargeable gains accruing after 6 April, 1965, on the disposal of all forms of assets including freehold and leasehold property, options and incorporeal hereditaments.

An asset may be disposed of by sale, exchange or gift. Disposal also includes part disposals and circumstances where a capital sum is derived from an asset.

A part-disposal arises not only when part of a property is sold but also when a lease is granted at a premium. By accepting a premium the landlord is selling a part of his freehold interest and the lessee is purchasing a profit rent. Premiums may thus be liable to income tax under the Income and Corporation Taxes Act, 1970, which deals with taxation of premiums and to capital gains tax under the Finance Act, 1965. The Act contains provisions for avoiding double taxation on any part of the premium.

A capital sum is derived from an asset when the owner obtains a capital sum from it. Thus it would include payments received to release another owner from a restrictive covenant or to release him from the burden of ancient lights and would also include compensation received for injurious affection on compulsory purchase.

It also includes capital sums received under a fire insurance policy, although if the money is wholly or substantially applied to restore the asset no liability will arise.

### (d) Exemptions and reliefs affecting property.

1. Owner-occupied houses.

Exemption from capital gains tax is given to an owner in respect of a gain accruing from the disposal of a dwelling-house (including a flat) which has been his only or main residence, together with garden and grounds up to one acre or such larger area as may be appropriate to the particular house. The exemption does not apply, however, if the intention of the transaction was to realise a capital gain (Finance Act, 1968, Schedule 12, para. 2).

The degree of exemption is proportionate to the period of owner-occupation during ownership. Full exemption is given if the owner has lived in the house throughout the whole of his period of ownership. To cover the circumstances where a house is vacant after the owner has moved and is looking for a purchaser, the exemption includes the last twelve months of ownership. Certain other periods of absence have also to be disregarded under the Act.

Thus, if a property is sold and was not owner-occupied for the whole period of ownership, the degree of exemption depends upon the ratio between the period of owner-occupation (including in any event the last twelve months of ownership) and the total period of ownership.

If, therefore X buys a house on 1 April, 1966, and lives in it for two years until 1 April, 1968, when he lets it, subsequently selling the house on 1 April, 1972, the proportion of any capital gain which is exempt from capital gains tax is:

$$\frac{2+1}{6} = \frac{1}{2}$$

Where premises are used partly as a dwelling and partly for other purposes, the exemption applies only to the residential part and it will be necessary to apportion any capital gain on the whole property between the two portions.

The exemption also applies to one other house which is occupied rent free by a dependent relative and also where trustees dispose of a house which has been occupied by the beneficiary under the trust.

2. Replacement of business assets.

Where trade assets, including fixed plant and machinery and goodwill are sold and the whole of the proceeds devoted to the replacement of the assets, the trader may claim to defer any capital gains tax which ordinarily may have been payable on the sale. Section 33 provides that instead, he may choose to have the actual purchase price of the replacement assets written down by the amount of any capital gain on the sale of the original assets. This process may be repeated on subsequent similar transactions so that tax on the accumulated capital gain will not be paid until the assets are sold and not replaced. To qualify for this relief, the acquisition of the new assets must be within a period commencing twelve months before and ending twelve months after the sale of the old assets. Section 33 also deals with circumstances where not all the proceeds of sale are re-invested.

*Example*

X purchases a freehold shop in 1967 for £8,000, the expenses of acquisition being £300 and commences trading as a grocer. In 1971, he sells this shop for £10,000, his expenses of sale being £400. He immediately purchases a new shop for £11,000, incurring expenses of £600 and continues in business in the same trade.

X may claim relief from the payment of tax in 1971 on the sale for £10,000 but the cost of acquisition of the new shop will be dealt with as follows:

|  | Sale price | ... | ... | | £10,000 |
|---|---|---|---|---|---|
| *Less* | 1967 Cost ... ... ... | | ... | £8,000 | |
| | Expenses of purchase ... | ... | ... | 300 | |
| | Expenses of sale ... | ... | ... | 400 | |
| | | | | | 8,700 |
| | Chargeable Gain ... | ... | ... | | 1,300 |
| | Cost of replacement asset | ... | ... | | 11,000 |
| *Less* | gain on sale of old asset | ... | ... | | 1,300 |
| | Notional cost of replacement asset ... | | ... | | £9,700 |

If the replacement shop was sold in 1976 for £14,000, the expenses of sale being £800, the owner then ceasing to continue in business, liability to capital gains tax would then arise as follows:

|  | Sale price ... | ... | | £14,000 |
|---|---|---|---|---|
| *Less* | Notional acquisition price ... | ... | £9,700 | |
| | Expenses of acquisition ... | ... | 600 | |
| | Expenses of sale ... ... | ... | 800 | |
| | | | | 11,100 |
| | Chargeable gain... ... ... | ... | | £2,900 |

He may, however, be eligible for relief from this charge if he retired on the disposal (see 3 below).

3. Transfer of a business on retirement.

On retirement between the ages of 60 and 65, an owner may be exempted from capital gains tax on gains of up to £10,000 which accrue to him from the disposal by way of sale or gift of a family business or of shares or securities in a family trading company. He must have been in the business for ten years or more. The full exemption of £10,000 is only given if the owner is 65 years of age or over. A sliding scale operates between 60 and 65 years of age.

(e) *Computation of gains.*

The general rule applicable to the disposal of non-wasting assets, which include freeholds and leases with more than 50 years unexpired is that in arriving at the net chargeable gain certain items of allowable expenditure are deductible from the consideration received on disposal. These items are:

(1) the price paid for the asset together with incidental costs wholly and exclusively incurred for the acquisition.

(2) expenditure wholly and exclusively incurred in disposing of the asset. This includes legal and surveyor's fees, stamp duty, advertising costs and any capital gains tax valuation fees.

(3) additional expenditure to enhance the value of the asset and reflected in the asset at the disposal date, including expenditure on establishing, preserving or defending title.

Any item allowed for revenue taxation cannot be allowed and thus only items of a capital nature are deductible. Special rules apply where expenditure has been met out of public funds.

Certain of the above-mentioned items will need to be apportioned in the case of a part disposal.

A capital loss might arise as a result of a disposal and would be allowable if a gain on the same transaction would have been chargeable. The loss would normally be set off against gains accruing in the same year of assessment but if in a particular year losses exceed gains, the net loss can be carried forward and set off against gains accruing in the following year.

*(f) Part disposals.*

The rule for calculating any gain or loss on a part disposal is that only that proportion of the allowable expenditure which the value of the part disposed of bears at the date of disposal to the value of the whole asset can be set against the consideration received for the part. Thus it is necessary to value the whole asset and this necessitates a valuation of the retained part. The proportion disposed of is then:

$$\frac{\text{Consideration on part disposal}}{\text{Consideration on part disposal} + \text{value of retained part}}$$

Thus if X buys an asset in 1967 for £10,000, including costs and later sells part of it for £6,000, no disposal costs being involved, the first step is to value the part retained, say £9,000. The proportion of the asset disposed of is:

$$\frac{£6,000}{£6,000 + £9,000} \text{ or two-fifths.}$$

Allowable expenditure is two-fifths of £10,000 or £4,000 and the chargeable gain is £6,000 less £4,000 = £2,000.

In April 1971 a new alternative basis of calculating the cost of a part disposal of an estate for capital gains purposes was introduced by the Board of Inland Revenue.[1] This alternative avoids having to value the unsold part of the estate. Under this alternative basis the

[1] See The Estates Gazette for 1 May, 1971.

part disposed of will be treated as a separate asset and any fair and reasonable method of apportioning part of the total cost to it will be accepted, e.g., a reasonable valuation of that part at the acquisition date. Where the market value at 6th April, 1965, is to be taken as cost, a reasonable valuation of the part at that date will be accepted.

The cost of the part disposed of will be deducted from the total cost of the estate (or from the balance) to determine the cost of the remainder: this avoids the total of the separate parts ever exceeding the whole.

The tax payer can always require the general rule to be applied except in cases already settled on the alternative basis but if he does so it will normally be necessary to adhere to the choice for subsequent part disposals.

This alternative basis will not apply to part disposals between 6th April, 1967, and 22nd July, 1970, where development value was involved. In other cases the Board reserve the right to apply the general rule if they are not satisfied that the apportionments claimed are fair and reasonable.

### (g) *The market value rule on certain disposals.*

In a normal case the actual sale price will be treated as the consideration received on disposal. On certain occasions, however, the Act provides for a deemed sale at market value at the date of disposal. The rule on market value operates in the case of gifts.[2] It also applies in the case of other dispositions not by bargain at arms length, such as transfers between closely related or associated persons. The rule applies to both transferor and transferee so that if X gives a property to his son worth £10,000, he will be deemed to have sold for that sum and will be assessed for capital gains tax accordingly. The son can then adopt £10,000 as his cost of acquisition on a subsequent disposition. Market value is the price which the asset might reasonably be expected to fetch on a sale in the open market, the valuation generally being made in accordance with the statutory rules applicable to valuations for estate duty (Section 44).[3] Thus no reduction is to be made if the price likely to be obtained on the notional sale will be lower on the assumption that the whole property is placed on the market at one time. Any depreciation in the value of the property attributable to the death of the owner can, however, be taken into account.

---

[2] Until the Finance Act, 1971, the rule also operated in the case of notional disposals which arose on death and periodically in the case of land heed by trustees. These cases were abolished in respect of deaths occurring before 31 March, 1971.

[3] See Chapter 15.

(*h*) *Assets owned on 6 April, 1965.*

Capital gains tax is designed to tax any increase in value accruing since 6 April, 1965. Where assets disposed of were acquired before this base date, it is necessary to ascertain the amount of any gain or loss which is attributable to the period since 6 April, 1965.

The normal rule is one of time apportionment. Any gain is deemed to have accrued at a uniform rate from the date of acquisition to the date of disposal. Where the date of acquisition was before 6 April, 1945, it will be deemed to have been acquired at that date.

Thus if an asset was purchased on 6 April, 1955, for £3,000 and seventeen years later, on 6 April, 1972, is sold for £6,400, the total gain is £3,400 but the chargeable gain would be that proportion of the whole gain accruing in the seven years from 6 April, 1965, that is £1,400.

The owner may elect for an alternative basis of computation, in which case he would be treated as having sold and re-purchased the asset on 6 April, 1965, at market value. The chargeable gain is then the excess of the disposal price over that figure. He would elect for this basis if it would produce a lesser gain or a greater loss. The election must be made within two years of the date of disposal and cannot be revoked.

Valuers are frequently called upon to make valuations as at 6 April, 1965. This has obvious problems: in many cases imagination is required by the valuer to put himself back to this date. Regard must be had to the circumstances then obtaining. Thus a cottage may be sold in say 1971 with vacant possession but in April 1965 it may have been worth only a fraction of the then vacant possession value if it was then occupied by a controlled tenant. Where appropriate the tenant's possible bid in April 1965 may be taken into account. Similarly land may be sold in 1971 with planning consent but in April 1965 no permission would have been granted. In this case the possibility of obtaining consent on appeal or in the future may take effect to give substantial "hope value".

If the disposal price of land includes development value so that the price obtained exceeds existing use value, the time apportionment basis is not applicable and the gain is calculated by reference to the market value of the land on 6 April, 1965. Special provisions in the Act deal with unfair results from the operation of this rule. Thus, for example, the chargeable gain must not exceed the actual gain made during the whole period of ownership.

(*i*) *Sale of leasehold interests.*

A long lease, that is a lease with more than 50 years unexpired, is not treated as a wasting asset and the whole of the original acquisition cost and other expenditure can be set against the consideration received on the sale of the lease.

A lease with 50 years or less to run, however, is treated for capital gains tax purposes as a wasting asset and on the sale of such an interest the whole of the acquisition cost and other expenditure cannot be deducted. Instead, it is deemed to waste away at a rate which is shown in a table of percentages in paragraph 1 of the 8th Schedule of the Act. Only the residue of the expenditure which remains at the date of disposition can be set against the consideration received.

The table of percentages is derived from the Years Purchase 6 per cent Single Rate table, although as they are concerned with depreciation of a leasehold interest, a dual rate table would have been a more logical basis. The Y.P. for 1 to 50 years is multiplied by a constant factor that makes the Y.P. for 50 years 100. Thus against 40 years the figure is 95·457 and against 25 years, 81·100. If, therefore, a lease having 40 years unexpired was purchased for £5,000 and sold for £8,000 when it had only 25 years to run, the whole of the expenditure of £5,000 would not be allowable, but only that part of it that has not notionally wasted away. In this case it is:

$$\frac{81 \cdot 100}{95 \cdot 457} \times £5,000$$

If a lease which has more than fifty years to run is purchased, the appropriate percentage at acquisition will be 100 and it will commence to be a wasting asset when it has less than fifty years unexpired.

(*j*) *Premiums for leases granted out of freeholds or long leases.*

The receipt of a premium on the grant of a lease is treated as a part disposal of the larger interest out of which the lease is granted. Against the premium may be set the appropriate part of the price paid for the larger interest and any other allowable expenditure as determined by the formula applicable to part disposals.[4]

Where a lease for a period of fifty years or less is granted at a premium a part, at least, of the premium will be liable for income tax under Schedule A.[5] To avoid double taxation the part of a premium for a lease which is thus chargeable to income tax is excluded from liability to capital gains tax. This necessitates a modification to the normal formula applicable to ascertain allowable expenditure on part disposals.

*Example*

X purchased a freehold shop for £10,000 (inclusive of costs) in 1967. In 1972, he grants a 21-year lease at £800 per annum net, taking a premium of £2,500.

---

[4] See section (*f*) of this Chapter.
[5] See Part 2 of this Chapter.

*Step* 1.   Calculate the amount taxable under Schedule A.

The amount taxable is the whole premium less 2 per cent of the premium for each complete year of the term except the first year.   £1,500 (£2,500 − 40% of £2,500) is thus taxable.   This £1,500 is excluded from any capital gains tax liability, leaving £1,000 as the amount of premium on which to base capital gains tax.

*Step* 2.   Allowable expenditure is then to be considered in accordance with the part disposal formula[6] but there is to be excluded from the consideration in the numerator of the fraction (but not in the denominator) that part of the premium taxable under Schedule A.

The application of the formula involves a valuation of the interest retained, which includes the capitalised value of the rent reserved under the lease:

| | | | |
|---|---|---:|---:|
| Rent reserved ... | ... | £800 | |
| Y.P. 21 yrs. @ 6½% | ... | 11·28 | |
| | | | 9,024 |
| Reversion to estimated full rental | | | |
| value (net) | ... | £1,150 | |
| Y.P. perp. deferred 21 yrs. @ 7% | | 3·45 | |
| | | | 3,967 |
| | | | £12,991 |
| Value of Retained Interest | ... ... ... say | | £13,000 |

Using the modified part disposal formula, the chargeable gain is

$$£1,000 - \left(£10,000 \times \frac{£1,000}{£2,500 + £13,000}\right)$$

£1,000 − £645

Chargeable gain £355.

*(k) Premiums for sub-leases granted out of short leases.*

As the larger interest is a wasting asset, the normal part disposal formula does not apply.   Only that part of the expenditure on the larger interest that will waste away over the period of the sub-lease in accordance with the table of percentages[7] can be set against the premium received.

Thus if a person acquired a 40 year lease for £5,000 and when the lease had 30 years to run, he granted a sub-lease for 7 years at the head lease rent, taking a premium of £6,000, the following percentages from the table are required:

40 years  95·457 (percentage when interest acquired);
30 years  87·330 (percentage on grant of sub-lease);
23 years  78·055 (percentage on expiration of sub-lease).

---

[6] See section (*f*) of this Chapter.
[7] See section (*i*) of this Chapter.

The percentage for the 7 years of the sub-lease is therefore $9 \cdot 275$ and the expenditure which is allowable against the premium of £6,000

$$\text{is } £5,000 \times \frac{9 \cdot 275}{95 \cdot 457} = £486$$

(*N.B.*—The allowable expenditure has to be written down if the sub-lease rent is higher than the head lease rent.)

The capital gain is therefore £6,000 − £486 = £5,514.

In this case 12 per cent of the premium is not taxable leaving £5,280 liable to income tax under Schedule A. The method of avoiding double taxation is different in this case. The amount of the premium chargeable to income tax is deducted from £5,514 and only the balance £234, is subject to capital gains tax.

### (*l*) *Land with development value.*

The Land Commission Act, 1967, imposed a Betterment Levy whenever development value was realised on or after 6 April, 1967. There were six acts or "cases" which could have led to the realisation of development value. The three main ones were Case A, which related to the sale of a freehold or leasehold interest, Case B, which arose on the grant of a lease and Case C which applied on the commencement of a project of material development.

To avoid double taxation on development value, the scope of capital gains tax on transactions on or after 6 April, 1967, was, by Section 33 and the 14th Schedule of the Finance Act, 1967, restricted to increases in the value of the land for its current use only.

Thus Betterment Levy applied to any development value "realised", broadly any increase over a value related to its current use, and capital gains tax to any increase in current use value arising on a disposal.

Betterment Levy is not payable in respect of chargeable acts or events taking place after 22 July, 1970, and development value realised from land transactions after that date is to be dealt with through the normal system of taxation of profits and capital gains.

In order to revert to the position prior to the Land Commisssion Act the provisions in the Finance Act, 1967, restricting capital gains tax to increases in current use value had to be repealed. This was done in the Finance Act 1971. A capital gain, whether it relates to an increase in development value or in current use value is now dealt with in the same way under the normal capital gains tax rules.[8]

There are, however, a number of points which must be stressed. The first is that existing capital gains tax legislation does not embrace

---

[8] But see (h) of this Chapter.

all the cases which might have led to levy liability. Thus the commencement of a project of material development, Case C, is not a disposition within the meaning of capital gains tax legislation and liability will be deferred until the asset is disposed of. Also the grant of a lease for development purposes at a full development value ground rent is similarly not a disposition, although Betterment Levy would have been payable under Case B on the development value realised on the transaction. The grant of a lease only constitutes a disposal within capital gains tax rules if a premium is taken and it is then only a part disposal to the extent of the amount of the premium taken. Thus it will no longer be necessary to pay a levy based on capitalised future income. On the other hand gifts are dispositions within the capital gains tax rules although they did not fall within the Betterment Levy cases.

Secondly, there is a basic difference between the two concepts of taxation. The Betterment Levy was directed at any increase over the price paid or a base value related to current use value. Capital gains tax, on the other hand, will tax any increase in value over the price paid if acquired on or after 6 April, 1965, or, if acquired before that date, over a base value, the value on 6 April, 1965, which may well include development value. Thus, if an owner disposes of land which he owned on 6 April, 1965, the use for which the land was allocated in the Development Plan at that date will be particularly important as the market value on 6 April, 1965, will reflect all its development potentialities. It will be remembered that the time apportionment formula does not apply to land sold at a price including development value.

A further important point is the exemption of owner-occupiers of houses from capital gains tax liability. Such an exemption did not apply to Betterment Levy, the only relief being that in certain circumstances the base value was twelve tenths instead of eleven tenths of the current use value. As the exemption extends to gardens and grounds up to one acre or such larger area as may be appropriate to the particular house, this may represent a very considerable saving to the owner.

Other factors which may reduce liability are that the capital gains tax rate is 30 per cent as against 40 per cent (although a company pays tax on capital gains at Corporation Tax rate, at present 40 per cent) and that losses can be set off against gains on other transactions. Further, the rules governing allowable expenditure are more liberal than those which were applicable to levy. There are also no difficulties regarding the adoption as a base value of a price paid in the "interim" period.

## 2. INCOME TAX ON PROPERTY

SCHEDULE A.

Income tax is charged under Schedule A of the Income and Corporation Taxes Act, 1970, on income from rents and certain other receipts from property after deductions have been made for allowable expenses.

A former charge to tax under Schedule A had been abolished in 1963. It related to the payment of income tax on annual value arising from the ownership of landed property. Liability to income tax now only arises from the receipt of income from property, so that the value of beneficial occupation to owner-occupiers or to occupying lessees enjoying a profit rent is not now subject to tax, as it was at one time.

Liability under Schedule A extends to rent under leases of land and certain other receipts such as rent charges. Premiums receivable on the grant of a lease for a term not exceeding fifty years are also subject to taxation under Schedule A. The amount of the premium taxable is the whole premium less 2 per cent for each complete year of the lease, except for the first year.[9]

Deductions from the gross rents receivable may be made in respect of allowable expenses incurred including cost of maintenance, repairs, insurance, management, services, rates and any rent payable to a superior landlord. Items of a capital nature, such as expenditure on improvements, additions or alterations, cannot be deducted except for percentages of the cost of certain specific categories. These include expenditure on the provision or improvement of agricultural or industrial buildings. A deduction may also be made if a premium has been paid to a superior landlord in consideration for the grant of a lease for a term not exceeding fifty years.

Rents receivable from furnished lettings are similarly chargeable to income tax on the gross rents less allowable expenses. A writing-down allowance may be claimed in respect of furniture and any other items provided. As an alternative to this, the taxpayer may choose to deduct the expenses of renewing these items.

SCHEDULE B.

If woodlands are occupied and managed on a commercial basis with a view to the realisation of profits, income tax is charged under Schedule B unless the taxpayer elects otherwise. The assessment under Schedule B is one-third of the annual value of the land if let in its natural and unimproved state.

The charge to tax under Schedule B is thus low and this basis is particularly advantageous when profits are being made from the sale of timber after a plantation has been established for some years.

---

[9] See Part 1 (3) (j) and (k) of this Chapter for Capital Gains Tax provisions concerning premiums.

The alternative is that the taxpayer may elect to be assessed under Schedule D, Case I on the profits from carrying on a trade or business. Election will be advantageous if there are current losses which can be carried forward against future profits. This will arise in the earlier years after a plantation has been established.

Once election for Case D is made it applies as long as the same person owns the land. A normal arrangement, therefore, is for a plantation in its early years to be assessed under Schedule D and when profits begin to flow for it to be transferred to a company so that it may then be assessed under Schedule B.

# Chapter 18

## The Town and Country Planning Acts
## A. Control of Development

### 1. INTRODUCTION

THE POWERS of local planning authorities to control development
in their areas depend on the provisions of the Town and Country
Planning Acts, 1962 to 1968, and on Regulations made under
them.

Before considering these powers, however, reference may usefully
be made to the code of planning law which they replaced, the basis of
which was the *Town and Country Planning Act*, 1932.

The central feature of this earlier planning code was the making,
by local planning authorities, of compulsory town planning schemes
for their areas. Essential steps in the procedure were (i) the resolution to prepare a scheme, (ii) the preparation of a draft scheme,
(iii) the approval and coming into operation of the scheme.

In practice a very considerable time might elapse between the
date when the resolution to prepare the scheme was approved by
the Minister and the date when the scheme came into operation.
This was known as the "interim period". Few schemes under the
Act advanced beyond this interim stage.

During this "interim period" it was necessary to obtain the
local planning authority's consent to any proposed development,
otherwise the owner might be required to alter or demolish buildings
or works without compensation if they were subsequently found
to contravene the provisions of an operative scheme. *The Town
and Country Planning (Interim Development) Act*, 1943, by providing that all land not already under planning control was to be
deemed to be subject to a resolution to prepare a town planning
scheme, extended this system of "interim development" control to
all land in the country. But certain types of development could be
carried out under the authority of General Interim Development
Orders without specific application to the planning authority.

Other Acts forming part of the planning code were:—

*The Restriction of Ribbon Development Act*, 1935, under
which highway authorities might, subject to the owner's right
to compensation, impose restrictions on development (i) within
220 feet on either side of a "classified" road, or (ii) within a

prescribed "standard width" for a road—being the width to which the road would ultimately be widened.

*The Town and Country Planning Act,* 1944, which, in addition to making certain amendments to the existing planning law, gave local authorities far-reaching powers for the acquisition and redevelopment of areas of extensive war damage or obsolete development.

## 2. PRESENT SYSTEM OF PLANNING CONTROL

As from 1 July, 1948, the above code of planning law was replaced by the provisions of the Town and Country Planning Act, 1947, an outline of which was given in Chapter 10.

The whole of the provisions of the Town and Country Planning Acts of 1932 and 1943 were repealed together with those provisions of the Restriction of Ribbon Development Act, 1935 referred to above and the greater part of the Town and Country Planning Act, 1944, including the provisions as to "blitzed" and "blighted" areas. Matters formerly dealt with under the latter two Acts now came within the general system of planning control established by the Act of 1947, now consolidated and amended by the Town and Country Planning Acts, 1962 to 1968.

Under the provisions of the 1947 Act every local planning authority was required, within three years from 1 July, 1948, to prepare and submit for the approval of the Minister[1] a Development Plan in respect of its area showing the manner in which it was proposed that land in the area should be used and the stages by which any such development should be carried out. These development plans were subject to amendment at least once every five years.

Amongst other provisions a development plan might "define" certain land as the site for some specific development—e.g., a new road, public building, or airfield; it might also "allocate" (or "zone") certain areas for some general form of development—e.g., residential, commercial, or industrial.

Under a new planning procedure introduced by the Town and Country Planning Act, 1968, the "development plan" for an area will ultimately be replaced by a "structure plan"—in the making and content of which both the Secretary of State and the local planning authority will be concerned—and one or more "local plans"—which will mainly be the concern of the local planning authority.

Until the coming into operation of the new system in a particular area, the existing "development plan" will continue in force, but no proposals for its amendment may be submitted without the approval of the Secretary of State.

---

[1] Now the Secretary of State for the Environment.

As from 1 July, 1948—with some exceptions—planning permission has been required for any development of land or buildings, irrespective of whether or not such development is in accordance with the provisions of the Development Plan or any subsequent amendment of it.[2]

In most cases such permission must be obtained from the local planning authority. But under the Town and Country Planning (General Development) Order, 1963 (S.I., 1963, No. 709), development of any of the classes specified in the First Schedule to the Order can, in general, be carried out on the authority of the Order itself and without specific application to the local planning authority; although subsequent directions by the Secretary of State or the local planning authority may withdraw such general permission in regard to development in a particular area or in regard to any particular development falling within a certain class.

There are also certain cases of proposed development already authorised under previous planning control, where permission will be deemed to have been granted (see 13th Sch. paras. 7 and 8 of the 1962 Act).

This necessity for the grant of town planning permission for any "development" is a most important factor in valuation practice. If a particular operation on or use of land does not amount to "development", no planning permission is necessary and it follows that any additional value due to the possibility of carrying out such an operation or commencing such a use may fairly be reflected in the market value of the land. If, on the other hand, planning permission is necessary, it is probable that such additional value will not be readily realisable in the open market until such permission has been obtained.

The precise statutory meaning of "development" is therefore of considerable importance to the valuer.

Section 12 (1) of the Town and Country Planning Act, 1962, defines "development" as meaning "the carrying out of building engineering, mining or other operations in, on, over, or under land, or the making of any material change in the use of any buildings or other land".[3]

But Section 12 Sub-section (2) specifies a number of *operations* or *uses* of land which are not to be classed as "development" and which do not therefore require planning permission. Among these may be mentioned:—

    (i) Works of maintenance, improvement or other alterations

---

[2] Town and Country Planning Act, 1962, Sec. 13.
[3] Many of the terms used in this definition are further defined in Sec. 221 (1), to which reference must be made in order to determine the precise application of Sec. 12 to any particular "operation" or "use".

to the interior of a building which do not materially alter its external appearance.[4]

Provided, of course, that such works are not accompanied by some change of user which would itself amount to "development".

(ii) The use of any buildings or other land within the curtilage of a dwelling-house for any purpose incidental to the enjoyment of the dwelling-house as such.

But the erection of any new building on the land—such as a garage—would not come within this exception.[5]

(iii) The use of any land, or of any building occupied with it, for the purposes of agriculture or forestry.

Provided, again, that no new buildings are erected.

(iv) Where buildings or other land is used for a purpose of a specified class—its use for another purpose falling within the same class.

For example, the Town and Country Planning (Use Classes) Order, 1963 (S.I. No. 708), specifies eighteen classes of use—"Shops", "Offices", "Light Industrial Buildings", etc., etc. Where a building or other land is used for a purpose falling within one of these specified classes, its use for another purpose of the same class does not involve "development".

Even where the proposed use falls within a different class to the present user, it will not amount to "development" unless it involves a "material change" in the use of the premises.

Sub-sections (3) and (4) of Section 12 expressly bring within the term "development" certain uses about which doubt might otherwise have arisen—including the use as two or more separate dwelling-houses of any building previously used as a single dwelling-house.

To conclude this very brief outline of the system of planning control first instituted by the Town and County Planning Act, 1947, and now governed by the Act of 1962, as amended in some particulars by the Act of 1968, it must be noted that if development is carried out in contravention of the system—i.e., without the necessary planning permission or contrary to conditions imposed on the grant of permission—the local planning authority can secure the removal or modification of the offending works or the discontinuance of the offending use without payment of compensation by serving an "enforcement notice" on the owner and occupier.

---

[4] But this exception does not extend to the alteration of a building by the provision of additional space below ground if the work was begun after 6 December, 1968—T. & C.P. Act, 1968, Sec. 74.

[5] See definition of "use" in Sec. 221 (1).

## B.  Compensation for Loss of Development Value
### 1.  INTRODUCTION

Under the system of planning control instituted by the Town and Country Planning Act, 1932, any owner whose property was depreciated in value by the coming into operation of a town planning scheme or by the doing of work under it was—subject to a number of important exceptions—entitled to compensation, which might include loss suffered by restrictions on development imposed during the interim period.  Compensation was also payable in respect of a number of other matters connected with the coming into operation or enforcing of schemes.

On the other hand, the responsible authority were entitled to recover 75 per cent of any increase in value due to an operative town planning scheme.  But, owing to the very small number of schemes actually in operation and to the difficulty of determining what increases in value were directly attributable to a scheme, this provision for the recovery of "betterment" was, in practice, a dead letter.

The Town and Country Planning Act, 1947, dealt with this "compensation—betterment problem", as it is often called, on entirely different lines.  An outline of the Act is given in Chapter 10, but certain of its financial provisions require re-examination at this stage.  The guiding principle of the Act was that, as from 1 July, 1948, all "development values" in land should be under the control of, although not actually vested in, the State, and that, as a consequence, transactions in land should in future take place on a basis of "existing use value" only.

The Act sought to achieve this by means of provisions to the following effect:—

   (i) If planning permission was refused, or granted subject to conditions, then—unless the proposed development came within Part 2 of the Third Schedule to the Act—no compensation was payable for any consequent loss of development value to the owner.

   (ii) If permission to develop was granted, then—with certain exceptions, including development within the scope of the Third Schedule or covered by the Development Charge Exemptions Regulations, 1948—a "development charge" was levied equal to 100 per cent of any increase in value due to the permission.

   This charge was based on the amount by which:—

      (a) the value of the land with permission to carry out the proposed works or change of use ("consent value") *exceeded*

      (b) the value of the land without that permission ("refusal value").

Both (a) and (b) were valuations of the fee simple in possession of the land, irrespective of the interest held by the particular developer. If permission was given for a limited period only, the charge was adjusted accordingly.

(iii) If land was acquired compulsorily or by agreement, under statutory powers, the basis of compensation was (with a few exceptions) the "existing use value" of the owner's interest—i.e., its market value assuming that planning permission would only be given for those forms of development listed in the Third Schedule to the Act.

As regards development value existing at 1 July, 1948, and which might be lost to the owner in consequence of these provisions, the owner was entitled to submit a claim under Part VI of the Act based on the difference between (a) the value of his interest in the land if restricted to existing use development only ("Restricted Value"), and (b) the value his interest would have had if the Act had not been passed ("Unrestricted Value"). Both valuations were based on prices current immediately before 7 January, 1947. Such claims were to have been met out of the "£300 million Fund" established under the Act and already referred to in Chapter 10 [Section 2 (viii)].

The above financial provisions of the 1947 Act were substantially amended by the Town and Country Planning Acts of 1953 and 1954.

The Act of 1953 abandoned the attempt to collect increases in value due to the grant of planning permission by abolishing the levying of Development Charge as from 18 November, 1952.

The Act also suspended the distribution of the "£300 million Fund" established under the 1947 Act—which was due to take place in July, 1953—leaving it to the Town and Country Planning Act, 1954, to introduce new provisions on the subject of compensation for loss of development value.

The guiding principles underlying these provisions of the Town and Country Planning Act, 1954, were:—

(i) that, as a general rule, no compensation should be payable to an owner for loss of development value accruing since 1 July, 1948;

(ii) that, as regards development value existing at 1 July, 1948, *which was the subject of an established "Part VI Claim" under the 1947 Act*, compensation should be payable in the circumstances specified in the Act but subject to a maximum figure dependent, in the first instance, on the amount of the "Part VI Claim".

Until 1 January, 1955, the right to secure any payment dependent upon a Part VI claim was known under the Act as a "claim holding" and was a purely personal right.

On and after 1 January, 1955, the value of any "claim holding" (or holdings) still existing in respect of any property was converted into a figure of "original unexpended balance of established development value" which thereafter is attached to the land itself and is not the personal property of any one owner.

There were three distinct classes of case in which payments were provided for under the Town and Country Planning Act, 1954, in respect of development value existing at 1 July, 1948:—

(1) Cases where, before 1 January, 1955, transactions in land were based on the 1947 Act principles that development values were vested in the State, subject to owners' claims on the £300 million Fund.

Payments in these cases were made under Parts I and V of the Act and were limited by the value of the "claim holding". They are now so much a matter of history that it is not proposed to make any further reference to them. Should the reader require further details they can be found on pages 289–291 of the Fifth Edition of this book.

(2) Cases where, on or after 1 January, 1955, planning permission should be refused or granted subject to conditions. Payments in these cases are now made under Part VI of the 1962 Act and are still limited by the amount of the "unexpended balance" attached to the land. They are considered in detail in Chapter 19.

(3) Cases where, on or after 1 January, 1955, land should be acquired or injuriously affected under the exercise of statutory powers.

Up to 29 October, 1958, payments in these cases were made under Part III of the 1954 Act and were also limited by the amount of the unexpended balance. They are considered in Chapter 23. As from 30 October, 1958—under the provisions of the Town and Country Planning Act, 1959, later incorporated in the Land Compensation Act, 1961—compensation in these cases has been based on the value of the land in the open market and no payment has been made in respect of any "unexpended balance" (see Chapter 21).

In the following Sections of this Chapter it is proposed to consider in rather more detail—(i) the nature and basis of the "Part VI claim" under the 1947 Act; (ii) the relation between the "Part VI claim" and the "claim holding" under the 1954 Act; and (iii) the conversion of "claim holdings" into figures of "unexpended balance of established development value".

## 2. CLAIMS UNDER PART VI OF THE 1947 ACT

(a) *Basis of the claim.*—Unlike the case of valuation for determining development charge, the valuer was concerned here with a particular interest in land—e.g., that of a freeholder, lessee or sub-lessee.

The claimant might choose the unit of land to which his claim related—e.g., his claim might relate to the whole of a particular piece of land in which he had an interest, or to part only.

The basis of claim was the amount by which the "restricted value" of the claimant's interest in the land on 1 July, 1948, was less than its "unrestricted value". The difference between those two figures was the "development value" for loss of which the owner was claiming.

*Restricted Value* meant the market value of the interest in land on the assumption that planning permission would be granted for development of any class specified in the Third Schedule to the Act, but would not be granted for any other development [Section 61 (2) (a)].

*Unrestricted Value* meant the market value of the owner's interest in the land assuming the Act had not been passed [Section 61 (2) (b)].

The general tendency of the provisions of the Act regarding (i) planning control, (ii) development charge, and (iii) compensation for compulsory purchase, were to reduce the market price of land to its existing use value. But in calculating "unrestricted value" the valuer had to assume that these provisions did not exist and that the land could be valued with the benefit of all potential development, subject only to such statutory or other restrictions as existed prior to the coming into operation of the Act. The latter would, in general, include any restrictions imposed under the Town and Country Planning Acts, 1932 and 1943, or under the Restriction of Ribbon Development Act, 1935.

The two principal rules governing the calculation of both "restricted" and "unrestricted" values were as follows:—

(i) Subject to the statutory assumptions referred to above, the value of the claimant's interest was the price it might be expected to realise if sold in the open market by a willing seller—value to one particular purchaser[6] and value due to illegal or unhealthy user to be ignored.

(ii) Except in certain special cases, the interest was to be valued as it existed on 1 July, 1948, subject to all incidents, restrictive covenants, easements, public or other rights affecting it at that date. *But the valuation was to be made by reference to prices current immediately before 7 January, 1947.*

---

[6] In December, 1950, however, the Chancellor of the Exchequer authorised the Central Land Board to take this factor into account in assessing claims in respect of land suitable for the extension of existing buildings. This act was legalised by the 1954 Act (Sec. 1 and First Sched., para. 10).

(b) *Exclusion of small claims.*—No claim for loss of development value could be entertained unless the development value, averaged over the land, exceeded £20 per acre and also exceeded one-tenth of the restricted value.

(c) *Making and Determination of Claims.*—Claims for loss of development value under Part VI of the 1947 Act had to be made to the Central Land Board by 30 June, 1949.

After a claim had been made, the Central Land Board (acting in practice through the Land Valuation Department of the Inland Revenue) considered the claim and eventually served a notice on the claimant stating what they considered to be the "development value" and the amounts of the "unrestricted" and "restricted" values.

The claimant might object, stating the grounds of his objection and specifying the amounts which in his opinion should be substituted. The Board then considered the objection and finally determined the "development value" (and the "unrestricted" and "restricted" values).

If the claimant disputed the amount of the claim as finally determined by the Board, he might appeal to the Lands Tribunal.

*A Part VI claim agreed with the Central Land Board or determined by the Lands Tribunal, in default of agreement, was known under the 1954 Act as an "established claim".*

(d) *Person entitled to claim.*—The right to a Part VI claim vested in the person who was the owner of the particular interest on 1 July, 1948. But that right could be transferred by operation of law (e.g., on death) or by assignment, which had to be notified to the Central Land Board.

(e) *Exemptions.*—No claim could be made for loss of development value in the case of land certified as "ripe for development" under Section 80 of the 1947 Act; nor—subject to the conditions specified in Sections 82-85—in the case of lands of local authorities, statutory undertakings or charitable trusts.

There was corresponding exemption from development charge in these cases.

(f) *Example.*—The following example illustrates the lines on which a Part VI claim might be made. The facts stated are those assumed to exist at 1 July, 1948, related to 1947 prices.

*Example.*—A rectangular area of land of 2 acres has a frontage of 400 ft., depth 220 ft. At the rear is a field of 5 acres. The whole was used for agricultural purposes on 1 July, 1948. In 1947, it is estimated that the value of the front land was £10 per foot frontage and that it would be four years before it could be developed due to licensing restrictions. The value of the 5 acres for building purposes was £500 per acre.

As agricultural land the holding was worth £50 per acre.

The valuation for loss of development value would be:—

*Unrestricted Value—*

| | | | | | |
|---|---|---|---|---|---|
| Agricultural value, say | ... | ... | ... | £14 p.a. | |
| Y.P. 4 years @ 4% | ... | ... | ... | 3·63 | £51 |
| | | | | | |
| 360 ft. (allow 40 ft. for access road to land at rear) @ £10 per ft. | ... | ... | £3,600 | |
| 5 acres @ £500 per acre | ... | ... | ... | £2,500 | |
| | | | | £6,100 | |
| P.V. £1 in 4 years @ 5% ... | ... | ... | 0·81 | £4,941 |
| | | | | | £4,992 |

*Restricted Value—*

| | | | | |
|---|---|---|---|---|
| 7 acres @ £50 per acre | ... | ... | ... | £350 |

| | | | | |
|---|---|---|---|---|
| *Development Value, say* | ... | ... | ... | £4,640 |

*Note*—In this case the same period of deferment is taken for the back land as for the front land, the difference in value being due to the development costs.

(*g*) *Special Payments in respect of War-Damaged Land.*—These were authorised by a scheme prepared by the Treasury under Section 59 of the 1947 Act and known as the Planning Payments (War Damage) Scheme, 1949.

They are now a matter of history and it is not proposed to make any further reference to them. Details can be found, if required, on pages 286 and 287 of the Fifth Edition of this book.

### 3. "Established Claims" and "Claim Holdings"
### (Parts I and IV of 1954 Act)

Under the 1954 Act the term "established claim" meant a claim for loss of development value which was agreed with the Central Land Board, or determined by the Lands Tribunal under Part VI of the 1947 Act; while the "benefit of an established claim" meant the prospective right to a payment in respect of that claim.

In some cases, however, the "benefit of an established claim" might have become split up between two or more persons since the claim was originally agreed or determined. The 1954 Act therefore used the following expressions in relation to rights existing in respect of an established claim during the period 1 July, 1948, to 31 December, 1954:—

"*Claim holding*" = "benefit of an established claim".

"*Area of claim holding*" = the land which forms the subject of the claim holding.

"*Value of the claim holding*" = the whole or part of the original claim of which the "claim holder" has the benefit.

*Example.*—X is the owner-occupier of the area of freehold land ABCD shown below. X submitted a "Part VI claim" which was agreed at £1,200.

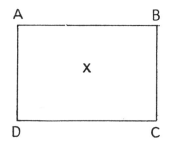

Provided no rights under the claim were assigned, until 1 January, 1955, X was the "holder" of a "claim holding" the area of which was ABCD and the value of which—subject to the possible deductions referred to later—was £1,200.

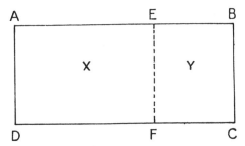

Supposing, however, that in March, 1951, X sold his freehold interest in part of the land (EBCF) to Y, together with such part of the established claim as was reasonably apportionable to it (say £500). Then the position under the 1954 Act from that date up to 1 January, 1955, would have been as follows:—

X would be the "holder" of a "claim holding" whose "area" was AEFD and whose value was (£1,200—500) £700.

Y would be the "holder" of a "claim holding" whose area was EBCF and whose value was £500.

*Example.*—"Greenacre" is a large house standing in about 3 acres of land, 2 acres of which could profitably be developed by the erection of six smaller houses.

B, who holds the property on a long term lease, submitted a "Part VI claim" in respect of his leasehold interest which was agreed at £1,400. A, the freeholder, succeeded in establishing a claim for £300 in respect of the freehold reversion.

In this case, immediately before 1 January, 1955—subject to any of the deductions referred to later—there would have been two claim holdings existing in respect of Greenacre:—

    (i) A's "claim holding"—value £300

    (ii) B's "claim holding"—value £1,400

each of which would at that stage have been the personal property of the particular "claim holder".

There were a number of cases under the 1954 Act in which the value of a claim holding might be reduced or extinguished altogether. These are now so much a matter of history that it is not thought necessary to refer to them in detail.

## 4.　Unexpended Balance of Established Development Value

(Sections 17 and 18 of the 1954 Act, now re-enacted in Sections 89–95 of the Town and Country Planning Act, 1962)

Broadly speaking, what is known under these Acts as the "original unexpended balance of established development value" in relation to any particular piece of land consists of eight-sevenths of the value of any claim holding, or holdings, subsisting in that land immediately after 1 January, 1955. The additional one-seventh corresponds roughly to interest at $3\frac{1}{2}$ per cent for the period 1948-55, less tax at the standard rate.

*Example* 1.—ABCD is the area of a single claim holding subsisting at 1 January, 1955, whose value was £1,400.

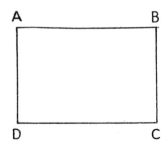

The "original unexpended balance of established development value" attaching to the land as from 1 January, 1955, would be:—

£1,400 × eight-sevenths = £1,600.

*Example* 2.—Taking the same area of land as in Example 1, assume that X the freeholder had a claim holding of £800 and Y the lessee had a claim holding of £1,300, both in respect of the whole area ABCD.

Then the "original unexpended balance of established development value" attaching to ABCD as from 1 January, 1955, would be:—

(800 + £1,300)    £2,100 × eight-sevenths = £2,400

It must again be emphasised at this point that, whereas the "claim holding" was a species of personal property belonging to the "claim holder", the "original unexpended balance of established development value" is not the subject of separate ownership. It is, in effect, a fund attached to the land from which, and until it is exhausted, any persons now or hereafter entitled to an interest in the land—irrespective of whether or not they themselves made a Part VI claim—may still be paid compensation under the provisions of the 1962 Act in respect of future planning decisions.

One obvious result of this is that the compensation payable to any one owner out of this common fund is a matter of concern not only to himself but to all the other owners. It also follows that whenever an occasion for compensation under the Act arises in the future it will be necessary to determine the amount of the "unexpended balance" existing at that particular date.

This may be the "original" unexpended balance—e.g., the £1,600 or £2,400 in Examples 1 and 2—or it may be that figure less any compensation paid on previous occasions, since 1 January, 1955, to one or more persons interested in the land.

A further deduction which may have to be made from the "unexpended balance" is the value—at the date when the unexpended balance has to be calculated—of any "new development" for which planning permission has been given. For instance, if, in, say, 1962, development (other than Third Schedule development) was carried out on Blackacre and later, in, say, January, 1967, permission for further development was refused, it would be necessary, in finding the unexpended balance available for compensation at the later date, to deduct the value of this previous new development. This value will be assessed as at January, 1967—not at 1962 when the development was initiated.

Under Section 95 and the Sixth Schedule of the 1962 Act, the value of the new development has to be calculated on the assumption that—

(a) the development has not been carried out and the land has remained in the state in which it was immediately before the development was initiated[7] (except that if the development involved clearing the site, the state of the land before development means the site after it had been cleared but before development had begun) and

(b) the development could be lawfully carried out (apart from the 1947 and 1962 Acts) at the time when the value of the development is being calculated.

The "value of the development"—i.e., the sum to be deducted from the unexpended balance—will then be the amount by which in these circumstances—

(a) the value of the land with unconditional permission for the new development (or subject to any conditions which were in fact imposed) granted immediately before the valuation date,
*would have exceeded*

(b) its value if permission had been refused immediately before that date, and it could be assumed that permission for that and any other "new development" would be refused on a subsequent application.

It would appear from the wording of the Act that the two valuations are to be based, not on the interest in the land of the particular developer, but on that of an assumed freeholder in possession.

If the development was initiated subject to a condition expressed by reference to a specified period (e.g., a consent for a limited term) then in the calculation of the value of the development, the conditions to be assumed attaching to the planning permission are deemed to include a like requirement for the same duration (beginning at the valuation date) as the period originally specified.

The value of the development has to be found by reference to prices current at the date of the valuation which—as has already been noted—may be several years after the time when the development was initiated.

If the development, the value of which has to be calculated, was not completed at the time when the value has to be ascertained, the calculation is to be made by construing references to permission for the development as references to permission for so much of the development as has been completed at the date of the calculation.

As in other cases under the Act "value" is to be estimated on the

---

[7] New development shall be taken to be initiated:—
    (a) if the development consists of the carrying out of operations, at the time when these operations are begun;
    (b) if the development consists of a change in use, at the time when the new use is instituted;
    (c) if the development consists both of the carrying out of operations and of a change of use, at the earlier of the times aforesaid. [1962 Act, Sec. 221 (5).]

basis of the price which the land might be expected to realise if sold in the open market by a willing seller.[8] Value attributable to illegal or unhealthy user is to be disregarded; but for the purpose of the Fourth Schedule, value to one particular purchaser may be taken into account.

If "new development" is carried out partly on land having an unexpended balance and partly on other land, it will be necessary for purposes of deduction, to estimate what proportion of the value of the development can properly be attributed to the land with the unexpended balance.

*Example*—A is the freeholder of 4 acres of land about a mile from the centre of a town of 50,000 inhabitants. The land was used for grazing until December, 1962, when planning permission was granted for its use as a caravan site for a term of ten years.

A claim under Section 58 of the Town and Country Planning Act, 1947, was submitted and agreed: Unrestricted Value £2,000. Restricted Value £250.

On obtaining planning permission, A let the land to B at a rent of £100 per annum, tenant paying all outgoings. By 1967, the value for this purpose had increased to £150 per annum.

It is required to find the amount of the unexpended balance of established development value in 1967.

*Original unexpected balance of established development value*
Claim under Section 58 of the Town and Country

| | | | | | |
|---|---|---|---|---|---|
| Planning Act, 1947 | ... | ... | ... | ... | £1,750 |
| Add one-seventh | ... | ... | ... | ... | £250 |
| | *Original unexpended balance* | | | | £2,000 |

*Deduct* value of new development in 1967:—
Value of land in 1967 with permission
to use it as a caravan site for ten
years:—

| | | | | |
|---|---|---|---|---|
| Rental Value | ... | ... | ... | £150 p.a. |
| Y.P. @ 6% for 10 years | ... | ... | 7·36 | £1,104 |
| | | | | |
| Reversion to value as grazing land | | | | |
| in 1977, say, | ... | ... | ... | £400 |
| P.V. £1 in 10 years @ 5% | | ... | 0·61 | £244 |
| | | | | £1,348 |
| *Less* Value of land in 1967 had the | | | | |
| above permission been refused ... | | | £400 | £948 |
| *Amount of unexpended Balance of* | | | | |
| *Established Development Value in* 1967 | | ... | | £1,052 |

---

[8] See Sec. 117 of 1962 Act.

It has already been noted that when compensation becomes payable on some future occasion under the Act—e.g., an adverse planning decision—the effect will be to reduce or extinguish the unexpended balance on the land. If the particular act or decision affects only part of the land, the unexpended balance on the whole will have to be apportioned, and compensation will only be payable out of such part of the balance as is properly attributable to the land affected.[9]

Apart from occasions arising under the Act, it may be desirable to know whether or not land, which is perhaps the subject of some private transaction, has an unexpended balance attaching to it, since this may well have a bearing on market value. Information on this point was formerly obtainable from the Central Land Board in the form of a certificate under Section 48 of the 1954 Act.

The Central Land Board was dissolved as from 1 April, 1959, and the information is now obtainable from the Department of the Environment.[10] The certificate is only bound to show the original unexpended balance attaching to the land, together with a statement of what was taken to be the state of the land on 1 July, 1948. But the Secretary of State may, at his discretion, include additional information as to acts or events which may result in a deduction from this figure. Failing such information, the applicant must ascertain such facts or events for himself and work out the appropriate deductions to arrive at the current figure of unexpended balance.

If "new development" has been carried out, it will in any case be impossible to arrive at a precise figure of unexpended balance by means of such a certificate because the appropriate deduction in respect of such development can only be calculated at the date of an occasion under the Act; until then—owing to the possibility of changing values—only the roughest of estimates can be made.

---

[9] See Sec. 98 (2) of 1962 Act.
[10] See now Sec. 99 of the 1962 Act.

# Chapter 19

## The Town and Country Planning Acts (cont.)

### C. Compensation for Adverse Planning Decisions.

1. DECISIONS AFFECTING THIRD SCHEDULE DEVELOPMENT
(*Secs.* 123, 127 *and* 128—*Town and Country Planning Act*, 1962)

WHERE, on appeal from a local planning autitrity's decision, or, on reference of the application to him, the Secretary of State refuses permission for any type of development specified in *Part 2 of the Third Schedule to the* 1962 *Act*,[1] or grants it subject to restrictions, any owner of the land whose interest is depreciated in value in consequence may claim compensation, provided he does so within six months.

The basis of compensation will be in effect the difference between:
  (i) the value of the interest if permission had been granted subject only to the condition imposed by the Schedule to the Town and Country Planning Act, 1963,[1a] restricting the use of additional floor space for any purpose, and
  (ii) its value subject to the refusal of planning permission or its grant subject to conditions, as the case may be.
The valuation will be made in accordance with rules contained in Section 5 of the Land Compensation Act, 1961, ignoring any mortgage to which the interest may be subject.

In making the valuation it is to be assumed that any similar application in the future would be treated in the same way; but regard must be had to any alternative development for which the Secretary of State may have undertaken to grant permission. An example of this type of case is given in Section 7 of this Chapter.

Where the Secretary grants development permission subject to conditions, he may, in effect, direct that no compensation shall be payable in respect of any such conditions regulating the design, external appearance, size or height of buildings if, having regard to local circumstances, he considers it reasonable to do so.

No compensation is payable where the refusal or the restrictions relate to the two types of development specified in Part 1 of the Third Schedule—i.e., rebuilding, or the use as two or more dwelling-houses of a building previously used as a single dwelling-house.

---

[1] But no compensation is payable where the application involves an increase in the cubic content of a building erected after 1 July, 1948, or any extension of the use of part of such building—Town and Country Planning Act, 1963, Sec. 1 (2) (see Appendix B (2)).
[1a] See Appendix B (2).

The owner's only remedy in such a case is to try to compel the compulsory acquisition of his land by means of a " purchase notice," as described in Section 5 of this Chapter.

## 2.   DECISIONS AFFECTING " NEW " DEVELOPMENT
### (*Part VI of the Town and Country Planning Act,* 1962)

(*a*) *Generally.*—" New " development means any development other than development of a class specified in the Third Schedule to the 1962 Act.

The general effect of this Part of the 1962 Act is that where planning permission for " new development " on land having an unexpended balance of development value is refused, or is granted subject to conditions, then—subject to the important exceptions referred to later in this Chapter—compensation for any depreciation in value due to the decision will be payable by the Secretary of State up to the limit of the unexpended balance attached to the land affected.

If no part of the land affected has an " unexpended balance " there is no right to compensation, and the owner's only possible remedy is the service of a purchase notice under Section 129 of the Act if the adverse planning decision renders the land incapable of reasonably beneficial use.

Where—as sometimes happens in practice—proposals for certain works, such as the construction of a service road by the would-be developer, are included in a planning application because the applicant has reason to think that without them he is unlikely to get planning permission for his proposed development, then, if permission is given and the Secretary of State certifies that he is satisfied that the work in question was only included in the application for the above reason, the applicant may get compensation as though the doing of that work had been made one of the conditions of the grant of permission.[2]

Where an application for an " industrial development certificate " is refused by the Department of Trade and Industry under Section 38 of the 1962 Act, the local planning authority may now be required to inform the applicant whether planning permission for the proposed industrial development would have been refused even had the certificate been granted. If they do so inform him, this will amount to a refusal of planning permission for the purposes of the Act.[3]

It may conveniently be noted at this point that the right to compensation under Part VI of the 1962 Act is not confined (as it is under Section 123 of the Act) to cases where the planning decision is given on a direct reference to the Secretary of State, or on appeal to him. It arises when an adverse decision is given by the

[2] Sec. 104.
[3] Sec. 40 (1) and 105.

local planning authority—although, as will be noted later in this Chapter, the local planning authority's decision may subsequently be amended by the Secretary of State, with a consequent reduction in the amount of compensation ultimately payable.

(b) *The right to compensation. (Section* 100).—To entitle a person to compensation under Part VI of the Act: —

- (i) he must own an interest in the land to which the adverse planning decision relates, or in land which includes that land;
- (ii) the whole or part of the land affected by the decision must have an unexpended balance attached to it;
- (iii) the owner's interest in the land affected must be depreciated in value by the adverse decision.

But even if these conditions are satisfied, the right to compensation may be excluded under Sections 101 and 102 of the Act either on account of (i) the type of restriction or the reason for its imposition, or (ii) the fact that planning permission is available for certain other forms of development.

(c) *Exclusion of Compensation.*—Under Section 101 no compensation is payable under Part II of the Act in respect of the following types of adverse planning decisions: —

- (i) *Refusal of permission* for any development which consists of or includes the making of any material change in the use of buildings or other land[4]—for example, refusal of permission to carry out structural alterations for the purpose of converting a dwelling-house into offices.
- (ii) Any decision in regard to the display of advertisements.
- (iii) *Imposition of conditions* in respect of the following matters: —
  - (a) the number or disposition of buildings on the land;
  - (b) the dimensions, design, structure or external appearance of any building or the materials to be used in its construction;
  - (c) the manner in which any land is to be laid out for the purposes of the development, including the provision of parking, loading and fuelling facilities on the land;
  - (d) the use of any buildings or other land;
  - (e) the location or design of any " means of access to a highway,"[5] or the materials to be used in its construction;
  - (f) the winning and working of minerals.

---

[4] Under Sec. 221 (1) of the 1962 Act, " use " in relation to land does not include the use of land by the carrying out of building or other operations thereon. For example, the erection of a dwelling-house on land formerly used as agricultural land, with planning permission to use it as a dwelling-house when erected, is not development including a change of use.

[5] This does not include a service road.

(iv) *Refusal of permission* on the grounds that the development is " premature " having regard to (a) the order of priority (if any) for development indicated in the development plan for the area, (b) any existing deficiency in the provision of water supplies or sewerage services and the period within which any such deficiency may reasonably be expected to be made good.

But if seven years have elapsed since the last application, the development cannot again be held to be " premature " on the same grounds.

(v) *Refusal of permission* on the grounds that the land is unsuitable for the proposed development because of its liability to flooding or subsidence.

*Note.*—If permission to develop land is granted subject to a condition prohibiting development of a specified part of the land, this must be treated as a decision refusing permission as respects that part. (Sec. 101 (6)).

So that if permission were given to erect houses on a particular estate provided no building was done on two hectares of the land which were liable to flooding, this would amount to a refusal of permission in respect of the two hectares but, under (v) above, would not entitle the owner to compensation.

Under Section 102 compensation for *refusal of planning permission* is also excluded if, immediately before the Secretary of State gives notice of his findings in respect of the claim, there is a grant of, or undertaking by him to grant, planning permission for some alternative form of " development of a residential, commercial or industrial character, being development which consists wholly or mainly of the construction of houses, flats, shops or office premises, or industrial buildings (including warehouses) or any combination thereof." For example, no compensation would be payable for refusal of planning permission to erect a garage on a particular piece of land if the Secretary of State were to grant, or undertake to grant, planning permission for the erection of shops on the site, either unconditionally or subject to such conditions as are referred to in (iii) (a) – (e) above.

(*d*) *Procedure in making claims* (*Secs.* 25, 108 *and* 109).—A claim for compensation under Part VI of the Act must be made within six months of the date of the planning decision which gives rise to it, or within such extended time as the Secretary of State may allow in any particular case.

The procedure is governed by the Town and Country Planning (Compensation and Certificates) Regulations, 1963.

The claim is made to the local planning authority who must forward it to the Secretary of State together with the information required by the Regulations.

The Secretary of State may notify the claimant that, in his opinion, no compensation is payable. But, except where a claim is withdrawn, he must give notice of the claim to every other person who appears to have an interest in the land to which the planning decision relates.

Except where claims are withdrawn, the Secretary of State may review any planning decision giving rise to a claim and may substitute a decision "more favourable"[6] to the claimant, or may give permission for some other form of development. But before making such a direction he must give the local planning authority and the claimant (or claimants) an opportunity of being heard.

It follows that, although a party may have what may be called a prima facie right to compensation when the local planning authority gives the adverse planning decision, the actual compensation (if any) to which he may be entitled will be determined having regard to any direction given by the Secretary on his review of that decision.

(e) *Amount of Compensation (Secs. 106 and 107).*—For the purpose of these sections land which has an unexpended balance of development value is referred to as "qualified land".

Broadly speaking, the amount of compensation payable will be—either

> (i) the depreciation in the value of the claimant's interest, so far as it subsists in "qualified land,"

or

> (ii) the amount of the unexpended balance—*whichever is the less.*

Since the amount of the unexpended balance is derived from values in 1947/8, it is almost always found in practice, due to the increase in values during the last two decades, that compensation is (ii) above.

If there is more than one claimant with an interest in the "qualified land" and the aggregate of the claims does not exceed the "unexpended balance" on the land, then each party will receive as compensation the depreciation in the value of his interest. But if the aggregate of the claims exceeds the "unexpended balance", then the latter—which is the limit of compensation payable—must be divided between the claimants in proportion to the depreciation in the value of their respective interests.

*Example*—A's interest in the land affected by an adverse planning decision is depreciated to the extent of £700. The depreciation

---

[6] "More favourable" means:—

    (a) in relation to a refusal of permission—a decision granting permission either unconditionally or subject to conditions, and either as respects the whole or part of the land; and

    (b) in relation to a grant of permission subject to conditions—a decision granting the permission applied for unconditionally or subject to less stringent conditions.

in the value of B's interest is £300. The " unexpended balance " on the land is £800. The compensation payable to the parties under Part II of the Act will be—

$$A \qquad £800 \times \frac{700}{1,000} = £560$$

$$B \qquad £800 \times \frac{300}{1,000} = £240$$

*Note.—Special rules[7] prescribed by Section 106—have to be applied where:—*
  (i) *part of the land affected by a planning decision is not " qualified land "—i.e., land which has an unexpended balance;*
*and/or*
  (ii) *one or more interests in the land affected relate to part only of that land.*

The depreciation in the value of the claimant's interest will be taken to be the amount by which—
  (i) the value of the claimant's interest at the time of the " relevant decision," and taking into account the effect of that decision, *is less than*
  (ii) the value it would have had if the decision had been to the contrary effect—i.e., if it had been granted instead of refused, or if it had been granted subject only to the type of conditions already referred to, which do not attract compensation.

" Value " is to be determined in accordance with Rules 2 to 4 of Section 5 of the Land Compensation Act, 1961.

In making the calculation, regard must be had to any grant of, or undertaking to grant, planning permission made after the decision giving rise to the claim and in force immediately before the Secretary of State gives notice of his findings on the claim. It must also be assumed that (apart from such grant or undertaking to grant permission) planning permission after the date of the " relevant decision " would only be given for Third Schedule development.[7a]

(f) *Apportionment and Registration (Sec.* 112).—If the compensation exceeds £20 and it appears practicable to the Secretary of State to do so, he must apportion the amount of the compensation between different parts of the land to which the claim relates according to the way in which he thinks those parts are differently affected by the decision.

---

[7] For a detailed explanation of these rules see Lawrance and White's " Guide to the Town and Country Planning Act, 1954 " (Estates Gazette) at pp. 67–68.
[7a] Third Schedule as modified by Town and Country Planning Act, 1963 —see Appendix B (2).

Details of any compensation exceeding £20 (together with any apportionment) are registered with the local authority in the register of local land charges and are known as " compensation notices ".

(*g*) *Determination of Claims (Sec. 27).*—Under the Town and Country Planning (Compensation and Certificates) Regulations 1963, notice of the Secretary of State's findings as to the compensation payable to any claimant must be given (i) to the claimant himself, and (ii) to all other claimants in respect of the same planning decision. Each of the parties concerned will therefore know the amount of the compensation proposed to be awarded to any other party interested in the land affected.

Details of any apportionment will appear in the Secretary's findings and must be given not only to the claimants but also to any other person whose interest in the land may be materially affected.

There is a right of appeal to the Lands Tribunal against the Secretary's findings or against any apportionment of the compensation over the land affected.

(*h*) *Effect of Payment of Compensation on Unexpended Balance* [*Sec.* 94 (1)].—The amount of any compensation payable under Part VI will be deducted from the amount of the unexpended balance when next it becomes necessary to determine the amount (if any) of the balance still attaching to the land.

(*i*) *Recovery of Compensation on Subsequent Development (Secs.* 113 and 114).—When a " compensation notice " is registered in respect of land, no " new development " of the types specified below may be carried out on that land until an appropriate sum in respect of that compensation has been repaid to the Secretary of State or secured to his satisfaction. The repayment may take the form of a lump sum, or a series of instalments of capital and interest, or a series of other annual or periodic payments, at the discretion of the Secretary.

" New development " is development other than that covered by the Third Schedule, and the types of " new development " which may involve repayment of compensation are : —

    (i) development of a residential, commercial or industrial character;

    (ii) the winning and working of minerals; or

    (iii) development whose probable value is such that in the opinion of the Secretary of State the provision as to repayment ought to apply.

But where, in the opinion of the Secretary, development is likely to be discouraged by the obligation to repay compensation, he has discretion to remit the whole or part of any sum which would otherwise be recoverable.

Also, where compensation was paid on account of planning permission being given subject to conditions, no question of repayment will arise when development is carried out in accordance with those conditions.

If the area on which "new development" is to be carried out—known as "the development area"—is the same as, or includes, the whole of the land comprised in the "compensation notice," the whole of the sum specified in the notice will be recoverable. If "the development area" comprises or includes part only of the land comprised in the "compensation notice," the amount recoverable will be an appropriate part of the sum specified in the notice.

What is "an appropriate part" in the latter case will depend on whether or not the Secretary of State's decision on compensation included an apportionment. If there is no apportionment, the compensation is assumed to be distributed rateably over the whole area—e.g., if a quarter of the area is to be developed, a quarter of the compensation will be repayable. If there is an apportionment, then the amount repayable will depend on the sums allocated by the apportionment to the part or parts of the area to be developed.

Once compensation has been repaid under these provisions, no further sum will be repayable in respect of further development at a later date, with the possible exception of those cases where the Secretary of State has previously remitted part of the sum repayable.

Where compensation has been repaid and it subsequently becomes necessary to determine the unexpended balance (if any) attached to the land, no deduction will be made in respect of so much of the original payment of compensation as was attributable to that land, since this has, in effect, been cancelled out.

The effect of the above provisions on value would appear to be that a prospective purchaser of land for development purposes will certainly inquire as to the existence of any "compensation notice" and that the price he will be prepared to pay will be influenced by the liability for repayment which he is likely to incur under it.

### 3. REVOCATION OR MODIFICATION OF PLANNING PERMISSION
*(Sections* 27, 118–122, 127 and 128—*Town and Country Planning Act,* 1962)

Under Section 27 of the 1962 Act a local planning authority may, by means of an order confirmed by the Secretary of State, revoke or modify a planning permission already given, provided they do so:—

(a) Before building or other operations authorised by the permission have been completed, in which case work already done will not be affected by the order, or

(b) before any change of use authorised by the permission has taken place.

Notice of the proposed Order must be given to the owner and occupier of the land affected and to any other person who, in the opinion of the local planning authority will be affected by the Order.

Any such person is entitled to object to the Order and to be heard by a person appointed by the Secretary of State.

In the event of the Order being confirmed, Section 118 of the 1962 Act provides for the payment of compensation under the following heads: —

(i) Expenditure on work which is rendered abortive by the revocation or modification—including the cost of preparing plans in connection with such work or other similar matters preparatory thereto.

But no compensation will be paid in respect of work done before the grant of the relevant planning permission —e.g., in anticipation of such permission being granted.

(ii) Any other loss or damage directly attributable to the revocation or modification.

No compensation was payable under Section 22 of the 1947 Act for depreciation in the value of land unless either (a) a development charge had been paid, or (b) the land was exempt from the charge under Part VIII of that Act.

But where the order for revocation or modification is made on or after 1 January, 1955, compensation for depreciation in the value of the claimant's interest in the land may be payable, under Section 118 of the 1962 Act, whether or not the original planning decision related to "new development" and irrespective of whether or not the land has an unexpended balance of development value.

In accordance with the provisions of Section 127 of the 1962 Act, compensation for depreciation in the value of an interest in land will be calculated on a market value basis as now prescribed by Section 5 of the Land Compensation Act, 1961, ignoring any mortgage to which the interest may be subject. The measure of compensation will be the amount by which the value of the claimant's interest with the benefit of the planning permission exceeded the value of that interest with the planning permission revoked or modified. In calculating such depreciation it is to be assumed that planning permission would be granted for development within the Third Schedule (as modified by the Town and Country Planning Act, 1963).

The above provisions as to compensation also apply where planning permission given by a Development Order is withdrawn—whether by the revocation or modification of the Order or by a direction made under it[8]—and, on an express planning application being made, permission is refused or is granted subject to conditions other than those imposed by the Development Order.

Disputes as to the compensation payable under Section 118—including any sum for depreciation in the value of land—are referable to the Lands Tribunal.[9]

---

[8] E.g., a "direction" made by the Secretary of State or the local planning authority under Article 4 of the General Development Order, 1963.

[9] Sec. 128 (1).

Revocation or modification of planning permission previously given may entitle the owner to serve a purchase notice under Section 129 of the Act.[10]

As in the case of claims under Part VI of the Act, provision is made[11] for the apportionment of compensation for depreciation in value exceeding £20 between different parts of the land, where practicable, and for the registration of the " compensation notice " as a land charge.

Also—as under Part VI of the Act—compensation so registered will be repayable in whole or in part if permission is subsequently given for " new development " on the whole or part of the land affected by the revocation order, except where the registered compensation was paid in respect of a local planning authority's order modifying planning permission previously given and the subsequent development is in accordance with that permission as modified.[12]

Where the circumstances are such that, had the original planning decision been to the same effect as the order for revocation or modification, compensation would have been payable by the Secretary of State under Part VI of the Act, the Secretary may pay to the local planning authority a sum equal to such compensation as, in his opinion, would have been payable. Provided that the amount of such contribution shall not exceed:—

 (*a*) the amount of compensation for depreciation paid by the local planning authority; or
 (*b*) the amount of the unexpended balance at the date when the order for revocation or modification is made.[13]

Any sum so paid may be deducted from any unexpended balance attached to the land. But interested parties must be notified of the Secretary's intention to make such a payment and may object that no compensation would, in fact, have been payable under Part VI or that the amount of the compensation would have been less than the proposed contribution. There is a right of appeal on this point to the Lands Tribunal.[14]

### 4. INTERFERENCE WITH AUTHORISED USES OR WORKS[15]
(*Sections* 28, 124 *and* 127—*Town and Country Planning Act*, 1962)

By means of an order confirmed by the Secretary of State, a local planning authority may at any time require the discontinuance or

---

[10] Sec. 135. See also Sec. 5 of this Chapter.
[11] Sec. 120.
[12] Sec. 122—for meaning of " new development " see Appendix B (2).
[13] Sec. 121.
[14] Town and Country Planning (Compensation and Certificates) Regulations, 1963.
[15] Where uses or works are " unauthorised," i.e., have been begun or carried out without the grant of planning permission or contrary to conditions attached to such permission, the local planning authority may proceed by means of an " enforcement notice " under Sec. 15 of the T. & C.P. Act, 1968 and no compensation is payable. They must, however, do so within four years of the development or breach of condition.

modification of an authorised use of land or the alteration or removal of authorised buildings or works.

Any person who suffers loss in consequence of such an order, either through depreciation in the value of his land, or by disturbance, or by expense incurred in complying with the order, is entitled to compensation provided his claim is made within six months. An example of this type of case is given in Section 7 of this Chapter. As an alternative to claiming compensation for depreciation in the value of his land, the owner of the interest may be able to serve a purchase notice (see next Section).

### 5.  PURCHASE NOTICE[15a]

*(Sections 129-137—Town and Country Planning Act, 1962)*

If, in any case, planning permission is refused, either by the local planning authority or by the Secretary of State, or is granted subject to conditions, then if the owner[16] of the land claims that it is incapable of reasonably beneficial use:—

  (i) in its existing state;

  (ii) if developed in accordance with conditions imposed;

  (iii) if developed in any other way for which permission has been, or is deemed to be, granted under the Act, or for which the Secretary of State or the local planning authority have undertaken to grant permission;

he may, within six months[17] of the planning decision in question, serve a " purchase notice " on the local authority for the district requiring them to purchase his interest in the land.

The Council on whom a purchase notice is served shall within three months of such service themselves serve a counter-notice on the owner to the effect either : —

  (a) that they are willing to comply with the purchase notice; or

  (b) that another specified local authority or statutory undertakers have agreed to comply with it in their place; or

  (c) that, for reasons specified in the notice, neither the council nor any other local authority or statutory undertakers are willing to comply with the purchase notice, and that a copy of the purchase notice has been sent to the Secretary of State on a date specified in the counter-notice together

---

[15a] The circumstances in which an owner/occupier may require the purchase of his interest, under Secs. 138 and 139 of the Act, are dealt with in Chapter 22, Section A (2).

[16] " Owner " means the person entitled to receive the rack rent of the land, or who would be entitled to receive it if the land were so let—Sec. 221 (1).

[17] Town & Country Planning (General) Regulations, 1948.

with a statement of the reasons for their refusal to purchase.

In cases (a) and (b) above, the Council on whom the purchase notice was served, or the specified local authority or statutory undertakers, as the case may be, will be deemed to be authorised to acquire the owners' interest in the land and to have served a notice to treat on the date of the service of the counter-notice.

In case (c), where the purchase notice is forwarded to the Secretary of State, the following courses of action are open to him:—

  (i) to confirm the notice, if satisfied that the land is in fact incapable of reasonably beneficial use in the circumstances specified in Section 129; [17a]

  (ii) to confirm the notice, but to substitute another local authority or statutory undertakers;

  (iii) not to confirm the notice, but to grant permission for the required development, or to revoke or amend any conditions imposed;

  (iv) not to confirm the notice, but to direct that permission shall be given for some other form of development;

  (v) to refuse to confirm the notice, or to take any action, if satisfied that the land has not in fact been rendered incapable of reasonably beneficial use.

" Reasonably beneficial use " is rather a vague term and the question has naturally arisen whether what is " reasonably beneficial " is to be judged in relation to the possible present use of the land or by comparison with the use to which it might have been put but for the adverse planning decision—e.g., the use of land for agricultural purposes may be " beneficial ", but is it " reasonably beneficial " compared with the purposes to which it might be put?   It is now provided that in considering whether or not the use of any land is " reasonably beneficial " the Secretary of State shall not take account of the possibility of any development outside those types specified in the Third Schedule of the 1962 Act.[18]

Before taking any of the steps enumerated above—including refusal to confirm—the Secretary must give notice of his proposed action to the person who served the purchase notice, the local authority on whom it was served, the local planning authority and any other local authority or statutory undertakers who may have been substituted for the authority on whom the notice was served.   He must also give such person or bodies an opportunity of a hearing if they so desire.   If after such hearing it appears to the Secretary to be expedient to take some action under the

---

[17a] But even in this case the Secretary is not obliged to confirm under certain special circumstances relating to land, forming part of a larger area, which has a restricted use by virtue of a previous planning permission— Town and Country Planning Act, 1968, Sec. 32.

[18] As now modified by the Town and Country Planning Act, 1963—see Appendix B (2).

Section other than that specified in his notice he may do so without any further hearing.

If the Secretary confirms the purchase notice, or fails to take any action within six months, the local authority on whom it was served will be deemed to be authorised to acquire the land compulsorily and to have served a notice to treat on such date as the Minister may direct, or at the end of the period of six months as the case may be.

Any party aggrieved by the decision of the Secretary on a purchase notice may, within six weeks, make an application to the High Court to quash the decision on the grounds that either (i) the decision is not within the powers of the Town and Country Planning Act, 1962, or (ii) the interests of the applicant have been substantially prejudiced by a failure to comply with any relevant requirements.

If the Secretary's decision is quashed, the purchase notice is treated as cancelled; but the owner may serve a further purchase notice within six months.

Where the Secretary, instead of confirming the purchase notice, directs that permission shall be given for some alternative development, then if the value of the land for such alternative development is less than its " existing use value "[19] the owner is entitled to compensation equal to the difference between these two values. But this is subject to any direction by the Secretary excluding compensation in respect of any conditions as to design, external appearance, size or height of buildings, or number of buildings to the acre.

Where a purchase notice takes effect—i.e., the authority are deemed to have served a notice to treat—after 29 October, 1958, the compensation payable to the owner will be assessed, as in any case of compulsory acquisition, under the provisions of the Land Compensation Act, 1961. (See Chapter 21.)

### 6.   OTHER CASES

Compensation on account of planning requirements may also be payable in connection with the following matters under the 1962 Act: —

> (i) Tree preservation orders (Sections 29 and 125 of the Town and Country Planning Act, 1962).
>
> (ii) Building preservation orders (Part V of the Town and Country Planning Act, 1968).
>
> (iii) Cost of removal of advertisements in certain cases (Sections 34 and 126 of the Town and Country Planning Act, 1962).

---

[19] i.e., the value assuming planning permisson would only be given for the forms of development specified in the Third Schedule to the 1947 Act, as originally enacted, but subject to the modifications prescribed by the Town and Country Planning Act, 1963.

## 7. EXAMPLES

*Example—Claim for refusal to permit Third Schedule (Part II) development (Section 1 of this Chapter).*

A freehold factory is situated in the outskirts of a large town in an area predominantly residential, the buildings comprise a two-storey office block and a single-storey factory. The total internal floor space is 1,000 m². The total cubical content is 5,000 m³. The premises were erected in 1927 and were purchased by the present occupier a few years ago for £40,000. At the side of the factory there is a plot of land between the factory and adjacent houses in the same road, with a frontage of 20 m and a depth of 40 m. Owing to the expansion of the business carried on, the premises have become very congested and the occupier has had plans prepared for the erection of a single-storey loading bay for packing, loading and unloading of goods. The building is to be erected on the vacant plot and will have a total floor space of 90 m² and a total cubical content of 450 m³.

An application for planning consent has been refused by the planning authority on the grounds that the factory is in an area allocated for residential use in the relevant development plan, and that no further extension should be permitted.

On appeal to the Secretary of State, the refusal is confirmed. You are asked to advise on the claim that should be submitted under Section 123 of the Town and Country Planning Act, 1962.

*Calculation of Compensation—*

The proposed extension is within the limits prescribed by Part II of the Third Schedule as modified by the 1963 Act, i.e., the addition to the cube and, presumably, the gross floor space is less than 10 per cent. Therefore, Section 123 claim is justified.

Assuming no change in value since the date of purchase value now is equivalent to £40 per m².

As a result of an inspection it is considered that the new loading facilities will enhance the value of the property to an extent that if the development were carried out, the property might reasonably be valued at £42 per m².

*Value with extension—*

|  |  |  |  | m² |  |  |
|---|---|---|---|---|---|---|
| Present area | ... | ... | ... | 1,000 |  |  |
| Extension | ... | ... | ... | 90 |  |  |
| Total area | ... | ... | ... | 1,090 at £42 | £45,780 |

| | | | | | |
|---|---|---|---|---|---|
| *Deduct* cost of extension, say | ... | ... | £2,750 | |
| *Add* for fees and contingencies, say | | ... | 250 | |
| | | | | 3,000 |

| | | | | | |
|---|---|---|---|---|---|
| Value | ... | ... | ... | ... | £42,780 |
| Value at present without permission to develop | ... | ... | ... | ... | 40,000 |
| Claim | ... | ... | ... | ... | £2,780 |

*Example—Compensation for refusal of planning permission for " new " development [Section 2 of this Chapter].* A parcel of 8 hectares of land lies on the edge of a suburb about fifteen miles from a town. The land forms part of a farm and has an unexpended balance of established development value of £16,000. The most profitable development for the land today would be by the erection of dwelling-houses at a density of 20 houses per hectare but for some time it has been known that the land lies within a " green belt ".

The owner has applied to the local planning authority for permission to develop the land by erecting 160 houses, but permission has been refused. The value today with the benefit of the planning permission applied for would be £15,000 per hectare and the value now, after the refusal, is £500 per hectare. It is required to assess the compensation payable under Part VI of the Town and Country Planning Act, 1962.

*Compensation*

The amount of compensation payable is the lesser of : —

(i) *The depreciation in the value of the free-holder's interest:—*

| | | |
|---|---|---|
| (a) | Value had permission been granted— 8 hectares @ £15,000 per hectare | £120,000 |
| less (b) | Value taking account of the refusal— 8 hectares @ £500 per hectare ... | £4,000 |
| | | £116,000 |

*or (ii) The unexpended balance of established development value:—*          £16,000

| | |
|---|---|
| *Compensation* | £16,000 |

*Example—Claim for discontinuance of an existing use—[Section 4 of this Chapter].*

A chemical factory has been established in its present building for many years. The building was constructed 50 years ago and the accommodation is on two floors, each of 300 m². There are no offices other than " works offices " and the site is fully covered. The process is one which brings the building into the " special industry " class and affects the amenities of the area by noise, smell and dirt.

The area is a residential one and is allocated for this use in the development plan for the area. The local authority, following objections by inhabitants of private residences in the locality, has ordered that it shall cease to be used for its present purpose.

It is required to assess the compensation payable under Section 124 of the Town and Country Planning Act, 1962, in respect of the discontinuance of the authorised use. No other premises are available in this area.

The planning authority has indicated that consent would be given for the erection of a single dwelling-house on the site.

*Calculation of compensation:—*

|  |  |  |  | *Total* |  |
|---|---|---|---|---|---|
| Value of premises as a factory— |  |  |  |  |  |
| Ground floor—300 m² @ £6 p.a. ... | ... | | | £1,800 | p.a. |
| First floor—300 m² @ £4 p.a. | ... | | ... | £1,200 | p.a. |
| Estimated net rental value ... | ... | | ... | £3,000 | p.a. |
| Y.P. in perpetuity ... | ... | ... | ... | 9 | |
| | | | | £27,000 | |
| Value of site with planning consent to erect a single dwelling-house, say ... ... ... ... | | | £2,500 | | |
| *Less:* Cost of demolition of existing buildings, say ... ... ... | | | £200 | £2,300 | |
| Depreciation in value of freehold interest ... ... ... ... | | | | £24,700 | |

*Note—*In addition, the freeholder would be entitled to claim for incidental losses due to " disturbance ", such as are discussed in Chapter 22.

*Example—Compensation following refusal of Secretary of State to confirm a purchase notice [Section 5 of this Chapter].* A site having a frontage of 10 m and a depth of 25 m stands on the inside of a sharp bend in a main road carrying heavy traffic. A shop with upper part on three floors was erected on the land in 1910 and was entirely destroyed by fire last year. The freeholder immediately applied for town planning permission to build another shop and upper part on the site but permission was refused on the grounds that the re-erection of the premises would obstruct the view of traffic approaching the corner.

The freeholder served a purchase notice on the County Council which came before the Secretary of State who refused to confirm it. He indicated in his decision that he would permit a lock-up shop to be erected on the corner to be set back so that the effective site depth would be only 15 m.

It is required to assess the compensation payable.

If the original premises were to be reinstated on the site, they would have a net rack rental value of £900 per annum. The lock-up shop for which permission would be granted would be worth only £400 per annum.

*Compensation*
  *" Existing use " value, i.e., value of site with per-*
    *mission to erect a shop and upper part worth*
    *£900 per annum:—*

| | |
|---|---:|
| 10 m frontage @ £600 per metre frontage | £6,000 |

  *Value of site for erection of lock-up shop worth*
    *£400 per annum:—*

| | |
|---|---:|
| 10 m frontage @ £360 per metre frontage | £3,600 |
| *Compensation* | £2,400 |

# Chapter 20

## Principles of Compulsory Purchase and Compensation

### 1. GENERALLY

THERE ARE numerous Acts of Parliament under which Government departments, local or public authorities, or statutory undertakings, may carry out schemes for the general benefit of the community involving the acquisition of land or interference with owners' proprietary rights.

Where an owner's property is taken under statutory powers he is entitled to compensation as of right, unless the Act which authorises the acquisition expressly provides otherwise. Where no interest in land is taken but a property is depreciated in value by the exercise of statutory powers, the owner's right to compensation depends on the terms of the Act under which these powers are exercised.

For a detailed account of the law on this subject the reader should consult some standard text-book such as Cripps's "Compulsory Acquisition of Land"[1]. The present chapter is confined to such a brief outline of the law as will provide the necessary background to the principles involved in compulsory purchase valuations.

It will be convenient to consider first the general position where land is acquired, and then to discuss the rights of those owners whose property is injured by the exercise of statutory powers.

In the majority of cases power to acquire land compulsorily is derived from some general Act of Parliament, which authorises a certain class of public body to acquire land for undertakings of a certain type—e.g., local authorities to acquire land for housing, or highway authorities to acquire land for road construction or improvement.

Authority to take land having been given in general terms, the public body for whose purposes a particular piece of land is wanted, must then follow a certain specified procedure in acquiring it. In most cases this involves the making of what is known as a Compulsory Purchase Order giving the necessary compulsory powers in relation to the particular undertaking.

Except where a Government department is itself acquiring the land, the Compulsory Purchase Order must first be made by the

---

[1] See also "Compulsory Purchase and Compensation", Fourth Edition, by Lawrance, D. M. (Estates Gazette, Ltd.).

acquiring body in question and then submitted to an appropriate Minister or Secretary of State for confirmation.

In the great majority of cases the making and confirming of Compulsory Purchase Orders is now regulated by the provisions of the Acquisition of Land (Authorisation Procedure) Act, 1946, under which the proposed Order must be advertised, notices served on interested parties, and opportunity given to inspect the Order, together with the plans and schedules of the land to which it relates, and to make any objections. Where objections are made the Minister concerned may order a public local enquiry to be held before confirming the Order. If the Order is confirmed, with or without modifications, the confirmation must again be advertised and notices served on interested parties.

The Act or Order from which compulsory powers derive in any particular case may conveniently be referred to as the "Special Act".

In 1845 Parliament passed a code of law known as the Lands Clauses Consolidation Act, 1845, designed to regulate the procedure in connection with all questions likely to arise between owners and acquiring bodies in cases where land should be authorised to be acquired compulsorily for public or semi-public purposes.

This Act and certain short amending Acts which followed it, are generally referred to as the "Lands Clauses Acts", and ever since 1845 have been incorporated in every Act or Order which confers powers of compulsory purchase, except in so far as certain sections of the code may be expressly or impliedly modified or excluded by the terms of the "Special Act".

Since 1st January, 1966, in all cases where the making and confirmation of the compulsory purchase order is governed by the Acquisition of Land (Authorisation Procedure) Act, 1946, the provisions of the Lands Clauses Act, 1845, are replaced by those of Part I of the Compulsory Purchase Act, 1965. But since—with certain exceptions—the provisions of the latter Act are substantially the same as those of the 1845 Act, this does not involve any appreciable change in the general law governing the exercise of compulsory powers.

The Lands Clauses Acts, and the interpretation of their provisions by the Courts in a number of important cases, may, therefore, be said to form the basis of the existing law of compensation, and for a considerable number of years governed all valuations for compulsory purchase purposes.

In 1919, however, a statutory distinction was drawn between cases where land was authorised to be taken by some semi-public body trading for profit, and cases where land was taken for some purely public purpose—e.g., housing, roads, public health purposes, etc.—by a public body employing public funds and not reaping any private profit out of the enterprise.

It was felt that bodies of the latter type should be able to acquire land on the most favourable terms possible, and it was doubted whether the Lands Clauses Acts, which were in many respects favourable to owners, could be relied on to ensure this.

Accordingly a further general code of law was passed by Parliament under the name of the Acquisition of Land (Assessment of Compensation) Act, 1919, which introduced certain modifications in the existing basis of compensation and prescribed a special procedure for assessing it in all cases where land was authorised to be acquired compulsorily by a Government department or local or public authority.

Later its application was extended, by the Town and Country Planning Act, 1947, to the compulsory acquisition of land by statutory undertakers.

As from 1st August, 1961, the provisions of the 1919 Act are re-enacted in Part II of the Land Compensation Act, 1961, and made applicable to *all* cases of compulsory acquisition. Any Act or Order, therefore, which gives compulsory powers will incorporate not only the Lands Clauses Acts or the corresponding provisions of the Compulsory Purchase Act, 1965, but also the Land Compensation Act, 1961, and the provisions of the latter code will overrule those of the former wherever the two are inconsistent.

The temporary modifications of the code of compensation under the 1919 Act made by the Town and Country Planning Acts, 1947–1954, and also the present basis of compensation prescribed by the Land Compensation Act, 1961, will be considered at length in subsequent Chapters.

The remainder of the present Chapter is devoted to a further consideration of the legal aspects of compulsory purchase.

## 2. COMPULSORY PURCHASE PROCEDURE

Save in the cases referred to in the concluding paragraphs of this Section, the first step in the procedure, after the acquiring body has obtained its compulsory powers, is the service of a notice to treat on all parties having an interest in the land to be acquired. This notice will indicate, usually with the help of a plan, the property to be taken and will state that the acquiring body are willing to treat with owners as to the purchase price and compensation. It will also demand particulars of the owner's interest and of his claim. The notice has an important bearing on subsequent proceedings, since compensation can only be claimed in respect of such interests in the land as existed at the date of the notice to treat and the acquiring body's burdens cannot be increased by the creation of fresh interests after that date.[2]

---

[2] *Mercer v. Liverpool, St. Helens & S. Lancs. Railway*, [1904] A.C. 461; *Corporation of Birmingham v. West Midlands Baptist (Trust) Association*, [1969] R.V.R. 484; Estates Gazette, 2 and 9 April, 1969.

In some cases the quantum of interest may be fixed even earlier than the date of notice to treat, for under the provisions of the Acquisition of Land (Authorisation Procedure) Act, 1946, the Lands Tribunal in assessing compensation may ignore the effect of any work done or interest created if it is satisfied that the creation of the interest or the doing of the work was not reasonably necessary and was with the object of obtaining or increasing compensation.

On receipt of notice to treat, the owner or his advisers, having satisfied themselves that the notice is in order and the property correctly described, will no doubt consider the preparation of a notice of claim.

Section 4 (2) of the Land Compensation Act, 1961, requires that the owner's notice of claim shall state the exact nature of the interest in respect of which compensation is claimed and give details, distinguishing the amounts claimed under separate heads, and showing how the amount claimed under each head is calculated. If this detailed claim is not made within a reasonable time the owner may be penalised in the matter of costs, should the case go to the Lands Tribunal. When such notice of claim has been delivered, the acquiring authority may, at any time within six weeks from the delivery thereof, withdraw any notice to treat served in respect of the property, but will be liable to pay compensation for any loss or expense suffered by an owner in consequence of the service of the notice to treat and its subsequent withdrawal.[3]

If the claimant fails to deliver a detailed statement of claim, the acquiring authority may withdraw their notice to treat within six weeks after the claim has been determined. In this case no compensation is payable to the claimant for any loss or expense incurred after the time when, in the opinion of the Lands Tribunal, a notice of claim should have been delivered.[4]

In preparing a claim for compensation, a valuer acting for the owner must give careful attention to the following principal points:—

   (i) The type of acquiring body.

   (ii) The purpose for which the land is to be taken—since if part only of a property is to be acquired the nature of the undertaking may considerably affect the extent to which the remainder is likely to be depreciated in value.

   (iii) The provisions of those sections of the Special Act relating to the taking of land by agreement or compulsorily.

   (iv) The precise terms and effect of the compulsory purchase order.

Points (iii) and (iv) are of vital importance, since the provisions of the Special Act, or of any Order made under it, may modify the

---

[3] Land Compensation Act, 1961, Sec. 31 (1) and (3).
[4] *Ibid.*, Sec. 31 (2) and (3).

general procedure and basis of compensation prescribed by the Lands Clauses Acts (or Compulsory Purchase Act, 1965) and the Land Compensation Act, 1961.

For instance, all Orders made under the Acquisition of Land (Authorisation Procedure) Act, 1946, contain provisions regarding the taking of part only of a property which may influence the preparation of the claim for the land taken.

The claim having been prepared and submitted, negotiations will follow between the acquiring body and the owner, and in a considerable number of cases a settlement by agreement may be reached.

It is, indeed, possible for negotiations for purchase to be carried through without the service of a formal notice to treat. The advantage of such a notice from the acquiring body's point of view, however, is that it enables compulsory powers to be exercised at once, should negotiations prove unsuccessful. Where no agreement is reached, compensation must be assessed by the Lands Tribunal established under the Lands Tribunal Act, 1949.[5]

It is beyond the scope of this book to consider details of the procedure before the Tribunal, but a brief reference to the question of costs is desirable since the statutory provisions on this point, although they do not affect the basis of compensation, may well influence the course of negotiations between the parties.

It is usual for the acquiring body to make an unconditional offer of compensation to the claimant before assessment proceedings commence. If the claimant accepts the offer, that is the end of the matter. If he rejects it, the offer is usually handed to the Tribunal in a sealed envelope which is not opened until after the case has been heard and the Tribunal has come to its decision as to the compensation payable.

The Lands Tribunal may order the claimant to bear the acquiring body's costs as well as his own if the sum awarded is the same or less than the unconditional offer, or if the claimant fails to submit a detailed statement of claim within a reasonable time. On the other hand, if the claimant makes an unconditional offer to accept a sum of compensation and also submits a detailed statement of claim and the amount awarded is the same or more than the offer, the acquiring body may be ordered to pay the claimant's costs incurred since the offer was made.[6]

In those cases where a settlement by agreement is negotiated it is the usual practice for the claimant's legal costs and the fees of the valuer advising him to be paid by the acquiring body as part of the agreed compensation.

---

[5] Land Compensation Act, 1961, Sec. 1; and Lands Tribunal Act, 1949, Sec. 1 (3) (a).

[6] Land Compensation Act, 1961, Sec. 4.

Under Sec. 30 of the Town & Country Planning Act, 1968, an acquiring authority may—as soon as a compulsory purchase order has come into operation—execute a "general vesting declaration", vesting the land in itself. The effect is that notices to treat will be deemed to have been served on all persons entitled to them, as from the date when the declaration was made, and the ownership[7] of the land will vest in the authority without formal conveyance.

Notice of the compulsory purchase order having been made must in these cases contain an invitation to owners to submit details of their interest in the land. They will then receive notice of the vesting declaration and will be entitled to submit their claims to compensation.

### 3.　POWER TO TAKE PART ONLY OF A PROPERTY

It frequently happens that an acquiring body requires part only of an owner's property—e.g., a strip of garden attached to a house or part of a forecourt in front of trade premises—for the purpose of its undertaking.

Under Section 92 of the Lands Clauses Act, 1845—which may still apply without modification in a few cases—an owner served with a notice to treat in respect of part only of a "house or other building or manufactory" might insist on the acquiring authority either taking his interest in the whole of the premises or else withdrawing its notice to treat.

In interpreting Section 92 "house" has been held to include not only a dwelling-house but any premises—e.g., a hospital or an inn—adapted to a particular use and occupation; while "part of a house" includes any portion of the premises, however inconsiderable, which would pass on a conveyance of the house or which is ordinarily used and enjoyed with it.

Similarly, part of a "manufactory" includes the whole of premises —land or buildings—used in a particular process involving the production of a finished article from raw materials.

Thus, service of a notice to treat in respect of a small piece of garden would under Section 92 entitle the owner to require the whole of a large house to be taken. Or the taking of a small piece of waste land used for the deposit of ashes from furnaces might involve the acquisition of the whole of a considerable manufactory.

The inconvenience of this section to acquiring bodies led to the insertion in later compulsory purchase acts of a "material detriment clause" either replacing Section 92 or considerably modifying the operation of it. Where, as is nearly always the case nowadays, the compulsory purchase order is made under the Acquisition of Land (Authorisation Procedure) Act, 1946, the procedure will be governed

---

[7] Town & Country Planning Act, 1968, Sec. 30.

by Section 8 of the Compulsory Purchase Act, 1965. This provides in effect that no person shall be compelled to sell a part only of any house, building or manufactory, or of a park or garden belonging to a house, except where the Lands Tribunal is of the opinion that the part can be taken without material detriment to the remainder or, in the case of a park or garden attached to a house, without seriously affecting the amenity or convenience of the house.

Whether the circumstances of a particular case justify a plea of "material detriment" is purely a question of fact. It is necessary to consider: (a) the physical effect of the taking of the part, and (b) the effect on value.

If it seems likely that the property could well be occupied in the same way as formerly without material damage to the convenience and amenity previously enjoyed by the owner, and if the loss of the part can fairly be met by payment of reasonable compensation, there can be little doubt of the acquiring body's right to take part only under a "material detriment" clause. But where the taking of part only would render the rest of the property less useful or less valuable in some significant degree, the owner may well be justified in claiming that the whole should be taken.

In a recent case[8] the Lands Tribunal expressed the view that . . . "the question should be whether it is reasonable to subject the owner against his will to a truncation of his property (with compensation) rather than make a clean sweep by taking the whole".

Extreme cases of material detriment occur where the amenities and identity of a property are destroyed so that it can no longer be reasonably occupied. Thus the whole must clearly be taken if a house loses a portion of the structure, necessitating the rebuilding of the parts in a restricted way and on a different plan, or where the whole of the structure is destroyed. In practice, the problem is often one of expediency. If the damage is serious the acquiring authority will usually take the whole property, if required, and recoup such part of the cost as is possible after the works are completed. This will frequently be cheaper than contesting the right of the owner to compel the taking of the whole as, even if the authority succeeds, the owner will still be entitled to be adequately compensated for the anticipated damage for the reduced value of the portion left.

### 4. Compensation for Injurious Affection

(a) *Generally*.—The term "injurious affection" implies some injury to an owner's property due to the exercise of statutory powers. Claims for injurious affection in connection with compulsory purchase, fall into two distinct classes:—

    (i) Claims for injurious affection to land formerly held with land taken.

---

[8] *Ravenscroft Properties Ltd. v. London Borough of Hillingdon* (Ref./198/1967).

    (ii) Claims for injurious affection due to the exercise of statutory powers on land not owned by the claimant.

It is proposed to consider briefly the legal principles governing the *right* to compensation in these two cases.

The practical considerations involved in the actual preparation of claims for compensation are considered in a later Chapter.

(*b*) *Injurious Affection to land held with land taken.*—Where part only of an owner's property is taken he is entitled to compensation not only for the loss of the part taken, but also for severance and other injury which may result to other land formerly held with it.

For instance, if part of the garden of a house is taken for the construction of a major road, the owner will be entitled to claim both for the loss of his land and also for further depreciation in the value of the house and the remaining land likely to arise from the presence of a road on the part taken.

The expression "held with" is not necessarily limited to land which is held under the same title deeds or which immediately adjoins that taken. It is enough to show that prior to the acquisition the lands were so near together or so situated in relation to each other that the possession and control of each gave an enhanced value to the whole.[9]

Thus the term has been held to extend to two portions of a building estate separated from each other by a public road and held under separate title deeds, but subject to one general scheme of development.

Claims for injurious affection in this type of case may include all injury likely to result either from the execution of the acquiring body's works or from their subsequent user on the land taken. For instance, the construction of a by-pass road across a country estate may result in certain fields being severed from the rest of the agricultural land and farm buildings and thereby depreciated in value, while the noise, fumes and loss of privacy likely to result from the use of the land as a busy thoroughfare may seriously reduce the value of the mansion. Both these items may properly be included in the claim.

Where the owner of a property consisting of a house and some surrounding land held an option to purchase some adjoining fields, part of which was acquired for the construction of a road, it was held that the option constituted an interest in the land taken entitling him to notice to treat and that, since his property was "held with" this land within the meaning of the Lands Clauses Act[10] he was entitled to compensation for the depreciation it would suffer from the user of the land taken as an arterial road.[11]

---

[9] *Cowper Essex v. Acton Local Board* (1889). 14 A.C. 153.

[10] Or, in most cases now, the corresponding Section of the Compulsory Purchase Act, 1965.

[11] *Oppenheimer v. Minister of Transport* (1941), 58 T.L.R. 86.

Compensation is, however, limited to what is done on the land taken. So where a road was widened for the purposes of a tramway system and land taken from the front garden of a house was used for the construction of the footpath, the owner was not allowed to claim for possible loss of value to the house due to the running of the trams on that part of the road which already belonged to the local authority.[12] While in a more recent case[13]—which concerned the taking of two small parcels of land, forming part of a house, for the purpose of a new road—it was held that the owner was only entitled to compensation for injury resulting from the construction and proposed user of the new road on the portions of land taken from him and not on the whole course of the road as it passed his house.

The claim is also restricted to injury likely to result from the proper exercise of the acquiring body's statutory powers. Injury caused by some unauthorised act on the land taken may give a right to damages at common law when it is actually suffered, but cannot be the subject of a claim for compensation.

(c) *Injurious Affection to land no part of which is taken.*—Where no part of an owner's property is taken, but he claims that it is depreciated in value by the carrying out of a statutory undertaking on other land, his right to compensation, if any, will be derived from the incorporation in the Special Act of Section 68 of the Lands Clauses Act, 1845, or more usually Section 10 of the Compulsory Purchase Act, 1965.

Typical examples of this type of case are where a right of light or way or other easement attached to a property is interfered with by a statutory undertaking carried out on adjoining land, or where the exercise of the acquiring body's statutory powers involves the breach of some restrictive covenant imposed for the benefit of neighbouring property.

No notice to treat will be served on the aggrieved owner and no right to compensation can arise until his rights have actually been interfered with. When the injury has been suffered, but not before, the owner may be entitled to submit a claim to the acquiring body stating the nature of his interest and the amount of his claim.

The right to compensation for injurious affection in this type of case is limited by the application of four rules approved by the Courts in *McCarthy v. Metropolitan Board of Works*[14] and other cases in which the correct interpretation of the section was exhaustively examined.

To entitle the owner to compensation his claim must pass all four

---

[12] *R. V. Mountford*, ex parte *London United Tramways* (1901), Ltd., [1906] 2 K.B. 314.
[13] *Edwards v. Minister of Transport* (1964), 2 Q.B.D. 134.
[14] (1874) L.R. 7 H.L. 243.

of the tests prescribed. If it fails on any one of them, there can be no right to compensation.

The following is a brief summary and explanation of the four rules.

### Rule 1.—*The damage or loss must result from an act made lawful by the acquiring body's statutory powers.*

If there is a wrong done which is not authorised by the powers conferred by Parliament the claimant must seek a remedy by action for damages at common law, and not a claim for compensation under the Act. Also if statutory powers are exercised in a careless or unreasonable manner the remedy will be by action, not by a claim for compensation.

So where, owing to negligence in construction, a new sewer bursts and adjoining land is flooded, the owner of such land cannot claim compensation from the local authority under Section 68 of the Lands Clauses Acts or Section 10 of the Compulsory Purchase Act, 1965, although he may have a remedy in damages at common law.

### Rule 2.—*The damage must arise from something which would have been actionable if the acquiring body had not been protected by statutory powers.*

In other words, there must be an interference with the owner's legal rights in connection with the property.

Thus a mere fear of injury gives no right to compensation nor do acts—such as obstruction of modern lights or a view, or interference with privacy, or interference with underground water running in undefined channels—which would not in any case have been actionable. But obstruction of a right of light or other easement attached to property, or breach of a restrictive covenant, or interference with a public right whereby the owner suffers some injury different in kind to that suffered by the public generally, are matters which would have given a right of action if the acquiring body had not been protected by their statutory powers, and are, therefore, subjects for compensation.

### Rule 3.—*The damage must be an injury to land, not a mere personal or trade injury.*

For a claim to succeed it must be shown that the property as a property has been depreciated in value by the act in question. Loss of trade or custom by reason of works not otherwise directly affecting the house or land in or upon which a trade has been carried on, is not by itself a proper subject for compensation.

In the case of shops, public houses and other trade premises, any interference with the trading prospects is almost certain to react on the value of the premises themselves. Here the success or failure of a claim for compensation may depend on the form in which the claim is made. For example, a claim based on loss of trade to a public house owing to interference with a right of access to it, would certainly fail. But a claim based on the reduced rental and capital value of the premises due to less convenient access should succeed.

*Rule 4.—The damage must be caused by the execution of the works and not by their subsequent user.*

Once the works are executed the acquiring body will not be liable for injury which may result from the normal use of them in the manner authorised by Parliament, although they would be liable to action or an injunction if they used their statutory powers in a negligent manner.

Thus, apart from any express provision which may be inserted in the Special Act, an owner from whom no land is taken is not entitled to compensation for injury caused by noise, smoke or vibration from passing trains once railway works are constructed, nor for noise, fumes and other inconvenience arising from a heavy volume of traffic on an arterial road.

An example of a case which would clearly pass the above four tests is where the execution of the acquiring body's works on adjacent land interferes with a right of light attached to office premises and so depreciates their value.

On the other hand, property may suffer serious depreciation in value for which the owner has no claim whatever. For instance, the construction of a by-pass road may divert traffic from a town and depreciate the value of a garage and petrol station on its main street; or the erection by a local authority of a big block of flats may depreciate the value of fair-sized residential property in the immediate neighbourhood. In neither of these cases is there any right to compensation, since there is no interference with any public or private right attached to the property in question and the claim, therefore, fails to pass Rule 2 above.

Once the owner's right to compensation has been established, the measure of compensation will be the total depreciation in the value of his property caused by the injury of which he complains. Thus, where an acquiring body obstructed lights, to which the claimant had a legal right, and also others to which the claimant had no legal right, it was held that both should be the subject of compensation. The interference with ancient lights clearly passed the four tests laid down in *McCarthy v. Metropolitan Board of Works*, and, the case having thus been brought within the compensation clauses of the Act, the interference with modern lights might be included in the claim, although it would not, by itself, have given a right to compensation.[15]

---

[15] In *Re London, Tilbury, etc., Rail Co. v. Gower's Walk Schools* (1889), 24 Q.B. 326.

# Chapter 21

## Valuations for Compulsory Purchase and Compensation

### A. Introductory

THE BASIS of compensation for land compulsorily acquired has from time to time been affected by the provisions of the following statutes:—

(a) *The Lands Clauses Act*, 1845.—The compensation provisions of this Act were somewhat vague. But certain general principles were established as the result of judicial decisions based on those provisions.

Since 1 January, 1966, in the majority of compulsory purchase cases, the provisions of the Lands Clauses Act, 1845, are replaced by corresponding provisions in the *Compulsory Purchase Act*, 1965. But since there is little change in the wording, these new provisions do not appear to affect the general principles established by the courts in their interpretation of the 1845 Act.

(b) *The Acquisition of Land (Assessment of Compensation) Act*, 1919.—Section 2 of this Act prescribed six rules governing the compensation payable for interests in land acquired compulsorily by any Government department, local or public authority or statutory undertaking.

The general basis prescribed was the price the land might be expected to realise if sold in the open market by a willing seller—known in practice as "open market value".

(c) *The Town and Country Planning Act*, 1944.—During the period 17 *November*, 1944, *to* 6 *August*, 1947, "open market value" for compensation purposes was to be estimated by reference to prices ruling at 31 March, 1939.

(d) *The Town and Country Planning Acts*, 1947–54.—These Acts applied to compensation payable under notices to treat served *after* 6 *August*, 1947, *and before* 30 *October*, 1958.

The general basis of compensation was "existing use value"—i.e., open market value assessed on the assumption that planning permission would only be given for such limited forms of development as were specified in the Third Schedule to the 1947 Act.

(e) *The Town and Country Planning Act*, 1959.—This replaced the Town and Country Planning Acts, 1947–54, in the case of notices to treat served *on or after* 30 *October*, 1958.

It restored "open market value", as defined by the 1919 Act, as the basis of compensation subject to certain additional rules, and subject also to certain prescribed assumptions as to the forms of development for which planning permission might reasonably be expected to be obtained.

(*f*) *The Land Compensation Act*, 1961.—As from 1 *August*, 1961, this Act incorporates and re-enacts the Acquisition of Land (Assessment of Compensation) Act, 1919, and the basic compensation provisions of the Town and Country Planning Act, 1959.[1] The new Act applies to all cases where land is authorised to be acquired compulsorily.

It will be clear from the above summary that the code of law *now* governing the basis of compensation for all interests in land compulsorily acquired consists of:—

    (i) Those general principles established by judicial decisions based on the provisions of the Lands Clauses Act, 1845.

    (ii) The provisions of the Land Compensation Act, 1961.

This code of law is examined in detail in this Chapter. Chapter 22 deals with certain compulsory purchase matters, involving questions of valuation, which are governed by Town and Country Planning legislation and also gives practical examples of valuations for compensation. While Chapter 23 gives a brief outline of the compensation provisions of the Town and Country Planning Acts, 1947–54, which can now only apply to a very limited number of cases where notice to treat was served before 30 October, 1958.

## B.   General Principles of Compensation

The general principles, established by judicial decisions under the Lands Clauses Act, 1845, and which apply to *all* cases of compulsory purchase, unless expressly or impliedly excluded by Statute, may be briefly summarised as follows:—

    (i) Service of the acquiring body's notice to treat fixes the property to be taken and the nature and extent of the owner's interest in it. No compensation is payable in respect of fresh interests created after the notice to treat has been served which increase the burden on the acquiring body.

    (ii) For just over 100 years—following the case of *Penny v. Penny* (1868)—it was assumed that the value of the property acquired must also be assessed as at the date of notice to treat. But in the recent case of *Corporation of Birmingham v. West Midlands Baptist (Trust) Association*[2] the House of

---

[1] Those parts of the 1959 Act which are incorporated are Sections 1–13, 16–21, 31 (4) (f), the 1st, 2nd and 3rd Schedules and one part of the 7th Schedule.
[2] [1969] R.V.R. 484; [1969] 3 All. E.R. 172.

Lords held that this supposed "rule" was without foundation, and expressed the view that the appropriate date for assessing the value of the land is either

(a) the date when compensation is agreed or assessed, or
(b) the date when possession is taken (if this is the earlier).

(iii) If the owner can prove that he has suffered loss between the date of service of notice to treat and the date at which compensation is assessed—for instance, through uncertainty of tenure created by the notice to treat—he may include this loss in his claim.[3]

(iv) Compensation must be based on the value of the land in the hands of the owner, not its value to the acquiring body.[4] Any increase in value due to the scheme involving the acquisition must be disregarded.[5]

(v) Covenants affecting the land, whether favourably or otherwise, must be considered in assessing compensation. For instance, the property may enjoy the benefit of a covenant restricting building or other works on adjoining land, or it may itself be subject to such a covenant and be less valuable in consequence.

In the case of restrictive covenants, however, it would seem that the possibility of their removal or modification under Section 84 of the Law of Property Act, 1925 as amended, is a factor which might properly be taken into account.

(vi) Where a lessee has a contractual or statutory right to the renewal of his lease that right will form part of the value of his leasehold interest; but the mere possibility of a lease being renewed is not a legal right existing at the date of notice to treat and cannot be the subject of compensation.

(vii) An owner is entitled to compensation not only for the value of the land taken but also for all other loss he may suffer in consequence of its acquisition.[6] For example, the occupier of a private house compulsorily acquired will be put to the expense of moving to other premises and will suffer loss in connection with his fixtures. An occupier of trade premises will suffer similar losses and in addition may be able to claim for loss on sale of his stock or for injury to the goodwill of his business. It will be convenient to

---

[3] *Cranwell v. The Mayor of London* (1870), L. R. 5 Ex. 284.

[4] *Corrie v. MacDermott* (1914), A.C. 1056; *Cedar Rapids Manufacturing Co. v. Lacoste* (1914), A.C. 569; In *Re Lucas and Chesterfield Gas and Water Board* (1909), 1 K.B. 16.

[5] *Pointe Gourde etc. Transport Co. Ltd. v. Sub-Intendent of Crown Lands* (1947). A.C. 565.

[6] *Horn v. Sunderland Corporation* (1941), 2 K.B. 26; *Venables v. The Department of Agriculture* (1932), S.C. 573.

discuss the compensation payable under these heads in the next Chapter. But it is important at this point to recognise them as part of the compensation to be paid to the owner for the compulsory taking of his interest in the land.

(viii) Where part only of an owner's land is taken, Section 63 of the Lands Clauses Act, 1845, and the corresponding provision in Section 7 of the Compulsory Purchase Act, 1965, make it quite clear that the owner is entitled not only to the value of land taken, but also to compensation for severance or injurious affection to other land held with the land taken.

These questions will be considered in detail in Chapter 24. In this Chapter we are dealing solely with the question of compensation for land actually taken.

## C.   The Land Compensation Act, 1961

### 1.   Six Basic Rules—Section 5

Section 5 of this Act (re-enacting with some slight amendments Section 2 of the 1919 Act) prescribes six rules for assessing compensation in respect of land acquired. Five of these rules relate to the valuation of land and interests in land: the sixth reaffirms the owner's right to compensation for disturbance and other loss suffered in consequence of the land being taken from him.

*Rule 1.—No allowance shall be made on account of the acquisition being compulsory.*

In assessing compensation under the Lands Clauses Act it had become a generally recognised custom to add 10 per cent to the estimated value of the land on account of the acquisition being compulsory. This addition was no doubt intended originally to cover the cost of reinvesting capital and other incidental expenses to which the owner might be put and in that sense may be regarded as part of the value of the land to him. There was nothing in the Act which expressly authorised such an allowance nor did it ever receive the direct sanction of the Courts. It is now expressly excluded.

*Rule 2.—The value of land shall, subject as hereinafter provided, be taken to be the amount which the land if sold in the open market by a willing seller might be expected to realise.*

The chief effect of this rule is to remove the old assumption of the willing buyer and the unwilling seller which underlies the interpretation by the Courts of the Lands Clauses Acts. It places compensation for interests in land on a basis which is at once more definite and more restricted than that of "value to the owner".

Where interests in land are of a purely investment nature there is probably no difference between value to owner and value in the open market. But in other cases the rule will operate to exclude from the valuation any element which would have no effect on the price obtainable for the property under normal conditions of sale and purchase.

The meaning of the words "amount which the land if sold in the open market by a willing seller might be expected to realise" was fully examined by the Court of Appeal in the case of *Inland Revenue v. Clay and Buchanan.*[7]

"In the open market" implies that the land is offered under conditions enabling every person desirous of purchasing to come in and make an offer, proper steps being taken to advertise the property and let all likely purchasers know that it is in the market for sale.

"A willing seller" does not mean a person who will sell without reserve for any price he can obtain. It means a person who is selling as a free agent, as distinct from one who is forced to sell under compulsory powers.

"Might be expected to realise" refers to the expectations of properly qualified persons who are informed of all the particulars ascertainable about the property and its capabilities, the demand for it and likely buyers.

In assessing compensation, then, it must be assumed that the owner is offering the property for sale of his own free will, but is taking all reasonable measures to insure a sale under the most favourable conditions. The compensation payable will be that price which a properly qualified person, acquainted with all the essential facts relevant to the property and to the existing state of the market, would expect it to realise under such circumstances.

An estimate of market value on this basis will take into account all the potentialities of the land, including not only its present use but also any more profitable use to which, subject to the requisite planning permission, it might be put in the future.

For example, if land at present used as agricultural or accommodation land is reasonably likely to become available for building in the future, the prospective building value may properly be taken into account under Rule 2 provided that it is deferred for an appropriate number of years. Again, if buildings on a well-situated site have become obsolete or old fashioned, so that the rental value of the property could be greatly increased by capital expenditure on improvements and alterations, compensation may properly be based on the estimated improved rental value, provided that the cost of the necessary works is deducted from the valuation.

---

[7] (1914), 3 K.B. 466—In that case the judgment of the Court was directed to almost identical words used in the Finance (1909–1910) Act, 1910.

It should be emphasised, however, that in the case of land capable of further development, the price which it might be expected to realise under present-day conditions of strict planning control depends very largely on the kind of development for which planning permission has already been obtained, or is reasonably likely to be given having due regard to the provisions of the development plan for the area.

In practice, a prospective purchaser in the open market would probably obtain permission for his proposed development before deciding the price he was prepared to pay. This factor is absent in compulsory purchase cases, and the Land Compensation Act, 1961, therefore provides that, besides taking into account any existing planning consents, certain assumptions shall be made as to the kinds of development for which planning permission might reasonably have been expected to be granted but for the compulsory acquisition. These assumptions are considered in detail in Section 3 of this Chapter.

In general compensation will be based on the value—as at the date of assessment or of entry on the land—of the interests existing at the date of the notice to treat. But in all cases to which the Acquisition of Land (Authorisation Procedure) Act, applies[8] the Lands Tribunal may ignore any interest in land, or any work done on it, if they are of the opinion that the creation of the interest or the doing of the work was not reasonably necessary and was done with a view to obtaining or increasing compensation.

In the case of leasehold interests there seems no doubt that their value should be determined by reference to the length of the unexpired lease at the date when the valuation is made.

*Rule 3.—The special suitability or adaptability of the land for any purpose shall not be taken into account if that purpose is a purpose to which it could be applied only in pursuance of statutory powers, or for which there is no market apart from the special needs of a particular purchaser or the requirements of any authority possessing compulsory purchase powers.*

Under the Lands Clauses Acts if land could be shown to be specially suited or adapted to a particular purpose so that anyone requiring it for that purpose might be expected to pay a higher

---

[8] These are cases of compulsory purchase.
   (i) Under public general Acts in force before 18 April, 1946, which authorise the taking of land by local authorities, or by the Minister of Transport for highway purposes;
   (ii) Under Local Acts in force before 18 April, 1946, which authorise the taking of land by local authorities—but only if the Minister of Housing and Local Government orders that the Act shall apply;
   (iii) Under any Act passed since 18 April, 1946, in which the Act is expressly incorporated.

price on that account, this "special adaptability" might be regarded as giving the land a special value in a certain limited market and thereby increasing its value in the hands of the owner.

Thus in *Manchester Corporation v. Countess Ossalinski*[9] the fact that land was specially suitable and adaptable for the construction of a reservoir for a town's supply was held to enhance its value to the owner; and, in later cases under the Lands Clauses Acts, it was held that such "special adaptability" might properly be considered even where the land could only be used for the purpose for which it was best suited by bodies armed with statutory powers.

It is obvious that Rule 3 considerably restricts the application of this doctrine of "special adaptability". For instance, the circumstances existing in *Manchester Corporation v. Countess Ossalinski* could not now affect the compensation payable for land, if there were no likelihood of its being used for the purpose of a reservoir except under statutory powers. Again, the exceptional price which one particular purchaser might be willing to pay for premises because of their special convenience to him will not now affect the assessment of their market value under Rule 2.[10]

But the word "purpose" in Rule 3 means some use, actual or potential, of the land itself and does not extend to a purpose connected with the use of the products of the land—e.g., mineral deposits—elsewhere. Also it implies some physical use of the land and would not extend, for example, to the possibility of a merger of a leasehold interest in the land with the freehold.[11]

> *Rule 4.—Where the value of the land is increased by reason of the use thereof or of any premises thereon in a manner which could be restrained by any Court, or is contrary to law, or is detrimental to the health of the inmates of the premises or to the public health, the amount of that increase shall not be taken into account.*

The general purpose of this rule seems clear and requires no further comment.

> *Rule 5.—Where land is, and but for the compulsory acquisition would continue to be, devoted to a purpose of such a nature that there is no general demand or market for land for that purpose, the compensation may, if the Lands Tribunal is satisfied that reinstatement in some other place is* bona fide *intended, be assessed on the basis of the reasonable cost of equivalent reinstatement.*

---

[9] Heard in Q.B.D. of the High Court on 3 and 4 April, 1883, but not reported.

[10] In *Inland Revenue v. Clay and Buchanan* (1914), 3 K.B. 466, it was held that the special price offered for a house by the adjoining owner who wanted the premises for the extension of his nursing home was properly taken into account in assessing market value" for the purposes of the Finance (1909–10) Act, 1910.

[11] *See Pointe Gourde, etc., Transport Co. Ltd. v. Sub-Intendent of Crown Lands*, [1947] A.C. 565; and *Lambe v. Secretary of State for Air*, [1955] 2 Q.B. 612.

There are certain types of property which do not normally come upon the market and whose value cannot readily be assessed by ordinary methods of valuation, such as that of estimating the income or annual value and capitalising it. Such properties include churches, alms-houses, schools, hospitals, public buildings and certain classes of business premises where the business can only be carried on under special conditions.

Under the Lands Clauses Acts compensation in such cases was commonly assessed on the basis of the cost of providing the owner, so far as reasonably possible, with an equally suitable site and equally suitable buildings elsewhere.

Rule 5 gives statutory authority to this practice—as an alternative to assessment on the basis of market value—provided that:

> (i) the land is devoted to a purpose for which there is no general demand or market for land;
> (ii) compensation is limited to the "reasonable cost" of equivalent reinstatement; and
> (iii) the Lands Tribunal is satisfied that reinstatement in some other place is *bona fide* intended.

"Equivalent reinstatement" would seem to imply putting the claimant in the same position, or in an equally advantageous position, as that which he occupied when his land was acquired.

In certain cases the only practical method of reinstatement may be the provision of a new site and new buildings. But where, for instance, claimants are using an old building which has been adapted to their purposes, the term "equivalent reinstatement" might cover the cost of acquiring another similar property, if that is possible, together with the expenses of any necessary adaptations.

In a recent case the point at issue was whether the cost of reinstatement should be assessed as at the date of notice to treat—agreed at £50,025—or as at the earliest date when the work might reasonably have been begun—agreed at £84,450. It was unanimously decided by the House of Lords—confirming the decision of the Court of Appeal and reversing a decision of the Lands Tribunal, that the latter figure was the proper basis for compensation.[12]

*Rule 6.—The provisions of Rule 2 shall not affect the assessment of compensation for disturbance or any other matter not directly based on the value of land.*

The purpose of this rule is to reserve to the owner his right under the Lands Clauses Acts to be compensated not only for the value of his land but for any other loss he suffers through the land being taken from him.

---

[12] *West Midland Baptist (Trust) Association (Incorporated) v. Birmingham City Corporation,* [1969] R.V.R. 484; [1968] 1 All E.R. 205.

Thus, in *Horn v. Sunderland Corporation*,[13] Lord Greene, M.R., said that Rule 6 "does not confer a right to claim compensation for disturbance. It merely leaves unaffected the right which the owner would, before the Act of 1919, have had in a proper case to claim that the compensation to be paid for the land should be increased on the ground that he had been disturbed".

In the same case this right was described as "the right to receive a money payment not less than the loss imposed on him in the public interest, but on the other hand no greater".

It is true that, in practice, the value of the land itself will be assessed in accordance with Rule 2 and another figure for disturbance may be arrived at under Rule 6. But these two figures are, in fact, merely the elements which go to build up the total figure of price or compensation to which the owner is fairly entitled in all the circumstances of the case and which should represent the loss he suffers in consequence of the land being taken from him.

It follows that an owner cannot claim a figure of compensation for disturbance which is inconsistent with the basis adopted for the assessment of the value of the land under Rule 2.

For instance, in *Mizzen Bros. v. Mitcham U.D.C.* (1929)[14] it was held that claimants were not entitled to combine in the same claim a valuation of the land on the basis of an immediate sale for building purposes and a claim for disturbance and consequential damage upon the footing of interference with a continuing market garden business, since they could not realise the building value of the land in the open market unless they were themselves prepared to abandon their market garden business.

On the other hand, where a valuation on the basis of the present use of the land, plus compensation for disturbance, may exceed a valuation of the land based on a new and more profitable user, the owner has been held entitled to claim the former figure.

*Example.*—Land having prospective building value and containing deposits of sand, limestone and gravel was compulsorily acquired for housing purposes. The owner occupied the land as farm land, chiefly for the rearing of pedigree horses.

The owner claimed the market value of the land as a building estate ripe for immediate development and also a substantial sum in respect of the disturbance of his farming business.

The official arbitrator awarded a sum of £22,700 in respect of the value of the land as building land, but disallowed any compensation in respect of disturbance of the claimant's business on the grounds that the sum assessed could not be realised in the open market unless

---

[13] (1914), 2 K.B. 26; 1 All E.R. 480.
[14] Estates Gazette Digest, 1929, p. 258; reprinted "Estates Gazette", 25 January, 1941, p. 102.

vacant possession were given to the purchaser for the purpose of building development.

It was held by a majority of the Court of Appeal that the arbitrator's award was right in law provided that the sum of £22,700 equalled or exceeded—(i) the value of the land as farm land, plus (ii) whatever value should be attributable to the minerals if the land were treated as farm land, plus (iii) the loss by disturbance of the farming business.

If, however, the aggregate of items (i), (ii) and (iii) exceeded the figure of £22,700 the claimant was entitled to be paid the excess as part of the compensation for the loss of his land. [*Horn v. Sunderland Corporation* (1941), 1 All E.R. 480.]

Claims for disturbance must relate to losses which are the direct result of the compulsory taking of the land and which are not remote or purely speculative in character. Loss of profits in connection with a business carried on on the premises and which will be directly injured by the dispossession of the owner is a permissible subject of claim. But where a speculator claimed, in addition to the market value of building land, the profits which he hoped to make from the erection of houses on the land, the latter item was disallowed.[15] Again, where an owner of business premises compulsorily acquired was also the principal shareholder in the company which occupied the premises on a short-term tenancy, a claim in respect of the depreciation in the value of her shares which might result if the acquiring body gave the company notice to quit was held to be too remote for compensation.[16]

Where a tenant's interest is no greater than that of a yearly tenant and he is required to give up possession before the expiration of his interest, the right to compensation for disturbance is governed by Section 20 of the Compulsory Purchase Act, 1965, or Section 121 of the Lands Clauses Act, 1845, both of which provide that the tenant is entitled to compensation for the value of his unexpired term and for other incidental losses.

But there may be cases where an occupier has no legal right to compensation either under Rule 6 of Section 5 of the Land Compensation Act, 1961, or under Section 20 of the Compulsory Purchase Act, 1965, or Section 121 of the Lands Clauses Act, 1845.

For instance, where a tenancy will shortly expire, or can be terminated by notice to quit, it may be possible for an acquiring body to purchase the landlord's interest and then allow the tenancy to run out, or give the tenant the notice to quit to which he is entitled, without being liable to compensation for disturbance.

This may well cause hardship, and certain enactments, such as

---

[15] *Collins v. Feltham U.D.C.*, W.N. 27, November, 1937.
[16] *Robert v. Coventry Corporation* (1947), 1 All E.R. 308.

the Housing Act, 1957, enable acquiring bodies, at their discretion, to make certain payments in such cases.

Without prejudice to such provisions under other enactments, Section 30 of the Lands Compensation Act, 1961, now provides that in any case where land is compulsorily acquired, or sold by agreement to an authority possessing compulsory purchase powers, the acquiring authority may pay such reasonable allowances as they think fit in respect of removal expenses, or loss by disturbance of trade or business, to persons displaced from any house or other building.

In estimating loss to trade or business the authority must have regard to the period for which the party might have been expected to remain in possession and also to the availability of suitable alternative accommodation.[17]

Certain practical valuation points in connection with claims for disturbance are dealt with in Section B of Chapter 22.

## 2. FURTHER RULES OF ASSESSMENT—SECTIONS 6, 7 AND 9

These Sections prescribe three additional rules to be applied in assessing market value for compensation purposes.

(a) *Ignore increase or decrease in value due to development under the acquiring body's scheme* [*Section 6 and First Schedule*].

This gives statutory authority to a principle already established under the Lands Clauses Acts as regards the exclusion of increases in value, and confirms its natural corollary that decreases in value due to the same cause must also be ignored.

In assessing compensation in any of the cases referred to in Table A below no account is to be taken of any increase or decrease in the value of the interest to be acquired due to development of the kind noted against that particular case.

"Development"—which includes the clearing of land—refers both to development which may already have taken place and also to proposed development—being in either case development which would not have been likely to be carried out except for the compulsory acquisition or [in cases (ii)–(iv)] if the areas mentioned had not been defined or designated as indicated.

In case (i) of Table A the rule would apply to the effects on value of the development, or the prospects of development, of other land acquired under the same compulsory purchase order or Special Act. In the remaining cases, which deal with large-scale undertakings, the rule extends to actual or prospective development of other land within the defined area of the scheme.

---

[17] A similar provision applying to agricultural holdings is contained in the Agriculture (Miscellaneous Provisions) Act, 1963, Section 22.

TABLE A

| Type of case | Ignore increase or decrease in value due to: |
|---|---|
| (i) All cases where the purpose of the acquisition involves development of any of the land to be acquired. | Development, for the purposes of the acquisition, of any land authorised to be acquired, other than the land to be valued. |
| (ii) Where any of the land to be taken is in an area defined in the current development plan as an area of comprehensive development. | Development of any other land in that area in accordance with the plan. |
| (iii) Where on the service of notice to treat any of the land to be taken is in an area designated as the site of a New Town, under the New Towns Act, 1965.[18] | Development of any other land in that area in the course of the development of the area as a New Town. |
| (iv) Where any part of the land to be taken forms part of an area defined in the current development plan as an area of town development. | Development of any other land in that area in the course of town development within the meaning of the Town Development Act, 1958. |

(b) *Set off increase in value of adjacent or contiguous land in same ownership* [*Section 7 and First Schedule*].

Where land is acquired compulsorily it may well be that other adjoining land belonging to the same owner is increased in value by the carrying out of the acquiring body's undertaking on land taken. Neither the Lands Clauses Acts nor the Acquisition of Land (Assessment of Compensation) Act, 1919, made any provision whereby the acquiring authority might benefit from this increase in value. But a number of special Acts, including the principal ones under which land is taken for road works, expressly provide that, in assessing compensation for land taken, any increase in the value of adjoining and contiguous lands of the same owner due to the acquiring body's scheme shall be deducted from the compensation payable.

The Land Compensation Act, 1961, now applies this principle of "set off" to all cases of compulsory acquisition.

The effect of Section 7 is that where, at the date of notice to treat, the owner has an interest in land contiguous or adjacent to the land acquired, any increase in the value of that interest due to development under the acquiring body's scheme is to be deducted from the compensation payable for the interest in land acquired.

As under Section 6, "development" refers to either actual or prospective development under the acquiring body's scheme which

[18] See Part II of the First Schedule for special provisions applying where notice to treat is served on or after the date on which the new town development corporation ceases to act. See also Section 2 of the New Towns Act, 1965.

would not be likely to be carried out but for the compulsory acquisition. In this case, however, the prospect of development on the land acquired must be considered as well as development on other land taken under the same compulsory purchase order, or special Act, or included in the same area of development.

The following table, based on the First Schedule to the Act, may help to make the position clear:—

TABLE B

| Type of case | Set off increase in value of contiguous or adjacent land of same owner due to:— |
|---|---|
| (i) All cases where the purpose of the acquisition involves development of any of the land to be acquired. | Development, for the purposes of the acquisition, of any land authorised to be acquired including the land to be valued. |
| (ii) Where any of the land to be taken is in an area defined in the current development plan as an area of comprehensive development. | Development of the land taken, or any other land in the area, in accordance with the plan. |
| (iii) Where, on the service of notice to treat, any of the land to be taken is in an area designated as the site of a New Town. | Development of the land taken or any other land in the area as a New Town. |
| (iv) Where any part of the land to be taken forms part of an area defined in the current development plan as an area of town development. | "Town development" on the land taken or on any other part of the area. |

The above provisions as to "set off" do not apply to acquisitions under certain existing Acts—specified in Section 8 (7)—which already provide for "set off", nor to acquisition under any local enactment which contains a similar provision. In these cases the question of "set off" will be governed by the express provisions of the particular Act. But any provision in a local enactment which restricts "set off" to any increase in "the existing use value" of contiguous or adjacent land will cease to have effect.

Under the above provisions as to set off, the compensation payable to an owner may be *reduced* by the increase in the value of his interest in adjacent land. But there are also cases where the compensation for land taken will be *increased* on account of the injurious affection to other land held with it due to the acquiring body's scheme. In either case, if such adjacent land is subsequently acquired, the operation of Section 6, which requires increases or decreases in value due to the scheme to be ignored, might result in an owner either being paid a certain amount of compensation twice over or deprived of it on two occasions.

Section 8 (1)–(4) therefore provides as follows:—

(i) If, either on a compulsory purchase or a sale by agreement, the purchase price is reduced by setting off (under Section 7 or any corresponding enactment) the increase in the value of adjacent or contiguous land due to the acquiring body's scheme, then if the same interest in such adjacent land is subsequently acquired that increase in value (which has served to reduce the compensation previously paid) will be taken into account in assessing compensation and not ignored as it otherwise would have been under Section 6.

(ii) Similarly, if a diminution in the value of other land of the same owner due to the acquiring body's scheme has been added to the compensation payable for land taken, then if the same interest in that other land is subsequently acquired that depreciation in value (for which compensation has already been paid) will be taken into account in assessing compensation and not ignored as it otherwise would have been under Section 6.

If in either of the above cases part only of the adjoining land is subsequently acquired a proportionate part of the set off or injurious affection will be taken into account.

Section 8 (1) also ensures that where several adjacent pieces of land of the same owner are acquired at different dates—although perhaps under the same compulsory purchase order—an increase in value due to development under the acquiring body's scheme which has already been set off against compensation on one occasion shall not be set off again on the subsequent acquisition of a further part of the lands in question.

(c) *Ignore loss of value due to threat of acquisition—Section* 9 (6).

Section 51 (3) of the Town and Country Planning Act, 1947, provided that in assessing compensation no account should be taken of any depreciation in the value of the claimant's interest due to the fact that the land had been designated for compulsory purchase in the development plan. Section 9 of the Lands Compensation Act, 1961, extends this principle to depreciation in value due to any proposals involving the acquisition of the claimant's interest, whether the proposals are indicated in the development plan—by allocation or other particulars in the plan—or in some other way. For instance, no account should be taken of depreciation in the value of land due to its inclusion in a compulsory purchase order which has been publicised under the Acquisition of Land (Authorisation Procedure) Act, 1946.

3. ASSUMPTIONS AS TO PLANNING PERMISSION—SECTIONS 14–16

These sections of the Act prescribe certain assumptions as to the grant of planning permission which are to be made in assessing the market value of the owner's interest in the land to be acquired.

They are without prejudice to any planning permission already in existence at the date of the notice to treat—whether, for instance, given by the local planning authority or under a General Development Order.

The valuer must make such one or more of the prescribed assumptions as are applicable to the whole or part of the land to be acquired, and compensation will be related to whichever of these assumptions is most favourable from the point of view of value in the open market.

But the fact that, under the Act, land may be assumed to have the benefit of planning permission—e.g., for residential purposes—does not necessarily imply a demand for that land for the purpose in question. It is not planning permission by itself which increases value; it is planning permission coupled with demand. In some cases normal demand—apart from the acquiring authority's scheme— might be so far distant as to warrant only a "hope" value for development.[19]

Again, the fact that these assumptions are to be made does not imply that planning permission for other forms of development would necessarily be refused. So the possibility that prospective purchasers might be prepared to pay a higher price for land in the hope of being able to obtain permission for a certain form of development may be a factor in assessing market value, even although the permission in question is not covered by the assumptions to be made under the Act. But in deciding whether permission might reasonably have been expected to be granted— and might therefore influence the price a prospective purchaser might be expected to pay—regard is to be had to any contrary opinion expressed in any certificate of "appropriate alternative development" which may have been issued under Section 17 of the Act.[20]

In applying these provisions of the Act one must also have regard to the possible incidence of other town planning legislation.

If, for instance, compensation has already been paid under the Town and Country Planning Acts of 1954 or 1962, in respect of an adverse planning decision, or the revocation of permission previously granted, then the fact that such compensation will be repayable if permission for "new development"—such as might be covered by one of the statutory assumptions—is given in the future will certainly affect the price which a prospective purchaser might be expected to pay for the land.

---

[19] *Camrose and Another v. Basingstoke Corporation. Times,* 26 May, 1966.
[20] Such certificates are considered in Section 4 of this Chapter.

Again, although any "unexpended balance of development value" does not form part of the compensation payable for land acquired, its existence may have an indirect effect on market value through the compensation provisions of the Town and Country Planning Acts, in regard to adverse planning decisions. Thus, cases may arise where no development of land to be acquired, other than of an "existing use" type, can be assumed under the terms of the 1961 Act, and yet if planning permission for "new development" were in fact refused, or granted subject to conditions, the owner might be entitled to compensation under Part VI of the 1962 Act not exceeding the amount of the unexpended balance attached to the land. Here, if the possibility of such compensation might fairly be assumed to affect the price which a prospective purchaser might be prepared to pay for the land, there seems no reason why this factor should not be taken into account in assessing market value under Rule 2 of Section 5 of the 1961 Act. Although such an imaginary purchaser would obviously pay very special attention to the limitations on the right to compensation imposed by Sections 101 and 102 of the 1962 Act.

The assumptions to be made under Sections 14–16 of the Land Compensation Act, 1961, may be described broadly as (1) general assumptions and (2) assumptions related to current development plans.

(1) *General assumptions as to Planning Permission.*

  (i) **Where the acquiring authority's proposals involve development of the whole or a part of the land to be acquired, it shall be assumed that planning permission would be given for such development in accordance with the authority's proposals. (Section 15 (1) and (2).)**

  But where a planning permission for the proposed development is already in force at the date of the notice to treat, its terms will take the place of any assumed permission, unless it is personal only and does not enure for the benefit of all persons interested in the land.

  As a general rule, then, the possibility of carrying out the type of development for which the land is acquired may be reflected in the compensation payable. For instance, if the local authority require the land for housing, it will be assumed that planning permission is available for the kind of housing development which the local authority propose to carry out.

  But where the proposed development is one to which the land could only be applied in pursuance of statutory powers, the assumption of planning permission will not necessarily affect the compensation, since this element of value may well be excluded by Rule 3 of Section 5 of the Act.

(ii) **It shall be assumed that planning permission would be granted for any form of development specified in the Third Schedule of the Town and Country Planning Act, 1962. [Section 15 (3) and (4).]**[21]

But this rule is subject to the following exceptions to avoid compensation being paid twice over:—

(a) Where at any time before service of notice to treat planning permission was refused, or was granted subject to certain conditions, in respect of some form of development in Part II of the Third Schedule and compensation has become payable under Section 123 of the 1962 Act, planning permission shall not be assumed for that particular development, or shall only be assumed subject to the conditions already imposed, as the case may be.

(b) Where before the date of notice to treat an order was made under Section 28 of the 1962 Act, for the removal of any building or the discontinuance of any use, and compensation became payable under Section 124 of that Act, it shall not be assumed that planning permission would be granted for the rebuilding of that building or the resumption of that use, as the case may be.

(iii) **It shall be assumed that planning permission would be granted for development of any class specified in a "certificate of appropriate development" which may have been issued under Part III of the Act. [Section 15 (5).]**

But this assumption is governed by the terms of the certificate, which may indicate that planning permission would not be granted until some date in the future and/or subject to certain conditions.

The cases in which such certificates may be issued and the procedure in connection with them are considered in detail in Section 4 of this Chapter.

(2) *Assumptions as to Planning Permission related to current Development Plans. (Section 16.)*

Where at the date of notice to treat land to be acquired is comprised in a current development plan—whether the original plan or some amended form of it—certain assumptions as to planning permission are to be made according to how the land, *or any part of it*, is dealt with in the plan.

---

[21] The text of the Third Schedule together with the modification made in it by the Town and Country Planning Act, 1963, will be found in Appendices B (1) and B (2).

In some cases land may be "defined" in the plan as the site for some specific development—e.g., a new road, a public building, a public park. In other cases land may be "allocated" (or zoned) for some more general purpose—e.g., for agricultural, residential or industrial user. Or, again, the land may be defined in the plan as an "area of comprehensive development" or "action area"—i.e., one which, in the opinion of the local planning authority, should be developed or redeveloped as a whole.

In all the cases set out below the assumptions made as to planning permission must be subject to:—

(a) any conditions which might reasonably have been expected to be imposed on the grant of the planning permission in question; and

(b) any indication in the development plan—whether on any map or in the written statement—that such permission would only be granted at some future time, thus suggesting that the benefit of the assumed permission should be deferred for an appropriate period.

Cases (i)–(iii) below refer to land which is not in an area of comprehensive development.

(i) **Land defined in the development plan as the site for development of a specific description. [Section 16 (1).]**

In this case it is to be assumed that planning permission would be given for the particular development.

In many cases, where the land is defined as the site of development for which there is no demand except by bodies armed with statutory powers, this assumption will have no effect on the market value of the land. In such cases the owner may be advised to apply for a certificate of "appropriate alternative development" under Part III of the Act (see Section 4 of this Chapter).

(ii) **Land allocated in the development plan for some primary use. [Section 16 (2).]**

In this case it is to be assumed that planning permission would be given for any development which:—

(i) is within the specified primary use; and

(ii) is of a form for which planning permission might reasonably have been expected to be granted but for the compulsory acquisition.

For example, land may be zoned primarily for "residential purposes", a term which may include a number of different forms of development—e.g., houses or blocks of flats, with varying densities per ha. Here planning permission must be assumed for the type of residential development for which it might reasonably have been expected to be granted had the land not been acquired compulsorily.

In some cases there may be a reasonable possibility that permission would have been given for the development of the whole or part of the land for some purpose ancillary to the purpose for which the area is primarily zoned—e.g., a terrace of shops in an area zoned for residential use. In such a case it would seem that, although definite planning permission can only be assumed for the specified primary use, it would be permissible to consider any possible effect which the reasonable expectation of planning permission for the ancillary use might have had on the open market value.

(iii) **Land allocated in the development plan primarily for two or more specified uses. [Section 16 (3).]**

In this case it is to be assumed that planning permission would be given for any development which:—

    (i) is within the range of uses specified in the development plan; and

    (ii) is of a kind for which planning permission might reasonably have been expected to be granted but for the compulsory acquisition.

(iv) **Land defined in the development plan as an area of comprehensive development. [Section 16 (4) and (5).]**

An area of comprehensive development is one which, in the opinion of the local planning authority, should be developed or redeveloped as a whole.[22] The development plan, in addition to defining the area in question, will also indicate the various uses to which it is proposed the different parts of the area should be put on redevelopment.

In this case, in assessing compensation for the land to be acquired, regard is to be had to the range of uses proposed for the area, but the proposed distribution of those uses under the development plan must be ignored, together with any development which at the date of notice to treat has already taken place in the area in accordance with the plan.

The open market value of the land in question must then be assessed on the assumption that planning permission would be granted for any form of development—*within the range of uses proposed for the area*—for which permission might reasonably have been expected to be granted if the area had not been defined as an area of comprehensive development.

---

[22] Town and Country Planning Act, 1962, Sec. 4 (4).

### 4. CERTIFICATES OF APPROPRIATE ALTERNATIVE DEVELOPMENT—PART III, SECTIONS 17–22

Where an interest in land is proposed to be acquired by an authority possessing compulsory powers and that land, or part of it, does not consist or form part of an area:—

(a) defined in the current development plan as an area of comprehensive development; or

(b) shown in the current development plan as allocated primarily for residential, commercial or industrial uses, or a combination of any of those uses with other uses,

either the owner of any interest to be acquired, or the acquiring authority, may apply to the local planning authority for a certificate stating what development (if any) might reasonably have been expected to have been permitted if the land had not been subject to compulsory purchase. When the certificate is issued, planning permission for such development as is indicated in the certificate will be assumed in assessing the market value of any interest in the land for compensation purposes [see Section 3 (1) (iii) of this Chapter].

This provision is intended to cover cases where no definite guidance is given by the development plan as to the kind of development for which planning permission might have been expected to be given.

Typical cases where such a certificate might be applied for are:—

(i) where land is defined in the development plan as the site for some purely public development—e.g., a sewage disposal works or a public open space;

(ii) where land is not allocated in the plan for any form of development—e.g., land in a green belt or "white area";

(iii) where the area is not covered by a current development plan.

The right to apply for a certificate arises where land is "proposed to be acquired", i.e.:—

(a) where any required notice in connection with the acquisition is duly published or served; or

(b) where notice to treat is "deemed to have been served"; or

(c) where an offer in writing is made on behalf of an acquiring authority to negotiate for the purchase of the owner's interest in the land.

Provisions as to the issue of certificates and appeals therefrom are contained both in the Act and in the Land Compensation Development Order, 1963. The following is a summary of the procedure.

The application for a certificate, accompanied by a plan or map, may be made at any time before the date of any reference to the

Lands Tribunal to determine the compensation in respect of the applicant's interest in the land. But it cannot be made after that date except with the written consent of the other party or by leave of the Tribunal.

The applicant must specify one or more classes of development which in his view would be appropriate for the land in question if it were not being acquired compulsorily. He must also state the date on which a copy of the application has been or will be served on the other party. Not earlier than twenty-one days from this latter date, but within two months from the receipt of the application, the local planning authority must issue a certificate to the applicant stating either:—

(a) that in their opinion planning permission for development of one or more specified classes (which may or may not be classes specified in the application) might reasonably have been expected to be granted if the land were not proposed to be acquired, or

(b) that in their opinion planning permission could not reasonably have been expected to be granted for any development other than the development (if any) which the acquiring authority propose to carry out.

Where, in the opinion of the local planning authority, the permission referred to in (a) above would only have been granted subject to conditions or at some future time, or both subject to conditions and at some future time, the certificate must say so.

The local planning authority are not necessarily bound by the provisions of their development plan in determining what sort of development might reasonably have been permitted on the land in question.

If a certificate is issued for development other than that specified in the application, or contrary to written representations made by the owner of the interest or the acquiring authority, the local planning authority must give their reasons and also state the right of appeal to the Secretary of State.

When a certificate is issued to either owner or acquiring authority a copy must be served on the other interested party. A copy must also be sent to the local authority in whose area the land is situated.

Either owner or acquiring authority may appeal against a certificate to the Secretary of State for the Environment who, after giving the parties and the local planning authority an opportunity to be heard, may either confirm the certificate, or vary it, or cancel it and issue a different certificate in its place.

Appeal may also be made to the Secretary of State if the local planning authority fail to issue a certificate within two months of an application to them to do so, although this time may be extended by agreement of the parties. In this case the appeal will proceed as though the local planning authority had issued a certificate to the effect that planning permission could not normally have been expected to be granted for any development other than that which the acquiring authority propose to carry out.

Appeals to the Secretary of State must be made within one month of the date of issue of the certificate, or the expiry of the time limit of two months (or extended time), as the case may be.

Section 19 of the Act contains special notes for applying the procedure in respect of certificates of appropriate alternative development to cases where an owner is absent from the Kingdom or cannot be found. Section 21 gives the right to challenge the validity of a decision given by the Secretary of State on appeal by means of an application to the High Court.

## 5. Special Cases

(a) *Houses Unfit for Human Habitation—Section* 10 *and Second Schedule.*

Under the Housing Act, 1957, where houses unfit for human habitation are compulsorily acquired, compensation is assessed on a bare site value basis.

The provisions of this Act, as amended by the Second Schedule to the Land Compensation Act, 1961, are considered in detail in a later Chapter.

We are concerned here with certain other special cases where— subject to an order declaring a house to be unfit for human habitation and incapable of being rendered so at reasonable expense— compensation will be assessed on a bare site value basis.

These are cases of compulsory acquisition under:—

  (i) Part V of the Town and Country Planning Act, 1962,[23] or

 (ii) Section 6 of the Town Development Act, 1952, or

(iii) Part VIII of the Town and Country Planning Act, 1962[24]— which enables certain types of owner-occupier to compel the purchase of property which has been "blighted" by the prospect of future acquisition for public purposes, or

 (iv) an Order under Section 1 of the New Towns Act, 1965, designating land as the site of a new town, or

  (v) under the New Towns Act, 1965, or under any enactment as applied by the provisions of that Act, being acquisition by a development corporation or a local highway authority or the Minister of Transport.

---

[23] Secs. 67 and 68 of that Act are now replaced by Secs. 28 and 29 of the T. & C.P. Act, 1968.
[24] Secs. 139–151 as amended by T. & C.P. Act, 1968.

The procedure in all the above cases is for the local authority to submit the unfitness order to the Secretary of State for the Environment, at the same time serving a notice on every owner and mortgagee of the land, or part of it, stating the effect of the order and the time within which objections to it may be made. The Secretary must consider any objections and must hold an enquiry if any objector or the local authority so desires.

Provided the order declaring the house to be unfit is confirmed by the Secretary the basis of compensation will be the open market value of the cleared site ignoring the value of any buildings on it.

In certain circumstances, specified in the Housing Act, 1957, the owner may also be entitled to a supplementary payment as an "owner-occupier" or in respect of a "well-maintained" house. These payments are considered in detail in the Chapter on that Act.

It is quite possible, however, that the open market value of the site, cleared of buildings and available for development, may exceed the value of the unfit house as it stands, for the latter figure would have to take into account such items as existing cost of maintenance, difficulty of securing possession from existing tenants, and the cost of demolishing dilapidated buildings.

Paragraph 1 (2) of the Second Schedule therefore provides, in effect, that the maximum compensation payable for an "unfit" house shall be the market value of the property as it stands estimated in accordance with the general provisions of the Land Compensation Act, 1961. But this is subject to a proviso that in the case of an owner-occupier of a private dwelling the compensation for his interest—including any "well-maintained" or "owner-occupier" supplement, but excluding compensation for disturbance, injurious affection or severance—shall not be less than the gross value of the house as shown in the current valuation list. Where part only of the house is owner-occupied the gross value must be apportioned by the valuation officer for the district.

Where an "unfit" house had sustained war damage the whole of which had not been made good at the date of the notice to treat, the compensation payable was increased by the value, at the date of the notice to treat, of the prospective right to receive such payment under the War Damage Act as might reasonably have been expected to be made but for the compulsory acquisition.

### (b) Land of Statutory Undertakers—Section 11.

Under the Town and Country Planning Acts, 1947–54, the compensation for certain special types of property was assessed on the assumption that planning permission would be granted for development whereby the use of the land could be made to correspond with that prevailing generally on contiguous and adjacent land.

The properties in question were those held by local authorities for general statutory purposes, operational land of statutory undertakers, land held and used for charitable purposes and specified land of the National Coal Board.

This "prevailing use basis", as it was called, was abolished by the Town and Country Planning Act, 1959, and now, under the Land Compensation Act, 1961, compensation in these cases will, in general, be assessed on the same basis as for any other type of property.

But where land is acquired from statutory undertakers who themselves have acquired the land for the purpose of their undertaking, compensation will be assessed in accordance with certain special rules contained in Section 171 of the Town and Country Planning Act, 1962.

It may conveniently be noted here that nothing in the 1961 Act shall apply to any purchase of the whole or part of a statutory undertaking under any enactment which prescribes the terms on which such a purchase is to be effected. (Section 36.)

(c) *Outstanding Right to Compensation for Refusal, etc., of Planning Permission—Section* 12.

It has already been noted (see Section C.3 of this Chapter) that where a right to compensation exists in consequence of some planning decision or order already made—e.g., a refusal of permission, or its grant subject to conditions, or the revocation or modification of a permission already given—the fact that this compensation, or part of it, may be repayable under Section 113 of the 1962 Act if permission for "new development" is given in the future will naturally affect the assessment of market value if the land is compulsorily acquired.

The liability to repay actually only arises under Section 113 provided that a "compensation notice" has been registered as a land charge. But the effect of Section 12 of the 1961 Act is that the factor of liability for repayment of compensation can be taken into account in the assessment of "market value" whether a "compensation notice" was registered before the notice to treat or on or after that date, and whether or not a claim for compensation in respect of the adverse planning decision has yet been made.

It follows, therefore, that if no claim for compensation in respect of the adverse decision has in fact been made, the owner should proceed with it in spite of the fact that his land is being acquired.

(d) *War Damaged Property—Section* 13.

In general, war-damaged property was assessed under the 1961 Act on an open market basis which took into account the condition of the property and the benefit of any "cost of works" or "value" payment to which the owner may be entitled under the War Damage Act, 1943.

But where war-damaged property attracting a "cost of works" payment would, if undamaged, have been devoted to a purpose for which there is no general demand or market for land, compensation might by virtue of Rule 5 of Section 5 of the Land Compensation Act, be assessed on a "reinstatement" basis.

In such cases, the reasonable cost of equivalent reinstatement was estimated by reference to the state of the land immediately before the occurrence of the war damage.

6. ADDITIONAL COMPENSATION IN RESPECT OF SUBSEQUENT PLANNING PERMISSION—PART IV SECTIONS 23–29 AND THIRD SCHEDULE

N.B.—These provisions no longer apply where land is acquired in pursuance of a notice to treat served, or contract for sale made, on or after 1 January, 1967[25].

(a) *When Payable.*—Subject to the above note an owner whose interest in land has been compulsorily acquired, or sold to an authority possessing compulsory powers, may be entitled to further compensation if, within five years of the vesting of the interest in the acquiring body, planning permission[26] is given for "additional development" of any of the land comprised in the acquisition or sale.

The term "additional development" means any development of the land in question other than:—

(i) development for the purposes for which the interest in land was acquired;

(ii) development for which planning permission was in force at the date when the notice to treat was served or the contract of sale made;

(iii) development for which, following the provisions of Sections 14–16 of the Act, it was assumed—in assessing the compensation or price—that planning permission would be granted.

These, of course, are all cases where the prospect of the development in question will already have been reflected in the original purchase price or compensation.

No compensation is payable in respect of land, which—(i) consists or forms part of an "area of comprehensive development";

---

[25] Land Commission Act, 1967, Sec.86.

[26] The permission in question may be conditional or unconditional, it may relate to land previously taken or to an area which includes such land, it may be granted either on an ordinary or an outline application, or it may be deemed to have been granted (Sec. 29 (2)). Sec. 25 contains special provisions governing cases where under any enactment planning permission is deemed to be granted or where it is granted under a development order.

or (ii) was acquired by a development corporation under the New Towns Act, 1946, either as being within the area designated as the site of a new town, or because the development corporation were required to purchase it under Section 6 (4) of that Act; or (iii) was acquired by a local authority as consisting or forming part of an "area of town development".

In all these cases it is probable that the new permission implements, rather than changes, the purpose of the acquisition.

In the event of death or sale the right to compensation will pass to the previous owner's personal representative or successor in title; but a mortgagee of the owner's interest is not entitled to claim.

(b) *Basis of Compensation.*—The general basis on which additional compensation can be claimed is the amount by which:—

  (i) the compensation or purchase price previously payable was *less than*

  (ii) the compensation which would have been payable in respect of a compulsory acquisition of the interest in question with the benefit of planning permission for the "additional development".

In other words, the owner will be entitled to claim the additional compensation (if any) which he would have received if the new permission had existed at the date of the notice to treat or contract of sale. Regard will, of course, be had to any conditions which may be attached to the new planning permission. Any mortgage to which the land may be subject is to be ignored.

The original figure of compensation will, in appropriate cases, have included compensation for (a) disturbance and (b) severance and injurious affection to other land held with the land taken. Or the compensation for land taken may have been reduced by a set off of the increase in the value of adjacent or contiguous land of the same owner (see Section C.2 (b) of this Chapter).

In valuation (ii) the question of what compensation, if any, is to be included for disturbance, or for severance and injurious affection, or what deduction from the value of the land taken is to be made for set off, must be determined in the light of the new planning decision giving rise to the claim for additional compensation.

Cases may occur where a claim for injurious affection in the original assessment of compensation would have been replaced by a reduction in the compensation on account of set off if the new planning decision had then been in force. Or the exact opposite may be the case.

In any event it should be emphasised that in valuation (ii)—with the benefit of the new planning permission—not only the value of the land acquired, but any compensation for severance or injurious affection or deduction from compensation in respect of set off, must all be based on prices current at the date of the notice to treat.

It may happen that, before the date of the new planning permission, the owner has sold the whole, or some part, of adjacent land which in the original assessment was the subject of additional compensation for injurious affection or a reduction of compensation on account of set off. In this case any such addition to, or deduction from, the compensation must either be excluded from both valuations (i) and (ii)—if the whole of such land has been sold—or confined to so much of such adjacent land as the owner still retains at the date of the new planning permission.

(c) *Making of Claims.*—If the person whose interest in land is acquired gives the acquiring authority an address for service, the authority must notify him at that address of any planning permission for the carrying out of "additional development" given, or deemed to be given, within five years of the completion of the acquisition.

The claim for additional compensation, to be effective, must be made within six months from the above notice of the decision or—in cases where the owner has not given an address for service—within six months from the date of the decision or the determination of any appeal thereon.

The provisions of the Land Compensation Act, 1961, apply to the assessment of compensation for additional development in the same way as they apply to the assessment of compensation for compulsory acquisition.

## 7. SUMMARY OF GENERAL BASIS OF COMPENSATION

It may be useful at this point to summarise briefly and in very general terms the basis of compensation for land taken prescribed by the 1961 Act.

Essentially it is the best price which the owner's interest might be expected to realise if voluntarily offered for sale in the open market. But in many cases it may be necessary to make two or more estimates of the value of the property, each based on different assumptions permitted by the Act, in order to determine what that "best price" is.

The possible bases for these estimates of value are as follows:—

> (i) The value of the property as it stands, but having regard to the possibility of any future development within the limits of the Third Schedule of the 1962 Act,[27] and taking into account also the terms of any planning permission already existing at the date of notice to treat, but not yet fully implemented by development.

---

[27] As modified by the Town and Country Planning Act, 1963.

In the case of a very large number of properties, both in built-up and in rural areas, this will represent the highest price obtainable in the open market.

(ii) The value of the land, as in (i), but with the assumption that planning permission would be given for the development which the acquiring body propose to carry out.

This may or may not give a higher value than (i) according to whether permission to carry out this kind of development would be of value (a) to purchasers generally or (b) only to bodies armed with statutory powers or one particular purchaser—in which case the element of value might be excluded under Section 5 Rule 3 of the Land Compensation Act, 1961.

(iii) The value of the land subject to such of the prescribed assumptions as to planning permission—based on the provisions of the current development plan—as are applicable to the particular case.

This does not necessarily rule out of consideration the possibility that purchasers might be prepared to pay a higher price in the *hope* that permission might be obtainable for some other form of development.

(iv) The value of the land subject to the assumption that planning permission would be given for one or more classes of development specified in a "certificate of appropriate alternative development"—in cases where the development plan gives little or no guide to the kind of development which might be permitted.

In all the above cases the valuation will exclude any increase or decrease in the value of the land attributable to actual or prospective development under the acquiring body's scheme, either on the land taken or on other land, also any decrease in value due to the threat of acquisition.

Where the owner has an interest in other land held with that taken, additional compensation for severance and injurious affection may be payable under the provisions of the Lands Clauses Act, 1845, or, in the great majority of cases, the corresponding provisions of the Compulsory Purchase Act, 1965.

Where he has an interest in land adjacent or contiguous to that taken, any increase in the value of such land due to actual or prospective development under the acquiring body's scheme, either on the land taken or on other land, is to be deducted from the compensation.

If a dwelling-house is certified as unfit for habitation, compensation will, as a general rule, be based on the value of the bare site.

# Chapter 22

## Valuations for Compulsory Purchase and Compensation
## (contd.)

### A. Further Miscellaneous Matters

1. LONG STANDING NOTICES TO TREAT—TOWN AND COUNTRY
PLANNING ACT, 1959, SECTIONS 14–16

THESE PROVISIONS—of a transitional nature only—related to notices to treat served before 6th August, 1947, with some exceptions.

Such notices automatically ceased to have effect unless: —

    (i) the acquiring body, before 17 February, 1960, served on the owner a " notice of intention to proceed "; and

    (ii) such notice having been served, compensation was settled, or proceedings for its determination were begun, or the authority entered on the land, within one year of the notice.

Compensation under a notice to treat served before 6 August, 1947, would probably fall to be assessed on the basis of prices current at 31 March, 1939. But the owner served with " notice of intention to proceed " might, in a detailed statement of claim served within six months of the " notice of intention ", elect that compensation should be assessed as if the original notice to treat had been served on 1 January, 1958—that is to say, on the basis prescribed by the Town and Country Planning Acts, 1947-54 (see Chapter 23).

The acquiring body, on receipt of the owner's detailed statement of claim, might withdraw their notice to treat, in which case compensation to the owner in respect of such withdrawal was limited to: —

    (a) loss or expense incurred after the service of the "notice of intention to proceed "; and

    (b) expenses reasonably incurred before the service of that notice in preparing and supporting a claim for compensation in respect of the acquisition.

## 2. Rights of Owner-Occupiers Affected by "Planning Blight"
### Town and Country Planning Act, 1962
### Sections 138–152[1]

Planning proposals which will eventually involve the compulsory acquisition of land may very well depreciate the value of a property, or even make it virtually unsaleable.

It is true that such depreciation will be ignored—under Section 9 of the Land Compensation Act, 1961—in assessing the compensation when the property is actually acquired. But this will not help the owner if, in the meantime, he wants to sell his property in the open market.

For instance, the owner-occupier of a house affected by such proposals may, for personal reasons, be obliged to move elsewhere and may suffer considerable hardship if he has to sell at a very much reduced price.

In partial mitigation of such cases, the 1962 Act enables a strictly limited class of owner-occupier to compel the acquisition of his interest in land if he can prove that *he has made reasonable efforts to sell his interest, but has been unable to do so except at a price substantially lower than he might reasonably have expected to obtain but for the threat of compulsory acquisition inherent in the proposals.*

The case must be one in which the land in question is:—

(a) indicated in a "structure plan" either as land which may be required for the functions of a government department, local authority, statutory undertaking or the National Coal Board; or

(b) allocated for the purposes of such functions by a "local plan" or defined in such a plan as the site of proposed development for any such functions; or

(c) is land in respect of which a compulsory purchase order is in force but notice to treat has not yet been served; or

(d) is land on which the Secretary of State has given detailed notification of his intention to provide a trunk road or special road; or

(e) indicated in a development plan as land for a new, improved or altered highway; or

(f) authorised by a special enactment to be compulsorily acquired; or

(g) on or adjacent to the line of a highway proposed to be constructed, improved or altered, as shown in an order or scheme under Part II of the Highways Act, 1959; or

---

[1] As amended by Sections 33-38 and 4th Sched. of Town and Country Planning Act, 1968. This type of case must be clearly distinguished from that in which an " owner " is entitled to serve a " purchase notice " under Section 129 of the 1962 Act. The latter type of case was dealt with in Chapter 19, Section 5.

(h) shown on plans approved by a local highway authority as land comprised in the site of a highway to be constructed, improved or altered; or

(i) included in a declaratory order made under Section 1 of the Town and Country Planning Act, 1944. (13th Sched. para. 3 of the 1962 Act).

The party who serves the blight notice must be:—

(a) A " resident owner-occupier " of the whole or part of a hereditament which (in whole or part) falls within any of the above cases; or

(b) the " owner-occupier " of the whole or part of any such hereditament the annual value of which does not exceed a certain prescribed limit (at present £750);[2] or

(c) the " owner-occupier " of the whole or part of an agricultural unit—e.g., a farm—which (in whole or in part) falls within any of the prescribed cases.

The term " owner-occupier " in relation to (b) and (c) above is defined in some detail in Section 149 of the 1962 Act, as now amended by Section 37 of the 1968 Act. There are certain qualifying periods which entitle a person or body to be regarded as an " occupier " and they must also during these periods have had an " owner's interest " in the land—i.e., the freehold or a lease with at least three years to run.

The term " resident owner-occupier " is defined in Section 149 (3) and refers to the occupation of a private dwelling-house. Here again, during the qualifying periods, the occupier must also have had an " owner's interest " in the land. In this case the annual value of the property is immaterial.

The notice to purchase the owner-occupier's interest must be in prescribed form[3] and must be served on the authority who, it appears from the proposals, will be acquiring the land.

In certain circumstances, specified in Section 34 of the 1968 Act, a notice to purchase may be served by a mortgagee.

It must relate to the whole of the party's interest in the land.

Within two months of the receipt of the claimant's notice, the appropriate authority may serve a counter notice of objection on any of the following grounds: —

(a) that no part of the hereditament or agricultural unit is land of any of the specified descriptions;

---

[2] Town and Country Planning (Limit of Value) Order, 1963.
[3] Town and Country Planning (Prescribed Forms of Notices) Regulations. 1959.

(b) that they do not, unless compelled, propose to acquire any part of the hereditament, or of the area of the agricultural unit, affected by the proposals;[4]

(c) that they propose to acquire a part of the affected area but do not, unless compelled, propose to acquire any other part of that area.

(d) that the claimant is not entitled to an interest in any part of the hereditament or agricultural unit;

(e) that the claimant's interest is not such as to entitle him to protection under the Act—e.g., he is not an " owner-occupier ";

(f) that he has not made " reasonable endeavours " to sell; or that the price at which he could sell is not " substantially lower " than that which he might reasonably have expected to get but for the planning proposals.

Within two months of the counter notice, the claimant may require the authority's objection to be referred to the Lands Tribunal who may uphold the objection or declare that the claimant's original notice is a valid one. If the authority's objection is upheld, or is accepted by the claimant, in case (c), they will, of course, have to purchase the part referred to in the counter notice.

Where no counter notice is served, or where the claimant's notice is upheld by the Lands Tribunal, the appropriate authority will be deemed to be authorised to acquire the claimant's interest in the hereditament, or (in the case of an agricultural unit) in that part of the unit to which the proposals which gave rise to the claim relate.

In general, notice to treat will be deemed to have been served at the expiration of two months from the service of the claimant's notice or—where an objection has been made—on a date fixed by the Lands Tribunal.

The general basis of compensation, where an authority are obliged to purchase an owner-occupier's interest under the 1962 Act, will now be that generally prescribed by the Land Compensation Act, 1961.

Except where the authority have already entered and taken possession under their deemed notice to treat, a party who has served a blight notice may withdraw it at any time before compensation has been determined, or within six weeks of its determination. In this case any notice to treat deemed to have been served will be deemed to have been withdrawn.

---

[4] In certain cases, specified in Section 35 (1) of the 1968 Act, objection may be on the ground that the appropriate authority do not propose to acquire during a period of 15 years (or longer) from the date of the counter notice.

### 3. ADJUSTMENT OF UNEXPENDED BALANCES—TOWN AND COUNTRY PLANNING ACT, 1962, SECTION 96

Since neither the 1959 nor the 1961 Act affected the provisions of Part II of the 1954 Act (now Section 106 of the 1962 Act) in regard to the basis of compensation for adverse planning decisions in relation to " new development ",[5] it follows that the existence and amount of any unexpended balance of development value attached to land may still be a matter of practical importance.

The 1962 Act therefore provides for the adjustment of unexpended balances of development value where compensation is paid for land taken or injuriously affected in connection with acquisitions by, or sales to an authority possessing compulsory powers.

The question of adjustment of balances on lands injuriously affected is dealt with in Chapter 24. We are concerned here only with the case of land taken.

If, as is usually the case, the compulsory acquisition or sale deals with all interests in the property, leaving no outstanding interest greater than that of a yearly tenant, then the unexpended balance attached to the land will be treated as extinguished by the payment of compensation.

But if, after acquisition or sale, an outstanding interest still remains, then the amount of the balance attributable to the interest or interests acquired must be ascertained, and the unexpended balance on the land will in future be reduced by this amount.

In these rare cases the amounts attributable to the interest or interests acquired and to the outstanding interest respectively are found by applying the same rules as were prescribed under the Town and Country Planning Act, 1954, when, on a compulsory purchase of land, it became necessary to find the proportion of the unexpended balance payable to each party in addition to the existing use value of his land.

These rules—formerly contained in the Fifth Schedule to the 1954 Act—are now re-enacted in the Seventh Schedule to the 1962 Act. In their simplest form they are described and illustrated in Chapter 23, Section 2B (e). Their application to more complicated cases is dealt with in Appendix D.

### B. Practical Points in Claims for " Disturbance "

The general principles governing the right to compensation for " disturbance " were discussed in Chapter 21, Section C.1, in relation to Rule 6 of Section 5 of the Land Compensation Act, 1961. It is now necessary to consider some of the practical points which may arise in connection with such claims.

---

[5] See Chapter 19, Section 2 (e).

## (a) PRIVATE HOUSES

Where a dwelling-house is compulsorily acquired, the occupier, if he be a freeholder, or a lessee sitting at an appreciable profit rent, will be entitled to compensation based on the value of his interest in the property, estimated in accordance with the statutory provisions already described. If he be a lessee or tenant holding under a contractual tenancy and paying approximately the full rack rental of the premises, the value of his interest in the land will be negligible, but he will be entitled to some measure of compensation for being forced to quit before the expiration of his term —similarly, when the interest is no greater than that of a yearly tenant and the tenant is required to give up possession before the expiration of his interest. No definite basis can be prescribed for these types of cases; but where the lease still has a number of years to run, a figure of one year's rent is often allowed for what may conveniently be called " extinction of lease ".

In addition to the value of his interest in the land, or a suitable allowance for the termination of that interest, the occupier will also be entitled to compensation in respect of (i) fixtures, (ii) cost of removal, and (iii) other incidental expenses.

*Fixtures.*—The occupier may remove any fixtures to which he is entitled, or he may insist on the acquiring body taking them as part of the premises. If he moves them he is entitled to compensation for any depreciation they are likely to suffer in the process of removal and fixing elsewhere—in practice an allowance of 50-75 per cent of their value is often adopted as a convenient basis for this item. If the fixtures are taken with the premises, the owner is entitled to their fair value as fixtures to an incoming tenant.

*Cost of Removal.*—This item will include not only the actual cost of moving the owner's furniture to other premises but also any other expense incidental thereto, such as temporary storage of furniture, cost of adapting various items of furnishing, such as blinds and curtains, to the new premises, change of address on stationery, etc.

*Incidental Expenses.*—In addition to cost of removal, there may be other incidental expenses incurred by an owner-occupier in consequence of being dispossessed of his premises.

In *Harvey v. Crawley Development Corporation,*[6] ROMER, L.J., summarised the principle governing the inclusion of such items in the claim as follows: " The authorities . . . establish that any loss sustained by a dispossessed owner (at all events one who occupies his house) which flows from a compulsory acquisition may properly be regarded as the subject of compensation for disturbance provided, first it is not too remote and secondly, that it is the natural and reasonable consequence of the dispossession

[6] (1957) 1 Q.B., 485.

of the owner ". In the case in question the claimant, who was required to give up possession of her house, was held entitled to recover legal costs, surveyor's fees and travelling expenses incurred in finding another house to live in, together with similar expenses incurred to no purpose in connection with the proposed purchase of a house on which she received an unfavourable report from her surveyor.

Legal and other professional fees incurred after notice to treat in connection with the preparation of the owner's claim are also recoverable under Rule 6 of Section 5 of the Land Compensation Act, 1961.

### (b) BUSINESS AND PROFESSIONAL PREMISES

Like the householder, the occupier of business premises will be entitled to compensation for (i) the value of his interest in the land *or* for " extinction of lease," (ii) loss of or injury to fixtures, and (iii) cost of removal. In addition, a trader or business man may have a claim for loss on stock and trade disturbance.

*Compensation for Interest in Land.*—As in the case of house property, if a lessee is sitting at a substantial profit rent he will be entitled to compensation for loss of his leasehold interest based on the ordinary principles of compulsory purchase valuation.

It is submitted that a claim of this kind is not affected by the provisions of the Landlord and Tenant Act, 1954. For although under that Act the tenancy will automatically continue after the termination date, the landlord, by serving the necessary notice under the Act, can ensure that the new tenancy shall be at a rent at which (having regard to the other terms of the tenancy) the holding might reasonably be expected to be let in the open market.

Where the rent already paid under the lease is approximately the full rack rental value of the premises, the additional security of tenure given by the Landlord and Tenant Act, 1954, would appear to strengthen the tenant's claim for compensation for " extinction of lease ", although it must be remembered that this factor may well be reflected in the claim for " injury to goodwill " or " trade disturbance ".

In the case of tenants from year to year, or any lesser interest—whose right to compensation depends on Section 121 of the Lands Clauses Act or Section 20 of the Compulsory Purchase Act, 1965—Section 39 of the Landlord and Tenant Act, 1954, expressly provides that no additional compensation shall be payable in respect of the tenant's right to obtain a new tenancy under that Act. But the total compensation paid to him is not to be less than that which, in certain circumstances, he might have received under Section 37 of the Act if a new tenancy had been refused—i.e., an amount equal to the rateable value, or twice the rateable value where the tenant or his predecessors in business have been in occupation of the holding for the past 14 years.

*Fixtures.*—The occupier will probably insist on these being taken with the premises, since the possibility of adapting them to other premises usually is somewhat problematical.

*Cost of Removal.*—This will usually be substantial, including in the case of industrial premises such items as the cost of moving machinery and its reinstallation in new premises.

*Incidental Expenses.*—These will include notification of change of address to customers, new sign writing, stationery, etc. As in the case of private houses, there is authority for the inclusion of legal and surveyor's fees incurred in connection with the acquisition of new premises and also legal and other professional fees incurred in connection with the preparation of the claim.[7]

*Loss on Stock.*—This may consist either of depreciation in the process of removal to other premises, or loss on forced sale in those cases where no other premises are available, or where the trade likely to be done in new premises will be of a somewhat different class, or where the stock will not bear removal.

Loss on depreciation may be expressed as a percentage of the value in the trader's books, but is often covered by the cost of taking out an insurance policy before the move. Loss on forced sale is likely to be high—possibly 33–50 per cent on retail prices.

*Trade Disturbance.*—" Trade disturbance " or " injury to goodwill " is the term applied to the loss of profits likely to result from a trader or business man being dispossessed of his premises.

It will be convenient to discuss the nature of this loss in relation to retail trades and then to see to what extent the same considerations apply to the wholesale trader, the manufacturer or the professional man.

The " goodwill " of a business has been defined as the probability of that business being carried on at a certain level of profit. Where a trader has been in business in certain premises for a number of years he will have attached to himself a circle of regular customers on whose patronage he can rely; he will also be able to count on a fairly steady volume of casual custom. As a result, by striking an average over three or four normal years he can make a fairly accurate estimate of his annual profits. It is the probability of those profits being maintained, or even increased, in the future which constitutes the " goodwill " of the business.

The various factors which go to make goodwill can usually be divided into two classes—(i) those which, being of a personal nature, do not depend on the situation of the premises, e.g., the name and reputation of the firm or the personality of the proprietor; (ii) those which are dependent on situation, e.g., the advantage

---

[7] See *London County Council v. Tobin*, [1959] 1 W.L.R. 354; also *Rowley v. Southampton Corporation*, [1959] 10 P. & C.R., 172.

derived from being on the main shopping street of a town or in a street or district which is the recognised centre for businesses of a particular type.

When business premises are taken under compulsory powers the tradesman's goodwill is not necessarily destroyed, but it may be seriously damaged. How seriously depends upon whether the goodwill is mainly personal in character or largely dependent upon the situation of the premises.

The usual method of assessing this class of loss is by multiplying the average annual net profits by a figure of Years' Purchase which varies according to the extent of the injury likely to be suffered. In most cases the figure of net profits is based on the past three years' trading as shown by the trader's books. The accounts are often supplied to the valuer by the claimant's accountant.

Usually, however, the figure given will not have taken into account interest on the capital employed in the business, and as the trader could earn interest upon his capital by investing it elsewhere, the annual profit due to the business is really not the figure taken from the books, but that figure less interest on capital. The tenant's capital would comprise the value of the fixtures and fittings, stock, etc., and the necessary sum to be kept in hand for working expenses. The latter item would obviously be larger in the case of a credit business than in a cash business. The valuer needs, therefore, to examine the figure supplied to him as the average net profits and to make a deduction for interest on capital if that has not already been done.

He must also ascertain what rent has been charged in the books. Usually the actual rent paid is charged in the accounts, and if the valuer estimates that the property is worth more than the rent paid, he must deduct the estimated profit rent. While in the case of a freehold, if no rent has been charged, the estimated annual rental used for arriving at the value of the property must be deducted.

The wages of assistants employed in a firm will naturally be deducted in finding the net profits. But it was held by the Lands Tribunal in *Perezic v. Bristol Corporation*[8] that there was no evidence that it was customary to deduct a sum in respect of the remuneration of the working proprietor of a one man business.

In a later case—*A. V. Speyer v. City of Westminster*,[9] the Tribunal expressed the view that whether such a deduction was appropriate or not must depend on the effect of the disturbance on the earning capacity of the claimant.

Such of these deductions as are applicable having been made, and true net profits having been found, the next step is to fix the multiplier which should be applied to this figure in order fairly to compensate the trader for injury to his goodwill.

[8] [1955] 5 P. & C.R. 237.
[9] (1958) 9 P. & C.R. 478.

Where the taking of the premises will mean total extinction of trade the full value of the goodwill may be allowed as compensation. In the case of retail businesses, this does not normally exceed 3 Years' Purchase of the net profits. The figure used will be influenced, amongst other things, by whether the profits appear to be increasing or decreasing.

Where the trade will not be totally lost but may be seriously injured by removal to other premises, a fair compensation may be about half what would be paid for total extinction. But a much lower figure will be given where the trade is likely to be carried on almost as profitably as before.

A cash tobacconist adjoining the entrance of a busy railway station may lose the whole trade if the premises upon which the trade is carried on are taken from him. In such a case, up to the full value of the business may be appropriate compensation—possibly 3 Years' Purchase of the net profits.

A milkman, on the contrary, knowing all his customers by reason of delivery of milk daily at the houses, may face removal with little risk of loss of that portion of his trade, and a baker or family butcher may be much in the same category, although any of these may suffer loss of some casual custom, and also in respect of items sold over the counter. In such cases a half-a-year's profits would often be proper compensation.

It is obvious that since the variety of trades is so great and the circumstances of each case may vary so widely, every claim of this sort must be judged on its merits. But the following are amongst the most important considerations likely to affect the figure of compensation:—

(i) The nature of the trade and the extent to which it depends upon the position of the premises.—For instance, a grocer or confectioner or draper whose business is done entirely over the counter will suffer considerable loss if he has to move to premises in an inferior trade position. Probably $1\frac{1}{2}$-2 Years' Purchase of his net profits would not be excessive compensation. On the other hand, a credit tailor would be far less likely to be injured by removal since his customers might be expected to follow him.

Where the trade is partly cash and partly credit, the valuer may think it proper to separate the profits attributable to the two parts and to apply a higher figure of Years' Purchase to the former than to the latter.

(ii) The prospects of alternative accommodation.—For instance, in many cases a shopkeeper turned out of his present premises will find it impossible to obtain a shop elsewhere in the town and a claim for total loss of goodwill may be justified. Or, again, the fact that the only alternative accommodation available is on a secondary shopping street may considerably affect the figure.

(iii) The terms on which the premises are held.—The compensation payable to a trader holding on lease with a number of years to run will probably be substantially the same as that of a claimant in similar circumstances who owns the freehold of his premises—particularly in view of the additional security of tenure now enjoyed by lessees under the Landlord and Tenant Act, 1954.

But a shopkeeper who holds on a yearly tenancy only can scarcely expect as high a level of compensation—especially since Section 39 (1) of the 1954 Act expressly provides that compensation in his case is to be assessed without regard to his right to apply for a new tenancy under the Act.

The question of the compensation payable to wholesale traders and manufacturers involves similar considerations to those already discussed. It will usually be found, however, that the probable injury to trade is much less than in the case of retail businesses, since profits are not so dependent upon position. Provided other suitable premises are available, the claim is usually one for so many months' temporary loss of profits during the time it will take to establish the business elsewhere, rather than for any permanent injury to goodwill.

In this type of case the sum claimed for temporary loss of income, since it forms part of the capital sum payable for the owner-occupier's interest in the land, will not be subject to income tax. It was therefore held in *West Suffolk County Council v. Rought Ltd.*,[10] that the Lands Tribunal, in assessing the compensation payable for temporary loss of profits, should have deducted their estimate of the additional taxation which the claimant company would have had to bear if it had actually earned the amount which the interruption to its business prevented it from earning.

But, in a case where the claim was for loss of profit due to service and subsequent withdrawal of notice to treat, it was held by the Lands Tribunal that, since the compensation—not being in this case part of a " consideration for sale "—was liable to income tax in the hands of the claimant, no tax should be deducted in computing it.[11]

In the case of professional men, such as solicitors or surveyors, the goodwill of the business is mainly personal and is not very likely to be injured by removal. But the special circumstances of the case must be considered, particularly the question of alternative accommodation. For instance, a firm of solicitors in a big city usually requires premises in the recognised legal quarter and in close touch with the courts, although this consideration might be of less importance to an old-established firm than to a comparatively new one.

---

[10] [1957] A.C. 403—following a decision of the House of Lords in *British Transport Commission v. Gourley*, [1956] A.C. 185.
[11] *Merediths Ltd. v. London County Council*, [1957] P. & C.R. 128.

In some cases of trade disturbance a basis somewhat similar to that of reinstatement is used in making the claim.

Thus, a claimant forced to vacate his factory, shop, etc., may show that he is obliged to move to other premises, which are the only ones available, and will base his claim for trade disturbance on the cost of adapting the new premises plus the reduced value of his goodwill in those premises.

The latter figure may be due to reduction in profits on account of increased running costs (other than rent) in the new premises. For instance, heating and lighting may cost more, transport costs may be higher, it may be necessary to employ more labour owing to the more difficult layout of a production line.

Or, again, the new position may not be so convenient for some customers as was the old. Or it may involve some change in the nature of the business which tends to make the profits rather less secure. For instance, in *L.C.C. v. Tobin*[12] the Court approved a figure of compensation for trade disturbance although it appeared that the profits in the new premises were likely to be higher than in the old. The compensation was based on the difference between the value of the profits in the old premises multiplied by 3 Y.P. and those in the new premises multiplied by $1\frac{1}{2}$ Y.P., the lower figure being justified by changes in the general circumstances of the business in the new premises.

To justify a claim based on the reinstatement of the business in other premises a claimant must show that he has acted reasonably and taken only such premises as a prudent person would take in order to safeguard his interests and mitigate his loss.

If there are no premises to which he can remove, except at a cost much out of proportion to what he is giving up, he may be justified in taking those premises; but he may in certain circumstances, particularly in the case of a trader, be compelled to allow a set-off from the cost of so reinstating himself in respect of the improved position he enjoys.

An acquiring body may sometimes offer alternative accommodation with a view to meeting a claim for trade disturbance.

Thus, if a retail trader claims that his business will suffer complete loss by the taking of the premises in which it is carried on, it is open to the acquiring authority to indicate premises which can be acquired for the reinstatement of the trade, or even to offer to build premises on land belonging to themselves, available for the purpose, and to transfer such premises to the claimant, in reduction of his claim. Arrangements of this kind are usually a matter of agreement between the parties. A claimant cannot be forced to accept alternative accommodation, although he may find it difficult to substantiate a heavy claim for trade disturbance in cases where it is offered.

---

[12] [1959] 1 W.L.R. 354.

## C. Practical Examples of Compulsory Purchase Valuations

*Example.*—Premises in a provincial town, occupied by a draper, consist of a shop and upper part. They are held from the free-holder on a 99 years building lease granted 58 years ago at a ground rent of £25 per annum.

The head-lessee let to the draper for 14 years four years ago at £500 per annum. The present rental value is £700 per annum.

The tenant's net profits over the last three years have been:— £2,900, £2,800 and £3,300 per annum after charging rent paid. Stock is worth £5,000. Fixtures £450. No suitable alternative premises are available. Acquired for road widening this year. The premises are in an area allocated for shopping purposes.

*Valuation*

*Freeholder*

| | | | |
|---|---|---:|---:|
| Freehold ground rent | ... ... | £25 p.a. | |
| Y.P. 41 years at 6% | ... ... | 15·14 | £378 |
| | | | |
| Reversion to | ... ... ... | £700 p.a. | |
| Y.P. in perp. at 8% deferred 41 years | ... ... ... ... | ·53 | £371 |
| | | | |
| | *Compensation,* say | | £750 |

Plus Surveyor's fees and legal costs.

*Head Lessee*

| | | | |
|---|---|---:|---:|
| Rent reserved | ... ... ... | £500 | |
| *Less:* Freehold ground rent | ... | 25 | |
| | | | |
| Net income ... | ... ... ... | £475 | |
| Y.P. 10 years at 7½% and 2½% (Tax @ 38.75%) | ... | 4·5 | £2,137 |
| Reversion to | ... ... ... | £700 | |
| *Less:* Freehold ground rent | ... | 25 | |
| | | | |
| Net income ... | ... ... ... | £675 | |
| Y.P. 31 years at 8½% and 2½% deferred 10 years (Tax @ 38.75%) | ... ... | 3·7 | £2,498 |
| | | | |
| | *Compensation,* say | | £4,635 |

Plus Surveyor's fees and legal costs.

The above is the " conventional " method of capitalising the varying incomes[13].

---

[13] See Chapter 6 (²) and Appendix A.

*Draper* (*Sub-lessee*)

| | | | | |
|---|---|---|---|---|
| Lease Profit rent ... ... ... | £200 | | |
| Y.P. 10 years at 9½% and 2½% ... | 4·2 | | |
| (Tax @ 38.75%) | ——— | | £840 |
| *Fixtures* (Assumed left) ... ... | | | 450 |
| *Stock* Loss on forced sale, say ... | | | £1,500 |
| *Goodwill* | | | |
| Average profits ... ... ... | £3,000 | | |
| *Less:* Profit rent ... ... ... | 200[14] | | |
| | ——— | | |
| " Goodwill " profits ... ... ... | £2,800 | | |
| Y.P., say ... ... ... ... | 2 | | £5,600 |
| | | | |
| Compensation | | | £8,390 |

Plus Surveyor's fees and legal costs.

Where development properties are acquired under the compensation provisions of the Land Compensation Act, 1961, the problem is mainly one of the choice of basis most favourable to the claimant. The following examples illustrate the choices available:—

*Example.*—Open land under grass acquired for housing and allocated as such in development plan, programmed 1–5 years. Housing value £18,000 per ha.

  *Compensation  —  £18,000 per ha.*

Note:—The value for purpose acquired and for allocation in development plan are the same.

*Example.*—Suppose the same land is acquired for allotments.

  *Compensation  —  £18,000 per ha.*

Note:—The value for allocation in the Development Plan gives the higher figure.

*Example.*—As above but programming 6–20 years. Acquired for school purposes.

*Compensation.*—£18,000 per ha deferred for length of time market would allow. For example, this could be three years if the programming is likely to be accelerated. It could alternatively be 15 years if (say) no drainage is available until then.

Note:—Here again the value is that for the allocation in the development plan since the value for school purposes is unlikely to be as great. In many cases school value is small.

---

[14] It is assumed that interest on capital and the draper's own services have been allowed for.

*Example.*—Open land under grass acquired for housing. Land is shown in a " white area " on the development plan.

*Compensation* — Housing value, say £18,000 per ha.
(Value for purpose acquired).

*Example.*—Open land under grass allocated in development plan for school purposes and acquired for use as such. The land is in the middle of a residential area in the development plan.

*Compensation*

In this case the claimant should apply to the local planning authority for a certificate of appropriate alternative development, asking for a certificate to be granted for residential development.
If granted—Compensation £18,000 per ha.
(Value for certified purpose).

If refused—" School value " or existing use value.

*Example.*—Land as before, but local planning authority's certificate states that planning permission could not reasonably have been expected except for school purposes. The land has an unexpended balance of established development value of £720, and " School Value " is taken in this case to be less than agricultural value (£500 per ha.).

*Compensation.*—£500 per ha plus £720 (discounted for time and trouble of collection) since this is a case where the owner could have claimed compensation up to £720 under the Town and Country Planning Act, if the planning permission for residential development had been refused, as seems probable.

*Example.*—Land in a " white area " is to be acquired as a recreation ground. There is some possibility that the development plan might be changed to a residential allocation on review. The agricultural value is £500 per ha. Recreation ground value £2,500 per ha. A speculator would give £4,000 per ha. in the hope that the allocation will be changed.

*Compensation* — £4,000 per ha.

In practice in the absence of direct evidence of recent comparable sales in the same area it is difficult to prove " hope value."

*Example.*—1 ha. of land in a green belt is to be acquired for housing. Compensation, equal to the original unexpended balance of established development value of £2,000 was paid for planning refusal in 1956.

*Compensation.*—Housing value, say £15,000 less £2,000 which would be repayable if planning permission for housing were now to be granted, i.e., £13,000.

*Example.*—A freehold building used until recently as a private house is to be acquired compulsorily: it is in an area of comprehensive development. It is now vacant. The development plan shows that the area is to be redeveloped for industrial and shopping purposes. If converted into a shop, the premises would be worth £600 per annum—the cost of conversion would be £1,400. The site area is 240 m². Industrial land is worth £10 per m².

(i) *Value with permission to convert into a shop:*—

| | | |
|---|---|---|
| Net rental value ... ... ... | £600 p.a. | |
| Y.P. ... ... ... ... | 12 | |
| | £7,200 | |
| *Less:* Cost, etc., say ... ... | £2,000 | (to include fees, profit, etc.) |
| *Compensation*, say | £5,200 | |

*OR*

(ii) *Value as industrial land* ... ... £2,400

*OR*

(iii) *Value as a house*, say ... ... £4,000

In this case basis (i) would be chosen by the claimant. Here the claimant is entitled, in any case, to the existing use value of £4,000. He could only claim £5,200 as compensation if he could show that planning permission for conversion to a shop might reasonably have been expected to be granted if the area had not been defined as an area of comprehensive development.

# Chapter 23

## Valuations for Compulsory Purchase and Compensation (contd.)

### The Town and Country Planning Acts, 1947–54

NOTE—Although the compensation provisions of these Acts have been superseded first by those of the Town and Country Planning Act, 1959, and now by the Land Compensation Act, 1961, they are still applicable to any case where land may have been acquired compulsorily by any Government department, local or public authority or statutory undertaking under a notice to treat served before 30 October, 1958. Also to any case of a "long standing notice to treat" when, under Section 15 of the 1959 Act, a notice to treat is deemed to have been served on 1 January, 1958. (See Chapter 22, A.1.)

It has therefore been thought appropriate to include a very brief outline of them in this book; although any reader desiring to study them in more detail is advised to refer to the Fourth or Fifth Edition.

1. THE TOWN AND COUNTRY PLANNING ACT, 1947 (Part 5)
[*Notices to Treat served between* 6 *August,* 1947, *and* 1 *January,* 1955]

(*a*) *Basis of Value* [*Sections* 50 (1) *and* 51 (1)]—As from 6 August, 1947, the 1939 standard of values prescribed by the Town and Country Planning Act, 1944, was abolished.

In future compensation was to be assessed in accordance with the Rules contained in Section 2 of the Acquisition of Land (Assessment of Compensation) Act, 1919—now Section 5 of the Land Compensation Act, 1961—by reference to prices current at the date of the notice to treat. But, *except where the cost of equivalent reinstatement was adopted as a basis in suitable cases*, the application of those Rules was subject to the following important modifications.

(*b*) *Exclusion of Development Value* (*Section* 51).—The market value of any interest in land was to be assessed on the assumption that planning permission would only be granted for such forms of development as were specified in the Third Schedule[1] to the Act.

The effect of this provision was to restrict compensation to what was described as the "existing use value" of the land and to exclude most elements of development value which, prior to the Act, might properly have been taken into account in assessing market value under the 1919 Act.

---

[1] Now the Third Schedule to the T. & C.P. Act, 1962.

Where, before service of notice to treat, planning permission had already been given for some development outside the scope of the Third Schedule which had not yet been carried out at the date when the notice was served, compensation was to be assessed as though that permission had not been given—i.e., any additional value due to the planning permission was to be ignored.

In the case of certain special types of property including (a) lands held by local authorities for general statutory purposes, (b) operational lands of statutory undertakers and (c) land held and used for charitable purposes, compensation could be assessed on the assumption that planning permission would be given for any development corresponding to that prevailing generally on contiguous and adjacent land. This was known as "prevailing use value". In these special cases, too, the land could be valued with the benefit of any planning permission already given but not yet implemented at the date of the notice to treat. [Sections 82 (5), 84 (4), 85 (4).]

Special provisions were made in regard to War Damaged Property (Sections 53 and 56), Requisitioned Land (Section 54) and Unfit Houses (Section 44 and Schedule 11).

## 2. THE TOWN AND COUNTRY PLANNING ACT, 1954
### [*Notices to Treat served on or after* 1 *January*, 1955, *and before* 30 *October*, 1958][2]

(*a*) *Existing Use Basis.*—In general, compensation continued to be assessed on an existing use basis under the provisions of the Acquisition of Land (Assessment of Compensation) Act, 1919, as modified by Section 51 of the Town and Country Planning Act, 1947.

No change was made in the special provisions of the 1947 Act relating to *War-damaged Property* (Section 53), *Requisitioned Land* (*Section* 54) *and Unfit Houses* [*Section* 44 (4)].

Nor to the special provisions whereby certain types of land were assessed on a "prevailing use" basis.

But where land acquired had attached to it an *unexpended balance of established development value*, then—unless "reinstatement" or "prevailing use value" was the basis adopted—compensation payable included this unexpended balance as well as existing use value.

The provisions of the Act on this point are examined in more detail in the following paragraphs.

(*b*) *Compensation in respect of Unexpended Balance* [*Section* 31]— Where compensation was assessed on an "existing use basis" and any part of the land to be acquired had an "unexpended balance of

---

[2] Compensation in these cases was subject to the joint effect of the 1947 and the 1954 Acts.

development value" immediately before the service of notice to treat, the compensation payable would include a sum in respect of that unexpended balance.

Special provision was made to meet possible cases of hardship where no unexpended balance existed owing to failure to submit what would have been a justifiable Part 6 claim.

Where the interest to be acquired was the only interest in the land —other than yearly tenancies or less—then, as a general rule, the whole of the unexpended balance would be added to the compensation payable to the owner.

But where there were two or more interests in the land—other than yearly tenancies or less—it was necessary to apportion the unexpended balance between the interests in question in order to determine the compensation which each owner ought to receive.

This question of the apportionment of the unexpended balance is dealt with in paragraph (e) below. First it will be convenient to note some further compensation provisions of the 1954 Act.

(c) *Additional Compensation for Works* [*Section* 32].—This Section referred to buildings or works erected by an owner, either on the land acquired or other land, between 1 July, 1948, and service or notice to treat, the value of which would not be adequately reflected in the assessment of compensation on an existing use basis.

For instance, work such as the construction of roads and sewers on what was formerly agricultural land might have been begun, but not completed, on the strength of a planning permission to develop for building. If notice to treat were now served, the effect of Section 51 (4) of the Town and Country Planning Act, 1947, would be that the benefit of that planning permission must be ignored in assessing compensation. As a result, the works—which would have formed an important part of the value of the completed development— might add little or nothing to the "existing use value" of the land, or might even depreciate it.

Under Section 32 the additional compensation payable in respect of such works was the amount by which (i) the value of the relevant interest immediately before the notice to treat, with the benefit of any planning permission in force at that time, exceeded (ii) the value it would have had at that time if the buildings or works had not been erected or constructed, but subject to:—

(a) the addition of any decrease in the existing use value due to the presence of the works; or

(b) the deduction of any increase in the existing use value due to their presence.

(d) *Protection for Prospective Purchasers* [*Section* 33].—It has already been noted that under Section 51 (4) of the 1947 Act, with some exceptions, the assessment of compensation on an existing use basis did not include the benefit of planning permission obtained but not yet implemented at the date of the notice to treat.

A purchaser who bought property at its full development value on the strength of planning permission obtained would therefore run the risk of receiving compensation only on an existing use basis if his newly purchased property were subsequently acquired before the development was carried out.

Section 33 of the Act therefore provided that where land was acquired compulsorily within five years of a notice obtained from the local authority to the effect that no compulsory purchase was contemplated within that period, the compensation payable would include the benefit of any planning permission in force at the date of that notice. An owner who claimed the benefit of this provision was not entitled to any payment in respect of the unexpended balance.

(e) *Apportionment of Unexpended Balance*—As stated in (b) above, this became necessary under the 1954 Act in cases where there were two or more interests in the land to be acquired—other than yearly tenancies or less—in order to determine the proportion of the unexpended balance properly payable to each owner by way of compensation in addition to the existing use value of his interest.

The apportionment was governed by rules contained in the Fifth Schedule to the Act (now re-enacted as the Seventh Schedule to the Town and Country Planning Act, 1962). These rules were complicated by the introduction of adjustments designed to cover special cases where the property was subject to rents or rentcharges in excess of what was called "the existing use rental". Detailed consideration of them has therefore been relegated to Appendix D of this book and the present chapter is confined to the normal, straightforward case of two or more interests subsisting in the land—e.g., freeholder, lessee, sublessee—none of the rents reserved being in excess of the "existing use rental" of the land.[3]

In apportioning the unexpended balance between the various interests in a case of this kind it was first necessary to find the "reversionary development value" (hereafter referred to as "R.D.V.") of any interest in reversion, e.g., that of a freeholder or head lessee. The R.D.V. of each such interest consisted of the amount of the unexpended balance deferred for the period extending from immediately before service of notice to treat to the date of the termination of the interest on which the reversion was expectant. The unexpended balance was then apportioned as follows:

---

[3] i.e., the amount of the rent which might reasonably be expected to be reserved if the land acquired were let on terms which permitted only the carrying out of "Third Schedule" development.

Freeholder — got R.D.V. of his interest.

Owner of a tenancy in reversion — {  got R.D.V. of his interest *less* R.D.V. of the interest immediately expectant on the termination of his own.

Owner of tenancy not in reversion — {  got the unexpended balance *less* the R.D.V. of the interest immediately expectant on the termination of his term.

*Example.*—At date of service of notice to treat A was the freeholder of land which he had leased to B for a term having 35 years unexpired. B had sublet to C for a term having 10 years unexpired. None of the rents reserved exceeded the fair rental value of the land for its existing use. The unexpended balance was £1,000.

In apportioning the unexpended balance it was first necessary to find the R.D.V. of A's and B's interests. Using a 6% basis (no specific rate was prescribed in the Act):—

R.D.V. of A's interest = £1,000 × P.V. £1 in 35 years at 6%
= £1,000 × 0·130 = **£130**

R.D.V. of B's interest = £1,000 × P.V. £1 in 10 years at 6%
= £1,000 × 0·558 = **£558**

The unexpended balance would then be apportioned as follows:

| | | | |
|---|---|---:|---:|
| A (Freeholder) | ... ... ... | | £130 |
| B (Head-lessee) R.D.V. | ... | £558 | |
| less A's R.D.V. | ... | 130 | |
| | | | 428 |
| C (Sublessee) Unexpended balance £1,000 | | | |
| less B's R.D.V. ... | ... | 558 | |
| | | | 442 |

**Total unexpended balance £1,000**

But a lessee or sublessee whose interest was acquired was not entitled to any payment in respect of the unexpended balance if, at the time of notice to treat, he was prohibited by the terms of his lease from carrying out any "new development" of the land.[4]

At the present day, with compensation based on the market value of the land under the Land Compensation Act, 1961, no payment is made in respect of any unexpended balance attached to the land.

Where—as is usually the case—all interests in the land are acquired the unexpended balance is deemed to be extinguished. But if after acquisition some outstanding interest still remains, then the

---

[4] Proviso to Sec. 31 (1), "New development" means any development other than development of a class specified in the Third Schedule.

amount of the unexpended balance attributable to the interest or interests acquired must be ascertained and the unexpended balance will in future be regarded as reduced by this amount. In these exceptional cases resort would have to be made to the rules of apportionment described above.

### 3.  Compensation for Injurious Affection Under the Town and Country Planning Act, 1954

The principles governing the legal right to compensation for injurious affection were examined in Chapter 20, Section 4.

The assessment of such claims at the present day is considered fully in Chapter 24.

Certain special rules governing compensation for injurious affection were contained in Section 36 of the Town and Country Planning Act, 1954. It is felt that reference should be made to them here. But since they would only apply if the claim arose from a compulsory acquisition under a notice to treat served after 1 January, 1955, and before 30 October, 1958, it is proposed to give only an outline of the principles involved. Any reader who may require a more detailed account should refer to Chapter 23 of the Fourth Edition of this book.

Under the Town and Country Planning Act, 1947, compensation for severance and injurious affection was based on the permanent depreciation in the "existing use value" of the land affected. The guiding principle of Section 36 of the 1954 Act was that compensation should continue to be paid in full for depreciation in "existing use value", and that compensation for injury to "development value" might also be payable, but only up to the limit of any "unexpended balance of development value" attached to the land.

With this object in view, a somewhat elaborate valuation procedure was prescribed for distinguishing between "loss of development value" and what was called "loss of immediate value".

"Loss of development value" was found by contrasting the value of the claimant's interest before and after the "injurious act or event",[5] both valuations being made on the assumption that until such time as the land might reasonably be expected to become ripe for development, no use whatever could be made of it.

"Loss of immediate value" was found by deducting the above figure from the total depreciation in the value of the claimant's interest calculated in the normal way.

If a property did not offer any prospect of future development, then loss of immediate value was the same as the total depreciation in the value of the property.

---

[5] Presumably the service of notice to treat, where part of land is taken, or the interference with the claimant's legal rights when no part is taken.

The claimant was in any case entitled to full compensation for any "loss of immediate value". But compensation for "loss of development value" was only payable up to the limit of any "unexpended balance" attached to the land. For instance, if "loss of development value" amounted to £600 and the "unexpended balance" attached to the land was £500, the claimant would only receive £500, in addition to any loss of "immediate value".

If there were two or more claimants, each would receive compensation for "loss of immediate value" to his particular interest. But if the aggregate of their claims for "loss of development value" exceeded the "unexpended balance", then the latter had to be divided among them in proportion to the "loss of development value" suffered by each.

Any compensation paid for "loss of development value" due to severance or injurious affection—whether arising from a compulsory acquisition or a sale by agreement to a body with compulsory powers—would be deducted in calculating the "unexpended balance" (if any) existing on any subsequent occasion under the Act.

On the other hand, if the compensation paid, or—in the case of a sale by agreement—the sum included in the purchase price, in respect of "loss of immediate value" was less than the difference between the "existing use value" of the interest (a) before, and (b) after, the injurious act or event, the difference was in future treated as an unexpended balance attached to the land.

# Chapter 24

## Compensation for Injurious Affection

### 1. GENERALLY

THE PRINCIPLES governing the *right* to compensation for injurious affection were considered in Chapter 20 where a distinction was drawn between—

    (i) claims for injurious affection to land formerly " held with " land taken; and

    (ii) claims for injurious affection due to the exercise of statutory powers on land not owned by the claimant.

The right to compensation in both cases derives either from the Lands Clauses Act, 1845, or—in the majority of cases nowadays—from the corresponding provisions of the Compulsory Purchase Act, 1965. The relevant Sections are 63 and 68 of the 1845 Act and 7 and 10 of the 1965 Act.

For this reason the view is often expressed that compensation under this head is part of the loss suffered by the owner in consequence of his land being taken and is not affected by the provisions of the Land Compensation Act, 1961.

While this is undoubtedly true in regard to many items in the nature of disturbance which may arise where part only of land is taken, it is submitted that, in so far as the claim for compensation is based on depreciation in the " value " of land, it comes within the scope of Rule (2) of Section 5 of the Land Compensation Act, 1961.

The wording of Rule (6) of the same Section which provides that Rule (2) shall not affect the compensation for disturbance or any other matter *not directly based on the value of land*, certainly seems to imply that where compensation is so based Rule (2) will operate.

It is therefore assumed in this Chapter that, in all cases of compulsory acquisition pursuant to a notice to treat served after 29th October, 1958, compensation for injurious affection—in so far as it is based on the value of land—will represent the depreciation in the value of that land in the open market.

It would appear, however, that the assumptions as to planning permission to be made under Sections 14–16 of the 1961 Act, in the case of lands taken, do not apply to assessments of market value in the case of lands injuriously affected.[1]

---

[1] Compare Secs. 14–16 with the definitions of " relevant interest " and " relevant land " in Sec. 39 (2).

## 2. Compensation Where Part Only of a Property is Taken

Cases of this type frequently occur, particularly in connection with the construction of new roads or the widening of existing roads.

It is necessary to consider the principal losses likely to be suffered in connection with the land formerly " held with " the land taken and the bases on which claims for compensation should be prepared.

Compensation where part of a property is taken falls under three main heads—(a) land taken; (b) severance and other injurious affection to land held therewith; (c) other incidental loss resulting from the compulsory taking. Other matters which may have to be considered are (d) accommodation works, and (e) apportionment of rents.

The student may find it useful at this stage to revise Section 4 of Chapter 20 which summarises the legal principles governing the right to compensation for " injurious affection."

(a) *Land Taken*.—The area of land to be taken will usually be indicated on the plan accompanying the notice to treat. In the case of a road it will include not only the land required for the road itself but also that occupied by the slopes of any cuttings or embankments.

The compensation for the land taken will be assessed, in accordance with the principles prescribed by the Land Compensation Act, 1961. In the case of agricultural land its "value" will probably be estimated by reference to prices paid for small areas of land of the same type in the district.

In addition to the value of the land itself the owner is entitled to compensation for the loss of any buildings or fixtures or timber on the land, while the tenant or owner-occupier of agricultural land may also have a claim for " tenant-right ". The latter item will be discussed in more detail under the heading of " other incidental losses ".

(b) *Severance and Other Injurious Affection*.—The term " injury due to severance " is generally used to indicate the probable depreciation in value where lands formerly owned and occupied as one property are separated from one another by the construction of a statutory undertaking. A typical example is where part of a farm is separated from the rest of the farm, including the farm-house and farm buildings, by the construction of a road across the property.

In the case of agricultural land, severance is likely to result in increased working costs. For example, if the severed portion is arable land, there will probably be an increase in the cost of all the normal operations of ploughing, sowing, reaping, carting, etc., as well as additional supervision necessitated by the separation of the land from the rest of the farm. If the severed portion is pasture land, extra labour and supervision may be required in driving cattle to pasture as well as possible risk of injury to cattle, as for instance in crossing a busy new road. These additional expenses are likely to involve some reduction in the rental value of the land which, capitalised, will represent the injury due to severance.

The extent of the injury will naturally vary greatly according to the nature of the undertaking and other circumstances. Thus an undertaking, such as a railway, will usually cause a greater degree of severance than a road. While the effect of a new road running on the level will be less serious than that of one which is mainly in a cutting or on an embankment.

In addition to the injury caused to the lands which are severed, it is possible that the property as a whole may suffer some depreciation in value by reason of the fact that it can no longer be occupied and enjoyed as one compact holding.

The valuer must also be careful to include in the claim for compensation any injury likely to be caused to the rest of the property by the authorised user of the works on the land taken.

For example, the use, as a major road, of a strip of land across a residential estate may seriously depreciate the value of the mansion by reason of noise, fumes, and loss of privacy. While in the case of agricultural land, the possibility of crops being damaged by fumes or dust from a new road, or the yield of milk from pasture land being reduced by disturbance of cattle due to heavy traffic on the road, may result in loss of rental value.

Every head of damage which can reasonably be anticipated should be included in the claim, since no further claim can be made later for damage which might have been foreseen at the time when the land was taken.

The claim for depreciation in value will be based on the market value of the land, which will take into account the benefit of any planning permission already given.

It may be permissible, in some cases, to consider the effect on value of the possibility that planning permission might have been given, having regard to the terms of the development plan and other circumstances. But no certain assumptions of planning permission can be made as in the case of land taken.

(c) *Other Incidental Injury.*—In addition to the value of the land taken and injurious affection to other land held therewith, the owner is entitled to compensation for all other loss and expense which he may incur in consequence of the compulsory acquisition. Such losses will vary with the circumstances of each case, so that it would be misleading to attempt to suggest an exhaustive list of possible items. But a consideration of some of the principal heads of damage likely to arise in connection with the taking of a strip of land through an agricultural estate will indicate the general nature of the items included in this part of the claim. They may be briefly summarised as follows: —

(i) *Disturbance and Tenant-Right on the Land Taken.*—Either an owner-occupier or a tenant is entitled to compensation for any loss suffered through having to quit a portion of his land at short notice. Such loss may arise from the forced sale of stock which can no longer be supported on the reduced acreage of the farm, or from the forced sale of agricultural implements. He may also claim for other similar consequential losses, for example, temporary grazing and storage.

Improvements to the land made at a tenant's expense may have to be taken into account. Both owner-occupiers and tenants may claim for " tenant right ".[2]

(ii) *Damage During Construction.*—It is almost unavoidable that during construction a certain amount of damage should be caused to crops, etc., on land immediately adjoining the works. It is also likely that certain parts of the farm, particularly those portions which are to be severed, will be more difficult to work during this period, so that a claim for increased labour costs or total loss of rental value may be justified. If the works are being carried out close to the mansion or farmhouse, the disturbance to the occupier may be considerable and in extreme cases it may be necessary for him to obtain temporary accommodation elsewhere.

(iii) *Reinstatement Works.*—Owing to the construction of the undertaking on the land taken, the owner or occupier may be forced to carry out various works to the remaining land. For example, small awkward-shaped pieces of land may be left on either side of the works which it will be necessary to throw into adjoining fields by re-arranging fences, grubbing-up hedges, filling in ditches, etc.

(d) *Accommodation Works.*—In the case of railway undertakings the acquiring body was obliged, under Section 68 of the Railway Clauses Act, 1845, to provide certain " accommodation works " for the benefit of owners of land adjoining the undertaking. These included bridges and other means of communication between severed portions of land, the adequate fencing of the works, means of drainage through or by the side of the railway and provision of watering places for cattle.

These works tended to reduce the effect of severance and other injury likely to be caused by the construction of the railway and were, of course, taken into account in assessing compensation.

In the case of other undertakings there is no obligation on the acquiring body to provide accommodation works, or on the owner

---

[2] Additional compensation, up to four times the annual rent of the part taken, may also be payable under the Agriculture (Miscellaneous Provisions) Act, 1968.

to accept them in lieu of compensation. But in practice it is frequently agreed between the parties that the acquiring body will carry out certain " accommodation works " or " works of rein- statement," and that compensation shall be assessed on the basis of these works being provided.

For instance, where a new road is constructed across agricultural or accommodation land, the acquiring body will not only fence along the boundaries of the road, but will also provide new gates where convenient. If part of the front garden of a house is taken under a street widening scheme, the acquiring body will probably agree to provide a new boundary wall and gates, to plant a quick- set hedge to screen the house, to make good the connection to the house drains, and similar works.

All these are items which would otherwise have to be included in the claim. It is more convenient for both parties that the acquiring body should do them while the works are still in progress. Details of the works agreed upon will therefore be included in any settlement of compensation by agreement, or in case of dispute may be handed to the Lands Tribunal and considered by them in awarding compensation.

It is also important in road cases to come to an understanding as to the maintenance of slopes, banks and retaining walls, and as to the owner's right of access to the road.

The acquiring body will usually undertake responsibility for slopes, banks and retaining walls. Normally any retaining wall built to support a highway, or wall built to prevent soil from higher land falling on the highway, will be part of the highway.

The owner will usually stipulate for access to the new road across any intervening slopes or banks and the right to lay sewers, and also for public services such as gas and water mains, electric cables, etc., to be permitted in the soil of the road.

(e) *Apportionment of Rent.*—Where part of land subject to a lease is taken it may be necessary to apportion the rent between the part taken and that which is left. Naturally the lessee should not be required to continue to pay the same rent, particularly if the portion taken is considerable; but it is often difficult to agree on the amount of the deduction to be made.

The lessee can only demand a fair apportionment of the rent paid, not of the annual value of the property. Also, he cannot include in the reduction of rent any figure representing reduced value to the rest of the property. That loss should be met by compensation from the acquiring body.

In view of these difficulties it is a common practice, particularly where small portions of urban properties are taken for road widening purposes, to agree on a nominal apportionment of, say, 1p or perhaps one pound a year on the land taken. Under this arrangement the lessee will continue to pay the rent reserved under his lease for the balance of his term, but on the other hand will receive full compensation for the loss of rental value from the acquiring body; while the freeholder will be compensated for the injury to his reversion.

Where a freehold property is subject to a building lease at a ground rent and a sub-lease at the full annual value or rack rent, apportionment might be agreed on a basis of 1p per annum on the part taken as regards the rent under the ground lease and £1 per annum for the part taken as regards the rent under the sub-lease.

Any dispute as to apportionment of rent under a lease may be referred to the Lands Tribunal. But in that case the apportionment must be a true apportionment as distinct from a nominal one.

(f) *Example.*—A Highway Authority is about to acquire a strip of land through a farm of 80 ha for the construction of a road 30 m wide, running roughly north and south and likely to carry a considerable volume of traffic. Where the road first enters the farm at the north, it will run for approximately 100 m on an embankment of a maximum height of 3 m. For the remainder of its course it will be on the level. The total area of land acquired, including the slopes of the embankment, will be 3 ha.

The farm consists of 64 ha of pasture, 15 ha of arable, and the rest roads and buildings. It is occupied by the owner. Similar land in the neighbourhood but without buildings has sold recently for £750 per ha.

The new road will sever 24 ha of the best land from the homestead and interfere with the water supply and land drainage of three fields.

The Highway Authority will fence along the whole length of the road, and at two points will provide gates giving access from the fields on one side of the road to those on the other. They will provide adequate land drainage along the sides of the road and to the slopes of the embankment and will make good any interference with the water supply.

Notice to treat was served on 25th March last. Estimate the compensation payable to the owner-occupier.

*Valuation—*

*Land Taken—*

| | | |
|---|---|---|
| 3 ha at £750 per ha ... ... ... ... | £2,250 |

*Injury Due to Severance—*

24 ha will be severed from the farmhouse and buildings and extra labour and risk will be involved in driving cattle to and from those fields.

| | |
|---|---|
| Loss of value, say £75 per ha on 24 ha   ... | £1,800 |
| Disturbance on land taken, including possible loss on sale of stock, say   ...   ...   ...   ... | 50 |
| Tenant-right on land taken, say ...   ...   ... | 75 |
| Interference during construction of works— | |
| (i) Depreciation of rental value on 24 ha for, say 6 months at £5 per ha   ...   ... | 60 |
| (ii) Total loss of rental value on 8 ha immediately adjoining the works, say   ...   ... | 120 |
| Cost of re-arranging fences between fields and ploughing up small area of pasture   ...   ... | 35 |
| Re-arrangement of land drainage to three fields ... | 30 |
| Compensation | £4,420 |

Plus surveyor's fees and legal costs.

*Note.*—The works of fencing, draining, etc., which the Highway Authority have undertaken to provide come under the heading of " accommodation works " or " works of reinstatement ".

### 3.   WHERE NO PART OF THE LAND IS TAKEN

The four tests which govern the right to compensation in this type of case are fully discussed in Chapter 20, Section 4 (c).

Typical examples are where authorised development by the acquiring body on land taken deprives an adjoining owner of the benefit of some easement attached to his land—such as a right of light or a right of way—or is in breach of some restrictive covenant to the benefit of which the adjoining owner is entitled.

Once the legal right to compensation is established, it is then a question of determining the depreciation in the market value of the land due to the injury complained of.

The usual method is to make two valuations of the property— (i) as it previously stood, and (ii) after the interference with the legal right in question.

This " Before and After " method, as it is often called, can be used both in this type of case and also in cases where part of land has been taken. It is considered in detail in the next section of this Chapter.

### 4.   " BEFORE AND AFTER " METHOD OF VALUATION

Besides the case where no part of the owner's land is taken, this method is also used in many cases of the taking of part of a property where, in practice, it is often very difficult to separate the value of the land taken from the injurious affection likely to be caused to the rest of the land by the construction and use of the undertaking.

As applied to this latter type of case it will involve two valuations—(i) of the property in its present condition unaffected by statutory powers, and (ii) of the property as it will be after the part has been taken and the undertaking is constructed and in use. The amount by which valuation (i) exceeds valuation (ii) will represent the compensation payable both for the loss of the land taken and also for injurious affection to the remainder. In addition, the owner might be entitled to claim for injury during the carrying out of the works, and it would be necessary to come to an understanding as to the works of reinstatement which the acquiring body are prepared to provide.

An example is the taking of a strip of land forming part of the garden or grounds of a house. Here it is usually very difficult to assign a value to the strip of land taken without at the same time considering all the consequences of the taking. For instance, suppose that the strip forms part of a garden of a fair-sized house and is to be used in the construction of a new road, the following are some of the questions which will naturally suggest themselves in assessing the fair compensation to the owner:—

(i) Will the land remaining be reasonably sufficient for a house of this size and type? (ii) Will the proposed road be on the level, on an embankment, or in a cutting? (iii) Will it be visible from the house, and if so from what parts of it? (iv) What volume of traffic may be expected? (v) How close will the house be to the road and to what extent is it likely to suffer from loss of privacy, noise, fumes and other inconvenience?

It is obvious that the most realistic approach to the problem is that of comparing the value of the house as it now stands with its estimated value after a portion of the garden has been taken and the new road is actually in full use.

In theory, at any rate, there are two statutory obstacles to the use of this method—(i) the fact that the statutory assumptions as to planning permission apply to land taken, but not to land injuriously affected; (ii) the fact that Section 4 (2) of the Land Compensation Act, 1961, requires that the owner's statement of claim shall distinguish the amount claimed under separate heads and show how the amount claimed under each head is calculated.

Even so, it is probable that the valuer's first approach to a problem of this kind will be along the lines of the " before and after " method and that, having in this way arrived at what he considers a reliable figure, he will then proceed to apportion i t if necessary, as between compensation for land taken and compensation for severance and injurious affection to the remaining land.

*Example—*

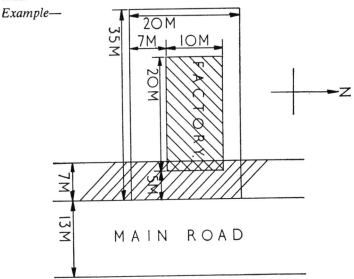

The factory illustrated above consists of a brick and slated building on two floors, in a reasonable state of repair and is held on ground lease having 41 years still to run, the ground rent being £15 p.a. The leaseholder-occupier is a manufacturer and the estimated rack rental is £1,200 (£3 per m²) p.a., landlord doing structural repairs. The total floor space is 400 m² and the apportionment of the ground rent on the land to be taken has been agreed at £3 p.a.

A Highway Authority are acquiring a strip of land 7 m wide on the west side of the main road for road-widening purposes and notice to treat was served on all interested parties in December last.

The forecourt is used for loading and unloading goods, the entrance doors being at present in the front. It may be assumed that the Highway Authority will not permit lorries to stand on the new road for these purposes, and that the claim put forward by the owners of the two interests concerned, that the whole of the premises should be acquired, will not be upheld.

It is required to assess the compensation payable and to list the probable " accommodation works " to be agreed.

*Valuation—*

*Note.*—The statutory assumptions do not appear to affect the case, and the " Before and After " method of approach is therefore adopted.

*Freeholder—*

Value of interest *before acquisition:*—

| | | | |
|---|---|---:|---:|
| Ground rent reserved | ... | £15 p.a. | |
| Y.P. 41 years at 6% ... | ... | 15·14 | |
| | | | £227 |
| Reversion to ... ... | ... | £1,200 p.a. | |
| *Deduct* for repairs, say | ... | 80 | |
| Net Income | | £1,120 p.a. | |
| Y.P. in perpetuity at 10% deferred 41 years ... | ... | ·20 | |
| | | | 224 |
| | | | £451 |

Value of interest *after acquisition:*—

| | | | |
|---|---|---:|---:|
| Ground rent reserved | ... | £12 p.a. | |
| Y.P. for 41 years at 6%, say ... | | 15 | |
| | | | £180 |
| Reversion to 360 m² at, say, £2·90 per m² | ... ... | £1,044 p.a. | |
| *Deduct* for repairs, say | ... | 74 | |
| | | £970 | |
| Y.P. in perpetuity at 11% deferred 41 years ... | ... | ·13 | |
| | | | £126 |
| | | | £306 |
| Compensation for land taken and injurious affection, say ... ... ... ... | | | £150 |

*Note.*—The Years' Purchase and rental value per square metre used in the " after acquisition " valuation are slightly lower than those used in the " before acquisition " valuation as the property will then be less desirable, e.g., no forecourt loading, and side entrance. The allowance for repairs is also less as the building will be smaller and will have a newly built front wall.

If it is required to divide this between the land taken and injurious affection the amount of the former could be obtained as follows:—

| | | |
|---|---:|---|
| Loss in ground rent ... ... ... ... | £3 p.a. | |
| Y.P. 41 years @ 6% ... ... ... ... | 15·14 | |
| | | £45 |
| Loss in rental value in reversion, 40 m² @ | | |
| £3, say ... ... ... ... ... | £120 p.a. | |
| *Deduct* for repairs ... ... ... ... | 10 | |
| | £110 | |
| Y.P. in perpetuity @ 10% deferred 41 years ... | ·20 | |
| | | 22 |
| Land taken, say ... ... ... ... ... | | £67 |
| Injurious affection ... ... ... ... | | 83 |
| Compensation as above, say | | £150 |

*Leaseholder—*

Value of interest *before acquisition:—*

| | | |
|---|---:|---|
| Rental value ... ... ... ... | | £1,200 p.a. |
| *Deduct* for repairs, say ... ... ... | £80 | |
| Ground rent ... ... ... ... | 15 | |
| | | 95 |
| Net Income | | £1,105 p.a. |
| Y.P. 41 years @ 11% and 2½% ... ... | | 7·5 |
| (Tax @ 38·75%) | | |
| Value of interest " before acquisition " | | £8,287 |

Value of interest *after acquisition—*

| | | |
|---|---:|---|
| Rental value ... ... ... ... ... | | £1,044 |
| *Deduct* for repairs, say ... ... ... | £70 | |
| Ground rent ... ... ... ... | 12 | 82 |
| Net Income | | £962 |
| Y.P. 41 years @ 12% and 2½% ... ... | | 6·98 |
| (Tax @ 38·75%) | | |
| Value of interest " after acquisition ", say ... | | £6,715 |

| | |
|---|---:|
| Compensation for injurious affection and land taken (£8,287–£6,715) ... ... ... | £1,572 |
| Cost of internal re-arrangement of factory due to entrance doors being at side and rear, say | 300 |
| Temporary loss of net profits, while production impaired, adjusted for income tax, say ... | 600 |
| *Total*, say | £2,475 |

*Note.*—If required, the sum of £1,572 mentioned could be apportioned between " land taken " and " injurious affection " in a similar manner to that done above in respect of the freehold interest.

*The accommodation works* would probably include:—

Demolition of existing front wall, erection of new wall and making good.

Making side entrances and rear yard fit for traffic, e.g.. tarmac surface, etc.

Any re-arrangement of drainage necessary.

Forming opening in side or rear wall and provision of entrance doors.

New front gates and boundary walls.

## 5. ADJUSTMENT OF UNEXPENDED BALANCE

### (TOWN AND COUNTRY PLANNING ACT, 1962—SECTION 97 (1) AND (2))

Where, in connection with a compulsory acquisition, or corresponding sale by agreement, compensation is paid for severance or injurious affection, in respect either of land held with land taken or land not so held, any unexpended balance which may attach to the land will in future be deemed to be reduced or extinguished by a sum equal to the amount by which:—

(i) the compensation payable
exceeds
(ii) the compensation which would have been payable had the value of the land been calculated on an "existing use" basis.[3]

In other words, the unexpended balance is reduced by so much of the compensation as represents injury to the development value of the land.

*Example.*—A sports ground with a total area of 3 ha is let by the freeholder to a club on annual tenancy at a rent of £240 per annum. The whole of the land is zoned residential at a density of 15 houses to the ha in the Development Plan and it was anticipated that development would commence in two years' time when the land would be worth £20,000 per ha. An original unexpended balance of £2,400 is attached to the land.

The freeholder has just been served with a notice to treat in respect of 1 ha of the land which is required for use as a car park and for the erection of public conveniences.

The acquisition will not delay development of the land not being acquired but it is considered that its value for residential development will be only £15,000 per ha and that as a sports ground it will let for £100 per annum.

---

[3] i.e., on the assumption that permission would only be granted for development within the Third Schedule and not for " new development."

Assess the compensation payable to the freeholder for the land taken and injurious affection to the remainder.

*Valuation.*—The most profitable assumption will be the value for the purpose for which the land is zoned and the claim will be made on this basis.

Value of interest *before acquisition*—
Rental value as sports
ground ...   ...   ...   £240 p.a.
Y.P. 2 years @ 5½%   ...   1·85   £444

Reversion to building value—
3 ha @ £20,000 per ha ... £60,000
P.V. £1 in 2 years @ 7% ...   ·87   £52,200 say £52,650

Value of interest *after acquisition*—
Rental value as sports
ground ...   ...   ...   £100 p.a.
Y.P. 2 years @ 5½%   ...   1·85   £185

Reversion to building value—
2 ha @ £15,000 per ha ... £30,000
P.V. £1 in 2 years @ 7% ...   ·87   £26,100 say £26,250

Compensation for land taken and injurious affection          £26,400

1. Compensation for land taken

Rental value as sports ground—
1 ha @ £80 per ha   ...   £80 p.a.
Y.P. 2 years @ 5½%   ...   1·85   £148

Reversion to building value—
1 ha @ £20,000 per ha ... £20,000
P.V. £1 in 2 years @ 7% ...   ·87   £17,400 say £17,550

2. Compensation for injurious affection   ...   ...   £8,850

*Effect of Acquisition on Unexpended Balance*—

Assume that the unexpended balance is spread rateably over the whole area.

The original unexpended balance on the land taken, £800, will be extinguished.

The original unexpended balance on the land not taken, £1,600, will be reduced on the next occasion when it becomes necessary to know whether or not a balance is attached to the land (e.g., if planning permission is refused in two years' time for the erection of houses and a claim is made for compensation), by the amount by which the compensation for injurious affection exceeds the depreciation in the existing use value.

| | | | |
|---|---|---:|---:|
| Compensation for injurious affection ... ... | | | £8,850 |
| Existing use value *before acquisition*— | | | |
| Rental value—2 ha @ £80 | | | |
| per ha ... ... ... | £160 p.a. | | |
| Y.P. perp. @ 5½% ... ... | 18 | £2,880 | |
| | | | |
| Existing use value *after acquisition*— | | | |
| Rental value—2 ha @ £50 | | | |
| per ha ... ... ... | £100 p.a. | | |
| Y.P. perp. @ 5½% ... ... | 18 | £1,800 | £1,050 |
| | | | |
| Excess ... ... ... | | | £7,800 |

The unexpended balance will, therefore, be extinguished.

*Note:* In calculating the compensation payable, allowance would have to be made for any compensation payable to the sports club under Part II of the Landlord and Tenant Act, 1954.

# Chapter 25

## Compensation under the Housing Acts[1]

### Introductory

THE " PRINCIPAL ACT " is the Housing Act, 1957, which consolidated a number of earlier Acts relating to Housing and which is now amended in part by the Housing Act, 1969.

Valuations for compensation purposes may be required in connection with the following matters dealt with in the principal Act: —

    (A)   Clearance Areas.

    (B)   Insanitary Houses.

    (C)   Obstructive Buildings.

    (D)   Provision of new Housing Accommodation.

As regards (A) and (D) an alternative method of procedure is available under the Town and Country Planning Act, 1962.

Thus, what is called a " clearance area " under the Housing Acts, might be designated for compulsory purchase in the local planning authority's development plan—or any subsequent amendment of it—as an " area of comprehensive development." It could then be acquired by the local authority under a compulsory purchase order, confirmed by the Minister, for purposes of general re-development.

The fact that alternative powers are available does not prevent a local authority from proceeding under the Housing Acts, and the latter procedure is still widely used. Since it presents a number of special features which directly or indirectly affect the valuation of houses in general it is dealt with in some detail in this Chapter.

### (A)   Clearance Areas[2]

#### 1.  GENERALLY

If in any area in a local authority's district the following conditions exist:—

    (a)   The houses are unfit for habitation or are dangerous or injurious to health because of their bad arrangement or the narrowness or bad arrangement of the streets; and

---

[1] This Chapter is confined to the question of compensation. For a comprehensive summary of the general law of Housing see " The Concise Law of Housing " by W. A. West. LL.B. The Estates Gazette, Ltd.).
[2] Housing Act, 1957, Part III, and Housing Act, 1969, Sec. 71.

(*b*)   the other buildings are dangerous or injurious to health for the like reason; and

(*c*)   the best solution is the demolition of all buildings in the area;

the local authority may define the area by means of a map, in such a way as to exclude from the area any building which is not unfit for human habitation or dangerous or injurious to health, and may pass a resolution declaring it to be a " clearance area ". A copy of the resolution must be sent to the Secretary of State for the Environment.

It should be noted that, in determining for any purpose of the Housing Act, 1957, and the Housing Act, 1969, whether a house is unfit for human habitation, regard shall be had to its condition in respect of the following matters, namely:—(*a*) repair; (*b*) stability; (*c*) freedom from damp; (*d*) internal arrangement; (*e*) natural lighting; (*f*) ventilation; (*g*) water supply; (*h*) drainage and sanitary conveniences; and (*i*) facilities for preparation and cooking of food and for the disposal of waste water;—and the house will be deemed to be unfit if, and only if, it is so far defective in one or more of these matters that it is not reasonably suitable for occupation in that condition.[3]

In practice the clearance area is defined on the "Area Map" by colouring it red. The area having been declared a "clearance area", the local authority may proceed to secure the clearance of it in one or other of the following ways, or partly in one of those ways and partly in the other—

(i)   by ordering the demolition of the buildings—effected by " demolition orders ".

(ii)   by acquiring the land and demolishing the buildings— effected either by agreement or by " compulsory purchase orders."

It should be noted, however, that local authorities are given power to postpone the demolition of houses acquired by them or made subject to clearance orders if, in their opinion, such houses can be rendered capable of providing accommodation of a standard which is adequate for the time being.[4]

## 2. CLEARANCE ORDERS

(*a*) *Procedure.*—The making of clearance orders does not as a general rule involve the acquisition of land.[5] Owners retain their sites, but are required to demolish the buildings—subject to the possibility of temporary postponement referred to above.

---

[3] Housing Act, 1957, Sec. 4.
[4] Housing Act, 1957, Secs. 46 and 48.
[5] For an exception to this general rule see Sec. 54 of the 1957 Act.

The properties to be dealt with in this way must be indicated on a Clearance Order Map and opportunity is given for the making of objections by interested parties. The order must be confirmed by the Secretary of State for the Environment, who, in case of objections, will first order a public local enquiry or a private hearing to be held. The whole procedure is governed by the Fifth Schedule of the Housing Act, 1957.

A clearance order can only relate to houses which are unfit for human habitation. But a building used partly as a dwelling-house and partly for other purposes may be included if the part used as a dwelling-house is unfit for habitation.

When a clearance order becomes operative, owners will be required to demolish their buildings within a stated period. In default, the local authority may enter on the land, demolish the buildings and sell the old materials. Any expense incurred by the local authority in excess of the sum realised by the sale of old materials is recoverable from the owner. Any surplus is payable to him. Demolition costs incurred in default by a local authority are registrable as local land charges.

After the order is made, the site can only be used for building, or otherwise developed, in accordance with such restrictions and conditions as the local authority may think fit to impose, subject to a right of appeal to the Secretary of State for the Environment If, after eighteen months from the date when the order becomes operative, any part of the land is undeveloped, the local authority may purchase that part either by agreement or by a compulsory purchase order confirmed by the Secretary of State.

(b) *Compensation.*—The owner is not entitled as a matter of right to compensation for the demolition of his building. But if the Secretary of State for the Environment is satisfied that the building has been well maintained he may order the payment of a certain sum in respect of it.

A local authority may also make an allowance for cost of removal and trade disturbance to occupiers displaced by a clearance order, or in respect of hardship suffered by retailers in the immediate neighbourhood.

The above payments may also be made in connection with the compulsory acquisition of land in a clearance area, and they are discussed at greater length in Section 3 (b) of this Chapter.

Where a local authority elect to acquire land which has been cleared under a clearance order and has remained undeveloped, the procedure is by way of compulsory purchase order confirmed by the Secretary of State for the Environment, and the normal basis of compensation for compulsory purchase will apply.

### 3. COMPULSORY PURCHASE ORDERS

(a) *Procedure.*[6]—The local authority may decide to acquire part or the whole of any land in a clearance area. They may also acquire any land surrounded by the area which is needed to secure a cleared area of convenient shape and size, and any adjoining land which is required for the satisfactory development or user of the cleared area.

If the local authority cannot acquire the land they want by agreement, they must apply to the Secretary of State for the Environment for confirmation of a compulsory purchase order. The order must be advertised and opportunity given for the making of objections. If any objections are raised, the Minister must hold a local enquiry, or give the objector an opportunity of being heard privately, before confirming, unless he is satisfied that the objections relate exclusively to matters which can be dealt with by the Lands Tribunal by whom the compensation is assessed.

The procedure is regulated by Schedule 3 of the Housing Act, 1957.

The compulsory purchase order and the map accompanying it must distinguish between : —

   (i) Unfit properties included in the clearance area—in practice coloured red or pink on the plans of the scheme;

   (ii) properties included in the clearance area only because of bad arrangement—usually coloured pink hatched yellow;

   (iii) properties not in the clearance area, but included in the scheme for the purpose of making it efficient—usually coloured grey.

If a person objects to a compulsory purchase order on the grounds that his property is not unfit for habitation, he is entitled to a written notice specifying the defects complained of at least 14 days before the local enquiry or private hearing is held.

The question of the category in which his property is placed on the map accompanying the compulsory purchase order is of considerable importance to the owner, since it will affect the amount of compensation to which he is entitled. He should carefully inspect the map as soon as the making of the order is advertised, since the only opportunity he will have of protesting against the inclusion of his property as unfit property will be at the local enquiry or private hearing held by the Secretary of State for the Environment. The point cannot be raised once the scheme is confirmed.

The compulsory purchase order, when confirmed by the Minister, will incorporate the Compulsory Purchase Act, 1965, and Sections 77-85 of the Railway Clauses Consolidation Act, 1845 (relating to mines and minerals under the land).

---

[6] Housing Act, 1957, Sec. 43 and Schedules 3 and 4—the Acquisition of Land (Authorisation Procedure) Act, 1946, does not apply to compulsory purchase under this part of the Act.

Part only of a house, building or manufactory may be taken if, in the opinion of the Lands Tribunal, it can be taken without " material detriment " to the remainder.

There is a general direction that any building erected or improvement or alteration made, or any interest in land created after the date on which notice of the order having been made is published, is to be ignored in assessing compensation if, in the opinion of the Lands Tribunal, it was not reasonably necessary and was carried out with a view to obtaining or increasing compensation.

Compensation will be assessed under the provisions of the Land Compensation Act, 1961, but its basis will be affected according to whether the property acquired consists of (i) houses in the clearance area unfit for habitation, or (ii) other property in or outside the clearance area.

(b) *Compensation for unfit houses in the clearance area.*[7]—In the case of houses in the clearance area unfit for human habitation the basis of compensation prescribed by Section 59 of the 1957 Act, is the value of the site cleared of buildings and available for development in accordance with building regulations.

The value of the site is to be estimated as at the date when the valuation is made.

Under the Land Compensation Act, 1961, the basis of compensation is the price which the bare site might be expected to realise if sold in the open market by a willing seller, having regard to the assumptions as to planning permission to be made under that Act.

In the case of land zoned for some valuable purpose, this basis might give a figure higher than the value of the unfit property as it stands. The 1961 Act, therefore, provides that the compensation payable under this part of the Housing Act, 1957, shall in no case exceed the compensation which would have been payable if it had not been assessed on a site value basis.[8]

In practice, the bare site value of a property is usually based on a figure of so much per unit of site area varying with the situation of the clearance area and the position of the particular site in the clearance area.

Where there are several interests in the property acquired, each party's interest must be valued as an interest in the bare site only. For example, if a house is held for a term of years at a ground rent and is let at weekly rents to a number of tenants, the freeholder's interest will be treated, for compensation purposes, as an unsecured ground rent receivable for so many years, followed by a reversion to the bare site value. Similarly, in estimating the lessee's compensation, the weekly rents must be ignored, since the site is assumed

---

[7] Housing Act, 1957, Secs. 59-61
[8] Land Compensation Act, 1961, Schedule 2.

to be cleared of buildings, and the lessee's profit rent (if any) will be deemed to consist of the difference between the ground rent payable to the freeholder and the rental value of the bare site. If the rental value of the site is the same as, or less than, the ground rent payable, the lessee will receive a purely nominal figure of compensation for the taking of his legal interest in the property although he may be in receipt of quite a substantial income from weekly rents.

### Well-Maintained Payments

Where the Secretary of State for the Environment is satisfied that a dwelling-house, although properly included in a compulsory purchase order or clearance order as unfit for habitation, has in spite of its sanitary defects been well maintained, he may direct the local authority to make a payment in respect of the building.[9] Before doing so, he will order the house to be inspected by an officer of the Department.

The payment made depends on whether the house is wholly or partially well-maintained.

*Wholly well-maintained houses*—Where formal slum clearance action was begun after 23rd April, 1968, the sum payable in respect of a wholly well-maintained house is an amount equal to four times the rateable value or such other multiplier as the Secretary of State may by order prescribe.

*Partially well-maintained houses*—Section 67 of the Housing Act, 1969, introduced the concept of a partially well-maintained house and provides for the case where either the interior or exterior, but not both, has been well-maintained. The most common example is where the tenant has done his best to maintain the interior but the landlord has neglected the exterior. Payments are made under this heading only where formal slum clearance action was begun after 25th August, 1969, and the amount of the payment is half that of the wholly well-maintained payment, at present twice the rateable value.

The amount of a wholly or partially well-maintained payment must not exceed the amount (if any) by which the full value of the house exceeds the site value. The full value of the house means the amount of compensation which would have been payable if the house had been purchased compulsorily but not as being unfit.

In general terms, the payment is made to the person to whose efforts the good maintenance of the house is attributable.

### Owner-Occupier Supplements

Section 68 and Schedule 5 of the Housing Act, 1969, makes provision for the payment of supplemental compensation to owner-

---

[9] Housing Act, 1957, Sec. 60 and Part I of Schedule 2; and the Housing Act, 1969, Secs. 65-67 and Schedule 4.

occupiers of certain premises if their interests are acquired at site value, or they are required to vacate their house under a demolition, closing or clearance order. Owner-occupiers are entitled to this supplementary payment in cases where clearance action was formally initiated by the local authority after 23rd April, 1968, provided the house was owner-occupied throughout the qualifying period which is defined as a period of 2 years ending with the date on which the local authority took action as set out in paragraph 5 of the Schedule. Where action was taken by the local authority before 22nd April, 1970, the qualifying period runs only from 23rd April, 1968, and ends with the date on which the local authority took action.

This requirement of a qualifying period was included to stop collusive sales between landlord and tenant in anticipation of clearance action to increase the amount of compensation. However, paragraph 1 (2) of Schedule 5 provides for payment in those cases where an owner-occupier bought within the qualifying period but was genuinely unaware of the likelihood of clearance action.

The additional compensation payable under these provisions is equal to the full compulsory purchase value of the interest less the compensation paid on a site value basis. In other words, the total compensation payable is equal to the full compulsory purchase value including disturbance.

The Housing Act, 1969, did not repeal the previous provisions for owner-occupier supplements under Part II of Schedule 2 of the Housing Act, 1957, as amended by the Housing (Slum Clearance Compensation) Act, 1965. These provisions with minor amendments continued to apply in any case where no payment fell to be made under Schedule 5 of the 1969 Act until they expired in December, 1970.

Provision is made for the payment of supplements of similar amount to owners of business premises where the owner was entitled to an interest in the premises and to the receipts from a business carried on there on 13th December, 1955, or for a qualifying period preceding the date on which the local authority initiated action. The original qualifying period of 10 years specified in Part II of Schedule 2 of the Housing Act, 1957, is reduced to 2 years by paragraph 3 of Schedule 6 of the Housing Act, 1969, to bring it into line with the other owner-occupier supplements.

*Discretionary Payments*

Any occupier of premises displaced by a clearance order or a compulsory purchase order may be paid such sum for cost of removal as the local authority think fit.[10]

Any person carrying on a trade or business on the premises may be given such allowance, if any, for trade disturbance, as the local authority think reasonable, having regard to the period for which

---

[10] Housing Act, 1957, Sec. 63.

the premises would probably have been available for the trade or business, and to the possibility of finding other premises.[11]

A local authority may also make such reasonable allowance as they think fit to retail shopkeepers in the locality of a clearance scheme who can prove that they suffer loss involving personal hardship owing to the diminution in the population of the locality caused by the clearance operation. In estimating this loss the local authority must have regard to the probable future development of the locality.[12]

" Owner " for the purposes of the above provisions may be either the freeholder or a lessee.

### Minimum Compensation

When a person owns and occupies a private dwelling-house at the date of the compulsory purchase order, and continues to own the interest at the date of the notice to treat, the compensation payable to him on a site value basis (including the amount of any well maintained allowance or any supplementary compensation under Schedule 2 of the 1957 Act) shall not be less than the gross value of the premises as shown in the current valuation list.[13]

(c) *Compensation for other Property.*[14]—In the case of (i) property not in the clearance area itself, and (ii) property included in the area only because of its bad arrangement in relation to other buildings, or on account of the narrowness or bad arrangement of the streets, compensation will be on the normal basis as prescribed by the Land Compensation Act, 1961, but subject to the following special rules contained in Part III of Schedule 3 to the Housing Act, 1957, as amended by the Town and Country Planning Act, 1959, and the Housing Act, 1969:—

(1) The Lands Tribunal is to ignore any enhanced rental due to the premises being used for illegal purposes or overcrowded.

(2) The Lands Tribunal may set off any increased value which will be given to other premises of the same owner.

(3) The Lands Tribunal must state in their award whether compensation has been reduced for any of the reasons (1) and (2) above and, if so, by what amount.

Occupiers may be given such allowance as the local authority think fit for cost of removal.

Persons carrying on any trade or business on the premises may also be given such compensation for trade disturbance as the local

---

[11] Housing Act, 1957, Sec. 63.

[12] *Ibid*

[13] Land Compensation Act, 1961, Second Schedule.

[14] Housing Act, 1957, Sec. 59 (4) and Part III of Schedule 3 (as amended by Town and Country Planning Act, 1959).

authority think fit, having regard to the period for which the premises would probably have been available for the trade or business and to the possibility of obtaining other suitable premises.

(d) *Rights-of-way, etc.*[15]—When land is acquired under this part of the Act all private rights-of-way and all rights of laying down, erecting, continuing, or maintaining any apparatus on, under, or over the land, and all other rights or easements in relation to the land are extinguished, and any such apparatus shall vest in the local authority.

Any person who suffers loss by the extinguishment or vesting of any such right or apparatus is entitled to compensation assessed in accordance with the Land Compensation Act, 1961.

This provision does not apply to statutory undertakers.

### (B)   Insanitary Houses[16]

If, in the opinion of the local authority, a house is unfit for human habitation,[17] but is capable of being rendered fit at a reasonable expense, a notice may be served on the person having control of the house specifying the work to be done and requiring him to execute it within a reasonable time.

If, on appeal against the notice to repair, the judge or court finds that the house cannot be made fit for human habitation at a reasonable cost, the local authority may purchase the house by agreement, or may be authorised to do so compulsorily by means of a compulsory purchase order confirmed by the Secretary of State for the Environment in accordance with Schedule 1 to the Act.

Compensation will be assessed in accordance with the Land Compensation Act, 1961, but the basis of assessment will be the value as a cleared site available for development in accordance with building regulations.

The compensation may include well-maintained payments and owner-occupier supplements both referred to in Section A 3 (b) of this Chapter.

Subject to a right of appeal to the county court, a local authority may require the demolition of any house which is unfit for human habitation and which, in their opinion, is not capable at a reasonable expense of being rendered so fit. The owner may offer to render the house fit for habitation or undertake not to use it for habitation until it has been rendered fit. But if no such offer or undertaking is made or accepted, or if an offer is not carried out, the local authority must serve a demolition or closing order or may purchase the house in lieu of making any such order. This power

---

[15]  Housing Act, 1957, Sec. 64 (3).
[16]  Housing Act, 1957, Secs. 9-11, 16, 17, 29 and 1st Schedule.
[17]  For the meaning of " unfit " see Section A 1 of this Chapter.

of purchase may be exercised when, in the opinion of the local authority, the house (in spite of its unfit state) is or can be rendered capable of providing accommodation of a standard which is adequate for the time being. Subject to the service of notices and a right of appeal to the county court, the local authority may then purchase the house by agreement or may be authorised by the Minister to acquire it compulsorily. Compensation will be on the same basis as in the case—referred to above—of a house unfit for habitation and incapable of being made so at reasonable expense.

### (C)   Obstructive Buildings[18]

An obstructive building is one which by reason only of its contact with, or proximity to, other buildings is dangerous or injurious to health. A local authority may order the demolition of the whole or part of an obstructive building after first notifying the owner of their intention and giving him an opportunity to be heard.

The owner or owners may offer to sell his or their interests to the local authority provided the acquisition of the interest or interests in question will enable the local authority to carry out the demolition.

The purchase-price will be assessed as if it were compensation for compulsory purchase subject to the rules prescribed by Part III of Schedule 3 of the Housing Act, 1957 (as amended), and already considered in Section A, 3 (c) of this Chapter.

If no offer to sell is made, the owner or owners must demolish the building within a given period, failing which the local authority will demolish it and sell the old materials.

Where the building is demolished, either by the owner or by the local authority, the local authority must compensate the owner or owners for any loss arising from the demolition. The general principles of compensation referred to above will apply, subject to the fact that the owner is being compensated not for the compulsory purchase of the property but only for the loss of the building.

### (D)   Provision of New Housing Accommodation[19]

(a) Procedure.—Local authorities are authorised to acquire any land, including any houses or other buildings thereon, as a site for the erection of houses.

They may also acquire houses, or other buildings which are, or may be made, suitable as houses, and have power to alter and adapt such houses and buildings as necessary.

Land may also be acquired for various ancillary purposes.

Failing agreement the land can be acquired compulsorily by means of a compulsory purchase order made and submitted to the

---

[18] Housing Act, 1957, Secs. 72-74.
[19] Housing Act, 1957, Part V and Schedule 7.

Secretary of State for the Environment and confirmed by him in accordance with the provisions of the Acquisition of Land (Authorisation Procedure) Act, 1946.

(*b*) *Basis of Compensation.*—Compensation will be assessed on the normal compulsory purchase basis as prescribed by the Land Compensation Act, 1961, but subject to the rules specified in Schedule 7 to the Act, which are similar to those set out in Section (A) 3 (c) of this Chapter.[20]

In assessing compensation the Lands Tribunal may disregard any increase in value due to interests in land created or work done on land if satisfied that the creation of the interest or the doing of the work, as the case may be, was not reasonably necessary and was undertaken with a view to obtaining or increasing compensation.[21]

*Example.*—A block of 22 unfit terraced houses was (after 23rd April, 1968) included in a Clearance Area and a Compulsory Purchase Order under the Housing Act, 1957, has recently been confirmed in respect of the whole block. The houses front on two parallel streets and each house stands on a site with a frontage of 3·658 m and a depth of 15·240 m.

Twenty of the houses in a block occupying a site 36·576 m by 30·480 m are held on ground lease with 22 years unexpired at a rent of £30 per annum. The houses are occupied by weekly tenants and are producing the maximum permitted gross income of £1,260 per annum.

The remaining two houses are owner-occupied by the freeholders. One purchased five years ago and has been in occupation since. The other purchased from the former landlord less than two years before clearance action was initiated but before purchase, he made enquiries from the local authority to ascertain if clearance action might be taken within two years and was informed that such action was unlikely.

Each house is assessed for rating purposes at G.V. £51, R.V. £28 and the rate is 50p in the £ including water.

All of the houses are in an area zoned for shopping purposes in the development plan.

The Secretary of State has directed that a well-maintained payment should be made in respect of the owner-occupied house purchased five years ago and that partially well-maintained payments should be made in respect of six of the leasehold houses, four relating to external condition and two relating to internal condition.

Notices to treat have just been served in respect of all interests. Assess the compensation payable.

---

[20] See page 405.
[21] Acquisition of Land (Authorisation Procedure) Act, 1946, 2nd Schedule, Part III.

*Valuations—*

   *Twenty Leasehold Houses*

     (i)  *Freeholder's Compensation.*—Value for purpose for which land zoned assuming a cleared site available for redevelopment in accordance with building regulations.

| | | |
|---|---:|---:|
| Next 22 years—ground rent ... | £30 p.a. | |
| Y.P. 22 years @ 6% ... ... | 12·04 | £361 |

| | | |
|---|---:|---:|
| Reversion—to value as shop site, say ... ... ... ... | £8,000 | |
| P.V. £1 in 22 years @ 7% ... | ·23 | £1,840 |
| | | £2,201 |
| | Say | £2,200 |

But the compensation payable must not exceed what would have been paid if the interest was not being acquired at site value. Thus, the compensation would be restricted to—

Ceiling Value—

| | | | |
|---|---:|---:|---:|
| Next 22 years—approx. as before ... | | ... | £361 |
| Reversion—to gross rentals ... ... | | £1,260 p.a. | |
| *Less* Rates ... ... | £280 | | |
| Repairs, say ... ... | 300 | | |
| Insurance ... ... | 30 | | |
| Management ... | 126 | 736 (58%) | |

| | | |
|---|---:|---:|
| Net income ... ... ... ... | £524 p.a. | |
| Y.P. perp. @ 12% deferred 22 years | ·69 | 362 |
| | | £723 |
| | Say | £725 |

     (ii)  *Lessee's Compensation—*

| | | |
|---|---:|---:|
| Ground rental value as shop site | £600 p.a. | |
| *Less* Ground rent payable ... | 30 | |
| Profit rent ... ... | £570 p.a. | |
| Y.P. 22 years @ 7½% and 2½% tax @ 38·75% | 7·6 | £4,332 |
| *Add* Partially well-maintained payments, say, 4 × 2 × R.V. £28 ... ... | | 224 |
| | | £4,556 |
| | Say | £4,550 |

*Ceiling Value—*

| | | | |
|---|---|---|---|
| Net income from houses | ... | £524 p.a. | |
| *Less* Ground rent ... | ... | 30 | |
| | | ——— | |
| Profit rent ... | ... | £494 p.a. | |
| Y.P. 22 years @ 14% | | | |
| and 2½% tax @ 38·75% | | 5·09 | £2,514 |
| | | ——— | |
| | Say | £2,500 | |

The lessee's compensation would, therefore, be restricted to £2,500.

(iii) *Tenants' Compensation.*—The tenants have no valuable interest in land but are entitled to be re-housed by the local authority and can receive discretionary payments from the authority towards, for example, costs of removal.

With regard to the two partially well-maintained payments relating to internal condition, it is evident from the earlier calculations that cleared site value is well in excess of the value of the standing house, therefore no partially well-maintained payment would be made.

## Owner-Occupied House Purchased Five Years Ago

The cleared site afforded here, 3·658 m by 15·240 m is too small for redevelopment for shop or residential purposes. This could mean that the value would be restricted to a " conventional " compensation value for small individual sites but it could be argued that " hope " value would attach because, even in the absence of compulsory acquisition, of the possibility that at some time in the future this site could be included in a larger redevelopment scheme. This hope must, however, spring from the possibility that redevelopment will at some time be undertaken by some agency other than the local authority and not from the action which the local authority is at present taking or any alternative action which the local authority might have taken— *Davy v. Leeds Corporation,* [1964] 16 P. & C.R. 24.

| | | | | |
|---|---|---|---|---|
| Site value, say ... ... ... ... | | | | £150 |
| *Add* Supplemental compensation—difference between full compulsory purchase value and site value. | | | | |
| Full value as house, say ... | ... | | £750 | |
| Disturbance, say ... ... | ... | | 100 | |
| | | | ——— | |
| Compulsory purchase value | ... | | £850 | |
| *Less* Site value ... ... ... | ... | | 150 | 700 |
| | | | ——— | ——— |
| | | | Total | £850 |

The well-maintained payment will not be made as the owner-occupier is already entitled to receive full compensation for his loss.

*Owner-Occupied House Purchased Less Than Two Years Before Action Initiated.*

Although the owner-occupier has not been in occupation as owner-occupier for the qualifying period of 2 years, it appears that this is only because the local authority advanced its slum clearance programme. In these circumstances the compensation paid would include the owner-occupier's supplement. Thus the computation would be on similar lines to the previous one but it is reasonable to assume that this house is in worse condition than the other.

| | | | |
|---|---|---:|---:|
| Site value, say    ...    ...    ...    ... | | | £150 |
| *Add*  Supplemental compensation— | | | |
| Full value as house, say ...    ... | | £700 | |
| Disturbance, say   ...    ... | | 100 | |
| | Compulsory purchase value | £800 | |
| *Less*  Site value    ...    ...    ... | | 150 | 650 |
| | Total | | £800 |

The owner-occupiers are entitled to be re-housed in the same way as tenants and no deduction should be made from their compensation for any " value " which might be said to attach to a local authority tenancy.

# Chapter 26

## Electricity Wayleaves, Sewer Easements and Pipe-Lines

### A. Electricity Wayleaves

#### 1. STATUTORY PROVISIONS

IN THE past there have been numerous electricity authorities and undertakings throughout the country concerned with the supply of electricity for light and power in particular areas.

Under the Electricity Acts, 1947–1958, the authorities now concerned in England and Wales are the Electricity Council, the Central Electricity Generating Board and 12 Area Electricity Boards. The Electricity Council is primarily a co-ordinating and advisory body and the functions of generation, transformation and transmission are performed by the other authorities.

It is proposed to summarise briefly the statutory powers vested in electricity authorities for the use of land for electricity purposes before considering the practical question of compensation likely to arise where these powers are exercised.[1]

Under Section 22 of the Electricity (Supply) Act, 1919, any authorised undertakers may place any electric line: —

    (*a*)   Below ground, across any land, and

    (*b*)   above ground, across any land other than land covered by buildings or used as a garden or pleasure ground.

Notice must first be served on the owner and occupier, who may give their consent on such terms as to compensation, etc., as may be agreed. But if they fail, within 21 days, to give consent, or will only do so on terms unacceptable to the undertakers, an application must be made to the Secretary of State for the Department of Trade and Industry for permission to lay the line.

The Secretary of State, after giving both parties an opportunity to be heard, may give consent either unconditionally or subject to such terms, conditions and stipulations as he thinks just. But any question of disputed compensation will be settled under the Land Compensation Act, 1961.[2]

Where an owner enters into an agreement with an electricity authority for a wayleave through or over his land, it is usual to reserve the right to terminate it at any time by twelve months'

---

[1] "Wires, Pipes, Pylons", a guide to landowners and their advisers, is published by the Country Landowners Association, 7 Swallow Street, W.1 (60p).

[2] *West Midlands Joint Electricity Authority and Minister of Transport v. Pitt and Others* (1932), 2 K.B.1.

notice.   But under Section 11 of the Electricity (Supply) Act, 1922, the authority may insist on retaining the line in position subject to the same procedure as though the line were being newly laid under Section 22 of the 1919 Act.   At any time while the line is so retained in position the authority may apply to the Secretary of State for a revision of the original terms and conditions, in which case also the matter will be treated as though the line were being newly laid.  In either case the Secretary of State will have no power to deal with any question of pecuniary compensation connected with the retention of the wayleave.

Under Section 9 of the Electricity Act, 1947, the Secretary of State may authorise any Electricity Board to purchase compulsorily any land which they require for any purpose connected with the discharge of their functions.  The expression " land " is expressly stated to include easements and other rights over land, and the Secretary of State may authorise any Electricity Board to purchase compulsorily a right to place an electric line across land, whether above or below ground, and to repair and maintain the line, without purchasing any other interest in the land.

The procedure in connection with the grant of these compulsory powers is governed by the Acquisition of Land (Authorisation Procedure) Act, 1946.   Compensation, if in dispute, will be assessed in accordance with the Land Compensation Act, 1961.

Under Section 34 of the Electricity (Supply) Act, 1926, an electricity authority may serve a notice requiring the lopping or cutting of any trees or hedges which obstruct or interfere with any electric line, subject to payment of the expense incurred in complying with the order.   Or, if the order is not complied with within 21 days, the authority may do the work itself.   Any owner or occupier is entitled to object to the terms of such an order within 21 days, in which case the matter is referred to the Secretary of State, who may make such order as he thinks fit and also determine what compensation (if any) and expenses are to be paid.

## 2.   CLAIMS FOR COMPENSATION

(a) *Generally.*—There are two main types of case which may arise under the Electricity Acts:—

(i) Where land is acquired compulsorily for the erection of generating stations, distributing stations, and other purposes;

(ii) where " wayleaves " are acquired, i.e., rights to carry electric lines under land, or over land by means of poles or pylons.

Case (i) does not differ in principle from any other case of compulsory acquisition where the compensation is governed by the Land Compensation Act, 1961.

The acquisition of " wayleaves " under case (ii) may include the following: —

(a) The carrying of overhead conductors[3] across land by means of supports erected on the land;

(b) the carrying of overhead conductors across land without any supports being erected on the land itself—sometimes referred to as " oversails ";

(c) the carrying of conductors underground.

The extent of the injury suffered by owners and occupiers will obviously differ according to the nature of the wayleave.

In (a) damage is likely to be caused when the line is erected, and thereafter certain parts of the land will be permanently occupied by the supports. The nature of these supports will vary according to the voltage to be transmitted. For the larger voltage lines, lattice-work steel towers are used with a base measurement of about 5 m × 5 m and upwards. The smaller voltage lines may be supported by smaller steel towers, by concrete towers or by double or single wood poles.

In (b) there is no actual occupation of the land itself, and in the case of purely agricultural land the presence of the oversail may have little, if any, effect on value, although the minimum height at which the conductor crosses the land is always a matter for consideration.

In (c) the damage during construction will be greater than in (a), but, on the other hand, the land will probably be little affected once the conductor is laid. Subject to fair compensation being paid for any injury done during the laying of the line or on any subsequent inspection or repair of it, annual rentals at the rate of 1p. per metre have commonly been agreed in this type of case. Conductors are not laid underground when it can be avoided, owing to the high cost of this method as compared with overhead lines.

Questions of compensation for overhead electricity wayleaves involve consideration of the following points: (i) The compensation to be paid for the wayleave itself, and (ii) the compensation to be paid for other loss suffered. It may also be necessary to distinguish between loss suffered by the owner and loss suffered by the occupier.

The first point for the owner to decide is whether he will grant a wayleave at an annual rent, or whether he will require a lump sum in full and final settlement. If the compensation is referred under the Land Compensation Act, 1961, it would seem that the Lands Tribunal is bound to award a lump sum of compensation.

In most cases, however. owners will probably be willing to enter into agreements on reasonable terms to accept an annual rent for

---

[3] The term " conductor " is used to indicate the wire or cable which conveys the current.

the wayleaves, provided a right is reserved to terminate the agreement at any time by, say, twelve months' notice or less. It is true that the right to determine will be subject to the authority's power, under Section 11 of the 1922 Act, to insist on the line being retained, but in that case the whole question of compensation is reopened and any changes in the circumstances of the land can be taken into account.

The terms of such agreements will provide for (i) a yearly rent or wayleave in respect of the use of the land and interference with agricultural operations caused by the presence of poles or towers, and (ii) compensation for any damage done in erecting the line and for any subsequent injury.

(*b*) *Compensation for Wayleave.*—Agreement has been reached with the Central Electricity Generating Board and the 12 Area Electricity Boards in England and Wales about rates of wayleave payment to be made to owners and occupiers for grid and distribution lines over agricultural land.

The rates are as follows:—

|  | Per annum p |
| --- | --- |
| (a) *Rent:* | |
| For each single pole, strut or stay ...  ...  ... | 10 |
| For each " A " or " H " pole  ...  ...  ... | 15 |
| For each tower with base dimensions over concrete at ground level of: | |
| Under 15′ × 15′  ...  ...  ...  ...  ... | 25 |
| 15′ × 15′ to 25′ × 25′  ...  ...  ...  ... | 47½ |
| 25′ × 25′ to 35′ × 35′  ...  ...  ...  ... | 62½ |
| 35′ × 35′ to 45′ × 45′  ...  ...  ...  ... | 95 |
| 45′ × 45′ and over  ...  ...  ...  ... | £1·25 |

(*b*) *Compensation for interference with agricultural operations:*

|  | Erected on Arable Land per annum p | Erected on Culti-vated Grass-land per annum p |
| --- | --- | --- |
| For each single pole ...  ...  ...  ... | 90 | 30 |
| "A" or "H" pole  ...  ...  ...  ... | £1·65 | 60 |
| Pole and stay...  ...  ...  ...  ... | £2·30 | 85 |
| "A" or "H" and stay  ...  ...  ... | £3·00 | £1·15 |

|  | | | | | p | p |
|---|---|---|---|---|---|---|
| Additional stay | ... | ... | ... | ... | 70 | 25 |
| Isolated stay ... | ... | ... | ... | ... | £1·40 | 55 |
| Under 8' 6" × 8' 6" ... | ... | ... | ... | £1·95 | 70 |
| 8' 6" × 8' 6" but under 12' 6" × 12' 6" | ... | £2·50 | 70 |
| 12' 6" × 12' 6" but under 17' 6" × 17' 6" | | £3·15 | 90 |
| 17' 6" × 17' 6" but under 22' 6" × 22' 6" | | £4·30 | £1·05 |
| 22' 6" × 22' 6" but under 30' 0" × 30' 0" | | £5·45 | £1·35 |
| 30' 0" × 30' 0" but under 35' 0" × 35' 0" | | £5·65 | £1·35 |
| 35' 0" × 35' 0" but under 40' 0" × 40' 0" | | £7·40 | £1·35 |
| 40' 0" × 40' 0" but under 45' 0" × 45' 0" | | £8·55 | £1·60 |
| 45' 0" × 45' 0" but under 50' 0" × 50' 0" | | £10·90 | £1·60 |
| 50' 0" × 50' 0" but under 55' 0" × 55' 0" | | £13·55 | £2·05 |
| 55' 0" × 55' 0" and over | ... | ... | £16·70 | £2·05 |

The compensation payments are intended to cover the costs of keeping the site of a pole or tower clean and of avoiding it in course of cultivations, the loss of profit on the area rendered unproductive and any diminution of crop immediately outside that area.

(c) *Other Compensation.*—In addition to any such annual sum as is suggested above, compensation may be payable for a number of other losses suffered by owner or occupier.

These may include loss of crops or tenant right on the land on which the towers are erected, together with any injury to crops and interference with agricultural operations on adjoining land while the work is being done. The above is based on the assumption that agreement has been or will be reached on these items and that fair compensation will be paid for any damage which may subsequently be caused by the Board's servants or by accident due to the presence of the cable

A line passing through woodlands generally requires the cutting of a ride 13 m wide; and compensation will be payable for the trees felled and for possible injury to the rest of the wood and to sporting rights.

In the great majority of cases electricity conductors are carried over open country—i.e., arable or grassland, or moorland.

If it were proposed to carry a line over ripe building land, the owner's best course would be to make representation to the Secretary of State offering an alternative route.

If the original proposal were persisted in, then the effect on the value of the estate of the erection of pylons on certain plots and the presence of high-voltage cables over other plots would have to be considered. In such a case a claim for depreciation in the value of the land affected could be made. The amount could be arrived at—by the "before and after" method—by valuing the estate before the line was placed over the land and deducting from this amount the value of the estate after the line had been erected.

In a case before the Lands Tribunal[4] a claim was successfully established for depreciation in the value of a manor house following the erection of pylons and the laying of overhead wires. The award included a sum for the value of the land taken and for legal and surveyors' fees prior to the reference.

## B. Laying of Sewers and Water Mains

### 1. STATUTORY PROVISIONS

Under the Public Health Act, 1936, a local authority may construct a sewer " in, on or over any land not forming part of a street, after giving reasonable notice to every owner and occupier of the land ". Similar powers may be exercised in respect of water mains.[5]

It is clear from the wording of the Act that the sewer or main may be carried below ground, or on the surface, or partly in one way and partly in another.

When the sewer is constructed it will vest in the local authority.[6]

The power to construct the sewer includes the provision of means of access or ventilation in the shape of manholes, ventilating shafts, etc.; and since the local authority is under obligation to maintain the sewer[7] there is an implied right of entry from time to time for purposes of inspection and repair.

An owner is, in general, entitled to claim " full compensation " for any damage he suffers through the exercise of an authority's powers under the Act.[8] But where compensation is claimed in respect of the construction of a sewer or the laying of a water main the tribunal which assesses compensation is directed to determine also by what amount, if any, the value to the claimant of any land belonging to him has been enhanced by the construction of the sewer or main, and the local authority is entitled to set off that amount against the amount of compensation awarded.[9]

Section 278 (2) of the Act provides that compensation for damage caused by the exercise of a local authority's powers shall be determined by arbitration—or by justices if the claim does not exceed £50 and either party so requires. But the case of *Thurrock, Grays & Tilbury Joint Sewerage Board v. Thames Land Company Ltd.*[10] appears to be authority for saying that, by virtue of the vesting in the local authority of that part of the land which comprises the pipe-

---

[4] *Radnor Trust, Ltd. v. Central Electricity Generating Board,* 1960 (Lands Tribunal—Ref./220/1959) 1 R. & V.R. 9.

[5] Public Health Act, 1936, Secs. 15 and 119. In London the power to construct sewers in private land is derived from the Public Health (London) Act, 1936, Sec. 17.

[6] Public Health Act, 1936, Sec. 20 (1) (b).

[7] *Ibid.,* Sec. 23.

[8] *Ibid.,* Sec. 278.

[9] *Ibid.,* Sec. 278 (4).

[10] (1925) 23 L.G.R. 648.

line, questions of disputed compensation for the laying of sewers or water mains should be determined under the Land Compensation Act, 1961—which now means that the case will be heard by the Lands Tribunal. From time to time, local authorities have questioned their liability to pay any compensation at all to a landowner for laying a pipe across his land. Landowners and their advisers now have the benefit of a number of Lands Tribunal decisions[11] which illustrate the amount of compensation payable in such cases. These cases support the view that owners are entitled to payment not only for permanent damage to the value of the surface land but also for the presence in the land of the pipe itself, implying as it does rights of entry for inspection and other purposes in the future.

## 2. CLAIMS FOR COMPENSATION

(a) *Temporary Damage.*—A certain amount of damage will almost certainly be caused by the actual laying of the sewer or main. In the case of agricultural land this may include such items as injury to fences, gates and land drainage, cost of making good the surface, loss of tenant right, and temporary interference with agricultural operations while the works are in progress. In the case of residential property damage might include the cost of reinstating flower beds, paths, lawn, etc., and temporary loss of amenity or rental value to the house. Except in so far as they may be made good by the local authority, the owner is entitled to compensation for all such items of " temporary " damage.

(b) *Permanent Depreciation in Value.*—Compensation may also be claimed for any depreciation in the value of the property due to the presence of the sewer or main in the land.

Even if the sewer is entirely underground, the owner is entitled to some compensation for the vesting of the subsoil in the local authority and for any inconvenience likely to be caused by the exercise of their rights of access for maintenance and inspection purposes. There may also be manholes, lampholes and ventilating

---

[11] *Eastleigh Borough Council,* Estates Gazette, 7 February, 1953; *T. C. Ward and the War Department,* Estates Gazette, 31 July, 1954; *Quartons (Gardens) Ltd. and the Scarborough R.D.C.,* Estates Gazette, 23 April, 1955; *Col. F. L. Orme, O.B.E., and the West Cheshire Water Board,* The Chartered Surveyor, September, 1956; *H. H. Russell and the Bradfield R.D.C.,* The Chartered Surveyor, January, 1958; *R. S. Frost and the Borough of Taunton,* Estates Gazette, 10 August, 1957; *The Trustees of Lord Emlyn's Marriage Settlement and The Trustees of the Will of Sir R. A. Morris, Baronet v. Swansea County Borough* (Ref. /134 and 5/1959); *R. G. N. Weston v. Bedford Rural District Council* (Ref. /134 and 5/1959) ; these cases being referred to in The Chartered Surveyor, November, 1960, Page 247.

See also The Chartered Surveyor, March 1963, Pages 503–8, " Water Mains, Sewers and other pipelines: compensation payable to the landowner."

See also *Lucey's Personal Representatives and Wood v. Harrogate Corporation, Lands Tribunal,* P. & C.R. Vol. 14 (1963) pp. 376–385.

shafts whose presence may cause some loss of value to the land. If the sewer is laid wholly or in part above ground the effect is likely to be more serious; not only will the strip of land occupied be quite unusable, but the use or amenities of the property as a whole may be substantially interfered with.

For many years it was common practice to claim compensation for what was described as the " pipe easement "—a misleading term to apply to a local authority's interest in the pipe line, since an " easement " can only exist as appurtenant to the ownership of a " dominant tenement ".

Compensation for the so-called " easement " was based either on the value of the strip of land occupied by the sewer or main or was taken at a figure of so much per yard run. Reference to the cases listed at footnote 11 above, indicates that a figure of so much per yard run seems to be preferred, the figure being usually between 12½p and 20p for agricultural land but more recently figures agreed are 25p to 37½p.

In the case of land ripe for building, the fact that no building may be erected over the sewer without the local authority's permission[12] may be a matter for serious consideration. When the pipe is laid above ground the loss of value will be much greater and may include injury to the rest of the property by severance or injurious affection. Water Companies will often undertake to move a pipe or to pay extra compensation if land is given consent for development after pipes have been laid.

A possible example in the case of a country estate might be depreciation in the value of the house due to a line of ventilating shafts across the park or a length of sewer carried above ground on an unsightly embankment.

On the other hand the provisions of the Public Health Act regarding " set off " must be borne in mind in cases where the owner will have a right of connection to the pipe line.

(c) *Manholes, Ventilating Shafts, etc.*—Compensation for these is usually taken at lump sum figures, the amount varying from £3-£4 to as much as £20 or over, according to the type of land in which they occur and the position in which they are placed.

For instance two or three manholes at intervals along the line of a hedge on agricultural land may be of little or no consequence, whereas a manhole or ventilating shaft close to a residential property may cause appreciable injury.

Again, a manhole in the middle of an arable field can be a potential danger to farm implements, and weeds tend to grow round them which will have to be removed from time to time.

Lampholes are usually taken at about half the figure for manholes or ventilating shafts.

---

[12] Public Health Act, 1936, Sec. 25.

Here, again, the present tendency is to regard conventional figures with suspicion and the valuer must be prepared to make out a good case for damage actually sustained.

*Example.*—An attractive country house of five bedrooms and three reception rooms stands in grounds of 5 ha, one of which forms the gardens, the remainder being used for the rearing of pigs and poultry by the occupier of the house. He purchased the whole a few years ago for £8,000 and has since spent about £3,000 on improvements to the property.

Nearly all the land is visible from the house. A sewer is to be taken through two of the fields, "Two acre" and "Four acre", for distances of about 240 and 164 m respectively. In "Two acre" there will be one manhole and the sewer will be underground at a depth averaging 6 m. In "Four acre" the pipe will be taken above ground at an average height of 1 m, and will divide the field into equal parts making access to the further half difficult. The pipe will be visible from the house and the subsoil is of a type likely to move after being disturbed. It is required to assess the compensation to be claimed.

| | | | £ | £ |
|---|---|---|---:|---:|
| *Answer*— | | | | |
| (i) *Area affected by presence of pipeline:*— | | | | |
| | (*a*) "Two acre" field, 240 m @ 30p per m ... ... ... ... | | 72 | |
| | (*b*) "Four acre" field, 164 m @ 35p per m ... ... ... ... | | 57 | |
| | | | | 129 |
| (ii) *Permanent depreciation:*— | | | | |
| | (*a*) In "Four acre" field, depreciation in capital value of 1 ha due to difficulty of access @ £100 per ha | | 100 | |
| | Depreciation in the remaining 1 ha @ £50 per ha ... ... | | 50 | |
| | | | 150 | |
| | (*b*) Depreciation in value of house ... | | 200 | |
| | | | | 350 |
| (iii) *Manhole* ... ... ... ... ... | | | | 15 |
| (iv) *Loss during construction of works* ... | | | | 15 |
| (v) *Repair of gaps in hedges* ... ... | | | | 20 |
| | | *Compensation* say | | £530 |

## C. Pipe-Lines

Under the provisions of the Pipe-Lines Act, 1962, compulsory purchase orders can be made for the acquisition of land and " compulsory rights orders " for the acquisition of rights over land required for the construction of private pipe-lines.

Where land is acquired under these provisions the Land Compensation Act, 1961, applies subject to minor modifications set out in the Third Schedule.

Where rights over land are acquired by a compulsory rights order the Act provides[13] that compensation can be claimed:—

(a) for any depreciation in the value of an interest in land which comprises or is held with land to which the order applies; and

(b) for any other loss suffered by reason of damage to, or disturbance in the enjoyment of, any land or chattels. This includes damage to land drainage, access roads and drives. Compensation is now generally paid to the owner or occupier in respect of his time and expenses dealing with contractors, statutory undertakers, etc., including secretarial expenses and telephone calls.

Generally speaking payments by Gas Boards and Oil Companies are 50p to 75p per m run although there is no reason why these figures should be greater than those paid for sewers and water mains.

---

[13] Section 14.

# Chapter 27

## Licensed Premises

### 1. GENERALLY

THE TERM " licensed premises " is a very wide one and includes all those properties which are licensed for the sale of intoxicating liquors, such as hotels, public-houses, beer-houses, refreshment rooms, restaurants and " off-licences ".

A valuation of this type involves not only a careful inspection of land and buildings but an enquiry into the nature and extent of the licensed trade carried on on the premises, and an estimate of the future prospects of that trade.

In practice this class of work is largely confined to specialists and only a very broad outline of the principles involved will be attempted here.

### 2. TYPES OF LICENCE

The retail sale of beer, wines and spirits can, with some exceptions, only be carried on under the authority of a licence granted by the Licensing Justices.

There are two principal types of licence—(i) the " on-licence ", which permits the sale of intoxicating liquors for consumption on or off the premises; (ii) the " off-licence ", which permits their sale for consumption off the premises only.

A full on-licence covers the sale of beers, wines and spirits; a beer and wine house licence, that of beer, cider and wine only.

Conditional forms of on-licences granted to Hotels and Restaurants are described as " a residential licence ", " a restaurant licence " or " a residential and restaurant licence ".

An on-licence first granted before the passing of the Licensing Act, 1904, is known as an " old licence ". It is for one year only, but its annual renewal is granted more or less as a matter of right unless the premises are unsatisfactory, or there has been some breach of the licensing laws, or the house is regarded as redundant. If renewal is refused on the grounds of redundancy the licensee is entitled to compensation for the loss of his licence. To provide a fund to meet such cases, the Compensation Authority has power to collect an annual payment, known as the "Compensation Levy", from the holders of all " old " licences in a particular licensing area.

Until 1959 the grant of a new on-licence was subject to payment of " monopoly value ", which was the difference between the value of

421

the premises with and without a licence. The payment of monopoly value was abolished by the Finance Act, 1959. Holders of new on-licences do not receive any compensation if renewal of their licence is refused, and they are not required to contribute to the Compensation Levy.

The obtaining of a new on-licence is a much more difficult matter than the renewal of an old one and may be subject to such conditions as the Licensing Justices think fit to impose in the public interest. The licence is renewable annually.

An off-licence may cover the sale of beers, wines and spirits for consumption off the premises. Or it may be limited to the sale of beer, cider and wine only.

### 3.  COMPENSATION FUND LEVY

This levy may be made under Section 17, Licensing Act, 1964, by the Compensation Authority for any licensing area to provide a fund out of which to compensate the owners of properties the renewal of the licence of which is refused on the grounds of " redundancy ", i.e., that there are more licences than the neighbourhood needs.

In those areas where the levy is made it is payable by the holders of all old on-licences, but is ultimately shared, by way of deduction from rent, by all parties interested in the licensed premises.

The levy is fixed yearly by the Authority up to a maximum of £100. The charge payable is an amount which bears to the sum fixed the same proportion as the charge in 1958 bore to the maximum charge which was or might have been imposed in that year.

The Act also prescribes the proportion of the levy which interested parties may deduct from their rent according to the length of their term. This varies from 100 per cent of the charge, in the case of a person whose unexpired term does not exceed one year, to 1 per cent of the charge where the unexpired term exceeds 55 but does not exceed 60 years. In no case may the amount deducted exceed half the rent.

### 4.  " FREE" AND " TIED " HOUSES

A " free " public-house is one in which the licensee is free to purchase his liquor from anyone he pleases. A "tied" public-house is one in which the licensee is bound to purchase his beers, and usually wines, spirits and even minerals, from a particular firm of brewers.

A " tied " house is created by a brewer obtaining a freehold or leasehold interest in licensed premises and putting in a tenant to run the business on the condition that he shall purchase his liquors from his landlord. Sometimes the tied tenant holds a lease of the premises from the brewer. More frequently he holds on a yearly tenancy.

The prices paid by tied tenants for certain types of alcoholic liquors are higher than those paid by free tenants. The difference consists of the extra discount a brewer or supplier may allow to free trade customers, who are those able to purchase liquors where they please. The tied tenant's trade is secured to the brewer by contract, whereas free trade must be obtained in competition with other brewers. Because of these discounts the tied rent will be less than the rent the premises would produce if let to a free tenant.

The value of a tied house to a brewer consists, therefore, partly in the tied rent and partly in the profits he may expect to make on the purchases from him secured by the tied tenancy.

Instead of letting to a tied tenant some houses are under the management of the brewer, thus securing the retail profits in addition to profits on supplies, or wholesale profits.

There are now very few free houses in the country, and whenever one with a good trade comes into the market it usually fetches a high figure by reason of the keen competition amongst brewers to secure an additional outlet for their supplies.

## 5. TRADE PROFITS

A valuation of licensed premises for whatever purpose will almost certainly involve some enquiry into the trade done and the actual or estimated profits.

(a) *Brewer's profits.*—In the case of a tied house it may be necessary to consider the profits which the brewer makes from the supply of liquor under the " tie ".

These vary, for there is no uniformity of practice regarding the terms on which tied houses are let. In some houses the tied rent may be low and the prices charged for liquor unusually high. In others the reverse may be the case.

The value of the beer trade also depends largely on the class of beers sold. Brewers earn a better profit upon higher priced beers, and consequently the value of such barrelage is more.

The figures of profits taken in the examples are to illustrate method and should not be regarded as representing actual profits in any particular case.

(b) *Tenant's profits.*—In some cases, for instance, in estimating the rental a tenant would be willing to pay, it may be necessary to inquire into the profits made by the licensee.

His gross profits will, of course, consist of the difference between purchases and sales. This may be found by reference to the accounts or may be estimated by taking a percentage on the purchase prices of beers, wines, spirits, etc.

The latter method requires a considerable amount of practical experience, but is often useful as a check on actual takings as shown by the books.

In either case it is desirable to consider the figures for a number of years in order to strike a fair average and to allow for any tendency towards appreciation or depreciation in the trade.

Gross profit having been found, a deduction for reasonable overhead and working expenses must be made to arrive at a figure of net profit.

Overhead and working expenses will include such items as rent, rates and water rate, share of compensation levy, wages and keep of staff, insurances, accountancy, tenant's share of repairs, lighting, heating and other incidentals, and interest on tenant's capital. The last item is usually calculated at about 10 per cent on the value of stock, fixtures and fittings and working cash capital.

## 6. PRINCIPLES OF VALUATION

A valuation of licensed premises may be required for various purposes—for sale or purchase, for mortgage, for probate, for grant or renewal of a lease, for rating, for compulsory purchase, for the purpose of estimating the compensation payable where renewal of an old on-licence is refused.

Valuations for rating and " referred " licences will be considered in later Sections of this Chapter.

It is proposed to deal here with estimates of capital value in the open market such as would be required for purposes of sale, mortgage, probate and compulsory purchase, and to illustrate the principles involved by reference to the case of the public-house with a full on-licence.

A valuation of a freehold or leasehold interest in a " free " house may be made by capitalising the retail net profits by an appropriate figure of years' purchase.

The result would reflect the value of the property in the open market to a free licensee. This method might be applied where the type of property is such that a large proportion of the business is in non-alcoholics such as catering and letting.

Where, however, by reason of the volume of sales in beers, wines and spirits the property is likely to prove attractive to a brewer a different method would be appropriate.

In such a case the value would be arrived at by capitalising the estimated brewer's profits on liquors and adding the capitalised estimated or actual tied rent (or capitalised net retail profits assuming the house would be under management).

An example of this type of valuation is as follows:—

| | | | |
|---|---|---|---|
| Estimated Brewer's profits from the sale of beers, wines and spirits (see page 430) ... ... ... ... | £1,300 | | |
| Years' purchase ... ... ... | 14 | | |
| | | £18,200 | |
| Estimated net tied rental ... ... | £225 | | |
| Years' purchase ... ... ... ... | 16 | | |
| | | £3,600 | |
| Market Value ... ... ... ... | | £21,800 | |

The appropriate figures of years' purchase will vary according to the age and type of house and the circumstances generally.

A further method would be to arrive at the capital value direct by reference to the weekly or yearly barrelage (one barrel equals thirty-six gallons).

The figure taken per barrel is based upon an analysis of sales of comparable properties. For example, a public-house with a trade of 4 barrels draught and bottled beer per week might be valued at £1,600 per barrel, giving a capital value of £6,400. As the price per barrel might vary between £1,200 and £3,000 the successful application of this method would clearly depend to a great extent upon the skill and experience of the valuer.

When dealing with a licensee's interest, he will often be found in practice to be holding on a short tenancy from a firm of brewers to whom he is tied for the supply of his liquors. In this case he may have no valuable interest in the property and in the event of his death, or a change of tenancy, all that would fall to be valued would be the loose effects and stock and such of the fixtures and fittings as may belong to him.

If the licensee holds the residue of a lease, an estimate of the rent which a tenant might reasonably be expected to pay for the premises may show that he is sitting at a profit rent. In this case, the capitalised profit rent, plus the value of his goodwill, based on so many years' purchase of his net profits according to the length of the term, plus the value of the stock, fixtures, and fittings, will represent the total value of his interest in the premises. Sometimes brewers make a loan to tenants which is repayable during the term of the lease. Any such sum still outstanding will, of course, be deducted from the above figure.

No definite rules can be laid down as to percentages in the valuation of licensed premises, as the security of the income is largely dependent upon the nature and prospects of the trade and wide variations are found in practice.

The valuer will naturally consider the character and situation of the house and its age and condition. He will have regard to the trading facilities—e.g., the number of bars, their type and accommodation, facilities for catering, the nature of the living accommodation and rooms for guests, the general layout of the house, cellarage, etc.  He will also consider the nature of the surrounding district, the density of the population, possible movements of population due to housing schemes and other causes, the extent of the competition from other licensed premises and similar factors. The possibility of the house being " referred for compensation " as being unnecessary and " redundant " to the neighbourhood must also be borne in mind.

An important element in the valuation will be the class of purchaser to which the property is most likely to appeal. It has already been pointed out that a free house will often command a very high price owing to the competition of two or more brewers anxious to secure the trade of the house by a profitable tie.

Freehold ground rents on licensed premises, unless very well covered, usually fetch a lower figure of years' purchase than those secured on other premises owing to the risk of the licence being lost and the security thereby diminished.  If a licence is lost on the grounds of redundancy only, the freeholder shares in the compensation; but if forfeited for misconduct on the part of the licensee, no compensation is payable.  Owners of ground rents may insure against this risk.

The following example of the compulsory purchase of tied licensed premises illustrates the method of valuing the landlord's and the licensee's interests respectively.  The additional items for removal, fixtures, etc., are similar to those met with in disturbance claims in other compulsory purchase cases.

*Example.*—The following property is to be acquired compulsorily by a local authority. You are acting for the freeholder, a brewer, and also for the lessee. Determine the compensation payable to all interested parties. The house was originally leased at £100 rent, but the property has since increased in value. The lease has 10 years to run. The lessee is tied for beers, wines and spirits and for the past few years the trade has varied very little.

Purchases last year amounted to £11,550 and takings to £15,400. The trade expenses, including the rent, were £2,265. The stock was recently valued at £700 and fixtures and fittings at £650. There is no brewer's loan on the property. The lessee pays for all repairs.

Details of purchases are as follows:—

| | |
|---|---|
| Draught Beer ... ... ... | 300 barrels |
| Bottled Beer ... ... ... | 3,600 doz. pints (150 barrels) |
| Wine ... ... ... ... | 80 gallons |
| Spirits ... ... ... ... | 120 gallons |

*Valuation—*
  *Lessee's Interest.*—This consists of two factors:—(i) his profit rent, (ii) his interest in the trade.
  (i) His profit rent is probably due to an improvement in the trade prospect of the " house " since the lease was granted. In order to ascertain the profit rent it is proposed to estimate, by reference to the trade, the rent which a tied tenant would be prepared to pay at the present day, assuming he held on the same conditions as to repairs, etc., as the lessee.

*Estimate of present tied rental value—*

| | | | |
|---|---|---:|---:|
| Gross profit ... ... ... | | | £3,850 |
| Deduct trade expenses ... ... | £2,265 | | |
| Less rent paid ... ... ... | £100 | | |
| | ——— | | |
| | | | £2,165 |
| | | | ——— |
| | | | £1,685 |

*Allow for " tenant's share ":*

| | | | |
|---|---|---:|---:|
| Stock ... ... ... ... | £700 | | |
| Fixtures and Fittings ... ... | £650 | | |
| Cash capital, say ... ... | £800 | | |
| | ——— | | |
| Interest on tenant's capital at 10% on £2,150 ... ... | | £215 | |
| Tenant's remuneration ... ... | | £1,200 | |
| | | ——— | £1,415 |
| | | | ——— |
| *Fair tied rent on lease* ... | | | £270 |
| | | | ——— |

*Lessee's Compensation.*
  (i) *Interest in lease:*

| | | | |
|---|---|---:|---:|
| Fair tied rent on lease ... | | £270 | |
| Rent reserved ... ... ... | | £100 | |
| | | ——— | |
| Profit rent | | £170 | |
| Y.P. 10 years at 7% and 2½% —allowing for Income Tax at 38·75% ... ... ... | | 4·64 | |
| | | ——— | £789 |

  (ii) *Trade:*

| | | | |
|---|---|---:|---:|
| Gross Profit ... ... ... | | £3,850 | |
| *Less:* | | | |
| Expenses ... ... ... | £2,265 | | |
| Profit rent ... ... ... | £170 | | |
| Interest on Capital ... ... | £215 | | |
| | ——— | | |
| | | £2,650 | |
| | | ——— | |
| Net | | £1,200 | |
| *Carried forward* | | | £789 |

| | | |
|---|---:|---:|
| *Brought forward* £1,200 | | £789 |
| Y.P. 10 years at 10% and 2½% —allowing for Income Tax at 38·75% ... ... ... | 4·15 | |
| | | £4,980 |
| Depreciation of value of fixtures and fittings, say 80% of £650 ... ... ... ... | | £520 |
| Loss on sale of stock, say 10% on £700 ... ... ... | | £70 |
| Cost of removal ... ... ... | | £50 |
| *Compensation to lessee*, say ... | | £6,400 |

*Brewer's Interest.*—This also will consist of two factors—(i) the tied rent; (ii) the profits from the tie.

(i) In valuing the tied rent we must consider (a) the rent of £100 reserved under the lease for the next 10 years, and (b) the rent receivable thereafter.

*Brewer's Compensation.*

| | | | |
|---|---:|---:|---:|
| Tied Rent for 10 years ... | | £100 | |
| Y.P. 10 years at 5% ... ... | | 7·7 | |
| | | | £770 |
| Reversion to full net rental value | | £270 | |
| (N.B.—This figure depends entirely on the trade being maintained and is not so well secured as the £100.) | | | |
| Y.P. perp. at 6% ... ... | 16·67 | | |
| Y.P. 10 years at 6% ... ... | 7·36 | 9·3 | |
| | | | £2,511 |

*Trade:* The brewer's profit may be accepted at the following figures:—

| | | |
|---|---:|---:|
| Draught Beer—300 barrels at £2·25 ... ... ... ... | £675 | |
| Bottled Beer—150 barrels at £3·50 ... ... ... ... | 525 | |
| Wines and Spirits—200 gallons at 50p. ... ... ... | 100 | |
| | £1,300 | |
| Y.P. perp. at 7% ... ... | 14 | |
| | | £18,200 |
| *Compensation*, say ... | | £21,475 |

It is assumed there is no value in the licence when put into suspense under Part 9 of the Licensing Act, 1964.

## 7. VALUATIONS FOR RATING

In valuing licensed properties for rating purposes, as in the case of all other properties, it is required to ascertain the rent which a tenant might reasonably be expected to pay from year to year on the terms of a yearly tenancy.

Obviously this will depend upon the profit which can be made by entering into a tenancy by competitive parties including licensees, brewers, and others, and the likely degree of competition is an important factor.

There was a fundamental change in the valuation of licensed premises for rating purposes following the decision of the House of Lords in *Robinson Bros. (Brewers) Ltd. v. Houghton and Chester-le-Street Assessment Committee.*[3]

Prior to that case the judgment of the High Court in *Bradford-on-Avon Union v. White*[4] had been followed for many years. The effect of this judgment was that, in assessing the rent a hypothetical tenant might be expected to pay for licensed premises, the possible competition of brewers could not wholly be excluded from consideration, but the rents they might be prepared to give, owing to special considerations relating to their trade profits, should be excluded, except so far as the possibility of such special rents being obtained might raise the market value generally.

It was found difficult to interpret the *Bradford* judgment in a practical way and as a general rule the competition of brewers does not appear to have been taken into account in rating assessments, at any rate quantitively. A quite common method of valuation was to estimate (a) the volume of trade the house was capable of doing, and (b) the gross profit obtainable assuming the house was " free "; working expenses were then deducted, leaving a balance to be divided between (i) tenant's remuneration and interest on capital, (ii) the fixed charges, viz., rates, water rate and licence duty, and (iii) the landlord's rent. In short, the object of the method was to find what profit a hypothetical free tenant, intending to occupy as licensee, could make, in order to estimate the rent he would be likely to bid.

The *Robinson* judgment established the principle that the hypothetical tenant may reasonably be expected to pay the rent which, in the letting market for such premises, would be offered as a result of the competition existing in that market. It is for the valuing authority to gauge both the extent of the competition in the market and the rent likely to be offered and accepted in that market.

Evidence of the rents which brewers would be prepared to pay for the tenancy of the house, whether they proposed to sub-let it to a tied tenant or to occupy it themselves by a manager, is both

---

[3] (1938), A.C. 321.
[4] (1898), 2 Q.B. 630.

competent and relevant in estimating the rent which the hypothetical tenant might be expected to pay. There is no justification
for including brewers among the competitors, but excluding from
consideration the rent they would offer.

Logically, therefore, it appears necessary in any particular case
to consider the profits which brewers might expect to receive by
securing the tenancy of the house. Usually the brewer would
sub-let to a tied tenant and his profit would consist of (i) the tied
rent, and (ii) the profit on the alcoholic goods supplied to the
tenant under the " tie ". It is out of the profits that he would make
his bid.

The proportion of his estimated income which a brewer might be
prepared to pay away in the form of rent depends on the volume of
the trade, the degree of local competition and other factors.

The following illustrates the method of valuation, known as the
Direct Method, which has been approved by the Lands Tribunal.

*Example.*—A fully licensed property occupied by a tied tenant.
The actual tied rent is £65 per annum. The average three years
trade was 120 Barrels Draught Beer, 80 Barrels Bottled Beer,
60 Gallons Wines and Spirits.

Estimated future maintainable trade—

| | |
|---|---:|
| Draught Beer—120 barrels at £2 profit per barrel | £240 |
| Bottled Beer—80 barrels at £3·50 profit per barrel | £280 |
| Wines and Spirits—60 gallons at 63p profit per gallon    ...    ...    ...    ...    ...    ... | £37 |
| Estimated Brewer's wholesale profit    ...    ... | £557 |
| Estimated fair Tied Rent, say    ...    ...    ... | £80 |
| Total Brewer's Income   ,   ...    ... | £637 |
| Brewer/Tenant Share 65 %    ...    ...    ... | £414 |
| Gross Value    35%    ...    ...    ... | £223 |

say £225 G.V.

### 8.  COMPENSATION FOR " REFERRED " LICENCES

Where renewal of an old on-licence is refused on the grounds of
redundancy the case is referred to the Compensation Authority for
the payment of compensation under the provisions of Section 14 of
the Licensing Act, 1964. The sum payable may be agreed upon
between the interested parties and approved by the Compensation

Authority, failing which it will be referred to the Commissioners of Inland Revenue for settlement.[5]

The Act provides that the compensation payable shall be the difference between:—

(i) The value of the premises as licensed premises, plus any depreciation in the value of the fixtures due to the refusal to renew the licence; and

(ii) The value of the premises without the licence.

The depreciation in the value of the trade fixtures due to the loss of the licence will usually be the difference between their value as part of a going concern and their value—probably " scrap " value—if removed and sold.

The unlicensed value is arrived at by valuing the premises for their most profitable permitted use and allowing for the cost of conversion.

In making the two valuations required by Section 14 of the Act, the valuer is not concerned with any particular party's interest, but with the value of the premises in the open market—(i) with the licence, and (ii) without it.

In the case of a tied house, the value with the licence will consist of the income from the tied rent plus the brewer's profits from the tie, both capitalised in perpetuity; to which must be added the depreciation in the value of the trade fixtures.

The practice in assessing compensation under the Act was brought before the Courts in the cases of *Ashby's Staines Brewery v. The Crown*, and *Ashby's Cobham Brewery v. The Crown*.[6] The following example illustrates this method:—

*Example.*—A brewery company are the freeholders of an 80-year old fully licensed house of which the licence has been referred as redundant. The premises are let to a tied tenant on a 7 years' lease, of which 4 years are unexpired, at a rent of £120 per annum. The trade done amounts to 130 barrels of beer, 2,880 dozen pints of bottled beer, 100 gallons of wines and spirits per annum. The fixtures are worth, in position, a sum of £250. The tenant's net trade profits are £750 a year. The premises are worth £110 a year without the licence, if £500 is spent to convert them into a house. Assess the compensation payable under the Licensing Act, 1964.

---

[5] In this case there is a right of appeal to the High Court.
[6] (1906), 2 K.B. 754.

*Valuation—*

(i) *Value as licensed premises, plus depreciation of fixtures.*
Profits from tie

| | | | |
|---|---|---|---:|
| 130 barrels of draught beer at £2·25 | ... | ... | £292 |
| 120 barrels of bottled beer at £3·50 | ... | ... | £420 |
| 100 gallons of wines and spirits at 50p. | ... | ... | £50 |

|  | |
|---|---:|
|  | £762 |
| Y.P.  ... | 8 |

|  | |
|---|---:|
|  | £6,096 |

Capitalised Tied Rent:

| | | | | | |
|---|---|---|---|---|---:|
| Tied rental ... | ... | ... | ... | ... | £120 |
| Y.P. perp., say | ... | ... | ... | ... | 16 |

|  | |
|---|---:|
|  | £1,920 |

|  | | |
|---|---|---:|
| Value licensed | ... | £8,016 |
| Depreciation of fixtures, 75% of £250 ... | ... | 187 |

|  | | |
|---|---|---:|
| *Value licensed plus depreciation of fixtures* | ... | £8,203 |

(ii) *Value unlicensed.*

| | | | | |
|---|---|---|---|---:|
| Rent as house | ... | ... | ... | £110 |
| Y.P. perp., say | ... | ... | ... | 16 |

|  | |
|---|---:|
|  | £1,760 |
| *Less* cost of conversion  ...   ...   ... | £500 |

|  | | |
|---|---|---:|
| *Value unlicensed* ...   ...   ...   ...   ... | £1,260 |

|  | | |
|---|---|---:|
| Compensation  ... | £6,943 |

The compensation payable out of the Compensation Fund having been ascertained, it must then be divided among the persons interested in the property. The Compensation Authority may fix the appropriate shares or may, at their discretion, refer the matter to the County Court. Very commonly the division of the compensation is agreed upon between the parties concerned.

A sum must first be set aside as compensation for the licensee. The Act provides that in fixing this regard shall be had to his conduct and to the length of time during which he has been the holder of the licence; and that in no case shall the licensee receive less than the amount he would be entitled to as a tenant from year to year of the licensed premises. Where, as is usually the case, the licensee is holding a yearly tenancy or shorter term, he will probably receive not less than one year's net trading profits.

A further sum is then set aside to cover depreciation of trade fixtures. This will be paid to the party who incurs this loss.

The remainder of the compensation, or " divisible balance ", is then apportioned amongst freeholder and other interested parties (if any) according to the extent of their interests in the property. Where there are several interests the sum total of the value of each party's interest will normally exceed the " divisible balance " so this has to be split up proportionally.

The following example illustrates the principles of apportionment between a freeholder and lessee.

*Example.*—Using the same facts and figures as in the previous example, apportion the compensation payable amongst the parties interested in the premises.

*Apportionments*

|  |  |  |
|---|---|---|
| Total compensation ... | | £6,943 |
| (i) Compensation to licensee, say 2 Y.P. of trade profits ... ... ... ... £1,500 | | |
| (ii) Depreciation of fixtures ... ... ... £187 | | |
| | —— | £1,687 |
| *Balance, Brewer's share* ... | | £5,256 |

## 9. LICENSING PLANNING

In areas where extensive war damage occurred special provisions were introduced and these are re-enacted in the Licensing Act, 1964, Part 7. Such areas were declared Licensing Planning Areas. It is the duty of Licensing Planning Committees to endeavour to secure that the number, nature and distribution of the licensed premises in the areas accord with local requirements.

Problems of valuations arise where licensed premises were physically totally destroyed, and where the licence, which has been in suspense, is granted a planning removal.

It is thought that the consideration of these special problems is beyond the scope of this book.

# Chapter 28

## Minerals

IN A BOOK of this nature it is only possible to give a brief outline on certain aspects of what is a specialised subject. There are, however, a number of surface minerals, for example, sand and gravel, brick earth, chalk and limestone, which can come within the province of general practice.

Valuations of minerals may be required for the purposes of assessing capital or rental values, compulsory purchase, rating, taxation, probate, planning refusals and restrictions. In addition, valuations are sometimes required on the basis of a going concern to include buildings and plant and machinery used in the undertaking.

The first essential in connection with any valuation of minerals is to have a sound knowledge of the particular industry and the problems encountered in the excavation and processing of the mineral and its marketing. Although at first sight two areas of mineral land may appear to be comparable, there can be factors which affect their respective ease of working and future rate of extraction which could have a marked effect on the value of one area as compared with the other.

The valuation of mineral-bearing land involves the valuation of an asset which is to be destroyed as excavations proceed and ultimately the land loses for all time its value so far as the mineral element is concerned. There may, however, be some residual value attaching to the land after the mineral has been worked and the site restored. In addition, there may be an interim surface value for, say, agricultural purposes on part of the land while the excavations proceed.

Planning control has an important bearing on a valuation of mineral land and it is necessary for the valuer to explore the planning position on any land with which he is concerned.

Due to the effect on amenities that can be caused by mineral extraction and also the destruction of what may be productive agricultural land, difficulty is often experienced in obtaining permission. Most permissions are usually subject to stringent conditions regulating the method of working and the later restoration of the land. Such conditions can have an effect on the value of the land and need careful consideration.

### 1. METHODS OF VALUATION

When dealing with any capital valuation the best evidence of value is usually to be found in comparable property. However, with minerals it is sometimes difficult to find evidence which is sufficiently comparable to be of real assistance.

It is clearly relevant to establish whether the sale of a comparable property was with the benefit of planning permission for mineral extraction. There may be instances where, even in the absence of a valid permission an enhanced price was realised, thus reflecting the purchasers anticipation that the necessary consents could be obtained.

In some areas where the market for the particular mineral is not restricted there may be sufficient evidence of current transactions to justify the valuer adopting a valuation on a basis related to the area of the land.

The particular circumstances of a prima facie comparable transaction should, however, be investigated. For example, it may be found that unduly high prices have been paid for land by a mineral operator whose existing reserves are on the point of exhaustion. The operator may have efficient plant that has been fully written down and rather than face the heavy capital expenditure that would be involved in establishing new plant and buildings on an alternative site he may be prepared to pay an exceptionally high price to keep his existing works in production.

Conversely there are still cases where agricultural land is bought by mineral operators from owners who may not be aware of the mineral potential.

In some cases sales may not represent arms length transactions. Sale prices in the above circumstances will probably afford little assistance for purposes of comparison.

It will be readily appreciated that two adjoining areas of apparently comparable land may have widely differing mineral contents per hectare and detailed investigation may indicate that one may be a better economic proposition to exploit than the other.

The valuer must be satisfied as far as possible as to the mineral content of the land and its quality. In appropriate cases the mineral should be proved by means of borings or trial holes and, in some instances, an electrical resistivity survey is employed in conjunction with conventional borings. The provings should indicate the amount of overburden overlying the mineral and any major faults in the deposit. The term "overburden" signifies topsoil and other strata above the mineral seam. The question of the proving of the land is a specialist matter and an inadequate number of boreholes in an unsatisfactory pattern could give a very misleading impression as to the true content of mineral in the site, which in turn would have a marked effect on the valuation. It is necessary to be satisfied as to the quality and suitability of the mineral for the proposed product. Where the geological formation is uncertain it is desirable for comprehensive tests to be taken.

Although land may contain a seam of high-quality mineral, it can have little or no value if it is so situated that the market is too distant or if the market is already adequately served from existing sources of supply with ample reserves.

For example, there are large tracts of land containing chalk but much of this land does not at the present time possess any special mineral value.

On the other hand, where the supply of a particular mineral-bearing land is limited, as is the case, for example, with sand and gravel, in certain districts there is an urgent demand from the gravel industry for further reserves. Planning control in some areas aggravates the shortage and enhances land values.

## 2. FACTORS AFFECTING VALUE

The value of minerals ultimately depend on the profit that a mineral operator can make from their exploitation.

The main factors to consider when making a valuation of mineral land are:

(1) The quantity of mineral in the land.
(2) Its quality and suitability for the market that it will serve.
(3) The ease or difficulty of its winning and working.
(4) The likely output that the potential market would justify.
(5) The estimated profitability bearing in mind the capital that is required to be employed in the venture.

## 3. ROYALTY METHOD OF VALUATION

An alternative method of approach which is sometimes employed, particularly where no evidence of capital transactions is available, is to capitalise the estimated revenue that the land should yield during the estimated life of the minerals. This is known as the royalty method of valuation, a royalty being the amount, under the terms of a mining lease, of the payment by the lessee to lessor in respect of each unit of mineral output. The units of measure usually adopted in the past were tons or cubic yards or, in the case of clay workings for brickworks, the royalty is often based upon a price per thousand bricks.

With metrication the increasing use of the tonne is to be anticipated.

This method of valuation is dependent upon a number of assumptions which have to be made by the valuer and it is important to try and check the answer produced by this approach from comparable capital transactions whenever possible.

The valuer must first make an estimate of the probable future rate of output from the undertaking and can then determine the estimated life of the minerals in the site having regard to the estimate of total content. This involves a careful appraisal of the market potential, bearing in mind the level of existing and prospective output from similar concerns in the area.

When the mineral is required for an extension of workings, guidance can be obtained from the present rate of output. The prospect of additional output over and above the estimated normal demand due to exceptional requirements for specific projects, should be taken into account. For example, a large road construction programme or a new reservoir might call for large quantities of gravel in a particular area for a limited period.

Particular care is needed in determining the appropriate royalty value for the unit of mineral, and regard should be had to any evidence available on current royalties paid in the locality. The valuer may have to adjust the figure having regard, for example, to the situation of the property, the quality of the mineral and the estimated cost of working. If overburden is unusually deep or there are expensive restoration conditions attached to the planning permission, a prospective lessee would clearly pay less by way of royalty than he would for a deposit where such difficulties and expense were not present. Similarly, if the undertaking is further from the market the additional transport costs will reduce the royalty value. The distance of the quarry from the market is particularly important in the case of heavy and relatively low-cost minerals due to the high cost of transport.

## 4. CAPITALISATION OF ROYALTIES

The capitalisation of the estimated annual royalty is usually carried out using dual rate valuation tables making allowance for tax on the sinking fund instalment, even where a freehold capital valuation is being made.

Minerals are a wasting asset and their valuation involves similar considerations as apply to the valuation of a leasehold interest in other types of property. Therefore, even in the case of a royalty valuation of a freehold interest, provision should be made whereby part of the terminable income represented by the annual royalty payment is set aside and invested in a sinking fund to replace the capital value of the mineral. Income-tax adjustment should be made in the normal way as the sinking fund instalment has to be set aside out of taxed income. Where immediate working is not anticipated, a suitable deferment factor must also be applied.

The choice of interest rates requires careful consideration, bearing in mind all the risks involved.

*Example.—*

6 hectares of chalk.
Estimated total mineral content 750,000 tonnes.
Estimated rate of working 25,000 tonnes per annum.
Estimated royalty value 5p per tonne.
Total life 30 years.

| | | |
|---|---|---|
| Annual Royalty Value 25,000 tonnes @ 5p | £1,250 | |
| Y.P. 30 years @ 12 and 3 per cent | 6·48 | |
| Tax @ 38·75% | | |
| | **£8,100** | |

This is equivalent to £1,350 per hectare, which should be considered in relation to available evidence of sales of comparable land.

In view of the number of assumptions that will have been made it is important to carefully consider the figure resulting from a royalty valuation in terms of capital values. Due to the taxation liabilities attaching to a royalty lease, so far as the freeholder is concerned, minerals are frequently disposed of on a freehold basis rather than the mineral being made available under a royalty lease. As a result the valuer may find difficulty in obtaining comparable royalty evidence although the taxation liability has been reduced by the Finance Act, 1970, to which brief reference is made later.

The valuation of a freeholder's interest subject to a mineral lease proceeds in a similar manner to the capital royalty valuation described above.

In addition to the reservation of a royalty under a mineral lease, it is frequently provided that the lessee will pay a minimum rent (sometimes referred to as a dead rent or certain rent) irrespective of whether working takes place in any year or not. This ensures that the lessor will receive a certain level of income during the currency of the lease irrespective of output. It also guards the lessor against the risk that the lessee may postpone the working of his land and makes less attractive the practice whereby a mineral operator takes a lease to lock up land with a view to reducing the risk of competition. It is normally provided that the royalty based on output merges with the minimum rent. For example, if the royalty is 5p per tonne and the minimum rent is £1,000 per annum, the minimum rent ceases to apply once the output exceeds 20,000 tonnes per annum.

In such cases there is usually a short-workings clause whereby if the rate of output falls short of the output prescribed by the minimum rent, the deficiency can be set off in subsequent years against royalty payments in excess of the minimum rent. In the example given above, if in the first year of working the output was only 15,000 tonnes then the lessee would pay the minimum rent of £1,000 but would be entitled to carry forward £250 short-workings. If in the second year's working the output increased to 30,000 tonnes his payment would be £1,500−£250 = £1,250.

Sometimes a surface rent is also payable by the lessee to compensate the lessor for the loss of agricultural land during the period of excavation. This is normally a sum based on the agricultural rental value of the land.

## 5. Residual Value

Apart from considering the value of the mineral itself it is necessary to consider whether any additional value attaches to the land having regard to the potential future use or development of the land after the mineral has been extracted. In many instances it is intended that the land will revert to agricultural use and no other development potential exists. Much will depend upon the deferment factor that is likely to arise before the land has been restored to agricultural use. In such cases any residual value there may be will probably represent a fairly insignificant item and make little difference to the open market value. In some cases, however, the excavations may have considerable value for filling purposes when the land is situated close to a large urban area where the demand for these facilities is considerable. In such cases it may be necessary to make a suitable addition to the value to reflect this potential. Permission may be obtained for the prior extraction of the mineral before the site is developed for some other purpose and in such cases a substantial allowance may need to be made to reflect the residual value. It would be necessary to estimate the deferment that is likely to be involved before the land would be suitable and available for its ultimate development.

In other cases the extraction of the minerals will result in the formation of lakes where the natural Water Table is high. With suitable landscaping treatment such lakes can become attractive amenity features and may be used for a variety of recreational purposes. Activities such as sailing, angling and water ski-ing are becoming increasingly popular and the potential value for such uses must be considered.

The Countryside Act, 1968, empowers Local Authorities to acquire land for recreational purposes and to provide adequate facilities for their enjoyment. Apart from this there is an increasing demand from private clubs and individuals for use of such facilities.

## 6. Valuations for Rating

On the general principles reference should be made to Chapter 16.

Mineral producing properties are rateable and the current statutory provisions flow from two principal sources. The Poor Relief Act, 1601, made coal mines expressly rateable and as only coal was mentioned, other minerals were held not rateable.

This anomalous situation was changed by section 3 of The Rating Act, 1874, which extended rateability to mines of every kind not mentioned in the 1601 Act and Section 7 prescribed the method of assessing tin, lead and copper mines.

The current statutory provisions are to be found in Sections 16, 35 and 36 of the General Rate Act, 1967. The Mines and Quarries (Valuation) Order, 1971, has been made under Section 35.

## Tin, lead and copper mines

Where a tin, lead or copper mine is occupied under a lease the rateable value, broadly speaking shall be taken to be the aggregate of " (a) the annual amount of the whole of the dues payable in respect of the mine during the year ending with December 31st falling between 3 and 15 months before the beginning of the rate period and (b) the annual amount of any fixed rent reserved for the mine which may not be paid or satisfied by such dues."

Where the mine is owner occupied the rateable value will be based on the rent that might reasonably have been expected.

## Coal.

Coal mines vested in the National Coal Board are assessed on a formula basis under the National Coal Board (Valuation) Order, 1963, and the Mines & Quarries (Valuation) Order, 1971. These Orders flow from Section 3 of the Rating and Valuation Act, 1961, re-enacted as Section 35 of the General Rate Act, 1967.

## Other minerals.

The valuer will normally be dealing with sand, gravel, clay, chalk, limestone, etc.

The rateability of such mineral producing hereditaments is covered by Section 16 (d) of the General Rate Act, 1967, which refers to " mines of every other description other than a mine of which the royalty or dues are for the time being wholly reserved in kind ".

Mineral properties are assessed direct to Net Annual Value. The method of assessment follows the recommendations of the former Central Valuation Committee and their Resolution No. 63 dated 22 March, 1929, on Mineral Producing Hereditaments is worthy of study.

A suitable royalty is decided upon having regard to the considerations referred to earlier in this chapter and this is applied to the actual estimated output. To this is added the Net Annual Value of the rateable plant and buildings if any.

The purpose is to ascertain the rent at which the property might reasonably be expected to let from year to year having regard to the rating hypothesis and the definition of Net Annual Value (General Rate Act, 1967, Section 19 (3)).

The factors affecting royalty values should be considered to enable comparisons to be made between different mineral properties in the same locality.

Any royalty information should be considered with the following factors in mind:

(1) Any royalty evidence should be analysed to ensure that it is up to date and to check whether a premium was paid.

(2) Up to 1963 royalties were fixed in the knowledge of industrial derating which was finally abolished in England and Wales in 1963.

(3) There is a tendency for minerals to be let on a tender basis. It is suggested that royalties fixed as a result of a tender are suspect from the rating point of view as the successful tenderer may have overbid his nearest rival by a large amount and if negotiations had been carried on with the normal " higgling of the market " such a high figure might not have been paid.

Following the Central Valuation Committee's recommendation assessments are revised annually and the Inland Revenue Valuation Office sent out statutory forms of return requiring information on the preceding year's output. Assessments are dealt with by the Mineral Valuer who revises the assessments on the up-to-date output and reflects any alterations to the rateable plant and buildings.

Once the hypothetical royalty has been agreed at the time of a Revaluation this is applied for the period of the Valuation List subject to any variations for changes in working conditions, etc., which may give rise to arguments for an upward or downward adjustment.

The royalty basis on any new hereditaments assessed for the first time within the normal quinquennial period of the Valuation List must conform to the statutory tone of the List procedure by virtue of Section 20 of the General Rate Act, 1967.

In some small undertakings there is no rateable plant and the deposit may be worked by portable machinery. Where, however, there is a permanent plant the effective capital value of the rateable parts has to be ascertained and to this a suitable percentage applied to arrive at the Net Annual Value on the contractors basis. An addition is made for the rental value of any buildings plus the rental value of the plant site.

There are two usual methods of dealing with rateable plant:

(1) The plant may not be used to full capacity and an optimum capital value based on total capacity is agreed and suitably adjusted each year to reflect any partial use having regard to the output.

(2) A static figure of effective capital value is agreed which remains a constant addition on any annual review of the assessment subject to any alterations and additions.

*Example:* The following example indicates the method outlined in (1) above.

A gravel pit has a processing plant capable of dealing with 130,000 tonnes per annum and the optimum capital value of the rateable plant is £20,000.

The previous year's output was 65,000 tonnes and it is assumed that a fair royalty is 15p per tonne.

Optimum value of plant £20,000 @ 5% = £1,000.

The plant can deal with 130,000 tonnes, but in the year under consideration only dealt with 65,000 tonnes. The value is, therefore, discounted to give an effective Net Annual Value as follows:—

Plant Element

$$\frac{65,000 \text{ tonnes}}{130,000 \text{ tonnes}} \times £1,000 \quad \ldots \quad \ldots \quad = \qquad £500$$

Buildings ... ... ... ... ... say     £100

Gravel output:

65,000 tonnes @ 15p ... ... ... ...     £9,750

Total N.A.V.     ...     £10,350

Section 35 (2) (b) of the General Rate Act, 1967, empowers the Secretary of State for the Environment to prescribe the method of determining the rateable value of any hereditament which consists of or includes a mine or quarry.

*Mines & Quarries (Valuation) Order, 1971.*

This Order, made under Section 35 of the General Rate Act, 1967, came into force on 31st March, 1971.

Prior to this the assessment of land occupied for the winning and working of minerals had been based following decisions of the Courts on the assumption that royalty payments made by occupiers of land to mineral owners were wholly in the nature of a rent. In other words the Net Annual Value and Rateable Value were identical.

The above Order now prescribes that the assessments on such land shall be made on the assumption that only one half of the royalty is to be treated as rent with consequent adjustments to Rateable Values.

The Order relates to that part of mineral hereditaments used for the winning and working, grading, washing, grinding and crushing of minerals.

The Order has only recently come into force and opinions vary on its interpretation. The unimproved value of a plant site is clearly entitled to relief, although for simplicity this has been ignored as a separate factor in the following example where it has been assumed that such site value is included in the hypothetical royalty:

|  |  | N.A.V. | R.V. |
|---|---|---|---|
| Plant element $\frac{65,000 \text{ tonnes}}{130,000 \text{ tonnes}} \times £1,000$ |  | £500 | £500 |
| Buildings ... ... | say | £100 | £100 |
|  | C/Fwd. | £600 | £600 |

|  | B/Fwd. | £600 | £600 |
|---|---|---|---|
| Gravel output: |  |  |  |
| 65,000 tonnes @ 15p ... | £9,750 | £9,750 |  |
| Less 50% to give effect to the Mines & Quarries (Valuation) Order, 1971 ... ... | £4,875 |  |  |
|  | £4,875 |  | £4,875 |
| Total N.A.V. ... |  | £10,350 | R.V. £5,475 |

The Order makes special provision for modification of the assessments of tin, lead and copper mines and of mine properties and opencast workings of the National Coal Board.

### 7. COMPENSATION FOR COMPULSORY PURCHASE AND PLANNING RESTRICTIONS

*Compulsory Purchase*

The general provisions relating to compulsory purchase and the assessment of compensation are, as for other types of property, to be found in the Land Compensation Act, 1961, and the Compulsory Purchase Act, 1965.

It should be noted that the " Mining Code " contained in Sections 77–85 of the Railway Clauses Consolidation Act, 1845, may be applied to a particular acquisition by the Compulsory Purchase Order. Briefly, this code enables an Acquiring Authority to buy land without the inclusion of the minerals but if the owner subsequently gives notice of his intention to work, the Acquiring Authority have the option to pay compensation to secure the sterilisation of the minerals.

Broadly speaking, the basis of compensation under the 1961 Act is current market value having regard to the various planning assumptions described in Chapter 21.

Minerals call for no special comment except that mineral-bearing land is generally situated in white areas (that is to say, without notation) or in the Green Belt in Development Plans. Mineral working, however, is not necessarily an inappropriate use in the Green Belt, or, for that matter, in areas of high landscape value. In such cases the certificate procedure in Part III of the Land Compensation Act, 1961, may be useful. The existence of a planning permission for mineral working does not necessarily preclude a claim in respect of some other form of surface use provided it can be shown that such potential is reflected in the open market value.

Consideration should also be given to the market value of restored land following mineral extraction for other surface uses such as building or playing fields. In suitable cases a claim could be based on the value of land for mineral extraction together with the value for surface development of the same area following restoration. Much will depend upon the speed at which restoration is possible following the extraction of the mineral and the period potential purchasers would allow for deferment for consolidation of the restored land before development could take place. A factor to consider would be the additional costs of construction likely to result from building on filled land although in some cases this could be offset by the revenue to be received from tipping charges while the excavations are being filled. Such revenue can itself be substantial in some areas in view of the growing scarcity of suitable sites available for the reception of filling material.

There is an increasing use of water areas for recreational purposes, e.g., sailing, angling, etc., and consideration should be given to the potential value of such areas when formulating a claim in cases where lakes are likely to result from the extraction of the mineral.

Minerals are the subject of special regulations under the Town & Country Planning Act, 1962, which adapt and modify certain provisions of that Act relating to compensation for planning restrictions or for the revocation or modification of planning permissions.

*Planning restrictions*

Claims for compensation arising as a result of planning refusals or conditions attached to planning permissions are governed by Part VI of the Town & Country Planning Act, 1962.

No claim can arise unless the land concerned has an unexpended balance of established development value. The general principles underlying such claims as described in Chapter 19 apply to minerals, the basis of compensation being the difference between the value of the land with and without the planning permission subject to the ceiling of the unexpended balance of established development value attaching to the land. A suitable reduction must be made from the unexpended balance to allow for the value of new development which is valued on the basis of the Sixth Schedule to the 1962 Act having regard to the current values at the date of the planning decision.

No compensation is payable in respect of conditions attached to a planning permission for mineral working unless the condition in effect prohibits the working of a specified part of the land (Section 101 (6) of the 1962 Act), For example, conditions may be imposed restricting the working of minerals within a specified distance from neighbouring development or from a highway boundary or limiting the depth of excavation.

The provisions of Section 102 of the 1962 Act apply so that in the event of alternative permission being available for residential commercial or industrial purposes no compensation is payable.

Regulation 9 of the Town & Country Planning (Minerals) Regulations, 1971, provides for the creation of separate claim holdings where since 1 July, 1948, the freehold in the minerals has been severed from the freehold interest in the remainder of the land. The claim holding or the unexpended balance of established development value is apportioned between the minerals and the remainder of the land whereupon the minerals and the remainder of the land are treated as separate claim areas.

### Revocation or Modification of Planning Permission

The position with minerals is similar to other forms of property in that full compensation is payable. Not only can compensation be claimed in respect of the full market value of the land but, in addition, compensation is payable for abortive expenditure and other loss or damage. It should, however, be noted that Regulation 5 of the Town & Country Planning (Minerals) Regulations, 1971, enables the Lands Tribunal to sever a claim in respect of buildings, plant or machinery from the remainder of the claim.

The above Regulation makes it the duty of the claimant to show that the buildings, plant and machinery cannot be used except at the loss claimed. As an example, if a revocation considered by itself would virtually render the buildings, plant and machinery associated with the mineral land valueless and subsequently the claimant is able to acquire further mineral land which can be processed in the existing plant, then this fact will be taken into account in assessing the loss or damage resulting from the revocation. This provision could well reduce or extinguish the claim in respect of the buildings, plant and machinery.

### Land Commission Act, 1967.

During the currency of this Act a landowner of mineral bearing land became liable to Betterment Levy under Case A or B in the event of a sale or lease in the same way as other transactions in property.

Mineral undertakers were accorded certain important exemptions in respect of the payment of Betterment Levy under Case C, and these were set out in the various Minerals Regulations made under the Act.

### 8. CAPITAL ALLOWANCES ACT, 1968

Section 60 of this Act (which replaces Section 37 of the Finance Act, 1963) provides that tax allowances will be granted to mineral operators in respect of sums laid out on the purchase of mineral bearing land or rights to work minerals. These depletion allowances will be given in respect of minerals worked after 4 April, 1963, whether the minerals were acquired before that date or in the future.

The total allowance that can be obtained will not exceed the capital expenditure incurred less any residual value that the land may have after the mineral has been extracted. In the case of minerals which were acquired and partially worked before April 1963 it has to be assumed that allowances had been made in the earlier years of working.

The allowances are calculated as a fraction of the royalty value of the output in the basis year but it should be noted that the royalty value is the amount which might reasonably have been expected to be charged as royalty if at the date of acquiring the land the operator had taken a lease instead of purchasing outright. The fraction of the royalty value which is allowed depends upon the period that has elapsed from the first working to the end of the basis year in question. For the first ten years working the scale is one-half of the notional royalty value—for the second ten years one-quarter—and thereafter one-tenth.

At the date when work ceases a balancing allowance or a balancing charge will be made. This will be arrived at by comparing the total of the allowances actually given with the original cost of the land less any residual value it may have at the date when work ceases. If part of the original area has been sold the amount realised will be deducted from the original cost. In calculating the residual value it is to be assumed that the operator will already have carried out any restoration work which is obligatory or which he might reasonably be expected to carry out in any event.

It is important to note that the depletion allowance can only be claimed by the person who has actually incurred the expenditure and who works the minerals concerned.

*Minerals Workings Act*, 1951.—This Act set up a fund to secure the restoration of land following open-cast iron-ore working. Operators are required to pay contributions to the fund and in turn are entitled to receive payments, when carrying out restoration under the terms of a planning permission.

*Finance Act*, 1970.

Prior to 5th April, 1970, payments made by the occupiers of land to a mineral owner in the form of a royalty were regarded wholly as income in the hands of the mineral owner and accordingly subject to tax.

The Finance Act, 1970, altered this situation and provided that only one half of the payments should be treated as income, the balance being treated as a receipt of capital. The capital element is subject to the rules regarding capital gains.

# Chapter 29

## VALUATIONS FOR BETTERMENT LEVY[1]

### 1. INTRODUCTION

BETTERMENT LEVY was introduced by the Land Commission Act, 1967. The Act established the Land Commission which was given two primary functions. That relating to land-dealing has already been referred to in Chapter 10. The other function is for the assessment and collection of betterment levy and it is the valuation implications of this levy function that will be considered in this Chapter.

Betterment has attracted the attention of legislators for many years. Its definition is not simple, and can even prove misleading when actual schemes for applying a charge on betterment are looked at in detail. At its simplest, betterment represents the enhancement in value of a person's land by the activities of a public body. Examples are the higher values that result from the building of a motorway whereby land becomes more accessible, or from the provision of services to an area so that development becomes possible.

Even at this relatively simple level acute problems arise both in identifying the area which benefits from the body's activities and in separating the value effects of such activities from other events that are taking place simultaneously—particularly in a highly developed country such as Britain. Evidence of these problems can be seen in the abortive efforts to collect payment for betterment created by certain major road improvements in London at the beginning of this century.

The introduction of a comprehensive planning system in 1947 served to attract greater attention to betterment while increasing the problems. The control of planning has become equated with the other activities of a public body and out of this has grown the view that increases in the value of land that flow from a favourable planning decision are a further form of betterment. Whether this view be correct or not, all schemes for the recoupment of betterment since 1947 have been closely related to planning control.

---

[1] For a comprehensive study of betterment levy the reader is advised to refer to "Betterment Levy and the Land Commission", by Harris and Nutley, published by Butterworths under the auspices of the Royal Institution of Chartered Surveyors.

For a less comprehensive work which concentrates on the valuation aspects of levy calculations the reader is advised to refer to "Calculations for Betterment Levy", by T. A. Johnson, B.Sc., A.R.I.C.S., published by the College of Estate Management.

The schemes established by Acts prior to the Land Commission Act, 1967, have been outlined in Chapter 10. This Chapter will be devoted to the Land Commission Act scheme which operated in respect of various transactions taking place between the 6 April,1967, and the 22 September, 1970, inclusive.

*General Scheme of Betterment Levy*

The provisions for the assessment of levy are contained within Part III of the Act in conjunction with several Schedules to the Act.

The opening words of Part III state that betterment levy shall be charged on the development value of land when it is realised. This immediately establishes the twin essentials for betterment levy to become payable, namely, that development value must exist, and that such development value must actually be realised.

The ways in which development value in land can be realised are set out in the Act in groups of related events known as Cases. There are 6 in all, these being:

*Case* A   The *Sale* of either a freehold interest, or a leasehold interest originally granted for not less than 7 years. Sales of leases originally granted for less than 7 years may be treated as a Case A event at the discretion of the purchaser.

*Case* B   The *Grant of a Lease* of not less than 7 years. Where leases are granted for less than 7 years, they may be treated as a Case B event at the discretion of the lessee.

*Case* C   The *Development* of land when there is started a project of material development. The meaning of a project of material development is explained below, but it broadly relates to development schemes which realise the development value in land.

*Case* D   The receipt of *Compensation* for adverse planning decisions paid under Part VII of the Town and Country Planning Act, 1962, being compensation for revocation or modification of planning permissions; compensation arising out of an order discontinuing the existing use of land; and compensation for the refusal of development contained in the General Development Order, 1963, which has become the subject of an Article 4 Direction. The provisions relating to the assessment of such compensation are set out in Chapter 18.

*Case* E   Any *Payment* made for the grant of an easement, or the release of an easement or restrictive right.

*Case* F   This Case covers various types of transactions not included in the other Cases, and comprises:—
   (*a*)   any *Payment* in relation to the grant of a wayleave;
   (*b*)   the receipt of *Compensation* for injurious affection where no land is taken; and

(c)  the *Renewal of* or *Variation in* the terms of an existing lease.

Where any transactions take place on or after the 6 April, 1967 ("the first appointed day") and before the 23 July, 1970, falling within the scope of the above Cases then there is a prima facie liability to pay betterment levy. If they do not fall within their scope then no betterment levy liability can arise.

The method of determining the levy liability depends upon into which Case the transaction falls since there are separate valuation rules for each Case. Before considering these it is appropriate to outline the process by which levy becomes payable.

*Procedure for Payment of Levy*

The essential pre-requisite for any liability to levy is that development value must be realised within the scope of the 6 Cases. Once such an event arises, a "chargeable event", the Land Commission must be notified of its occurrence and this sets in motion the levy collection machinery. In each of the Cases other than Case C there are two parties involved. One party will be liable to pay any levy due: the other party will have the duty of notifying the Commission (except in Case E).

Thus: in Case A, the purchaser notifies the Land Commission and the vendor will be liable to pay the levy.

in Case B,  the lessee notifies, the lessor pays.

in Case D,  the compensating authority notifies, the person receiving the compensation pays.

in Case E,  the person giving the consideration notifies, the person receiving pays. (Unlike the other Cases, notification is at the discretion of the person giving the consideration).

in Case F,  the authority granting the wayleave or paying the compensation, or the landlord, as appropriate to each situation, notifies, the grantor of the wayleave, the person receiving the compensation, or the tenant, pays.

In Case C special rules apply. The developing owner, if there is one, notifies, the owners of assessable interests pay. Unlike the other Cases, more than one person may be liable for payment of levy in Case C. An assessable interest is one where:—

(a)  The interest exists at the time development commences, and

(b)  The interest is either freehold, or leasehold of more than a year or year to year, and

(c)  The interest is a reversionary interest with not more than 98 years to reversion. Further qualifications to the determination of what is an assessable interest can be found in Section 32.

When notified, the Commission determines whether development value has been realised.  If so, the levy payer is issued with a notice of assessment to which he may object, disputes being determined by the Lands Tribunal.  In practice, the assessment of any development value is made by the District Valuer, acting on behalf of the Commission, and levy payers commonly agree the development value before any formal notice of assessment is issued.

## Exemptions from Payment of Levy

Certain bodies are exempt from liability to pay levy including public bodies such as central government bodies and local authorities; statutory undertakers in respect of their operational land; charities in respect of land which forms part of their permanent endowment.

In certain other instances relief from levy is granted. Under the Finance Act, 1969, where the levy payer under any of the Cases is liable to pay levy in a financial year which does not exceed in aggregate £1,500 having regard to the total liabilities he has incurred in that year, then the levy liability is reduced to nil.

Another relief from levy under Case C is given by the Land Commission Act in the case of certain developments where the interest was owned by the developing owner before the 23 September, 1965.

## Development Value

Once an assessment has been agreed or confirmed then levy is payable at a rate prescribed by Order, currently fixed at 40 per cent of the development value realised.  Development value is not defined in the Act.  Instead, there is provided an extensive set of valuation rules for each Case whereby a scheme of calculations is set out.  If these schemes of calculations produce a positive end sum, then such a sum will be regarded as "development value realised". Development value is therefore a matter of valuations rather than straightforward legal definition.

The broad theory underlying the calculations is that development value is any value above that attributable to the property in its current state.  The value in its current state is known as its *current use value*.  Such a theory corresponds closely with the determination of development value under the Town and Country Planning Act, 1947 (see Chapter 10).

## Calculation of Development Value

The procedure for determining development value is dependent on into which Case the chargeable event falls since the schemes of calculations vary with each Case.

Before considering the valuation approach to the determination of development value within each of the Cases it is useful to set out some of the factors which are common to all Cases and thereby avoid needless repetition.

## 2. COMMON VALUATION FACTORS

### (a) Consideration Received

In all Cases other than Case C the leviable act will normally be marked by money being paid by one party to the other. This consideration forms the starting point for all calculations. It is, however, subject to certain modifications.

Firstly, Schedule 6, Para. 1 of the Act provides that the value of any matter associated with the disposal which was taken into account in determining the consideration shall be added to the consideration passing. For example, if land is sold where the vendor reserves a right of way over the land, or requires the purchaser to pay his costs of sale; or where the purchaser gives the vendor some other property in addition to money; then in all these situations it is clear that the price actually agreed for the land will reflect these matters. It is necessary therefore to determine their value and add them to the consideration.

Secondly, where any consideration includes payment for a chattel then such payment shall be deducted from the consideration. "Chattel" includes not only such things as furnishings, or plant and machinery, but also goodwill.[2]

Thirdly, Schedule 6, Para. 19, as amended by the Finance Act, 1969, allows a deduction to be made from the consideration for fees and expenses incurred in relation to the disposition such as agents' and solicitors' fees, advertising costs, and stamp duty, together with any valuation fees incurred in determining the levy liability.

### (b) Current Use Value

This value lies at the heart of all levy calculations. It is the value of the interest at the "relevant date" for the Case (the date at which the transaction giving rise to levy arose) on the assumption that planning permission would not at any time be given for material development but would be given for any other development.

"Material development" is any development which is not: (a) development included in Schedule 3 of the Town and Country Planning Act, 1962, subject only to the limitation of Section 1 (4) of the Town and Country Planning Act, 1963, which limits the application to the original building; (b) any development included in the General Development Order, 1963, and (c) development contained in Regulations issued by the Minister.

### (c) Expenditure on Improvements and Ancillary Rights

Schedule 4, Part V of the Act, provides that any expenditure on improvements or ancillary rights—allowable expenditure—may be brought into account in determining the development value.

---

[2] See Land Commission Practice Note No. 11.

The expenditure is categorised in Para. 42 and is broadly of two types:—

(i) any expenditure on works since the 1 July, 1948, which increased the market value or consideration for the disposition;

(ii) any expenditure on buying easements or restrictive covenants, or paying for their release, which occurred between 1 July, 1948, and 29 December, 1965, or on or after the 6 April, 1967 and which were notified under Case E.

Typical examples of (i) include the running in of services to land, improvements to the structure, and demolition and clearance in preparation for development.

The expenditure must have been incurred by the person liable for the levy, and does not include expenditure for which compensation or payment from another source, such as a government grant, has been given.

The actual expenditure is subject to an adjustment. Where the expenditure results in a higher current use value at the time of disposition than would otherwise exist, such an increase in value is deducted from the expenditure; contrariwise, any decrease is added to the expenditure. Exceptions to this rule will be noted later.

### (d) Consideration for Last Relevant Disposition

As an alternative to the general principle noted above that development value is that value lying above current use value, the Act provides that the levy payer may have the levy assessed on the difference between the price paid by him when purchasing his interest and the consideration received at sale (similar to the approach adopted for capital gains tax). The provisions relating to this alternative are found in Schedule 5 and will be referred to as the Schedule 5 Base Value (= consideration for the last relevant disposition).

The Schedule 5 Base Value applies where the levy payer purchased his interest in the "antecedent period"—1 July, 1948, to 22 September, 1965—or on or after the 6 April, 1967. Where the purchase occurred on or after the 6 April, 1967, the price paid has to be adjusted for changes in current use value between the times of the purchase and the subsequent chargeable event, any increases being added to the price and decreases being deducted. The reason for this is to avoid double taxation since changes in current use value are the subject of capital gains tax.

*Example 1.*—A freehold interest was purchased in 1968 for £10,000 when the current use value was £2,000. The interest was sold in July 1970 for £14,000 when the current use value was £2,500.

Hence *Schedule 5 Base Value:*

| | | | | | |
|---|---|---|---|---|---|
| Price paid in 1968... | ... | ... | ... | ... | £10,000 |
| Current Use Value 1970... | ... | ... £2,500 | | | |
| „ „ „ 1968... | ... | ... £2,000 | | | |
| ∴ Increase in CUV | ... | ... | ... £500 | | |
| *Add* Increase ... | ... | ... | ... | ... | 500 |
| ∴ Schedule 5 Base Value | ... | ... | £10,500 | | |

One further point to note is that where the Schedule 5 Base Value arose in the antecedent period, the adjustments to Expenditure on Improvements and Ancillary Rights for the effects on current use value (see page 454) do not apply.

The Finance Act, 1969, introduced two exceptions to the rule that purchases in the interim period 23 September, 1965, to 5 April, 1967, inclusive cannot rank as Schedule 5 Base Values. These are, first, where the purchase was for the purpose of erecting a single dwelling-house and, second, where the purchase was for a consideration of £2,500 or less.

(*e*)  Related Tenancies

In some instances the levy payer may have enlarged his interest by acquiring an inferior interest to which he held the reversion, the inferior interest then merging with the reversion. The cost of acquiring such inferior interests, known as "related tenancies", is allowable as an expenditure in computing the development value. However, the related tenancies must have been acquired either within the antecedent period, or on or after the 6 April, 1967, and notified to the Commission.

Where the acquisition was on or after the 6 April, 1967, the price paid has to be adjusted by deducting from it the current use value of that interest at the time of acquisition. In this way only the development value that was "purchased" is set against the subsequent chargeable event.

(*f*)  *Credits Carried Forward*

Under the original betterment levy scheme, where a negative development value arose from the calculations it was treated as being nil. However, in certain circumstances negative development values were to be carried forward and set off against subsequent chargeable events. These allowances were known as credits carried forward. Since betterment levy is not payable on events taking place after the 22 September, 1970, these credits are no longer of importance.

The foregoing general factors apply to the calculation of the development value for all of the Cases. The specific calculations for each Case now follow. It will be seen that a pattern of calculations applies to each Case.

### 3. CASE A

This Case applies to the sale of a freehold interest or the sale of a leasehold interest with an original term of 7 years or more. Sales of leases of shorter original terms than this only constitute a chargeable event if the purchaser chooses to notify the Land Commission.

The calculations have the following sequence:

1 Market Value
2 Current Use Value
3 Severance Depreciation
4 Base Value
5 Related Tenancies
6 Improvements and Ancillary Rights
7 Net Development Value

These can now be considered in turn.

1. *Market Value.* This is not a valuation but is the consideration passing for the sale (see Consideration Received on page 453). Thus if the consideration is greater or less than market value it will still constitute Market Value for the purposes of Case A.[3]

There may be deducted from the consideration any sums expended on achieving the sale together with valuation fees paid to a valuer for agreeing the levy valuations.

*Example 2.*—Green Produce Ltd. sold the freehold interest in 1·20 hectares of land in December 1969 to a developer for £45,000. The developer proposes to carry out residential development. The site forms part of a smallholding of 32 ha which the company has used for many years as a market garden. The agents' fees for effecting the sale were £700 and the solicitors' fees £250. In the conveyance the company retained a right of way from the main road to the land they are retaining at the rear of the site.

| | | |
|---|---:|---:|
| *Market Value* Consideration Received ... ... | | £45,000 |
| *Add* for value to company of right of way retained, say ... ... ... ... | | 1,000 |
| | | £46,000 |
| *Less* Fees incurred in disposal: | | |
| Agents ... ... ... ... | £700 | |
| Solicitors ... ... ... ... | 250 | |
| Levy Valuation Fees (estimated) ... | 150 | |
| | | 1,100 |
| ∴ Market Value ... ... ... | | £44,900 |

---

[3] See *Pennington v. Land Commission,* 1970, J.P.L., 399.

2. *Current Use Value.* The rules for assessing this value were described above. (See page 453.) It is essential to consider the full range of development for which it is deemed planning permission would be granted since this may on occasion have a substantial value. For example, the tolerances of Schedule 3, ignoring the restriction on floor area tolerance of the Town and Country Planning Act, 1963, may well give a substantial value, particularly in locations where values of floor areas are high relative to building costs. Any outstanding planning permissions for material development which have not been acted upon must of course be ignored.

> *Example 3.*—Assume the facts given in Example 2. The value of the land for horticultural use is £1,250/ha.
>
> *Current Use Value* 1·20 ha @ £1,250/ha   =   £1,500

Where the land has an unexpended balance of established development value the amount of such balance will normally be added to the current use value since the assumption that permission for material development would never be granted generally coincides with the grounds for payment of compensation for refusal of "new development".

3. *Severance Depreciation.* Where the sale results in the current use value of any land held with the land sold being depreciated in value due to the sale, such depreciation is to be assessed for inclusion in the calculation. The reason for this is that on any subsequent realisation of development value on the land retained, the development value will be increased by the amount of the depreciation. Thus double levy is avoided.

> *Example 4.*—Assume the facts given in the previous examples. The land retained by Green Produce Ltd. will be depreciated by the sale since it is a less viable unit and also because the future proximity of residential development has an adverse affect.
>
> *Severance Depreciation:*
>
> | | |
> |---|---:|
> | Value of land retained before sale—30·80 ha @ £1,250/ha   ...   ...   ...   ...   ... | £38,500 |
> | *Less* Value of land retained after sale—30·80 ha @ £1,000/ha   ...   ...   ...   ...   ... | 30,800 |
> | ∴ Severance Depreciation   ...   ... | £7,700 |

4. *Base Value.* There are two alternative Base Values that need to be determined.

> (a) *Schedule 4 Base Value.* In this case the Base Value involves a simple calculation. The current use value, as determined, is increased by $\frac{1}{10}$ and to this is added any severance depreciation. The aggregate figure represents the Base Value. As an

exception to this approach, the Finance Act, 1969, provides that, in the case of the sale of a dwelling-house which is the vendor's sole or main residence and which does not exceed $\frac{1}{4}$ acre in extent where the consideration is £10,000 or less, the current use value is to be increased by $\frac{1}{5}$. There are provisions for marginal relief where the sale exceeds £10,000.

*Example 5.*—Assume the facts given in Examples 2, 3, and 4.

| | | | | | |
|---|---|---|---|---|---|
| Current Use Value | ... | ... | ... | ... | £1,500 |
| *Add* $\frac{1}{10}$ | ... | ... | ... | ... | 150 |
| Severance Depreciation | | ... | ... | ... | 7,700 |
| ∴ Schedule 4 Base Value | | | ... | ... | £9,350 |

(*b*)  *Schedule 5 Base Value.* The basis of determining the Schedule 5 Base Value was explained above (see page 454).

5.  *Related Tenancies.* Any sum in respect of payment for Related Tenancies is added to the Base Value. The basis of determining such payments was explained above (see page 455).

6.  *Improvements and Ancillary Rights.* The basis for determining any expenditure allowed in respect of works or ancillary rights was explained above (see page 453).

7.  *Net Development Value.* This value, on which the levy will be assessed, is found by deducting from the Market Value the aggregate of the Base Value, sums for Related Tenancies, and any Expenditure on Improvements and Ancillary Rights.

*Example 6.*—(The full levy calculations in respect of the facts adopted in the previous examples will be used). Hence:
Green Produce Ltd. sold the freehold interest in 1·20 ha of land in December 1969 to a developer for £45,000. The developer proposes to carry out residential development. The site forms part of a smallholding of 32 ha which the company has used for several years as a market garden since purchasing the land for £12,000 in 1950. The agents' fees for effecting the sale were £700 and the solicitors' fees £250. In the conveyance the company retained a right of way from the main road to the land it is retaining at the rear of the site. Prior to the sale the company demolished a glass-house on the land at a cost of £2,000.

Assess the betterment levy payable under Case A.

1  *Market Value:*

| | | |
|---|---|---|
| Consideration Received ... | ... | £45,000 |
| *Add* for value of right of way | ... | 1,000 |
| C/Fwd. | | £46,000 |

|  | | | | |
|---|---|---|---|---|
| B/Fwd. ... | | £46,000 | |
| *Less* Expenses of Sale: | | | |
| Estate Agents ... | £700 | | |
| Solicitors ... ... | 250 | | |
| Levy Valuation Fees | 150 | | |
| | —— | 1,100 | |
| | | | £44,900 |

2 *Current Use Value:*
1·20 ha @ £1,250/ha ... ... £1,500

3 *Severance Depreciation:*

| | | |
|---|---|---|
| Value of 30·80 ha before sale @ | | |
| £1,250/ha ... ... ... | £38,500 |
| *Less* Value of 30·80 ha after sale | | |
| @ £1,000/ha ... ... | 30,800 |
| ∴ Severance Depreciation... | £7,700 |

4 *Base Value:*

(*a*) *Schedule* 4. Current Use

| | | |
|---|---|---|
| Value ... | £1,500 |
| *Add* ⅒ ... ... | 150 |
| | 1,650 |
| *Add* Severance Depre- | |
| ciation ... ... | 7,700 |
| ∴ Sch. 4 Base Value... | £9,350 |

(*b*) *Schedule* 5. Whole land
purchased in
antecedent period for
£12,000, i.e., say £375/
ha
∴ 1·20 ha @ £375/ha = £450

∴ Adopt Schedule 4 Base Value    £9,350

5 *Related Tenancies:*
None in this case.

6 *Improvements and Ancillary Rights.*
Glass-houses demolished before
sale. Presumably value of land
cleared of buildings greater than
before. Hence market value increased, hence expenditure allowance.

| | | | |
|---|---|---|---|
| ∴ Cost of demolition ... | £2,000 | | |
| C/Fwd. ... | £2,000 | £9,350 | £44,900 |

| | | | | |
|---|---|---|---|---|
| B/Fwd. ... | | £2,000 | £9,350 | £44,900 |
| Current Use Value without demolition of glasshouses, say 1·20 ha @ £2,000/ha ... ... ... | £2,400 | | | |
| Current Use Value after demolition (as above) ... | £1,500 | | | |
| ∴ Decrease in Current Use Value ... ... ... | £900 | | | |
| Add Decrease ... ... | | 900 | 2,900 | 12,250 |

7 *Net Development Value* ...                                    £32,650

Betterment Levy is therefore payable
at 40% of £32,650 ...     ...     ...         =     £13,060

## 4. CASE B

This case applies to the grant of a lease of 7 years or more. The Levy calculations have the following sequence:

1   Consideration for the Disposition
2   Current Use Value
3   Reversionary Value
4   Proportion
5   Current Use Value Realised by Disposition
6   Severance Depreciation
7   Base Value Realised by Disposition
8   Related Tenancies
9   Improvements and Ancillary Rights
10  Net Development Value by Disposition.

These can now be considered in turn.

1. *Consideration for the Disposition.* The calculation of the Consideration involves a valuation since the grant of a lease gives rise to the payment of an annual rent whereas levy is assessed on a capital sum. Hence the calculation required is to determine the capital value of the rent. The Act's provisions for capitalising the rent have led to problems of interpretation but it seems to be generally agreed that the rent should be capitalised using a dual rate years' purchase even where the rent is payable to a freeholder who is also entitled to the reversion, contrary to normal valuation practice. A further departure from normal practice is the Act's requirement that where the grantor is himself a lessee, the capital value of the rent payable under the grantor's lease (for the term of the sub-lease the subject of the Case B event) shall be deducted from the capital value of the rent receivable—instead of the normal valuation of the profit rent.

In addition to the capital value of the rent, any premiums payable are brought into account together with any other items of Consideration (see Consideration Received on page 453). Expenses of sale and fees are deductible as for "Market Value" under Case A (see page 456).

*Example 7.*—Hippy Products Ltd owns the freehold site of a factory recently destroyed by fire. The site was let in May 1970 to the Optimum Property Co. Ltd. at a ground rent of £5,000 p.a, plus a premium of £20,000 for the erection of shops with offices above. The lease is for 60 years and provides for rent reviews at 10–year intervals. The agents' fees were £1,000 and the Solicitors' £500.

*Consideration for the Disposition:*

| | | | | |
|---|---|---|---|---|
| Rent receivable ... ... ... | | | | £5,000 p.a. |
| Y.P. 60 years @ 7½ and 2½% ... | | | ... | 11·49 |
| (tax @ 38·75%) | | | | |
| | | | | £57,450 |
| *Add* premium ... ... ... ... | | | | 20,000 |
| | | | | £77,450 |

*Less* Expenses of sale:

| | | | |
|---|---|---|---|
| Agents ... ... ... | £1,000 | | |
| Solicitors ... ... ... | £500 | | |
| Levy Valuation Fees | | | |
| (estimated) ... ... | £500 | | |
| | | £2,000 | |
| | | | £75,450 |

*Example 8.*—Assume the same facts as in Example 7 but further assume that Hippy Products Ltd. hold the site under a lease expiring in 80 years' time at a rent of £500 p.a. without provision for rent review.

*Consideration for the Disposition.*

| | | | |
|---|---|---|---|
| Rent receivable ... ... | £5,000 p.a. | | |
| Y.P. 60 years @ 8 and 2½% | | | |
| (tax @ 38·75%) ... ... | 10·87 | | |
| | | £54,350 | |
| *Less* Rent payable ... ... | £500 p.a. | | |
| Y.P. 60 years at 10 and 2½% | | | |
| (tax @ 38·75%) ... ... | 8·93 | | |
| | | £4,465 | |
| | | £49,885 | |
| *Add* Premium ⎱ as in last Example | | | |
| *Less* Expenses ⎰ = net addition | | | |
| of Sale ⎰ of ... ... ... | £18,000 | | |
| | | | £67,885 |

N.B. The difference in yields adopted in capitalising the two rents is to reflect the different qualities of each. The £500 p.a. is fixed for a long term and therefore attracts a higher yield than the £5,000 p.a. which has regular reviews.

2. *Current Use Value.* The current use value is assessed for the whole interest out of which the lease is granted but immediately before the grant of the lease. The determination of current use value has been described above (see page 457).

*Example 9.*—Assume the facts in the Example 7. The current use value is of a site with the assumption that planning permission would be granted for the rebuilding of the factory in accordance with Para. 1 of Schedule 3 of the Town and Country Planning Act, 1962.

*Hence:* Industrial Site Value, say ... ... £25,000

The valuation of the site has been made by direct comparison.

3. *Reversionary Value.* The Act requires the value of the reversion to the lease to be determined assuming the land to be in the same state as it was before the grant of the lease.

Thus the valuation is made on the assumption that the current values and situation would obtain on reversion disregarding any proposals of the lessee, including any current development schemes.

*Example 10.*—Assume the facts in the Example 7. The current development value of the site for development with shops and offices is £5,000 p.a. plus the annual equivalent of the premium of £20,000, say £1,600 p.a. Hence current development value is £6,600 p.a.

∴ Reversion after 60 years to full rental value    £6,600 p.a.
     Y.P. in perp @ 8% ... ... ...    12·5

                              £82,500
× P.V. £1 in 60 years @ 8% ... ...    0·01

                                £825

*Example 11.*—Assume the facts in the Example 8. In this case the reversion is to an unexpired term of 20 years.

Reversion after 60 years to profit rent of    £6,100 p.a.
     Y.P. 20 years @ 9 and 2½% (tax @
       38·75%) ... ... ...    6·50
     P.V. £1 in 60 years @ 9% ...    0·01

                                0·065

                                £400

4. *Proportion.* This calculation is required for application to subsequent figures. The proportion is determined by the following formula:

$$\frac{\text{Consideration for Disposition}}{\text{Consideration for Disposition} + \text{Reversionary Value}}$$

This "proportion" may be said to represent the proportion of the total development value being realised by the grant of the lease. As will be seen the same proportion of the current use value and other items is set against the consideration for the disposition illustrating the logic of the calculations.

*Example 12.*—Assume the facts in Examples 7 and 10 Hence,

$$\text{Proportion} = \frac{77,450}{77,450 + 825} = 99\%$$

5. *Current Use Value Realised by Disposition.* This is simply determined by applying the Proportion to the Current Use Value, both previously calculated.

6. *Severance Depreciation.* The depreciation due to the grant of the lease in the current use value of other land held with the land the subject of the lease is calculated in a similar manner to that described in the calculations for Case A (see page 457).

7. *Base Value Realised by Disposition.* The calculation of the Base Value under either Schedules 4 or 5 is basically the same as described in the calculations for Case A (see page 457). The main differences are that, for Schedule 4 Base Value, the $\frac{1}{10}$ increment applies to the Current Use Value Realised by the Disposition; the Schedule 5 Base Value once determined, and adjusted if necessary for changes in current use value, is then adjusted by applying the Proportion as previously calculated. The higher of the two Base Values under the respective Schedules is then adopted as the Base Value Realised by the Disposition.

8. *Related Tenancies.* Any sum in respect of payment for Related Tenancies is added to the Base Value Realised by the Disposition. The basis of determining such payments was explained above (see page 457).

9. *Improvements and Ancillary Rights.* The basis for determining any expenditure allowed in respect of works or ancillary rights was explained above (see page 453). Once the allowance has been determined in the normal way it is adjusted by applying the Proportion as previously calculated.

10. *Net Development Value Realised by Disposition.* This value, on which the levy will be assessed, is found by deducting from the

Consideration for the Disposition the aggregate of the Base Value Realised by the Disposition, Sums for Related Tenancies, and any Expenditure on Improvements and Ancillary Rights.

*Example. 13*—(The same facts will be adopted as for Examples 7, 9 and 10. Hence:

Hippy Products Ltd. owns the freehold site of a factory recently destroyed by fire. The site was let in May 1970 to the Optimum Property Co. Ltd., at a ground rent of £5,000 p.a. plus a premium of £20,000 for the erection of shops with offices above. The lease is for 60 years and provides for rent reviews at 10-year intervals. The agents' fees were £1,000 and the solicitors' £500.

The site value on the basis of rebuilding the former factory is £25,000. The company purchased the freehold interest in 1968 for £60,000 when the factory stood on the site. The value as a factory, ignoring development value for other purposes, was £50,000 at that time.

1 *Consideration for Disposition:*

| | | |
|---|---|---|
| Rent receivable ... ... ... | | £5,000 p.a. |
| Y.P. 60 years @ 7½/2½% (tax @ 38·75%) | | 11·49 |
| | | 57,450 |
| *Add* premium ... ... ... | | 20,000 |
| | | 77,450 |
| *Less* Expenses of sale: | | |
| Agents ... ... | £1,000 | |
| Solicitors ... ... | 500 | |
| Levy Valuation Fees, say | 500 | |
| | —— | 2,000 |
| | | £75,450 |

2 *Current Use Value:*

| | |
|---|---|
| Industrial site value ... ... ... | £25,000 |

3 *Reversionary Value:*

| | |
|---|---|
| Reversion after 60 years to full rental value ... ... ... ... ... | £6,600 |
| Y.P. in perp. @ 8% ... ... | 12·5 |
| | £82,500 |
| × P.V. £1 in 60 years @ 8% ... ... | 0·01 |
| | £825 |

4 *Proportion:*
$$\frac{77,450}{77,450+825} = 99\%$$

C/Fwd   ...    £75,450

5 *Current Use Value Realised by Disposition:*

£25,000 × 99% ...     ...     ...     £24,750        B/Fwd.   £75,450

6 *Severance Depreciation:* assume nil.

7 *Base Value Realised by Disposition:*

(a) Sch. 4.   Current Use Value Realised ...   ...   ...   £24,750

      *Add* $\frac{1}{10}$   ...   ...   ...   2,475

      ∴ Sch. 4 Base Value   ...   £27,225

(b) Sch. 5 Purchase Price in '68...   £60,000

      Current Use Value in '68     £50,000

      Current Use Value at Letting     25,000

      ∴ Decrease in Current Value   ...   £25,000

      *Deduct* Decrease   ...   ...   25,000

                          £35,000

      × proportion @ 99%   ...   0·99

      ∴ Sch. 5 Base Value...   ...   £34,650

      ∴ Adopt Sch. 5 Base Value realised ...   ...   ...       £34,650

8 *Related Tenancies:* None in this case.

9 *Expenditure* on Improvement and *Ancillary Rights:*

      None in this case   ...   ...       —

                                £34,650

10 *Net Development Value Realised by Disposition:*   ...   ...       £40,800

      Betterment Levy is therefore payable at 40% of £40,800 =       £16,320

## 5. Case C

This case applies to the development of land. Levy liability arises under this Case upon the start of a project of material development. A project of material development is as described above (see page 453). The project is deemed to start upon the carrying out of certain specified operations as defined in Section 64 of the Land Commission

Act, 1967, and relating broadly to the start of actual construction works such as the digging of a foundation trench or running in pipes. Where the development involves only a change of use, the time at which the change takes place constitutes the start.

Unlike all other Cases, more than one interest may be an assessable interest under Case C so that levy may be payable by several persons. The meaning of assessable interests was given above (see page 451). As a typical example, where a lessee with a lease of less than 98 years starts a project, not only the lessee but also his landlord may be liable for levy under Case C.

The calculations for levy have the same sequence as for Case A, as previously described. The differences between Case C and Case A will be noted below, otherwise the calculations follow the Case A approach.

1. *Market Value*. In Case C, since there is no consideration passing at the start of the project, the market value has to be determined by valuation.

The basic criteria for such valuations laid down by the Act are as follows. The "full market rent" of the land the subject of the development must first be determined. This is broadly the ground rental value of the site assuming a lease for 99 years with the lessee covenanting to carry out the project of material development. It is further assumed that planning permission for the project exists but any further permissions for material development must be ignored.

Once full market rent is determined, the assessable interest is valued following normal valuation practise with the full market rent being treated as full rental value. This capital value is then "Market Value". Valuation fees for assessing the levy can be deducted from the Market Value.

> *Example 14.*—Optimum Developments Ltd. owns the freehold interest in a site of 2000 m² in the centre of a large town. It commenced development of the site in 1969. The development comprises the erection of a supermarket with offices above. The value of the site at that time was £200,000.

> *Market Value:*
> > *Full Market Rent.* Capital value of site is £200,000. Hence ground rental value, at say 8%, is £16,000 p.a.

| | | | |
|---|---|---|---|
| ∴ Full Market Rent ... ... ... | £16,000 p.a. |
| × Y.P. in perp. @ 8% ... ... | 12·5 |
| *Market Value* ... ... | £200,000 |
| *Less* Levy Valuation Fees (estimated) ... | 2,000 |
| | £198,000 |

N.B. In practice, if evidence exists of the freehold site value, the valuation would probably be made direct to this value.

*Example 15.*—As for Example 14 but assume that the company holds under a lease with 60 years to run at £2,000 p.a.

In this situation the freeholder would also have an assessable interest. Hence,

1 *Optimum Developments Ltd.*

| | | |
|---|---|---|
| Full Market Rent ... ... ... | £16,000 p.a. | |
| *Less* Rent payable ... ... ... | 2,000 | |
| | £14,000 p.a. | |
| Y.P. 60 years @ 9 and 2½% ... | 9·80 | |
| (tax @ 38·75%) | | |
| *Market Value* ... ... | £137,200 | |
| *Less* Valuation Fees, say ... ... | 1,500 | |
| | £135,700 | |

2 *Freeholder.*

| | | |
|---|---|---|
| *Term.* Rent reserved ... ... ... | £2,000 p.a. | |
| Y.P. 60 years @ 7% ... ... ... | 14·04 | |
| | | £28,080 |
| *Reversion* to full market rent ... ... | £16,000 p.a. | |
| Y.P. in perp. deferred 60 years @ 8% ... | 0·12 | |
| | | £1,920 |
| Market Value ... ... ... | | £30,000 |
| *Less* Valuation fees, say ... ... ... | | 500 |
| | | £29,500 |

The above comments and examples relate to development of land. Where the development constitutes the extraction or winning of minerals, special rules apply in relation to the anticipated life of the mineral sources. Since these are specialised cases, and in any event subject to various exemptions from levy, they will not be covered in detail here. Nevertheless the general approach of the Case C calculations will apply.

2. *Current Use Value.* The general approach noted in Case A applies in Case C. However, in some cases an unusual situation will emerge in that a lease will previously have been granted to a developer reflecting development value. In such cases the rent payable will exceed the current use rental value. Such a negative profit rent is treated as nil. Further, the landlord will be entitled to a considerably smaller rent on reversion than he obtains under the lease. In such cases the lease rent may be valued on the dual rate basis following normal valuation practice.

*Example 16.*—Assume the facts in Example 14 and assume the current use value of the site to be based on the right to rebuild small shops with flats above which were previously on the site. Value on this basis assumed to be £20,000.

Hence, Current Use Value ... ... ... ... £20,000

*Example 17.*—Assume the facts in Examples 15 and 16. Hence,

*Current Use Value of Optimum Developments Ltd.'s Interest:*

| | | |
|---|---|---|
| Current Use Value ... ... ... | £20,000 freehold |
| Rental value, @ say 8% ... ... | 0·08 |

| | | |
|---|---|---|
| Current Use Value ... ... ... | £1,600 p.a. |
| *Less* Rent payable ... ... ... | 2,000 p.a. |

| | | |
|---|---|---|
| ∴ Profit rent say ... ... | Nil |
| *Hence* Current Use Value ... ... | Nil |

*Current Use Value of Freeholder's Interest:*

| | | |
|---|---|---|
| *Term.* Rent reserved under lease ... | £2,000 p.a. |
| Y.P. 60 years @ 7% ... ... ... | 14·04 |
| | £28,080 |
| *Reversion* to Current Use Value rental ... | £1,600 p.a. |
| Y.P. in perp. def'd. 60 years @ 8% ... | 0·12 |
| | 192 |

| | | |
|---|---|---|
| Current Use Value ... ... | £28,272 |

N.B. In valuing the freeholders interest, Regulations under the Land Commission Act provide that the term rent can be regarded as secure, although above rental value. The fall in income may be reflected by adjusting the yield or valuing partly with a dual rate Y.P., if thought necessary.

3. *Severance Depreciation.* The general approach noted in Case A applies to Case C in relation to depreciation in the current use value of other land caused by the development.

4. *Base Value.* The two alternative approaches of Schedule 4 and Schedule 5 apply as in Case A except that under Schedule 4 Base Value, where the land the subject of the development includes existing buildings which will not be affected by the project, the $\frac{1}{10}$ or $\frac{1}{5}$ increment will not be applied to the current use value of such existing buildings but only to the value of the remainder of the site.

*Example 18.*—Assume the facts given in Example 16. Further assume that the interest was purchased in 1966 for £25,000.

*Sch. 4 Base Value:*

| | | | | |
|---|---|---|---|---|
| Current Use Value (as above) | ... | ... | **£20,000** |
| Add $\frac{1}{10}$          ...     ...     ... | ... | ... | 2,000 |
| | | | **£22,000** |
| Severance depreciation      ...     ... | ... | Nil |
| ∴ Sch. 4 Base Value         ...     ... | ... | **£22,000** |

*Sch. 5 Base Value.* The purchase in 1966 was in the interim period and is not therefore relevant, hence there is no Sch. 5 Base Value.

∴ Base Value = £22,000.

---

**5.   *Related Tenancies.*** Any sum for related Tenancies is added to the Base Value.   The basis for determining such payments was explained above (see page 455).

**6.   *Improvements and Ancillary Rights.*** The basis for determining any expenditure allowed in respect of works or ancillary rights was explained above (see page 453).

**7.   *Net Development Value.*** This value, on which the development value will be assessed, is found by deducting from the Market Value the aggregate of the Base Value, Sums for Related Tenancies, and any expenditure on Improvements and Ancillary Rights.

*Example 19.*—Assume the facts in Examples 15 and 17. Hence, Optimum Developments Ltd. owns the freehold interest in a site of 2000 m² in the centre of a large town. It commenced development of the site in 1969. The development comprises the erection of a supermarket with offices above. The value of the site at that time was £200,000. The company holds under a lease with 60 years to run at a rent of £2,000 p.a. It purchased the lease in 1966 for £25,000. The freeholders purchased their interest in 1957 for £30,000.

Both the company and the freeholders have assessable interests. The full market rent is valued at £16,000 p.a., i.e., 8% of capital value.

A *Optimum Developments Ltd.'s Net Development Value.*

| | | | | |
|---|---|---|---|---|
| 1 *Market Value.*  Full Market Rent | ... | £16,000 p.a. |
| *Less* Rent payable          ...     ... | ... | 2,000 p.a. |
| Profit rent          ...     ... | ... | £14,000 p.a. |
| Y.P. 60 years @ 9 and 2½% <br> (tax @ 38·75%) | ... | ... | 9·80 |
| | | £137,200 |
| *Less* Valuation Fees, say      ...     ... | 1,500 |
| | | £135,700 |

2 *Current Use Value*

| | | | |
|---|---|---|---|
| Freehold Current Use Value | ... | ... | £20,000 |
| Assume rental value @ 8% | ... | ... | 0·08 |

| | | | |
|---|---|---|---|
| ∴ Current Use Value ... | ... | ... | £1,600 p.a. |
| *Less* Rent payable | ... | ... | 2,000 |

| | | | |
|---|---|---|---|
| ∴ Profit rent say | ... | ... | Nil |
| Hence Current Use Value | ... | ... | Nil |

3 *Severance Depreciation.* Assume none in this case.

4 *Base Value:*

(*a*)  *Sch.* 4. Since both Current Use Value
and Severance Depreciation are ...    Nil
∴ Sch. 4 Base Value    ...    ...    Nil

(*b*)  *Sch.* 5. Purchase of lease in interim
period,    ...    ...    ...    ...
∴ Sch. 5 Base Value    ...    ...    Nil

5 *Related Tenancies.* Assume none in this case.

6 *Improvements and Ancillary Rights:*
Assume none in this case...    ...    ...    —    —

7 *Net Development Value* ...    ...    ...    £135,700

Levy would be payable at 40% on £135,700 =  £54,280

B *Freeholder's Net Development Value.*

1 *Market Value*

| | | | |
|---|---|---|---|
| *Term* Rent reserved ... | ... | £2,000 p.a. | |
| Y.P. 60 years @ 7% | ... | 14·04 | |
| | | | £28,080 |
| *Reversion* to full Market Rent | | £16,000 p.a. | |
| Y.P. in perp. def'd. 60 years | | | |
| @ 8% ... | ... | ... | 0·12 | |
| | | | 1,920 |
| | | | £30,000 |
| *Less* Valuation Fees, say | ... | | 500 |
| C/Fwd. | | | £29,500 |

|  |  | B/Fwd. |  | £29,500 |
|---|---|---|---|---|

**2** *Current Use Value*

    *Term* Rent reserved   ... £2,000 p.a.
        Y.P. 60 years @ 7%...  14·04
                           ————   28,080

    *Reversion* to Current Use
        rental      ...     ... £1,600 p.a.
        Y.P. in perp. def'd. 60
        years @ 8%     ...  0·12
                           ————      192

                                   £28,272

**3** *Severance Depreciation.*
    Assume none in this case.

**4** *Base Value*

    (*a*)  *Sch.* 4. Current Use Value
        Term      ...     ...      £28,080
        Reversion ...     ...   192
        *Add* $\frac{1}{10}$   ...     ...    19
                           ———    211

                                  £28,291

    (*b*)  *Sch.* 5.  Price paid in ante-
        cedent period     ...     ... £30,000

        ∴ Base Value     ...     ...        £30,000

**5** *Related Tenancies.*
    Assume none in this case.              —

**6** *Improvements and Ancillary Rights.*
    Assume none in this case.     ...    ...     —     30,000

**7** *Net Development Value* ...    ...    ...    minus   £500
    No levy is therefore payable by the
    freeholders.

### 6. CASES D AND E

Although these two Cases deal with different situations the calculations for each Case are identical so they can be dealt with jointly.

Case D arises on the payment of compensation under Part VII of the Town and Country Planning Act, 1962. Case E arises where an easement is purchased or where an easement or restrictive covenant is released, for valuable consideration.

The scheme of calculations is as follows:

1　Amount of Compensation (Case D)
　　or Consideration for the Disposition (Case E)
2　Current Use Value
3　Base Value
4　Improvements and Ancillary Rights
5　Restricted Value
6　Appropriate Deduction
7　Adjusted Compensation (Case D)
　or Adjusted Consideration (Case E).

The following matters should be noted in respect of each of these calculations.

1. *Amount of Compensation. Consideration for the Disposition.* In Case D, where the Amount of Compensation needs to be determined, this is the depreciation in the value of the interest payable in respect of an Order under Section 27 or Section 28 of the Town and Country Planning Act, 1962. Hence any compensation in respect of other heads of claim such as abortive expenditure or disturbance must be ignored.

In Case E, where the Consideration for the Disposition needs to be determined, this will be the actual consideration passing for the grant or release of the easement or covenant, in the same way that market value under Case A means the consideration passing—including consideration not in terms of cash (see page 453). In both cases the fees in respect of the levy valuations may be set off against the levy.

*Example 20.*— Melior Developments Ltd. owns the freehold interest in 2 hectares of farmland which were acquired in 1964 for £10,000. In 1966 planning consent was granted for the residential development of the land. In 1968 when development was about to begin the planning consent was revoked. Compensation under Part VII of the Town and Country Planning Act, 1962, was agreed as:

| | | |
|---|---|---:|
| Value with consent, 2 ha @ £20,000/ha... | ... | £40,000 |
| *Less* Existing Use Value, 2 ha @ £500/ha | ... | 1,000 |
| | | |
| Compensation for Depreciation in Interest | ... | £39,000 |

*Case D*

| | | |
|---|---|---:|
| *Amount of Compensation* (as payable) | £39,000 | |
| *Less* Levy Valuation fees, estimated, | | |
| say　　　... | 200 | |
| | | |
| | £38,800 | |

2. *Current Use Value.* The rules for determining this value were set out above (see page 453). The time of valuation is immediately

before the Order was made (Case D) or the grant or release of easement or restriction took effect (Case E). Thus it is the before-Order
or before-disposition current use value.

3. *Base Value.* The rules for determining this value under
Schedule 4 or Schedule 5 were set out above (see page 457). Base
Value in these Cases does not include sums for Severance Deprecia-
tion.

4. *Improvements and Ancillary Rights.* The rules for determining
this value were set out above (see page 453).

5. *Restricted Value.* This is the Current Use Value of the interest
where the valuation is made immediately after the Order is made
(Case D) or after the grant or release of easement or restriction (Case
E). Thus it is the post-Order or post-disposition current use value.

6. *Appropriate Deduction.* This sum derives from the calculations
previously made and is determined by deducting the Restricted Value
from the aggregate of the Base Value and any sum for Improvements
and Ancillary rights.

7. *Adjusted Compensation. Adjusted Consideration.* This sum, on
which levy is assessed, is determined by deducting the Appropriate
Deduction from either the Amount of Compensation (Case D) or
the Consideration for the Disposition (Case E).

*Example 21.*—Assume the facts in Example 20

1. *Amount of Compensation*

| | | |
|---|---|---|
| Compensation for Depreciation in interest | £39,000 | |
| *Less* Levy Valuation fees, say ... ... | 200 | |
| | | £38,800 |

2. *Current Use Value*
Value as farmland
∴ 2 ha @ £500/ha ... ...    £1,000

3. *Base Value*

| | | |
|---|---|---|
| *Sch.* 4 Current Use Value ... | £1,000 | |
| Add 1/10 ... ... | 100 | |
| *Sch.* 4 *Base Value* ... | £1,100 | |

| | | |
|---|---|---|
| *Sch.* 5 Price Paid Antecedent Period ... ... | £10,000 | |
| ∴ Base Value... ... | | £10,000 |

4. *Improvements and Ancillary Rights*
Assume none in this case ...                 —

| | |
|---|---|
| | £10,000 |
| C/Fwd ... | £38,800 |

|  | B/Fwd | ... | ... | £10,000 | £38,800 |
|---|---|---|---|---|---|

5. *Restricted Value*
Value as farmland ...
∴ 2 ha @ £500/ha ... ... | | | | 1,000

6. *Appropriate Deduction* ... ... ... | | | | | 9,000

7. *Adjusted Compensation* ... ... ... | | | | | £29,800

Hence betterment levy will be payable @
40% of £29,800 ... ... ... ... | | | | | £11,920

## 7. CASE F

Case F arises in three broad categories, and the assessment of levy depends on the category concerned.

### a. *Grant of a wayleave*

Consideration for the grant of a wayleave is similar to that for the grant of an easement. As such the calculation of levy follows the same procedure as for Case E, as described above.

### b. *Compensation for Injurious Affection when No Land is Taken*

This compensation is equated with compensation under Part VII of the Town and Country Planning Act, 1962, for depreciation in the value or an interest. Hence the calculation follows the same procedure as for Case D, as described above.

### c. *Renewal, Extension or Variation of a Lease*

In these circumstances, the new lease that arises may be equated with the grant of new lease. Hence the calculation of levy follows the procedure as for Case B, as described above. However, the calculation is subject to two adjustments in relation to Consideration for the Disposition and Base Value.

1. *Consideration for the Disposition* (see page 453). The adjustment required by Case F is to determine what is known as the additional amount. The determination of the additional amount depends on whether the original lease was purchased from the original lessee or taken direct from the landlord. In either situation it is the price paid or premium paid, less, in the case of purchases of leases or grants of leases after the 5 April, 1967, the current use value of the interest at the time of purchase or grant.

2. *Base Value Realised by Disposition* (see page 457). The adjustment required by Case F is two-fold.

   Firstly, the additional amount determined for consideration for the Disposition is also added to the Base Value Realised.

   Secondly, there is added the difference between the value of the landlord's interest at the time of variation of the lease subject to the lease, less the value of the landlord's interest assuming the tenancy did not exist. Apart from these adjustments the calculations follow the Case B scheme of calculations.

## 8.  CASE A AND COMPULSORY PURCHASE

The acquisition of an interest under compulsory purchase powers, despite the special rules surrounding it, is still nonetheless the purchase of an interest that constitutes a Case A chargeable event. However, because of the special factors involved, the Case A scheme of calculations is subject to special rules that justify separate attention. These rules are found in Schedule 9 of the Land Commission Act.

The general scheme of calculations and the methods of determining each of the sums within Case A were explained above (see page 456) but the following special additional points should be noted.

1.  *Market Value.* The compensation for compulsory acquisition falls under various heads of claim but Market Value is limited to that compensation for the interest in the land plus any compensation for severance or injurious affection to land held with the land taken. It also includes compensation for disturbance other than payment for fees and incidental expenses, effectively limiting the disturbance compensation to goodwill.

In those cases where compensation for severance or injurious affection is received, an extra deduction from Market Value is permitted. This deduction is a calculation of what would have been the Appropriate Deduction under Case D if the payment of compensation for injurious affection had been a Case D chargeable event. (See page 473 for calculation of the Appropriate Deduction.) This is illustrated in the following example.

*Example 22.*—Arable Farmers Ltd. owned a freehold farm of 230 hectares. The farm was purchased in 1945. 10 ha of this land were acquired compulsorily in May 1970 and the compensation payable was:

| | | | |
|---|---|---|---|
| 1. Land Taken, 10 ha @ £700/ha ... | = | | £7,000 |
| 2. Injurious Affection to 30 ha of adjoining land | | | |
|     Before value—30 ha @ £700/ha | = | £21,000 | |
|     After value—30 ha @ £600/ha | = | £18,000 | |
|         Injurious Affection ...     ... | | | £3,000 |
| Hence, under Case A, | | | |
| *Market Value* | | | |
|     Compensation for Land Taken ...     ... | | | £7,000 |
|     Compensation for Injurious Affection ... | | | £3,000 |
|         C/Fwd     ... | | | £10,000 |

|  | B/Fwd. | | £10,000 |
|---|---|---|---|

*Less*

1 "Appropriate Deduction" on "land
held with"

    *a. Current Use Value*
       30 ha @ £700/ha    ...    ...   £21,000

    *b. Base Value*
       (i) Sch. 4 Current Use Value   £21,000
          *Add* $\frac{1}{10}$   ...    ...    ...     2,100

                                £23,100

       (ii) *Sch.* 5 NIL
          ∴ Base Value ...    ...   £23,100

    *c. Allowable Expenditure*
       Assume nil in this case     ...    —

                                £23,100

    *d. Restricted Value*
       Current Use Value after Sale
          30 ha @ £600/ha   ...     18,000

    *e.* Appropriate Deduction     ...       £5,100

2 Fees for Levy Valuations (estimated) say      200
                                                           5,300

                 ∴ Market Value    ...     ...     ...     £4,700

*NOTE:* It seems that compensation for goodwill may be deducted
from Market Value where included in the compensation,
applying the general rule that sums paid for chattels are
deducted since goodwill may be regarded as a chattel.

2. *Current Use Value.* In determining this value, the valuation
must adopt Rules 2, 3 and 4 of the Land Compensation Act, 1961,
Section 5, and must also ignore certain capital sums and rentcharges.
Apart from these, the method of determining Current Use Value is
adopted (see page 453).

3. *Severance Depreciation.* Any sum under this head is omitted
from the Case A scheme of calculations where compensation for
severance or injurious affection is payable.

4. *Base Value.* There is added to the Base Value as determined
under Schedule 4 and Schedule 5 any compensation for disturbance
that would have been payable had the land been purchased on an

existing use basis. This will operate in a situation where the rule in *Horn v. Sunderland*[4] applies and the interest is being acquired at a development value so excluding any claim for compensation for disturbance.

5. *Related Tenancies.* The method of determining any sum for Related Tenancies is unaffected by compulsory acquisition (see page 455).

6. *Improvements and Ancillary Rights.* Expenditure on these items is allowed in the usual way (see page 453).

7. *Net Development Value.* This is determined in the usual way.

*Example 23.*—Stacked Products Ltd. owns an old warehouse which it purchased in 1954 for £20,000. In 1969 the premises were acquired under compulsory powers by the local authority for £100,000 on the basis of industrial site value. The value as a warehouse at that time was £30,000 and the disturbance claim would have been £20,000 had it been payable.

1 *Market Value:*

| | | |
|---|---:|---:|
| Compensation for land taken ... ... | £100,000 | |
| *Less* Levy valuation fees (estimated) ... | 400 | |
| | | £99,600 |

2 *Current Use Value:*

| | |
|---|---:|
| As a warehouse ... ... | £30,000 |

3 *Severance Depreciation:*
Assume none in this case.

4 *Base Value:*

1 *Schedule* 4

| | |
|---|---:|
| Current Use Value ... ... | £30,000 |
| *Add* $\frac{1}{10}$ ... ... ... | 3,000 |
| | £33,000 |

2 *Schedule* 5

| | |
|---|---:|
| Price Paid in 1954 ... ... | £20,000 |

| | |
|---|---:|
| ∴ Base Value ... ... | £33,000 |
| *Add* for Disturbance that would have been payable ... | £20,000 |

| | | |
|---|---:|---:|
| C/Fwd. | £53,000 | £99,600 |

[4] See page 338.

|  | B/Fwd. | £53,000 | £99,600 |
|---|---|---|---|
| 5 *Related Tenancies:* | | | |
| Assume none in this case. | | | |
| 6 *Improvements and Ancillary Rights:* | | | |
| Assume none in this case. | | — | 53,000 |

| 7 *Net Development Value* ... ... ... | £46,600 |
|---|---|

Betterment Levy would be payable @ 40% of £46,600 = £18,640

It should be noted that where the Land Commission purchased an interest the compensation payable by the Commission was assessed as for any general compulsory purchase case but the betterment levy payable was assessed at the time of purchase and deducted from the compensation.

# APPENDIX A

## THE MATHEMATICS OF VALUATION TABLES

### 1. GENERALLY

An understanding of the mathematical principles upon which the tables are based will be found to be of assistance in using the tables correctly, and to their best advantage.

The tables dealt with in this Appendix are described in Chapter 5.

It is beyond the purview of this book to examine the theory of interest. It is sufficient to accept the fact that the valuation of future sums receivable is based upon compound interest. If it is desired to value an amount receivable in the future, the assumption is made that a purchaser would give such a sum as would accumulate at compound interest, during the period that elapses before it is received, to the amount receivable. The rate per cent at which the accumulation is to take place will depend upon the risks attendant upon the investment.

The justification for this method of approach is not based on theoretical considerations, but on the fact that future sums receivable do, in the market, command prices which are found to accord with calculations made on this basis.

### 2. THE AMOUNT OF £1 TABLE

To find the amount to which £1 will accumulate at compound interest in a given time.

Let the interest per annum of £1 be i.

Then the amount at the end of 1 year will be $(1 + i)$ ;

,,        ,,        ,,     2 years    ,,    $(1 + i)^2$;

and so on.

By similar reasoning the amount in n years will be $(1 + i)^n$. The total interest paid on £1 in n years will be $(1 + i)^n - 1$.

### 3. THE PRESENT VALUE OF £1 TABLE

To find the present value of £1 receivable at the end of a given time.

Since £1 will accumulate to $(1 + i)^n$ in n years, the present value of £1 due in n years equals $\dfrac{1}{(1 + i)^n}$.

### 4. ACCUMULATIONS AT LESS THAN YEARLY INTERVALS

It is assumed in the foregoing sections that interest is paid **yearly**.

If it is desired to take into account the payment of interest and its reinvestment at more frequent intervals, i and n must be modified.

Let the number of payments in 1 year be m. Then the total number of payments is mn. As the annual rate of interest is i, the rate of interest for one period is $\frac{i}{m}$, and the amount of £1 in n years equals $(1 + \frac{i}{m})^{mn}$.

The present value of £1 correspondingly will be $\dfrac{1}{(1 + \frac{i}{m})^{mn}}$.

## 5. THE AMOUNT OF £1 PER ANNUM TABLE

The amount to which £1 per annum invested at the end of each year will accumulate in a given time.

It is conventional to assume that interest is not paid until the end of the first year, hence the first payment of £1 will accumulate for n – 1 years if the period of accumulation is n years.

The second payment will accumulate for n – 2 years and so on year by year.

The amount to which the first payment accumulates will (from 2) be $(1 + i)^{n-1}$; the second $(1 + i)^{n-2}$; and so on.

Let the amount of £1 per annum in n years be A.
Then $A = (1 + i)^{n-1} + (1 + i)^{n-2} + (1 + i)^{n-3}$ ........................
$(1 + i)^2 + (1 + i) + 1$; or more conveniently
    $A = 1 + (1 + i) + (1 + i)^2 ............ (1 + i)^{n-1}$.
These terms form a geometrical progression for which the general expression is $S = \dfrac{a(r^n - 1)}{r - 1}.$ Substituting therein $S = A$;
        $a = 1$;   $r = 1 + i$;

    Hence $A = \dfrac{(1 + i)^n - 1}{i}$

## 6. ANNUAL SINKING FUND TABLE

To find the sum which, if invested at the end of each year, will accumulate at compound interest to £1.

Let the annual sinking fund be S and the period n years, then, as indicated in Section 5, the first instalment will accumulate to $S (1 + i)^{n-1}$; the second to $S (1 + i)^{n-2}$; and so on.
    Hence $1 = S (1 + i)^{n-1} + S (1 + i)^{n-2}$......
      $S (i1 + {}^2 + S (1 + i) + S$; or more conveniently
      $1 = S + S (1 + i) + S (1 + i)^2 ......S (1 + i)^{n-1}$.

The sum of the series shown by the method in Section 5 will be: $-1 = \dfrac{S\,[\,(1+i)^n - 1\,]}{i}$ therefore $S = \dfrac{i}{[\,(1+i)^n - 1\,]}$

It will be observed that S is the reciprocal of A in Section 5.

It will be noted that investment of the sinking fund takes place at the end of each year. This is convenient when dealing with the income from real property, which is commonly assumed to be receivable yearly at the end of each year.

In comparing sinking fund tables with amounts payable under a sinking fund policy it must be remembered that under a policy the premium is payable at the beginning of each year.

By similar reasoning to the above in this case

$$S = \frac{i}{(1+i)^{n+1} - 1}$$

### 7. Present Value of £1 per Annum or Years' Purchase Table

To find the value of £1 per annum receivable at the end of each year for a given time allowing compound interest.

As shown in Section 3 the present value of the first instalment of income is $\dfrac{1}{1+i}$, that of the second $\dfrac{1}{(1+i)^2}$, the third $\dfrac{1}{(1+i)^3}$, and so on.

Let the present value be V and the term n years, then

$$V = \frac{1}{1+i} + \frac{1}{(1+i)^2} \cdots \frac{1}{(1+i)^{n-1}} + \frac{1}{(1+i)^n}.$$

Hence summing the series

$$V = \frac{1}{1+i}\left\{ \frac{\dfrac{1}{(1+i)^n} - 1}{\dfrac{1}{(1+i)} - 1} \right\}$$

changing the sign in the numerator and denominator

$$V = \frac{1 - \dfrac{1}{(1+i)^n}}{i}$$

This expression has a three-fold aspect. V has been shown in this Section to represent the present value of a series of future payments allowing compound interest.

It also represents the sum upon which an income of £1 per annum will yield simple interest at i per annum and provide a sinking fund at i to accumulate to V at the end of n years, as shown in the following Section.

**8.**

The amount of simple interest on V is V.i, the sinking fund to replace V in n years is $V \dfrac{i}{(1 + i)^n - 1}$ (as shown in Section 6). If these together are assumed to be equal to £1 then:

$$1 = V.i + V \frac{i}{(1 + i)^n - 1}$$

$$1 = V.i \left(1 + \frac{1}{(1 + i)^n - 1}\right) = V.i \frac{(1 + i)^n}{(1 + i)^n - 1}$$

$$V = \frac{(1 + i)^n - 1}{i (1 + i)^n}$$

Dividing numerator and denominator by $(1 + i)^n$

$$V = \frac{1 - \dfrac{1}{(1 + i)^n}}{i}$$

which accords with the expression derived in Section 7.

**9.**

The general expression in Section 7 also represents the loan which can be repaid by equal annual instalments of capital and interest, allowing interest on outstanding annual balances, thus:—

Let the loan be V to be repaid in equal annual instalments of £1 in n years with interest at i on outstanding balances. Then from Section 7

$$V = \frac{1 - \dfrac{1}{(1 + i)^n}}{i}$$

Let $p = \dfrac{1}{(1 + i)}$ so that $V = \dfrac{1 - p^n}{i}$

During the first year the loan outstanding is V, which equals $\dfrac{1 - p^n}{i}$, and the interest thereon at the end of year is $i . \dfrac{1 - p^n}{i} = 1 - p^n$.

As the annual amount is £1, the capital repayment will be $1 - (1 - p^n) = p^n$.

In the second year the capital outstanding will equal

$$\frac{1 - p^n}{i} - p^n$$

$$= \frac{1 - p^n - ip^n}{i}$$

$$= \frac{1 - p^n (1 + i)}{i}$$

$$= \frac{1 - p^{n-1}}{i}$$

Hence the interest payable will be $1 - p^{n-1}$, and the capital repayment $p^{n-1}$.

In the third year the capital outstanding will be $\dfrac{1 - p^{n-1}}{i} - p^{n-1}$, which by similar reasoning will be seen to be equal to $1 - p^{n-2}$ and the corresponding capital repayment $p^{n-2}$.

The capital repayments will constitute a series
$$p^n + p^{n-1} + p^{n-2} \ldots\ldots p.$$
This series is seen to be identical with the series shown in Section 7 as $p = \dfrac{1}{(1+i)}$

That is to say, the annual payments of £1, after providing for interest yearly on outstanding capital reconstitutes the amount $V$ over the period n.

It will be observed that this aspect of the years' purchase or annuity table corresponds with the ordinary Building Society basis for repayment of loans.

In American practice terminable investments are sometimes regarded from this point of view. In England the aspect of the tables developed in Section 8 is the more common viewpoint. For the individual investor the repayment of capital by small annual instalments over the period of the investment would create difficulties in reinvestment. It is more usual to regard the income as a flat yield throughout the term, with sufficient margin to permit of capital being reinstated at the end of the term.

## 10. The Dual Rate Tables

The practical difficulties involved in finding a sinking fund investment yielding the same rate as the investment have led to the growth in the use of dual rate tables.

To find the present value of £1 per annum for a given number of years, allowing simple interest at i per annum on capital and the accumulation of an annual sinking fund at s per annum.

As before, let the present value be $V$, then each annual instalment will consist of simple interest on $V$, that is $V.i$, and a sinking fund instalment equal to $V . \dfrac{s}{(1+s)^n - 1}$.

$$1 = V.i + V . \frac{s}{(1+s)^n - 1}$$

$$V = \frac{1}{i + \dfrac{s}{(1+s)^n - 1}}$$

This corresponds with the formula for $\text{Y.P.} = \dfrac{1}{i + S}$

when $S = \dfrac{s}{(1+s)^n - 1}.$

## 11. Years' Purchase for Perpetuity

In the general expression $V = \dfrac{1 - \dfrac{1}{(1+i)^n}}{i}$ (Section 7),

if n is infinity then $\dfrac{1}{(1+i)^n} = 0$ and $V = \dfrac{1}{i}$

## 12. Income Receivable at Other than Yearly Intervals

In Section 4 the application of the equations for the amount of £1 and the present value of £1 for periods other than yearly was explained. In a similar way the equations for the amount of £1 per annum, sinking fund and the present value of £1 can be adapted for other than yearly intervals.

As in Section 4 let the number of payments in one year be m, the total number be mn. If the annual rate of interest be i then

$$V = \frac{1 - \dfrac{1}{(1 + \dfrac{i}{m})^{mn}}}{i}$$

## 13. Recurring Payments

From the general equation for the present value of £1 per annum an expression can be derived from the present value of a series of equal regularly recurring premiums.

Let the amount of each payment be £1, the interval between the payments be n years, the first premium be deferred m years, and the total number of premiums be t.

As in Section 9, let V be the present value of the series and

$p = \dfrac{1}{1 + i}.$

Then
$$\begin{aligned}
V &= p^m + p^{m+n} + p^{m+2n} \ldots\ldots p^{m\,(t-1)n} \\
&= p^m (1 + p^n + p^{2n} \ldots\ldots p^{(t-1)n}) \\
&= p^m \left\{ \frac{1 - p^{tn}}{1 - p^n} \right\} \text{ (from Section 7).}
\end{aligned}$$

This corresponds with the usual formula:

V = P.V. of £1 deferred the term of the first premium

$$x \; \frac{\text{Y.P. for the total term}}{\text{Y.P. for the interval between the payments}}$$

as will be seen by dividing the numerator and denominator by i.

Thus:
$$V = p^m \left\{ \frac{\dfrac{1 - p^{tn}}{i}}{\dfrac{1 - p^n}{i}} \right\}$$

## 14. Diminishing Incomes

In many cases in practice it may be considered that the income from a property may alter in the future. The methods of valuation to be adopted are discussed fully in Chapter 6 on the basis that the income remains constant for fixed periods.

In some cases it may be considered that an income receivable may progressively diminish year by year. For example, a building newly erected may be considered to have a useful life of 60 years; as it becomes older and compares more and more unfavourably with comparable premises of less age, the rental value is likely to diminish.

It might be possible to make a forecast of the diminution at the beginning of the term of the income, and years' purchase tables have been constructed on the assumption of a gradual diminution of income from 100% at the commencement to a proportion at the end of the term, or even to nil.

The difficulties involved in making estimates of future changes of income of this character are very great. It is to be doubted if sufficient data exists for such estimates to be other than entirely speculative.

Such adjustments of the normal years' purchase equations are, it is suggested, unnecessary, as the rate per cent yield from various types of property investment reflects the possibilities of changes in income in the future; where the risk of a future reduction in income is high the rate per cent will be high. The rate used will have been derived from the analysis of the sales of similar properties; as indicated in Chapter 8 the methods of analysis used usually assume continuance of income for a term and accordingly the year's purchase and rate per cent derived from the analysis take into account the risks attaching to the particular investment in question.

If diminution of income were to be taken into account by a modification of the tables, the analysis of past sales would have to be on the same basis. In view of the great difficulties inherent in estimating a rate of diminution, it is to be doubted if any greater accuracy in valuations would be achieved.

## 15. Valuation of Variable Incomes

It was pointed ont in Section 2 of Chapter 6 that the usual method employed to calculate the capital value of a leasehold interest, where the income varies during the term of the lease, is incorrect because of the use of the dual rate tables. The method envisages more than one sinking fund being taken out to provide for the redemption of capital whereas in practice a purchaser would in all probability take out a single policy to cover the whole term. The concept of a variable sinking fund is not in itself incorrect and a valuation could be made on this basis if a method were employed which would enable the varying instalments to compound to the required amount over the full unexpired term.

The normal method of approach used in the valuation of varying incomes for a limited term does not allow for the correct compounding of the sinking fund accumulations. This type of valuation is made in two or more stages, so that each separate sinking fund instalment will be based on the number of years in the appropriate stage of the valuation and will not be based over the full length of the term. Consequently the sum provided by these sinking funds over the full length of the term will not equal the capital sum required for the redemption of capital.

The following examples illustrate the error which occurs when the normal method of valuation is used:—

Example A.—The valuation of a leasehold interest on an 8 and $2\frac{1}{2}$ per cent basis. The lease has an unexpired term of 10 years and produces a profit rent of £1,000 p.a.

| | Profit Rent | £1,000 p.a. |
|---|---|---|
| Y.P. 10 years @ 8 and $2\frac{1}{2}$% ...    ... | | 5·908 |
| | Capital Value | £5,908 |

Example B.—If the unexpired term of 10 years in Example A is considered in two stages of say, 4 years and 6 years the valuation will take the following form:—

| | | Profit Rent | £1,000 p.a. | |
|---|---|---|---|---|
| Y.P. 4 years @ 8 and $2\frac{1}{2}$% ...    ... | | | 3·117 | £3,117 |
| | | Profit Rent | £1,000 p.a. | |
| Y.P. 6 years @ 8 and $2\frac{1}{2}$% ... | 4·227 | | | |
| P.V. £1 in 4 years @ 8% ... | 0·735 | | 3·107 | £3,107 |
| | | Capital Value | | £6,224 |

In these two examples the profit rental of £1,000 p.a. has been capitalised in each case for a total period of 10 years at the same remunerative rate of 8%; each example should therefore produce the same result. The difference of £316 is caused by the error which arises in Example B. The method of valuation used in this example is based on the dual rate basis and is made in two stages; an incorrect sinking fund instalment will therefore be implicit in the valuation and will introduce an error into the calculation.

The degree of error which occurs in Example B is approximately +5¼%. If the 10-year term had been divided into three stages (with the income varying in the third and sixth year) the error would increase to over 8%.

*The effect of Tax.*—If the incidence of income tax on the sinking fund element is taken into account this must have some effect on the degree of the error. In the following valuations the figures of Years' Purchase used in Examples A and B are adjusted to allow for the effect of income tax:—

*Example A (t)*—

| | | |
|---|---|---|
| | Profit Rent | £1,000 p.a. |
| Y.P. 10 years @ 8 and 2½% ... ... | | 4·43 |
| (Tax at 38·75%) | | |
| | Capital Value | £4,430 |

*Example B (t)*—In this example the 10-year term is again considered in two stages:—

| | | | | |
|---|---|---|---|---|
| | Profit Rent | | £1,000 p.a. | |
| Y.P. 4 years @ 8 and 2½% ... ... | | | 2·113 | £2,113 |
| (Tax at 38·75%) | | | | |
| | Profit Rent | | £1,000 p.a. | |
| Y.P. 6 years @ 8 and 2½% ... | | 2·98 | | |
| (Tax at 38·75%) | | | | |
| P.V. £1 in 4 years @ 8% ... | | 0·735 | 2·19 | £2,190 |
| | | Capital Value | | £4,303 |

These examples illustrate that when an allowance is made to reflect the incidence of tax, it will not always increase the error which exists, although this is often thought to be the case. They show that in making the allowance for income tax, the adjustment has had a compensatory " pull " on the degree of the error which is reduced in the last example to approximately −3%.

In many instances the effect of the tax adjustment will be more marked and will usually over-compensate for the " normal " error to such an extent that a much greater inaccuracy will be introduced. In some cases an error which is well in excess of 10 per cent may be involved.

*The Double Sinking Fund Method.*—The following method enables this form of valuation to be made without involving any significant error. An attempt has been made to use the conventional methods of valuation and to avoid any involved mathematical approach.

*Example C.*—In this example the same leasehold interest is again considered and the term is divided into two stages as in Example B. It should be noticed that the dual rate principle is not used.

Let the Capital Value＝P.

| | | |
|---|---|---|
| Profit Rent | £1,000 p.a. | |

*Less* a.s.f. to replace P in 10 years
@ 2½% ... ... ... ·0893P

Spendable Income £1,000 – ·0893P
Y.P. 4 years @ 8% ... ... 3·312

£3,312 – ·2958P

Spendable Income £1,000 – ·0893P
Y.P. 6 years @ 8% ... 4·623
P.V. £1 in 4 years @ 8% 0·735 3·398

£3,398 – ·3034P

£6,710 – ·5992P

*Plus Repayment of the capital replaced by the Single Rate S.F.
P × P.V. of £1 in 10 years @ 8% ... ... + ·4632P

Capital Value £6,710 – ·136 **P**

$$\therefore P = £6,710 - ·136P$$
$$1·136P = £6,710$$
$$P = £5,907$$

The spendable income has been valued on the single rate basis. This means that the "capital" has been replaced by allowing for a sinking fund at 8% in the capitalisation. Thus two "capital recoupments" have taken place one at 2½% and one at 8%.

* As the valuation has been reduced by allowing for the capital to be replaced twice, a figure equal to the deferred capital value has been added back to the valuation.

If the result is compared with the capital value of £5,908 (the result in Example A) it will be seen that the difference is negligible and would not occur if a sufficient number of decimal places were taken.

*Tax Adjustment.*—The Double Sinking Fund Method can easily be adjusted for tax. This is shown in the following valuation which is of a more practical nature than the previous examples. It also shows how a reduction in the remunerative rate can be made in the valuation when the income is more secure during part of the term.

*Example D.*—The valuation of a leasehold interest which has an unexpired term of 10 years at a rent of £100 p.a. The property is sub-let for the next two years at a rent of £200 p.a. The full rental value is £300 p.a. and the leasehold rate is 12%.

Let the Capital Value = P.

| | | |
|---|---|---|
| Rent Rec'd. | £200 p.a. | |
| *Less* Rent Paid | £100 | |
| Profit Rent | £100 p.a. | |
| *Less* a.s.f. to replace P in 10 years @ 2½% (tax @ 38·75%) ... | 0·146P | |
| Spendable Income | £100 – 0·146P | |
| Y.P. 2 years @ 11% | 1·71 | £171 - 0·25P |
| *2nd Term* Rev. to | £300 p.a. | |
| *Less* Rent Paid | £100 | |
| Profit Rent | £200 p.a. | |
| *Less* a.s.f. as above | 0·146P | |
| Spendable Income | £200 – 0·146P | |

| | | | |
|---|---|---|---|
| Y.P. 8 yrs. @ 12% | 4·97 | | |
| P.V. £1 in 2 yrs. @ 12% | ·797 | 3·96 | £792 – 0·578P |
| | | | £963 – 0·828P |

| | | | |
|---|---|---|---|
| *Plus* Repayment of the capital replaced by the Single Rate S.F. | | P | |
| P.V. £1 in 8 yrs. @ 12% | 0·404 | | |
| × P.V. £1 in 2 yrs. @ 11% | 0·812 | | |
| | | 0·328 | +0·328P |
| Capital Value | | | £963 – 0·5P |

$$\therefore \ P = 963 - 0·5P$$
$$1·5P = 963$$
$$P = 642$$

Capital Value £642

## 16. CAPITAL APPRECIATION

The preference of some investors for a capital gain rather than an increase in income and the possibility of making some allowance for this by using the present value of £1 adjusted for tax were referred to in Chapter 5. This method of adjustment is probably adequate when applied to capital sums receivable in the future but is incorrect when applied to capital gains arising from increases in income.

*Example.*—Value the interest of the freeholder in a shop in a first class position let to a multiple on full repairing and insuring lease with five years unexpired at a rent of £10,000 per annum. The full rental value now is £15,000 per annum.

A normal valuation without allowance for capital appreciation would be:—

*Term*—

| | | | | |
|---|---|---|---|---|
| Rent reserved ... ... ... | £10,000 p.a. | | | |
| Y.P. 5 years @ 5% ... ... | 4·3 | | | £43,000 |

*Reversion*—

| | | | | |
|---|---|---|---|---|
| To full rental value ... ... | £15,000 p.a. | | | |
| Y.P. in perpetuity @ 6% ... | 16·67 | | | |
| | £250,000 | | | |
| P.V. £1 in 5 years @ 6% ... | ·75 | | | £186,000 |
| Present Capital Value | | | | £229,000 |

A valuation allowing for capital appreciation by adjusting the present value of £1 for tax at 38·75% would be:—

*Term*—

| | | | |
|---|---|---|---|
| As before ... ... ... | | | £43,000 |

*Reversion*—

| | | | | |
|---|---|---|---|---|
| To full rental value ... ... | £15,000 p.a. | | | |
| Y.P. in perpetuity @ 6% ... | 16·7 | | | |
| P.V. £1 in 5 years @ 6% adj. tax @ 38·75% ... | | ·83 | 13·9 | £208,500 |
| | | | | £251,500 |

Thus the adjustment turns a capital gain of £21,000 (£250,000–£229,000) into a capital loss of £1,500 (£251,500–£250,000). This is because the capital appreciation is assumed to have risen on the whole of the reversionary income £15,000 per annum, instead of on the increase in the income on reversion, £5,000 per annum.

*The Split Reversion Method.*—The simplest method of confining the adjustment to the increase in income on reversion is to split the full rental value as follows:—

*Term*—
   As before ...    ...    ...    £43,000

*Reversion*—
   To full rental value split

| | | | | |
|---|---|---|---|---|
| (i) | | £10,000 p.a. | | |
| | Y.P. perp. @ 6% def'd. 5 yrs. | 12·4 | £124,000 | |
| (ii) | | £5,000 p.a. | | |
| | Y.P. perp. @ 6%  16·7 | | | |
| | P.V. £1 in 5 yrs. @ 6% adj. tax @ 38·75% | ·83 | 13·9 | £69,500  £193,500 |

Present Capital Value    £236,500

*The "Layer" Method.*—Another method which overcomes the difficulty but which is rather more complex is that described on Page xxiii of the Eighth Edition of Parry's Valuation Tables. As applied to the example under consideration the calculation would be:—

*Preliminary Calculations*—

| | | | | |
|---|---|---|---|---|
| (i) | Rental value   ...   ... | £15,000 p.a. | | |
| | Y.P. perp. @ 6% ...   ... | 16·7 | £250,000 | |
| (ii) | Existing rent   ...   ... | £10,000 p.a. | | |
| | Y.P. perp. @ 5% ...   ... | 20 | £200,000 | |
| (iii) | Capital value of "marginal" income | | £50,000 | |

(iv)   The marginal income is therefore a

$$\frac{5,000}{50,000} \times \frac{100}{1} = \frac{10\% \text{ risk}}{}$$

*Valuation*—

| | | |
|---|---|---|
| "Hard core" income | £10.000 p.a. | |
| Y.P. perp. @ 5% | 20 | £200,000 |
| "Marginal" income | £5,000 p.a. | |
| Y.P. perp. @ 10%  10 | | |
| P.V. £1 in 5 yrs. @ 10% adj. tax @ 38·75%  ·74 | 7·4 | £37,000 |

Present Capital Value    £237,000

It will be noted that no attempt has been made to allow for the effect of capital gains tax. While it is possible to produce a mathematical computation to allow for this, as the liability for this tax does not arise until realisation and there are a number of exemptions and reliefs, the practical value of such a calculation is doubtful.

Notes on the use of some tables adjusted for income tax are to be found on pages xxv to xxx of the Ninth Edition of Parry's Valuation Tables.

# APPENDIX B (1)

## TOWN AND COUNTRY PLANNING ACT, 1962

### THIRD SCHEDULE
#### DEVELOPMENT NOT CONSTITUTING NEW DEVELOPMENT

#### PART I

*Development not ranking for compensation under section 123*

1. The carrying out of any of the following works, that is to say—

   (a) the rebuilding, as often as occasion may require, of any building which was in existence on the appointed day, or of any building which was in existence before that day but was destroyed or demolished after the seventh day of January, nineteen hundred and thirty-seven, including the making good of war damage sustained by any such building;

   (b) the rebuilding, as often as occasion may require, of any building erected after the appointed day which was in existence at a material date;

   (c) the carrying out of works for the maintenance, improvement or other alteration of any building, being works which affect only the interior of the building or which do not materially affect the external appearance of the building and (in either case) are works for making good war damage,

so long as (in the case of works falling within any of the preceding sub-paragraphs) the cubic content of the original building is not exceeded—

   (i) in the case of a dwelling-house, by more than one-tenth or seventeen hundred and fifty cubic feet, whichever is the greater, and

   (ii) in any other case, by more than one-tenth.

2. The use as two or more separate dwelling-houses of any building which at a material date was used as a single dwelling-house.

#### PART II

*Development ranking for compensation under section 123*

3. The enlargement, improvement or other alteration, as often as occasion may require, of any such building as is mentioned in sub-paragraph (a) or sub-paragraph (b) of paragraph 1 of this Schedule, or any building substituted for such a building by the carrying out of any such operations as are mentioned in that paragraph, so long as the cubic content of the original building is not increased or exceeded—

   (a) in the case of a dwelling-house, by more than one-tenth or seventeen hundred and fifty cubic feet, whichever is the greater, and

   (b) in any other case, by more than one-tenth.

4. The carrying out, on land which was used for the purposes of agriculture or forestry at a material date, of any building or other operations required for the purposes of that use, other than operations for the erection, enlargement, improvement or alteration of dwelling-houses or of buildings used for the purposes of market gardens, nursery grounds or timber yards or for other purposes not connected with general farming operations or with the cultivation or felling of trees.

5. The winning and working, on land held or occupied with land used for the purposes of agriculture, of any minerals reasonably required for the purposes of that use, including the fertilisation of the land so used and the maintenance, improvement or alteration of buildings or works thereon which are occupied or used for those purposes.

6. In the case of a building or other land which, at a material date, was used for a purpose falling within any general class specified in the Town and Country Planning (Use Classes for Third Schedule Purposes) Order, 1948, or which, having been unoccupied on and at all times since the appointed day, was last used (otherwise than before the seventh day of January, nineteen hundred and thirty-seven) for any such purpose, the use of that building or land for any other purpose falling within the same general class.

7. In the case of any building or other land which, at a material date, was in the occupation of a person by whom it was used as to part only for a particular purpose, the use for that purpose of any additional part of the building or land not exceeding one-tenth of the cubic content of the part of the building used for that purpose on the appointed day, or on the day thereafter when the building began to be so used, or, as the case may be, one-tenth of the area of the land so used on that day.

8. The deposit of waste materials or refuse in connection with the working of minerals, on any land comprised in a site which at a material date was being used for that purpose, so far as may be reasonably required in connection with the working of those minerals.

## PART III

### Supplementary provisions

9. Any reference in this Schedule to the cubic content of a building shall be construed as a reference to that content as ascertained by external measurement.

10. Where, after the appointed day, any buildings or works have been erected or constructed, or any use of land has been instituted, and any condition imposed under Part III of this Act, limiting the period for which those buildings or works may be retained, or that use may be continued, has effect in relation thereto., this Schedule shall not operate except as respects the period specified in that condition.

11. For the purposes of paragraph 3 of this Schedule—

    (a) the erection, on land within the curtilage of any such buildings as is mentioned in that paragraph, of an additional building to be used in connection with the original building shall be treated as the enlargement of the original building; and

    (b) where any two or more buildings comprised in the same curtilage are used as one unit for the purposes of any institution or undertaking, the reference in that paragraph to the cubic content of the original building shall be construed as a reference to the aggregate cubic content of those buildings.

12. In this Schedule " at a material date " means at either of the following dates, that is to say—

    (a) the appointed day, and

    (b) the date by reference to which this Schedule falls to be applied in the particular case in question;

Provided that sub-paragraph (b) of this paragraph shall not apply in relation to any buildings, works or use of land in respect of which, whether before or after the date mentioned in that sub-paragraph, an enforcement notice served before that date has become or becomes effective.

# APPENDIX B (2)

SUMMARY OF
## THE TOWN AND COUNTRY PLANNING ACT, 1963

*(Modifications in the application of the Third Schedule of the T. & C.P. Act, 1962)*

1. *Generally*—In all cases where either (i) the value, or (ii) the depreciation in value, of an interest in land falls to be determined on the assumption that planning permission would be granted for any of the classes of development specified in the Third Schedule to the Town and Country Planning Act, 1962, the 1963 Act makes important modifications in paragraphs 1, 3 and 7 of that Schedule.

These modifications are summarised in paragraph 2 below, and their effect on other sections of the 1962 Act is considered in paragraph 4.

2. *Modifications of the Third Schedule*—(1963 Act, section 1 and Schedule.)

(i) *Rebuilding or Alteration.*

(a) Where the building to be rebuilt or altered is " the original building ", Paras. 1 and 3 of the Third Schedule must now be read as subject to a further condition that the gross floor space which may be used for any purpose in the building as rebuilt or altered must not exceed by more than 10 per cent the amount of gross floor space last used for that purpose in " the original building." For example, if " the original building " was used for office purposes, a rebuilding or extension of the premises will only be within the Third Schedule provided neither the cubic content of the original building, nor the gross floor space used for office purposes therein is increased by more than 10 per cent.

(b) Where the building to be rebuilt or altered is not " the original building ", the new condition to be read into Paragraphs 1 and 3 of the Schedule is that the gross floor space to be used for any purpose in the rebuilt or altered building does not exceed the amount last used for that purpose in the previous building.

(c) Where a building was first erected after 1st July, 1948, or was erected after that date as a replacement of an original building, Paragraph 3 of the Schedule no longer applies, so that any increase in cubic content due to enlargement, improvement or other alteration will be outside the Third Schedule.

(ii) *Extension of user of part of land or buildings.* In the case of buildings erected after 1st July, 1948, Paragraph 7 no longer applies and any extension of a particular user to a further part of the building will be outside the Third Schedule.

In determining the purpose for which floor space was last used in any building no account shall be taken of any use in respect of which an effective enforcement notice has been or could be served, or, in the case of a use which has been discontinued, could have been served immediately before the discontinuance.

" Gross floor space " is to be ascertained by external measurement; and where different parts of buildings are used for different purposes floor space common to those purposes shall be apportioned rateably.

3. *"The Original Building"*—For the purposes of both the 1962 and the 1963 Acts, it would appear that "original building" means:—

(i) A building existing at 1st July, 1948, or before that date but after 7th January, 1937; or

(ii) a building erected for the first time since 1st July, 1948, and in existence at the time when the Schedule falls to be applied; or

(iii) in the case of a war-damaged building—the building as it existed before the damage was sustained.

Section 1 (4) of the 1963 Act expressly provides that where a building is rebuilt after 1st July, 1948, the previous building—not the one which replaces it—is "the original building."

4. *Application to other sections of the Town and Country Planning Act, 1962.*

(i) *Section 123—(see Chapter 19, section 1).*

(a) No compensation will be payable for an adverse planning decision relating to works involving an increase in the cubic content of a building erected after 1st July, 1948. [1963 Act, section 1 (2)].

(b) In determining the extent to which the value of the owner's interest is less than it would have been if permission had been granted, regard must be had to the conditions on floor space imposed by the 1963 Act. [1963 Act, section 1 (1) (a)].

(ii) *Section 129 (see Chapter 19, section 5).* In determining whether the conditions for the service of a purchase notice are fulfilled, no account shall be taken of any prospective development within the Third Schedule which would contravene the new conditions as to floor space imposed by the 1963 Act. [1963 Act, section 1 (1) (b)].

(iii) *Section 134 (see Chapter 19, section 5).* "Existing use value" for the purposes of this section means the value of the land assuming that planning permission would only be given for those forms of development within the Third Schedule of the Town and Country Planning Act, 1947, as originally enacted, but subject to the modifications prescribed by the 1963 Act. [1963 Act, section 1 (5)].

5. *"New Development"*—In section 12 (5) of the Town and Country Planning Act, 1962, "new development" is defined as any development other than development of a class specified in Part I or Part II of the Third Schedule to that Act. The 1963 Act does not affect the meaning of this term as applied to those provisions of Part VI of the 1962 Act which govern the right to compensation for adverse planning decisions relating to "new development", or the recovery of such compensation when permission for "new development" is subsequently given. [1963 Act, section 1 (3) and see Chapter 19, section 2 (a) and (i)].

But as applied to the repayment of compensation previously paid under Part VII of the 1962 Act for the revocation or modification of planning permission, the term "new development" must be interpreted by reference to the Third Schedule of that Act as modified by the provisions of the Town and Country Planning Act, 1963 [see Chapter 19, section 3].

6. *Operation of the Act.*—The Act was passed on 10th July, 1963, but is deemed to have come into force on 25th February, 1963.
But it does not affect:—

(i) Any determination arising out of a notice to treat served before 25th February, 1963;

(ii) Any determination arising out of a notice to treat served at any time in respect of a " purchase notice ", or notice requiring purchase served before 25th February, 1963, under sections 129 or 139 of the Town and Country Planning Act, 1962;

(iii) Any other determination under the 1962 Act in respect of or arising out of a " purchase notice " served before 25th February, 1963;

(iv) Any claim for compensation for depreciation of value under sections 118 or 123 of the 1962 Act, or under sections 18 (i) or 20 of the 1947 Act, which arose before 25th February, 1963.

In relation to any time before 1st April, 1963—the date when the 1962 Act came into operation—any reference in the Town and Country Planning Act, 1963, to an enactment contained in the 1962 Act shall be construed as a reference to the corresponding enactment repealed by the 1962 Act. [1963 Act, section 4 (2)].

# APPENDIX C

## (1) LAND COMPENSATION ACT, 1961

PART II.—SECTIONS 5–9

### PROVISIONS DETERMINING AMOUNT OF COMPENSATION

GENERAL PROVISIONS

*Rules for assessing compensation*

**5.** Compensation in respect of any compulsory acquisition shall be assessed in accordance with the following rules:

(1) No allowance shall be made on account of the acquisition being compulsory;

(2) The value of land shall, subject as hereinafter provided, be taken to be the amount which the land if sold in the open market by a willing seller might be expected to realise;

(3) The special suitability or adaptability of the land for any purpose shall not be taken into account if that purpose is a purpose to which it could be applied only in pursuance of statutory powers, or for which there is no market apart from the special needs of a particular purchaser or the requirements of any authority possessing compulsory purchase powers;

(4) Where the value of the land is increased by reason of the use thereof or of any premises thereon in a manner which could be restrained by any court. or is contrary to law, or is detrimental to the health of the occupants of the premises or to the public health, the amount of that increase shall not be taken into account;

(5) Where land is, and but for the compulsory acquisition would continue to be, devoted to a purpose of such a nature that there is no general demand or market for land for that purpose, the compensation may, if the Lands Tribunal is satisfied that reinstatement in some other place is bona fide intended, be assessed on the basis of the reasonable cost of equivalent reinstatement;

(6) The provisions of rule (2) shall not affect the assessment of compensation for disturbance or any other matter not directly based on the value of land;

and the following provisions of this Part of this Act shall have effect with respect to the assessment.

*Disregard of actual or prospective development in certain cases*

**6.**—(1) Subject to section eight of this Act, no account shall be taken of any increase or diminution in the value of the relevant interest which, in the circumstances described in any of the paragraphs in the first column of Part I of the First Schedule to this Act. is attributable to the carrying out or the prospect of so much of the development mentioned in relation thereto in the second column of that Part as would not have been likely to be carried out if—

(*a*) (where the acquisition is for purposes involving development of any of the land authorised to be acquired) the acquiring authority had not acquired and did not propose to acquire any of that land; and

(*b*) (where the circumstances are those described in one or more of paragraphs 2 to 4 in the said first column) the area or areas referred to in that paragraph or those paragraphs had not been defined or designated as therein mentioned.

(2) The provisions of Part II of the First Schedule to this Act shall have effect with regard to paragraph 3 of Part I of that Schedule.

(3) In this section and in the First Schedule to this Act—
" the land authorised to be acquired "—

(*a*) in relation to a compulsory acquisition authorised by a compulsory purchase order or a special enactment, means the aggregate of the land comprised in that authorisation; and

(*b*) in relation to a compulsory acquisition not so authorised but effected under powers exercisable by virtue of any enactment for defence purposes, means the aggregate of the land comprised in the notice to treat and of any land contiguous or adjacent thereto which is comprised in any other notice to treat served under the like powers not more than one month before and not more than one month after the date of service of that notice;

" defence purposes " has the same meaning as in the Land Powers (Defence) Act, 1958;

and any reference to development of any land shall be construed as including a reference to the clearing of that land.

### *Effect of certain actual or prospective development of adjacent land in same ownership*

**7.**—(1) Subject to Section 8 of this Act, where, on the date of service of the notice to treat, the person entitled to the relevant interest is also entitled in the same capacity to an interest in other land contiguous or adjacent to the relevant land, there shall be deducted from the amount of the compensation which would be payable apart from this section the amount (if any) of such an increase in the value of the interest in that other land as is mentioned in subsection (2) of this section.

(2) The said increase is such as, in the circumstances described in any of the paragraphs in the first column of Part I of the First Schedule to this Act, is attributable to the carrying out or the prospect of so much of the relevant development as would not have been likely to be carried out if the conditions mentioned in paragraphs (*a*) and (*b*) of Subsection (1) of Section 6 of this Act had been satisfied and the relevant development for the purposes of this subsection is, in relation to the circumstances described in any of the said paragraphs, that mentioned in relation thereto in the second column of the said Part I, but modified, as respects the prospect of any development, by the omission of the words " other than the relevant land ", wherever they occur.

### *Subsequent acquisition of adjacent land and acquisition governed by enactment corresponding to Section 7*

**8.**—(1) Where, for the purpose of assessing compensation in respect of a compulsory acquisition of an interest in land, an increase in the value of an interest in other land has, in any of the circumstances mentioned in the first column of Part I of the First Schedule to this Act, been taken into account by virtue of Section 7 of this Act or any corresponding enactment, then, in connection with any subsequent acquisition to which this subsection applies, that increase shall not be left out of account by virtue of Section 6 of this Act, or taken into account by virtue of Section 7 of this Act or any corresponding enactment, in so far as it was taken into account in connection with the previous acquisition.

(2) Where, in connection with the compulsory acquisition of an interest in land, a diminution in the value of an interest in other land has, in any of the circumstances mentioned in the first column of the said Part I, been taken into account in assessing compensation for injurious affection, then, in connection with any subsequent acquisition to which this subsection applies, that diminution shall not be left out of account by virtue of Section 6 of this Act in so far as it was taken into account in connection with the previous acquisition.

(3) Subsections (1) and (2) of this Section apply to any subsequent acquisition where either—

(a) the interest acquired by the subsequent acquisition is the same as the interest previously taken into account (whether the acquisition extends to the whole of the land in which that interest previously subsisted or only to part of that land); or

(b) the person entitled to the interest acquired is, or derives title to that interest from, the person who at the time of the previous acquisition was entitled to the interest previously taken into account;

and in this Subsection any reference to the interest previously taken into account is a reference to the interest the increased or diminished value whereof was taken into account as mentioned in Subsection (1) or Subsection (2) of this section.

(4) Where, in connection with a sale of an interest in land by agreement, the circumstances were such that, if it had been a compulsory acquisition, an increase or diminution of value would have fallen to be taken into account as mentioned in Subsection (1) or Subsection (2) of this Section, the preceding provisions of this Section shall apply, with the necessary modifications, as if that sale had been a compulsory acquisition and that increase or diminution of value had been taken into account accordingly.

(5) Section 7 of this Act shall not apply to any compulsory acquisition in respect of which the compensation payable is subject to the provisions of any corresponding enactment, nor to any compulsory acquisition in respect of which the compensation payable is subject to the provisions of any local enactment which provides (in whatever terms) that, in assessing compensation in respect of a compulsory acquisition thereunder, account shall be taken of any increase in the value of an interest in contiguous or adjacent land which is attributable to any of the works authorised by that enactment.

(6) Where any such local enactment as is mentioned in Subsection (5) of this Section includes a provision restricting the assessment of the increase in value thereunder by reference to existing use (that is to say, by providing, in whatever terms. that the increase in value shall be assessed on the assumption that planning permission in respect of the contiguous or adjacent land in question would be granted for development of any class specified in the Third Schedule to the Town and Country Planning Act, 1947. but would not be granted for any other development thereof), the enactment shall have effect as if it did not include that provision.

(7) References in this Section to a corresponding enactment are references to any of the following, that is to say,—

    (*a*) Section 13 of the Light Railways Act, 1896;

    (*b*) Sub-paragraph (C) of paragraph (2) of the Schedule to the Development and Road Improvement Funds Act, 1909;

    (*c*) Subsection (6) of Section 222 of the Highways Act, 1959;

    (*d*) Paragraph 4 of Part III of the Third Schedule to the Housing Act, 1957;

and, in Subsection (1), include references to any such local enactment as is mentioned in Subsection (5).

*Disregard of depreciation due to prospect of acquisition by authority possessing compulsory purchase powers*

**9.** No account shall be taken of any depreciation of the value of the relevant interest which is attributable to the fact that (whether by way of designation, allocation or other particulars contained in the current development plan, or by any other means) an indication has been given that the relevant land is, or is likely, to be acquired by an authority possessing compulsory purchase powers.

FIRST SCHEDULE

ACTUAL OR PROSPECTIVE DEVELOPMENT RELEVANT FOR

PURPOSES OF SECTIONS 6 & 7

PART I

*Description of Development*

| *Case* | *Development* |
|---|---|
| 1. Where the acquisition is for purposes involving development of any of the land authorised to be acquired. | Development of any of the land authorised to be acquired, other than the relevant land, being development for any of the purposes for which any part of the first-mentioned land (including any part of the relevant land) is to be acquired. |
| 2. Where any of the relevant land forms part of an area defined in the current development plan as an area of comprehensive development. | Development of any land in that area, other than the relevant land, in the course of the development or redevelopment of the area in accordance with the plan. |
| 3. Where on the date of service of the notice to treat any of the relevant land forms part of an area designated as the site of a new town by an order under the New Towns Act, 1946. | Development of any land in that area, other than the relevant land, in the course of the development of that area as a new town. |
| 4. Where any of the relevant land forms part of an area defined in the current development plan as an area of town development. | Development of any land in that area other than the relevant land, in the course of town development within the meaning of the Town Development Act, 1952. |

*Assumptions as to planning permission*

**14.**—(1) For the purpose of assessing compensation in respect of any compulsory acquisition, such one or more of the assumptions mentioned in Sections 15 and 16 of this Act as are applicable to the relevant land or any part thereof shall be made in ascertaining the value of the relevant interest.

(2) Any planning permission which is to be assumed in accordance with any of the provisions of those sections is in addition to any planning permission which may be in force at the date of service of the notice to treat.

(3) Nothing in those provisions shall be construed as requiring it to be assumed that planning permission would necessarily be refused for any development which is not development for which, in accordance with those provisions, the granting of planning permission is to be assumed; but, in determining whether planning permission for any development could in any particular circumstances reasonably have been expected to be granted in respect of any land, regard shall be had to any contrary opinion expressed in relation to that land in any certificate issued under Part III of this Act.

(4) For the purposes of any reference in this Section, or in Section 15 of this Act, to planning permission which is in force on the date of service of the notice to treat, it is immaterial whether the planning permission in question was granted—

    (*a*) unconditionally or subject to conditions; or

    (*b*) in respect of the land in question taken by itself or in respect of an area including that land; or

    (*c*) on an ordinary application or on an outline application or by virtue of a development order;

or is planning permission which, in accordance with any direction or provision given or made by or under any enactment, is deemed to have been granted.

*Assumptions not directly derived from development plans*

**15.**—(1) In a case where—

    (*a*) the relevant interest is to be acquired for purposes which involve the carrying out of proposals of the acquiring authority for development of the relevant land or part thereof, and

    (*b*) on the date of service of the notice to treat there is not in force planning permission for that development,

it shall be assumed that planning permission would be granted, in respect of the relevant land or that part thereof, as the case may be, such as would permit development thereof in accordance with the proposals of the acquiring authority.

(2) For the purposes of paragraph (*b*) of the preceding Subsection, no account shall be taken of any planning permission so granted as not to enure (while the permission remains in force) for the benefit of the land and of all persons for the time being interested therein.

(3) Subject to Subsection (4) of this Section, it shall be assumed that planning permission would be granted, in respect of the relevant land or any part thereof, for development of any class specified in the Third Schedule to the Town and Country Planning Act, 1947 (which relates to development included in the existing use of land).

(4) Notwithstanding anything in Subsection (3) of this Section—

(*a*) it shall not by virtue of that Subsection be assumed that planning permission would be granted, in respect of the relevant land or any part thereof, for development of any class specified in Part II of the said Third Schedule, if it is development for which planning permission was refused at any time before the date of service of the notice to treat and compensation under Section 20 of the said Act of 1947 became payable in respect of that refusal;

(*b*) where, at any time before the said date, planning permission was granted, in respect of the relevant land or any part thereof, for development of any class specified in the said Part II, but was so granted subject to conditions, and compensation under the said Section 20 became payable in respect of the imposition of the conditions, it shall not by virtue of the said subsection (3) be assumed that planning permission for that development, in respect of the relevant land or that part thereof, as the case may be, would be granted otherwise than subject to those conditions;

(*c*) where, at any time before the said date, an order was made under Section 26 of the said Act of 1947, in respect of the relevant land or any part thereof, requiring the removal of any building or the discontinuance of any use, and compensation became payable in respect of that order under Section 27 of that Act. it shall not by virtue of the said subsection (3) be assumed that planning permission would be granted, in respect of the relevant land or that part thereof, as the case may be, for the rebuilding of that building or the resumption of that use.

(5) Where a certificate is issued under the provisions of Part III of this Act, it shall be assumed that any planning permission which, according to the certificate, might reasonably have been expected to be granted in respect of the relevant land or part thereof would be so granted, but, where any conditions are, in accordance with those provisions, specified in the certificate, only subject to those conditions and, if any future time is so specified, only at that time.

*Special assumptions in respect of certain land comprised in development plans*

**16.**—(1) If the relevant land or any part thereof (not being land subject to comprehensive development) consists or forms part of a site defined in the current development plan as the site of proposed development of a description specified in relation thereto in the plan, it shall be assumed that planning permission would be granted for that development.

(2) If the relevant land or any part thereof (not being land subject to comprehensive development) consists or forms part of an area shown in the current development plan as an area allocated primarily for a use specified in the plan in relation to that area, it shall be assumed that planning permission would be granted, in respect of the relevant land or that part thereof, as the case may be, for any development which—

(*a*) is development for the purposes of that use of the relevant land or that part thereof; and

(*b*) is development for which planning permission might reasonably have been expected to be granted in respect of the relevant land or that part thereof, as the case may be.

(3) If the relevant land or any part thereof (not being land subject to comprehensive development) consists or forms part of an area shown in the current development plan as an area allocated primarily for a range of

two or more uses specified in the plan in relation to the whole of that area, it shall be assumed that planning permission would be granted, in respect of the relevant land or that part thereof, as the case may be, for any development which—

(a) is development for the purposes of a use of the relevant land or that part thereof, being a use falling within that range of uses; and

(b) is development for which planning permission might reasonably have been expected to be granted in respect of the relevant land or that part thereof, as the case may be.

(4) If the relevant land or any part thereof is land subject to comprehensive development, it shall be assumed that planning permission would be granted, in respect of the relevant land or that part thereof, as the case may be, for any development for the purposes of a use of the relevant land or that part thereof falling within the planned range of uses (whether it is the use which, in accordance with the particulars and proposals comprised in the current development plan in relation to the area in question, is indicated in the plan as the proposed use of the relevant land or that part thereof, or is any other use falling within the planned range of uses) being development for which, in the circumstances specified in the next following Subsection, planning permission might reasonably have been expected to be granted in respect of the relevant land or that part thereof as the case may be.

(5) The circumstances referred to in the last preceding Subsection are those which would have existed if—

(a) the area in question had not been defined in the current development plan as an area of comprehensive development, and no particulars or proposals relating to any land in that area had been comprised in the plan; and

(b) in a case where, on the date of service of the notice to treat, land in that area has already been developed in the course of the development or redevelopment of the area in accordance with the plan, no land in that area had been so developed on or before that date;

and in that subsection " the planned range of uses " means the range of uses which, in accordance with the particulars and proposals comprised in the current development plan in relation to the area in question, are indicated in the plan as proposed uses of land in that area.

(6) Where in accordance with any of the preceding Subsections it is to be assumed that planning permission would be granted as therein mentioned—

(a) the assumption shall be that planning permission would be so granted subject to such conditions (if any) as, in the circumstances mentioned in the Subsection in question, might reasonably be expected to be imposed by the authority granting the permission; and

(b) if, in accordance with any map or statement comprised in the current development plan, it is indicated that any such planning permission would be granted only at a future time, then (without prejudice to the preceding paragraph) the assumption shall be that the planning permission in question would be granted at the time when, in accordance with the indications in the plan, that per-mission might reasonably be expected to be granted.

(7) Any reference in this Section to development for which planning permission might reasonably have been expected to be granted is a reference to development for which planning permission might reasonably

have been expected to be granted if no part of the relevant land were proposed to be acquired by any authority possessing compulsory purchase powers.

(8) In this Section " land subject to comprehensive development " means land which consists or forms part of an area defined in the current development plan as an area of comprehensive development.

## (2) COMPULSORY PURCHASE ACT, 1965

*Measure of compensation in case of severance*

7. In assessing the compensation to be paid by the acquiring authority under this Act regard shall be had not only to the value of the land to be purchased by the acquiring authority, but also to the damage, if any, to be sustained by the owner of the land by reason of the severing of the land purchased from the other land of the owner, or otherwise injuriously affect-that other land by the exercise of the powers conferred by this or the special Act.

# APPENDIX D

## APPORTIONMENT OF UNEXPENDED BALANCE ON COMPULSORY ACQUISITION

### Town and Country Planning Act, 1962, section 96 and Seventh Schedule
(formerly T. & C.P. Act, 1959—Sixth Schedule)

This Schedule contains the rules governing the apportionment of the unexpended balance between two or more interests (other than " excepted interests "[1]) in land compulsorily acquired.

The circumstances in which such an apportionment becomes necessary are referred to on page 378 of the text.

*Determination of relevant area.*—In order to apply these rules the area of land having the unexpended balance must, if necessary, be divided into such number of separate areas as will ensure that:—

(a) every interest subsisting in that area relates to the whole of that area; and

(b) any rent-charge on the area in question is charged on the whole of it.

The rules of the Schedule must then be applied separately to each of these " relevant areas."

*Preliminary calculations.*—These are required (i) in establishing the basis for the apportionment of the unexpended balance among the several interests; and (ii) for making certain deductions, where appropriate, from the amount apportioned to each interest.

The latter deductions are applicable where either (a) the amount of a rent-charge on freehold land, or (b) the rent reserved under a tenancy, exceeds the " existing use rent."

The following are the calculations required:—

(1) **" The existing use rent."**—This is the amount of the rent attributable to the relevant area which might reasonably be expected to be reserved if the land acquired were let on terms which permitted only the carrying out of " Third Schedule " development.

(2) **" Rental liability."**—*In the case of a fee simple subject to a rent-charge*—this means the capital value of the right to receive, for the remaining period of the rent-charge, so much of the rent-charge applicable to the relevant area as exceeds " the existing use rent ". For example, if a rent-charge of £20 is payable in perpetuity on an area whose existing use rent is £15, the " rental liability " on a 4 per cent basis would be £5 × 25 years' purchase = £125.

*In the case of a tenancy*—it means the capital value of the right to receive for the remainder of the term so much of the rent reserved applicable to the relevant area as exceeds " the existing use rent ". For example, if A has a lease from B for a term having ten years still to run at a rent of £350, " the existing use rent " being £250, then the " rental liability " of A's interest will be the capital value of the right to receive £100 per annum for ten years.

*Note:* In the case of the freehold interest it would appear that there can be no " rental liability " unless the property is subject to a rent-charge.

(3) **" Rental increment."**—In the case of an interest in reversion—e.g., that of a freeholder or head lessee who has granted a lease or sub-lease —means the capital value, at the time of the notice to treat, of the right

---

[1] An " excepted interest " is one no greater than that of a tenant for a year or from year to year.

507

to receive for the remainder of the tenancy so much of the rent reserved, applicable to the relevant area, as exceeds the existing use rent.

*Note:* It would, therefore, appear that, in the second example in (2) above the " rental liability " of A's interest and the " rental increment " of B's interest will be calculated on the same figure of excess of rent paid over " existing use rent ".

No attempt is made here to discuss the problems, which must inevitably arise in practice, of the rate per cent to be used in such calculations and whether they should be on a single rate or dual rate basis.

(4) **" Reversionary development value."**—Applies to any interest in reversion and means the capital value at the time immediately before the service of notice to treat of the right to receive a sum equal to the unexpended balance of the relevant area payable at the expiration of the tenancy upon which the interest is immediately expectant.

For example, if A has leased to B for a term having fifteen years unexpired at the time of the notice to treat, and the unexpended balance of the area in question is £500, " the reversionary development value " of A's interest on a 5 per cent basis would be: £500 × ·481 (present value of £1 in 15 years) = £241.

*Note*: 5 per cent is used for purposes of illustration only. No rate is prescribed by the Act.

*Apportionment of unexpended balance between interests.*—This involves (i) the division of the unexpended balance between the different interests in the land, and (ii) a possible deduction from the amount allotted to one or more of those interests in respect of the amount by which any " rental liability " of that interest exceeds any " rental increment " of the same interest.

The reason for the deduction would appear to be that in the case of a " rental liability " the compulsory acquisition will relieve the party from the future obligation to pay rent in excess of the existing use rent.

In relation to the relevant area, the sum attributable to the various interests will be : —

(a) *Interest in fee simple.*—The reversionary development value *less* the amount (if any) by which any " rental liability " exceeds any " rental increment ".

(b) *Tenancy in reversion.*—The R.D.V. of the interest *less:*—

(i) the R.D.V. of the interest in reversion immediately expectant on the termination of the tenancy; and

(ii) the amount (if any) by which any " rental liability " exceeds any " rental increment ".

(c) *Tenancy not in reversion.*—The amount of the unexpended balance *less :*—

(i) the R.D.V. of the interest in reversion immediately expectant on the termination of the tenancy;

(ii) any rental liability.

# APPENDIX E

FINANCE ACT, 1969

SCHEDULE 17

ESTATE DUTY

PART I

### DETERMINATION OF AMOUNT OF ESTATE DUTY ON ESTATE

The amount of the state duty on an estate—

(*a*) if the aggregate principal value of all property comprised in the estate does not exceed £12,500[1], shall be nil;

(*b*) in any other case, shall be an amount equal to the aggregate of—

    (i) 25 per cent of any amount by which that aggregate principal value exceeds £12,500[1] but does not exceed £17,500; and

    (ii) 30 per cent of any amount by which that aggregate principal value exceeds £17,500 but does not exceed £30,000; and

    (iii) 45 per cent of any amount by which that aggregate principal value exceeds £30,000 but does not exceed £40,000; and

    (iv) 60 per cent of any amount by which that aggregate principal value exceeds £40,000 but does not exceed £80,000; and

    (v) 65 per cent of any amount by which that aggregate principal value exceeds £80,000 but does not exceed £150,000; and

    (vi) 70 per cent of any amount by which that aggregate principal value exceeds £150,000 but does not exceed £300,000; and

    (vii) 75 per cent of any amount by which that aggregate principal value exceeds £300,000 but does not exceed £500,000; and

    (viii) 80 per cent of any amount by which that aggregate principal value exceeds £500,000 but does not exceed £750,000; and

    (ix) 85 per cent of any amount by which that aggregate principal value exceeds £750,000,

but not exceeding an amount equal to 80 per cent of that aggregate principal value.

---

[1] Finance Act, 1971, Section 61. In respect of deaths occurring before 31st March, 1971, the sum was £10,000.

# TABLE OF CASES

# TABLE OF CASES

# INDEX

*(Page numbers in italics indicate a page in the Appendix)*

## A

# E

# F

# G

## M

## N

## O

## P

## Q

## R

# T